T0323684

# Cognitive Capitalism

Nations can vary greatly in their wealth, democratic rights and the wellbeing of their citizens. These gaps are often obvious, and by studying the flow of immigration one can easily predict people's wants and needs. But why are there also large differences in the level of education indicating disparities in cognitive ability? How are they related to a country's economic, political and cultural development? Researchers in the paradigms of economics, psychology, sociology, evolution and cultural studies have tried to find answers for these hotly debated issues. In this book, Heiner Rindermann establishes a new model: the emergence of a burgher-civic world, supported by long-term background factors, furthered education and thinking. It initiated a reciprocal development changing society and culture, resulting in past and present cognitive capital and wealth differences. This is an important text for graduate students and researchers in a wide range of fields, including economics, psychology, sociology and political science, and those working on economic growth, human capital formation and cognitive development.

HEINER RINDERMANN is Professor of Educational and Developmental Psychology at Chemnitz University of Technology, Germany. He has published approximately 150 articles and books, and is a fellow of the Association for Psychological Science (APS). His research focuses on cognitive human capital from an interdisciplinary perspective, bringing together ideas on cognitive competence, cognitive development, productivity, politics and culture on individual and national levels.

# Cognitive Capitalism

*Human Capital and the Wellbeing of Nations*

Heiner Rindermann

*Chemnitz University of Technology*

CAMBRIDGE
UNIVERSITY PRESS

# CAMBRIDGE
## UNIVERSITY PRESS

University Printing House, Cambridge CB2 8BS, United Kingdom

One Liberty Plaza, 20th Floor, New York, NY 10006, USA

477 Williamstown Road, Port Melbourne, VIC 3207, Australia

314–321, 3rd Floor, Plot 3, Splendor Forum, Jasola District Centre,
New Delhi – 110025, India

79 Anson Road, #06–04/06, Singapore 079906

Cambridge University Press is part of the University of Cambridge.

It furthers the University's mission by disseminating knowledge in the pursuit of
education, learning, and research at the highest international levels of excellence.

www.cambridge.org
Information on this title: www.cambridge.org/9781107050167
DOI: 10.1017/9781107279339

First published 2018

Printed in the United Kingdom by Clays, St Ives plc

*A catalogue record for this publication is available from the British Library.*

*Library of Congress Cataloging-in-Publication Data*
Names: Rindermann, Heiner, 1966– author.
Title: Cognitive capitalism : human capital and the wellbeing of nations /
Heiner Rindermann.
Description: Cambridge, United Kingdom ; New York, NY : University Printing
House, 2018. | Includes bibliographical references and index.
Identifiers: LCCN 2017024439 | ISBN 9781107050167 (hardback) |
ISBN 9781107651081 (pbk.)
Subjects: | MESH: Quality of Life | Cognition | Intelligence |
Socioeconomic Factors | Education–economics | Capitalism
Classification: LCC QP363.3 | NLM WA 30 | DDC 612.8/2339–dc23
LC record available at https://lccn.loc.gov/2017024439

ISBN 978-1-107-05016-7 Hardback
ISBN 978-1-107-65108-1 Paperback

# Contents

# Figures

# Tables

# Preface

Why are we much richer today than our ancestors? Why in the last centuries so many nations have developed towards liberty, rule of law and peace? And why are some nations still on average much richer, freer and safer than others which lag behind? Why do countries and populations progress or regress, prosper or fail, fall or rise?

People as individuals as well as nations had and have to face large differences in given political and economic conditions. And peoples themselves, from historical and cross-country comparisons, largely differ in habits, values, preferences and, less known but importantly, in competences. All these characteristics are connected. Of course they are connected; simple correlational studies show empirical relations. However, mere descriptions of various indicators of development and of their usually positive associations are intellectually unsatisfactory. We want to *understand* why peoples and societal conditions are how they are, why they are interrelated, what causes are at work and what we can learn to *improve* the fate of societies. Big questions!

Big questions call for big theories. Nevertheless, for solid answers in the search for reasons and causes we need the nitpicky work on numbers led by epistemic rationality. This is even more important, as these questions are tangential to religious, cultural, ethical and political worldviews. In classical German philosophy and social science such worldviews were termed *Weltanschauungen* (Jaspers, 1919). They shape our perceptions of what happens around us and also influence our judgement in epistemic questions; in those questions in which answers have to be solely judged according to their approximation of truth and not according to their affinity to our likes and dislikes.

We consider 'cognitive capital' to be crucial for economic growth, especially in modernity. Cognitive capital is conceptualised as the *ability to think*, to solve problems by cognitive means, to reason inductively and deductively, to deal with abstraction, to understand and construct meaning, to learn, to acquire and use true and relevant *knowledge*. In psychology, this cognitive capital is termed intelligence, cognitive ability or cognitive competence. Cognitive capital has driven and continuously drives technological and cultural modernisation. For these macro-social processes, the level of high ability *cognitive classes* is especially important, shaping an intellectual climate, working through innovation and management, expressing itself in technology and companies, in law and politics, in science and the arts.

In historic development and in cross-cultural comparison, cognitive ability and its rise are related to the emergence of a burgher-civic world, supported by cultural factors furthering education and intelligence. Such a development includes mediated reciprocal effects, from culture via physical, societal and psychological environments to ability and back to environment and culture. This has led in the past and present to differences in cognitive capital and wealth.

However, this is not the only approach developed in the field. What impact do the accidental determinants of geography, climate and mineral resources and the less accidental circumstances of history, politics and power structures have? And what about evolutionary factors? The quality of political and economic institutions? The contribution of a scientific model cannot be sufficiently evaluated by mere empirical proof using data, statistics and causal modelling, but also needs a careful comparison to alternative, complementary or rival scientific approaches.

I hope this book will stimulate discussion and scientific progress. I could not have written it without the help of many others. First of all, every study is built on the work of many predecessors, whose work and discoveries enriched our understanding and thinking. Colleagues helped me through their research and stimulating, sometimes critical, comments. There is a vivid international scene; we remain close by reading the publications of our colleagues, by email and by exchanges at annual meetings. My work benefited from receiving stimulating ideas and extensive data sets. The best way to honour such contributions is by referring to and working with them. In particular, I give thanks to David Becker, Gregory Christainsen and Justus Sänger, who carefully checked earlier drafts of the book and contributed many valuable suggestions. Erich Weede and Garett Jones read my final drafts, which then turned out to be very preliminary versions as they were greatly improved by their advice.

Phil Good and Chris Harrison from Cambridge University Press supported me a lot with their always helpful and appreciative comments from the beginning to the end of the writing and editing of this book and my copyeditor, Kevin Hughes, made my book readable – thanks to you all! We do not come out of nowhere. My parents, Dr Karin and Dr Wigbert Rindermann, had a hard time educating a frequently difficult boy. Also, I remember the attic of my grandfather, Dr Joseph Rindermann, whom I never met; he died around the time of my birth. The attic was full of ancient books on science, humanities and philosophy. In the evening, after his daily strenuous work as a physician, he was an intellectual. Last, but not least, I want to thank my wife and our children for all their contributions to transforming mere existence into life.

# 1 Large Wealth Differences across Time and Nations

Large income and wealth differences across time and between nations are described. We start by presenting economic production and income measures indicating wealth. We will finish by showing limitations and possibilities for improvement.

Living conditions largely differ for people depending on when they were born and where they live. If a child is born in a modern, well-developed country, he or she will receive proficient health care, before, during and after birth and throughout childhood and youth. Many will grow up in large and well-constructed houses. Others in former times, and still in some regions of the world, grew up in huts, maybe in what appear to us as picturesque lodges, but many in dark and wretched shacks. Some will have access to clean and fresh running water, others regrettably not. Modern indoor plumbing, electricity, heating, air conditioning, refrigerators and stable doors and windows provide a comfortable, healthy and secure life. That is not a result of the merit of the individual child, but is given to him by parents, and the parents themselves are embedded in different neighbourhoods and societies providing very different opportunities.

## 1.1 Measures of Production, Income and Wealth

International comparative statistics show the above-mentioned differences in a systematic and largely comparable manner: *Gross national product* (GNP) describes the sum ('gross') of all the goods and services that are produced by a country (precisely by its citizens) during one calendar year. Products are those things and services that can be sold and bought on the market. Products are negotiable and have prices. *Gross domestic product* (GDP) represents the sum of a country's goods independent of the citizenship of the owners of enterprises. *Gross national income* (GNI) additionally considers all transfers coming from abroad (and subtracting everything going out) as foreign aid or remittances from relatives working overseas. Whereas GNI is a better indicator of consumable wealth, especially for smaller countries, GDP is a better indicator of what a society is capable of producing. GNP is less important or clear because ownership and citizenship are rather arbitrary categories. Usually, GDP or GNI are used, but most data – for the most countries in contemporary or historical comparisons – are given for GDP.[1]

The distinctions between the mentioned variables are conceptually interesting; however, empirically the distinctions are less important: the variables are highly correlated across countries. To be precise, the *differences* between countries in these variables are highly correlated: countries that have higher values in GDP also have higher values in GNI. The main reason is that national income is largely based on produced goods.[2] The same is true for differences across time with respect to historical development. Countries that produced less in the past had poorer inhabitants.

More important is to distinguish between country and per capita measures to give a more accurate picture: if GDP was not scaled down to individuals, countries with larger populations would be perceived as being richer. They have larger markets and they are, all other things being equal, more powerful, but we do not know their average level of affluence. Therefore, we always and only use per capita ('/c') estimates. These per capita estimates represent the *annual* income.

The crucial problem to be dealt with is *comparability* across countries and time: first of all, comparisons across countries have to be based on one common scale, that is, currency. Usually US Dollars are chosen. But selecting one currency is not sufficient to achieve comparability. Cross-country differences in price levels are not adequately reflected by exchange rates: they are frequently fixed and influenced by politics, they are more volatile (varying between years) and they are too often based on small sets of goods (e.g. traded mineral resources). Therefore, all wealth indicators are adapted for 'purchasing power parity', in short 'ppp'.[3] Comparisons across time expressed in monetary units additionally need to be corrected for inflation and – though it is very difficult – for change in quality of goods.[4]

In their narrow meaning, GDP and GNI are indicators for *production* and *income*, but not for given wealth, which also comprises existing stocks and real

---

[1] These terms are not always used consistently by researchers and organisations. For example, GNP and GNI are often used synonymously.

[2] GDP presented by Penn and GNI by HDR correlate with $r = .95$ ($N = 197$ nations; GDP-Penn 2010, HDR-GNI 2010, both per capita and ppp; Heston, Summers & Aten, 2012; UNDP, 2010).

[3] Purchasing power parity adaptations reduce economic differences between developed and developing countries. They increase between twofold and nearly tenfold the economic estimates for developing countries (e.g. for China from 1,100 to 4,990 $US, for India from 530 to 2,880 $US, for Ethiopia from 90 to 710 $US; Komlos & Snowdon, 2005, pp. 7–8).

[4] 'Relative' correlational analyses (comparing country differences) including regressions and path analyses (if they present results in standardised units) do not need across-time corrections. Similarly, corrections are not necessary for present-day correlational comparisons, if, for example, GDP/c in US Dollar and GDP/c in international currency units are correlated.

estate and their quality. However, because income is based on production and given wealth on previously achieved production of wealth, it is not unusual to use GDP and GNI as proxies for *wealth*.

Current production, income and wealth are based on *past economic growth*. Wealth is the result of middle- and long-term growth based on all the positive factors discussed in economic science, such as economic freedom (e.g. trade and property rights), geography (e.g. mineral resources and proximity to markets), politics (e.g. rule of law and peace) and human capital (e.g. cognitive ability and conscientiousness). For research, wealth measures (from GDP to those wealth indicators in the narrow sense as provided by Credit Suisse) are more reliable criteria than growth measures: wealth measures are less volatile (short-term growth heavily depends on business cycles) and there is no negative effect of achieved wealth on present wealth as there is for wealth on present growth: Less developed countries can learn from more developed countries. Following cleared paths and avoiding others' mistakes is easier than exploring and clearing new paths. Catching up is faster than inventing new products and production processes. Imitation is easier than innovation. Economic growth at lower development levels is easier than at higher development levels – therefore, growth is usually higher in poorer countries, termed in economics as advantages of backwardness, beta or $\beta$-convergence.[5]

However, factors increasing wealth can work only via stimulating growth. Why did some countries in certain eras grow faster than others? In a longitudinal design we can control current for previous wealth. An analysis will show that the change of wealth is influenced by growth factors. Of course, the simple maintenance of wealth also needs production that depends on favourable economic, geographic, political and human capital factors. So growth as well as wealth are both useful criteria when studying economic factors.

Producing and obtaining income and wealth (GDP/c, GNI/c) is expressed in monetary units, usually in US Dollars. But numerically identical increases at different levels have a different meaning: a $5,000 income increase (or difference between countries) from $5,000 to $10,000 means much more improvement for standard of living and quality of life than a $5,000 income increase from $30,000 to $35,000. At the poorer level, the $5,000 increase has an essential impact on nutrition, health and housing quality. In some countries, education would be enabled, e.g. paying transport to school or school fees, and buying school uniforms and school books. And children would no longer form the necessary workforce at home and in the fields. At the richer level, income increase means something like a bigger house, more trips to more distant countries and the yearly update of smart phones. The increase at the lower

---

[5] Gerschenkron (1962), Cohen & Levinthal (1990).

level has much more impact on living quality. Therefore, we usually use the *logarithm* of wealth indicators (natural logarithm of GDP/c, GNI/c) in statistical analyses.[6] Numerically, this transformation reduces the increases at the upper levels. It transforms nonlinear, exponential increases in 'currency units' to linear increases in more realistic 'living quality units'. However, GDP-logs do not give understandable units. For communication of the meaning of certain income levels, straightforward numbers are more useful.

GDP per capita in raw numbers or logged is by far the most used indicator of production, productivity, income and wealth. Its economic meaning changes somewhat with its use: as a *dependent* variable, GDP/c stands for productivity and production – how much are people capable of producing? As an independent variable, GDP/c stands for wealth effects – what are the effects of prosperity on peoples' destiny, e.g. on democracy or human capital development? In its narrow sense in economics, GDP/c is merely a production indicator. However, this production leads to income being indicative of wealth. When we speak henceforth of production, income or in a broader sense of wealth, GDP per capita is the chosen indicator. If we more precisely compare production and income, GDP/c stands for production and GNI/c for income. And if we compare annually produced income with given wealth, GDP/c stands for the yearly income and wealth for existing assets.

## 1.2    Some Country Examples

Results from different historical epochs and different regions today show large wealth differences expressed in comparable monetary units. However, any categorisation, by centuries, by developed vs. emerging and developing countries, by regions according to geographical or cultural criteria and even by nations is somewhat arbitrary. Historical developments are continuous. There is large heterogeneity within continents, cultures and nations. Nevertheless, such rough categories provide the basis for all perceptions and, carefully used, they help to understand differences and developments.

Let us look first at different epochs and continents (see Table 1.1).

Around the year zero the majority of people lived from hunting and gathering, animal husbandry and/or subsistence farming. Their income was defined by Maddison (2007, 2008) as '$400 in 1990 international $'. Only a few regions, such as Rome and the Mediterranean coastal regions (today single countries), other ancient advanced civilisations and regions influenced by the advanced, achieved higher production, income and wealth shown in their equivalent current country divisions: Italy $809, Greece $550, Egypt $600,

---

[6] Natural logarithm is the logarithm to the base *e* (Euler's number, 2.71828 . . .).

Table 1.1 *Income differences across time and continents (annual per capita GDP and GNI in comparable units)*

| | GDP 0001 Maddison | GDP 1500 Maddison | GDP 1820 Maddison | GDP 1913 Maddison | GDP 2010 Maddison | GDP 2010 Penn | GNI 2010 HDR |
|---|---|---|---|---|---|---|---|
| **Africa (total/North)** | 472 | 414 | 420 | 637 | 1,934 | 3,468 | 3,873 |
| Kenya | – | – | – | – | 1,141 | 1,246 | 1,628 |
| **America (North)** | 400 | 400 | 1,081 | 4,874 | 27,716 | 39,243 | 42,881 |
| USA | 400 | 400 | 1,257 | 5,301 | 30,491 | 41,376 | 47,094 |
| **America (Centr-S)** | 400 | 416 | 691 | 1,494 | 7,324 | 11,848 | 10,109 |
| Brazil | 400 | 400 | 646 | 811 | 6,879 | 8,325 | 10,607 |
| **Asia** | 456 | 568 | 581 | 695 | 9,316 | 14,963 | 13,567 |
| India | 450 | 550 | 533 | 673 | 3,372 | 3,477 | 3,337 |
| **Australia-NZ** | 400 | 400 | 459 | 5,155 | 22,235 | 34,448 | 32,065 |
| New Zealand | (400) | 400 | 400 | 5,152 | 18,886 | 27,788 | 25,438 |
| **Europe** | 457 | 669 | 1,064 | 2,598 | 14,753 | 23,202 | 25,197 |
| Germany | 408 | 688 | 1,077 | 3,648 | 20,661 | 34,085 | 35,308 |

*Notes:* GDPs per capita per year from Maddison in 1990 international $ (Maddison, 2008; 2010 from Bolt & van Zanden, 2013). For non-Western countries only a small amount of data are available, e.g. for Africa 1820 no single country, 1913 only four countries, Egypt, Ghana, Morocco and South Africa, continental averages are based on estimations for larger country samples; GDP Penn 2010: in 2005 constant prices, ppp international dollar per capita, Laspeyres (Penn World Table V7.1, Heston, Summers & Aten, 2012); GNI 2010 HDR: in 2008 ppp, US dollar per capita, HDR: Human Development Report (UNDP, 2010, pp. 143–147); continental averages based on identical weighting of all countries (countries with larger populations do not have larger impact); Brazil 0001 estimated by taking the value from Mexico; New Zealand 0001 as Australia (NZ was first settled in the thirteenth century by Polynesians); Centr-S: Central-South.

Turkey $550, Iraq $500, Iran $500, India $450, China $450. The further away from those centres, the poorer were the people, e.g. Spain with $498, France with $473 or the Netherlands with $425. The comparatively high values in Table 1.1 for Africa and Asia are misleading, because they are based on selected regions (North African strips settled by Romans; China and India) for which data are provided by Maddison.

Around the year 1000 the situation was no different, except that formerly 'rich' regions in Europe had become poorer (see Maddison, 2007, 2008). However, by *1500* they had recovered. With $669 Europe is now the richest region in the world; within Europe, Italy again is the highest with $1,100 (within Italy the hot spots have moved up to the north) and then the future leading region, Western and Northern Europe (Belgium $875, here Flanders as hot spot, Netherlands $761, France $727 and Britain $714). Nevertheless, the average annual economic growth in Europe between 0 and 1500 reached only 0.025 per cent! China and India also improved with $600 and $550, respectively, and Japan achieved $500 (up from around $400), but these countries developed noticeably less.

In *1820* the pattern was more pronounced. Within Europe, the hot spots moved to the north west (Netherlands $1,838, Great Britain $1,706, Belgium [Flanders] $1,319, Denmark $1,274). This becomes obvious when changing the rather rough continental perspective to a more precise regional-cultural perspective (Table 1.2). North American income resembles that of its Northern and Western European ancestral roots (United States $1,257). China and India have not improved ($600 and $533), and Japan only slightly ($669).

This was the situation before the peak of the industrial revolution in the nineteenth century. By *1913* the gap between 'developed' and 'not developed' regions became much wider: within Europe there were large differences between Western, Northern and Central Europe on the one hand (see Table 1.2, these three regions simply averaged $3,455) and Eastern Europe ($1,783) or Southern Europe ($1,555) on the other hand. The regions settled by the British (North America, Trans-Tasman, averaged: $5,015) resemble Western, Northern and Central Europe, especially Great Britain ($4,921). Latin America ($1,494) is close to Southern Europe ($1,555) and the two mother countries Spain and Portugal ($2,056 and $1,250). Asia and Africa developed too ($695 and $637), especially Japan ($1,387). However, China and India even deteriorated or only weakly improved ($552 and $673). Their 1913 position was in sharp contrast to their past economic and cultural achievements.

This pattern seems to be repeated at a much higher level in the year 2010 (see also Figures 1.1 and 1.2): Western, Northern and Central Europe (all results simply averaged at the level of regions, GDP 2010 Penn: $39,900, GNI

Table 1.2 *Income differences across time and regions (annual per capita GDP and GNI in comparable units)*

| | GDP 0001 Maddison | GDP 1500 Maddison | GDP 1820 Maddison | GDP 1913 Maddison | GDP 2010 Maddison | GDP 2010 Penn | GNI 2010 HDR |
|---|---|---|---|---|---|---|---|
| **Africa (sub-Sahara)** | 418 | 414 | 420 | 637 | 1,436 | 2,989 | 3,352 |
| Kenya | – | – | – | – | 1,141 | 1,246 | 1,628 |
| **N-Africa M-East (ArM)** | 522 | 590 | 607 | 1,042 | 7,945 | 19,885 | 19,655 |
| Egypt | 600 | 475 | 475 | 902 | 4,267 | 4,853 | 5,889 |
| **America (North, Engl)** | 400 | 400 | 1,081 | 4,874 | 27,716 | 39,243 | 42,881 |
| USA | 400 | 400 | 1,257 | 5,301 | 30,491 | 41,376 | 47,094 |
| **America (Latin, C-S)** | 400 | 416 | 691 | 1,494 | 7,324 | 11,848 | 10,109 |
| Mexico | 400 | 425 | 759 | 1,732 | 7,716 | 11,940 | 13,971 |
| **Asia (Central-South)** | 450 | 500 | 469 | 783 | 4,254 | 4,296 | 3,743 |
| India | 450 | 550 | 533 | 673 | 3,372 | 3,477 | 3,337 |
| **East Asia** | 425 | 525 | 644 | 1,016 | 27,847 | 27,847 | 24,035 |
| China | 450 | 600 | 600 | 552 | 8,032 | 7,746 | 7,258 |
| **Southeast Asia, Pacific** | 420 | 565 | 621 | 935 | 8,845 | 9,756 | 9,386 |
| Philippines | – | – | 584 | 988 | 3,024 | 3,194 | 4,002 |
| **Australia-NZ (English)** | 400 | 400 | 459 | 5,155 | 22,235 | 34,448 | 32,065 |
| New Zealand | (400) | 400 | 400 | 5,152 | 18,886 | 27,788 | 25,438 |
| **Western Europe** | 599 | 797 | 1,234 | 3,687 | 23,025 | 34,843 | 35,607 |
| United Kingdom | 400 | 714 | 1,706 | 4,921 | 23,777 | 34,267 | 35,087 |
| **Scandinavia** | 400 | 613 | 919 | 2,886 | 25,024 | 37,796 | 37,788 |
| Norway | 400 | 610 | 801 | 2,447 | 27,987 | 50,491 | 58,810 |

Table 1.2 (cont.)

| | GDP 0001 Maddison | GDP 1500 Maddison | GDP 1820 Maddison | GDP 1913 Maddison | GDP 2010 Maddison | GDP 2010 Penn | GNI 2010 HDR |
|---|---|---|---|---|---|---|---|
| **Central Europe** | 419 | 676 | 1,128 | 3,793 | 23,263 | 47,062 | 48,867 |
| Germany | 408 | 688 | 1,077 | 3,648 | 20,661 | 34,085 | 35,308 |
| **Eastern Europe** | 400 | 499 | 769 | 1,783 | 10,290 | 13,906 | 14,698 |
| Russia | 400 | 499 | 688 | 1,488 | 8,660 | 15,062 | 15,258 |
| **Southern Europe** | 577 | 700 | 922 | 1,555 | 11,146 | 16,923 | 20,565 |
| Italy | 809 | 1,100 | 1,117 | 2,564 | 18,520 | 28,381 | 29,619 |

*Notes*: Wealth indicators, see Table 1.1; regions due to culture and evolutionary background of people; within regions retaining heterogeneity such as Israel in the Middle East or 1913 South Africa in sub-Saharan Africa; N-Africa M-East: North Africa, Middle East; ArM = Arab-Muslim; North, Engl: North, English; C-S: Central-South; identical weighting of all countries; for Maddison, if not given, regional data calculations based on single country reports and averaging (East Asia: China, Japan, Korea, Taiwan, Hong Kong, Singapore; Maddison, Singapore 1820 obvious error '83' corrected as '830'); Penn, Romania missing year numbers assigned; minor deviations between Maddison's and my country-region-classifications and averages (e.g. considering the size of populations).

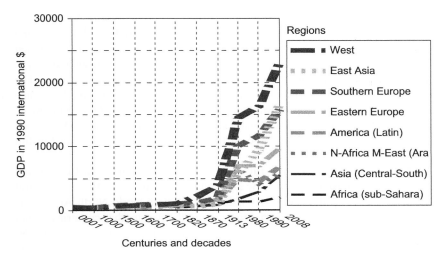

Figure 1.1 Income (annual GDP/c) development in different regions from
0001 to 2008 (data from Maddison, 2008)
We finished the depiction with the year 2008, because the Maddison project published
data for fewer countries for 2010 than for 2008 ($N_{2008}$ = 159 vs. $N_{2010}$ = 117).
Southeast Europe is included in Eastern Europe.

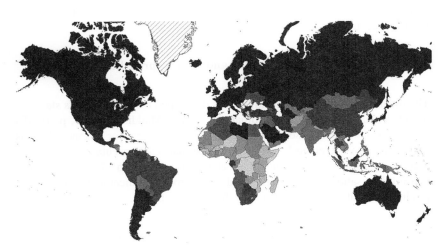

Figure 1.2 Wealth around the world (annual GDP 2010, Penn V7.1, per capita
ppp, $N$ = 188 countries), darker means higher, shading accentuates
differences at the poorer levels (similar to using logarithm)

2010 HDR: $40,754) and the former British colonies, North America and Trans-Tasman (GDP 2010 Penn: $36,846, GNI 2010 HDR: $37,473) are the richest regions. But East Asia was catching up: first Japan and Korea, and then smaller Chinese-populated offshoots, Hong Kong, Macau, Taiwan and Singapore, then later China and to a lesser extent countries in Southeast Asia. The largest gap between West and East occurred around 1980 and has since decreased (see Figure 1.1). And there are very rich Arabian Gulf economies, based on mineral resources (oil and gas), with smaller populations. As a result of such mineral resources, large differences exist among Arabian-Muslim countries.

Within Europe, there are still gaps between Western-North-Central and Southern and Eastern Europe. Scandinavia caught up with Western-Central Europe in the twentieth century. Within the Western world North America is leading. The gap between Latin America and the two mother countries, Spain and Portugal, compared to 1913 is now clearly larger (Latin America GNI 2010: $10,109; Spain and Portugal: $29,661 and $22,105). However, since the 1990s the gaps have been narrowing.

All regions in the world improved in terms of income and wealth during the twentieth century, as did those Arabian-Muslim countries without mineral resources, South and Central Asia and sub-Saharan Africa. For sub-Saharan Africa, average GDP in 2010 was *five times* that of 1913. In Maddison's 2008 statistics (in 1990 international $, 2008: $2,272, in his own Africa average $1,780) it is three to four times. And as will be shown below, these monetary income units underrate real wealth and living standard increases as indicated by life expectancy.

## 1.3      Problems of Current GDP and GNI Approaches – and Possible Solutions

The older the Maddison data and the less developed a country and its statistics the more shaky are the GDP estimations. Angus Maddison (2001, p. 191ff.) always explicitly expressed this; he wrote in his reports, for instance: 'It was assumed', 'proxy element', 'the available estimates are speculative', 'assumed that African per capita income did not change from 1500 to 1700'. Frequently, mere urbanisation ratios were used as a rough indicator for economic production. But even for newer data there are problems.

### 1.3.1      Differences between Various Sources of the Same Indicator

We have presented only one result for each measure (GDP or GNI, both annually and per capita) and historical era. However, there are different data pools, for example, the already introduced Maddison and the Penn statistical collection or the ones from the IMF, CIA, World Bank, HDR and OECD.[7] Their values differ.

One example is GDP per capita ppp in the year 2000 from Maddison (2008) and Penn (Penn V7.1; Heston et al., 2012). Maddison presents only one set of statistics, Penn various; we took the first.[8] Both Penn and Maddison are given for the year 2000; however, they differ in one aspect: Maddison uses 1990 dollars, Penn 2005 dollars. Due to inflation, Penn's numbers should always be somewhat higher than Maddison's – but they are not.

Across 156 common countries the difference goes in the expected direction; GDPs are $3,744 higher in the Penn estimates (see Table 1.3). Across all regions Penn estimates are higher. This cannot distort a standardised correlation (mean differences are irrelevant for correlations). The correlation for 156 countries between Maddison's and Penn's GDPs is $r = .87$.[9] It is high, but for an identical characteristic it is astonishingly low – we expected something like $r > .95$.

The richer (the more productive) a country, the larger are the differences: $GDP_{Maddison}$ correlates with the difference at $r = .54$, $GDP_{Penn}$ with the difference $r = .89$. That means, the higher the GDP of a country, the more Maddison underestimates and the more Penn overestimates the GDP. Across

---

[7] *Penn*: The Penn World Tables contain different econometric data. Initially, they were calculated by the Center for International Comparisons of Production, Income and Prices at the University of Pennsylvania (Philadelphia, USA). Today, further research groups are involved. *IMF*: International Monetary Fund, organisation for the support of the international payment system. The IMF also researches and presents economic statistics (World Economic Outlook Database). *CIA*: Central Intelligence Agency, US secret service. The CIA publishes country reports including econometric data (The World Factbook). *World Bank*: The World Bank supports countries by providing loans and consultations. It has a larger research unit presenting econometric data. *HDR*: The Human Development Report is a yearly published report by the United Nations Development Programme (UNDP) describing the developmental status of nations. They publish economic statistics based on IMF and World Bank data. *OECD*: The Organisation for Economic Co-operation and Development supports trade and development. It has a research department that publishes economic statistics.

[8] *Maddison*: ppp converted GDP per capita, 1990 International Geary-Khamis dollars). Roy C. Geary (1896–1983) was an Irish economist working in Ireland, the UK and the US. Salem Hanna Khamis (1919–2005) was a Palestinian-Christian economist working for the UN and FAO. 'Geary-Khamis dollars' (one international dollar = 1 US dollar) stands for a method of comparing the purchasing power of different currencies.

*Penn*: ppp converted GDP per capita (Laspeyres), derived from growth rates of c, g, i, at 2005 constant prices, unit: 2005 International dollar per person (2005 I$/per person) (rgdpl). Ernst Laspeyres was a German-Huguenot economist (1834–1913). 'Laspeyres' stands for a method of calculating prices and their development of a selected and fixed class of goods and services. It is used to compare the purchasing power of different currencies.

Price indices and their contents (basket of consumer goods) vary – different people (across wealth levels, countries, time) buy different goods at different prices. Quality differences of statistically identical goods (e.g. a car) are difficult to estimate.

[9] For the 2010 measures (Maddison 2010 is developed by Bolt & van Zanden, 2013) the correlation between GDP Maddison and Penn is even smaller: only $r = .72$ ($N = 116$).

Table 1.3 *Differences in GDP ppp per capita 2000 between Maddison and Penn*

| | GDP 2000 Maddison | Difference (Penn-Madd) | GDP 2000 Penn |
|---|---|---|---|
| **Regions** | | | |
| **Africa (sub-Sahara)** | 1,669 | 698 | 2,334 |
| **N-Africa M-East (Arab-Muslim)** | 5,635 | 8,787 | 14,445 |
| **America (North, English)** | 25,478 | 11,127 | 36,604 |
| **America (Latin, Central-South)** | 5,406 | 2,098 | 9,806 |
| **Asia (Central-South)** | 2,136 | 203 | 2,454 |
| **East Asia** | 11,569 | 4,189 | 18,201 |
| **Southeast Asia, Pacific** | 5,861 | 1,804 | 8,218 |
| **Australia-New-Zealand (English)** | 18,989 | 10,013 | 29,001 |
| **Western Europe** | 21,028 | 11,142 | 32,171 |
| **Scandinavia** | 22,139 | 12,195 | 35,003 |
| **Central Europe** | 20,703 | 12,764 | 41,383 |
| **Eastern Europe** | 6,734 | 2,418 | 9,153 |
| **Southern Europe** | 9,418 | 5,828 | 14,887 |
| **Average in 156 common countries** | 6,406 | 3,744 | 10,150 |
| **Countries with large positive or negative differences** | | | |
| Qatar | 9,844 | 52,703 | 62,547 |
| Norway | 25,102 | 20,203 | 45,305 |
| USA | 28,467 | 11,177 | 39,644 |
| China | 3,421 | −247 | 3,174 |
| Estonia | 11,710 | −719 | 10,991 |
| Syria | 7,368 | −3,985 | 3,383 |

*Notes*: GDP 2000 Maddison expressed in 1990 dollars, GDP 2000 Penn expressed in 2005 dollars. Difference = $GDP_{Penn} - GDP_{Maddison}$. Differences are only calculated for countries having information in both statistics. Thus calculated differences are not identical to the differences of means of regions. The difference measure based on complete pairs is more reliable.

all regions Penn GDP estimates are higher; however, for Europe and the West they are the highest. This is another reason why logarithmised data should be used for statistical analyses. Taking the logarithm reduces differences at higher levels. Penn also includes smaller countries such as Antigua-Barbuda, Bhutan, Brunei, Iceland, Luxembourg and Cyprus, Maddison does not. Maddison also includes North Korea, but Penn does not. This biases comparisons at the level of regions, but not the calculated differences based on pairs of countries.

The largest overestimation by Penn compared to Maddison can be found in oil-producing countries (Qatar, other Gulf countries and Norway); the largest overestimation by Maddison compared to Penn can be found in former socialist countries (e.g. Syria, Estonia and China).

Why are there these differences? What are the 'true', or at least better, estimates? Are there some simple 'spreadsheet errors' as sometimes detected in economics?[10] We found only a few (see notes for Table 1.2). However, why were they not detected before? Many researchers arrange these tables and even more use them. Maybe there are more undetected errors. But they cannot be the main reason for differences.

Per capita estimates are calculated based on two variables, on *GDP* divided by *population size*. Thus, if population size is differently gathered, even identical GDP estimates would lead to different per capita results. Usually, researchers do not collect data by themselves, they do not travel to countries and measure annually produced wealth and count people. They receive their data from national statistics or other researchers; only occasionally do they make their own estimations. Typically, econometric teams work on these issues; the numbers are a product of collaborative work. By such an approach, individual errors should be minimised. Sometimes identical years are hidden behind different years; due to missing data, the information from the preceding year is taken for one country (e.g. the GNI 2010 measure for Malta; UNDP, 2010). Alternatively, missing values are estimated by taking values from neighbouring countries (e.g. the GNI 2010 measure for Andorra by Spain or for Liechtenstein by Switzerland; UNDP, 2010).

Finally, the correlation with cognitive human capital varies, depending on used data: the cognitive ability average (see Chapter 2 and appendix Table A.2) correlates with Maddison's 2000 GDP at $r = .74$, but with Penn's 2000 GDP at $r = .61$ (corrected IQs[11], identical country sample $N = 156$). The difference between $r = .74$ vs. .61 is *not* negligible.

Due to these differences between measures of identical constructs and the lack of information on crucial quality differences between them (we do not know which source represents a 'truer' value) statistical analyses should apply robustness checks: are the theories also backed up when different data are used? If yes, a theory receives additional support.

### 1.3.2    *Hardly Believable Large or Small Values*

In a similar way to strange gaps between different sources of the same indicator there are barely believable large or small values for certain countries. Luxembourg has GDP/c Penn 2010 of $75,590 – are people in Luxembourg really so rich? Is Cuba ($11,509) richer than Bulgaria ($10,589), Venezuela

---

[10] E.g. the case discussed in the media, 'Growth in a time of debt' by Carmen Reinhart and Kenneth Rogoff. A general overview of spreadsheet errors in economics is given by Panko (1998).

[11] IQ: intelligence quotient, a measure of intelligence and cognitive ability, see Chapter 3.1.

($9,071), Brazil ($8,325) and Montenegro ($7,315)? Once these countries are visited, somebody will call into question these numbers.

### 1.3.3    Differences between GDP and GNI: Rich Countries Transfer Income and Poor Receive

GDP and GNI are not the same; the first stands for produced income, the other for received income, however, mainly by production. On average, GNI/c (2010, HDR) is only $13 higher than GDP/c (2010, Penn; across 180 common countries). GDP and GNI can differ for single countries due to transfers, but not in a worldwide average. The negligible difference of $13 supports this claim. Additionally, both measures are highly correlated ($r = .95$, $N = 180$), much higher than the different indicators of the single concept GDP mentioned above (Maddison and Penn 2000).

Furthermore, there are *systematic* and plausible differences between GDP/c and GNI/c according to the level of wealth: the richer (more productive) a country, the more negative is the difference (Difference = $GNI_{HDR} - GDP_{Penn}$; $GDP_{Penn}$ and difference $r = .53$, $GNI_{HDR}$ and difference $r = -.22$). That means that richer countries produce more goods than they consume as income. They transfer money to poorer countries that produce less and receive more. This is also true for within-Europe comparisons; e.g. Southern and Eastern Europe have positive differences (they earn more than they produce, $2,052 and $793, respectively), compared to Northern, Western and Central Europe with $-$1,510. Foreign workers transfer income home to their relatives; countries give development aid or pay more to supranational organisations (European Union, World Bank, IMF), which redistribute means.

But that is not true for all regions. Some oil-producing countries have higher GNI than GDP (Kuwait: +$55,719 vs. +$41,244, similarly Norway, Equatorial Guinea and Saudi Arabia). However, among the biggest spenders there are also oil-producing countries in which GDP is higher than GNI (GDP > GNI: Qatar: $-$56,885 and Emirates $-$2,126). Paradoxically, Latin America is among the spenders ($-$344) and the United States is among the receivers (+$5,718). The US dollar is used as a reserve currency: middle and upper class people from Latin America and funds managing money from those countries, in particular, use the US dollar as a safe harbour against inflation, devaluation and political interference. Additionally, important US companies avoid taxes by officially settling offshore (e.g. Amazon-Europe in Luxembourg and Apple and Google-Europe in Ireland). GDP measures become biased (Ireland and Luxembourg both have higher GDP than GNI: $-$1,824 and $-$24,481, respectively).

Except for outliers, GDP/c should be a better indicator for the effects of cognitive human capital than GNI/c: GDP does not include transfers; therefore it should be more sensitive towards cognitive effects. But that is not the case: cognitive ability correlates higher with GNI ($r = .62$) than with GDP ($r = .53$, corrected IQs, $N = 158$ same countries). The differences are not correlated with IQs ($r = .01$). One reason could be that past GNI has a stronger effect on cognitive ability than past GDP; in other words, wealth reaching people and influencing their life is more important for cognitive development than produced wealth.

Another, maybe even more important reason is that being able to convince other nations, their political classes supported by media and advocacy groups, to spend money for the own country is also an indicator of smartness. For instance, Cyprus, in spite of having one of the wealthiest peoples in Europe (ECB, 2013, p. 76), receives large guarantees and credits (in the long run transfers) from the European Union (indirectly, for example, by Germany and Finland, with, according to the statistics, poorer people; see next paragraph). Or Israel's military budget is largely supported by the United States (with, at the present, about $118 billion dollars) and Germany (providing free weapons or direct or indirect grants for military purposes; Sharp, 2013; Steinmetz, 2002).

Taking the 'receivers' internationally (GNI/c > GDP/c), IQs and gains (GNI$_{HDR}$ − GDP$_{Penn}$, both per capita) are positively correlated ($r = .23$, $N = 126$). The smartness-hypothesis is backed up. Thus a positive difference between GNI/c and GDP/c, stemming from transfers from nationals working abroad, from multinational companies or politically or ethically justified aid seems to also be an indicator of clever people. This is one more reason to use both indicators.

### 1.3.4    Comparison with ECB and Credit Suisse Indicators of Wealth (Wealth in the Narrow Sense)

In early summer 2013, the European Central Bank surprised the public by presenting data on average private household wealth for countries in the European Union (ECB, 2013, p. 76, median net wealth in Euro): measured by household assets (real estate, vehicles, deposits, funds, bonds, etc.), income and indicators of consumption minus liabilities (residence mortgages, credit cards, etc.) the average Cypriot (€266,900), Spaniard (€182,700), Italian (€173,500) and Greek (€101,900) private households were much wealthier than the average German (€51,400) and Finnish (€85,800).

If we compare per capita GDP Penn and GNI HDR with the ECB-wealth measure (all 2010 or 2009), the correlations are very weak: $r = .56$ and $r = .34$.[12] Annual production-income (GDP) and income (GNI) are not identical

---

[12] $N = 15$ countries, ECB medians being used; if ECB means are used, the correlations are even lower: $r = .49$ vs. $r = .31$.

with existing wealth. Additionally, the ECB has calculated the wealth per household, but household size varies across countries. An alternative measure of wealth was presented by Credit Suisse (2013a, b). Its unit of analysis is individuals – individuals and not families or households are the owners of assets. Adults (20 years old and older) are taken as individuals since children usually have little wealth. Per capita results were additionally presented.

Credit Suisse (CS) defined wealth as the marketable value of financial assets plus non-financial assets (principally housing and land) less debts. The measurement is based on household balance sheet data or household survey data; estimates were made for countries without data. Information on wealth distribution was taken into account, and the data were rated according to data quality. International comparisons are based on official exchange rates and not on ppp converted units. The argument used by Credit Suisse is that the cross-country trade of assets is also based on exchange rates. Results for 2000 and 2010 are presented in Table 1.4.[13]

The ECB results for 2010 only correlate at $r = .44$ (median) or $r = .43$ with the Credit Suisse measures (mean, always fifteen European countries). Because ECB lists per household and Credit Suisse per adult, and household sizes vary across countries, the comparison across different units is not accurate. Therefore, Credit Suisse (2013b, table 1, p. 17) has converted, for comparison, the ECB household results to per adult values. For the same units the correlation is only somewhat higher ($r = .54$).

Comparing both ECB and CS with GDP/c (Penn for 2010) reveals that for the same fifteen European countries there is a considerably higher correlation between GDP and the Credit Suisse measure of wealth (ECB: $r = .56$ or .49 for median and mean, Credit Suisse: $r = .73$ or .73 for per adult or per capita). Also, in a larger cross-country comparison there is no difference between Credit Suisse per adult or per capita measures ($N = 172$, $r = .72$ and .72). The magnitude of the correlation remains remarkably stable across different country samples and units. If instead of production an income measure is chosen (GNI 2010 HDR), the ECB-CS pattern is accentuated (ECB around $r = .32$, Credit Suisse around $r = .81$).

A correlation of $r = .54$ for two measures of the same theoretical construct – wealth per adult – is much too low. Behind these different measures stand monetary institutions with large research staff. Following the higher correlations with GDP and the assumption that economic production leads to wealth, the Credit Suisse measure seems to be more valid. However, a scientifically convincing judgement should be based on a theoretical analysis of concepts

---

[13]  This procedure is questionable: instead of measuring national levels of upper classes' (minority) wealth accurately by using exchange rates, it is more important to cover the average wealth of ordinary (majority) people by using the purchasing power parity transformation (ppp).

Table 1.4 *Wealth means and differences across regions (assets from Credit Suisse per adult in 2013 US dollar)*

|  |  | Wealth 2000 |  | Wealth 2010 |  |
|---|---|---|---|---|---|
| **Africa** (sub-Sahara) |  | 2,709 |  | 5,867 |  |
|  | Kenya |  | 1,029 |  | 1,700 |
| **N-Africa M-East** (ArabM) |  | 20,022 |  | 35,579 |  |
|  | Egypt |  | 7,097 |  | 10,353 |
| **America** (North, English) |  | 150,432 |  | 242,521 |  |
|  | USA |  | 192,399 |  | 247,247 |
| **America** (Latin, C-South) |  | 10,085 |  | 16,103 |  |
|  | Mexico |  | 17,484 |  | 34,338 |
| **Asia** (Central-South) |  | 2,110 |  | 5,907 |  |
|  | India |  | 2,036 |  | 5,304 |
| **East Asia** |  | 76,293 |  | 103,998 |  |
|  | China |  | 5,672 |  | 18,182 |
| **Southeast Asia, Pacific** |  | 12,350 |  | 26,367 |  |
|  | Philippines |  | 2,744 |  | 5,906 |
| **Australia-NZ** (English) |  | 75,450 |  | 241,452 |  |
|  | New Zealand |  | 47,748 |  | 146,096 |
| **Western Europe** |  | 122,530 |  | 232,254 |  |
|  | United Kingdom |  | 162,999 |  | 250,633 |
| **Scandinavia** |  | 131,058 |  | 229,646 |  |
|  | Norway |  | 110,805 |  | 319,143 |
| **Central Europe** |  | 149,467 |  | 275,243 |  |
|  | Germany |  | 89,770 |  | 184,060 |
| **Eastern Europe** |  | 7,261 |  | 22,480 |  |
|  | Russia |  | 1,711 |  | 13,477 |
| **Southern Europe** |  | 41,205 |  | 76,510 |  |
|  | Italy |  | 119,773 |  | 243,407 |

*Notes*: Data from Credit Suisse databook (2013a, their tables 2-1 and 2-4, pp. 22–25, 74–77, per adult in US Dollar).

and measures. Apart from the unit of analysis, both concepts are comparable; the problems have to be in their measurement. But even the Credit Suisse Research Institute relies in its argumentation on plausibility arguments:

It seems implausible that non-financial assets in Cyprus are worth three times as much as in Germany or the Netherlands, or that Cyprus has double the financial assets of Italy ... This does not square with everyday experience. (2013b, p. 18)

As a result, it should be recorded that different data resources for wealth do not necessarily come to converging results. Credit Suisse data seem to be more valid measures for economic wealth. For measuring economic wealth it is recommendable to use three statistical indicators: annual GDP and GNI per capita and wealth per adult.

### 1.3.5    Differences between Statistical Indicators and Observations: Cuba and the United States as Examples

At a closer look and considering "everyday experience" as mentioned by Credit Suisse, some country estimates seem to be rather strange.[14] Many countries could be mentioned, but let us focus on two: Cuba and the United States.

According to Penn 2010, Cuba ($11,509) is richer than Bulgaria ($10,589), Venezuela ($9,071), Brazil ($8,325) and Montenegro ($7,315). GNI data cannot be included, because HDR does not report this value for Cuba (UNDP, 2010, p. 138). Having visited all mentioned countries (altogether around 45 weeks), I get the impression that Cubans are considerably poorer than Bulgarians, Venezuelans, Brazilians and Montenegrins. For example, in Santiago de Cuba it was observable that car owners painted their car with wall paint. They had no gloss paint. Cars were usually in terrible condition, e.g. after 30 minutes driving a 5-minute repair was necessary (in Santiago and Havana). The Sierra Maestra villages usually had no electricity. In cities, electricity power failures were rather the rule than the exception. In the Sierra de Purial, men were riding oxen as a daily means of transport – in Europe, they were replaced by horses in the Middle Ages. People in the Sierra Maestra had no intact socks and shoes. In the big cities, ordinary people had problems getting milk, butter and meat, especially beef. Fruits, vegetables and meat were usually of low quality: oranges were sour and stringy, garlic was very small and peel-loaded, meat contained bone splinters, due to the work of amateur butchers, and often as tough as old boots. In the other countries, all these mentioned indicators of low production and poverty were not possible to observe – except for some ethnic-social minorities and groups (Indígenas/Indians, Roma/gypsies, impoverished in the streets). The one economically positive thing that could be said for Cuba was that extreme misery, as observable in the 1980s in Brazil, e.g. families living in the streets, was not seen. Other sources, such as data from Maddison or HDR 2013, report considerably lower values for Cuba than for the mentioned comparison countries.

Assuming that the Penn 2010 GDP for Cuba is a kind of single outlier, the statistical results for the United States are consistently high across years, measures and sources (Penn 2010 GDP: $41,376, HDR 2010 GNI, $47,094, Maddison 2008 GDP 31,178, Maddison 1950 GDP $9,561). The values are higher than for Switzerland, Netherlands or Denmark (Penn 2010 GDP: $39,986, $38,190, $33,717, HDR 2010 GNI: $39,849, $40,658, $36,404). According to these numbers, Americans' standard of living must be really

---

[14] We should be careful basing an opinion on information only received from media. They frequently show what the *zeitgeist* in their home countries expects to see.

high. However, on visiting this country (2006–2017) a traveller does not always get this impression. E.g. if somebody enters the United States via Philadelphia airport, the new arrival is met by one to two hour queues. Public services seem to be underdeveloped. At other airports the situation is similar. Admittedly, this single public service indicator is not a really informative gauge of wealth. However, for the traveller wishing to take a connecting flight through Philadelphia, based on observations from 2010, only old, somewhat ruined armchairs with torn imitation leather and sunken cushions were available to sit on. Very loud alarms sounded repeatedly but nobody cared. If flights were cancelled, travellers had to organise their trip for themselves (e.g. no transport to hotel, no payment for transport or hotel). Again, it can be objected that this is only one airport, which is also a public building, and that private wealth is not covered. However, if you enter Singapore, travellers get a totally different impression at the airport. In other US airports it is possible to see joking employees having nothing to do (Washington, baggage reception, 2010). There is no hint of very productive human capital. Atlanta city centre (this is Atlanta, which has Coca-Cola and CNN, and hosted the Olympic games in 1996, rather than an outlier such as Detroit), with its many poor people and beggars, looks more like a third-world city (2008). During a hotel stay there was a fire in the kitchen. For the fire to be extinguished by the fire brigade, all guests needed to leave the hotel. Private houses, including in the Northeast, owned by middle-class and rich people, have thin walls. Usually, windows in hotels and private houses have only one pane. Devastating effects of tornadoes on buildings (flimsy housing without cellars in regions with tornadoes, even in so-called tornado alley) back up such observations.

Are these only non-representative observations on isolated phenomena? Are they contradicted by indicators of large production, income and wealth as shown by the successful software and aircraft industries, huge cars and high house ownership rates? Objectively measured indicators of peoples' standard of living, height and life expectancy (see Chapter 2) back a more sceptical view: on average, the Dutch, Swedes and Danes are taller than the Americans; Americans also have shorter lives than Dutch, Danes or Swiss (and many other Europeans; Komlos & Baur, 2004).[15]

Inferring from these data and observations there seems to be a gap between *average per capita wealth as calculated by dividing countries' annual GDP and GNI by population* and that seen in *everyday life.*

---

[15] Using height data from Wikipedia (Retrieved 11 September 2013 http://en.wikipedia.org/wiki/Human_height), Swiss men and women are also taller than US men and women.

### 1.3.6    Validity Issues and What We Want to Know?

Different sources for the same indicators (e.g. Maddison-GDP vs. Penn-GDP), different measures (produced GDP vs. earned GNI), different concepts (annually produced or given per capita country estimates) and different approaches to assessing wealth (numerical-currency country estimates vs. observations vs. corporeal indicators) come to diverging results.

We must always keep in mind that in addition to statistical problems leading to different results from different organisations for the same countries, there are important conceptual problems:

1. GDP/c only adequately covers the production *tradeable and transacted at markets* and *official* income. Many things are difficult to include in this measure: free public service (usually police, defence, education, health), living in one's own house, the informal economy, subsistence and home production, services produced for oneself, bartering and black markets. Therefore, using GDP and then deriving GNI leads to overestimations of wealth differences between first and third world countries. An alternative indicator such as average height of people could be an answer (Komlos & Snowdon, 2005).

2. Everything that results in production and income is covered by GDP; this even accounts for *recovery costs* following man-made accidents, environmental pollution or natural disasters. In common statistics a hurricane or climate change would stimulate production and therefore economic growth leading to 'increasing wealth'. Household-based or individual wealth indicators are necessary. Using GNI is a first step in this direction.

3. The *quality of service* is hardly covered, e.g. accessibility, waiting periods, guarantees, counselling, corruption and administrative efficiency. Two different haircuts are not the same, but are difficult to rate qualitatively against each other.

4. *Negative external effects* such as pollution and accidents are not adequately covered. Again, household-based or individual wealth indicators are necessary. Corporeal indicators such as height and life expectancy are also useful.

5. *Within-country heterogeneity* is not covered by statistical means. For example, a few very rich people can bias wealth estimates. Medians (the 50 per cent rank) are not influenced by the values of outliers. They are alternative statistics. *Gini* coefficients describe income and wealth differences. A measure such as height is also less influenced by the presence of a few rich people in a country.

6. Finally, *quality of living* does not only comprise goods, products and assets and their increase or decrease but also other aspects of life such as health and life satisfaction (Stiglitz, Sen & Fitoussi, 2010). Alternative complementary indicators such as the Human Development Index (HDI) have been developed. These concepts of wellbeing of nations and individuals will be examined in the next chapter.

# 2    The Wellbeing of Nations

The wellbeing of nations comprises more than just economic wealth. It includes health, environmental, psychological, social, political and cultural attributes of societies. National development is given a normative frame – what is good and what is aimed at.

## 2.1    Health: Height and Life Expectancy

As shown in Chapter 1, economic indicators of societal wellbeing, like production-income (GDP), income (GNI) and assets (Credit Suisse measure), show statistical and theoretical problems. In general, they can be criticised as being one-sided and narrow concepts. If something is criticised, alternatives have to be presented. An important extension is the perspective of health, a biological standard of living. The two most promising indicators so far are height and life expectancy.

Komlos and Snowdon (2005) suggested *height*, the average height of humans measured from foot to head, as an indicator for the standard of living and wellbeing of a country. Height is not only a physical-biological feature but also an outcome measure of the quality of life. Height is an indicator of long-term quality nutrition in childhood (proteins, vitamins, minerals). GDP (production) as well as GNI (income) are only inputs into this quality. Mean height also is a sensible way of measuring wealth distribution, because wealth gains in the upper strata have almost no effect on average height, whereas wealth growth (or decline) in the lower strata does. Thus height indirectly covers what the Gini coefficient as an economic heterogeneity indicator directly measures. However, height is also a sensible measure of 'consumption ability', the societal competence to spend given money in a sensible way.

Wikipedia presents data for a larger set of countries.[1] Data are continuously updated by different anonymous contributors. The usual scientific quality control mechanisms by peer review and indirectly by university education

---

[1] en.wikipedia.org/wiki/Human_height and here 'average height around the world'. Data retrieved September 11, 2013, (21.30 CEST).

and university employment of authors and their reputation are not implemented. However, scientists may also anonymously contribute, most of the original data are based on scientific studies and contributions are frequently controlled by other contributors. Finally, height is a much less politically sensitive topic.

An estimate used more often internationally, with a corresponding better data base, is *life expectancy* (average length of life, age of death, life expectancy at birth). Usually, the life expectancy of people born in the reference year is inferred from the present typical length of life (precisely: inferred from age-specific death rates). Women usually live around five years longer than men. Whereas height is determined during youth, longevity is also strongly influenced by occurrences in later developmental stages through the whole lifespan. Thus it covers more broadly life quality.

Unlike GDP, GNI and assets, both biological indicators, height as well as life expectancy, have the advantage of being measurable on an *objective yardstick*, easily comparable across time and countries. Height and longevity can be used for very long historical comparisons by examining skeletons and obituary columns. And data for countries such as North Korea and Cuba are given.

However, older statistics and statistics from developing countries on dates of birth of ordinary people (the relevant population) are not always reliable. And child mortality rates heavily influence life expectancy calculated from birth onwards. Additionally, both depend not only on the quality of life, but are also influenced by genetic determinants. For example: Men are taller but not thereby richer, men live shorter but are not thereby poorer. Genetic factors could stand behind long-term historical changes or cross-country differences. They are observed for the Americas between 1500 and 1800 or for East Asians vs. East Africans. Finally, is more always better? Is there an optimum height or longevity? Being taller than around two metres entails some corporal disadvantages and living as a sick and demented elderly person is certainly not an indicator of life quality.[2]

Economic wealth indicators (per capita GDP, GNP and CS-assets) are correlated with height ($r = .53$, $.54$ and $.52$) and life expectancy ($r = .74$, $.75$ and $.63$), height and life expectancy are only weakly correlated ($r = .33$, all correlations in the same country sample of $N = 105$). Following the theoretical argument (longevity depends on wealth across lifespan, height on wealth in youth) and the empirical correlations, longevity seems to

---

[2] Alternative measures would be *disability-free life expectancy* (DFLE) or *health adjusted life expectancy* (HALE). However, we need data for countries, and, for longitudinal comparisons, data from further decades. Information on life expectancy is much more accessible and, of course, will be highly correlated with DFLE, HALE or life expectancy minus DALY.

be the better wealth indicator. Compared to height, long-term health and as its resultant life expectancy also rely more on careful behaviour, on one's own behaviour and the behaviour of others, which are positively influenced by cognitive ability (e.g. Gottfredson, 2004a; Whalley & Deary, 2001).

People in the First World (Europe, West) are not only more productive and richer, they are also taller and longer living (see Table 2.1). There are also stable north-south patterns within Europe and America. However, all these measures cannot be understood as pure wealth indicators; particularities are given such as small stature in Japan (1.623m) in spite of high GNI ($34,692 HDR 2010) and high life expectancy (82.67 years). Similar outliers are very small Guatemalans or tall Montenegrins; Costa Ricans live 'too' long relative to GNI, South Africans die 'too' early. For height, the influence of specific evolutionary-genetic factors is obvious. Nevertheless, we should not forget that both, height as well as life expectancy, are intended to be long-term, even cross-generational wealth measures. Unsurprisingly, due to relatively new mineral resources people in oil-rich countries (Qatar, Bahrain, UAE or Equatorial Guinea) are richer than they are tall or long living.

Life expectancy data are documented by the UN back to 1950 (see Table 2.1). Historical height data (nineteenth century and earlier) are only given for selected countries (e.g. Hatton, 2014); the same is true for life expectancy (e.g. Kenny, 2005). Single historical reports, e.g. for the West, indicate life expectancies of around 20 to 25 years in the Ancient World and Middle Ages (Maddison, 2007, p. 69). In the past century in Europe, average height increased per decade by 1 cm (NCD, 2016). Backing the validity of wealth indicators, these height increases are correlated to GDP increases and they only slightly vary with country sample and timespan ($r = .42$ to $.46$, $N = 66$ to $185$, from 1913 or 1950 to the 1990s). What we need are systematic historical collections and inferences for height and life expectancy, similar to Maddison's GDP data and estimates back to the year 0. Using human skeletons, data could go even further back.

Just looking at the life expectancy trends from 1950 to 2010, two things are obvious: (1) on average, people are living longer everywhere, from 1950/55 $M = 49.89$ years to $M = 68.75$ years in 2005/10 ($N = 188$ same countries); (2) the differences between countries are becoming smaller (from $SD = 12.23$ years to $SD = 9.75$ years). This means that during the last decades former 'short-life countries' have made greater improvements (e.g. Yemen from 25 to 62 or Bhutan from 26 to 66 years) than 'already long-life countries' (e.g. Sweden from 72 to 81 or Australia from 69 to 82 years). This is also true for sub-Saharan Africa. However, this region has still not caught up (see Figure 2.1, from 38 to 55 years).

Table 2.1 *Height and life expectancy*

| | Height (in metres, 2003) | | Life expectancy (in years, 1950–55) | | Life expectancy (in years, 2005–10) | |
|---|---|---|---|---|---|---|
| **Africa (sub-Sahara)** | 1.652 | | 38.32 | | 55.45 | |
| Kenya | | 1.659 | | 42.30 | | 57.23 |
| **N-Africa M-East** | 1.649 | | 46.78 | | 73.21 | |
| Egypt | | 1.644 | | 41.14 | | 69.92 |
| **America (North, English)** | 1.693 | | 68.74 | | 79.33 | |
| USA | | 1.691 | | 68.58 | | 78.13 |
| **America (Latin)** | 1.624 | | 53.33 | | 72.94 | |
| Mexico | | 1.640 | | 50.69 | | 76.26 |
| **Asia (Central-South)** | 1.612 | | 43.03 | | 66.66 | |
| India | | 1.578 | | 36.19 | | 64.93 |
| **East Asia** | 1.628 | | 51.38 | | 76.18 | |
| China | | 1.628 | | 44.59 | | 74.44 |
| **Southeast Asia, Pacific** | 1.597 | | 47.76 | | 70.21 | |
| Philippines | | 1.571 | | 55.43 | | 67.80 |
| **Australia-NZ (English)** | 1.711 | | 69.56 | | 80.96 | |
| New Zealand | | 1.711 | | 69.68 | | 80.23 |
| **Western Europe** | 1.714 | | 68.51 | | 79.96 | |
| United Kingdom | | 1.692 | | 69.28 | | 79.65 |
| **Scandinavia** | 1.735 | | 70.69 | | 80.21 | |
| Norway | | 1.742 | | 72.66 | | 80.6 |
| **Central Europe** | 1.721 | | 67.28 | | 80.28 | |
| Germany | | 1.723 | | 67.53 | | 79.76 |
| **Eastern Europe** | 1.706 | | 61.59 | | 72.67 | |
| Poland/Russia | | (P) 1.699 | | (R) 58.52 | | (R) 67.17 |
| **Southern Europe** | 1.711 | | 61.71 | | 77.56 | |
| Italy | | 1.710 | | 66.32 | | 81.48 |

*Notes*: Height based on Wikipedia entry 'human height'. Corrections by the author (HR) for differences in age (younger persons are taller), year of measurement (more recent measurements lead to higher results) and missing data for men (missing data lead to underestimations of country averages) or women (lead to overestimations). Several measurements for countries or country regions were averaged. For Russia, Belarus and Ukraine there are no data on height; here Poland was used. Mean measurement year 2003. Life expectancy data are taken from UN (2013).

Finally, countries at poor economic levels today have reached higher life expectancy levels than present-day rich countries have in the past at comparable economic levels. This means that today's wealth buys more health. For instance, US-Americans and British in 1913 with around $5,200 GDP per capita (1990 international dollar) had a life expectancy of 52 to 54 years, whereas people in Ghana, India, China and Peru in 1998 with GDPs between $1,200 and $3,700 live around 59 to 70 years (Goklany, 2007, pp. 33–37). Progress in knowledge achieved in modern countries transferred to developing

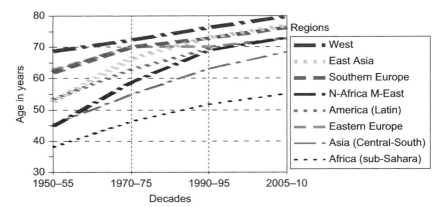

Figure 2.1 Life expectancy development in different regions from 1950 to 2010 (data from UN, 2013)

countries in the form of hygiene, water and food quality management, medicine, medical education and medical care has made this possible.

Today's wealth not only buys more health per monetary unit, but also more real wealth, with declining gaps between the rich and poor: while in the past only a few people had glass windows and this had been true from the Middle Ages for centuries, today nearly everybody has glass windows. Modern technology spreads faster and faster to all classes. While, for instance, the use of electricity needed 46 years from its invention in 1873 to reach mass use by a quarter of the US population, television only needed 26 years from 1926 and mobile phones 13 years.[3] Today in developing countries, mobile phones compensate for the absence of wired devices, computers and cameras, even sometimes for banks and help illiterate persons. Wealth differences due to income differences are declining (Kenny, 2005, p. 9), health differences between the rich and the poor within modern societies are small compared to a century ago (Costa, 2015).

## 2.2    The Human Development Approach

The Human Development Index (HDI) is a combined measure of *wealth* (GNI), *longevity* (life expectancy at birth) and *education* (average years of schooling, expected years of schooling). Values vary between 0 (low) and 1 (high). They are presented by the Human Development Report, which has been published and updated every year since 1990 by the United Nations

---

[3] Kurzweil, www.singularity.com/charts/page50.html.

Development Programme (UNDP).[4] The HDI was developed by the Pakistani economist Mahbub ul Haq (1934–1998).[5] Economic production outcomes (GDP) were seen to be a too narrow measure for national quality of life. An additional measure, introduced in 2010, is the Inequality-adjusted Human Development Index (IHDI). The IHDI, an HDI taking account of inequality, should more accurately reflect the quality of life of an average person in a society. In addition, older data going back to 1870 are provided for the HDI.

The results based on human development indices are similar to the results based on various wealth and health measures. This is somewhat inescapable because HD indices also contain wealth and health measures.[6] The West (at the top Trans-Tasman, Australia and New Zealand) places first, then the Eastern and Southern parts of Europe and East Asia, followed by the Arabian-Muslim world and Latin America, Asia and Africa.

The pattern similarity was criticised as redundancy of the HDI by Cahill (2005). But if education, wealth and health are correlated, this also has a meaning: maybe they depend on each other? Another problem is that the way in which the Human Development Indices are *mathematically* defined (0 to 1) leaves not much headroom for advanced countries (e.g. in Scandinavia). On the other hand, this reflects that improvements at the higher levels lead to smaller improvements in the general standard of living. Possibly, there is also a turning point where higher GNI or longevity or better education means lower ratings in other important areas of life quality.

What is clearly observable in the data is a twentieth-century upward trend (Table 2.2, Figure 2.1). This also includes the least developed countries such as in sub-Saharan Africa. Again, today's 'poor' countries are richer than today's rich countries were one or two centuries ago. The current HDI of less developed countries is higher than the HDI of present-day rich countries was one and a half centuries ago. For instance, GDP per capita

---

[4] The data are based on collections of other institutions, e.g. United Nations Department of Economic and Social Affairs, UNDESA, (life expectancy), United Nations Educational, Scientific and Cultural Organization, UNESCO, (education), World Bank (GNI). Measures used vary somewhat across time, with a 2010 larger modification (GNI, formerly GDP; education, formerly also adult literacy rates).

[5] The development of the HDI was supported by further economists such as Amartya Sen (Indian-US economist, *1933).

[6] The correlations are: GDP 2010 and HDI 2010 $r = .77$, and IHDI 2010 $r = .81$, GNI 2010 and HDI $r = .81$, IHDI $r = .84$; CS-assets 2010 and HDI $r = .63$, IHDI $r = .67$ (all for the same country sample with $N = 133$). Height and HDI $r = .51$, and IHDI $r = .59$; life expectancy and HDI $r = .91$, IHDI $r = .90$ (same country sample, $N = 100$). GNI correlates higher (GNI is part of the HDI, not GDP and not assets). Life expectancy correlates higher (life expectancy is part of the HDI, not height). IHDI correlates higher than HDI; this is especially true for height, which tends to better cover effects of inequality, which IHDI also tries to measure.

Table 2.2 *Human development indices 1870–2010*

|  | HDI 1870 | HDI 1913 | HDI 1950 | HDI 2010 | IHDI 2010 |
|---|---|---|---|---|---|
| **Africa (sub-Sahara)** | – | – | .27 | .41 | .25 |
| Kenya | – | – | – | .47 | .32 |
| **N-Africa M-East** | – | – | .34 | .70 | .52 |
| Egypt | – | – | .29 | .62 | .45 |
| **America (North, English)** | .50 | .64 | .79 | .90 | .81 |
| USA | .51 | .64 | .80 | .90 | .80 |
| **America (Latin)** | – | .37 | .48 | .68 | .51 |
| Mexico | – | .27 | .48 | .75 | .59 |
| **Asia (Central-South)** | – | .14 | .31 | .55 | .45 |
| India | – | .14 | .25 | .52 | .37 |
| **East Asia** | .25 | .47 | .45 | .78 | .59 |
| China | – | – | .23 | .66 | .51 |
| **Southeast Asia, Pacific** | – | – | .43 | .62 | .43 |
| Philippines | – | – | .50 | .64 | .52 |
| **Australia-NZ (English)** | .52 | .70 | .79 | .92 | .86 |
| New Zealand/Australia | (A) .52 | .71 | .80 | .91 | (A) .86 |
| **Western Europe** | .48 | .62 | .75 | .87 | .80 |
| United Kingdom | .50 | .64 | .77 | .85 | .77 |
| **Scandinavia** | .42 | .60 | .76 | .89 | .83 |
| Norway | .45 | .63 | .78 | .94 | .88 |
| **Central Europe** | .44 | .59 | .75 | .87 | .80 |
| Germany | .46 | .61 | .74 | .89 | .81 |
| **Eastern Europe** | – | .45 | .66 | .76 | .68 |
| Russia | – | .35 | .69 | .72 | .64 |
| **Southern Europe** | .28 | .45 | .58 | .79 | .69 |
| Italy | .27 | .49 | .67 | .85 | .75 |

*Notes*: Data from 1870 (*N* = 17 countries), 1913 (*N* = 30) and 1950 (*N* = 76) by Crafts (2002), from 2010 (*N* = 169, HDI, or *N* = 139, IHDI) by UNDP (2010); scale 0 to 1 (high).

(in 1990 $ppp, Maddison) for the United States in 1820 was $1,257 and for Germany $1,077, but in 2008 for India it was $2,975, for Latin America $6,787 and for sub-Saharan Africa $2,272. The same is true for the Human Development Index: in 1870 for the United States it was .51 and for Germany .46, but in 2010 for India it was .52, for Latin America .68 and for North Africa and the Middle East .70. The exception is sub-Saharan Africa, due to AIDS and its still-low literacy rate: .41.

Theoretically, it is problematic to include education as a further criterion of life quality because it is a causal factor for both wealth and health. So determinants and criteria are combined. Among criteria, political and ecological aspects are missing. And, clearly, the carrying capacity of the earth is not taken into account. The present modern industrial economy is neither sustainable across time nor across nations, when extended to emerging and developing nations (Randers, 2012).

## 2.3  Psychological, Environmental and Holistic Approaches

For decades, economists were dissatisfied with a pure economic wealth measure as a criterion of the *wellbeing* of *nations* and their *people*. Wellbeing is more than economy, it also includes *health* as indicated by life expectancy and height. Health was integrated by the HDI but wellbeing also covers *political criteria* such as peace, security, liberty and autonomy. And it includes *psychological criteria* such as life satisfaction. Negative *side effects* such as environmental degradation have to be discounted. Researchers from the Indian subcontinent such as Mahbub ul Haq and Amartya Sen led this process. However, any criticism of mere production or income approaches was far from new. Already, the founding father of the modern econometric approach to welfare measurement, Simon Kuznets, stated in 1934 (p. 6f.):

Economic welfare cannot be adequately measured unless the personal distribution of income is known. And no income measurement undertakes to estimate the reverse side of income, that is, the intensity and unpleasantness of effort going into the earning of income. The welfare of a nation can, therefore, scarcely be inferred from a measurement of national income.

### 2.3.1  Gross National Happiness (GNH)

In 1972, the then Bhutan-Buddhist king, Jigme Singye Wangchuck, suggested an alternative concept termed '*gross national happiness*': GNH as an explicitly *normative* concept comprises sustainable development, preservation and promotion of general and local cultural values, conservation of the natural environment and good governance. In detail, the following nine domains are combined: *Psychological wellbeing* stands for life satisfaction, emotional balance and spirituality. Further attributes are *health*, *education* including values, *culture*, a reasonable *use of time* including for fulfilling work and sleep, good *governance* with political participation, *community vitality* (a social network of family and friends, security, low crime rates), living in a healthy *environment* with ecological diversity and finally a sufficient *living standard* comprising income, assets and housing quality (Ura, Alkire, Zangmo & Wangdi, 2012, p. 13ff., 42).

Whereas GNH results are listed for different regions within Bhutan, no data are given for countries. Thus it is not possible to use GNH for international comparisons. However, it is theoretically stimulating and has inspired other research groups as described in the next section.

### 2.3.2    The Stiglitz–Sen–Fitoussi Approach

In 2008, then French president Nicolas Sarkozy invited three economists (Joseph E. Stiglitz, Amartya Sen and Jean-Paul Fitoussi) to form a research group, the Commission on Measurement of Economic Performance and Social Progress, to develop a new approach defining, describing and measuring the wellbeing of nations.

Central to their approach (Stiglitz et al., 2010) is to look at households (usually families), life quality and sustainability. In detail: Production (GDP) should not be measured, but rather income (GNI), and within this the income that is actually reaching households as the means for consumption, including public service and production by households. Public services such as health insurance, education and police are usually underrated in their positive effect on household welfare. Savings reduce consumption; the use of assets increases it. The distribution of income and assets in a society needs to be considered, as does the 'marketing' of formerly within-family services – education of children, care of the sick or elderly. Depreciation and depletion through normal use or accidents and catastrophes need to be discounted. Leisure time, economic and personal security are further wellbeing indicators. Very similarly to the Bhutan approach, psychological wellbeing (here: 'hedonic experiences'), health, social nets, environment and sustainability should be considered.

However, despite consisting of 'big names' from important research institutions, being backed by the highest political support and a friendly media reception, the project did not provide data. Similarly to the Bhutan GNH approach and others (e.g. Nussbaum, 2011), it is theoretically stimulating, but until now not empirically usable. There is a gap between theory and empirical work.

### 2.3.3    Happy Planet Index (HPI)

The *Happy Planet Index* (HPI) could be seen as an empirical answer to the Bhutan and French theoretical approaches. The New Economics Foundation,[7] a British private non-profit institution, proposed this wellbeing index consisting of life satisfaction (psychological), life expectancy (biological) and ecological footprint (environmental) in 2006. Psychological *wellbeing* or *life satisfaction* is taken from the Gallup World Poll ("ladder of life question", 2006–2011), *life expectancy* at birth from the Human Development Report 2011 and *ecological footprint*, the demand of natural resources relative to their

---

[7] Formerly founded as the 'Ernst Friedrich Schumacher Society'.

supply and renewal, from the Global Footprint Network. Roughly speaking, *HPI* is the average happy life years achieved per unit of natural resource use:

$$HPI = \frac{\text{Life satisfaction} \times \text{Longevity}}{\text{Ecological footprint}}.$$

Not only current life satisfaction is considered, but also the number of happy life years and, by using the ecological footprint, the wellbeing of future generations.[8]

Using the HPI reveals a different pattern of results to GDP/c and assets (see Table 2.3): the highest HPI (last column) is found in Latin America, then in Trans-Tasman and Central-South Asia. The lowest HPIs are found in Eastern Europe and Africa. For the subindices: the highest life satisfaction is given in Scandinavia followed by North America (for Bhutan no values are reported). The lowest are in Asia and Africa. The most happy life years can be observed in Scandinavia and Trans-Tasman, the fewest in Asia and Africa. A totally different measure is the ecological footprint, with lowest (best) in sub-Saharan Africa and Central-South Asia and the highest (worst) in North America and Central Europe.

Using personality questions (life satisfaction) in cross-country studies is always tricky, because self-ratings are influenced by cultural frames of reference. With whom do they compare? Do they have high or low aspirations?[9] Thus correlations are frequently strange: in PISA 2006, self-reported student interest and enjoyment of science negatively correlated with competence in science across countries ($r_{\text{Nat}} = -.77$ and $-.74$, $N = 40$).[10]

Even more problematic is the ecological footprint: it turns out to be an indicator of low technological-economic development. The ecological footprint is a kind of non-development index.[11] Only if wealth is considered (partialled out, so countries at similar wealth levels are compared) it is a positive ability indicator of coping with environmental challenges. Finally, political criteria are not included in the HPI.[12]

---

[8] Statistical adjustments are left out in this formula (see Abdallah, Michaelson, Shah, Stoll & Marks, 2012). OECD (2013a) also presents data on a holistic perspective of people's wellbeing. However, their *Better Life Index* covers only 36 nations.

[9] For personality scales Schmitt et al. (2007, p. 206) mentioned a confounding 'by different response styles ... with respect to cultural norms'. Thus their cross-national estimates for the Big Five personality scales (e.g. extraversion, neuroticism and conscientiousness) do not correlate (on average $r = .01$, $N = 36$ countries) with the results of another study on the same subject (Terracciano et al., 2005). See overview on cross-country personality measurement problems by Meisenberg (2015a).

[10] At the individual level of $N = 398.570$ students' interest and enjoyment of science correlate positively with science competence: $r_{\text{Ind}} = .20$ vs. and .24. See Täht, Must, Peets & Kattel (2014, table 2, p. 265).

[11] Abdallah et al. (2012, p. 10).    [12] Abdallah et al. (2012, p. 14).

Table 2.3 *Happy Planet Index 2012 and three subindices*

| | Life satisfaction | | Happy life years | | Ecological footprint | | HPI 2012 | |
|---|---|---|---|---|---|---|---|---|
| **Africa (sub-Sahara)** | 4.25 | | 30.94 | | 1.51 | | 33.45 | |
| Kenya | | 4.26 | | 31.74 | | 0.95 | | 38.00 |
| **N-Africa M-East (ArabM)** | 5.17 | | 46.38 | | 3.42 | | 43.08 | |
| Egypt | | 3.88 | | 38.55 | | 2.06 | | 39.64 |
| **America (North, English)** | 7.41 | | 63.79 | | 6.81 | | 40.45 | |
| USA | | 7.16 | | 61.29 | | 7.19 | | 37.34 |
| **America (Latin)** | 6.17 | | 52.03 | | 2.58 | | 52.58 | |
| Mexico | | 6.80 | | 57.96 | | 3.30 | | 52.89 |
| **Asia (Central-South)** | 4.99 | | 40.41 | | 1.57 | | 46.16 | |
| India | | 4.99 | | 40.06 | | 0.87 | | 50.87 |
| **East Asia** | 5.41 | | 50.44 | | 4.45 | | 40.05 | |
| China | | 4.65 | | 43.11 | | 2.13 | | 44.66 |
| **Southeast Asia, Pacific** | 5.46 | | 46.79 | | 2.30 | | 48.93 | |
| Philippines | | 4.94 | | 41.83 | | 0.98 | | 52.35 |
| **Australia-NZ (English)** | 7.31 | | 64.42 | | 5.50 | | 46.77 | |
| New Zealand | | 7.22 | | 63.38 | | 4.31 | | 51.56 |
| **Western Europe** | 7.09 | | 62.45 | | 5.86 | | 43.41 | |
| United Kingdom | | 7.03 | | 61.78 | | 4.71 | | 47.93 |
| **Scandinavia** | 7.44 | | 64.62 | | 6.30 | | 43.41 | |
| Norway | | 7.63 | | 66.25 | | 4.77 | | 51.43 |
| **Central Europe** | 7.17 | | 63.23 | | 6.40 | | 43.40 | |
| Germany | | 6.72 | | 60.04 | | 4.57 | | 47.20 |
| **Eastern Europe** | 5.27 | | 46.71 | | 3.90 | | 38.68 | |
| Russia | | 5.46 | | 44.68 | | 4.40 | | 34.52 |
| **Southern Europe** | 5.49 | | 51.24 | | 4.09 | | 42.25 | |
| Italy | | 6.35 | | 58.81 | | 4.52 | | 46.35 |

*Notes*: Data from 2012 and somewhat earlier (if no 2012 data given). Life satisfaction: self-rated life satisfaction (psychological wellbeing), 2011 or earlier, scale 0–10 (lowest in Togo, 2.81, highest in Denmark, 7.77); Happy Life Years: wellbeing multiplied by life expectancy divided by 10, scale equivalent to years (lowest in Central African Republic, 24.33, highest in Switzerland, 66.55); Ecological Footprint: demand for natural capital, global hectares per capita, empirical values between 0.5 (Afghanistan) and 11.7 (Qatar); HPI 2012: Happy Planet Index 2012, based on wellbeing, life expectancy and low ecological footprint; scale theoretically between 0 and 100, empirically between 23 (Botswana) and 64 (Costa Rica). Source: Happy Planet Index 2012 report (Abdallah et al., 2012).

However, living a life in considerable happiness is a positive attribute per se. By weighting life satisfaction with longevity a useful statistical indicator was achieved. Theoretically complementing measures such as the former *Index of Sustainable Economic Welfare* (ISEW) and the present *Genuine Progress Indicator* (GPI) have advantages: they cover private consumption and distribution, value of non-market services, low crime rates, family stability, education, ecological variety, clean environment and low resource consumption, but they do not give comparable data for larger country samples or for historical analyses.

## 2.4    Including Political and Sociological Criteria

The wellbeing of peoples (as aggregated individuals) and nations (as social, cultural or ethnic entities) comprises more than economic wealth indicated by production, income, assets or biological criteria such as longevity and height. Wellbeing has to include psychological, political and sociological criteria.

There are *theoretical* approaches which have conceptually included a wider range of criteria (Skidelsky & Skidelsky, 2012; Stiglitz, Sen & Fitoussi, 2010). They are complemented by different *measurement* approaches:

- *Newsweek's list of World's Best Countries* based on five criteria (education, health, quality of life, economic competitiveness, politics);
- *Legatum Prosperity Index* built upon eight sub-indices (economy, entrepreneurship, governance, education, health, safety, freedom and social capital);
- and *Lynn and Vanhanen's Index of the Quality of Human Conditions* comprising five aspects (GNP, literacy, education, life expectancy and democracy).[13]

All these measures cover important aspects of national wellbeing. What causes theoretical and empirical problems is that all indices confound possible determinants with criteria of wellbeing. Of course, the wellbeing aspects may influence each other, e.g. politics and wealth, but they should not be combined with a theoretically central determinant such as education. For understanding national development and differences, determinants and outcomes need to be distinguished.

How can we find relevant aspects of national wellbeing? First of all, they can be derived from *individual preferences* that are aggregated for nations. Economic criteria are relevant (income and wealth and related indicators for them such as height and life expectancy); crucial is health (a good indicator is life expectancy); also important are psychological (happiness, trust) and political criteria (autonomy, participation, freedom, security).

Second, they need to be accompanied by *genuine macrosocial* aspects such as rule of law, peace, low crime rates and (gender) equality.

Third, *empirical research* at the level of individuals or nations on determinants and consequences of wellbeing has to be considered.

Finally, a *normative concept* is needed to give reasons for any wellbeing criterion. Norms can be supported by cross-cultural preference studies, but majority opinions can be misleading. Imagine an opinion poll in 1914 in

---

[13] See overview on international wellbeing indices by Vanhanen (2011).

European countries on national wellbeing or in 1212 at the time of the Children's Crusade on aims of life. Rational arguments have to undergird criteria of wellbeing. We include in our national wellbeing sum value the following criteria:

(1) *Economic wellbeing*: GDP 2010 Penn, GNI 2010 HDR (both per capita) and assets 2010 Credit Suisse (per adult). Production leads to income and assets; they are highly correlated ($r = .95$, $.72$ and $.79$); different sources correct single survey outliers. Nearly all people across different ages and cultures positively value income and wealth for themselves and their families and the more the better. Higher wealth leads to better life conditions and therefore healthier and longer lives with more developmental options and fewer risks. Positive effects outweigh negative side effects such as growing stress, complexity, fear of loss and robbery, ecological damage or the necessity of means to control them.

(2) *Biological wellbeing* (health): Life expectancy (2005–2010, source UN) and height are good health and indirect wealth indicators. On height, the data basis is less reliable, genetic causes (evolutionary differences) may influence height. Finally, height itself is not an important good. It may be objected that healthy longevity is more important than longevity, and, of course, people prefer a healthy longer life, but the data base on disability-free life expectancy is less reliable. To live is the basis for any wellbeing; it is the ultimate quality of life criterion and does not only cover the quality of the health system and wealth, but also peace, security and low crime rates.

(3) *Psychological wellbeing*: Personal wellbeing (satisfaction, 2006–2011 from Gallup World Poll/HPI) and interpersonal trust (1997–2008 from World Value Survey) are central criteria for a happy life. Many 'sophisticated' philosophies of life do not regard happiness as a fulfilling aim of life; however, as for wealth and health, the majority of people feel it is worth striving for. Trust and wellbeing are theoretically and empirically related (Algan & Cahuc, 2014). Complementarily for humans as social beings, we added interpersonal trust from the World Value Survey.[14] People feel more secure and happy where they can trust each other ($r = .50$, $N = 111$). In many religions trustworthiness is a highly regarded value. Honesty, trustworthiness and reliability are important values (and also supporting factors for wealth[15]).

---

[14] People were asked: 'Generally speaking, would you say that most people can be trusted or that you need to be very careful in dealing with people?' $N = 117$ countries, surveys between 1997 and 2008 (mean around 2005); values below 100 indicates that a majority of people does not trust others, values above 100 that the majority trusts others. Source: Díez-Medrano (2014).

[15] Trust is essential for economic transactions and supports growth and income. In a study of Algan & Cahuc (2010) trust and income were correlated at the country level with $r = .73$ and changes in trust and income between 1935–2000 with $r = .66$ (their figures 3 and 4).

(4) *Sociological 'society' wellbeing* (security, peace and stability): murder is the most serious crime. Low murder rates indicate a safe society. Peace is a similarly important criterion, more so at the level of the nation. Low corruption is a measure of law-abiding behaviour in administration, economy and society. A low divorce rate is an indicator of social stability (e.g. *The Wellbeing of Nations* by OECD, 2001).[16]

(5) *Political wellbeing*: Participation, freedom and rule of law stand for a burgher-civic society, gender equality for equal rights and opportunities of both sexes. They are all also indicators for cultural and social modernity. All are founded in values of civil rights and liberties and enlightenment.[17]

What might still be missing is *environmental quality* (clean water, clean air, safe food, wilderness, species protection, biodiversity); however, I found no sum index. Another important criterion is *human rights*; however, rule of law, political freedom, democracy and low homicide rates cover this aspect. Education and intelligence should not be included because they are important contributing factors, similarly government effectiveness, economic freedom, innovation and technology. *Social cohesion* and *quality of neighbourhoods* are largely covered by interpersonal trust. Not covered are *autonomy and self-determination of nations* (e.g. Basques, Scots, South Tyrolean, Palestinian, indigenous peoples). We do not have data for this aspect. Also *richness of culture* (e.g. let us say Tuscany compared to Oregon) is not covered. *Homogeneity* aspects such as economic homogeneity (low Gini coefficient standing for equal distribution of income) or ethnic homogeneity (low ethnic diversity) are not unambiguous positive criteria: it causes no harm to people that some are rich; it does not damage other Swedes that Ingvar Kamprad has 23 Billions.[18] And as Ludwig von Mises (1996/1927) has mentioned, the rich are even beneficial for others as they stimulate economic progress by their consumption. Somebody has to start buying 4K Ultra HD resolution

---

[16] Source for *murder* rates 2008–2011 (intentional homicide count and rate per 100,000 population); $N = 178$ countries: UNODC (2012).

Source for *war*, 1995–2012 (taken for a longer period because war is usually a rare incident but with long-term effects); $N = 166$ countries: Marshall (2013).

Source for *corruption*, 2010–2012; $N = 183$: Transparency International (2012).

Source for *divorce* rates, 2001; $N = 79$: Kurian (2001, p. 52).

[17] *Participation-democracy*: mean of 2007–2012; $N = 190$, statistical data from Vanhanen & Åbo Akademi (2013) and estimations from Polity (Marshall, Gurr & Jaggers, 2013).

*Political freedom*: mean of 2008–2012; $N = 196$, Freedom House (2013).

*Rule of law*: mean of 2009–2011; $N = 200$, Kaufmann, Kraay & Mastruzzi (2010).

*Gender equality*: mean of 2006–2011; $N = 135$, Hausmann, Tyson & Zahidi (2011).

[18] Gregory Mankiw (2013, p. 22): 'If we can make some people better off without making anyone worse off, who could possibly object?'

technology in TV, cameras and storage media or new safety technology in luxury cars such as Mercedes (ABS brake, traction control, Electronic Stability Program) before the innovations spread and become cheaper and available to the average consumer.[19] On the one hand, ethnic homogeneity supports trust, on the other hand, ethnic heterogeneity bears the potential of division of labour and innovation (e.g. Jews and Parsi) and could be valued as 'multiculturalism' (e.g. diversity of festivals and food).[20]

To calculate one national wellbeing index, first within the five categories (economy, health, psychology, society, politics) the different indices were standardised and averaged, and second those means were averaged across the five categories.[21] The final wellbeing index was standardised setting United Kingdom at 100 and using a standard deviation of 10. Results are given for 202 countries. The index highly correlates with the Legatum Prosperity Index (2009–2013) with $r = .94$ ($N = 142$).

On top of the world (see Table 2.4 and Figure 2.2) in national wellbeing are smaller Central and Northern European countries: Liechtenstein (114), Norway (110), Sweden (106), Switzerland (106) and Denmark (105). They are followed by Australia (104), Finland (104), Luxembourg (103), Netherlands (103), Canada (102), Iceland (102) and New Zealand (101). Taken together, Scandinavian, Central European and Commonwealth nations settled and modelled by the British are leading. At the end are mainly countries from sub-Saharan Africa: Somalia (61), Congo (Zaire, 63), Sudan (65), Central African Republic (68), Chad (68), South Sudan (68), Angola (68), Ivory Coast (68) and Burundi (70). Afghanistan (68) and Burma (Myanmar, 71) have the lowest values outside Africa. Bhutan reached 83.

The small Arabian Oil Emirates (e.g. Qatar) illustrate some outliers – their values in the wealth indicator are considerably higher than in the other four indicators of national wellbeing. A similar outlier is Equatorial Guinea. In longevity, African countries form negative outliers (Sierra Leone, Lesotho, Botswana, Swaziland, Zimbabwe, Mozambique) – mainly due to AIDS but also due to war; in psychological wellbeing, negatively Togo and Cape Verde;

---

[19] Goklany (2007, p. 77): 'The rich are not better off because they have taken something away from the poor, rather the poor are better off because they have benefit from the technologies developed by the rich, and their situation would have been further improved had they been better prepared to capture the benefits of globalization.' Economic heterogeneity within the upper half may be beneficial, but probably not within the lower half, decreasing economic growth (Cingano, 2014).

[20] On diversity effects see Sections 12.2.3 and 13.3.3.

[21] The homogeneity of the national wellbeing index is Cronbach-$\alpha = .86$; the average correlation between the five measures is $r = .55$. A factor analysis reveals one factor with 64 per cent variance explained; the factor loadings vary between $\lambda = .44$ (security, peace and stability) and $\lambda = .70$ (wealth). There is a strong $G$ factor of national wellbeing. For 154 countries there is information from all five subcategories; for 48 countries only from between one and four subcategories.

Table 2.4 *National wellbeing index (around 2010)*

|  | National wellbeing 2010 | |
| --- | --- | --- |
| **Africa (sub-Sahara)** | 74.92 | |
| Kenya | | 74.96 |
| **N-Africa M-East (ArabM)** | 84.43 | |
| Egypt | | 79.79 |
| **America (North, English)** | 100.41 | |
| USA | | 98.39 |
| **America (Latin, Central-South)** | 87.21 | |
| Mexico | | 87.13 |
| **Asia (Central-South)** | 77.76 | |
| India | | 71.89 |
| **East Asia** | 87.99 | |
| China | | 85.07 |
| **Southeast Asia, Pacific** | 85.01 | |
| Philippines | | 77.01 |
| **Australia-NZ (English)** | 102.75 | |
| New Zealand | | 101.4 |
| **Western Europe** | 100.53 | |
| United Kingdom | | 100.00 |
| **Scandinavia** | 101.85 | |
| Norway | | 109.66 |
| **Central Europe** | 105.08 | |
| Germany | | 100.50 |
| **Eastern Europe** | 87.20 | |
| Russia | | 80.09 |
| **Southern Europe** | 91.69 | |
| Italy | | 97.43 |

*Notes*: Information on data construction see text and footnotes.

in sociological wellbeing, negatively India, Sudan, Congo, Somalia, Columbia, Afghanistan, Iraq and Burma. Singapore is a positive outlier here. In political wellbeing, Muslim countries and North Korea form negative outliers (Somalia, Yemen, Turkmenistan, Sudan, Saudi Arabia, Emirates, Qatar). Singapore is an anomaly with a low political wellbeing score and a high general national wellbeing level; the same is true for Liechtenstein. However, in both countries rule of law is very high.[22]

---

[22] Using factor analysis instead of averaging, a general or *G*-factor of national wellbeing can be calculated. Comparing results in the wellbeing average used (Table 2.4) with the *G* factor, *small* Caribbean and European countries form outliers in the standard average value. Due to missing values, the averaging procedure seems to be more sensible for outliers. Missing values were substituted by means in the *G* factor procedure.

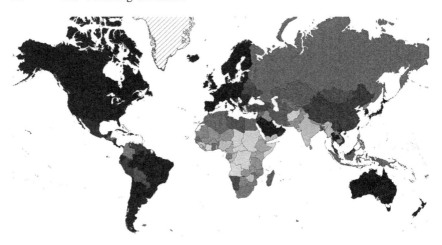

Figure 2.2 National wellbeing around 2010 (built upon wealth, health, psychology, security-stability, politics), darker means higher, shading accentuates differences at the poorer levels; no data for Greenland.

## 2.5    Why Still Use GDP?

In spite of its theoretical narrowness and empirical flaws GDP per capita remains an indispensable indicator of national wealth and wellbeing. There are two very simple reasons why:

(1) Whereas many alternative constructs also seem plausible in theory, they lack sufficient data. We can work only with *data* we have – GDP is available for *nearly all countries* and for many countries in the *past*. We have data from one source for longitudinal analyses (Maddison).

(2) GDP per capita *highly correlates* with national wellbeing. The Penn 2010 GDP used in this chapter correlates with the final wellbeing average at $r = .76$ ($N = 189$), the related income indicator HDR GNI 2010 at $r = .82$ ($N = 183$), and the Maddison GDPs, usable for longitudinal analyses, even at $r_{2008} = .86$ ($N = 159$) or $r_{2010} = .89$ ($N = 117$).[23]

---

[23] If only using countries (Penn GDP, HDR GNI, Maddison GDP 2008, Maddison GDP 2010) for each of the four country samples ($N = 189, 183, 159, 117$) which are also present in the other indicators, i. e. in all samples ($N = 112, 112, 112, 112$), the correlations with national wellbeing are $r = .75, .84, .90$ and $.89$. The correlations and differences in them do not depend on country sample variations. The Maddison source was not used for calculating the national wellbeing index. Wellbeing indices of other authors show even higher correlations with GDP/c, e.g. Jones & Klenow (2016) report $r = .96$ to $.98$ for their welfare index and GDP.

The production indicator GDP is a proxy for achieved income and wealth. But in comparison to GNI or GNP, *GDP is less affected by fluctuations* caused by arbitrary variations of import and export prices and exchange rates. In modernity, the relevant production is for markets. However, theoretical and measurement limits should never be ignored since wellbeing is more than just the economy. And longitudinal GDP increases can both overestimate or underestimate wealth increases: negative developments such as increasing pollution and positive developments such as rising quality of goods are not covered. An indicator is not the 'thing-in-itself'.

# 3     Human Capital, Cognitive Ability and Intelligence

The concepts of human capital, cognitive ability and intelligence are introduced. We compare different ways to measure them. Development, causes for development and for differences, and furtherance approaches are outlined.

## 3.1     Terms and Definitions

*Human capital* is defined as everything within a person that helps to be productive in economic action. It comprises *physical-bodily* and *psychological abilities* as well as *personality* attributes; e.g. health and the ability to walk, see and hear; to understand and cognitively perceive and solve problems; to be diligent, reliable and motivated. Human capital is part of the broader *production factors* concept, factors that help to produce goods. They are not wanted for themselves but for achieving goods, which are themselves valued. Capital is, along with land and labour, one of the three main factors of production. Within capital, physical capital (e.g. buildings, machines and money) is distinguished from human capital.

Adam Smith (*1723, †1790) was one of the first to describe human capital as 'the acquired and useful abilities of all the inhabitants or members of the society'.[1] And more precisely, Smith highlighted the crucial role of cognitive abilities and burgher virtues:

The qualities most useful to ourselves are, first of all, superior *reason* and *understanding*, by which we are capable of discerning the remote *consequences of all our actions*, and of *foreseeing* the advantage or detriment which is likely to result from them: and secondly, *self-command*, by which we are enabled to abstain from present pleasure or to endure present pain, in order to obtain a greater pleasure or to avoid a greater pain in some future time. In the union of those two qualities consists the *virtue of prudence*, of all the virtues that which is most useful to the individual.[2]

---

[1] Wealth of nations (1982/1776, p. 377; Book II, Chapter I).

[2] Theory of moral sentiments (2004/1759, p. 248; Part IV, Chapter I).

Without the closer psychological perspective applied by Smith 'human capital' would remain a fuzzy term. Imagine using 'kangaroo capital' for the ability to make large leaps or 'cheetah capital' for the ability to run fast. A precise description of the essential attributes of persons who can productively work is needed. The first person who explicitly introduced the concept of *intelligence* to economics was the German-US economist Friedrich List. In 1841 (published in English in 1909), he stated: 'Everywhere and at all times has the well-being of the nation been in equal proportion to the intelligence, morality, and industry of its citizens; according to these, wealth has accrued or been diminished' (p. 87).

List also saw an interaction with institutional quality – that human capital cannot show its potential under restrictive conditions. On closer inspection of human capital theories and research (Walsh, 1935; Mincer, 1958; Schultz, 1961; Becker, 1993/1964; Barro, 1991; Heckman, 2000) two main psychological traits can be found, resembling the two Smith attributes, reason and self-command: first, *cognitive ability* and second a broader personality dimension standing for *industrious discipline* (diligence, commitment, conscientiousness, self-discipline, self-monitoring, agreeableness, robustness; Sackett & Walmsley, 2014). Further human capital attributes that are also relevant but less stressed in research are *physical* conditions (e.g. health, eyesight, hearing ability), further *personality attributes and attitudes* (e.g. agreeableness, ethical orientation, assertiveness) and noncognitive *competences* (e.g. social competence). They are all important for the working process itself, but less relevant for explaining differences.

In statistical analyses of job performance, cognitive abilities show the highest predictive validity by far. Depending on job performance criteria and applied correction formula for low reliability and variance restriction, the relationships range between $r/\beta/\rho = .23$ and $.64$ (Salgado et al., 2003; Schmidt, 2012).[3] This is true for different countries, including developing countries (Meisenberg et al., 2006). In more complex jobs, from office jobs onwards, the predictive validity is even higher (corrected $\rho_{lowCompl} = .40$ vs. $\rho_{highCompl} = .58$, Kuncel & Hezlett, 2010; $\rho_{lowCompl} = .51$ vs. $\rho_{highCompl} = .64$, Salgado et al., 2003). Next to job performance, intelligence also predicts income, cross-sectionally as well as longitudinally, i.e. current and future wage differences (Irwing & Lynn, 2006; Kramer, 2009). Cognitive ability is the most important and most robust concept for predicting success in economic criteria for individuals.

But why?

---

[3] $r$: the standard not corrected bivariate correlation, Pearson correlation; $\beta$: path or regression coefficient (other predictors are included in a model and usually make single effects smaller, usually $\beta < r$); $\rho$: corrected bivariate correlation (corrected for low reliability or restricted variance or both, leads to higher correlations, usually $\rho > r$).

One technical reason is that ability tests are more *reliable* and *valid* psychological instruments than personality tests. A further reason is that people *differ more* in cognitive predictors. Differences are a prerequisite for correlational predictivity. Thus a fundamental condition for successful job performance such as visual ability is not predictive because blind people are rare and frequently excluded *a priori* (e.g. from becoming a pilot). And cognitive differences are *related* to other relevant attributes such as conscientiousness.

Even more important is that requirements in the world of employment call for cognitive abilities because tasks in this world are better solvable by using thinking and knowledge. *Job requirements* are cognitively demanding, e.g. understanding instructions, orders and security risks; prioritizing tasks; coming to a decision; dealing with people; processing, integrating and evaluating information for solving problems, such as for accountants, businessmen, physicians, engineers, managers, scientists etc. (Gottfredson, 2003). Especially in modernity and more complex jobs, *learning* is a prerequisite to becoming an effective worker (Schmidt & Hunter, 1998). Cognitive ability is not only helpful to *pass the educational selection* and *competence building process* in schools, but also to successfully cope with requirements in employment and beyond: in everyday life, e.g. driving a car, managing income and property, finding a mate, raising children and conducting life in a healthful and sensible way.[4]

How should this mental capacity be named and defined?

*Economists* use the terms 'skill' or 'skills'. *Psychologists* use the terms 'intelligence', '*g*', 'IQ', 'mental ability' or 'cognitive ability'. *Educational researchers* use 'literacy' or 'competence'.

Names are more than sound and smoke: 'Skill' connotes a narrow ability; however, intelligence, cognitive ability and human capital are not narrow. 'Intelligence' stresses thinking but usually excludes knowledge. However, all problem-solving processes and tests cover at least some knowledge. Only a broader concept of intelligence including 'crystallised intelligence' would comprise such knowledge. '*g*' implies no definition or theoretical construct; it is only the first unrotated factor of a factor analysis. Without a definition, anything could be factor analysed, from climate indicators to personality attributes. A theoretical definition is indispensable. 'IQ' is initially only a scale metric with $M = 100$ and $SD = 15$. Only when enriched by an intelligence definition is it a useful short term. 'Literacy' connotes only reading and dealing with text, which is too narrow for covering what is necessary to solve cognitive problems and what is measured by mental tests. 'Human capital', 'ability' or 'competence' are extremely broad concepts covering, e.g., also eyesight,

---

[4] Economic 'Human capital' research has included in its research agenda such broader effects as well (e.g. Becker & Becker, 1998).

strength and health. They need a qualifying attribute – 'cognitive'. 'Mental' is too broad connoting psychological health.

We recommend using the term *cognitive ability*. It comprises the ability to think (intelligence), knowledge (the store of true and relevant knowledge) and the intelligent use of this knowledge. 'Cognitive competence' can be interchangeably used. 'Cognitive human capital' covers the application of 'cognitive ability' or 'cognitive competence' in (economic) prediction and explanation studies. We use cognitive human capital as an umbrella term also comprising educational measures.

*Intelligence is the ability to think*, a rather knowledge-reduced mental capacity, ideally free of specific knowledge. Intelligence comprises:

- *problem solving*: to solve new problems by thinking (no simple knowledge recall),
- *reasoning*: to infer (to conclude and reason, to draw inductive and deductive-logical conclusions including finding patterns in information, to correctly generalise, to apply rules for new examples and to solve syllogisms),
- *abstract thinking*: to categorise, to form concepts, to sort out less relevant information, to process abstract information in the form of verbal and numerical symbols, in the form of abstract figures and in the form of general rules,
- *understanding*: to recognise and construct relationships, structures, contexts and meaning, to have insight.

Intelligence as thinking ability includes the ability to change cognitive perspectives, to make plans and use foresight; finally, learning depends on intelligence and on previously acquired knowledge facilitated by intelligence.

This concept of *intelligence* does not include basic cognitive processes and abilities such as mental speed, concentration, memory span and working memory. It does not include memory, the ability to store and retrieve information, and it does not include knowledge, the disposal of true and relevant information. And it does not comprise cognitive creativity (imaginativeness and invention of important and useful ideas). However, the broader concept *cognitive ability* comprises all these more or less complex cognitive abilities.

This understanding of cognitive ability is similar to what economists such as Nelson and Phelps (1966, p. 69) understand as the effect of education: 'Education enhances one's ability to receive, decode, and understand information.'

All used terms bear no statement on development of individual and national levels and differences. We do not use the terms 'talent' or 'gift' because they connote a given, largely genetically determined trait. And we also do not use 'skill' or 'literacy'. The narrow skill and literacy approaches ignore the broader paradigms of intelligence research, be it the psychometric, the Piagetian or the everyday life analysis tradition (see Chapter 4).

## 3.2     Paradigms and Measurement Approaches

### 3.2.1     *Education as a Proxy for Ability*

Education is frequently used as a proxy for human capital, and indirectly for cognitive ability. To do so in empirical research, education has to be operationalized and quantified. Three indicators are taken: *years spent attending school* (from primary to tertiary, from elementary school to university), *highest achieved degree* (primary, secondary, tertiary, PhD) or *literacy rate*. The first two are purely formal measures and are hence burdened with problems:

- It is assumed that the effects of one year of education at different levels of education are the same (e.g. one year more up to four years has the same effect as one year more on top of 12 years). However, there are certainly diminishing returns.
- In many countries, children only erratically attend school, are frequently absent or interrupt school attendance for some months to years (Glewwe & Kremer, 2006).
- Similarly, it is assumed that degrees are comparable in achieved abilities across countries. This is not the case, as student assessment studies have shown.
- Across countries and time, educational degrees are difficult to compare, for instance the educational levels of German speaking countries with their tradition of vocational training are underrated compared to countries with the same professions educated at universities.
- There are mistakes in national statistics, for example in dealing with grade retention (e.g. according to Beaton et al., 1996a, p. 14, Norway has a 116 per cent attendance rate in secondary schools).
- Sometimes fraud distorts national statistics, for instance because schools receive more money when they report more pupils (e.g. Yemen; Barro & Lee, 1993, p. 366f.).
- Theoretically, it is not formal levels of education that are decisive, nor titles, but what persons are able and willing to do; education is only a proxy of the relevant ability and personality.
- Finally, education is only one important determinant of cognitive and other human capital; their development depends on more factors, from genes to family education, the health system and culture.

The third measure, literacy (Romer, 1990), is an alternative to pure formal attendance and degree measures. But, for modernity, literacy as the ability to read and write texts is a much too basic competence.

Not surprisingly, for predicting national development as economic growth, these three educational measures usually show lower correlations compared to more complex ability measures.[5] For all these reasons Hanushek and Kimko (2000) recommended the use of adequately measured outcome variables of education: *student assessment test results*. Before we discuss them, two older paradigms, frequently applied in cross-cultural research, will be presented.

### 3.2.2   Psychometric Intelligence Tests

Psychometric intelligence tests measure 'intelligence', 'cognitive ability', 'IQ' or '*g*'. In the standard version, a *paper-and-pencil test* is applied. Usually, *several shorter tasks* (called 'items') are combined to form one of the different *dimensions* (or scales) such as figural, verbal or numerical intelligence.

Depending on the chosen model and specific test, dimensions are differently related to knowledge. The most used test in cross-cultural research is the 'Raven', a figural intelligence test with abstract figures (abstract thinking) in which rules have to be detected (inductive reasoning; pattern detection and concept formation as part of abstract thinking) and applied (deductive reasoning) for finding the correct solution (see three examples in Figure 3.1).[6]

*Factor analysis* is a frequently used statistical method within the psychometric paradigm. Basically, correlations between many items are reduced to a few, usually one, two or three factors or, in Carroll's (1993) overview including many different tests, to eight factors. Ideally, these factors form theoretically substantiated dimensions explaining the correlations between items.

Theoretically, three main approaches can be distinguished:

(1)  *Raymond Bernard Cattell*'s (1987/1971) differentiation of fluid and crystallised intelligence: *Fluid intelligence* means a culture-reduced intelligence, pure reasoning. It is comparable to what in this book is defined as intelligence. *Crystallised intelligence* covers knowledge and the use of

---

[5] However, education and cognitive ability are substantially correlated. Education is the best proxy for cognitive ability at the individual and the national level. If cognitive ability measures are not given, education is the best indicator.

[6] The Raven is given in three versions: (1) Coloured Progressive Matrices (CPM) for children around 3 to 6 years. (2) Standard Progressive Matrices (SPM) initially for youth and adults, but today best for children around 6 to 12 years and groups with lower ability. (3) Advanced Progressive Matrices (APM) for youth and adults at average to higher ability levels. All are figural, culture-reduced tests of fluid intelligence. The test was developed by John C. Raven in 1936.

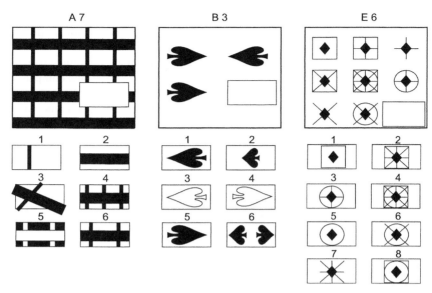

Figure 3.1 Raven Matrices-like tasks

knowledge. Cattell's dichotomy is tied to a developmental theory: fluid intelligence steeply rises due to maturation in childhood until age 15 to 25. Crystallised intelligence is invested fluid intelligence plus experience, learning by experience in everyday life and school, which could increase until old age. Fluid intelligence depends on age (genetically driven maturation) and a biologically healthy environment, and crystallised intelligence depends on invested fluid intelligence and the stimulation quality of the cultural environment.

(2) Related to the first theory is the *mental speed* theory, one important supporter is Arthur Jensen (last summary 2006a). Similar to fluid intelligence, mental speed is a basic cognitive ability, but comparatively more basic and less complex and more dependable on *neurological efficiency*. Mental speed increases through maturation in childhood and decreases from around age 15 to 25 years and onwards. Mental speed development depends on age and a biologically healthy environment. Similarly to mental speed, *working memory* increases in childhood and decreases, somewhat later, from young adulthood onwards. Working memory is the ability to store, retrieve and process around seven units in a central executive.[7]

---

[7] Mental speed is correlated with working memory capacity at around $r = .28$ (Conway et al., 2002, their Table 2), speed and intelligence at $r = .30$ (manifest, latent $r = .51$; Grudnik &

(3) Finally, there is a kind of statistics-driven 'theory', the *g* factor. Again, one important supporter is Arthur Jensen (1998), while the first was Charles Spearman (1904), who detected a positive manifold leading to *g*: results of different tests are correlated. Factor analyses of correlations between items and dimensions across the differences between individuals always reveal a strong first unrotated factor. This means that one person shows more or less similar results across different tests: individuals who, relative to other persons, solve many tasks in a verbal test scale also solve many tasks in a numerical and figural scale relative to others. Individuals who are slow in mental speed tasks also have a weak memory.

A theory is needed to explain this empirical-statistical evidence. There are different theories behind the *g* factor; one relates to a common effect of *generalist genes* (Plomin & Kovas, 2005), which shape generally effective neurological structures; one of these could be *mental speed* and its general effects on intelligence (Jensen, 2006a). Another theory stresses *reciprocal causation* among different cognitive processes and subdimensions within a person (Maas et al. 2006). *Environment has global effects*, as educated parents and good schools not only support verbal, but also maths and general cognitive development (Rindermann, 2007a). Finally, *cognitive tasks*, *abilities* and *processes* to solve different items and dimensions of tests are *similar* (Rindermann & Baumeister, 2015).

For most psychometric variables such as intelligence there are no 'natural' scales. That is to say, a ratio dimension with an absolute zero cannot be used in the same way as for measuring life expectancy or height. Hence, results need to be standardised using a meaningful and representative group. Results are presented in an age-neutral 'IQ' scale with a mean of 100 and standard deviation of 15.[8] Thus, five-year-old children have a mean IQ of 100 and so do 25-year-old adults, but comparing raw scores (and real world behaviour), the adults are much more intelligent. And in 1930 the mean IQ was 100 as it was in 2010; however, people today are more intelligent than in the past. As a result, IQs mask development across time, in individual lives as well as in

---

Kranzler, 2001), and working memory capacity and intelligence at $r = .48$ (latent, Ackerman, Beier & Boyle, 2005). Correlations at the manifest data level are lower than those corrected for error at the latent level. Because working memory is cognitively more similar to intelligence the explanative value of speed for intelligence is higher (we can theoretically better explain B2 with A than with B1).

[8]   Some tests use other norms, such as Z norms ($M = 100$, $SD = 10$), T norms ($M = 50$, $SD = 10$) or C norms ($M = 5$, $SD = 2$). All these norms can be easily transformed, as metre to foot or Celsius to Fahrenheit. Percentiles are different, as they express differences on a percentage scale: percentile 43 means, 42 per cent (exactly $42.\overline{9}$ per cent) have lower values, 56 per cent ($56.\overline{9}$ per cent) have higher values. Percentiles numerically stress differences in an average range of results and numerically reduce them in the extremes. Therefore, percentiles cannot be used in usual statistical analyses.

history. As if UK's GDP/c across time would be always $10,000. Also, any changes in homogeneity or heterogeneity are not depicted.[9] It should not be ignored that the final result represents the individual outcome compared to others in that ability – it is an individual differences measurement, not one of intelligence itself.

Two very important research issues are *bias susceptibility* and the *nature vs. nurture issue*. Coaching, test experience, stereotype threat as part of any suggestibility, test anxiety and specific knowledge are not unimportant, but usually they do not change ranks of individuals and groups (Jensen, 1980; Sackett, Hardison & Cullen, 2004).[10] Different twin design and adoption studies show that individual differences (not individual values) depend more on genetic factors (which one and how they work is yet unknown) than on environmental factors such as family influence or specific individual experiences and that with increasing age in childhood the impact of genes rises to 80 per cent in young adulthood (Johnson, 2010). Genes can explain 50–80 per cent of differences between individuals, and the rest can be more or less explained by idiosyncratic experiences.

### 3.2.3    Piagetian Cognitive Development

A similarly old, but theoretically totally different, paradigm is the cognitive development approach of the Swiss-French biologist, psychologist and philosopher Jean Piaget (1896–1980). He developed a complex theory of *cognitive development* called '*genetic epistemology*'. In this case, 'genetic' means developmental. The ability to rationally understand the world ('epistemology') develops in a process of *assimilation* and *adaptation*. This means cognitive schemata are being constantly formed during the developmental interaction between subject (child) and object (world). Schemata mainly assimilate (integrate) new experiences, but they also adapt, change, develop, become more differentiated and get substituted.

Unsuccessfully integrated experiences lead to a state of *disequilibrium*, which motivates cognitive development. This cognitive development goes through *four stages*:

(1) *Sensorimotor stage*: from age 0 to 2 years, precognitive, cognition based mainly on senses and reflexes.

---

[9] A solution would be to use mental speed tests with a defined zero point. But they do not measure the more relevant complex cognitive abilities.

[10] Bias susceptibility as part of the broader validity question as well as the nature vs. nurture issue are empirical questions we will deal with in this book. Stereotype threat as explanation for low intelligence test results of African Americans was introduced into research by Steele & Aronson (1995).

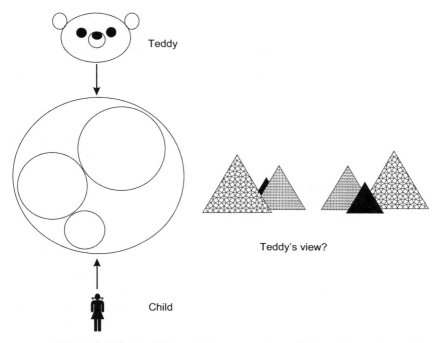

Teddy

Teddy's view?

Child

Figure 3.2 Sketch of Piaget's three mountains task (the task was done with real, three-dimensional material, not paper-pencil)

(2) *Preoperational stage*: from 2 to 6 years, characterised by fast learning of language and norms, irrationalities such as cognitive egocentrism, no perception of logical contradictions, anthropomorphic and magical thinking, finalism and animism.

(3) *Concrete operational stage*: from 7 to 11 years, children start to think logically (hierarchical classification, conservation of mass, number and volume, decentring) but in a concrete, on obvious aspects fixed way.

(4) *Formal operational stage*: from age 11 onwards, persons develop abstract and hypothetical thinking, metacognition (thinking about thinking), understand syllogism and think in an epistemically rational way like a scientist should.[11]

Piaget summarised this development of thinking as an advancement from cognitive egocentrism to decentred thinking (Piaget, 2001/1947). He developed and examined the theory by observing children in everyday life cognitive scenarios. He did not use paper-and-pencil tests and statistics. One famous task is the three mountains task, as demonstrated in Figure 3.2, which was applied

---

[11] The reported ages refer to children in modernity.

in a real world setting with a Teddy bear: the child sees three mountains in a miniature landscape. A Teddy sits on the other side. The child is asked to construct with three paper mountains what the Teddy is seeing. This task measures the ability of *perspective taking* (vs. cognitive egocentrism). Children in the preoperational stage (2 to 6 years) think the Teddy sees the world like the child; children in the concrete operational stage can take the perspective of the Teddy.

There are no standardised results for populations. Piaget's research was focused on the study of general cognitive development as a kind of becoming an objective and rational person. However, age differences (in which age certain stages are reached) or stage differences (whether stages are fully or partially achieved in a given age) can be correlated with results of psychometric and educational tests as well as achievements (degrees etc.). The average correlations between Piagetian tasks (across individual differences) and intelligence tests are $r = .49$ (Jensen, 1980, p. 674), with student achievement tests $r = .55$ (Jensen, 1980, p. 674) and with scholastic achievement $r = .54$, and with maths even $r = .73$ (Hattie, 2009, p. 43).[12] The correlations are within the spectrum of correlations among various psychometric intelligence tests and between psychometric and student achievement test results.

These high correlations do not undermine the theoretical value of the Piagetian approach at all. They only show the homogeneity of cognitive development across individual differences. Age results can be compared across time and countries. The development of individuals and over historical time is not masked by different standardisation. However, the use of Piagetian scenarios in large scale studies is not really possible, because, at least originally, they are single person tests.

Another example of real world tasks similar to the Piagetian ones are questions used by Alexander Luria (1976/1974) in his Central Asia study. For example peasants were asked:

'In the far north, where there is snow, all bears are white. Novaya Zemlya is in the far north and there is always snow. What colour are the bears?' (Logic reasoning, syllogisms, formal operational stage.)

Or 'Here we have four things: a hammer, a saw, a log, and a hatchet. Please group together those that were similar or can be designated by one word.' (Categorisation, concrete operational stage.)

Tasks similar to those in everyday life are used as measures of cognitive ability. In anthropological approaches, usually no tasks are presented; typical behaviour is observed (e.g. Hallpike, 1980).

---

[12] In my own, yet to be published study with Piagetian tasks and a Raven Matrices test (CPM) the correlation was $r = .49$ ($N = 40$ children in kindergarten in Styria/Austria).

The most important advantage of the Piagetian approach is not in measurement, but in theory. It shows a large heuristic value for understanding people's thinking in former times and in cross-cultural comparison, e.g. understanding phenomena such as animism, trials against animals, magic and cruelty (Hallpike, 1980; Oesterdiekhoff, 2009b, 2012a, 2014b). The Piagetian approach was widely received in sociology, philosophy and in philosophy of history. While for many the psychometric approach was too technical, focused on differences between persons and peoples and hereditary, the reception of 'genetic epistemology' benefited from its theoretical complexity and focus on advancement.

### 3.2.4   Educational Achievement

The measurement of educational achievement is a less homogenous approach than the psychometric or Piagetian ones. At first, the simple use of marks given by teachers, results of central exams and student achievement tests like PISA have to be distinguished. Researchers use all of them, but the terminology is not distinctive: terms used are 'scholastic aptitude', 'scholastic achievement', 'student achievement', 'student assessment', 'student competence' or 'literacy'. Among student achievement tests, tests with a pure diagnostic or scientific purpose have to be distinguished from tests for selection purposes such as the SAT (United States, since 1926) and the ACT (American College Testing, United States, since 1959).[13]

Traditionally, tests are used by psychologists or teachers to test single students or classes, e.g. measuring orthography or arithmetic ability. Large-scale student assessment tests, by contrast, take representative samples or measure entire populations, e.g. NAEP (National Assessment of Educational Progress, United States, since 1969), TIMSS (Trends in International Mathematics and Science Study, internationally, developed following NAEP, since 1995), PISA (Programme for International Student Assessment, internationally, since 2000) or PIRLS (Progress in International Reading Literacy Study, since 2001).[14] In the internationally applied large-scale student assessment tests the results are standardised at $M = 500$ and $SD = 100$. One widely recognised published task from the PISA reading literacy scale is the Lake Chad task (see Figure 3.3).

After presentation of the figures students were asked

(1) 'What is the depth of Lake Chad today?' (multiple choice, one correct answer to be marked is hidden among several not correct ones),

---

[13] The SAT changed its label nearly every two decades: Scholastic Achievement Test, then Scholastic Aptitude Test, then Scholastic Assessment Test, now it has no meaning, purely 'SAT'.

[14] There are more student achievement tests, older and regional ones. See appendix.

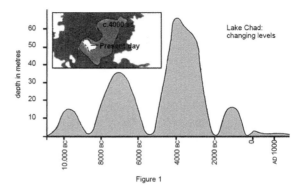

Figure 1

Saharan rock art and changing patterns of wildlife

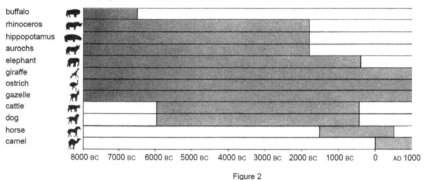

Figure 2

Figure 3.3 PISA 2000 Lake Chad task (sketchy; OECD, 2006)

(2) 'In about which year does the graph in Figure 1 start?' (open format, needs to be written down),
(3) 'Why has the author chosen to start the graph at this point?' (open format),
(4) 'Figure 2 is based on the assumption that …' (four choices, one correct, e.g. 'the artists were highly skilled' or 'the animals were present at that time') and
(5) 'For this question you need to draw together information from Figure 1 and Figure 2. The disappearance of the rhinoceros, hippopotamus and aurochs from Saharan rock art happened …' (four choices, e.g. 'after the level of Lake Chad had been falling for over a thousand years' or 'at the beginning of the Ice Age', one correct).

This task measures the ability to read text, figures and numbers (1–5), to retrieve (1, 2, 5) and understand information (4, 5), to conclude/infer/reason (3, 4, 5) and to take others' perspective (3).

Researchers stress the distinctness of different achievement fields: of literacy (reading, writing, verbal, language) versus mathematics versus natural science. Initially, student achievement tests were intended to measure in a school-like way the knowledge acquired at school and its typical school-like application. TIMSS is such a curriculum-orientated test. Tasks are short and similar to school exams. PISA and PIRLS follow a different aim; they want to measure comprehension, the application of knowledge, the ability to understand real-life tasks and to solve problems embedded in real world contexts. This leads to longer tasks with overlapping domains: reading tasks include geography and biology contents (science); maths and science tasks include longer texts; science tasks overlap with mathematics. This mixture of domains enlarges the correlations between the results of different student achievement scales (Rindermann & Baumeister, 2015).

Theoretically, achievement test results are seen as the outcome of structured knowledge that has been accumulated across time through learning opportunities within school. Common theories describe in detail processes of comprehension while reading texts, figures and tables or solving mathematical problems (Kintsch, 1998; Mayer & Hegarty, 1996). The student achievement approach picked up the threads of expertise research (Ericsson, Krampe & Tesch-Romer, 1993) and of a social science view on cognitive ability (for an overview: Frankish & Ramsey, 2012).

Empirically, results (a) of different scales within student achievement tests and (b) of student achievement tests and other cognitive tests highly correlate. The positive manifold is present everywhere. Students who are good at reading relative to others are also good in mathematics. Relatively intelligent students are also good in school.

According to Schiefele et al. (2004, p. 171f.), average correlations between PISA scales at the individual data level using measured data are around $r_m = .65$. Using latent data, the theoretically error-free level, they reach $r_l = .80$. These correlations are *higher* than usually observed correlations between different scales within psychometric intelligence tests (around $r = .50$) or grades in different school subjects (around $r = .55$). PISA and CogAT scales[15] correlate around $r_m = .65$ or at the latent level $r_l = .74$.[16] According to Sonnleitner et al. (2013, p. 301) PISA-tasks in reading, maths and science highly load on a reasoning $g$ factor (average loadings $\lambda = .50$ and $.51$). This is not at all a specific PISA phenomenon. Other, more traditional student achievement tests also show high correlations with intelligence tests,

---

[15] CogAT, Cognitive Abilities Test, is a psychometric test that consists of a figural (culture reduced, fluid), a verbal and a numerical scale (two rather crystallised intelligence scales).

[16] Latent (theoretically free of error): personal communication of Cordula Artelt, 6 February 2004, manifest (as the given data are): calculated by the author.

e.g. the Kaufman Test of Educational Achievement and the Woodcock-Johnson intelligence-test correlate at the level of *g* factors with $r = .83$ (Kaufman et al., 2012). In PIAAC, the 'adults' PISA', the correlation between literacy and numeracy even reaches $r = .87$![17]

The description of high correlations is *not* meant as a critical statement. As aforementioned, the correlations are around $r = .50$ between psychometric IQ and Piaget tests. Common causes (genes, health, neurological structure, basic cognitive processes and abilities, physical environmental quality, psychological and cultural environmental quality, attitudes) and similar demands in solving different cognitive tasks unavoidably lead to high correlations, in the case of PISA's real-life tasks only boosted by similar item content.

### 3.2.5    *Cognitive Behaviour in Everyday Life and Its Sediments*

Until now we have presented tests and scenarios suitable for measuring cognitive ability. Why not directly look at what people are doing in everyday life: in family, jobs and leisure time? How they speak, think, educate, solve or avoid problems, read and write? How they organise their life, spend their time and means and how they communicate; what they have produced; what they believe and their values, worldview and way of understanding their life, their meaning of life.

Tests are easier to apply than analyses of everyday life behaviour. They are checked for psychometric criteria (objectivity, reliability, validity), they have norms. So why use other indicators? First of all, we cannot apply tests for people who lived in the past – they are dead. Even more important, the ultimate criterion of any ability and its estimation is *practised* ability. And this can be observed in everyday life and in 'sediments' of past cognitive behaviour, e.g. in written texts, in created art or in produced and used technologies. Test results were frequently criticised for lacking validity and cross-cultural comparability. As a reply, let us directly look at behaviour and its sediments.

Such an analysis needs to start with a *definition of cognitive ability,* of *intelligence, knowledge* and the *intelligent use of knowledge*: As suggested, intelligence is the ability to think, to solve problems in a cognitive way, to inductively and deductively reason, to think abstractly and to comprehend and understand the world. Knowledge is true, important and useful information. The intelligent use of knowledge is to use information for solving problems, reasoning, abstract thinking and comprehension. Taken together, this is cognitive ability.

---

[17] PIAAC, Programme for the International Assessment of Adult Competencies (OECD, 2013b, p. 85).

This concept, similarly to the Piagetian approach, needs to be guided by a normative theory of truth and a normative theory of rationality and, additionally, by a normative theory of education and of cognitive production. They all answer the question of what is correct thinking and true knowledge and why thinking and knowledge are important.

*Truth* can be found in statements. Statements need to be logical (especially consistent); they should correspond to the actual state of affairs (outside and inside people, in things, incidents, experiences and statements), they should avoid unfoundedly contradicting well-established theories (coherence; if contradicting well-established theories, a larger amount of evidence and arguments is necessary). Finally, a set of statements should not be selective, but contain the relevant aspects of a phenomenon.[18]

*Rationality* is an attitude, an ability and a way of practice that comprises consistency (no self-contradiction), uniformity (like cases are treated alike), coherence (actions themselves, and actions, attitudes and statements are related), simplicity (following Ockham: needless complications are avoided), and economy (efficiency) (Rescher, 1988, p. 16). Within rationality, for *action* instrumental rationality and for *thinking* epistemic rationality are distinguished: *instrumental rationality* (or means-end rationality, purposive rationality) means using suitable means for reasonable ends. *Epistemic rationality* describes an attitude guided by logicality, empiricity and argumentativity. Epistemic rationality, being orientated towards truth and recognition, is the ethics of thinking.[19]

'*Bildung*' (intellectual education) tries to impart true and important knowledge, thinking, the intelligent use of knowledge, an attitude that is interested in knowledge and thinking and rationality. To know more is better than to know less.

Finally, *actions* and *products* themselves can be assessed. Criteria are correctness, complexity (difficulty), coherence, invention and (incremental) innovation, functional and aesthetic quality. Rationality and results of modern science need to be applied to assess products according to these criteria. E.g. praying on a ship to avoid death by drowning is less intelligent and rational than learning to swim, or, at the institutional level, ensuring crew competence, security standards and shipping laws. Animism is an indicator of a lower cognitive ability level in contrast to a rational-empirical worldview. Here we see an affinity with the Piagetian approach.

---

[18] E.g. if somebody describes a car as an artificial product with a horn, lighting and a radio, all single statements are true, but they miss the central characteristics of a car (a motor vehicle usually with four wheels to transport humans). 'Das Wahre ist das Ganze.' ('The truth is the whole.'; Hegel, 1999/1807, p. 19).

[19] Similarly, but more narrow Jean Piaget (1948/1932, p. 404): 'Logic is the morality of thought just as morality is the logic of action.'

This can be assessed for individuals, but also for societies and cultures and for former times.[20] However, similar to the test approach, single items (here single behaviours, products and incidents) are not enough; larger samples of behaviours, products and incidents are necessary and they have to be as representative as possible.

## 3.3     Contentious Issues

### 3.3.1     Fragmentation and Compartmentalisation in Science

As previously mentioned, an *independence* of constructs, dimensions and measures was claimed that empirically is not given – the underlying abilities are highly correlated; causes of development are similar; contents, cognitive demands and processes are alike.

For research, having such a variety of approaches is a big advantage because information from different theory and measurement traditions can be used. But the given similarities are often ignored. On the one hand, that is a typical effect of paradigms, a kind of cognitive narrow-mindedness and strategic ignorance. People only read certain journals, understand and appreciate only 'their' methods, attend 'their' conferences and cite the work of 'their' colleagues (Fleck, 1979/1935; Kuhn, 1962). This attitude is also not alien to researchers in economics. There is an iron curtain inside the brain. But this is not a disadvantage in so far as different researchers and disciplines independently and recip-rocally confirm results of research, for instance, that the average ability level of one's peers and class has a positive effect on cognitive development (Dar & Resh, 1986; Sacerdote, 2011). Educationalists, economists and psychologists independently working at different planets came to the same results!

On the other hand, intentionally ignoring important contributions and the work of others is epistemically irrational and does not represent ethical integrity. In extreme cases this ignorance is motivated by interests, guarded by ideology and reinforced in a circle of false consciousness. One example is the relationship between parental SES and their children's results in one of the three achievement scales that is always mentioned in OECD reports on PISA (e.g. OECD, 2013d, pp. 38f.). To start with, it is misleading to do the analysis with a *single* scale (mathematics). This deludes the readers into believing that it is a specific relationship and not a general one between parental SES and

---

[20] Authors who have done this can be assigned to the Piagetian approach (e.g. Christopher Hallpike, Georg Oesterdiekhoff) or, not focused on cognitive ability, to the French history of mentalities (e.g. Lucien Febvre, Jacques Le Goff). Also, researchers vaguely affiliated to the psychometric paradigm have applied the everyday behaviour analysis approach, e.g. Robert Gordon, a sociologist.

children's cognitive competence. Scientifically even more deceptive is that any mention of *genetic* effects is missing. Research, e.g. by Kovas et al. (2005), has shown that the environmental family impact is much smaller than the genetic parental impact, here with $h^2 = .64$ on children's mathematics performance assessed by teachers.[21] Additionally, the largest genetic effect on mathematics was from one common genetic factor for *g* and reading. Or, according to Trzaskowski et al. (2014), the correlation between parental SES and children's IQ is at 75 per cent of genetic origin.[22] Higher cognitive ability leads to higher SES (e.g. Deary et al., 2005) and because parents are akin with their children, it would be impossible to find a zero correlation between parent's SES and children's cognitive competence in any country. Leaving out all this important information comes close to telling lies.

However, a purely psychometric IQ and individual differences approach has its own limits. The method of age-related standardisation incidentally underrates the growth of thinking and knowledge during childhood. The focus on individual differences, which show a high stability from youth to old age (e.g. from age 11 in 1932 to age 77 in 1998 $r = .63$; Deary et al., 2000), tempts one to mix up *relative* stability (the stability of individual differences) with *absolute* stability (that there are no increases or decreases across time). The individual differences approach also leads to overlooking the huge historical changes in average intelligence. The general level escalated while individual differences still remained.

Nevertheless, the psychometric approach became a kind of hoover research absorbing other paradigms on cognitive ability and opening itself to other perspectives and thus becoming an integrative paradigm: the variability of intelligence, e.g. as its secular rise was described several times (Flynn, 2012a; Lynn, 2013), student achievement test results are integrated (e.g. Lynn & Vanhanen, 2012), the Piagetian approach is welcomed (Oesterdiekhoff, 2012b), economists can publish in the psychology journal *Intelligence* and do it regularly (e.g. Belasen & Hafer, 2012).

### 3.3.2  Political-Scientific Concerns and Epistemic-Ideological Confoundings

Intelligence research is still ignored by student achievement research. PISA, PIRLS and TIMSS reports do not mention related and convergent results from

---

[21] According to Kovas et al. (2005, their table 2), the correlation between monozygotic twins (MZ) in mathematics was $r = .75$, between dizygotic twins (DZ) $r = .43$. According to the heritability formula (Falconer's formula) $h^2 = 2(r_{MZ}-r_{DZ})$ heritability is $h^2 = 2(.75-.43) = .64$. Environmental effects can be here at maximum .36.

[22] The study of Trzaskowski et al. (2014) was conducted in Great Britain, and the children were 7 or 12 years old. The correlation between SES and IQ was $r = .32$, and the genetic part of this correlation is around $r = .23$.

intelligence or Piagetian research. Maybe there is some political and ideological influence. This, although never explicitly expressed in science, could
be the main reason: psychometric intelligence research was inclined towards
a genetic-hereditarian point of view from the beginning, starting with the
famous work of Francis Galton in 1869, *Hereditary Genius*. Francis Galton,
cousin of Charles Darwin, was a genius himself, a polymath who worked on
anthropology, geography, meteorology, photography, fingerprints, genetics,
statistics, giftedness, mental speed and intelligence; additionally he was an
explorer and travel writer.[23] In particular, due to his work on cognition,
statistics and genetics he became the founder of psychometrics and differential psychology.[24]

Because Galton (he was married, but childless) assumed that cognitive
ability and genius are largely based on genetic factors, because parents and
children are akin and because he valued high cognitive ability resp. genius as
an important good for persons themselves, their parents and society, he
developed the concept of 'eugenics'. All three premises are backed by empirical research: genetic factors contribute to, but do not exclusively determine,
intelligence and genius; parents and children are genetically related; high
intelligence and genius have more positive than negative aspects. The positive
valuation of intelligence and genius could be substantiated by their consequences for individuals, others, society and culture and is most probably
shared by the majority of people. Therefore, the consequence, to support the
spread of healthy and beneficial genes, is intellectually and ethically convincing. The chosen ways could be wrong or good (assessed according to
standards of functionality and ethics), could be worse or better compared to
others, but the main idea as described in the three premises and the conclusion
could hardly be rejected.

Galton's idea was picked up by many researchers in the realms of statistics
and psychometrics (Karl Pearson, 1857–1936, Galton Chair of Eugenics at the
University of London), of psychometrics and giftedness (Lewis M. Terman,
1877–1956, developer of the Stanford-Binet-Test, initiator of the most important study on high ability, professor at Stanford, president of the American
Psychological Association, APA) and of psychometrics and dysgenics
(Richard Lynn, *1930, University of Ulster, one of the discoverers of the

---

[23] Both Darwin and Galton were independent researchers, living from their inheritance. They
never worked as professor or scientist at a university. They did not depend on income from
lectures, books or talks. They were not dependent on anybody's consent. They did not apply for
research grants. This guaranteed their independence (see also Hayek, 2011/1960, chapter 8,
'Employment and Independence'). Retirement seems to have a similar effect today, liberating
researchers from zeitgeist constraints.

[24] Differential psychology: research on individual differences in ability and personality.

secular rise of intelligence, initiator of international intelligence comparisons, research on dysgenics, e.g. Lynn, 1996).

Finally, Francis Galton is an initiator for studies on racial differences in cognitive ability. 'Race' is defined as an evolutionary differentiation of a species into subgroups, a correlated pattern of phenotype and genotype, usually called 'subspecies' (for humans this is also known as 'genetic clusters' or 'ancestry'). In the past, scientific studies were frequently accompanied by older expressions for subspecific evolutionary groups (e.g. 'Negro' or 'Mongoloid') and comments that are seen as disparaging today. Also, more modern research in psychology (e.g. Jensen, 1969; Rushton, 1997/1995; Lynn, 2006) and in economics (e.g. Neal, 2006) have frequently dealt with 'racial' differences, 'race' used as a pure descriptive category or as a historical-cultural or evolutionary-genetic causal variable.

After the second world war, 'eugenics' and 'race' were associated with the politics of National Socialism. And opponents of intelligence research additionally have associated intelligence research, because 'eugenics' and 'race' were among other topics of research, with National Socialist or right-wing research. For instance, the French sociologist Pierre Bourdieu (1993/1978) polemicised in a paper 'The racism of intelligence' against intelligence research itself as racist:

I am thinking of IQ racism, the racism of intelligence ... The racism of intelligence is the means through which the members of the dominant class aim to produce a 'theodicy of their own privilege', as Weber puts it, in other words, a justification of the social order that they dominate. ... Having said that, I think one should purely and simply refuse to accept the problem of the biological or social foundations of 'intelligence', in which psychologists have allowed themselves to be trapped. Rather than trying to decide the question scientifically, one should to try to look scientifically at the question itself – and try to analyse the social conditions of the emergence of this kind of enquiry and of the class racism to which it points the way. (p. 177f.)[25]

Later Bourdieu (2001, p. 51) also denounced the economist and human capital researcher Gary Becker as a 'neo-Darwinist'. Similar accusations towards cognitive ability researchers can be frequently found on the Internet and Wikipedia. Two aspects are especially relevant in Bourdieu's critique.

First, Bourdieu overstretches the concept of 'racism'. 'Racism' is unsubstantiated schematic thinking towards a group and individuals (wrongly or correctly connected to an evolutionary background) leading to empirically wrong assertions with a negatively valued assessment or leading to empirically correct assertions with an unfounded negatively valued assessment resulting in

---

[25] The translation into English was paid for by the French government (French Ministry of Culture). Bourdieu received several honorary doctorates, honorary medals and awards from universities in different countries. So, who is a 'member of the dominant class'?

unjustified behavioural consequences. In spite of the possibility of assessing individuals by their individuality, they are only treated as a member of a group. Bourdieu sees racism as an attempt at self-justification of power. This is a different phenomenon and not 'racism'.

Second, Bourdieu opposes scientific research. According to him, biological or social determinants of cognitive ability, its development and differences should and must not be researched. It is best to answer him with his own words:

We would also need to note methodically all the cases where politicization functions as a compensatory strategy allowing an escape from the specific laws of the academic or scientific market, for instance all forms of political criticism of scientific studies which allow scientifically outmoded producers to give themselves – and to give their peers – the illusion that they transcend what transcends them. (Bourdieu, 1988/1984, p. 20)

It is ironic that an author can be refuted in such a devastating way with his own words, an indicator for a disorganised way of thinking: political criticism of scientific studies allows the scientifically outmoded the illusion that they transcend what transcends them. It is no speciality to politically attack a field or a person as Bourdieu has done against intelligence research and against Gary Becker. There had even been violent attacks in the past; the Berkeley psychologist Arthur Jensen needed to be guarded by the police; the Canadian psychologist Philippe Rushton was attacked by the Prime Minister of Ontario who called for his University to dismiss him; invited presentations of the Harvard psychologist Richard Herrnstein were denounced as 'fascist'; talks needed to be cancelled etc. (Herrnstein, 1973; Nyborg, 2003; Segerstråle, 2000).

One final example is Robert Sternberg. In 2013 he 'morally' attacked a paper and its author, Earl Hunt (2012). Statements and motives were projected into Hunt's article, where any such mentions and hints were missing in the original text. Two examples:

Some of the countries today that are congratulated by Hunt as high in IQ are repressive dictatorships (disguised as self-labeled 'democracies'). (p. 188)

Hunt admires the Spaniards, who conquered the Incas and Aztecs with their superior 'cognitive artifacts'. (p. 188)

Sternberg's comments attribute value judgements and motives to Hunt that he did not state, and they do so in a manner that leaves a disparaging impression of him (see also the critique by Coyle et al., 2013). Hereafter, an unethical and unsubstantiated criticism of scientists along with a feeling of moral superiority should be dubbed *to sternberg*.

It is also quite difficult to understand how Pierre Bourdieu, a frequently awarded and supported person by different universities and ministries, a member of the well-respected international scientific elite, published by highly reputed companies and frequently invited to presentations, can attack others as members and defenders of the ruling classes: other scientists even have difficulties presenting their work orally or in writing to the scientific and wider public. The opposite is true; the ruling classes in media and science attack the outsiders with epistemically, argumentatively and ethically unjustifiable means. Scientists such as Ignaz Semmelweis, who have challenged institutionally leading groups in science, even more so when they have touched the spirit of the times, were always unwelcome.[26]

Contradicting common beliefs, National Socialists were *opposed* to intelligence research (Becker, 1938; Jaensch, 1938): in their view, intelligence research would represent a 'supremacy of Bourgeoisie spirit' (Jaensch, 1938, p. 2); intelligence measurement would be an instrument 'of Jewry' to 'fortify its hegemony' (p. 3); selection in schools according to intelligence would stand for a 'system of examination of Jewish origin' (p. 4), especially the concept of intelligence as a 'one-dimensional dimension' (p. 3) and 'one common central factor' (Becker, 1938, p. 24). Because people differ and therefore intelligence differs (p. 4) they called for an 'intelligence measurement according to a national and typological point of view' (p. 15); for Germans they asked for a measurement of 'realism', 'conscientiousness' and 'actually of the character value of intelligence'. They were opposed to a measurement solely of 'theoretical intelligence', of 'intellectualism' (Becker, 1938, p. 22); instead they favoured 'practical intelligence' (p. 18) that should be measured. Nazi researchers were opposed to the methods of correlation and factor analysis (p. 23f.); general intelligence did not exist: 'In fact there is no general, qualitatively comparable and from type independent intelligence.' (Jaensch, 1938, p. 4)

If the term 'Jewish' were exchanged for 'dominant class' we would have the same critique as mentioned by Bourdieu, only 40 years earlier and developed by the National Socialists. And the critique from the 'left' of today against cross-cultural intelligence comparisons, incomparability, bias, $g$ factor etc. was also first mentioned by the National Socialists.

Of cause, this is all scientifically irrelevant, because statements cannot be disproved by showing who has said something too, before, simultaneously or later. Only logic, empirical data and content-based arguments count. If 'Jews' (or gentiles), 'ruling classes' (or suppressed people), 'Capitalists' (or workers),

---

[26] Ignaz Semmelweis (1818–1865) was a physician in Vienna who discovered that the incidence of puerperal fever could be drastically reduced by the use of hand disinfecting in obstetrical clinics. This discovery was rejected by the then leading medical community. Doctors felt offended by the allegation that they could be responsible for the death of young mothers. As a consequence, young mothers continued to die. *Semmelweis reflex* is a term for the reflex-like tendency to reject new or divergent theories because they contradict established concepts and norms held by important groups.

'Whites', 'Europeans' (or Africans) or somebody else benefits from intelligence or intelligence research, this does not make any statement more or less wrong or correct. It is true that in modernity and in at least partly meritoric societies the 'upper classes' have on average higher intelligence (intelligence helps to climb the social ladder; Deary et al., 2005; Saunders, 1997), and that 'Whites', 'Europeans', and 'Jews' have higher average intelligence and that 'Jews' are outstandingly represented in research including intelligence, but does this change the veridicality of statements?[27] If something like the intelligence concept is rejected due to ethnic or social contexts, with the same argument it would be possible to reject money, books, psychology or science itself. Scientific (epistemic) statements have to be evaluated by their approximation to truth and finding new truth. Political, ideological or ethical criteria cannot substitute criteria of truth.

Similar to National Socialism, in *Communism* intelligence research was condemned. Alexander Luria was unable to publish his pioneering cross-cultural study on cognitive ability before 1974, which he conducted four decades earlier in the 1930s in Uzbekistan.

It seems to be that once again *les extrêmes se touchent*, here in the National Socialist and Communist opposition against intelligence research. And it is another hint that intelligence is a *civic-burgher phenomenon*.

Because of such negative associations and political pressures, caution in the student achievement approach about adopting the results of intelligence research is instrumentally rational ('zweckrational'), e.g. facilitating receiving grants, getting manuscripts published and enhancing one's career. But it is not epistemically rational. Other terms such as 'literacy' or 'skill' may gain easier acceptance. 'Name is but sound and smoke'. Insofar as they are properly defined, not too narrow or broad and consistently used, there is no reason for being upset. But due to the missing reception of intelligence research there are other serious scientific shortcomings:

- *Environmentalism*: any research on heritability and genes is ignored, whether it used psychometric intelligence or student achievement tests or with school marks as indicators of cognitive ability (an overview on behavioural genetics e.g. Plomin et al., 2013a). Environmental correlations such as between parental SES, school quality and children's achievement are interpreted as mere

---

[27] Some researchers with Jewish origin in the broader field of cognitive ability research: Alfred Binet, Howard Gardner, Michael Hart, Richard Herrnstein, Paul Irwing, Seymour W. Itzkoff, Arthur Jensen, Lucien Lévy-Bruhl, Alexander Luria, Ulric Neisser, Steven Pinker, Peter Salovey, K. Warner Schaie, Otto Selz, Théodore Simon, William Stern, Robert Sternberg, Lev Vygotsky, David Wechsler, Robert Weissberg, Heinz Werner. My work and this book have benefited from the groundwork of many of them also, including in subjects other than intelligence research, e.g. from Norbert Elias, Lawrence Harrison, Lee Jussim, David Landes, Ludwig von Mises and Byron Roth.

environmental effects. This is fundamentally wrong, because environment and genes are related (Scarr & McCartney, 1983). In particular, the possibility of an individual and group shaping its environment is neglected: this can happen (1) passively, as genetically related parents transmit an adapted environment, (2) evocatively, as different people elicit different reactions of an environment, and (3) actively, as people select and create environments according to their ability and personality. The physical environment around us can be seen as the extended phenotype of genes in us (Dawkins, 2008/1992).[28]

- *Societism*: related or rooted in environmentalism is the view that society as a kind of independent external entity has created (frequently negatively valued) conditions of life for individuals and groups. However, society is influenced by individuals and past individuals, by their culture, by external influences (e.g. neighbouring countries), and by internal influences and of course by genetic factors.
- *Feasibility illusion*: related to environmentalism and societism is the idea of producibility of desired states of society by means of social engineering. However, society, culture and individuals, including their abilities, are empirically stable and multidetermined entities, not only determined by modifiable current conditions.
- *Schoolism*: schoolism is a part of the feasibility illusion that school education only needs to be adjusted properly and is accordingly changeable, and that by improvements in school an intended state of ability and ability distribution can be achieved. Other determinants of ability development are neglected.

### 3.3.3   Not All Relevant Aspects of Education Are Covered

Another critique deals with the narrow concept of education covered by the test approach. Student achievement studies measure competences, the ability to solve tasks in reading, mathematics and science.[29] However, the contents

---

[28] Dawkins (2008/1992, p. 200) described one example for an extended phenotype in detail, the landscape in which beavers live: 'A beaver dam is built close to the lodge, but the effect of the dam may be to flood an area thousands of square metres in extent . . . The lake may be regarded as a huge extended phenotype, extending the foraging range of the beaver in a way which is somewhat analogous to the web of the spider. As in the case of the spider web, nobody has done a genetic study of beaver dams, but we really do not need to in order to convince ourselves of the rightness of regarding the dam, and the lake, as part of the phenotypic expression of beaver genes. It is enough that we accept that beaver dams must have evolved by Darwinian natural selection: this can only have come about if dams have varied under the control of genes.' According to Kendler & Baker (2007), the average heritability of human environment attributes is $h^2 = .27$.

[29] Only marginally were other domains covered as problem-solving (PISA 2003) or the ability to use computers ('problem-solving in technology-rich environments', adult study PIAAC 2012).

of instruction and the aims of education are broader; they also include writing (orthography, grammar, sentence construction, structure, dramatic arc, style), oral presentations, foreign languages, music, art, sports, and not only knowledge and competences, but also preferences, interests and ethics. The scholastic test movement is the offspring of an empirically orientated approach to education developed in the United States. The broad, emphatically loaded concept of enlightened and neo-humanistic 'Bildung' (intellectual-ethical education) is not covered in its whole spectrum. The testing movement could lead to teaching to test and under certain circumstances to fraud (e.g. in Atlanta 2011; New York Times, 2011).

These critics are correct; however, we should not demand too much from an international test approach. There are limits of measurability. Usually, different aspects of educational quality and competences are correlated, but, of course, not perfectly. Education has to be founded on justified contents and aims, not on measurement. Standardised achievement tests cannot replace teaching, marking and the role of teachers. Education, especially self-education, contains more. This is true and should not be forgotten.

## 3.4     Cognitive Development and Its Determinants

### 3.4.1     Description of Development across Lifespan

The psychometrist Raymond B. Cattell (1987/1971) described for his model of fluid and crystallised intelligence a diverging development pattern (Figure 3.4): fluid intelligence increases up to age 20, crystallised until around age 50. Empirical support indicates that mental speed, as a part of fluid intelligence, declines at a younger age and that vocabulary, as a part of crystallised intelligence, in older age. Similarly, working memory, the number of units that can be stored and processed, increases in childhood and starts to decrease in younger adulthood, depending on mental speed (Fry & Hale, 1996).

The general pattern is confirmed by empirical studies (Baltes, 1997; Salthouse, 2013). It is also backed by studies on exceptional achievement that show an achievement peak between 30 to 40 years in science, engineering and chess (Bertoni et al., 2013; Lehman, 1966; Simonton, 1988).[30] This has serious consequences for an ageing society, with rising cognitive demands (see Section 12.2.1).

Unlike Cattell, Piaget did not assume any age decline in cognitive development. Student achievement research started with studies on adults

---

[30] Peak achievement according to age depends not only on cognitive factors on the part of the individual but also on part of the domain, e.g. complexity, innovation and competition by others.

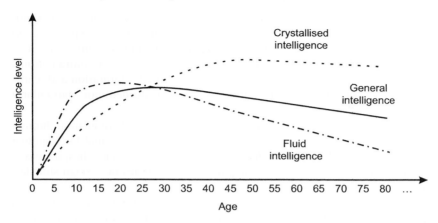

Figure 3.4 Development of fluid and crystallised intelligence according to the model of Cattell

in 2012 (PIAAC). Cross-sectional research shows a literacy and numeracy peak at age 25 to 35 years (OECD, 2013b, pp. 190ff.).[31] The psychometric intelligence research results are corroborated by the student achievement approach; they are slightly more similar to the results found for fluid intelligence.

### 3.4.2   Developmental Processes

Development can be controlled by *internal factors*, by *external factors* or by a *combination* of both. Factors influence development itself and differences in development. In the mental speed and working memory approaches, development depends on *biologically driven maturation*. Maturation means a neurological process, mainly the improved myelination of axons. This biological process is internally driven by genes, but needs support by a healthy environment. An unfed body cannot survive; poisons harm; proteins, vitamins and trace elements help.

---

[31] The age-related pattern is more accentuated in cross-sectional studies, in which age and cohort effects are confounded, than in longitudinal studies only measuring age effects. Cohort effects mean that today's older people had worse environmental conditions in their youth (e.g. less education, lower quality nutrition and less general stimulation), resulting in a general gap between the generations that biases the differences between today's young and old persons, which are therefore not only age differences.

Piaget's theory also followed the *maturation* concept, but in a *psychological* way: children need to be cognitively challenged by experiences in an average everyday life environment. By reaching one's cognitive limits – experiences do not fit into existing concepts, discovery of contradictions, failures of assimilation – development is stimulated. Maturation and learning are entangled. Special training is neither needed nor particularly helpful.

The *learning* concept is different: here, psychological stimulation through environment shaped by families, school and society is essential for cognitive development. In the student achievement and expertise approaches, increased cognitive competence is seen as acquired knowledge learnt through stimulating environments.

A further concept describes development as a *dynamic process* inside a person or as interaction between the person and environment, in which the environment and its relevance are selected and influenced by the person. Piaget's theory of cognitive development fits in this concept, as does the model of mutualism for intelligence by Maas et al. (2006): different internal cognitive processes interact, resulting in general intelligence. Also, interactions such as between cognitive ability and school anxiety belong to this concept: ability reduces through success detrimental anxiety and lower anxiety leads to better learning and better concentration ability.

Such dynamics can explain why people with increasing age differ more: given the same time and stimulation, more intelligent students will acquire more knowledge. Their reasoning abilities will be trained better; they will be more effective in finding stimulating environments, where they can improve their knowledge and competences. Gagné's (2005) empirical study demonstrates, with a test that is not age-standardised, this development (see Figure 3.5): while in form one (at age six to seven years) the standard deviation is $SD = 15$, it is in the same norm in form four (at age nine to ten) $SD = 28$ and in form nine (at age 14 to 15) $SD = 43$. While in form one the difference between the percentile ranks 16 and 84 is 30 IQ points, corresponding to around one year difference of school learning of average students in this test and sample, it is 55 'first form standardised' IQ points in form four, corresponding to around three to four years school difference and in form nine it is 83 'first form' IQ points, corresponding to around six years school difference. Every age-related standardisation conceals such spreading development.

This does not mean that external interventions or internal deliberate decisions would not have any impact: minor interventions may push long-running developments, leading in the end to very diverging states of individuals and societies (see Figure 3.6).

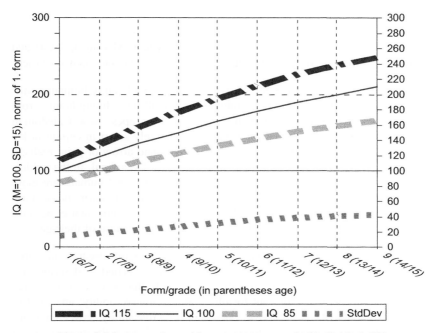

Figure 3.5 Increase of cognitive competences and of individual differences from form 1 to form 9 in the constant norms of form 1 (Iowa Tests of Basic Skills: average of reading, language, mathematics), results slightly smoothed (Gagné, 2005)

Figure 3.6 Illustration of positive or negative running, spiral-shaped, dynamical developments

### 3.4.3    Genes

Evidence for genetic effects on intelligence is old (e.g. Merriman, 1924) and frequently corroborated by various studies of different authors in many countries.

*Comparison of Species*    It is obvious that all healthy humans from around age two onwards are more intelligent than all other living beings from different species. Some non-human species such as apes, New Caledonian Crows, dolphins and Border Collie dogs are relatively smart in certain tasks. But no animal is able to use fire, construct a bow and arrow or paint realistic pictures in caves. This difference is clearly genetic. No animal, in the wilderness or educated by humans, has learnt these abilities. That humans are more intelligent is a result of genes that enabled them to invent, learn and develop cultures. The same is true for animal differences: dogs are not smarter because they are better educated than mice. They are smarter because of their genes.

*Molecular Genetic Evidence*    Molecular genetic research has three aims: first to find genes coding for cognitive ability; second to describe in a detailed way how such genes specify amino acids that lead to neurological structures and processes relevant for observable cognitive ability; and third to find those genes that can explain differences in cognitive ability between individuals and groups. A discovery of molecular genetic evidence is the most important step to corroborate a theory of genetic influence on intelligence. Genomewide association studies (GWAS) try to go in this direction. They correlate the expression of genes (alleles of genes, more specific: single-nucleotide polymorphisms, SNPs) with phenotypic cognitive attributes such as IQ test results. Another research option is to look for candidate genes, alleles of genes for which a causal theory exists or former research has shown associations with test results.

The results have been disappointing so far. There are not really robust findings from GWAS (Chabris et al., 2012). As Ian Deary (2012, p. 463) has summarised it:

Molecular genetics. With almost-equal justification, this section of the overview could be very long or very short: very long, because dozens of candidate genes have been reported as being associated with intelligence; very short, because almost none of them has been replicated.

Nevertheless, the work has started. And a variant of GWAS, the 'genome-wide complex trait analysis (GCTA)', meaning the correlation of genetic SNP (Single Nucleotide Polymorphism) similarity with phenotype similarity (Plomin et al., 2013b), supports genetic influence and here several SNPs correlated with intelligence were found and replicated (Piffer, 2013). Research and replication studies are continuing, with promising results (e.g. for DUF1220; Davis et al., 2015). After finding correlative evidence for single genes, molecular ways to amino acids, the nervous system and intelligence have to be found.

*Evidence from Animal Breeding Studies*   Breeding studies with rats from the 1930s and 1940s were undertaken by Edward Tolman, Robert Tryon and W. Heron (Heron, 1941; Innis, 1992): rats were divided into two groups and bred for learning ability (tested with a maze); on the one hand the smart learners were bred with smart learners, and on the other hand the slower learners with slower learners. After eight generations, the differences increased so much that there was no remaining overlap in intelligence between the distributions of the two lines.

A similar experiment, not with intelligence, but with tameness, was done with wild foxes in Russia (Trut, 1999): the silver fox became a psychologically different species after 30 to 35 generations of breeding for tameness: docile, without fear, feedable by hand, affectionate, friendly. The new foxes sought human contact. Their friendly behaviour was evident before the pups were one month old. Again, there was no remaining overlap to the old wild line.

Both studies unequivocally show that animal behaviour, here intelligence and tameness, is influenced by genes and could be fundamentally changed within a few generations. This knowledge, that behaviour is influenced by genes, can be transferred to humans. Of course, any conclusion by analogy is not secure, but why should any evolutionary principles be different for humans?

*Evidence from Behavioural Genetics*   For centuries, people have known that relatives resemble each other in behaviour: 'He's got that from his grandpa' or 'She has learnt it from her mother.' In scientific language, psychological traits of relatives correlate. However, parents and children do not only share genes but also environment. This connectedness was first described by Francis Galton (2005/1869, p. 81) and he offered a solution to disentangle them:

I must not compare the sons of eminent men with those of non-eminent, because much which I should ascribe to breed, others might ascribe to parental encouragement and example. Therefore, I will compare the sons of eminent men with the adopted sons of Popes and other dignitaries of the Roman Catholic Church.

For ethical reasons, breeding studies are not possible for humans, but the use of *natural experiments* is. Such an approach, the first idea came from Galton, was refined by behavioural genetic research:

- The comparison in phenotypic similarity of *monozygotic twins* (100 per cent of genes are identical, except for rare mutations) with the phenotypic similarity of *dizygotic twins* (on average 50 per cent of genes are identical, like usual siblings), both living in their families. If monozygotic twins are more similar, this larger similarity can be attributed to genes.
- Comparison in phenotypic similarity of *monozygotic twins reared apart*.

- Comparison in phenotypic similarity of *adopted children* with their *biological and their adoptive parents*.
- Comparison in phenotypic similarity of *adopted children* with their *biological siblings* and the *non-related children* of their adoptive parents.
- Comparison in phenotypic similarity of *children* with their *biological parents* (mother and father) and their *stepparents* (usually stepfathers) in patchwork families.
- Comparison in phenotypic similarity of *differently related children* in patchwork families.

These natural designs allow estimates of the 'heritability' of any biological or psychological trait such as height, political orientation, intelligence or school achievement. Heritability ($h^2$) is the percentage of *individual differences* attributable to genetic factors (additive genetic factors, also called 'A'). The other variance is due to environmental effects, which is again divided into the impact of 'shared' or 'common environment' (the family effect, shared/common for siblings, 'C') and of 'non-shared' effects (specific environmental effects inside and outside the family combined with 'error', statistically the rest, 'E'). The three factors can be estimated by mathematical formulas (e.g. Plomin et al., 2013a).[32]

For intelligence, the heritability is around $h^2 = .50$ to $.80$. There is no precise single number because heritability rises with age (from around $h^2 = .20$-$.30$ below age 3 to $h^2 = .50$ around age 10 and $h^2 = .80$-$.90$ for age 20 and older; Bouchard, 2004; Johnson, 2010). Accordingly, the numbers for environment decrease (see Figure 3.7).

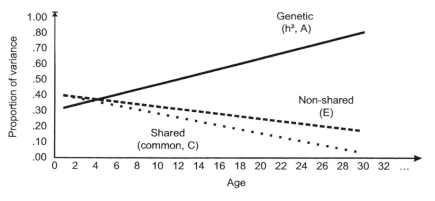

Figure 3.7 Proportions of variance attributable to genetic and shared and non-shared environmental effects depending on age in cognitive ability (schematically outlined, based on Bouchard, 2004, and Johnson, 2010)

---

[32] The model is simplified as interactions, covariances and assortative mating are not considered (see Jensen, 1998, p. 174).

There are further modifying factors for heritability and 'environmentality': the larger the variability in environmental quality, the higher its impact on individual differences. On the other hand, in a totally homogenous society and environment as drawn by different utopian approaches (Campanella's Città del sole, Marx' Communism, Zionist-Socialist Kibbutzim, Skinner's Walden II) all remaining minor differences could be only explained by genes (Herrnstein, 1973). Similarly, good environmental conditions decrease the explanative effect of remaining environmental conditions. According to the law of diminishing returns, a small improvement at low environmental quality level shows larger impact (Turkheimer et al., 2003; for the good environmental quality of adoptive parents: Stoolmiller, 1999). Assortative mating leads to underestimations of heritability (Vinkhuyzen et al., 2012).

The heritability concept has led to several misunderstandings. The limits of behavioural genetics should not be ignored: (1) First of all, heritability is only a *statement on differences*. Seventy per cent heritability does not mean that of an IQ of 100, 70 points belongs to genes and 30 to environment. (2) Second, it is only related to *differences* between *individuals*, not between groups (Bronfenbrenner & Ceci, 1994; Block, 1995). Concerning the latter, only plausibility considerations using analogy are possible; for instance, if genes are important for individual differences and for individual development, they seem to be also important for group differences and evolutionary development. (3) Third, we do not know by this design anything about *single genes* or *environmental determinants*, how they work and what we can do to improve cognitive ability. (4) Fourth, high heritability does not reduce the *effect of interventions*, e.g. myopia is heritable and genetically determined; however, its consequences can be easily remedied by using glasses. (5) Fifth, phenotypic attributes as having two ears are *genetically determined*, but their heritability is low, because there is no variability in genes and variation belongs only to environment (accidents or madness as van Gogh; Block, 1995; Sesardic, 2005).

Finally, there are some misleading allegations such as the 'Burt affair'. Cyril Burt (1883–1971) was a British psychologist who was one of the pioneers of twin and heritability research. He was accused of having falsified his data, e.g. correlations across his different samples would have been too similar to be true (e.g. Hearnshaw, 1979). Others such as Joynson (1989) did not see any fraud. However, from a scientific viewpoint, to find answers on the genetic and environmental determinants of intelligence it is irrelevant whether Burt has or has not done any fraud, because independent research by others in several countries using different methods has convincingly found the same pattern of results.

In other realms of cognitive ability research, forgery has been unquestionably proved and researchers were sentenced and imprisoned by courts for their fraud – for example, Rick Heber and his colleagues from the Milwaukee

Project, who have 'shown' that intelligence could be improved by education in preschool age by about 20 to 30 IQ points.[33] Nevertheless, further research (e.g. Perry Preschool Program or Abecedarian) has shown positive effects of preschool education, including midterm effects on IQ. Nobody doubts their effects because some other person has acted fraudulently.

A second rehashed allegation deals with twin research undertaken by National Socialist physicians in concentration camps (Josef Mengele). They performed cruel medical experiments. However, as medical research, e.g. in Harvard, is not related to medical research in concentration camps, twin research in Minnesota is not related to twin research in Auschwitz and scientifically there is no relationship or impact at all for cognitive ability research. Opponents of science try to associate what they do not like in science with political phenomena; they criticise in an unethical way by using bogus ethical reasons; they 'sternberg' other scientists (see Section 3.3.2).

*Evidence from Everyday Life Experience*    Some scientifically weak evidence for genetic effects comes from everyday life experience. Relatives resemble each other not only in their appearance but also in their behaviour, attitudes and thinking. But nature and nurture are interwoven. Variability among siblings is striking and meaningful. As many parents have observed, their children, in spite of the same parents and family, differ and they differ more than any plausible explanation can attribute to birth order, different class mates or friends. As the behavioural geneticist David T. Lykken has described:

The denial of genetically based psychological differences is the kind of sophisticated error normally accessible only to persons having Ph.D. degrees. Even the be-doctored tend to give up radical environmentalism once they have a second child. (Lykken, 1998)

*Summary on Genetic Factors*    Different scientific access, comparisons across species, animal breeding studies and behavioural genetics give robust evidence for strong genetic effects on cognitive ability. However, the most important proof, molecular genetic evidence explaining the genetic effects from genes to proteins, neurological structures and processes resulting in observable cognitive behaviour, is still missing. 'Genetic explanations' are, so far, black box explanations. Up to now, single environmental explanations, if proved in experimental designs, are more corroborated than single genetic effects and they can help to design beneficial interventions.

High heritabilities, especially that individual differences in adulthood are nearly only attributable to genetic factors and barely to family effects, are very

---

[33] http://en.wikipedia.org/wiki/Milwaukee_Project.

counterintuitive and psychologically difficult to accept. If genes are so decisive, are we still autonomous persons? And we cannot externalise our deficits anymore – it is not the bad behaviour of our parents and teachers or the unjust society. Every environmental impact is easier to observe and understand than any concealed genetic effect. Two final quotes should illustrate the provocative message of research on genetic effects:

> Environments most parents provide for their children have few differential effects on the offspring. Most families provide sufficiently supportive environments that children's individual genetic differences develop . . . To see the effects of having no parents (or parent surrogates), one would have to . . . see children trapped in crack houses of inner cities in the United States, locked in basements and attics by vengeful crazy relatives. (Sandra Scarr, 1992, p. 3)

> If you want to maximize your children's chances, you need to pay attention not to the social phenotype of your marriage partner but instead to his or her status genotype. That genotype is indicated by the social group your potential partner belongs to, as well as the social phenotype of their siblings, parents, grandparents, cousins, and so on to the *n*th degree of relatedness. Once you have selected your mate, your work is largely done. You can safely neglect your offspring, confident that the innate talents you secured for them will shine through regardless. (Gregory Clark, 2014b, p. 14f.)

Could this be true? Let us look at the environmental side.

### 3.4.4   Physical and Biological Aspects of Environment

Before we start describing the impact of physical and biological aspects of environment on cognitive ability, on development of ability and on differences in ability, four introductory remarks shall be given: to reach a solid knowledge we need experimental evidence and a theory explaining the way that the described determinants work. Here we have a problem because experimental studies with possible severe outcomes are (justifiably) not possible. So we frequently only have association studies in which it is necessary to deal with the problem of correlation versus causation. Second, the distinction between physical and biological versus psychological, social and cultural aspects is more a heuristic one. Culture, society and psychology can change physical and biological aspects of environment, and conversely, physical and biological aspects can make it easier or more difficult to develop beneficial psychological, social and cultural determinants. Third, the determinants are only risk or supportive factors; exceptions always exist, as there are long-living smokers and toreros. Finally, the relationship between possible determinants and cognitive effects is presumably not linear: more does not always mean better. Breastfeeding supports cognitive development, but not breastfeeding until age 18. Five hundred per cent of the recommended daily allowance in trace elements and vitamins will not boost intelligence, but may have negative consequences. There are threshold zones (no single values) and diminishing returns.

The journalist Hank Pellissier (2012) has presented a long list of possible determinants for cognitive development. Broadly speaking, everything that is good for healthy development is also good for cognitive development. Ultimately, dead persons cannot think. Let us have a look at some of the most important determinants:

- *Consanguineous marriages* reduce average intelligence; *exogamy* increases it, effects are around 2 to 3 IQ points (e.g. Jensen, 1983; Woodley, 2009). Genetic relationship between spouses enables recessive mutations to express negative effects ranging from physical to intellectual disadvantages. In infrequent cases of no mutations with negative effects, consanguineous marriages do no harm (e.g. the Rothschilds).
- *Healthy environments and behaviours during pregnancy* help to avoid health risks such as not consuming alcohol, drugs, cigarettes, smog, mercury, radiation, pesticides or malnutrition (in trace elements and vitamins). In my own Austrian study, maternal smoking during pregnancy (controlled for educational background) had a negative impact of $-6.93$ IQ points ($N = 169$ secondary school children between 10 and 18 years old; Perissutti & Rindermann, 2013); in a larger Estonian study with $N = 1,822$ children it was $-3.3$ IQ (Rahu et al., 2010). Alcohol, smoking and other toxins are detrimental for the uterus and child; the general development of the foetus is impaired; maternal malnutrition has similar effects for neurological development.
- *Breastfeeding* has a positive effect on intelligence, according to Victora et al. (2015) of around 4 IQ points at age 30.[34] Children who are not breast fed can be given long-chain polyunsaturated fatty acids (LC-PUFA) with somewhat smaller positive effects (Protzko et al., 2013).
- *Infectious diseases* and *parasites* (e.g. intestinal worms, Plasmodia leading to Malaria) harm health, with general effects including impaired cognitive ability (e.g. via Diarrhoea or school absence) and sometimes with special effects, e.g. Measles (Encephalitis) (Eppig et al., 2010).
- *Poisons* harm health, with general effects (smoking) including cognitive ability and sometimes special effects, e.g. lead (Hunt, 2012), mercury, mould (according to Jedrychowski et al., 2011: $-9.16$ IQ), alcohol, drugs, fluoride (Cheng & Lynn, 2013: $-6.9$ IQ).
- *Nutrition*: meat (because of proteins, trace elements and vitamins; Whaley et al., 2003), iron, zinc, vitamin B (Thiamine), iodine, phosphorus, calcium

---

[34] Further positive effects of breastfeeding include more years of education (around one year) and higher monthly income (around 100 Euro/Dollar in Brazil; Victora et al., 2015).

(for an overview see Eysenck & Schoenthaler, 1997) show general health effects supporting cognitive development.

### 3.4.5 Psychological Aspects of Environment – Family

For many researchers, the family is the most important factor for cognitive development, e.g. David Armor (2003, p. IX, p. 4):

'The most important environmental influences on a child's IQ take place in the family.'

'Family environment plays a key and possibly irreversible role in shaping a child's intelligence.'

A similar view can be found in econometric studies: for instance, for immigrants from devastated environments (refugee camps, war zones, i.e. Vietnam, Laos and Cambodia) Schoellman (2016) detected no relationship between children's age at arrival to the United States and their later human capital as adults. According to Schoellman's study, the individual family environment was crucial, not the general environment with its huge variation from unschooled misery to life and education in one of the richest countries of the world.

In every country, parental *socio-economic status* (SES) is associated with children's intelligence test results and student achievement (e.g. OECD, 2013d, p. 39). Even in a Communist regime such as Poland during the 1970s parental SES was associated with children's cognitive development (11 year olds, $r = .27$-$.29$; Firkowska et al., 1978). A meta-analysis with the majority of studies from the United States and Western countries revealed a mean correlation of $r = .29$ (Sirin, 2005). At school level, average SES is the most important single variable to explain student achievement, with an effect of around 50 to 100 SASQ or 7 to 15 IQ (Dronkers & Velden, 2013). A closer look distinguishing between parental indicators revealed that income or wealth is less important than *parental education*[35]: the mean direct effect of parental education was $\beta_{Ed} = .30$ to $.45$, but of income and wealth $\beta_{In} = .09$ to $.12$ ($N = 15125$, $k = 18$ samples). However, behind any parental effect of education, be it educational degrees, verbal behaviour or education practised in the family, environmental as well as genetic effects may be at work.[36] For example, (a) income has a larger

---

[35] Sixteen cross-sectional and three longitudinal samples in seven countries (United States, Austria, Germany, Costa Rica, Ecuador, Vietnam, Brazil), children aged 4 to 22, total $N = 15297$, children's cognitive ability was measured with different tests (mental speed tests, CFT, the Ravens, Stanford-Binet, PPVT-R, WET, CogAT, Piagetian tasks, AFQT, PIRLS, TIMSS, PISA) (Rindermann & Ceci, 2018).

[36] Scarr & McCartney (1983, p. 427): 'Genotype → environment effects arise in biologically related families and render all of the research literature on parent-child socialization uninterpretable. Because parents provide both genes and environments for their biological offspring, the

positive 'effect' on biological children than on adoptive children and (b) income produced by parents themselves generally has a more positive 'effect' than state-provided income (Mayer, 1997). These 'income effects' can only be explained (a) by genetic effects or (b) by an associated educational behaviour effect. The effects do not work only via psychological learning, but also via genes and by creating a supportive environment.

Let us have a look at some of the most important determinants:

- *Parental educational level* is together with *parental intelligence* the best non-child predictor for children's intelligence, student achievement and school marks (parental educational level: $r = .45$; parental IQ: $r = .43$, $\rho = .56$).[37] Better educated and more intelligent parents speak quantitatively more and qualitatively better to the child, have more books, read more to their children, spend their common time more on educational activities, smoke less, are more likely to be married (civic, burgher, middle-class family). They select higher quality educational institutions. Their children themselves are more likely to behave in ways which are supportive for cognitive development (such as own reading and self-discipline) (Rindermann & Ceci, 2018).
- A comparable, but less good, predictor is the *number of books* at home, with $r = .25$ and $\beta_{Bo} = .18$ (Rindermann & Ceci, 2018). Having books leads to parents and children reading them.
- *Quantity and quality of parents' speech* has a strong effect on children's cognitive development ($\beta_{LS} = .58$; Hart & Risley, 1995; Rindermann & Ceci, 2018). This parental behaviour increases verbal input and it is a role model.
- *Reading to the child* supports cognitive development (around 6 IQ, Protzko et al., 2013; $\beta_{RtC} = .18$; Rindermann & Ceci, 2018).

child's environment is necessarily correlated with [his or] her genes, because [his or] her genes are correlated with [his or] her parents' genes, and the parents' genes are correlated with the rearing environment they provide. It is impossible to know what about the parents' rearing environment for the child determines what about the child's behavior, because of the confounding effect of genetic transmission of the same characteristics from parent to child.' To neglect behind phenotypical correlations the possible genetic effects is termed the 'sociological fallacy' (Flynn, 2012b, p. 75ff.; Sesardic, 2005, p. 121ff.)

[37] According to a reanalysis of Plomin et al. (2013a, p. 76, based on a study of Th. Bouchard and a calculation of J. Loehlin) the parent-children IQ correlation is $r = .42$ ($N = 8433$) (manifest; true correlation using correction for attenuation is about $\rho = .49$, assuming a reliability of $r = .90$ and of $r = .80$ for parents and children); or according to Anger & Heineck (2008, Table 2, p. 24) it is $r = .44$ ($N = 450$, reported reliability of $r = .70$ results in a true correlation of $\rho = .63$); arithmetically combined, the true individual parent-children intelligence correlation is $\rho = .56$. This still underestimates the real correlation because both two parents' (mean) intelligence is the relevant causal variable. All correlations in this list were obtained in samples with children raised by their (usually) biological parents.

- *Married parents* have smarter children (around 4 IQ points, Armor, 2003; $d = 0.17$, Hattie, 2009, p. 64; $\beta = .17$, Rindermann & Ceci, 2018; Woessmann, 2016).
- An *authoritative parenting style* (compared to an authoritarian, permissive or neglectful one) is more beneficial for children's general development, including student achievement (Steinberg et al., 1994).
- *Adoption* can have a positive effect on intelligence of up to one standard deviation (15 IQ; van IJzendoorn, Juffer & Poelhuis; 2005; Nisbett, 2009). The effects were smaller in a Swedish study, with around 3 to 4 IQ points (Kendler et al., 2015). Of course, it is not adoption itself that creates positive effects, but the improved environmental quality in these cases. Because there cannot be a genetic effect, adoption effects are convincingly interpreted as causal.
- *Child abuse* and *violence* by parents generally harm children's development ($\beta = -.19$ on intelligence, high levels of domestic violence −8 IQ; Koenen et al., 2003).

### 3.4.6   Psychological Aspects of Environment – Neighbourhoods, Preschool and School

Families are not children's only environment. Neighbourhoods, classmates and friends, crèche, kindergarten and school are further important developmental environments. They are selected by parents and children, they are formed by them and environments react to them. Thus, external environments are not only external determinants. Again a list:

- *Violence in neighbourhoods* is associated with lower intelligence (in regression analyses controlled for other factors: $\beta = -.13$, Delaney-Black et al., 2002). Violence produces stress, which has negative neurological and psychological impacts on cognitive function and development.
- The attendance of *preschool* institutions has a positive impact on intelligence, at least in childhood and youth; more general effects on personality and economically relevant variables such as employment persist ($d = 0.47 \approx$ 7 IQ, Hattie, 2009, p. 58; around 5 IQ, Baumeister, Rindermann & Barnett, 2014; around 6 IQ, Protzko et al., 2013). Preschool education supports personality development (discipline and the like) and skill acquisition (such as using a pencil), both being relevant for school and learning, knowledge acquisition (numbers, words, concepts) and verbal ability (speaking, asking, understanding), having indirect and direct effects on intelligence.[38]

---

[38] Pre-K education (crèche, below age 3) can also have negative side effects on behaviour (e.g. Baumeister et al., 2014; Loeb et al., 2007).

- *School attendance* increases cognitive ability – one year at around 3 IQ (Ceci, 1991; Winship & Korenman, 1997). The effects are larger on crystallised than on fluid intelligence (factor 1.5, e.g. 4.5 IQ vs. 3 IQ; Stelzl et al., 1995). These effects were studied in convincing natural experiment designs such as comparing earlier or delayed school onset due to external conditions. Approximately two thirds of the age increase in intelligence could be attributed to school. The increases are probably smaller for older students. Instruction delivers knowledge, and dealing with abstract information trains intelligence including abstract thinking (Luria, 1976/1974).
- The *average competence* and *school level* indicated by classmates' cognitive ability improve individual cognitive development (positive modelling, fewer discipline problems in class, faster and more demanding instruction by teachers, efficient use of time) (Ding & Lehrer, 2007; Sacerdote, 2011; Hattie, 2009).
- *Teacher quality*: better teachers give more effective instruction and better manage their classes, resulting in better ability development (Ding & Lehrer, 2007; Ehrenberg & Brewer, 1994; Hanushek & Rivkin, 2006).
- *Certain aspects of instruction* support cognitive development: efficient use of class time for instruction and learning; direct instruction (efficient knowledge transport); class management (leads to efficient use of class time); open questions for the entire class (stimulates attention, training of thinking for all); structure and clarity (efficient use of class time, students understand the material); periodical tests (motivate to learn, results inform students, parents and teachers); targeted use of modern media and computer-assisted instruction (motivation, individualisation of learning, efficient use of attention, structure); problem-solving teaching (thinking, insight, argumentation) (Bishop, 2006; Brophy & Good, 1986; Hattie, 2009; Phelps, 2012). Good instruction also has positive effects for personality development.
- *Certain aspects of schools* support cognitive competence development: school autonomy (decisions based on local information); discipline education, high expectations and work with parents (all particularly relevant for lower ability students and students from less-educated parents); achievement orientation (directs attention and action towards learning); extension of class time; private schools (better efficiency as a result of local decisions, more discipline such as in KIPP, Knowledge Is Power Program, Charter and No-Excuses schools, additional creaming effect through selection of better students); class size has a small negative effect (Carter, 2000; Ehrenberg et al., 2001; Hanushek & Woessmann, 2011; Hattie, 2009).
- *Certain aspects of school systems* support cognitive competence development: central exams (more reliable competence measurement, define a minimum standard, signal achievement as being important, motivate to

learn, improve discipline, results inform students, parents, teachers and school administration); competition by private schools (competition leads to improvement); tracking (better adaptation of instruction to students' ability level, signals achievement as being important, increases average class ability for the better students supporting instruction and learning) (Bishop, 1997; Duflo et al., 2011; Koerselman, 2013).

For school, there are partially contradictory factors such as direct instruction and alternative instructional methods (e.g. problem-solving teaching and computer-assisted instruction). Depending on what students bring along, the teachers, schools and school systems need to adapt. For instance, for disciplined students with school-orientated parents, large classes work but they do not for students with the opposite characteristics.

Nevertheless, three main factors can be put on record: first, *time* is crucial, for example, formal school attendance and efficiently used class time for teaching and learning. This includes education at preschool, crèche, kindergarten, school, vocational school and university and also covers direct instruction, class management, average class competence level and private additional instruction. The other factor is *achievement-oriented structure*: it directs attention and behaviour to learning and achievement of all involved, not only of the students but also of parents, teachers and the administration. It covers class management, discipline education, high expectations, structure and clarity, periodical tests, central exams, private schools, competition and tracking. Finally, *competence begets competence*, be it from classmates or teachers, improving environmental quality as described above.

### 3.4.7   Individual Behaviour

Up to now, it has seemed that persons are at the mercy of their genes and given environments. However, that is a simplified view. Persons have influence, through their own behaviour, on the outcomes of their lives, including some impact on their cognitive development. Students and adults can *decide* to read, not to smoke and more generally to spend their time on meaningful action and aims. Some examples:

- *Reading* improves cognitive ability; it delivers knowledge and trains thinking (Cunningham & Stanovich, 1998; $\beta_{Read}$ = .14, Rindermann & Ceci, 2018).
- *Self-discipline* and *discipline* have positive effects on learning and through this on cognitive ability (Barton et al., 1998; Duckworth & Seligman, 2005; $\beta_{Dis}$ = .23, Rindermann & Ceci, 2018).
- Doing *homework* increases student achievement ($d$ = 0.29, Hattie, 2009, pp. 234ff.).

- *TV and media consumption* (computer, video, smart phones) have on average a negative effect ($d = -0.18$; Hattie, 2009, p. 67). However, depending on their use ('educational television' vs. 'commercial entertainment television'), they can also have positive effects.
- Voluntarily taking of *detrimental substances* causes harm – smoking tobacco or marijuana, taking alcohol or other drugs (for smoking, e.g. Ott et al., 2004).

For all these behaviours there are reciprocal effects with cognitive ability, e.g. more intelligent people stop or even do not begin smoking (Taylor et al., 2003; Zimmerman, 2003).

### 3.4.8    How We Can Bring This All Together: Natascha Kampusch and the Productive Imagination of Malleability

Natascha Kampusch was a ten-year-old Austrian girl living in Vienna, who was kidnapped for eight years until age 18 (1998 to 2006). She was probably constantly abused. She did not attend school during these eight years. Instead, she was held in a soundproofed $2.50 \times 2$ meters cellar without windows. Her educational input consisted of a few excursions with her kidnapper; 'occasionally' she was given newspapers, books, radio and video and instruction in reading and writing. She had only four years primary school education. Her parents were never married and lived separately; the mother was a tailor and the father was a baker.

According to the presented research regarding genes to environment her intelligence should not have reached average. Merely from taking into account missing school (eight years without the expected increase of approximately 3 IQ points per year) she should have an IQ of below 80 (optimistically, presuming an average of 100 IQ minus $8 \times 3$ IQ = 76 IQ). However, she is different. After her liberation and some treatment by psychologists she gave television interviews in which she showed high verbal ability. She was a talk show host and interviewed her guests with eloquence. After her liberation she completed secondary school with the best possible grades.[39] Was the treatment after her release so effective that it compensated for all deficits of the past?

Is her case not a refutation of all our research results? Did we overrate the impact of school and of childhood environment?

To start with, her case is only one *single case*. There are always exceptions; there are never pure categories. There are peaceful lions and aggressive female

---

[39] Sources in German: www.oe24.at/leute/Kampusch-schliesst-Hauptschule-mit-Vorzug-ab/324104 (14.06.2008), www.stern.de/wissen/mensch/natascha-kampusch-von-vorbildlichen-medien-erzogen-569955.html (13.09.2006), www.zeit.de/2010/03/Kampusch-03 (15.01.2010).

does.[40] All determinants have only a *probabilistic effect*. Single determinants may be *compensated* by other determinants. There are *interactions* among different determinants, making predictions of effects difficult. The genetic endowment is not the simple average of two parental genetic gifts in any single case, but rather an interactive product plus (rare benign) *mutations*.

The cases of the blind and deaf illustrate how strong the internal genetic factors and the effects of compensation by a beneficial environment could be: due to severe deprivation resulting from a biological handicap we expect that their intelligence is lowered. However, that cannot be confirmed by studies. Their intelligence level is average; there are only special and highly plausible differences for the blind: less knowledge, but better working memory (Rindermann, 2013; Vernon, 1968).

And how can we bring together the mentioned large heritabilities with the shown environmental effects? Are they methodological errors due to non-experimental designs? No. First, genes work through *shaping* the environment. Genetically endowed parents will create a similarly endowed developmental environment for their children (see Figure 3.8).

As the analysis of family and children data from 118 Austrian primary school pupils in grades 1 to 4 shows, better educated parents create an environment which is more beneficial for their children's development: education as proxy for cognitive ability has positive effects on completeness and stability of family (.27), number of books (.39), reading to the child (.35), children's reading (.14, totally .39) and income (.37); income is here not positively relevant for children's intelligence (−.09), but all the others have a positive impact on intelligence. Parents' effects work through shaping family environment.

Second, environmental improvement can improve cognitive ability; however, it rarely changes the rank order of differences between people. Ebb and flow influence small and big boats, but they do not transform aircraft carriers to canoes or dinghies to ocean liners. In correspondence, a very supportive developmental environment usually does not modify pupils with learning difficulties into the talented:

The average effects of treatments, such as adoption, seem to increase the mean IQ scores, but they do not seem to affect the rank order of the children's scores with respect to their biological parents, and it is on rank orders, not means, that correlations depend. (Scarr & McCartney, 1983, p. 430)

What treatments are successful?

---

[40] An example from National Geographic, a lioness has adopted an antelope, can be found in YouTube by searching for 'A lioness adopts a baby antelope'; an example of an aggressive female deer can be found in YouTube by searching for 'Saanich: aggressive deer'.

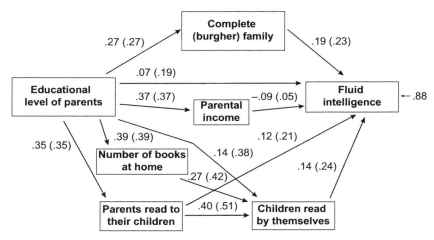

Figure 3.8 Determinants of cognitive ability of primary school students
($N = 118$, FIML, *CFI* = .97 and *SRMR* = .05; Austrian data)
On the arrows are standardised path coefficients (beta, usually between –1, 0 and +1),
correlations are in parentheses, error terms as unexplained variance on the right. FIML:
full-information-maximum-likelihood, no listwise deletion in the case of missing data.
CFI: Comparative Fit Index, a fit index, results should be CFI $\geq$ .95, SRMR:
Standardised Root Mean Square Residual, another fit index, results should be
SRMR $\leq$ .08. Intelligence was measured by the fluid-figural test CFT (Culture Fair
Intelligence Test; Cattell, 1987/1971). Total effects are calculated by adding direct and
indirect effects, here for education on child's own reading: .14 + (.39 $\times$ .27) + (.35$\times$.40) =
.3853, rounded .39.

## 3.5    Furtherance of Cognitive Ability

The answer can be simple: reduce the occurrence of negative expressions of
determinants and increase the occurrence of positive ones. However, as mentioned before, there are thresholds and diminishing returns. And there are
differences in the mutability of determinants and in the effect–cost ratio.
Any intervention has opportunity costs or side effects. For example, if cognitive training is offered in school, normal classes will be missed: Mathematics
cannot be learned at the same time. Teachers need to be trained, regrettably
creating costs, etc.

Below a shorter list of interventions is presented:

- When people are malnourished, a *micronutrient supplementation* with vitamins and minerals raises IQ by 3.5 IQ points (Eysenck & Schoenthaler,
  1997). The treatment is cheap and without side effects (normal application
  assumed).

- The *reduction of sugar and fat* and their replacement by salad, rice, pasta, fish, nuts and fruit are helpful in general, as well as specifically for cognition (Northstone et al., 2012).
- *Deworming drugs* in Africa improved health for treated and untreated pupils (due to reduced disease transmission) and school attendance rates increased by 25 per cent as a result (Glewwe & Kremer, 2006, p. 980f., 983f.). School attendance means instruction and learning, increasing cognitive ability. The treatment costs per year are only $3.50 and side effects are unknown (normal application assumed).
- The price of *infant formula* in a poor country such as the Philippines has a negative effect on intelligence at age eight. A *price reduction* by half would increase children's intelligence six to eight years later by 4.4 IQ points (Glewwe & King, 2001, p. 97). Negative side effects could be the replacement of breastfeeding or wrongful use (e.g. feeding animals) and less means for other projects.
- Very basic aids such as *glasses* for people with visual disabilities and *hearing aids* for auditory impaired ones help with receiving information and learning in school and everyday life (Gerstmeyer & Lehrl, 2004; Lehrl & Seifert, 2003).
- Different *cognitive training programmes* show positive effects on intelligence (Herrnstein et al., 1986; Irwing et al., 2008). The best-researched approach is the inductive reasoning training from Karl Josef Klauer. It does not only show positive effects on intelligence, but also on student achievement in school; its effects are stable and generalise to everyday cognitive behaviour (average $d = 0.59$; Klauer & Phye, 2008).
- Of course, *extend* and *improve education* inside and outside families and schools (see suggestions in Chapter 14).

And what about society and culture and worldviews? We will deal with them in Chapter 6.

## 3.6   Can We Praise or Blame People for Cognitive Ability?

Now, at the end of this chapter, let us turn to another perspective and ask an epistemic-ethical-functional question: can we praise or blame individuals or nations for being, relative to others, more or less intelligent and knowledgeable? This question has an *epistemic* aspect; are people responsible for their intelligence? It has an *ethical* aspect; should we treat them as if they were responsible for their intelligence? And finally for *functioning*; do praising and blaming them have any positive effect on their intelligence?

Let us reframe the question: can I be blamed for not being Einstein? Or you, the reader? Can we blame our mothers for not having married a smarter man?

Or our fathers for not having married a smarter woman? Or our grandparents? Whom we should blame for the physical, social and cultural quality of our developmental environments? Of course, we can read more, participate in training programmes, take any cognitive challenge such as looking at Brian Greene's 'Space, Time & The Universe'. But the largest part of our individual competence and of individual, as well as national, differences depends on barely controllable and modifiable genetic and environmental determinants.

However, maybe it is functional to criticise somebody or even a nation for bad results with the aim of improving the situation. This may stimulate ambition and reformative fervour. An even better strategy would be to stress the possibilities of change. This is the typical strategy of parents and teachers to somewhat overrate children, to criticise them for too low effort and to overestimate a little the range of malleability. This also gives hope and a better feeling. While we must not give up the epistemic struggle for truth in science – the orientation to truth is the ethics of science – erroneous overestimations and malleability beliefs may be helpful in everyday life. The tiger mother Amy Chua (2011) has exemplified this strategy and science has shown that the *belief* in intelligence as an incremental, malleable characteristic has a positive effect on effort and development (Dweck, 2000). Similarly, environmental explanations have a positive function; maybe they are wrong, but they are still helpful through initiating an improvement.

# 4　International Ability Differences and Their Development

For several decades, research has documented large differences in the results of cognitive ability tests – large differences between generations and between countries. Whether these differences reflect real cognitive ability differences is still a contentious issue. We document the results and give evidence for an interpretation of them as real world differences: they are backed by further statistical indicators of cognitive achievement and by comparisons with everyday life experiences in different regions of the world.

## 4.1　Historical Differences (FLynn Effect)

The seminal 1984 review paper 'The Mean IQ of Americans: Massive Gains 1932 to 1978' of the American–New-Zealand political scientist James Flynn made the secular rise of IQ test performance in science and media popular. The effect was later labelled the 'Flynn effect'. Other researchers have described the phenomenon too; the first was Edward Rundquist in 1936. In the 1980s, Richard Lynn (1982) described the same phenomenon for Japan. So two researchers, Lynn and Flynn, or Flynn and Lynn, have rediscovered the secular IQ rise, therefore we term it the 'FLynn effect'. The increase in Western countries across different decades of the twentieth century was around 3 IQ points per 10 years, more precisely according to the meta-analysis of Pietschnig and Voracek (2015) *dec* = 2.83 IQ points (*dec*: per decade). There is evidence for a decline of the FLynn effect or even its inversion in developed countries and for larger recent gains in the developing world.

Initially, James Flynn (1987), and today other researchers such as Jan te Nijenhuis and Henk van der Flier (2013), assumed that these increases were mere test increases, a kind of 'IQ inflation', not reflecting improvement in real-world problem-solving ability. Admittedly, older and younger generations differ in test results, but not in their cognitive abilities.

However, there is evidence for *increases in real-world problem-solving ability*:

- The *age of top chess players* has dropped, indicating rising cognitive ability or at least an acceleration of cognitive growth in youth and young adulthood (Howard, 1999).
- *Height* also increased, around 1.2 cm per decade (equivalent to $d = 0.17$ or $dec = 2.57$ 'IQ' scale points – very similar; Lynn, 1990).
- *Brain size* (and, as an indicator, head circumference) has also increased, equivalent to $d = 0.20$ (or $dec = 3.00$ 'IQ' – again similar, Lynn, 1990; 4.69g per decade, Miller & Corsellis, 1977).
- The best predictor at the individual level and one of the determinants of cognitive ability, *amount of education*, has also increased in the twentieth century (Meyer et al., 1992).
- Generally, *living conditions* were considerably improved (e.g. Moore & Simon, 2000), from health to cognitive stimulation, that make a real increase in intelligence and knowledge (except for memory) highly plausible.
- Much more people than in the past work today as *academics*, as physicians, lawyers, teachers, scientists, engineers or economists.
- In professions, *cognitive demands* have risen. Cognitive ability has to be elevated to deal with all these intellectual challenges, as described by Seymour Itzkoff (1994, p. 97) for farmers:

The modern farmer is an abstract symbolic analyst ... The modern farmer cares for a multitude of specialized machines, consulting manuals for maintenance and repair. Constant reading of weather and climate reports, governmental publications on new seed, fertilizer, anti-bacterial and pest treatments, study of the complex price support programs, as well as decision making about whether or when to take land out of production, feed cattle, or plant other crops, are all part of a modern farmer's job. The farmer has to plan next year's program, of necessity speculating on the commodity futures market in Chicago, prices at the storage bins in the area, as well as negotiate the usual yearly bank loans, now linked to the interest rates set on Wall Street.

The German sociologist Georg W. Oesterdiekhoff goes even further and claims that intelligence in modern countries has not just risen during recent decades, but rather over several centuries (i.e. before psychometric tests were established).[1] Based on the Piagetian cognitive approach and transferring individual development to historical development, Oesterdiekhoff has described a lot of evidence for rising intelligence in history. Generally, he sees progress from the second cognitive stage, *preoperational thinking*, in which the majority of people up to the nineteenth century thought, to the third and fourth cognitive stages of *concrete operational* and *formal operational thinking*, in which the majority of people in modern countries today think. There is

---

[1] The main works from Oesterdiekhoff are written in German; some English extracts can be found in Oesterdiekhoff (2009a, 2009b, 2012a, 2012b, 2014a, 2014b).

an increase of logical thinking, an increase in understanding of causality, chance and probability, and an increase in perspective taking.

To give only some examples, up to the seventeenth century people in Europe believed that witches existed. Women (mainly) were accused of sorcery. Fewer people today believe in magic and superstition. Cruelty has decreased. There were trials against animals up to the sixteenth century, e.g. rats were ordered to appear in court for having eaten major parts of the harvest. Celestial bodies were seen as conscious beings that could be communicated with and which influenced people's lives. In premodern societies, death was generally seen as being caused by other persons using witchcraft. The content of dreams stood for real experiences. Ordeals and oracles showed the truth; their results also overrode empirical evidence. Magic procedures could cure sickness. A further evidence is found in the increases of literacy and numeracy (for England since the Middle Ages: Clark, 2007, pp. 177ff.).

The development of thinking ability was crucial for cognitive progress in history, according to Oesterdiekhoff and the Piagetian tradition. Knowledge increases are secondary, a byproduct of cognitive growth. For understanding and insight, thinking is decisive.

A second contentious issue are the *causes* of the secular rise in test results and intelligence. Most probably there is no single cause. Various determinants work together, and depending on the stages of cognitive modernisation different determinants are relevant:

- *Test-wiseness*: some part of the rise in IQ test performance can be attributed to changes in test-taking patterns such as more guessing instead of leaving blank in cases where the answer is not known (Must & Must, 2013).
- *Cognitive patterns*: related, but not identical, is a kind of rather *simple rule learning* applicable for solving tasks in tests constructed according to a cookie-cutter approach (Armstrong & Woodley, 2014) or the acquisition of *'scientific spectacles'* to see the world differently and more abstractly as *en vogue* in modernity (Flynn, 2007b).[2]
- *Genetic health*: improved health by heterosis caused by modernisation (fewer consanguineous marriages; Mingroni, 2007).
- *Improved health* as a result of better nutrition, health care and generally improved environmental conditions and life styles (e.g. Lynn, 1990).
- *Increased quantity and quality of education* in families, preschool and school for individuals and cohorts (Meyer et al., 1992).

---

[2] However, what can be seen as only 'simple rule learning' or 'viewing through scientific spectacles' can be also interpreted as enhanced intelligence, as improved thinking ability. For example, for Piaget abstract categorisation is a crucial element of cognitive development. James Flynn has developed during recent decades his interpretation of the IQ test rise from mere IQ inflation to a real intelligence improvement phenomenon.

- *Modernisation*: technological, social and cultural modernisation with consequences for the cognitive quality and complexity of everyday life (Flynn, 2012a).
- *Virtuous circle*: a feedback loop between improving environmental conditions and cognitive ability leading to an upward trend (Meisenberg, 2014).[3]

The acceleration of development in childhood, stronger FLynn effects in early childhood than for teenagers or young adults (Lynn, 2013; Rindermann & Thompson, 2013) and general height and brain size increases point to a larger impact of biological than educational causes. This does not mean that educational conditions are without effects on historical cognitive development. But they are less directly cognitive effective (e.g. by delivering knowledge or training intelligence) but indirectly, e.g. by creating better physical, biological and psychological childhood environments. For example, knowledge delivered by education improves health relevant for cognitive development.

The FLynn effect seems to be petering out in modern countries. In Norway (stopped, Sundet et al., 2004), Denmark (decline, Teasdale & Owen, 2008), England (decline measured by Piaget tests, Shayer & Ginsburg, 2009), Australia (stopped, Cotton et al., 2005), Finland (decline, Dutton & Lynn, 2013; Heller-Sahlgren, 2015b), Austria (decline, Pietschnig & Gittler, 2015) and generally for Western countries in mental speed (decline, Woodley et al., 2013). In countries with negative trends, the average decline was about *dec* = $-2.44$ IQ points (Dutton, van der Linden & Lynn, 2016). Positive trends can go hand in hand with negative ones (co-occurrence; Woodley et al., 2015).

All these ups and downs underscore the malleability of intelligence, but they do not refute heritability and possible dysgenic effects. Heritability relates to individual differences, not to historical developments. Strong environmental improvements could compensate any possible dysgenic effect.

There seems to be a specific historical time frame for the FLynn effect. The deceleration of the FLynn effect in developed countries but its continuance in developing countries may lead to a narrowing of international gaps (Meisenberg & Woodley, 2013). The up and down of the FLynn effect and international differences could be related. Researchers have frequently compared them, to stress the dissimilarity or similarity of causes. For instance, Gerhard Meisenberg (2003, p. 197):

---

[3] Meisenberg (2014, p. 81) described such a feedback loop: small environmental improvements lead to minor increases in intelligence. Individuals and nations with (on average) higher intelligence are more likely to establish stimulating environments such as in family and school, leading to children's intellectual growth. Smarter children will later become smarter parents, further improving environmental quality for their children. This creates a transgenerational feedback loop between rising environmental quality (including economic growth) and rising intelligence.

High intelligence produces a high standard of living, which in turn raises intelligence even more ... This feedback loop between intelligence and standard of living can explain the great magnitude of the IQ differences between nations.

Individual differences, historical differences and national differences are dissimilar and their causes need an independent analysis. Nevertheless, causes found for historical and individual differences can be heuristically used for the search for causes of international differences. First, let us look at them.

## 4.2    National Differences

National differences in cognitive abilities in a test-based manner were first detected by old student assessment studies in the late 1960s and early 1970s. The results were collected in one summary table by Lee and Barro (2001) and cover 19 nations (description see Appendix). The quality of the older student assessment studies regarding sample size, sample collection, representativity, comparability of collection and testing procedures and task construction is lower than of the studies since the 1990s. The results for all 19 countries are presented in Table 4.1; regional averages are based on participating countries.

We have results for all our regions, but only for Trans-Tasman, Western Europe, Scandinavia and North-Africa-Middle-East do we have more than one country in each region. Thus the results are less convincing in addition to the study problems mentioned previously. Israel is not the typical country for the Middle East and Chile not for Latin America. Finally, in Communist countries (Hungary at that time) 'statistical creativity' was not an unknown pattern. Nonetheless, the correlation with our current cognitive ability measure is, with $r = .95$, astonishingly high!

At the top is East Asia followed by Trans-Tasman and Eastern Europe, and the lowest results are found in Latin America, Central-South-Asia and Africa. Comparing the older and newer data collections and measurements there is no large outlier observable (see Figure 4.1).[4]

The old means understood as absolute values are more problematic due to their standardisation on the newer values than their rank order and the relative size of differences. The high correlation of $r = .95$ is similar to the GDP stability, even slightly higher (Maddison, same 19-country sample with results for 1960 and 1970 averaged vs. 2008 and 2010, $r = .93$). International differences in cognitive ability are stable; the high correlations indirectly back their validity.

---

[4] The more recent data collection on national cognitive ability is based on SAS and psychometric IQ data. Only the psychometric IQ data also contain some older studies.

Table 4.1 *Results of older student assessment studies (SAS)*

|  |  | Average result in IQ scale |
|---|---|---|
| **Africa (sub-Sahara)** | | 63.12 | |
| | Malawi | | 63.12 |
| **N-Africa M-East (ArabM)** | | 89.80 | |
| | Iran | | 78.22 |
| | Israel | | 101.38 |
| **America (North, English)** | | 95.71 | |
| | USA | | 95.71 |
| **America (Latin, Central-South)** | | 85.82 | |
| | Chile | | 85.82 |
| **Asia (Central-South)** | | 82.62 | |
| | India | | 82.62 |
| **East Asia** | | 105.39 | |
| | Japan | | 105.39 |
| **Southeast Asia, Pacific** | | 89.57 | |
| | Thailand | | 89.57 |
| **Australia-NZ (English)** | | 101.48 | |
| | Australia | | 99.15 |
| | New Zealand | | 103.81 |
| **Western Europe** | | 97.58 | |
| | Belgium | | 97.93 |
| | France | | 97.75 |
| | Netherlands | | 96.80 |
| | United Kingdom | | 97.84 |
| **Scandinavia** | | 98.20 | |
| | Finland | | 98.49 |
| | Sweden | | 97.91 |
| **Central Europe** | | 99.32 | |
| | Germany | | 99.32 |
| **Eastern Europe** | | 101.21 | |
| | Hungary | | 101.21 |
| **Southern Europe** | | 94.76 | |
| | Italy | | 94.76 |

*Notes*: Collected for 19 countries in the 1960s and early 1970s in reading, mathematics and science, only students in secondary education. Standardised according to modern cognitive ability results. Entire list shown.

Modern ability test results are mainly based on two sources: the *psychometric intelligence test result collection* of Lynn and Vanhanen (2012) and *student assessment results*, mainly from PISA, TIMSS and PIRLS (in detail see Appendix). Lynn and Vanhanen (2012) have not conducted an international test survey such as PISA but collected published test results based on the psychometric approach (in a few of the surveys one of the authors was involved as co-author). The surveys were conducted with different tests

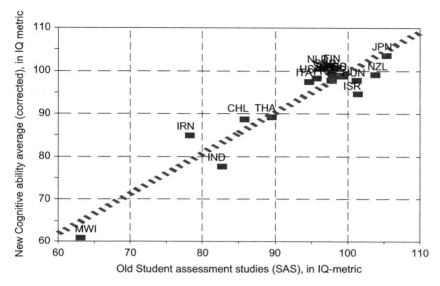

Figure 4.1 Comparison of older and newer data on cognitive ability levels of nations (*N* = 19, indicated by the three-digit ISO code for countries)

(e.g. the three Raven Matrices CPM, SPM, APM, the CFT, WISC[5]), in different age groups (usually children and younger adults), in different years (e.g. 1985 or 2000) and with differently large and representative samples. This looks a bit messy.

Test results were normed according to one common benchmark, the average of Britain 1979 called 'Greenwich-IQ'. This means the British IQ was set at 100 with a standard deviation of 15 and the ability levels of other countries are normed compared to Britain; higher resp. better test results receive values above 100 and lower resp. worse results below 100. For the different survey years, Lynn and Vanhanen applied FLynn corrections assuming a roughly homogenous historic trend in different countries (i.e. older results were adjusted upwards). Results of different test samples in one country were normed according to the Greenwich-IQ and then averaged. This increases the representativity (if samples are not systematically biased, e.g. groups, regions or tests with lower or higher achievement excluded) and the reliability of the country averages.

---

[5] Raven: figural, culture-reduced tests of fluid intelligence, CPM: Coloured Progressive Matrices, easiest test version for young children, SPM: Standard Progressive Matrices, APM: Advanced Progressive Matrices, most difficult version. Also figural: CFT: Culture Fair Intelligence Test. WISC: Wechsler Intelligence Scale for Children, a combination of fluid and crystallised scales.

Correlations between different tests across countries (the stability of country differences in various test measures) vary between $r = .94$ ($N = 45$ nations with at least two samples, 2002 compilation), $r = .93$ ($N = 65$ nations, 2006 compilation) and $r = .88$ ($N = 90$ nations, 2012 compilation; Lynn & Vanhanen, 2012, p. 30f.), altogether on average $r = .91$ ($N$-weighted mean). These reliability measures are high; such values are regarded at the individual level as being 'excellent'.[6]

For countries for which they have no psychometric IQ data, they estimated in the past values by using results from neighbouring countries. If we take the 2002 estimated but 2012 measured data, for 48 countries, the correlation is $r = .92$. Thus their former estimation procedure was highly reliable. In 2012, they used, if given, SAS results for estimations and, if not given, as before neighbouring countries. Finally, Lynn and Vanhanen compared their (pure) IQ measures with SAS measures and reached a correlation of $r = .91$ ($N = 87$).

The second important source are *student assessment studies* (SAS). Best known are TIMSS, PIRLS and PISA[7]:

- TIMSS, usually in fourth and eighth grade, consists of shorter, curriculum-related questions in mathematics and natural science; it started in 1995 and has been repeated with a growing country sample in all four years; the organiser is the IEA;
- PIRLS, usually in fourth grade, applies longer tasks in reading literacy; since 2001, it has been repeated with a growing country sample for all five years; organiser is the IEA;
- PISA, for 15-year-old students, has longer tasks intended to measure reading literacy, mathematics and natural science; it started in 2000 and has been repeated with a growing country sample all three years; organiser is the OECD.

All three studies use students (youth in regular schools) as probands and try to survey representative samples for a grade or age group. All three do not use (as usual for psychometric intelligence tests) complete tests, but only a fraction of tasks ('multi matrix sampling') and calculate ability estimates based on given achievement items and background information as attributes of students

---

[6] http://ctl.utexas.edu/services/test_scanning/results; see also Nunnally & Bernstein (1994, p. 264f.).

[7] Acronyms: TIMSS: Trends in International Mathematics and Science Study; PIRLS: Progress in International Reading Literacy Study, PISA: Programme for International Student Assessment; IEA: International Association for the Evaluation of Educational Achievement; OECD: Organisation for Economic Co-operation and Development; IAEP: International Assessment of Educational Progress; LLECE: Laboratorio Latinoamericano de Evaluación de la Calidad de la Educación; SACMEQ: Southern and Eastern Africa Consortium for Monitoring Educational Quality; MLA: Monitoring Learning Achievement; PASEC: Programme d'Analyse des Systèmes Éducatifs.

(e.g. sex), family (e.g. SES) and school (e.g. level). The procedure includes calculations for scales that were not measured at all, e.g. calculation of science from reading and mathematics. To avoid an overestimation of correlations between scales and with background variables, not just one value but five 'plausible values' for each person are calculated. This method is chosen because it is not the aim of all three student assessment studies to measure the ability of an individual student but of groups of students, mainly country groups, but also subgroups such as boys and girls, natives and migrants, low and high achievers, different ages (if grade design), different grades (if age design), different school types (e.g. private vs. public) and frequently different regions within countries such as Germany, Italy and Spain.

To come to highly reliable measures we averaged the results across different scales. Beforehand, an adaptation to a common scale is needed, as different grade- and age-groups, survey years, studies and study approaches are differently standardised. For comparison, it is also not possible to directly average for height results from studies given in metres and feet – before a transformation to a common yardstick is necessary.[8] If data were given this was not only done for the general means, but also for the subgroups of natives and migrants and low achievers (achievement at the 5 per cent level) and high achievers (achievement at the 95 per cent level).

Further older and regional student assessment studies were only used for countries without data in these SAS: IEA-Reading Literacy Study 1990–1991, IAEP-II Mathematics and Science 1991, both of 9-year-old and 14-year-old students, and LLECE 1997 and 2005–2006, a Latin American reading, mathematics and science study in third to sixth grade (see Appendix).

Student assessment studies were first standardised in the usual SAS scale ('SASQ') with $M = 500$ and $SD = 100$ representing the past mean of above average, overwhelmingly 'First World' countries and the individual differences deviation within them. Finally, we have put them on the conventional IQ scale, with UK natives on 100 IQ points (Greenwich norm, UK average is 99.60 IQ, UK migrant average 96.94).

---

[8] Different grade- and age-groups are differently standardised, also different studies (TIMSS vs. PIRLS vs. PISA) and approaches (grade IEA- vs. age OECD). However, different survey years are tried to be comparatively standardised using anchor items, items that are unchanged used in different survey years. Here a direct comparison based on given numbers is possible. However, because there are general historical trends (see FLynn effect), countries participating in older surveys would receive too low estimations. Additionally, the author is somewhat sceptical whether the results are really comparable across time. Finally, except for PIRLS, the single scales were not combined across time with the original values, but with the previously averaged results across scales and grades. For these three reasons data for combinations across time were restandardised.

The student assessment studies highly correlate:

- Across *scales*, e.g. within TIMSS 2011 fourth grade, mathematics with science: $r = .95$ ($N = 52$ countries), within eighth grade: $r = .93$ ($N = 46$), within PISA 2009 reading with mathematics: $r = .94$ ($N = 73$), reading with science: $r = .98$ ($N = 73$) and mathematics with science: $r = .97$ ($N = 73$).
- Across *grades*, within TIMSS 2011 fourth grade with eighth grade: $r = .95$ ($N = 35$).
- Across *time*, within TIMSS on average: $r = .93$ ($N = 23–50$), within PIRLS on average: $r = .95$ ($N = 24–34$), within PISA on average: $r = .96$ ($N = 33–63$).
- Across *different studies*: between TIMSS and PIRLS: $r = .94$ ($N = 54$), between TIMSS and PISA: $r = .89$ ($N = 58$), between PIRLS and PISA: $r = .82$ ($N = 49$).
- Across *different approaches* (grade vs. age, different scales, different organisations, curriculum orientated or general literacy) between IEA- and OECD-studies: $r = .88$ ($N = 61$).

And they also highly correlate with psychometric IQ: $r = .85$ ($N = 89$ countries). This means that countries with students achieving high results in reading also have students achieving high results in mathematics and science; results of countries in fourth grade are similar to the ones in eighth grade; country differences are stable across time, measurement methods and approaches; if a country's students are more intelligent, so are its youth and adults.

These high correlations can be illustrated by showing the results of a factor analysis (see Figure 4.2). The covariations between different cognitive ability scales can be statistically explained by one very strong $G$ factor, the first unrotated factor of a factor analysis; the average loadings are $\lambda = .95$ (for corrected estimates: $\lambda = .96$).

Finally, the IQ and SAS results were combined. SAS are weighted three times stronger than IQs – their samples are larger and more representative. For sub-Saharan African countries, we have data in student achievement studies from only a few countries, and the respective psychometric basis is also weaker (see Wicherts et al., 2010a).[9] To compensate these shortcomings to a certain extent, we added results from three regional African studies (SACMEQ, MLA, PASEC) measuring reading and mathematics in fourth to sixth grade. However, the problem of these African studies is that they did not use an internationally anchored scale and no single one First World country participated. As if height in Africa would be measured in a local, elsewhere

---

[9] International student assessment studies in Africa: Botswana, Ghana, Mauritius, South Africa. Mauritius is in the narrow sense not a sub-Saharan African country because the majority of its people are of Indian descent. The overlap between African regional studies and SAS is only three countries (Botswana, Mauritius, South Africa).

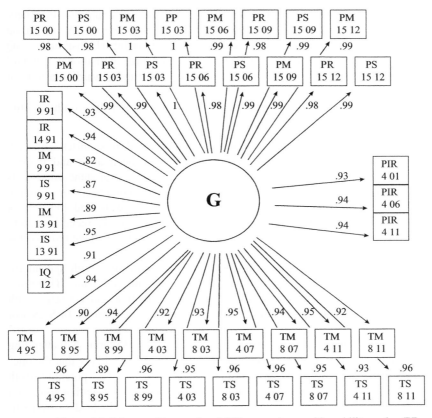

Figure 4.2 *G* factor of international differences in cognitive ability scales (PR: PISA Reading, PM: Math, PS: Science, PP: Problem solving; PIR: PIRLS; TM: TIMSS Math, TS: TIMSS Science; IR: IEA Reading, IM: IAEP Math, IS: IAEP Science; IQ: Lynn & Vanhanen; numbers: age or grade, survey year or publication year; on arrows loadings max. 1)

unknown scale. It was only possible to standardise them using the (corrected) psychometric IQ data: the results in regional African studies were rescaled according to the results of African countries having data in the Greenwich scale. Finally, we used results from the International Mathematical Olympiad (IMO) for countries for which we do not have any IQ and SAS data ($N = 8$ countries). IMO results are difficult to use because they measure only the mathematics ability of the best six students of a country. After all, they still correlate at $r = .68$ ($N = 83$ countries with having IMO and IQ data) with IQ and $r = .63$ ($N = 94$) with student achievement studies.

The final cognitive ability measure is given for 173 countries. It is very strongly correlated with IQ ($r = .96$, $N = 136$) and SAS ($r = .99$, $N = 108$), on which it is built on. The British average is 99.60 IQ points (British natives IQ 100), the international average is IQ 84.68 and the international standard deviation is 11.52. The standard deviation is orientated towards the SDs of the IQ and SAS measures.[10]

However, if taken as a cognitive ability estimate of students, youth or entire society this measure has some weaknesses:

- Countries *without any IQ and SAS data* are not equal to countries with such surveys. Whether such studies and testing have been done and if done whether they are published and on a usable international standard scale is an indicator.[11] We assume generally less favourable conditions for cognitive development for countries without data, e.g. civil wars and low school attendance rates. Therefore, their values should not be estimated by purely taking the mean IQ results of neighbouring countries. We have reduced the estimations in cases based on neighbours by 3 IQ.
- Students in grade studies (TIMSS, PIRLS) vary in *age*. With age intelligence matures and children have had more time to learn. Therefore, countries with older students need a down correction and countries with younger students an up correction. For each age year we took 14 SASQ or 2.1 IQ.
- Across countries different shares of age cohorts attend school. Not attending school affects cognitive development. Additionally, it is likely that the ones not getting into or leaving school are often those with less potential. Both effects, (1) a larger share not being schooled and (2) those getting education being partially selected for their cognitive abilities, will lead to overestimations if the results are taken as measures for the entire youth or society. Related to this issue is that differently large shares attend regular schools (not special schools for mentally handicapped children) and participate in the test. We assumed that in secondary school unattendees had an average reduced IQ by $-22.50$ and in primary by $-15.39$ points. This includes a

---

[10] The for population size weighted international average is 87.23 IQ points (see Section 13.2.6). China, in particular, with its large population, lifts the average.

[11] E.g. the African study SACMEQ has not published its results on an international scale. A paper of the *Center for Global Development* commented on it: 'Overlapping items were included in the African tests with the explicit purpose of facilitating international comparisons. It appears this *ex ante* push for comparability was abandoned *ex post*. To my knowledge, no reporting of SACMEQ scores on an international scale exists in the public domain. It is widely rumored that these results were withdrawn due to the political sensitivity of highlighting the enormous learning deficiencies in all fourteen SACMEQ countries relative to the global distribution' (Sandefur, 2016, p. 3).

reduction for not attending school, the selection effect and an assumption that further important conditions for cognitive development are affected in societies with low school attendance rates. Finally, countries with lower SAS values received a smoothed upward correction for fractions of youth not attending school (resulting in less reduction): in these countries the school quality is lower; losing more years in those schools leads to declining losses; the common biological level of cognitive ability and stimulation in everyday life buffer losses (see Appendix).

If cognitive ability measures are used to measure the quality of the educational system, uncorrected SAS values should be used. If cognitive ability measures are used to explain attributes and development of society, the corrected SAS-IQ-values (CA total corrected) have to be used.

Table 4.2 *Correlations between national measures of cognitive ability*

| | Psycho-metric IQ | Psym. IQ corrected | SAS | SAS corrected | CA total | CA total corrected |
|---|---|---|---|---|---|---|
| **Psychometric IQ** **(intelligence tests)** | 1 (136) | | | | | |
| **Psym. IQ corrected** | 1 (136) | 1 (200) | | | | |
| **SAS (student assessment)** | .85 (89) | .86 (108) | 1 (108) | | | |
| **SAS corrected** | .86 (89) | .86 (108) | .98 (108) | 1 (108) | | |
| **CA total (IQ+SAS)** | .96 (136) | .95 (173) | .99 (108) | .98 (108) | 1 | |
| **CA total corrected** | .96 (136) | .97 (200) | .97 (108) | .99 (108) | .99 (173) | 1 (200) |
| **Lynn-Vanh. SAS** | .91 (87) | .92 (108) | .94 (98) | .95 (98) | .97 (108) | .97 (108) |
| **Lynn-Vanh. total (IQ +SAS)** | .99 (136) | .99 (200) | .90 (108) | .91 (108) | .96 (173) | .98 (200) |
| **Hanushek-Woess (SAS)** | .83 (68) | .82 (77) | .92 (76) | .91 (76) | .90 (77) | .88 (77) |
| **Altinok et al. (SAS)** | .87 (100) | .89 (131) | .97 (104) | .96 (104) | .94 (130) | .94 (131) |

*Notes*: CA: Cognitive ability; correlations in first row, *N* in second (in parentheses); Lynn-Vanh. SAS: the mean of Lynn and Vanhanen (2012) calculated by using SAS studies; Lynn-Vanh. total: the mean of Lynn and Vanhanen (2012) calculated by using IQ and SAS studies; Hanushek-Woess: SAS data from Hanushek and Woessmann (2009, p. 25f., A2ff., A13ff., Excel table); Altinok et al.: SAS data from Altinok et al. (2013, Excel table 1); correlation of Lynn and Vanhanen SAS with Hanushek: $r = .90$ ($N = 77$), with Altinok: $r = .95$ ($N = 107$), Hanushek with Altinok: $r = .94$ ($N = 76$).

Correlations between psychometric IQ and SAS measures are high ($r = .85$ to .86). The pattern of international differences is nearly independent of chosen scales, sampling methods and sample sizes. The correlations slightly increase by applying corrections. Rank orders before and after corrections are identical ($r = .9848$ or $1.0000$). Student assessment studies correlate slightly more with the final total cognitive ability measure because their studies were three times stronger weighted than psychometric studies.

The values can be compared with other sources. There are four independent research groups who use student assessment studies for inferring national cognitive abilities. They do so either in combination (Lynn & Vanhanen, 2012; Rindermann, 2007a) or without (Altinok et al., 2013; Hanushek & Woessmann, 2009) psychometric IQ data.

At first we compare with the Lynn and Vanhanen combination of IQ and student assessment studies. Because we use their psychometric IQ data and later, like them, SAS (independently and differently combined), the correlations are very high ($r = .90$ to .99). Hanushek and Woessmann (2009) used an older SAS sample from 1964 to 2003; their combination is based on US NAEP-results and on an OECD country sample. In the same variable (but not identical years and studies), SAS, the correlation is $r = .92$. Altinok et al. (2013) used SAS from 1965 to 2010 and combined them using anchor countries. In the same variable (but not covering identical years and studies), SAS, the correlation is $r = .97$. When we use corrections for SAS, correlations with their data go down slightly ($r = .92$ vs. .91; $r = .97$ vs. .96). This is compelling because we alter the SAS results by corrections and Altinok et al. do not. If we look at the final means (CA total) the correlations are higher than $r = .90$, except for Hanushek, with Hanushek at least $r = .88$. Compared to GDP 2010 and the correlation of $r = .73$ ($N = 116$) between two sources of a theoretically identical measure, Penn and Maddison, *the cognitive ability correlations are much higher*, even between two measures frequently regarded as not being identical (psychometric and student achievement tests)!

The high correlations in SAS ($r = .90$ to .97) between four independent research groups (Altinok, Hanushek, Lynn, Rindermann) show the reliability of the data compilations.[12] They also underscore the quality of measures, their

---

[12] High correlations do not exclude some errors in detail; a mistake for Bosnia in Lynn and Vanhanen (2012, p. 20) was corrected by me (from 82.2 in Lynn-Vanhanen total to 93.1). Altinok et al. (2013) used a single country anchoring approach for combining data from two studies; the United States, or in Africa and Eastern Indian Ocean countries only South Africa, Botswana or Mauritius, different standard deviations are ignored. This makes combinations more volatile and less reliable. PISA data are ignored by Altinok if IEA study results are given. Altinok et al. have not made corrections of within-country regional data or exclusions of

reliability and validity. However, the last is only examined within a paper-and-pencil test approach.

Let us have a look at regional and selected country means (see Table 4.3 and map in Figure 4.3).

The highest test results are found in East Asia (around IQ 100 and higher). Mongolia is an East Asia outlier (IQ 91). Following East Asia there are five regions of occidental origin with similar results: Trans-Tasman, Scandinavia, Central Europe, Western Europe and North America (around IQ 99). There are some minor within-region differences, as Finland is better in student assessment than in IQ studies, and between countries, as Canada is better than the United States, but the general level is roughly robust. They form a Western pattern. Discernibly weaker are results in Eastern Europe (around IQ 95), mainly due to Southern East European countries in the Balkans.[13] Next is Southern Europe (around IQ 93). Northern Spain and Northern Italy are outliers here with IQs around 99 to 100, similar to Central Europe (e.g. Rindermann, Woodley & Stratford, 2012). Southeast Asia and the Pacific achieve around IQ 86. Singapore raises the results for Southeast Asia (IQ 105); culturally and cognitively it is an East Asian country. North Africa and the Middle East (around IQ 84) show slightly better results than Latin America (around IQ 79); however, Israel (IQ 95) raises the Middle East value.[14] Central-South Asia has a similar result (IQ 79). India has an astonishingly low result (around IQ 80 or lower). Sub-Saharan Africa shows the lowest results, with a cognitive ability level of around IQ 70.

In direct comparisons in same-country samples ($N = 89$) the standard deviations of student assessment studies are larger: for uncorrected psychometric

---

plausible mistakes (e.g. Shanghai for China, TIMSS 2007 Kazakhstan). Mistakes can also be found in other international statistics, e.g. in PISA 2012 for Albania in all native-immigrant categories 0 per cent of students (OECD, 2013d, p. 232, 236); the results for Belgium at the 5 per cent and 95 per cent levels in achievement differ between released reports and tables; Tunisia, Romania and Montenegro are supposed to have 100.00 per cent school enrolment rates etc. (OECD, 2013d, p. 210). We emailed the OECD-PISA researchers in March 2014 but never received an answer. Or, in econometric data, e.g. in Maddison for Ireland 1845 a GDP of $1 is listed (because a comma was used, not a decimal point as for all other values; Bolt & van Zanden, 2013). Of course, I might have committed similar lapses in this publication, despite trying to avoid them. During transformation procedures (e.g. combining SAS), updating tables and more complex statistical data analyses (path modelling) mistakes are always possible. Please feel free to contact me in case you detect anomalies. A comparison with the data and results of other authors is helpful.

[13] Hence we distinguish for future predictions in Chapter 13 between Northeast (more precisely: Eastnorth) and Southeast Europe (see Table 13.2).

[14] The chosen categorisation in regions is culturally heterogeneous (above all Israel and Singapore). For analyses of cultural effects other categorisations are necessary.

Table 4.3 *Cognitive ability estimates*

| | Psycho-metric IQ | SASQ 500 | SAS IQ | SAS IQ corrected | CA corrected |
|---|---|---|---|---|---|
| **Africa (sub-Sahara)** | 70.93 | 347.68 | 74.25 | 66.97 | 69.12 |
| Nigeria | 71 | 365 | 77 | 69 | 75 |
| **N-Africa M-East (ArabM)** | 84.63 | 399.00 | 81.95 | 78.80 | 84.24 |
| Egypt | 81 | 396 | 82 | 80 | 84 |
| **America (North, English)** | 99.00 | 519.47 | 100.02 | 99.80 | 99.45 |
| USA | 98 | 511 | 99 | 98 | 98 |
| **America (Latin, Central-S)** | 83.28 | 385.93 | 79.99 | 76.14 | 79.32 |
| Mexico | 88 | 436 | 88 | 81 | 86 |
| **Asia (Central-South)** | 80.80 | 390.24 | 80.64 | 76.06 | 79.41 |
| India | 82 | 369 | 77 | 69 | 78 |
| **East Asia** | 103.07 | 527.85 | 101.28 | 99.43 | 99.43 |
| China | 106 | 536 | 102 | 99 | 101 |
| **Southeast Asia, Pacific** | 88.70 | 457.40 | 90.71 | 86.50 | 85.16 |
| Philippines | 90 | 352 | 75 | 70 | 80 |
| **Australia-NZ (English)** | 98.50 | 517.40 | 99.71 | 99.34 | 99.06 |
| New Zealand | 99 | 516 | 100 | 99 | 99 |
| **Western Europe** | 97.90 | 515.87 | 99.48 | 99.20 | 98.83 |
| United Kingdom | 100 | 517 | 100 | 100 | 100 |
| **Scandinavia** | 99.00 | 510.68 | 98.70 | 98.80 | 97.06 |
| Norway | 100 | 493 | 96 | 97 | 98 |
| **Central Europe** | 99.83 | 517.27 | 99.69 | 98.58 | 98.85 |
| Germany | 99 | 515 | 99 | 99 | 99 |
| **Eastern Europe** | 95.29 | 492.66 | 96.00 | 94.57 | 95.54 |
| Russia | 97 | 506 | 98 | 97 | 97 |
| **Southern Europe** | 95.00 | 465.76 | 91.96 | 90.40 | 92.61 |
| Italy | 97 | 500 | 97 | 97 | 98 |

*Notes*: Information on data construction, see text and footnotes. Country results rounded. Instead of Kenya (no SAS), Nigeria. The UK average in SAS IQ, SAS IQ corrected and CA corrected is exactly 99.53. Results for all countries of our data base in Appendix, Tables A.1 and A.2.

tests $SD = 9.32$, for SAS $SD = 10.88$[15], for corrected $SD = 9.32$ and $SD = 12.90$. Student assessment studies measure more school dependent content compared to the predominantly used figural psychometric tests. Differences in school quality between countries boost given cognitive ability differences. However, they hardly affect the pattern of country differences – the correlations at around $r = .85$ are very high.

The corrected values are lower than the uncorrected ones – why? Because for the corrected values, young people not at school were included by using

---

[15] In the SAS scale (SASQ) with $M = 500$ and $SD = 100$ the observed standard deviation is $SD = 72.54$.

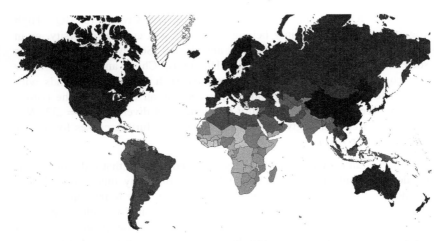

Figure 4.3 Cognitive ability levels around the world, darker represents higher values (including estimates for 27 countries, 173 measured)

assumptions and applying corrections and because in developing countries, where more children do not attend school and many are in grades older than in the international average, the corrections are larger.[16]

## 4.3     Methodical, Political and Cultural Objections

International cognitive ability research has provoked criticism. Critique can be grouped into methodical, political and cultural objections and is frequently backed by more general aloofness against cognitive ability research.

(1) First of all, and certainly true, is that country means hide *within-country heterogeneity*. Means represent averages, not more, not variability and not overlaps between populations. The heterogeneity can be shown by standard deviations or, as used here, by the difference between the 5 per cent and 95 per cent levels. This information is only given in student assessment studies. The countries with the largest 05–95 differences are South Africa (difference 53 IQ), Egypt (52 IQ), Malta, Qatar, Palestine and Trinidad (51 IQ), and Israel (50 IQ); the lowest are found in Vietnam (30 IQ), Macau (33), Honduras (35 IQ), Costa Rica, Estonia, El Salvador and

---

[16] The age- and school-attendance-corrections in SAS for developing countries are –4.86 IQ, for developed –0.46 IQ (data are always restandardised). E.g. for sub-Saharan Africa –7.28 IQ, for Scandinavia +0.10 IQ, for Western Europe –0.28 IQ, for Southern Europe –1.56 IQ.

China (36 IQ) and the Netherlands, Finland and Croatia (37 IQ). High cognitive diversity certainly belongs to ethnic and cultural diversity, as in the cases of South Africa, Qatar and Israel. Somewhat homogeneous societies such as Vietnam, Macau, Honduras, China and Finland show low cognitive diversity, whereas a country such as the Netherlands with quite a few immigrants (around 15 per cent) is an exception. The correlation between the cognitive ability difference and diversity is $r = .32$ ($N = 95$).[17] A correlation is given, but there have to be further causes for low or high cognitive diversity.

Within-country heterogeneity leads to the conclusion that individual ability does not only depend on nationality, but on many other, nevertheless frequently related, factors. Nationality is only one, very rough, predictor for an individual's ability. That does not make nationality useless. Without further information a population's trait average is a useful predictor for a randomly chosen individual from this population. For instance, Germans, on average, drink more beer than French people.[18] If you meet two persons from Germany and France and you have no further information about them it is rational to assume that the German will drink more beer than the French. Of course, there are exceptions: Germans, such as the author of this book, who do not drink beer and French people who drink a lot of beer and even more than wine. And men will drink on average more than women. The larger the heterogeneity the less informative is an average. If it is important and you have the possibility, simply ask the person. Because research at the macrosocial level is not focused on the level of individuals, this aspect is rather unimportant.

(2) A second objection deals with the age of the tested persons in international surveys: using cognitive ability results for predicting and explaining technological, economic, political and cultural development suffers from the fact that the cognitive ability samples are mainly composed of *young people in school*. But how can results from students who do not produce, research or vote be seen as causally relevant for production, innovation and politics? Is it not nonsense? The answer is no for three reasons.

---

[17] The diversity measure is based on four diversity measures from Meisenberg (2007): 'ethnic diversity', 'religious diversity', 'sectarian diversity' and 'racial diversity weighted by genetic distance'. A similar, but inverted measure 'ethnic homogeneity' by Kurian (2001, p. 56f.) correlates at $r = -.25$ ($N = 93$) with cognitive diversity, the same pattern results for 'ethnic heterogeneity' from Vanhanen (2012) with $r = .26$ ($N = 95$) and for 'ethnic fractionalization' from Alesina et al. (2003) with $r = .25$ ($N = 95$).

[18] Beer consumption per capita and year in 2010 (Brewers of Europe, 2012, p. 8): 107 litres in Germany, 30 litres in France.

First, international differences of student and adult competence levels correlate. We have one adult ability study from the Programme for the International Assessment of Adult Competencies, PIAAC 2012, but only for a high achieving country sample of 23. The correlation is $r = .67$ and the for range restriction corrected correlation is $r = .95$.[19] Thus we can infer at the country level from students' to adults' results. Only in the case of larger migrations or rapid historical changes would the inference be misleading.

Second, today's young generations will form the future adult ones. Longitudinal designs and predictions of future social development benefit from using student samples.

Third, within psychometric intelligence studies, adult samples are integrated too.

(3) Is there no *threshold value for intelligence and knowledge*, as for GDP, a certain national level of cognitive ability, values above which do not have noteworthy effects? So, if a sufficient ability level is achieved no further effort in increasing it is reasonable?

This is a double question, and the first is easier to answer than the second. There seems to be no lower or upper thresholds beyond which no or only negligible further positive effects arise. For instance, among the gifted, the top 1 per cent in maths in the US SAT, equivalent to an IQ of 135, the more intelligent achieve more than the less intelligent: more had doctorates and tenure and they had more peer-reviewed publications and patents and higher income (Robertson et al., 2010). Additionally, cognitive demands in everyday life are continuously increasing; the competent use of technology and generally any dealing with the rising amount of information become cognitively more complex. Every step forward in technology and administrative, social, cultural and scientific work becomes more challenging. There is a dynamic spiral-shaped process of intelligence and challenges because intelligence makes the world continuously more complex and this complexity calls for more intelligence.

---

[19] Correlation between our uncorrected SAS average of pupils and the by PIAAC authors adjusted average of adults in reading and mathematics (OECD, 2013b, p. 259, 264). 'Adjusted' for PIAAC means that the entire sample was used, including adults who were not able to provide enough background information because of specific language or general mental disabilities. The average ability mean in our SAS IQ in this 23-country sample is 99 IQ ($SD = 3$, lowest 91 IQ). In our total 108-country SAS sample the mean is 89 IQ ($SD = 11$, lowest 62 IQ). There is a strong range restriction of 10 IQ points. All countries participating in PIAAC are developed countries from Europe, North America, East Asia and Australia. The correction for range restriction was done using a conservative formula for direct range restriction (Schmidt et al., 2006, p. 284) resulting in $r = .95$. Applying the more correcting formula for indirect range restriction (Schmidt et al., 2006, p. 285f.) would result in $r = 1$ ($r = .9970$).

More difficult to answer is the question of the relationship between investment of time, means and effort in cognitive development and its outcomes. Life is not only achievement. Tiger mom and tiger child behaviour are not aims for everyone. Investment will achieve different outcomes for different persons and levels. We will come back to this issue at the end of the book.

(4) The achieved numerical results, especially in less developed countries and here in sub-Saharan Africa, have provoked doubts about the *meaningfulness* of such numbers; for instance, Richard Nisbett (2009, pp. 214f.) questioned them:

> Let's stop and think for a moment about what an IQ of 70 might mean, if we took it seriously as an actual indicator of intelligence of sub-Saharan blacks ... Given what we know about people with such low IQs in our society, the average African, then, might not be expected to know when to plant seeds, what the function of a chief might be, or how to calculate degrees of kinship. Obviously something is desperately wrong with these African IQ scores. They cannot possibly mean for the African population what they do for people of European culture.

Not only are the results of psychometric IQ tests astonishingly low, but so are the outcomes of studies in African countries measuring student achievement (in IQ metric 74 points; see Table 4.3). This number certainly needs to be corrected for youth not in school and overaged students, resulting in a value of 67 points. This number does not even include a correction for countries not participating.

Arthur Jensen (1998, pp. 367ff.) observed the same problem as Nisbett described: low IQ results seem to have a different meaning for people in the United States with European descent than for people with African descent. While for teachers white pupils with an IQ of 70 and lower seem to be mentally retarded, black pupils were not. However, the validity of IQ measures, e.g. for predicting achievement in school, was similar for both groups. Jensen explained the differently competent behaviour in cognitively less demanding situations – Black children being more successful – as an effect of different causes for low intelligence: while for white kids an IQ of 70 or lower is caused by a severe neurological handicap leading to general mental retardation, for black kids the low IQ is caused by a more normal variation from the mean.

Still, this does not answer the question whether the values in Africa are biased or true – further evidence, different from tests, is necessary such as observations of everyday life (see Section 4.4.3).

(5) Can we compare cognitive competences across different countries, cultures and times? This is the old and still up-to-date *cross-cultural comparison challenge*. It is not only a methodological question, but also a political

issue. The critique was ingeniously condensed in one sentence of a one-page article by Mallory Wober (1969, p. 488): 'How well can they do our tricks?' The main reproach is that cognitive ability tests (usually thought of psychometric IQ tests) measure a culturally restricted ability to handle tests, which is only predictive in a Western context. The concept of cognitive ability, its utility and its measurement were not transferable. Intelligence would mean in another society something different, would not be predictive for real world achievement and measurement results would be biased against members of other cultures.

There is also a political connotation, as usually people of other cultures come off badly in Western-developed cognitive ability tests. Tests, surveys, their results, interpretations and researchers are not uncommonly accused of being racists, either in a narrow sense of erroneously claiming a biological superiority of European (-descent) people or in a more metaphorical sense as the expression of a neo-colonialist, imperialist and predominant Western attitude. Many people, including researchers, feel uncomfortable in dealing with the empirically found pattern of ability results. Three examples:

(a)    'But from my presentation thus far, you can anticipate the uneasiness with which I greet conclusions that equate poor performance with lack or less of some general cognitive process.' (Cole, 1977, p. 478)

(b)    'Faced with the two temptations of condemning things which are offensive to him emotionally or of denying differences which are beyond his intellectual grasp, modern man has launched out on countless lines of philosophical and sociological speculation in a vain attempt to achieve a compromise between these two contradictory poles, and to account for the diversity of cultures while seeking, at the same time, to eradicate what still shocks and offends him in that diversity.' (Lévi-Strauss, 1952, p. 13)

(c)    'Since earliest times, nations, cultural groups, and other human collectivities have been trying to show that they are better than other comparable groups. Historically, the main way of doing this has been through wars. But in modern times, there is less violence, perhaps because there are diverse and less violent ways of proving our people are better than your people. Academics typically seek intellectual rather than physical battlegrounds, and psychological scientists, in particular, may choose to show the superiority of one nation or culture over another in psychological terms. Today, its latest manifestation is in the form of books and articles regarding comparative national intelligence.' (Sternberg, 2013, p. 187, quote shortened)

As the famous ethnologist Claude Lévi-Strauss described, modern people including modern scientists try to 'solve' discrepancies between desired versus empirical states by eradicating empirical observations: by an adaptation of perceptions to norms. Later, Bernard Davis (1978) called this epistemic mistake the '*moralistic fallacy*'. Following Jean Piaget's theory of cognitive development it is a cognitive failure, an insufficient assimilation, an over-stretched scheme, altogether signs of being stuck between cognitive stages, not reaching the formal level, which is epistemically necessary for dealing with constructs, distinctions, theories and contradictions. The formal level is necessary for reflecting epistemic-ideological confoundings, to value and self-control arguments by discourse integrity.

For political claims, there are three rather simple answers: first, East Asians in their countries of origin and in other countries, where they emigrated to, usually achieve better results than Westerners and natives (e.g. in the United States, Australia, Malaysia, Latin America etc.). Second, Jews, the old object of hate for traditional Western racists, usually achieve better results in cognitive ability tests and indicators of cognitive achievement. Third, even if the French are the inventors of the metre they are shorter than the Dutch. The rejection of a metre does not eliminate height nor differences in it. The refusal of a thermometer or the concept of heat do not change temperature.

The cross-cultural issue itself deals with the question of universalism. *Universalism* may represent a normative standard, in ethics as human rights or in epistemic questions as one common standard for finding truth, or it may represent an empirical assumption that all humans are factually equal, e.g. in thinking and thinking abilities as subliminally provided by the rational choice approach. Universalism is opposite to *relativism*: that for different people different norms have to be applied, concepts and ways of finding truth are different but equally true, or that people empirically differ across cultures and nations.

Cross-cultural research is based on the idea that there is one common reasonable concept of intelligence and one common standard for finding truth. If people empirically differ in certain aspects, they just differ in them. The last is 'accidental', not cogent; people may be also similar in any attribute including intelligence, e.g. Hungary and Slovakia, and any difference or similarity is subject to change across time.

How is this position to be justified? The first approach is a reference to *given realities* and *functionality*: because we live in modernity, a modernity that is essentially built upon Western principles, because most people want to live in such modern societies and because modernity can be successfully mastered and achieved with Western concepts of intelligence and knowledge, the use of Western standards, e.g. in cognitive ability research, is justified.[20] This parsimonious attempt avoids any theory on cognitive ability. Additionally, if cognitive ability would be paraphrased as 'literacy', 'skill', 'dealing with artefacts' or 'managing modernity', such a position could sidestep politically

---

[20] The argumentation of Earl Hunt (2012) tended in this direction.

delicate issues of intelligence differences. However, the argument of the West being important and desired by a majority is theoretically less convincing.

Let us have a closer look at the arguments of the relativistic position: it distinguishes an 'etic approach', positively using a universal standard, negatively using the standard of the culture of the researcher, and an 'emic approach', positively seeing the world and thinking by the standards of the investigated culture, negatively using a relativistic or no standard at all.[21]

An example for the emic approach is the study of the intelligence concept of Ganda people in Uganda by Mallory Wober (1974). The author interviewed people about their concepts of intelligence. In Ganda culture, intelligence is positively seen as a kind of mental order (p. 265), being slow, cautious, determined, sane. Educational aims stress obedience to adults and orientation towards tradition.[22] The mentioned 'mental order' is not so different to the structuralist approach of Piaget; 'circumspection' and 'caution' are elements and effects of intelligence and 'mental health' is a very basic condition for cognitive ability. Thus the traditional Ganda view is not so different to a Western concept of intelligence.

Even if the aspects were different, e.g. intelligence as obedience, knowing holy texts by heart, magic wisdom or acquisition of a traditional worldview, it would not undermine a concept of intelligence as thinking ability. The suitability of a concept does not depend on agreement with culturally varying views. It depends on clarity, logic, empirical connectedness and functionality for research. For instance, if in one culture height were defined as size from feet to head including hair of the head, this does not invalidate a concept based only on feet to head without hair. Because hair artificially varies with haircuts, fashion, gender and age, hair should not be included in height concepts and height measurement.

An answer to the universalism problem could be found also within intelligence research, by applying its understanding of thinking and cognitive development on science itself. Here the work of Deirdre Kramer (1983) is informative: she extended the Piagetian concept of formal operational stage and assumed a continuing cognitive development in adulthood. In this higher stage, (1) the realisation of the relativistic nature of knowledge is a preliminary and necessary step in cognitive development with (2) the aim of integration of relativistic and contradictory views towards a meaningful whole. Accordingly, it is important to see differences between viewpoints and their contradictions, but contradictory views cannot both be true, they can only be a part of a

---

[21] The etic–emic distinction was developed by Kenneth L. Pike and Ward Goodenough.

[22] Wober (1974, p. 263): 'Achievement is explicitly defined as successful service to existing norms and values ... These higher abilities are those which tend to maintain the essential structure of the system, rather than to question or challenge it.'

transitory stage. Applied to cognitive science, this means that critique has to be received but answered, leading to an improved, well-reasoned higher-order universalistic position.

Related to the conceptual issue is the measurement issue. Of course, command of a special language cannot be an indicator of intelligence, but command of the native language (and the ability to learn a new language) can. Tasks need to be related to cognitive ability, for intelligence as the ability to think. For example, mental speed, memory tasks or knowledge questions are less suitable for intelligence (however, achievement in these is correlated with intelligence). Tests should be applied in the native language and should cover a broad range of cognitive tasks. Best are figural tasks, as used in Raven Matrices (CPM, SPM, APM), Cattell's CFT and similar scales in many intelligence tests. But this is not enough; tasks such as logic and categorisation questions developed and used by Alexander Luria (1976/1974) or realistic tasks and categorisation questions developed by Jean Piaget (2001/1947) should be applied. They also enable study of thinking processes by thinking out loud and asking questions. But their use is laborious as – differently to paper-and-pencil tests – every person has to be tested individually. Student assessment tests (PIRLS, PISA and TIMSS) are also valuable sources. However, they include arithmetic and dealing with knowledge acquired in school, family and everyday life in modern societies. They are not pure measures of intelligence (similar to intelligence tests comprising verbal and numeric scales). They are mixed measures of crystallised and fluid intelligence.

Inasmuch as knowledge is included, a normative theory on knowledge is necessary (a 'Bildungstheorie', a philosophy of education). Knowledge has to be true and should be relevant and functional to be valuable to know. Psychologically, the pure amount of stored, structured and retrieved information such as on football teams, witchcraft or the number of blades of grass in one's yard is informative, but not from a perspective of reasonable education. The international student assessment studies are based on assumptions of competence and knowledge functionality in modernity.

If research finds differences in such tasks between peoples and countries, these differences do not refute the application of a concept of intelligence historically developed in Western culture. If swimming ability had been developed by Polynesians, this would not refute the concept itself for nineteenth-century Europeans, women or Bedouins, even when among them a smaller percentage of people can swim. However, it would be wrong to take swimming ability as the only indicator for physical fitness.

Another problem are cross-cultural differences in *test-wiseness* and *test-taking motivation*. In 2001, the author tried to test Yanomami Indians in Brazil with the SPM. It was impossible; they did not understand what was demanded, neither did young Yanomami men with knowledge of Portuguese and some modern experience gained by visiting Brazilian cities. The application of cognitive tasks in groups with no test experience is difficult. At least, the command of the local language by the test administrator and some test taking training for the test subjects are necessary. As research among indigenous, but illiterate, people shows, this is possible (e.g. Lacey, 1970; Luria, 1976/1974). It is reported that East Asian teachers, students and their parents see the participation in an international student assessment study as a kind of national contest. Sometimes they intone the national anthem before the test begins. However, in North America, East Asians also show good results – even without singing the anthem. They also excel in school achievement (Flynn, 1991). People who are highly motivated and disciplined in tests usually show similar behaviour in real-life situations and also acquire, by this behaviour in school, more knowledge and better train their cognitive abilities.

All this discussion does not answer the fundamental question whether intelligence (without knowledge and the use of knowledge) developed in Western culture is a reasonable concept and whether it is applicable for other cultures. Let us start looking closer at the term 'intelligence': it is based on the Latin *intellegere* (from *inter-legere*), meaning to understand, recognise, comprehend, grasp and correctly judge. *Legere* goes back to the Greek λεγειν, meaning to collect, speak and explain, and back to λογος, meaning reason, thought, speech, word, arithmetic, thinking ability. The oldest documented use of the term '*intelligentia*' is found in Cicero's *De inventione* around 2,100 years ago, describing an ability to understand. All these meanings are also covered by the contemporary concept of intelligence, but also by the literacy term used in student assessment studies. The meaning as a thinking ability is quite stable across centuries.

Analyses of historical origins of terms also do not answer the fundamental question whether intelligence is a reasonable concept. Two answers can be given:

Intelligence is a part of the *Enlightenment* ('Aufklärung') and of the ideas that emerged in this era such as cognition, truth and the human as a rational mind. The cognitive ability research streams of Jean Piaget, Lucien Lévy-Bruhl or Alexander Luria are explicitly based on the idea that true and rational access to the world, to the physical, social and mental world, and to oneself (self-reflection was, for example, studied by Luria) is the distinctive feature and important characteristic of humans. Intelligence accompanied by knowledge and the intelligent use of knowledge are the conditions for true and rational access to the world and oneself. To think and understand are valuable in themselves. Enlightenment is based on intelligence and supports intelligence.

Second, as frequently mentioned by different researchers and organisations (e.g. Linda Gottfredson, Earl Hunt, OECD), cognitive ability is *predictive* (correlated with) and *functional*, meaning being causally relevant (creating, supporting) to achieve positively valued states and aims such as health, longevity, economic productivity, power, good jobs, respect or social status.

Up to now, we have assumed that science and critique within science are based on the aim of approaching truth via statements. Argumentation, critique and justification, contentual, logical and empirical arguments are heard and serve in a two-way exchange to find the relatively truer and more informative statement. However, observing research, it seems that this is not always the case. As mentioned before, intelligence researchers reported unfair accusations and personal attacks and some were even attacked and needed protection by police, as in the cases of Arthur Jensen, Richard Herrnstein and Philippe Rushton (e.g. Gottfredson, 2010; Herrnstein, 1973; Nyborg, 2003; Segerstråle, 2000).

Frequently, ethically negative motives are alleged for which the epistemic statements are attacked indirectly; other researchers were sternberged, criticised by constructing ethical arguments in an unethical and unsubstantiated way: scientists would like to 'restore Western supremacy', they were 'racists' or 'neo-colonialists'. Even if these allegations were true, science does not deal with motives, but with the truth or falseness of statements. A devil's truth is as true as an angel's truth: $2 + 2 = 4$. Relevant is whether a statement is correctly describing and explaining the world, and second, if it is new. Somebody who says in summer that the coming winter will be cold is not a 'winterist', but, if true, a realist and if wrong, an errant or simply a person stating something wrong.

Scientific disputes with non-epistemic background are not all new. Scholars were also attacked in the past, Averroes, Galilei, Bruno, Spinoza, Darwin or Freud are good examples. Lines of conflict change; Darwin was blamed for Anti-Christian sentiment and today a similar position is blamed for racism. The same paradigm, for example evolution, can be attacked from the right (against the idea of evolution of humans) or the left (against the idea of evolution of individual or group differences among current humans). How can researchers deal with such ideological-political problems? There are various problematic attitudes:

(1) *Anxiety leading to avoidance.* People like to avoid problems; a comprehensible, useful attitude, especially for own progress.
(2) For some, research is not originally motivated by science, pursuing new knowledge orientated towards truth guided by epistemic rationality, but a *functional business* increasing wealth and reputation.
(3) Some sail with the *ideological winds* and use their positions as scientists to boost these winds.
(4) Some went so far as to explicitly *appreciate the unethical treatment of opponents* in scientific disputes ('proponents of race science, while entitled

to their freedom of inquiry and expression, deserve the vigorous disapprobation they often receive'; Turkheimer, 2007).

(5) *Oddity*: finally, there are some attracted by these research questions who like to shock others,[23] who like to celebrate a minority status, who have strange personalities or who are burdened with attitudes towards certain groups. Previous knowledge and attitudes could stimulate research and could be true or wrong (see Ashton & Esses, 1999), but they should not bias research results.

One example could be the book by Stephen Jay Gould (1981, pp. 50–69), '*The Mismeasure of Man*'. In this book, which is still credited to some extent by the public and by some 'scientists', Gould alleged different researchers had dishonest motives, particularly having cheated due to racist motives. One 'case' for him was Samuel George Morton (1799–1851), an American physician, natural scientist and anthropologist from Philadelphia. Using craniometry, Morton came to the result that Europeans have on average larger brains than Native Americans and Africans. Gould claimed that this result was based on an unconscious manipulation of data due to 'prejudices' ('finagling'). However, a student (Michael, 1988) has checked Morton's data and found no systematic error, only deficits in precision.[24] John Michael sent his results to Gould but he never reacted.[25] But dealing with the results of others and dealing with questioning and critique is essential for an epistemic attitude (searching truth) and scientific progress (finding new truth). And not dealing with them, except

---

[23] James Watson seems to belong to this provocative spectrum ('Avoid boring people').

[24] 'Morton's tables contain miscalculations and omissions of data, but his 1849 data are reasonably accurate and there is no clear evidence that he doctored these tables for any reason.' (Michael, 1988, p. 354) Michael's results were supported by Lewis et al. (2011, p. 3, 5), who found biased systematic errors in Gould's book, but only unsystematic errors in Morton's work. Those unsystematic errors actually led to decreased estimates of racial group differences – so if there still were any kind of (conscious or unconscious) prejudices involved, they could rather be an effect of some egalitarian agenda:

> Clearly, Morton was not manipulating samples to depress the 'Indian' mean, and the change was trivial in any case (0.3 in³). In fact, the more likely candidate for manipulating sample composition is Gould himself in this instance. In recalculating Morton's Native American mean, Gould reports erroneously high values for the Seminole-Muskogee and Iroquois due to mistakes in defining those samples and omits the Eastern Lenapé group entirely, all of which serve to increase the Native American mean and reduce the differences between groups . . . The summary table of Morton's final 1849 catalog has multiple errors. However, had Morton not made those errors his results would have more closely matched his presumed a priori bias. Ironically, Gould's own analysis of Morton is likely the stronger example of a bias influencing results. (references omitted)

[25] 'Gould ignored Michael's contribution completely. Michael personally sent him his article but Gould did not even mention it in the second edition of *The Mismeasure of Man*, despite its obvious relevance for the book's central theme.' (Sesardic, 2005, p. 42) Stephen Jay Gould (1941–2002) was a paleontologist at Harvard.

for time and cognitive constraints, hints to a non-epistemic attitude (pursuing other aims than truth).

Psychologically interesting is that Gould alleged that others were biased in their research; however, he was himself biased. Projection is an indicator of a poorly integrated cognitive system. E.g. Blinkhorn (1982, p. 506) on Gould:

The theme of this [Gould's] particular book is that since science is embedded in society, one must expect to find the prejudices of the age presented by scientists as fact. Most authors, given such a theme, would be content to document and catalogue instances in support of the proposition. Gould, however, goes one better by writing a book which exemplifies its own thesis. It is a masterpiece of propaganda, researched in the service of a point of view rather than written from a fund of knowledge.

Or Carroll (1995, p. 122), who sees Gould not only as prejudiced, but as producing prejudices:

His [Gould's] account of the history of mental testing, however, may be regarded as badly biased, and crafted in such a way as to prejudice the general public and even some scientists against almost any research concerning human cognitive abilities.

Others avoid scientific argumentation and entirely move to the political arena. Pierre Bourdieu, himself an example for this strategy (see earlier), described politicisation as a strategy to avoid an epistemic examination of reality allowing people to pretend to deal with science but to 'give themselves – and to give their peers – the illusion that they transcend what transcends them'. (Bourdieu, 1988/ 1984, p. 20). Bourdieu sees it as a power strategy; however, maybe it is also, or only, a cognitive simplification strategy, to bring order in a complex and confusing reality as described by Piaget's concept of assimilation.

'Et lux in tenebris lucet, et tenebrae eam non comprehenderunt.' (Ioannes, 1:5)[26]

## 4.4     Everyday Life Evidence and Sediments

### 4.4.1     Indicators of Cognitive Ability for Historical and International Analyses

There is no better source for assessing cognitive ability than professionally applied cognitive tests. Intelligence is *the* construct of psychology. There is no more extensive cross-cultural research than with cognitive ability tests, especially by student assessment studies. Tasks, the testing procedure and the interpretation of results are checked for objectivity, reliability and, most relevantly, for validity. Generally, the tests are economic, fair, useful and

---

[26] 'The light shines in the darkness, and the darkness has not understood it' (John 1:5).

provide normed and interpretable results. This is true for the measurement of individuals as well as of nations. Estimates are based on a variety of tasks. National estimates are usually the result of large samples; hundreds or thousands of persons are tested.[27]

However, results of test samples and interpretations based on them were sometimes criticised for being meaningless – they would be unrelated to real-life cognitive performance. There had been epochal qualitative, non-test studies analysing thinking itself such as from Alexander Luria (1976/1974) in Uzbekistan in the 1930s and internationally comparing overviews on old ethnological studies such as from Lucien Lévy-Bruhl (1923/1922). However, we are more interested in *contemporary* cognitive development levels. The past is insofar interesting as it may show the stability of patterns and the conditions of historical development.

What could be valid indicators of cognitive ability in everyday life and its sediments? The answer is simple: all behaviour and all results of behaviour based on the usage of cognitive ability. Especially relevant are *complex* tasks and operations. For instance, an explanation of a sickness and its therapy are more complex and therefore more informative than herding cattle. They can be assessed according to correctness (approximating truth), complexity (difficulty, invention and innovation), coherence, epistemic rationality (using logic, empirical evidence and arguments), instrumental rationality (functionality) and aesthetic quality.

Here we can distinguish between behaviour itself and its results (sediments; see Section 3.2.5), between indicators of average and high ability cognitive achievement and between past and present cognitive achievement. From a conventional scientific viewpoint, the reference to international statistics is a more convincing strategy than doing analyses on behaviour in everyday cognitive achievement situations. Such statistics are based on 'numbers' and are collected by others – both may help to persuade sceptics.

However, the everyday life approach has two important advantages: cognition and cognitive ability of people in past epochs can be determined. And we can support – or question – the validity of test results. Let us describe a list of possible sources.

Especially valuable sources are historical *behaviour patterns representing cognitive irrationality*. At the individual level, intelligence and rationality are highly correlated ($r = .70$; Stanovich, Toplak & West, 2016, p. 260). Because we assume a long-term cognitive rise (a slow FLynn effect since early Middle Ages), such patterns should have become less common. Typical examples, as

---

[27] Systematic deviations of samples from intended populations (e.g. students vs. entire youth) or sampling differences between countries (e.g. students in country A are older than in other countries or fewer children attend school) need to be corrected (see Appendix).

extensively described by the sociologist Georg W. Oesterdiekhoff (2007, 2009a, 2009b, 2012a, 2012b), are:

- *Magical thinking* and its manifestations such as belief in witchcraft, using ordeals to find the true answer on epistemic or juridical questions (why a person died and who is to be punished?), magic conceptions of health and illness, magic causality, astrology.
- *Anthropomorphous thinking* like assuming that animals can understand humans and their rules and that they can be guilty of bad behaviour (trials against animals).
- *Animist thinking* such as that natural beings (e.g. the sun or moon) behave like persons with their own intentions.
- *Problems with numbers, categorisation and logic.*
- The *excessive and personal use of cruelty* (lower perspective taking and empathy, lower developed stage of moral reasoning and behaviour).

Such behaviour was not only found in the European past, but was also extensively described by ethnologists for premodern societies outside Europe (Evans-Pritchard, 1976/1937; Everett, 2008; Frazer, 1922/1890; Hallpike, 1980; Lévy-Bruhl, 1923/1922; Signer, 2004).

The sociologist Robert Gordon (1997) described in 'Everyday Life As an Intelligence Test', with 118 pages the longest and most verbose paper ever published by the journal *Intelligence*, a naturalistic observation approach to estimate cognitive ability. He treated single non-test actions in everyday life in analogy to single test items, both evaluated for correctness. One example is the *belief in conspiracy rumors* (opposite to epistemic rationality); others, less close to cognition, were *delinquency, single parenthood, HIV infection* and *poverty* (functionality and ethics), which all were negatively correlated at the group level with intelligence.

The anthropologist John Baker (1974, p. 507f.) developed a list of 21 criteria of civilisation, of which many can be taken as indicators of cognitive ability development in history[28]: (1) Being clothed, (2) cleanliness, (3) no severe mutilation, (4) knowledge of building in brick or stone (if material available; criterion does not fit for Inuit), (5) city culture and travel ways, (6) agriculture, (7) animal husbandry, (8) metallurgy, (9) use of wheels, (10) use of money, (11) system of law, (12) accused persons are allowed to defend themselves, (13) no torture for extracting information or punishment, (14) no cannibalism, (15) religion includes ethics and not only superstition, (16) use of script, (17) abstract use of numbers, (18) use of accurate calendar, (19) intellectual

---

[28] John Baker (1900–1984) was professor at the University of Oxford; together with Michael Polanyi (1891–1976), professor in Berlin and Manchester, he founded the Society for Freedom in Science in 1940.

education of the young, (20) appreciation of fine arts, (21) knowledge and understanding are valued as ends in themselves. Some criteria are doubtful (e.g. the use of wheels for transport was forbidden in Tibet) and many are very basic and show only loose connection to cognitive ability (e.g. being clothed), but the last six (15–21) are important cognitive criteria.[29]

One example of a narrow, but cognitively informative, indicator is the *use and quality of cartography*. The better the quality (correctness, usability), the higher is the cognitive development stage (compare to Piaget's three mountains task in Figure 3.2):

Humanity's collective history of mapping the whole known world can be paralleled with the child psychologist Jean Piaget's threefold developmental theory of the individual. First, perceptions and representational abilities are not matched; only the simplest topographical relationships are presented, without regard for perspective or distances. Then an intellectual 'realism' evolves, one that depicts everything known with burgeoning proportional relationships. And finally, a visual 'realism' appears, advocating scientific calculations to achieve it. (Virga, 2007, p. 5)

Of course, not only the production of maps but also the reading of maps is informative – do people understand and more basically do people use maps at all? A similar indicator is the *understanding of time*, its *efficient use* and, more technological, the development and mastery of *time measurement* by clocks (Landes, 1983). Individually, people should understand the clock. One example: in the late 1990s I asked about 20 people in Cuba, all adults, how many times each day a broken analogue watch that stopped running with a dial and hands shows the correct time. This question is related to everyday life in Cuba, since many clocks were not working. About 75 per cent said 'never shows the correct time', 15 per cent 'once' and 10 per cent 'twice'. A Cuban teacher with better command of Spanish than me, came in her survey to a similar distribution. According to the Piagetian theory, the persons had not developed the last or the second last cognitive development stage enabling abstract-formal thinking and cognitive perspective taking.[30] Similar phenomena can be observed by displaying a map and asking people for the right way.

---

[29] A similar approach defines and measures cultural complexity of native people in premodern eras (Murdock & Provost, 1973). Excluding due to replacement immigration America and Trans-Tasman, the variable cultural complexity correlates with present cognitive ability at $r = .32$ ($N = 84$), adding Aborigines' and Maoris' cognitive ability averages (based on Lynn, 2006, pp. 104, 117, IQs 62 and 90) the correlation is $r = .34$ ($N = 86$). Another researcher, Morris (2013), uses for the 'measure of civilization' development indicators such as energy capture, organisation, information technology and war-making. However, no numbers are given for countries.

[30] For comparison, a German Hauptschul teacher (vocational track) asked the same question in April 2005: In seventh grade, 12 out of 26 pupils (46 per cent) knew the correct answer, in eighth grade 15 out of 27 pupils (56 per cent) and in tenth grade 4 out of 5 pupils (80 per cent). So Cubans would correspond to sixth or fifth vocational track graders in Germany (if there is no sampling error). This would correspond to an IQ in Greenwich norms of around 75 to 70.

Culturally, the efficiency of using time largely varies (Levine, 1997). The advice of Benjamin Franklin (2004/1964, p. 200) is famous: 'Remember that time is money.' Much older is the similar advice of the Italian Renaissance polymath Leon Battista Alberti, given in his book '*Della famiglia*' (2004/ 1441, Book III, p. 171f.):

My plan, therefore, is to make as good use as possible of time, and never to waste any ... I spend no more time on anything than is needed to do it well. And to waste no part of such a precious thing, I have a rule that I always follow: never remain idle, I avoid sleep, and I do not lie down unless overcome by weariness ... First thing in the morning, when I arise, I think to myself, 'What are the things I have to do today?' There are a certain number of things, and I run through them, consider, and assign to each some part of my time: this for the morning, this later today, and that this evening. In this way I find every task gets done in an orderly way, almost without effort ... Just remember not to waste time. Do as I do. In the morning I plan my whole day, during the day I follow my plan, and in the evening, before I retire, I think over again what I have done during the day.

Along with cognitive ability, an important precondition and effect of this time efficiency attitude is the development and use of timekeepers. Cognitive ability and culture work together in the improvement of time measurement. For the production of clocks, only very few raw materials are necessary. Transport is cheap. Clocks can be produced anywhere in the world. However, a lot of competence, discipline and technical precision is necessary to produce a clock. Time efficiency and punctuality need time competence, virtue and self-discipline:

Knowledge of the time must be combined with obedience – what social scientists like to call time discipline ...

No other project in applied science has ever drawn on so much intelligence and talent. (Landes, 1983, p. 2, 12)

However, the clock and time examples also show that indicators of cognition and cognitive ability are not pure indicators – they are commingled: they are also measures of burgher behaviour and burgher values. Let us start first with statistical indicators of cognitive ability in everyday life and its sediments and later come to qualitative data.

### 4.4.2   Quantitative Data for Statistical Analyses

Information needs to be comparatively measured to be useful for statistical analyses. The following variables and sources representing average and top cognitive achievement in the past and present can be used:

According to international data, the corrected cognitive ability estimate for Cuba is IQ 84 (Table A.2).

(1) The development and *adoption of technology* is one central indicator of cognitive achievement. Comin et al. (2010) provided adoption data (e.g. using the plough, compass, printing) for 1000 BCE, O CE, 1500 CE and 2000 CE. However, adoption is suboptimal because adoption is relatively simple and also depends on vicinity to innovative centres. Development is more challenging and would be more informative. Additionally, in America and Trans-Tasman the populations were replaced. Ancient countries were assigned to current ones (e.g. Rome to Italy). Data are given from 1000 BCE to 2000 CE for 112, 134, 123 and 133 countries. For Tables 4.4 and 4.5 of this book all data were standardised according to the international cognitive ability measure.[31]

(2) *Scientific excellence* from 800 BCE to 1950 CE in science (astronomy, biology, chemistry, earth sciences, physics, medicine), mathematics, and technology is measured by the eminence and number of important scientists in a country (an analysis of encyclopaedias by Murray, 2003, for 42 countries). The resulting number was related to modern population size, e.g. China needs more eminent scientists than Greece to come to the same level of eminence, and countries without eminent scientists were set at zero (all together $N = 198$). Charles Murray's assessment is correlated with the much shorter list of Michael Hart's assessment (2007) with $r = .72$ ($N = 198$, missing countries set at 0).

(3) Another supplementary past index, here for *intellectual* eminence, is the Enlightenment Index from Joel Mokyr (2005). He took the *Encyclopedia of the Enlightenment* and used as quantitative indicator the scope of entries per country, 'lines per million of 1750 population'. Data for 32 countries; countries without data set at zero ($N = 186$).

(4) Number of *patents* of a nation (sum of residents and non-residents), average annual patents per 1 million people 1991–2007 ($N = 76$ countries). Source is the World Intellectual Property Organization (WIPO, 2009). Patents stand for technological innovation – for development instead of adoption.

(5) *High-technology exports* as a percentage of total goods exports, 2007 or most recent year (Dutta & Mia, 2010, p. 392). This variable stands for the mastery of modern technology and its development.

(6) *Airline safety* in 2009 and 2010 (Wolf, 2010, 2011). Data for 37 countries. Problematic is that only the 60 safest airlines were ranked; all the unsafe ones are excluded. Additionally, this selection excludes many airlines from developing countries. This reduces differences between countries and reduces correlations. Airline safety presents the mastery

---

[31] For better comparability and comprehensibility, the same scale, mean and standard deviation in the common sample of countries for each variable was used, based on $M = 100$ and $SD = 15$.

Table 4.4 *Indicators of cognitive achievement in historical development*

| | Technology −1000 (Comin) | Technology 0 (Comin) | Technology +1500 (Comin) | Technology +2000 (Comin) | Eminent Scientists −800 to +1950 (Murray) | Enlightenment Index 18th cent. (Mokyr) |
|---|---|---|---|---|---|---|
| **Africa (sub-Sahara)** | 74 | 80 | 69 | 75 | 88 | 89 |
| Kenya | 77 | 97 | 68 | 77 | 88 | 89 |
| **N-Africa M-East (ArabM)** | 104 | 97 | 89 | 84 | 88 | 89 |
| Egypt | 102 | 97 | 91 | 79 | 88 | 89 |
| **America (North, English)** | 87 | 92 | 94 | 114 | 90 | 113 |
| USA | 86 | 90 | 91 | 116 | 91 | 113 |
| **America (Latin, Central-S)** | 81 | 80 | 84 | 82 | 88 | 89 |
| Mexico | 77 | 78 | 78 | 84 | 88 | 90 |
| **Asia (Central-South)** | 85 | 91 | 84 | 75 | 88 | 89 |
| India | 92 | 77 | 91 | 76 | 88 | 89 |
| **East Asia** | 88 | 88 | 91 | 89 | 88 | 89 |
| China | 102 | 97 | 96 | 77 | 88 | 89 |
| **Southeast Asia, Pacific** | 83 | 76 | 81 | 81 | 88 | 89 |
| Philippines | – | 76 | 83 | 79 | 88 | 89 |
| **Australia-NZ (English)** | 89 | 93 | 97 | 110 | 92 | 88 |
| New Zealand | – | 91 | 95 | 111 | 95 | 89 |
| **Western Europe** | 88 | 97 | 97 | 104 | 100 | 96 |
| United Kingdom | 87 | 97 | 101 | 104 | 114 | 110 |
| **Scandinavia** | 87 | 97 | 95 | 107 | 95 | 94 |
| Norway | 87 | 97 | 97 | 108 | 95 | 95 |
| **Central Europe** | 88 | 97 | 96 | 106 | 99 | 94 |
| Germany | 88 | 97 | 97 | 105 | 104 | 93 |
| **Eastern Europe** | 88 | 83 | 94 | 87 | 89 | 89 |
| Russia | 87 | 97 | 93 | 85 | 89 | 89 |
| **Southern Europe** | 100 | 89 | 97 | 90 | 91 | 90 |
| Italy | 106 | 97 | 97 | 99 | 97 | 92 |

*Notes:* All values rounded and corrected for population size. Normed in comparison to the current corrected total cognitive ability average. Those with no values in eminent scientists and Enlightenment were set to 0. Indicators described in text.

118

Table 4.5 *Indicators of cognitive achievement in modern times*

| | Patents 1991–2007 (WIPO) | High-tech exports 2007 (WEF) | Airline safety 2009–10 (AERO) | Innovation 2013 (WIPO) | Science Nobel Prizes 1901–2004 | High Citations 1987 (Cole) | Top universities 2010–2013 |
|---|---|---|---|---|---|---|---|
| **Africa (sub-Sahara)** | 88 | 80 | 94 | 75 | 80 | 83 | 75 |
| Kenya | – | 81 | – | 78 | 79 | 83 | 74 |
| **N-Africa M-East (ArabM)** | 89 | 80 | 92 | 82 | 80 | 85 | 82 |
| Egypt | 88 | 79 | – | 76 | 81 | 83 | 84 |
| **America (North, English)** | 101 | 95 | 99 | 106 | 102 | 112 | 110 |
| USA | 103 | 103 | 98 | 108 | 110 | 119 | 114 |
| **America (Latin, Central-S)** | 88 | 83 | 78 | 81 | 80 | 83 | 83 |
| Mexico | 89 | 94 | – | 84 | 80 | 83 | 91 |
| **Asia (Central-South)** | 89 | 81 | 89 | 75 | 80 | 83 | 79 |
| India | – | 83 | 89 | 83 | 80 | 83 | 93 |
| **East Asia** | 98 | 112 | 94 | 96 | 80 | 84 | 96 |
| China | – | 112 | 98 | 92 | 80 | 83 | 100 |
| **Southeast Asia, Pacific** | 99 | 96 | 91 | 85 | 79 | 83 | 87 |
| Philippines | 88 | 112 | 91 | 78 | 79 | 83 | 84 |
| **Australia-NZ (English)** | 112 | 82 | 98 | 101 | 92 | 96 | 100 |
| New Zealand | 119 | 82 | 95 | 102 | 93 | 96 | 97 |
| **Western Europe** | 92 | 98 | 99 | 105 | 105 | 98 | 102 |
| United Kingdom | 92 | 96 | 100 | 109 | 126 | 108 | 110 |
| **Scandinavia** | 96 | 93 | 97 | 106 | 115 | 104 | 97 |
| Norway | 102 | 83 | – | 103 | 118 | 94 | 96 |
| **Central Europe** | 92 | 92 | 100 | 105 | 114 | 113 | 101 |
| Germany | 93 | 93 | 100 | 103 | 117 | 98 | 103 |
| **Eastern Europe** | 90 | 86 | 99 | 89 | 81 | 83 | 85 |
| Russia | 92 | 80 | 99 | 84 | 81 | 83 | 95 |
| **Southern Europe** | 91 | 88 | 98 | 90 | 80 | 84 | 88 |
| Italy | 91 | 86 | 98 | 95 | 84 | 87 | 95 |

*Notes:* All values rounded and corrected for population size. Normed in comparison to the corrected total cognitive ability average. Smaller countries have an advantage in exports (smaller own market). WIPO: World Intellectual Property Organization; High-tech exports: High-technology exports as a percentage of total goods exports; WEF: World Economic Forum; AERO: Aero International.

of highly complex technology and all the management surrounding it (airport organisation, education of staff, etc.).

(7) *Innovation*: data come from the World Intellectual Property Organization (WIPO; Dutta & Lanvin, 2013). WIPO ranks countries according to their innovations in science, technology, economy and society based on seven pillars: institutions including politics, human capital covering education and research, infrastructure, market sophistication (credit and trade), business sophistication (knowledge workforce), knowledge and technology outputs, and creative outputs including arts. The Global Innovation Index (GII) is used for the year 2013 ($N = 142$ countries). This index is a broad measure of top cognitive achievement.

(8) *Nobel Prizes* in science (physics, chemistry, medicine and economics) 1901–2004 related to population size.[32] Mean correlations between the prizes in the four fields are around $r = .90$ ($\alpha = .97$, $N = 187$ countries, countries with no prizes set at zero). Similar to Murray's scientific excellence indicator, Nobel Prizes stand for top cognitive achievement.

(9) Number of *highly cited research articles* (more than 40 times) per million of population in 1987 (Cole & Phelan, 1999) in 93 countries. This indicator represents more modest top cognitive achievement.

(10) Information on the *quality of universities* was taken from three sources: Quacquarelli Symonds 2012 (QS 2012), Shanghai Ranking 2010 (ARWU, 2010) and Times Higher Education 2012–2013 (2013). The three agencies estimate the quality of around 500 to 700 'top' universities in the world somewhat differently (based on research, reputation, citations, faculty student ratio, papers published in prestigious journals, teaching and international staff and students). We took the values for the three best universities of a country and calculated one average. Ranks correlate with $r = .60$–.88 (average $\alpha = .88$). Ranks were only provided for 40 to 71 countries. Differences between countries are reduced and correlations tend to be lower. It is reasonable to assume that larger countries with unranked universities have low quality universities. Therefore, countries with more than 10 million people and without any rankings were set to zero. Data were given for 103 countries.

(11) Finally, we formed three *mean values*: one for mainly older achievement (Table 4.4), one for current achievement (Table 4.5) and one for both together ($r = .68$, $\alpha = .74$–.80).[33]

---

[32] Sources for Nobel Prizes: http://nobelprize.org/nobel_prizes/lists/all, http://en.wikipedia.org/wiki/List_of_Nobel_laureates_by_country.

[33] One methodological problem is how to deal with missing values: They represent no resp. low achievement or the country population is too small.

Results in all indicators depend on further factors than cognitive ability. For instance, Nobel Prizes do not only depend on individuals' cognitive ability: higher society ability levels lead to better universities, a more stimulating environment and networks of contacts to institutions which award prizes. Individuals with exceptional abilities surrounded by non-supportive conditions easily fail to show their potential. However, cognitive competence and its development remain crucial. As the Piagetian structure-genetic sociologist Georg W. Oesterdiekhoff mentioned:

> Basically, scientific progress does not base on 'accumulation of facts', on 'falsifications' or on 'methodologies'. It rather roots in the transformation of the psychostructural system respectively in the rise of the anthropological and developmental stages. (Oesterdiekhoff, 2013, p. 328)[34]

Cognitive ability differences are boosted and stabilised through their institutional effects ending in reinforcing feedback-loops (see Figure 3.6).

In technology, 3000 years ago Rome, Greece (not listed in Tables 4.4 and 4.5), Egypt and China were leading, and today the West and Japan (not listed). Eminent scientists are concentrated in Western and Central Europe (a more in-detail analysis would also include Northern Italy as a hot spot). Enlightenment is mainly a British and US-American phenomenon.

Innovation, technology and science are led by Western, Northern and Central Europe, North America and Trans-Tasman. East Asia is catching up, especially Japan, China and the 'smaller Chinese countries'. The lag in top science (Nobel Prizes, citations) is astonishing and not attributable to low top cognitive levels in East Asia. Except for East Asia in top science the regional distributions resemble the ones known from cognitive ability studies. Correlations will provide more clarity (see Table 4.6). Cognitive ability measures were used in their corrected (society) versions.

All cognitive achievement indicators, of past or current achievement, of more average or top achievement, are positively correlated to the current national cognitive ability measures. If we compare older and more current measures on technology adoption from Comin et al. (2010), the newer ones correlate more strongly, from around $r = .25-.50$ in 1000 BCE to around $r = .70-.80$ in 2000 CE. Rather astonishingly, the correlations for 1500 and 2000 are very similar. Countries with a high technological development level in 1500 have today the smartest people and students. The eminent science and intellectuals indicators (scientists, philosophers, Nobel Prizes, citations) correlate only modestly with cognitive ability measures (around $r = .35$ to .45). These values are based on very few individuals. And too many countries have a bottom value representing no eminence at all. There is no differentiation at

---

[34] Quote translated by the author (GWO); see also Piaget & Garcia (1989/1983).

Table 4.6 Correlations between cognitive ability estimates and indicators of cognitive achievement in past and present

| Cognitive ability estimates (in parentheses number of countries) | Technology –1000 (Comin) | Technology 0 (Comin) | Technology +1500 (Comin) | Technology +2000 (Comin) | Eminent Scientists –800 to +1950 (Murray) | Enlightenment Index 18th cent. (Mokyr) |
|---|---|---|---|---|---|---|
| CA corrected (max 197) | .48 | .36 | .82 | .77 | .37 | .34 |
| SAS mean corr (max 98) | .28 | .38 | .78 | .71 | .36 | .32 |
| SAS 95% corr (max 98) | .26 | .40 | .76 | .75 | .37 | .33 |
| SAS 05% corr (max 98) | .26 | .37 | .75 | .68 | .35 | .32 |

| | Patents 1991–2007 (WIPO) | High-tech exports 2007 (WEF) | Airline safety 2009–10 (AERO) | Innovation 2013 (WIPO) | Science Nobel Prizes 1901–2004 | High Citations 1987 (Cole) | Top universities 2010–2013 |
|---|---|---|---|---|---|---|---|
| CA corrected (max 197) | .49 | .52 | .53 | .83 | .37 | .44 | .74 |
| SAS mean corr (max 98) | .46 | .46 | .50 | .79 | .35 | .42 | .61 |
| SAS 95% corr (max 98) | .51 | .46 | .57 | .81 | .37 | .45 | .65 |
| SAS 05% corr (max 98) | .41 | .45 | .45 | .76 | .35 | .40 | .58 |

| | Cognitive achievement in history (until 1950) | Cognitive achievement in modernity | Cognitive achievement total average |
|---|---|---|---|
| CA corrected (max 197) | .53 | .72 | .69 |
| SAS mean corr (max 99) | .55 | .67 | .70 |
| SAS 95% corr (max 99) | .55 | .70 | .73 |
| SAS 05% corr (max 99) | .53 | .64 | .67 |

*Notes:* The three SAS measures mean, top ability level (95 per cent, intellectual classes) and low ability level (5 per cent) in the same country samples (in parentheses maximum number of countries); in history: Comin, Murray and Mokyr combined; in modernity: patents, high-tech exports, airline safety, innovation, science Nobel, high cites, top universities.

the bottom level reducing correlations. Top universities, a broader indicator, including a broad range of scientists, of various research fields, different areas of achievement from research and teaching to administration and management, show high correlations at around $r = .60–.75$. Cognitive ability measures are averagely correlated to patent rates, high-tech exports and airline safety (around $r = .50$).[35]

The highest correlations are found for the broad innovation indicator (WIPO, around $r = .80$). Analysing the tasks and the processes to solve them, innovations in science, technology, economy and society are so closely related to intelligence and knowledge that any progress seems to be impossible without a high national cognitive ability level.

Mostly, the cognitive ability total average ('CA corrected') is stronger correlated with top achievement than the other three cognitive measures. However, that is only an effect of the broader country sample in this variable. If we use only countries who have data in all variables ($N = 98$) and if we look at the mean variables in history, modernity and the total average, the maximum difference in correlations is |.013|. The correlations are identical for the total cognitive ability average and the student assessment average.

The correlations of the cognitive ability measures country mean, 95 per cent level (top ability level, intellectual classes) and 5 per cent level (bottom ability level) are not identical. The intellectual classes' levels always correlate more highly with top achievement than the bottom ability levels. On average, the intellectual classes' levels also correlate higher than the country mean; for the tech-science-achievement total variable: intellectual classes' level $r_{95\%} = .73$, mean level $r_{mean} = .70$, low ability level $r_{05\%} = .67$ ($N = 99$ same country sample). Two reasons may account for this pattern: the international differences in the 95 per cent level are more reliable than in the mean or in the 5 per cent level. It is reasonable to assume that nearly all top ability youth attends school; the SAS samples are entirely based on students. Thus there will be nearly no sampling errors. By contrast, the mean is based on the entire cohort and ability spectrum at school. Countries differ in enrolment rates (we tried to correct this). Also, at the lower achievement level more students will differ in test-taking behaviour. Therefore, it is convincing to assume that international ability differences at lower levels are less reliable.

The second more important reason is that top ability groups are responsible for technological, scientific and intellectual progress and its maintenance (e.g. Rindermann, 2012). Such an interpretation would be backed if there were also stronger low ability group correlations for societal attributes, which could be

---

[35] Indicators of high-tech mastery are replaceable, e.g. taking nuclear energy (number of plants relative to population size in countries with at least 5 million people), the correlations with cognitive ability (in the order of Table 4.6) are $r = .53, .51, .53, .50$ ($N = 107$ or $61$).

reasonably assumed that low ability groups are more responsible for them. These are phenomena like serious violations of ethic norms and laws, irrational and self-damaging behaviour or lifestyle indicators of average or plainer people. Felony or unprotected sex with many partners, increasing the probability of catching sexually transmitted diseases (STD) such as HIV, would be such examples. And they would be supported by higher correlations to possible causal factors of lower ability. The empirical evidence is supportive; for HIV, head lice, life speed, teacher salary, language identity (family and school), height, the two evolutionary indicators skin lightness and brain size and for consanguinity the lower ability level is more informative, but not for murder.[36]

One objection is that the relationship between national cognitive ability levels and cognitive achievement is due to wealth. Theoretically, this is less convincing because achievement in technology and science obviously depends on the ability to think and to acquire and process knowledge. But rich countries have the opportunity to attract highly competent people from all over the world. However, it is not only their wealth (which is also built upon cognitive ability) that attracts people but also their freedom and rule of law (e.g. in the past, the United States for Jews that were oppressed and persecuted in other countries). The correlation between top ability group and average cognitive

---

[36] Murder: Around 2010 (2008 to 2011), rate per 100,000 population, from Interpol, for 178 countries, source: UNODC (United Nations Office on Drugs and Crime), retrieved from www.unodc.orgdocumentsdata-and-analysisstatisticscrimeHomicide_statistics2012.xls. Correlations with cognitive ability measures: $r_{95\%} = -.51$, $r_{mean} = -.48$, $r_{05\%} = -.45$, $N = 94$. That is to say, the negative correlation between murder and cognitive ability is the highest for the ability level of intellectual classes, the cognitive elite ($r_{95\%} = -.51$). One obvious interpretation is that the impact of intellectual classes via institutions (law, police, criminal investigation, judiciary, administration) is crucial for reducing the severest crime, homicide. In-depth analyses have to check this interpretation.

HIV: HIV-infection rate 2003 for adults from UNAIDS/WHO (2003), $N = 147$. Correlations: $r_{95\%} = -.31$, $r_{mean} = -.34$, $r_{05\%} = -.32$, $N = 85$.

Lice: Prevalence of head lice from 2000 to 2008 from Falagas et al. (2008), $N = 27$. Correlations: $r_{95\%} = -.04$, $r_{mean} = -.07$, $r_{05\%} = -.15$, $N = 22$.

Life speed from Levine (1997) for 1992–1995, service speed at post office (how much time is needed to sell a stamp), walking speed and accuracy of clocks, for 31 countries. Correlations with cognitive ability measures: $r_{95\%} = .69$, $r_{mean} = .71$, $r_{05\%} = .71$, $N = 30$.

Teacher salary: see Section 10.5.2, $r_{95\%} = .32$, $r_{mean} = .36$, $r_{05\%} = .38$, $N = 40$.

Language identity (family and school use the same language): $r_{95\%} = .26$, $r_{mean} = .30$, $r_{05\%} = .32$, $N = 92$.

Human height: $r_{95\%} = .41$, $r_{mean} = .46$, $r_{05\%} = .47$, $N = 97$; data from NCD (2016).

Skin lightness: see Table 10.7, ability measures, $r_{95\%} = .694$, $r_{mean} = .738$, $r_{05\%} = .743$, $N = 96$.

Brain size (cranial capacity): see Table 10.8, ability measures, $r_{95\%} = .461$, $r_{mean} = .510$, $r_{05\%} = .517$, $N = 93$.

Consanguinity: see Table 10.9, $r_{95\%} = -.50$, $r_{mean} = -.53$, $r_{05\%} = -.56$, $N = 59$.

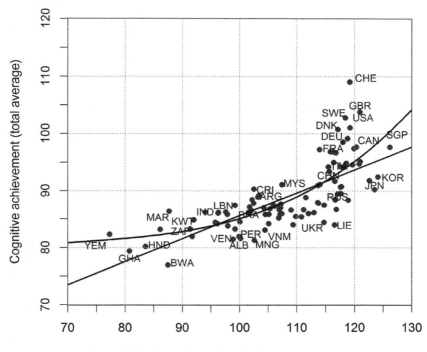

Figure 4.4 Top cognitive ability level and cognitive achievement across millennia for 99 countries, linear: $r = .73$, cubic: $r = .76$, countries indicated by three-letter country code (ISO 3166-1 alpha-3)

achievement is $r = .75$ ($N = 99$); partialled out, wealth using the three GDP/ GNI measures sees the correlations sink but they remain: $r_{p|GDP10Madd} = .26$, $r_{p|GDP10Penn} = .65$, $r_{p|GNI10HDR} = .61$. Because the Maddison indicator is most strongly correlated with cognitive ability (for the 95% level: $r_{GDP10Madd} = .77$, $r_{GDP10Penn} = .48$, $r_{GNI10HDR} = .55$) the downward correction is the largest. However, the positive correlations remain.

Summarising, international cognitive ability estimates are backed by high and stable correlations with quantitative cognitive achievement indictors. The international differences are validly measured.

Finally, are there outliers and is the relationship linear (as assumed by conventional correlational analyses)? A scatterplot provides information to assess this (see Figure 4.4). Switzerland (country code 'CHE') is a positive outlier – it has more top achievement than predicted by its intellectual classes' ability level. This is also true for other small countries such as Singapore, Sweden, Denmark and the Netherlands. Larger countries are maybe disadvantaged in exports (more inland trade) or in Nobel Prizes ('Oh no, not the US again'). But there are indicators, like technology adoption (Comin) or airline safety and innovations, where no bias is conceivable. And larger countries such as the United Kingdom, the United States and Germany are also positive outliers.

There seems to be a systematic *curvilinear* relationship (Figure 4.4) between cognitive ability and outcomes as assumed by cognitive ability theory: the higher the ability, the larger are the payoffs. A cubic regression leads to a higher correlation.[37] At least in cross-national comparisons and competition there are no diminishing returns for intelligence.

### 4.4.3    A Closer Look into Regions: A First Exercise in Cognitive Hermeneutics of Everyday Life

In this chapter, we deal with qualitative data itself. For many researchers, qualitative data have a bad reputation. In a field such as national cognitive differences, which is seen by some as controversial, a qualitative approach may be received with even more scepticism. Numbers are judged as being more able to represent aspects of reality. This is especially true for a science such as economics – numbers, statistics and quantitative models count, less so verbal statements as in literature or difficult to measure values and descriptions of behaviour itself. Deirdre McCloskey (2010, p. 291), a professor of Economics, History, English and Communication, has described this attitude: 'Many economists' – I add: also many psychologists – 'think that "empirical" is a fancy word for "numbers".' However, and of course, experience is more than numbers and all numbers themselves are based on original qualitative experience being later more or less objectively, reliably and validly transferred to numbers. 'The "mathematics" is merely a metaphorical language that economists understand.' (McCloskey, 2010, p. 411) Numbers are not the reality; they reflect it. What in reality happens is important, and this should be tried to describe.

There are important scientific books in the field of economics and in related studies of political and sociological science that extensively use qualitative

---

[37] Correlations are $r_{Linear} = .7454$ and $r_{Cubic} = .7796$. Numerically, this is only an increase of $r = .0342$. The increases in explained variance look somewhat larger, from 55.56 per cent to 60.78 per cent, a plus of 5.22 per cent. The relationship between two variables disproportionately increases with the size of correlations. This could be calculated by a Fisher $z$-transformation; here the linear correlation corresponds to a $z = 0.9625$ and the cubic correlation to a $z = 1.0443$, a difference of 0.0818.

data – inclusive descriptions of own experiences: Deirdre McCloskey (2006, 2010, 2016) uses them in her analyses of bourgeois values and their crucial impact on growth, wealth and development of modernity; similarly, David Landes (1972/1969, 1983, 1998, 2006), in his studies on poverty and wealth of nations and their historical development; Lawrence Harrison (2006, 2013), in his own books or ones edited together with Peter Berger (2006), Samuel Huntington (2000) or Jerome Kagan (2006), in which culture and its consequences for society, politics and economy were investigated; finally, the psychologist Robert Levine (1997) describing his experiences during a one-year trip around the world and the results of his measurements about how people deal with time. Even a bank, Credit Suisse (2013b, p. 18), which is inevitably focused on numbers, considers 'everyday experience' to scrutinise quantitative results.

All these studies enabled us to understand historical, cultural, political and institutional differences and how they influence economic growth and national wellbeing. However, our aim is not to replace the quantitative approach with a qualitative one. The aim is much more modest: qualitative descriptions should help us to understand the meaning of numbers and the effects of what they should represent: cognitive ability levels, differences of them between nations and across time and their effects. What does it mean to live in a country with an ability level of IQ 80 or 100? What does it mean to fly with an airline of one or the other country? What does it mean to speak with a typical person of the past centuries or of today? And looking at it the other way round: can we infer from the performance of institutions, politics and companies (sediments) to the average ability level of a society?

For this purpose, we will use information coming from the media and journalists, from other researchers or from our own experience. Information will contain descriptions of behaviour and descriptions of results of behaviour in certain environments, which are themselves not independent from the average attributes of the people of a society. Actions and products themselves can be observed and assessed without any detour on numbers. As mentioned, criteria for cognitive ability in those are correctness (approximating truth), complexity (difficulty, invention and innovation), coherence, epistemic rationality (using logic, empirical evidence and arguments), instrumental rationality (functionality) and aesthetic quality. Rationality and results of modern science need to be applied to assess products according to these criteria.

This can be assessed for individuals as for societies and cultures and for former times. Similar to the test approach, the use of single items (here behaviours, products and incidents) is not enough. And as observed for individuals, there is huge variety and variance within societies. But due to space constraints (remember, Robert Gordon's paper in *Intelligence* on

'Everyday Life as an Intelligence Test' was the longest ever published) it is impossible to reach sample sizes equivalent to those of tests and national surveys. However, many different authors have described informative aspects of cultures and societies and their qualitative data can be condensed into narrative reviews. Certainly, everyday life descriptions are also error-prone. What is a meaningful and typical everyday life occurrence? Not something that happens nearly everywhere, but a distinctive occurrence that is reasonably representative. Descriptions will contain particulars and details, stories and oddities. However, do stories really belong in a scientific book? Do oddities matter as much? Are interpretations not based on experiences too superficial and speculative?

Of course, there are no pure cognitive ability indicators – they are blended with the personality attributes as conscientiousness and the whole array of the burgher world (see Section 4.4.1 and Chapter 6; cf. McCloskey, 2006). However, the same is true for single items of cognitive ability tests: to be good at psychometric IQ tests or in PISA and TIMSS diligence and conscientiousness are helpful and are indirectly included in the measurement. Even though qualitative descriptions in general or the evidence presented here in particular have their weak points, qualitative data are necessary to demonstrate the significance of cognitive ability. Test values that do not correspond to real-life experience are wrong and meaningless. This applies to individual as well as national cognitive ability test results. We understand this as a first attempt, as an exercise testing the possibilities and limitations of a qualitative approach to cognitive abilities at the national level.

One problem is also a political one: the description of occurrences indicating low ability may be perceived as being impolite, disparaging and insensitive. However, the aim of an epistemic endeavour such as science is not to distribute compliments but true and informative statements. And what is problematic, the *occurrences themselves*, *their de*scription, *their possible wrong description* or the *wording*? What is more critical, the behaviour and incidents, that they are described, that they are incorrectly or incompletely described or the way in which they are described? Frequently, the fact itself is shocking, but the transmitter is blamed for it, relieving in this way for the recipient the tension between a desired and a real world. There is also a reflex of the old magical thinking that words make reality – speak of the devil and he doth appear (Malinowski, 1954/1948, p. 74/V.1): words would have a real effect; the use of words gives force to the named things. Therefore, persons should avoid bad words and use of euphemisms, e.g. not speaking about AIDS.

Finally, any individual attribute of a researcher is unimportant. Statements are only relevant in their contribution to a truth-finding process. Scientists are not criticisable for their opinion, only for their possible deviation from truth and the process of epistemic rationality.

*Africa (Sub-Sahara)*   There are numerous ethnological reports on *magical thinking* in Africa. According to Piaget, magical thinking is typical for the preoperational cognitive stage in early childhood until around age seven. Converted to IQ, this would indicate an IQ below 70 as measured by psychometric or student assessment tests. Here are some historical examples describing magical thinking: according to Evans-Pritchard (1976/1937, p. 181), the Azande, an ethnic group of Central Africa, used crocodile teeth for supporting the growth of banana plants because both are curved and new crocodile teeth grow if the old fall out. This is a typical expression of magical thinking, here in the form of the theory of signatures (similarities, 'similia similibus curentur').

Lévy-Bruhl (1923/1922) has described many behaviours based on magical thinking. For example, the Waschamba in Tanzania killed children born with their feet first – they are seen as a bad omen. A similar scheme – belief in bad omens – worked here: in the case of upper incisors coming first, the Makololo in Zimbabwe killed their children.[38] In a widespread belief there is no natural death; all deaths are supposed to be caused by witchcraft. Therefore, such persons, who were more or less indiscriminately accused of witchcraft, were killed. Lawsuits were solved by using ordeals, e.g. by taking poison; a person who survived was deemed innocent.

This is *not unique* for Africa, but indicative for the general premodern mentality in all cultures. Oesterdiekhoff (2007–2014) has described the same cognitive pattern for the European past, for instance belief in witchcraft, ordeals and trials against animals. However, it is indicative that magical thinking endured longer in Africa. Metallurgy was not invented in Africa, but imported from outside, the same is true for spinning, the wheel and domesticated animals (Baker, 1974, pp. 351, 352, 373, 376ff.).[39] Introduced domesticated animals were not profitably used:

The Dinka castrated one-third of their bulls. These castrated animals were useless, since, [un]like other cattle, they were not slaughtered for eating nor used for riding or transport. 'Ask the Dinka what good they get from their possessions of oxen,' wrote Schweinfurth, 'and they have ever the answer ready that it is quite enough if they get fat and look nice.' (Baker, 1974, p. 360)[40]

---

[38] Lévy-Bruhl took here a report from David Livingstone (1813–1873), the famous British explorer and medical missionary.

[39] Jared Diamond (2002, 1997, his chapter 9) argued that wild animals from Africa cannot be tamed. However, there is no reason why African animals are not domesticable, but Asian and European ones. Horses, aurochs and wolves were also quite dangerous. Foxes were tamed within a few years by Russian scientists (Trut, 1999). Zebra, antelope, gazelle, smaller cats and wild dogs are probably similarly domesticable as their relatives from outside Africa (Hart, 2007, p. 174ff.). The only sub-Saharan African animal that was domesticated is the Guinea fowl, which was domesticated twice but *outside* of sub-Saharan Africa, in Egypt and Europe.

[40] Dinka: people in South Sudan; Georg August Schweinfurth: 1836–1925, Baltic-German botanist, ethnologist and explorer.

The Neolithic revolution of agriculture happened around 7,000 years later in Africa than in the Middle East, probably spreading from the north (Neumann, 2003). The Great Zimbabwe monument (eleventh to fourteenth century) consists of pure walls; compared to buildings constructed earlier or at the same time in other cultures it is less sophisticated (Egyptian pyramids, Greek temples, Roman aqueducts, Mesoamerican pyramids, Islamic mosques, Gothic churches, Khmer Angkor Wat etc.). The same is true for rock and cave paintings such as in Brandberg (Namibia), Laas Geel (Somalia) or the Cederberg Mountains (South Africa), compared to the ones in Chauvet and Lascaux (France) or for stone-age artefacts (Renfrew, 2008).

*But is it not all old stuff?* The mentioned test results are from the present, so *present-day evidence* is necessary!

Different books and reports from ethnologists and journalists document the present-day prevalence of preoperational thinking in the form of associative thinking and thinking in similarities, of belief in magic causal relationships, of projections and animism, of sacrifices to gods to make them well-intentioned and ordeals: for example, the Swiss ethnologist David Signer (2004) described in a 450-page book the life and healings of an African sorcerer in the Ivory Coast. The practice of witchcraft is widespread – including academic circles. People believe in magic money duplicators. Because of similarity ('many offspring') Bakossi people in Cameroon use frog eggs as a remedy against infertility among humans (Gonwouo & Rödel, 2008). In Togo, the national football team was advised by a sorcerer in 2006.[41] African prostitutes in Europe are afraid of leaving prostitution because Marabus (sorcerers) in Africa have hair and nails belonging to them and can bewitch them if they do not follow their procurers.[42]

Another example is the frequent belief that AIDS is caused by supernatural powers (Caldwell, 2002). Such AIDS theories reach up to governments: According to Nattrass (2012, p. 89f.), in South Africa, the former President Thabo Mbeki and the former Health Minister Manto Tshabalala-Msimang questioned anti-retroviral therapy with consequences for people and unborn babies infected by HIV; around 400,000 more people died and were infected with HIV due to these anti-scientific politics. Contrary to a predominant conviction of modern people, magic thinking is *not* a kind of folkloristic phenomenon, but a thinking pattern with tormenting and lethal consequences. Documented by Fadera (2010), the president of Gambia from 1996 to 2017, Yahya Jammeh, claimed that he was a healer and could cure AIDS. Following a BBC report, South African's president, Jacob Zuma, mentioned in 2006 that taking a shower after sexual intercourse with an HIV-infected woman 'would minimise the risk of contracting the disease [HIV]'.[43] Dr Wangari Maathai, a Kenyan political activist, deputy minister and 2004 Nobel Peace Prize winner, is reported to have claimed in 2004, that HIV/AIDS was 'deliberately created by Western scientists to decimate the African population'.[44] After criticism she disputed these allegations (this is evidence for the beneficial effects of a well-informed and epistemically rational public including scientists). According to the *Wall Street Journal*, the Ghanaian politician Anita Sosoo explained the country's currency crisis in 2014 by the influence of dwarfs: 'These dwarfs, the black magic is what has made the cedi lose value.'[45]

Another example is described by a Nigerian woman, by Joana Adesuwa Reiterer (2009), who was suspected to be a witch, being a so-called '*Ogbanje*' ('water goddess'). There is a general belief that some persons, especially girls, are powerful embodiments of evil ghosts. Their mission is to make their parents suffer. Persons are suspected of witchcraft if somebody suffers from diseases or misfortune. Many children and adults in Western Africa are accused in this way. They have to be 'cleaned' and, if this procedure is not 'successful', they need to leave their family and home region. As evil forces, they are threatened by their relatives and some are killed. It is also believed that female circumcision protects against being obsessed by an evil spirit. The belief in these 'Ogbanjes' is part of the 'Juju-cult', which, again, is part of the traditional 'Voodoo' cult in Africa and in the Caribbean, especially in Haiti.[46]

Similar patterns of magic thinking are not only found in the African American cult Voodoo (in Haiti, Dominican Republic), but also in Macumba and Candomblé (in Brazil), Santería (Cuba) and Kumina (Jamaica).

All the mentioned indicators not only represent individual cognitive competence but also a collective and institutionalised cognitive competence influencing individual cognitive development via education and via modelling in families, school, the public and culture.

However, as mentioned for the cases of Wangari Maathai and Anita De Sosoo, both were publicly criticised for irrational statements. Cognitive modernisation is working. The social environment and its cognitive and rational level influence individual development. Initially, such critics will reduce the

---

[43] BBC, 5 April 2006, http://news.bbc.co.uk/2/hi/africa/4879822.stm.

[44] Radio Liberty, 10 December 2004, www.rferl.org/content/article/1056339.html.

[45] Wall Street Journal, 6 March 2014, http://online.wsj.com/news/articles/SB1000142405270230 4585004579417822045597450. Anita Desooso was criticised for her statement in Ghanaian media, e.g. http://graphic.com.gh/news/odd-news/17511-cartoon-anita-desooso-and-the-little-dwarfs.html – an indicator for intellectual progress!

[46] Reports more specifically on 'witch children' and 'witch women': Oppenheimer (2010), Houreld (2009) and on the Internet (search for 'Return to Africa's witch children' or 'Nigeria's child witch scandal: Children killed as witches' on YouTube; be careful, terrifying content).

public promulgation of irrationality. Usually, this will not lead to a really well-conceived and systematised thinking pattern, but to a rougher rule of thumb, which is, nevertheless, still more rational:

But the layman's ground for accepting the models propounded by the scientist is often no different from the young African villager's ground for accepting the models propounded by one of his elders. In both cases the propounders are deferred to as the accredited agents of tradition. (Horton, 1967, p. 186)

Expressions are not only based on individual understanding but also on adoption of 'what is said' due to social factors enlarging at the macrosocial level the correlation between cognitive ability and rationality, the 'hive mind' (Jones, 2016). But in the long run, environmental rationality influences, via shaping a climate of thinking, individual and cultural development itself.

The description has some limitations: we have not dealt with within-Africa differences such as between the city and the countryside, the more educated and less educated, more modern and premodern peoples (according to language, religion or evolutionary history), e.g. the Bantu, Nilotic, West African and Ethiopian versus Khoisan and Pygmies. As for all cultures, there is a huge variety within. Finally, because the general result indicates low cognitive ability some critics will be quick to allege racism. However, a political, ethical or attitudinal argument is no argument in an epistemic question. (See Sections 9.1, 3.3.2, 4.3 and 4.4.1). Using such 'arguments' means having none.

*Occident (the West)*    We unite here the so far distinguished regions of Western Europe, Scandinavia, Central Europe, Eastern Europe, Southern Europe and the regions in the world which were former British colonies and are settled by them: North America, Australia and New Zealand. Additionally, Israel is included. As is true for all categorisations there is heterogeneity within the group; some members are more prototypical and the borders are somewhat fluid.

There are many hints for a general low cognitive ability level in the past. In historical times, only a few people went to school, could read, write and calculate. Magical thinking was widespread, as shown by the use of ordeals, by the belief in witchcraft and astrology, by burning of witches and trials against animals (Oesterdiekhoff, 2007–2014).

However, there are also many clues for a rising trend:

- During the twentieth century the average test results rose by around 3 IQ points per decade (*FLynn effect*).
- Since the Middle Ages *education has spread* until reaching a near 100 per cent literacy level today.

- According to Clark (2007, p. 175ff.), historical documents such as obituary columns show an *increasing precision of age statements* from Roman times until the nineteenth century.
- Late medieval Scholastic theologians, especially Thomas Aquinas (1225–1274), show a *transition from authority-based thinking towards* thinking based on arguments and rationality, pioneering Renaissance, Enlightenment and cognitive modernity.

*Cognitive modernisation* is a long-term historical process. Additionally, there are many clues for a comparatively high cognitive development level in the past, such as the very early cave paintings in Chauvet (around 32,000 BCE), Lascaux (around 16,000 BCE) and Altamira (around 14,000 BCE), the earliest human figurative prehistoric art (Venus of Hohle Fels, around 35,000 BCE), the oldest fantasy sculpture (Lion human of the Hohlenstein Stadel, around 35,000 BCE), the earliest realistic representation of a human face (Venus of Brassempouy, around 23,000 BCE), all indicating symbolic communication (Conard, 2003). The oldest solar observatory (up to now) was found in Goseck (from around 5,000 BCE), the oldest portrayal of the sky and astronomical instrument comes from nearby (Nebra sky disk, around 2,000 BCE). Greek and Roman architectural, technological, scientific, philosophical, political and artistic achievements are well-known. In architecture and technology: temples, water pipes, streets and the dome. In science: the Pythagorean theorem, the calendar and the geocentric worldview. In philosophy: argumentation. In politics: democracy and law. In the arts: naturalistic sculpture, comedy (e.g. The Birds by Aristophanes) and epic (e.g. Iliad from Homer) (Hart, 2007; Murray, 2003). Cultural modernity began in Northern Italy around 1,300 CE.

Nevertheless, remnants of magic thinking are still being found today, such as the use of astrology, horoscopes, homeopathy and cartomancy. Remnants also remain in religion and political ideology. Usually, they are only practised as a kind of play, an add-on to a generally accepted scientific worldview. They are criticised, believers are not taken seriously and they are perceived as being odd or slightly mad.

The present state is not an entirely intelligent and rational one. The majority of people do not understand probability and make thinking errors (Dobelli, 2013). People follow heuristics that simplify complex problems too much. Even scientists have serious problems understanding statistics, especially significance testing (Gigerenzer, 2004). To a large extent, science is the product of tradition guided by *conformism* and *zeitgeist* schemes, susceptible to verbiage and authority (Fleck, 1979/1935; Gross & Levitt, 1994; Sokal, 2008). Political pressures on rationality are still strong. The two scientific journals, *Science* and *Nature*, recognised most by media and public, are not free of fraud (e.g. papers from the German physicist Jan Hendrik Schön, the

Dutch psychologist Diederik Stapel or the Korean stem cell researcher Hwang Woo-suk). Especially regarding intelligence research, those leading journals are inclined to a political bias, for example in the so called '*Lawrence Summers Affair*':

The past Chief Economist at the World Bank, then Harvard president and past Director of the White House National Economic Council Lawrence Summers discussed, in 2005, possible causes for the lower representation of women in science and engineering and came, after weighting the evidence, to the conclusion that a lower high end ability level, rather than discrimination and socialisation, was relevant (Summers, 2005). As a 'scientific answer' *Science* (Muller et al., 2005) published a letter signed by 73 prominent academics protesting against his statements. 'The list of seventy-three signers of the letter included prominent academic scientists and science administrators, it did not include any of the major figures who do research on individual differences in cognition.' (Hunt, 2010, pp. 399f.) Earl Hunt, an expert in intelligence research, also noted that the paper published by *Science* contained demonstrably false statements, e.g. claiming that cognitive ability test results cannot predict success in science careers or stating that if somebody says factor A contributes to outcome 1 this includes saying there are no further factors – simple errors in knowledge and thinking. *Science* accepted the letter, but did not publish a scientific study regarding this subject and additionally never published any paper on international intelligence differences and their impact on society. Scientific quality is replaced by ideology, by false consciousness.

However, suboptimal science is better than no science and critics are active and have contributed to strategies to improve the epistemic process (e.g. Albert, 1985/1968; Flynn, 2012b).

Core regions of human accomplishment within Europe were Northern Italy, the Northwest and Central Europe. In France, a hot spot is given for the Île-de-France (see Figure 4.5).

## Western Europe

Since the sixteenth century, the Netherlands, France and Great Britain have been the pioneers of modernity. There is a very long list of leading Dutch, French and British thinkers, philosophers and scientists, who shaped the worldview and modern world. To name a few: Erasmus, Descartes, Montesquieu, Pascal, Voltaire, Rousseau, Condorcet, Hobbes, Newton, Locke, Hume, Watt, Smith, Mill, Darwin, Galton, Russell, Comte, Pasteur, Fleming. The concepts of modern law, human rights, separation of powers, empiricism, liberty, reasonableness and of unassuming as well as powerful common sense were developed here. Industrialisation started here. The burgher culture, a civic middle-class culture, was first fully developed here. Leading universities educated powerful and smart elites. Prehistoric art and monuments document a long-term cognitive competence (Chauvet, Lascaux, Newgrange, Stonehenge). In France, *concours* and objective and blind central exams ensure purely merit-based selections in education.

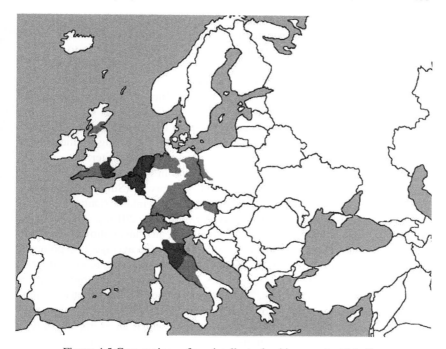

Figure 4.5 Core regions of top intellectual achievement within Europe
800 BCE to 1950 CE according to Murray (2003, p. 298; sketch; darker
means more contributions)

However, ideological violence was also invented here (English Civil War
and la Terreur in France), as were concentration camps (by the British in the
Second Boer War) and slavery was used but later its abolition started here
(William Wilberforce, French Revolution and Victor Schœlcher). Colonialism and wars have had terrible consequences for victims, and effects of
slavery are measurable in African regions until today (Nunn, 2014), but the
colonial age also brought along beneficial long-term consequences: the
longer a country was colonised by Britain or France, the higher is its GDP
today and the lower its child mortality rate, explained by the positive effects
of adopted institutions developed in the European mother country (Feyrer &
Sacerdote, 2009).

### Scandinavia
Finnish pupils constantly achieve the highest results in PISA in the
Western world. But Scandinavia did not lead in culture or science in the

past.[47] A millennium ago, the Vikings were a brutal, albeit definitely successful, warrior people with a penchant for looting and pillaging (Landes, 1998,
chapter 3). As Normans, they settled lands from Northern France to Southern
Italy. They founded Russia. They conquered England and parts of Syria. They
were the first Europeans to arrive in America. As these examples show,
competence is far from always connected to ethics. A modern example of
terror exemplifies this again: the most 'effective' (the term 'effective' is of
course without an ethical assessment!) one-man terror attack was perpetrated
by a Norwegian accompanied by an around 1,500 page-long political mani-
festo, compiled and written in a foreign language for the writer.[48]

Several studies have shown for the first time in history in Scandinavia an
end of the secular rise of intelligence, first for Norway (Sundet et al., 2004),
then for Denmark (Teasdale & Owen, 2008) and Finland (Dutton & Lynn,
2013, in student assessment studies Heller-Sahlgren, 2015b). The two later
studies even showed a decline. Additionally, Scandinavia shows very large
native-immigrant gaps in student assessment results (on average 7 IQ points; in
Finland more than 8 IQ points).[49] Finally, there are recurring reports of larger
unemployment, crime and violence rates, including riots by immigrants in
Sweden, Norway and Denmark.[50] The reasonableness of the countries' immigration policies is questioned by their own peoples.

In the last few decades, Scandinavia has represented an exemplary way of
organising a peaceful, homogenous and modern society with an equal distribution of wealth. Scandinavia is for many, for intellectuals as well as for
migrants, a kind of ideal world. Maybe it is a little bit of a colourless and
boring world, but being bored is a far better state than that endured by 99 per
cent of human history.

---

[47] Regarding science, it has to be mentioned that considering population size Scandinavian
countries lead in number of Nobel Prize winners (Sweden rank 2, Denmark rank 3, Norway
rank 6).

[48] As the 2011 example of Anders Behring Breivik shows, competences can be misused for
unethical aims. However, intelligence and knowledge are on average supportive determinants of
ethical development of individuals and societies (Piaget, 1948/1932; Kohlberg, 1987; Oesterdiekhoff, 2012a, 2012b; Pinker, 2011). E.g. according to Simonton (1984, p. 10) among
political leaders intelligence and morality are positively correlated ($r = .23$). E.g. better educated
persons and persons with a higher level of moral development (intelligence is for both
supportive) less frequently obeyed a torture order (25 per cent vs. 87 per cent or 13 per cent
vs. 75 per cent; Kohlberg, 1984).

[49] Native-immigrant gaps: results from PISA, TIMSS and PIRLS used and transformed to an IQ
scale, Scandinavia 7 IQ, Central Europe 7 IQ, Western Europe 5 IQ, Southern Europe 4 IQ,
Eastern Europe 5 IQ, North America 3 IQ, Australia and New Zealand 0 IQ (Table 10.2,
country results see Table A.2).

[50] Sweden, e.g. Stockholm in May 2013, Malmö in December 2008, in several cities in May
2016 and February 2017; Norway, e.g. violence and sexual crimes rates in Oslo; Denmark, e.g.
Jyllands-Posten cartoons and following violent protests and attempted murder (2005ff.). Similar
reports come from other countries such as France and Great Britain.

### Central Europe

Central Europe, here meaning the German-speaking countries,[51] perceived itself for more than ten centuries as the successor of the Roman Empire. However, until the fifteenth century technological, scientific, intellectual and cultural achievements were rather low.[52] The biggest Romanesque church in the world is the German Speyer Cathedral; however, the Northern Italian Romanesque churches are more sophisticated and beautiful (e.g. cathedral and Piazza dei Miracoli in Pisa). But around the sixteenth century a very rich intellectual and technological tradition started; here are some names and examples (Watson, 2010):

- Martin Luther (a university professor as founder of a religion, Protestantism).
- Johannes Gutenberg (invention of mechanical movable type printing).
- Composers and musicians (Bach, Handel, Mozart, Beethoven, Wagner, Kraftwerk, Rammstein).
- Philosophers (Leibniz, Kant, Schiller, Hegel, Marx, Nietzsche, Cassirer, Jaspers, Heidegger, Carnap, Popper, Wittgenstein, Adorno, Habermas).
- Scientists (Copernicus, Leibniz, brothers Humboldt, Liebig, Semmelweis, Mendel, Freud, Planck, Weber, Haber, Einstein, Elias, Heisenberg).
- Engineers and inventors (Siemens, Zeiss, Daimler, Benz, Diesel, Leitz, Bosch, Porsche, Braun).

Germany recovered from several devastations, most seriously in the Thirty Years' War and the Second World War.

However, Germany is also well-known for mental peculiarities usually judged as follies. Most terrible was the reign of National Socialism. However, and without any ethical connotation (see discussion above on the relation between competence or intelligence and ethics), it was a quite 'effective' regime of terror and military operations (Dupuy, 1977), which was only stopped by the unified endeavour of nearly all the rest of the world. Other lesser terrible or neutral follies such as Homeopathy (Hahnemann) and Anthroposophy (Steiner) have roots in magical thinking. Romanticism is anti-Enlightenment, the same is true for Nietzsche, Heidegger, Wagner, at least

---

[51] In a broader concept of Central Europe, Central-East European countries were included (Baltics, Poland, Bohemia/Czech Republic, Hungary, Slovenia).

[52] Stone-age exceptions are the oldest figurative art (Venus of Hohle Fels), oldest fantasy sculpture (Lion human of the Hohlenstein Stadel), the oldest solar observatory (Goseck) and the oldest portrayal of the sky and astronomical instrument nearby (Nebra sky disk). The German Roman Emperor Frederick II (1194–1250), the '*stupor mundi* ', a kind of scientist, author and political moderniser, is also an exception. However, he lived in Italy.

partly also for German idealism and Marx and Marxism.[53] Germany seems to fall every 50 years into irrationality expressed in different forms. In the nineteenth century, it was Romanticism and Marxism in intellectual circles. In the twentieth century, it was National Socialism. In all those movements, science as an endeavour pursuing objective truth was categorically denied. Mephistopheles, the devil in Goethe's Faust, said: 'Reason and Science you despise, ... And I'll have you, totally.' Today, many rate the 'Energiewende' (energy transition), the 'refugee' policies or the strict rejection of genetically modified crops as further examples of this tradition in irrationalism.

All these movements can be seen as the result of an anti-Enlightenment culture. Not from an ethical view, for in this realm there is a clear improvement across time, but from a purely cognitive perspective development has become even worse: while the Nazi movement was a fatal answer to existing problems (Treaty of Versailles, Great Depression, unemployment and unrest) and never won a majority in free elections, the present nuclear phase-out is a wrong answer to a non-existing incident (Fukushima nuclear 'catastrophe' with zero fatalities due to radiation exposure) shared in free elections by a majority.[54] Similarly irrational seems to be the 'refugee' policy. Applying conventional economic and political standards this policy is detrimental for Germany and Europe and the same amount of money spent to help refugees and other countries' poor people in those countries or in their neighbouring countries would have a much larger positive effect for the people in need. Outside Germany the most highly reputed economists and migration researchers, Paul Collier from Oxford and George Borjas from Harvard, heavily criticised

---

[53] Georg Lukács (1980/1954) described in detail these anti-enlightenment movements (except for Marxism, which has to be included). One general remark on references: a reference to an author's publication does not mean that all his remarks in the referred work nor in others, nor in talks, and in no sense all his/her actions are supported, e.g. in the case of Lukacs, the support for Stalin, his praise of communism, his opposition to criticism of communism regarding communist violation of human rights, his personal involvement in execution of opponents in Poroszlo. The reference relates only to the mentioned statement.

[54] From a United Nations report: 'No radiation-related deaths or acute diseases have been observed among the workers and general public exposed to radiation from the accident ... No discernible increased incidence of radiation-related health effects are expected among exposed members of the public or their descendants. The most important health effect is on mental and social wellbeing, related to the enormous impact of the earthquake, tsunami and nuclear accident, and the fear and stigma related to the perceived risk of exposure to ionising radiation.' (UNSCEAR, 2014, p. 10). However, because any increase in radiation leads to an increase in the probability of mutations some health effects, including deaths, are highly probable. But they are minor compared to the effects of the tsunami (around 18,000 fatalities) or of alternative energy production using fossil fuels and water power or to the effects of runaway costs resulting from the German energy transition. Similarly, there are no scientific results for any increased risks of genetically modified crops; however, they are banned in Germany (and Austria).

German refugee politics. The same is true for the Dutch migration researcher Ruud Koopmans who designated German refugee politics in foreign newspapers an 'absolute misperformance of Angela Merkel' not being able to 'assess the consequences of her decision'. At the same time, Koopmans stated that his research is ignored in Germany. Within Germany, the political scientist, professor of international relations and researcher in Islamic studies Bassam Tibi, himself from Syria, published his consternation at German immigration politics in a Swiss newspaper. Even the Dalai Lama has expressed his concerns about German refugee policies ('Germany can't become an Arabic country.').[55] Finally, these politics also infringe the law and even violate the constitution, a kind of governmental crime.[56] Reiterated, because it is important: this is not an assessment of ethical aspects in which, of course, Nazi politics were worse.

Similar irrationalities can also be exemplified in the lives of two scientists who are essential for this book: Max Weber and Werner Sombart. Weber suffered from psychological breakdowns and gave up his professorship. Sombart was refused a professorship in the 1890s in Baden because he was perceived to be too radically left-wing. In 1934 he signed a letter in favour of Hitler. There seems to be a deficit in *modest reasonableness*, in life as well as in thinking. This can be found in exemplary scientists as well as in politics and in intellectual currents.

This cannot be explained by a cognitive competence theory. In particular, Nazism and terror are negative exceptions for a historical cognitive development theory; the Neolithic astronomy achievements are positive ones; both are not possible to explain by the standard paradigm.[57] A qualitative approach helps to detect this.

---

[55] Sources:     www.welt.de/wirtschaft/article151603912/Ist-Merkel-schuld-an-Fluechtlingskrise-Wer-sonst.html,    www.faz.net/aktuell/wirtschaft/wirtschaftspolitik/migrationsforscher-george-borjas-eine-million-fluechtlinge-sind-gewiss-zu-viel-14031850.html?printPagedArticle=true#pageIndex_2; on migration effects see chapters 12 and 13, www.weltwoche.ch/ausgaben/2016–4/artikel/europa-nach-merkel-die-weltwoche-ausgabe-42016.html, quotes from Koopmans translated by the author (HR) from: www.huffingtonpost.de/2016/05/03/merkel-fluchtlingspolitik_n_9825772.html, www.nzz.ch/feuilleton/gespraech-mit-dem-soziologen-ruud-koopmans-assimilation-funktioniert-ld.13975,     www.dailysabah.com/syrian-crisis/2016/05/31/germany-cant-become-an-arabic-country-dalai-lama-says.

[56] Power plants were forced to shut down because of the tsunami in Japan, which is against the law     (www.faz.net/aktuell/wirtschaft/energiepolitik/rwe-schadensersatzforderung-was-das-schon-wieder-kostet-13994347.html); 'refugees' coming from secure neighbouring countries were received, violating the German constitution § 16a (www.gesetze-im-internet.de/englisch_gg/englisch_gg.html#p0085).

[57] An in-depth discussion on the relationship between cognitive development of society and National Socialism can be found in a book of Georg Oesterdiekhoff (2012c, chapter 4.5). Cognitive theory cannot explain Nazi irrationalities, but the quick, enduring and successful reforms after 1945.

## Eastern Europe

The Indo-European (or Indo-Aryan) peoples and languages have their origin in East-South Europe at the border with Asia, in the north of the Caucasus and around the Black Sea. Similarly, the Greeks most probably have their origin in East-South-Europe. Regarding the last few centuries, most prominent are high achievements in music, the arts and chess. Famous East European persons are Dostoyevsky, Tchaikovsky, Tolstoy, Pasternak, Chagall, Rand/Rosenbaum, Solzhenitsyn and Kasparov; among them, similarly for Germany, are many Jews (Slezkine, 2004; Solzhenitsyn, 2009/2001). The same is true for eminence in cognitive psychology (Vygotsky, Luria), mathematics (Kolmogorov, Perelman) and economics (Kondratjew, Leontief). Russia developed the first spacecraft, Sputnik, and is still leading (with the United States) in space travel.

In many countries (e.g. Bulgaria) there is a very strong cognitive elite, as observable for instance in results of Mathematical Olympiads. This can be confirmed by the experience of the author: I was hiking in 1995 in the Bulgarian Rhodope Mountains and first passed a Roma camp with children in terrible conditions. Later, I met, in the same valley, a Bulgarian burgher-intellectual family with all their members speaking different foreign languages perfectly, the adults being well informed about politics and philosophy, the children playing musical instruments. However, the same episode hints at large heterogeneity. As if Star Trek had beamed down people from different epochs in one valley.

Nevertheless, real breakthroughs in arts, science or philosophy were very rare. Eastern Europe was behind Western, Southern and Central Europe in philosophy, science, music and technology. Compared to current cognitive ability levels in other parts of Europe there is intellectual underachievement in Eastern Europe. Quantitative data show a more favourable picture than qualitative. More is expected for the future![58]

## Southern Europe

Modern civilisation was born in Greece, with the development of science (mathematics, physics, astronomy, anatomy), mastery of architecture and realistic sculpture (dome, aqueduct, canal, streets, naturalistic free-standing

---

[58] Seymour Itzkoff expects for Eastern Europe around 2050, compared to other regions of the world, an economic and cultural heyday (Itzkoff, 2003, p. 101): 'About the year 2050, Russia and Eastern Europe will be one of the few places in the world to be truly able to generate a peaceful political/economy having high standards of life for their people through internal growth, and economic independence. They will be undergirded by the current beneficent demography, the commitment to democratic and free market policies, the enormous fund of natural resources, grains, oil, natural gas, titanium, gold. The climate, while harsh, is varied, and around the Black Sea not too dissimilar from Silicon Valley. This historical setting will provide the context for high intellectual achievement.'

sculptures), the beginnings of philosophy (idealism, realism, using arguments and critique), flourishing literature (*epos*, comedy) and the onset of burgher culture and democracy. The Greeks paved the way for the later Roman empire. Important names are Homer, Democritus, Parmenides, Socrates, Plato, Aristotle, Diogenes, Archimedes, Pythagoras, Seneca, Ovid and Virgil among many others. They also had very successful military leaders such as Alexander and Caesar (without ethical judgement).

The Greek intellectual achievement has to be assessed as being exceptional considering the small population of around two to four million people, the frequent wars and the pioneering role: they could not benefit from others. They are the prodigy of history. However, cognitive analyses of the work of ancient scientists and authors (e.g. of Plato, Cicero and Plutarch) and especially cognitive analyses of the behaviour of average people and the leading classes show a somewhat different picture. Magical thinking seems to have prevailed, to give only some examples for ancient Greece and Rome (Oesterdiekhoff, 2012c; Piaget & Garcia, 1989/1983): belief in fate, use of ordeals, sun and moon as animate and conscious beings, seeing personal attributes in nature, offerings and sacrifices, the idea of mystical participation, fortune-telling, pleasure by observing other people suffering in arena games, sadistic practices, the absence of any serious ethical critiques by ancient philosophers. People liked to visit places to observe where others were tortured. Many of the Roman emperors are examples of human beasts, not only the usually known tyrants and lunatics ('furor principum', Caligula, Nero, Commodus, Elagabalus), but also Alexander, Augustus, Caesar and others.[59] This all reflects cognitive egocentrism. At least the Romans were not ahead of the Greeks; there was no progress.

The Roman-Italians were the only people who have twice been leading in history: during the Roman empire and in the Renaissance. The European and worldwide cognitive, scientific, artistic, technological, social and cultural modernity began in Northern Italy. Only to mention some of the most important persons:

- Petrarca (or Petrarch; poetry and detection of nature),
- Brunelleschi (architecture, dome, and inventions such as linear perspective),
- Leonardo (anatomy and other scientific studies, engineering and inventions, painting, organisation, aphorisms),

---

[59] Alexander the Great, for instance, killed the male population of Gaza and sold the women and children into slavery; he crucified the unsuccessful physician of one of his friends; with his own hands he killed an officer who had previously saved his life (Kleitos). Caesar used decimation (killing of every tenth Roman soldier) as punishment; he committed genocide against Germanic tribes during a cease-fire with them. Augustus ordered the killing of leading Romans, among them Cicero and senators; he was one of the main supporters of gladiatorial games.

- Michelangelo (sculptures, painting, architecture),
- Machiavelli (political theory),
- Galilei (principles of scientific research, mathematics, physics, and astronomy).

Modern thinking based on arguments was developed with the aid of Italian scholars (Thomas Aquinas) and was first fully developed as a rational lifestyle by Leon Battista Alberti. Alberti was, like Leonardo, an *uomo universale*, a polymath. He was an author on the arts, architecture, mathematics and satire, an architect and cryptographer. In his book *Della famiglia* he described a rational way of thinking, of education, of spending one's money and conducting one's life. He is the first descriptor of a rational-efficient burgher lifestyle, pioneering the coming middle classes. Later on, further eminent scientists and artists appeared (e.g. Volta, Verdi, Pasolini), but the other nations made up ground.

There is a substantial gap in achievements between Northern and Southern Italy, which is also reflected in today's cognitive ability differences. Qualitative and quantitative data match. The regional results of Northern Italy in PISA belong to the highest PISA results worldwide. For instance, in PISA 2012 Lombardi, Trento, Emilia, Friuli, Liguria, Piemonte, Veneto and Tuscany achieved a whopping average in mathematics of 522 SASQ (range 498–552, directly transformed representing 103 SAS-IQ points), whereas Campania, Sardegna, Puglia, Basilicata, Calabria and Sicilia achieved on average 471 SASQ (range 453–491 SASQ, 96 SAS-IQ; OECD, 2013c, p. 511).[60] There is no single northern region which falls in the range of the southern regions and no southern region which falls in the range of the northern ones.

In Southern Italy, the situation in public and private institutions is not always top-notch: e.g. Pompeii is prone to crumble due to lack of financial resources and 'mismanagement'.[61] On a new motorway (Autostrada A3, between Salerno and Cosenza, August 2013), there is a speed limit of 60 km/h (37 mph) for long distances, which does not make any sense and all motorists drive with around 120 km/h (75 mph) – except for places with fixed radar traps. Based on my own experience, in a pension a rickety wardrobe was not fixed to the wall with the consequence that when opening the door, a glass jug filled with water fell down (highly dangerous for small children). One week and also one year later the wardrobe was still not fixed. Construction workers claimed that they were repairing a collapsed street in the mountains

---

[60] Central Italy regions left out.
[61] Pompeii, March 2014, www.ansa.it/web/notizie/rubriche/english/2014/03/03/Pompeii-risks-falling-apart-warns-UNESCO_10174834.html.

manually. Only around two hours' work per day was observable; the rest was filled with the journey to and from the place, with breaks for breakfast, lunch and talking (all observations in summer 2013). Like all single behavioural observations they not only represent cognitive ability (e.g. here judgement, foresight) but also other attributes such as conscientiousness.

Compared to Italy, Spain and Portugal contributed less to developments in science, arts and technology. The most important Spanish explorer, probably the most famous 'Spaniard' ever, is an Italian – Christopher Columbus from Genoa; the most famous premodernist painter is a Greek – El Greco. There are important and famous artists (Goya, Picasso, Miró, Dalí), explorers (Gama, Magellan) and authors (Cervantes, Pessoa) and there is an important political reformer and progressive dictator – the Portuguese Marquis of Pombal (1699–1782). But the Iberian contribution to the development of modernity is rather small. Spain and Portugal conquered gigantic regions in Central and South America; however, the main factor of this 'success' was the vulnerability of the indigenous people to infectious diseases. Later, against the British, French and United States, all wars were lost. On the contrary, the easy conquests and raids led to a long-term decline – the 'Spanish disease'.

One scientifically probably informative approach would be to systematic- ally analyse the performance of international companies having branches in different countries. In this natural experiment the general set-up is similar; the differences are only due to local conditions, mainly based on human capital. Chains of supermarkets are one example, e.g. the discount stores Lidl and Aldi have shops in many countries. Based on personal observa- tions, while in Germany and Northern Italy mistakes only rarely occur at the checkouts, in a Madrid Lidl (August 2007) the prices of fruits were wrongly registered at the till (fruit prices frequently change and need to be renewed by the local staff), at 11 o'clock not all fruit in the shop was assigned with prices and trees in the car park were desiccated (there was an irrigation plant, but obviously not properly used). In the Aldi at Torrevieja (Costa Blanca, Spain, August 2007) information on price tags for cocoa and on the articles themselves differed (different weights); the saleslady could not help. The product was cheaper at the till than marked. Similarly, at Carrefour (another supermarket company from France with a larger and more expensive assort- ment) in Torrevieja (August 2007) the goods were cheaper at the till than marked. In a snack booth in Madrid the sandwich was marked outside with 3 Euro but only cost 2.40 Euro. Similar problems can be found in Lidl in Southern France (St Pons de Thomières, August 2007; Vaison-la-Romaine September 2012): shop assistants did not know the prices, there was a difference between price label and price in the till, there were goods on the receipt which were not bought (when the customer wanted to change it, this caused greater trouble) and price labels were hanging so low in the shop that a 1.84m tall person may hit his head.[62]

What can these episodes tell? They hint at management quality in ordinary jobs. They were no high-level cognitive tasks. If the experiences were representative they hint at cognitive problems of the salespersons but also of the managerial staff. Motivation and conscientiousness may also have an impact. Qualitative single observations cannot prove this but future studies using systematic sampling, test and analysis procedures could. Such qualitative studies may also include interviews – how the local staff perceives and assesses the situation? Use the disperse knowledge of the people in the field!

Compared to Italy, the cognitive competence test results in Spain and Portugal are somewhat lower (Italy 98, Spain 96, Portugal 95). Current test differences are smaller than the differences in past intellectual accomplishment. The North-South difference in Italy is mirrored in a similar North-South difference in Spain: In PISA 2012, mathematics scores were achieved in the Basque Country of 490, in Aragon 483, Galicia 474, Catalonia 483 and in Castile and Leon 513, while in Andalusia 455, Murcia 447 and in Extremadura 479 SASQ. The North-South difference is on average 489 vs. 460 SASQ, directly in IQ metric 98 vs. 94 SAS-IQ.

### North America

Since the twentieth century, the United States has been the leading nation in science, technological innovation and everyday life culture. Of course, the population size has to be taken into account, but US universities, for example, are leading with and without population corrections.[63] The second-ranked country in top universities is Great Britain and then Canada. The United States is frequently successful in attracting the best scientists, artists and inventors and provides conditions for them to become successful. In particular, Jews, who had been in danger in Europe were successful in the United States, e.g. Ayn Rand, Albert Einstein, Billy Wilder (together with I. A. L./Itek Diamond) or Jan Koum.

The leading US position has not come out of nowhere. At the beginning stood a remarkable intellectual-political elite shaping the political and cultural institutions. No other country was founded by such an intellectual elite. For instance, let us look at *Philadelphia*. Philadelphia was founded by William

---

[62] However, there are no 100 per cent homogenous categories, only percentage differences. Mistakes can also be found in Lidl and Aldi in Germany. The author perceives them as increasing in recent years.

[63] The United States leads in the absolute number of Nobel Prizes, but related to population size it is Switzerland and the United States is ranked ninth. However, the awarding of Nobel Prizes could also be subject to political considerations ('It's that country again!'). Population size corrections may overcorrect.

Penn (1644–1718), a Protestant Quaker and author, having studied in Oxford and London. The name of Philadelphia is based on Christian and Greek history. Penn introduced democracy and liberty in Pennsylvania and negotiated a peace treaty with the Native Americans. Philadelphia was the home of Benjamin Franklin (1706–1790), who was a polymath, inventor, author, *homme de lettres*, statesman and one of the founding fathers of the United States. Similarly well-educated was Thomas Jefferson (1743–1826), a philosopher of Enlightenment, architect, university and library founder and statesman. James Madison (1751–1836) studied in Princeton and was one of the fathers of the US constitution, a political theorist and statesman. John Marshall (1755–1755), home and self-schooled in classical education, statesman and chief justice at the supreme court, shaped the constitutional control of public institutions.[64] The American revolution established rule of law, political freedom, economic liberty and constitutional democracy. Coming back to Philadelphia, the city was the meeting place for the founding fathers; independence and the constitution were declared there; it served as the temporary US capital. According to an episode by the economist Friedrich Hayek (2011/1960, p. 285), even Philadelphia taxi drivers were sort of political philosophers, as exemplified by a statement from a taxi driver on Roosevelt's death in 1945: 'But he ought not to have tampered with the Supreme Court, he should never have done *that*!'

Later technological and scientific achievement in the nineteenth to twenty-first centuries was and is overwhelming, e.g. by Thomas Edison or Henry Ford, the high-tech companies and forces, the leading American universities and information technology (IBM, Apple, Microsoft, Amazon, eBay, Google, Facebook). The modern world is one shaped by American inventors and companies.

Today's experiences with Philadelphia, at least for foreigners such as me, are quite different. According to experiences in May 2010, the airport was in a miserable condition, people entering the country needed to wait more than an hour at passport control; armchairs were broken; repeatedly, nerve-wracking alarms went off without any official reaction; many people, including soldiers, were much too overweight; a large number of people were in wheelchairs. Taking up the thread of Hayek on taxi drivers in Philadelphia, in January 2014 there was no communication on political philosophy, but after paying with credit card, the credit card was misused (for a meal in a New York MacDonald's and shopping in Jamaica).

Further single observations: the excellent and free public museums in Washington are nearly only attended by tourists (December 2010). In Atlanta

---

[64] Jefferson, Madison and Marshall were not from Philadelphia, but from surrounding Northeastern states and worked and/or died in Philadelphia.

in December 2008, the free Martin Luther King National Historic Site was visited by nobody (except for Phil Rushton and his son), the educational Fernbank Museum of Natural History (with many stimulating texts to read and experiments to do) was not well-attended (except for a Jewish family and some white social workers with African American children); however, the expensive but less educational Georgia Aquarium (nearly no texts, only big fish in big tanks, some of which could be touched) was full of people, with many of them carrying food and soft drinks in their hands. The technological quality of many hotels and especially private houses is low (thin single-paned windows, thin walls); in an Atlanta hotel there was a fire in the kitchen, resulting in an evacuation of all guests (December 2008). Frequently, food is unhealthy (e.g. much too big ice creams, San Francisco May 2014) and it is sometimes difficult (e.g. in December 2012 in the centre of San Antonio to buy fruits) to buy healthy food; safety belts in taxis are out of order. Staff in the international hotels are challenged by rarer occurrences such as paying with an airline voucher (Marriott, Philadelphia, January 2014). In restaurants, different TVs are running with different programmes, making it impossible for the guests to focus (Marriott). For centuries, nearly every year tornadoes destroy houses and kill people – why are buildings and rules for their construction not adequately adapted to this predictable challenge? The usual TV programmes are not intellectually valuable; there is too much advertising, entertainment, twaddle or, if serious, religious content presented in an irrational way. In Detroit, corruption and crime by the mayor (elected in free elections by the citizens), sex with employees, residents putting corpses in the street to avoid funeral expenses etc. describe a situation worse than in average Third World cities.[65] American science is heavily influenced by ideological considerations, usually called 'political correctness' (e.g. described by Maranto, Redding & Hess, 2009; Wade, 2014).

There is a huge gap between classes, e.g. between the people attending scientific conferences and people working in the conference hotel, as observable in health, teeth and physique, in linguistic expression, in cultural and evolutionary background (European vs. African), in walking and movement speed (AEA, Marriott, Philadelphia, January 2014). The United States is like the first and third world combined in one country. It contains the top universities, but around 45 per cent of Americans believe in Creationism, 20 per cent in a geocentric world and only 25 per cent understand scientific concepts.[66] However, the competence gap between the 5 per cent and 95 per cent levels in

---

[65] News, Tagesschau, 11. January 2011, https://tsarchive.wordpress.com/2011/01/11/detroit186.
[66] 2012, www.huffingtonpost.com/2012/06/05/americans-believe-in-creationism_n_1571127.html; 2005, www.nytimes.com/2005/08/30/science/30profile.html?ex=1184990400&en=2fb126c313 2f89ae&ei=5070&_r=0.

student assessment studies in international comparison is average – an indicator for a successful educational homogenisation.

What does the presented information tell us? The last observations on scientific knowledge are closely connected to cognitive criteria and the ones mentioned before more loosely. All indicators are related to interests and attitudes but both are not independent from cognitive ability, and of course they constitute an integrative part of burgher values. While there is persuasive evidence for top achievement, the overall picture looks quite different.

### Australia and New Zealand (Trans-Tasman)

Australia and New Zealand are very similar to Great Britain. They not only drive on the left, but they also have similar institutions, student assessment and IQ test results. Peoples' attitudes and abilities resemble each other. All the same but less rainy and more sun. And Marmite is called Vegemite. The German Justus von Liebig invented it and the British adopted it like a Trojan Horse. However, it does not seem to be terrible enough to seriously harm the British or the Aussies. If there is any refutation of geographical theories on societal wellbeing differences or intelligence or anything else, here it is, at least for short to medium-term effects of geography and climate. On the other side of the world everything is similar. New Zealand has more sheep than men (about six to one).

### Israel

Definitely one of the most interesting cases is Israel. Geographically, *Palaestina* (an old Hebrew-Egypt-Greek-Roman term) belongs to the North-Africa-Middle-East region; however, culturally, at least in important aspects of the political and economic system, Israel belongs to the Western world. In the West and in the last two centuries, Jews formed a very important cognitive elite (e.g. Karl Marx, Albert Einstein, Sigmund Freud, Peter Singer, to name some non-economists too). Jews in Western countries have an above average IQ of around 110 points (Lynn, 2011, p. 29). In the past, American and Russian universities and schools reduced the share of Jews in their best educational institutions by quotas, tricks or affirmative action for gentiles (Karabel, 2005; Farron, 2010). German Nazi psychologists condemned intelligence concepts and testing as being Jewish (Becker, 1938; Jaensch, 1938). In chess, music, arts and the movies Jews excelled (e.g. Bobby Fischer, Viktor Korchnoi, Leonard Bernstein, Marc Chagall, Billy Wilder). It is not possible to seriously question high Jewish intelligence, only a qualification is feasible: we do not exactly know whether before around 1800 the cognitive ability level was similarly high, but the average was high if we draw conclusions from the professions back then practised by Jews. And among Jews, the *Ashkenazim* (originally meaning the 'German', then Western, European Jews) outrange the

*Sephardim* (initially the Iberian, then Southeast European Jews) and the *Mizrahim* (the Middle East, Arabian, Oriental Jews). The last two show only slightly above average intelligence compared to their neighbouring peoples.

The Western high ability pattern of Jews definitely contrasts with the results for Israel, which average around IQ 95 (corrected and uncorrected, in student assessment studies 482 SASQ). This is around one standard deviation below the Western Jewish average and lags far behind top performers in East Asia with around 105 IQ points (Singapore, Korea, Hong Kong, Japan etc.) Israel lags 'behind' countries such as Croatia and Portugal and only slightly 'outperforms' Ukraine and Bulgaria. Are those results real? And if real, what happened here?

Let us start with a look at older values for Israel from the 1960s (Table 4.1): here Israel clearly outperformed, with an IQ of 101 points, Western countries such as the UK (98), Finland (98) or the United States (96). Only Japan (105) and New Zealand were better (104). However, when we start from the well-established 10 IQ point advantage for Jews within Western countries, an IQ of 101 is a fair amount lower than 110 or 106 (past US 96 + 10 IQ). If we take it as a historical development, the results are declining from a whopping 110 to 101 and now 95 IQ points. Theoretically, there could be three reasons for this comparatively low result and negative development:

(1) Jews who immigrated to Israel had lower intelligence than those who lived in Western countries.
(2) Other groups with lower ability levels than the Ashkenazi Jews constitute a growing share of Israeli population.
(3) Conditions in Israel are adverse for cognitive development.

We do not have exact data on who emigrated to Israel and who did not. Generally, it was not only religious Jews that emigrated, but among Jews the more religious ones seem to be more motivated to come 'home'. Arabs constitute approximately 20 per cent of the Israeli population. Among Jews, around 12 per cent are Haredi (ultra-Orthodox).[67] However, usually their schools do not participate in student or intelligence assessment studies. Among Israelis, 42 per cent have Ashkenazi roots, 38 per cent have Sephardi and Mizrahi roots.[68] Further small groups are Ethiopian Jews, Druzes and others. If we take for Arabs an IQ of 86 (the average of the neighbouring Arabian countries, 84, and assuming a plus of 2 IQ due to better environmental conditions in Israel such as better health service), of Ashkenazi Jews

---

[67] According to the last OECD PISA report (2013e, p. 49), there is a strong increase of 'Arab-speaking and ultra-orthodox streams'. Lynn (2011, p. 173) described it similarly.
[68] Following Wikipedia (Haredi Judaism, 13-05-2014), the majority of Haredi are Ashkenazi.

110 and of Sephardi and Mizrahi together approximately 95,[69] then a cognitive ability level of IQ 100 for Israel results – this is still 5 IQ points too high. Only if the Ashkenazi IQ would be 99 would the equation result in a country IQ of 95. Lynn (2011, p. 175f.) assumes a lower IQ for European (Ashkenazi) Jews of 106, Oriental Jews of 91 and Arabs of 84, resulting in an IQ of 96 points for Israel. All these results would mean that either a skewed proportion of Ashkenazi Jews emigrated to Israel (which is not plausible) or, more plausibly, that the conditions in Israel for individual and national cognitive development are less favourable and this in an increasing way.[70] The Israeli observation of cognitive decline (according to test results) is corroborated by similar observations in the United States: Ron Unz (2012, p. 26f.) described a 'strange collapse of Jewish academic achievement' looking at data of US Maths Olympiads (the fraction of Jews going down from 40 per cent to 3 per cent) and Physics Olympiads (from 25 per cent to 5 per cent), of Putnam winners (from 40 per cent to 9 per cent) and in results of science talent search (from 22 per cent to 7 per cent).

However, low ability results in Israel are *inconsistent* with high Israeli achievements in technology, the military and science.[71] Only in high-tech exports (rank 35) is a lower position acquired. There is clear evidence for good intellectual achievement; however, not for top intellectual achievement as from Western Ashkenazi Jews.

And there is observational evidence from society and politics hinting at lower cognitive development levels. One example: the highly recognised Israeli Rabbi Ovadia Yosef has made (according to different sources) many irrational statements, e.g. the 'Holocaust victims were reincarnations of the souls of sinners, people who transgressed and did all sorts of things that should not be done';[72] Hurricane Katrina would be the result of US support for the

---

[69] Numbers for intelligence of different Jews according to Lynn (2011, p. 29). For Israeli Arabs, Lynn gives a somewhat higher estimate (p. 153) as we have used here (IQ 88 vs. 86). According to Shavit (1990), Ashkenazi and Oriental Jews differ in military ability tests at about $d = 0.75$ equivalent to 11 IQ.

[70] We do not deal with causal theories in this chapter, only with real-life evidence of statistical test data. On possible causes of Jewish accomplishment, ranging between cultural-environmental and genetic-environmental theories see Botticini and Eckstein (2012), Cochran and Harpending (2009), Lynn (2011), Van Den Haag (1969) and the introducing overview of Pellissier (2013).

[71] Examples for high Israeli achievements: nuclear power, successful high-tech military forces, in patents rank 11 of countries, in airline safety among the top 9 countries, in innovation rank 14, in science Nobel prizes rank 15, in high citations rank 4, top universities rank 17. Science Nobel prizes underestimate Israeli scientific achievement because Israel did not exist before 1948 and because many Israeli researchers have dual citizenship and frequently the assigned country is the country of residence.

[72] 2000,       www.independent.co.uk/news/world/middle-east/rabbi-says-holocaust-victims-were-reincarnations-of-sinners-711547.html.

Gaza disengagement and of general lack of Torah study by Blacks;[73] the 'sole purpose of non-Jews would be to serve Jews';[74] Arabs and Palestinians should be 'annihilated'.[75] Of course, people expressing odd ideas exist in every country, but usually they do not have a leading role in society and their funeral is not the most attended in a country's history (for Yosef, the attendance is estimated at 850,000 Israeli people).

Further examples: reports about the political elite, voted in through democratic elections by the people, frequently mention corruption and violence. Again, every country has some corruption and violation of law, but the degree among the elite is different. Some examples (according to official and media reports):

- Mosche Katzav, former President, was convicted in 2010 of rape, sexual harassment and obstruction of justice.
- The former Justice Minister Haim Ramon was convicted of indecent conduct and *then* became vice premier.
- Ehud Olmert, former Prime Minister, was convicted of bribery, fraud and corruption.
- The former Minister of Finance Avraham Hirschson was convicted of larceny and forgery.
- The former Health Minister Shlomo Benizri was convicted of accepting bribes. For Shlomo Benizri, not only are various different crimes reported, but also irrationality: according to them he blamed earthquakes on Israel's tolerance of homosexuality.[76]
- The former chief of the Israeli Police, Mosche Karadi, resigned due to allegations of involvement with the Mafia.

Statistics from Transparency International on corruption corroborate these political observations: while Scandinavian nations are leading in non-corruption, closely followed by (present and past) British and European countries, Israel comes at rank 37, after Botswana, Emirates and Chile.[77] At the international level, corruption and cognitive ability correlate with $r = -.56$ ($N = 182$); in a same-country sample the intellectual classes' ability level is more highly correlated with corruption than the average ($r_{95\%} = -.64$ vs. $r_{mean} = -.60$). At the individual level there is a positive correlation between intelligence and the ethical dimension of behaviour (average people:

---

[73] 2005, www.ynetnews.com/articles/0,7340,L-3138779,00.html.
[74] 2010,     www.haaretz.com/jewish-world/adl-slams-shas-spiritual-leader-for-saying-non-jews-were-born-to-serve-jews-1.320235.
[75] 2012,     www.jewishpress.com/news/breaking-news/rav-ovadia-yosef-we-must-pray-for-the-destruction-of-iran/2012/08/26.
[76] 2008, http://news.bbc.co.uk/2/hi/middle_east/7255657.stm.
[77] Low corruption, 2010–2012, Transparency International (2012).

around $r = +.60$, McNamee, 1977; political leaders: $r = +.23$, Simonton, 1984). These correlations make corruption indicative of cognitive ability, especially for the one of leading classes. Theoretical-psychologically, this is explained by the ability of role-taking, by insight in consequences etc. (see Section 7.1). Finally, cognitive ability, education, moral, foresight and delayed gratification (vs. time preference) are all also indicators of global background factors as of the burgher world.

Additionally, international law is frequently violated in the treatment of Palestine and Palestinians; enemies including disabled persons and, as side effects of the violence, families and children are killed, flouting human rights; politicians use hate speech regarding their opponents within and outside the country (documented e.g. by Chomsky, 1999; Finkelstein, 2003/1995).[78]

As already stated, irrational and lawbreaking persons can be found in all countries including in governments, but not in this concentration in a free and democratic country. The picture is contradictory; there might be a smart technological, scientific and military elite on the one hand, but the society lags further behind than expected, backing the astonishing low test results.

*Latin America (Central and South America)*   Latin America was first settled by American Indians (Native Americans or Indigenous peoples of the Americas). Due to low resistance to European-Asian-African infectious diseases, and due to slavery and expulsion they make up only a minority today (from approximately 0 per cent in Cuba and Uruguay to approximately 40 per cent in Peru and Bolivia). People of European, African and mixed Amerindian-European-African descent constitute the majority now.

Indigenous civilisations show impressive architectural achievements – pyramids in Mexico such as Teotihuacan or cities in Peru such as Machu Picchu. Agriculture was developed and domesticated animals were present (guinea pig, llama, alpaca, Muscovy duck, turkey). Metallurgy was invented and used. However, writing was only invented in Mesoamerica by the Maya. The wheel was not invented and used for transport. Compared to Asia and Europe the achievements lag behind.

Nowadays, magical thinking mixed with some Christian contents is still common (e.g. Macumba, Santería) and has some influence also for middle-class people with European background. For instance, in 1985 a Brazilian

---

[78] It is not possible to give an exhaustive overview; we guess there are around 50 to 100 books on Israeli treatment of Palestinians, dealing with rule of law, international law and human rights, and maybe 100,000 reports in the news. The message is: there is a clearly visible deviation from an optimum of cognitive ability *along* with a clearly visible deviation from an optimum of ethics – as theoretically assumed by Piaget, Kohlberg, Habermas and Oesterdiekhoff. Nevertheless, Israeli politics is at least somewhat instrumentally rational.

student, who had studied in Germany, was upset when the author lighted candles at the Copacabana Beach in Rio de Janeiro – they were set up by Brazilians and if another person lights them after they have been blown out by the wind this may cause misfortune. In the Bonfim church of Salvador do Bahia (1991), an army officer (man) crawled on his knees from the door to the altar. Its chapel is full of votive offerings. Throughout Latin America amulets are frequently used.

The mastery of technological modernity is not always present, e.g. in Cuba, Brazil or Venezuela in average houses approximately 5 to 10 per cent of doors cannot be closed or opened with a key (locks are broken, no keys etc.). The author had this experience in Brazil in 2010 twice in different modern houses with amusing consequences, but possibly dangerous ones in the case of fire. In Cuba, the majority of people asked do not know how many times each day a broken watch shows the correct time (see Section 4.4.1). Shower heads in Brazil, if they provide warm water, frequently are live, giving the person taking a shower a haunting experience. In 1985, in the remote Amazonian village São Gabriel da Cachoeira, I met a priest laying a cable who was continuously receiving mild electric shocks. Because the voltage level is only 110 V this is not too dangerous, but it is also no indication of technological bravura. The PISA Science scales contain items dealing with such electricity tasks (e.g. 2006 electric engines and wind farms), measuring according to the PISA approach a specific science literacy; however, due to similar cognitive demand, similar processes during resolving them and high correlations at all levels they represent a broad cognitive competence (see Section 3.2). Using these PISA science tests for Latin America (corrected for youth not attending school) an average of approximately 370 SASQ (student assessment points) or in Greenwich-IQ of 77 IQ points results. In Latin America, test-measured understanding of science is below standard, corroborating the qualitative observations, albeit the latter not being based on comparably large samples.

At home, books are rather rare. Here are some illustrative but extreme examples: a middle-class family with two children in Foz do Iguaçu in 1985, the father of which was a bank clerk, had only one book, a comic book bible. Another couple, both technicians or engineers in Salvador in 2010, had no books at all. In São Gabriel da Cachoeira in 1985, three girls of about five to ten years old had a book depicting the development of amphibians from eggs to tadpoles and finally to frogs. We studied the images together; however, the children were totally astonished and doubted the content. In TIMSS fourth grade one task measuring science literacy at a 'Low International Benchmark' deals exactly with this topic: 'Which box contains two animals that lay eggs?' – and depicted are different birds, mammals and fish (Martin et al., 2016, exhibit 2.4.1). The number of books is the third best parental indicator of children's intelligence ($r_{Bo} = .25$; Section 3.4.5) and at the international level the correlation is very high with cognitive ability ($r_{Bo} = .70$; Table 10.5) – much higher than any attribute of instruction or schools. The average number of books at home can be used as a proxy of national cognitive ability. Looking at the numbers taken from student assessment studies (see Appendix and Table A.3) the average for Latin America at home is 28 books, in Brazil 34 books, approximately a quarter to a third compared to Britain with 102 or Scandinavia with 111 books. Episodic observations correspond to statistical data but present a much more vivid picture. Quantitative and qualitative sources validate each other and both hint at possible causes of national differences in cognitive ability.

However, in Latin America there have been and still are eminent intellectuals (e.g. Mario Vargas Llosa, Gabriel García Márquez, Octavio Paz), scientists and reformers (e.g. Fernando Henrique Cardoso, Hernando de Soto). Influential ideas were developed in Latin America (e.g. liberation theology). Latin America shines in music and dance. There is a large within-society heterogeneity.

*North-Africa-Middle-East (Arabian-Muslim world)*   The region reaches from Morocco to Turkey and Arabia and ends in Pakistan and Bangladesh. The categorisation is mainly based on culture (Islam) and secondarily on geography and evolutionary background. Malaysia and Indonesia, despite having Muslim majorities, are not included (but could be). Ethnically, the region includes Arabs (with Egypt and Saudi Arabia as core countries), Turkic peoples (with Turkey as core), Iranian peoples (Iran) and Indians (Pakistan). Among Muslims, Sunnites can be distinguished from Shiites as the two main groups.

In Mesopotamia and the Fertile Crescent, civilisation began, writing and the calendar were first invented by the Sumer, the first epic was written down here (Gilgamesh), a complex society was developed with organised irrigation and an intellectual class (priests) emerged. The oldest human cities we know of were founded here (Çatalhöyük, Jericho, Babylon). The Indus Valley civilisation was also an advanced ancient civilisation. Ancient Egypt is impressive with its pyramids, obelisks, temples and beautiful paintings in sepulchres. Ancient Persian culture is also striking (Persepolis). The second heyday was between the eighth and thirteenth centuries. The Arabian-Persian culture absorbed classical Greek, Indian and Chinese intellectual achievement and passed it to Europe (e.g. Aristotle, Indian-Arabian numbers, paper originated in China). There were impressive intellectuals, e.g. Algoritmi or al-Khwarizmi (780–850, mathematician), Avicenna (980–1037, physician), Averroes (1126–1198, philosopher), Ibn al-Nafis (1213–1288, physician). Islamic architecture is very graceful (e.g. Isfahan, Samarkand, Taj Mahal). The medieval king Saladin was regarded as a wise king (but erroneously[79]). Islam refuses magic and belief in miracles. Beginning with Muhammad, the Arabs were very successful conquerors from the seventh to eighth centuries.[80]

However, the scientific and cultural contributions, seen in context, are far from being spectacular. According to Michael Hart (2007, p. 253.):

Arabs made no major discoveries in mathematics or science, nor did they make any major advances in applied sciences such as medicine and engineering. In fact, there was not a single important invention that originated in the Arab world. (By way of contrast, in the interval 650–1300 AD, spectacles were invented in Italy, and the Chinese invented printing, gunpowder, and the compass.) There is, of course, more to human culture than the arts and sciences. The growth of democracy, the abolition of slavery, the emancipation of women, the rise of religious tolerance, and the establishment of freedom of speech are advances that are more valuable than beautiful paintings, symphonies, or poems. Here too, however, the contribution of the Arabs was negligible.

Additionally, reports of anti-educational, irrational and anti-scientific attitudes are widespread and old. Landes (1998, p. 54) mentioned a 'Muslim hostility to learning':

Islamic science, denounced as heresy by religious zealots, bent under theological pressures for spiritual conformity ... For militant Islam, the truth had already been revealed. What led back to the truth was useful and permissible; all the rest was error and deceit.

During the conquest of Persia the leaders asked their soldiers to throw books into the water (p. 54). Later, the printing press was rejected (p. 401f.). Intellectuals were frequently prosecuted, books were banned and destroyed, the polymath Averroes was banished and the philosopher Suhrawardi executed. There was also an important external cause: the Mongols damaged Muslim culture in 1258; Baghdad, its Grand Library and the House of Wisdom were destroyed. However, education, thinking, science and rationality had already declined, as they were seen as being anti-Islamic. Literal interpretation of traditional writings was appreciated, not an own search for new truth.

A report from the United Nations (UNDP, 2003) described in various aspects present-day conditions being detrimental to cognitive development. For instance, in Arabian countries only a few new books are published, translated or written (pp. 3f., 76ff.), instruction in schools is not cognitively challenging, there is only a few modern research and media output is rather dull:

---

[79] Saladin put to death the philosopher Suhrawardi (1153–1191); after losing a battle Christian knights were executed, one by him personally (Battle of Hattin), and others were sold to slavery.

[80] The worldwide most 'effective' (without an ethical assessment!) terror attack was perpetrated by Arabs (September 11 2001). Its 'perfect' organisation was one reason for the development of conspiracy theories around 9/11.

Some researchers argue that the curricula taught in Arab countries seem to encourage submission, obedience, subordination and compliance, rather than free critical thinking. (UNDP, 2003, p. 53)

Research in advanced fields, such as information technology and molecular biology, is almost non-existent. (p. 70)

A review of media programmes and research indicates that light entertainment is the most common offering, and is predominantly superficial, repetitive in content, and promotes values that encourage consumerism and a depreciation of work ... The news is often presented as a succession of isolated events, without in-depth explanatory coverage or any effort to place events in the general, social, economic and cultural context. (p. 61)

One may doubt whether the media content is actually better in other countries. However, apart from media further indicators are given. Fundamentalist groups such as the Taliban and Boko Haram attack schools and kill students and teachers. Due to religious resistance, vaccination programmes in Afghanistan and Pakistan need military protection. Conspiracy or simply irrational theories are prevalent, about Jews, tsunamis, AIDS, earthquakes or September 11. For example, the Professor of Islamic Law, Fawzan al-Fawzan, from the Saud Islamic University in Riyadh said, according to the Washington Post, about the 2004 South Asia tsunami: "The tsunami, Fawzan declared, was God's punishment for allowing resorts where 'especially at Christmas, fornication and sexual perversion of all kinds are rampant.'"[81] Following a report by the Guardian, Egypt's military leaders announced in February 2014 that they have developed a device to detect and cure HIV/AIDS and Hepatitis C.[82] In several Arabian-Muslim countries in free elections religious-fundamentalist parties were elected by the majority of people (Turkey 1995 and 2002–2015, Palestine 2006, Tunisia 2011, Egypt 2011–2012, Iran in the early 1980s, Algeria in the early 1990s).

However, the picture is somewhat more heterogeneous, especially regarding *Iran*. Here, academics, physicians, physicists and philosophers became leading politicians (e.g. Gholam-Ali Haddad-Adel, Ali Larijani, and nearly all candidates in the 2013 presidency election). Iran has 'exported' important intellectuals to the West (e.g. Lotfi Zadeh, mixed Iran-Jewish background, developer of the fuzzy set theory). Iranian immigrants to the United States are well-educated (Feliciano, 2005). But as centuries ago, intellectuals are suppressed and killed, e.g. the highly gifted physician and poet Ramin Pourandarjani (1983–2009).

---

[81] www.washingtonpost.com/wp-dyn/content/article/2006/09/04/AR2006090401107_3.html.
[82] www.theguardian.com/world/2014/feb/28/egypt-unveil-device-detects-cures-aids,   http://egyptianstreets.com/2014/05/11/egypt-invents-devices-to-detect-worlds-deadliest-diseases.

Similar *suppression of intellectuals*, either by non-governmental or governmental groups, can be found in other Muslim countries, e.g. in Egypt the killings of Farag Foda (1946–1992) or Khaled Mohamed Saeed (1982–2010). Nasr Hamid Abu Zaid left Egypt after he was forced to divorce from his wife due to being accused of apostasy. Intellectuals have even been threatened in the West (e.g. Robert Redeker or Salman Rushdie). Several secularist authors and bloggers in Bangladesh have been killed in recent years by Islamists (e.g. in April 2016 Rezaul Karim Siddique, professor of English at the University of Rajshahi, and Nazimuddin Samad, law student at Jagannath University). There are only a few Arabian intelligence researchers, but one of them mysteriously disappeared (Omar Khaleefa from Sudan in 2012). It is not only intellectuals that are faced with such problems; problems with the rule of law and human rights are widespread.

A positive development is the general and large increase in literacy and school enrolment rates, e.g. in Morocco, Egypt and Iran, starting from below 50 per cent four decades ago and now reaching over 90 per cent. The Gulf states have founded international universities in co-operation with European and American institutions. However, competence levels according to international student assessment studies or more selective university student studies are still low, too low for meeting the challenges of technological and cultural modernity.[83]

*Central and South Asia*    India is the major country of this region and its culture has radiated to the surrounding countries. Hinduism and Buddhism emerged here and spread to the south, north and east. The religions of Zoroastrianism (Parsis) and Jainism originated here too. Buddhism shaped Central and East Asia and parts of Southeast Asia (Tibet, China, Japan, Thailand, Cambodia), and Hinduism the island of Bali. In India, the modern numerical system, including the number 0, was invented. The classical architecture is beautiful and impressive: most famous is the (Mughal) Taj Mahal, a sculpture of love. Decorative art and sculptures are realistic and beautiful. The cuisine is various and has spread to the West, similarly the East and Southeast Asian cuisine. Since 1974 India has been a nuclear power, and the same is true for Pakistan since 1998. India is participating in space travel, and is the largest institutional democracy in the world. Immigrants from India in the United States, in Latin America, in Africa or on the island countries in the Indian

---

[83] The student assessment results for the mentioned three countries, Morocco, Egypt and Iran, reached uncorrected averages at SAS-IQ 70 to 84, intellectual classes at SAS-IQ 94 to 107. In my own study, Emirati engineering university students reached an average IQ of 104. The result is above average, but certainly too low to cope with complex cognitive tasks common in engineering (Rindermann, Baumeister & Gröper, 2014).

Ocean constitute not only unproblematic minorities, but they are well-known for high achievement in commerce and computing. A Jain, Anshu Jain, was from 2012 to 2015 the head of the largest German bank, Deutsche Bank, the first foreigner to head a German bank.

However, looking back into the past, India was conquered five times by peoples from the Northwest, first around 1,500 BCE by people from Iran (Aryans), in the sixth century by Hephthalites (White Huns), in the eighth century by Muslim conquerors from Iran and Afghanistan, in the sixteenth century by Mongolian-Muslim conquerors (Mughal) and in the nineteenth century by the British, bringing institutions and language, but only temporarily settling there. Strangely enough, in each case very small minorities of foreigners ruled the subcontinent. There are inventions (stepwell, ruler, shadow play), but they were not revolutionary, except for mathematics (zero, Pascal's triangle, equations, etc.; e.g. Aryabhata, 476–550).

Cognitive ability test results for India are around IQ 80, which is astonishingly low. Psychometric measures showed higher results than student assessment studies; depending on corrections differences are around 5 to 13 IQ points. India never participated in the large PIRLS, PISA and TIMSS studies; only a few regions participated in later surveys (Das & Zajonc, 2010; Walker, 2011). Older assessments four decades ago corroborate the current low pattern (Table 4.1, SAS-IQ 83). Additionally, the indicators of cognitive achievement in modernity hover at 80 to 90 (Table 4.5).

The practised religion is very colourful, full of magical and anthropocentric thinking (e.g. Gods with anthropomorphous characters, sacrifices). Religious fanaticism is widespread, sometimes leading to eruptive violence. Three leading politicians were killed by religiously and politically motivated assassins. Abstract Buddhism has nearly vanished from India. Illiteracy rates are high (about 25 per cent). Among the Roma (Gypsies), most probably a people from India, a pattern of a non-burgher lifestyle is much more prevalent than among surrounding European societies.[84]

India is a very large country with around 1 billion people. The huge size of the population may skew the impression based on qualitative data from science, mathematics and art. Possibly, there is no larger than usual gap between top intellectual achievement and average people: simply, huge population size enables more extreme top achievement. Additionally, large

---

[84] Pattern of non-burgher lifestyle, indicators: low educational results, high illiteracy rates, e.g. among Roma in Romania about 50 per cent, low cognitive ability test results, e.g. in Serbia IQ of around 70 (Rushton, Cvorovic & Bons, 2007); many live on welfare or are day labourers in low-qualified jobs; low order and cleanliness, e.g. 2013 www.welt.de/regionales/duesseldorf/article115697608/Armutsfluechtlinge-sollen-abgeschoben-werden.html; property offences, e.g. 2009 http://news.bbc.co.uk/2/hi/8226580.stm, e.g. 1968 www.spiegel.de/spiegel/print/d-45465311.html. Usual official data not exist (no crime statistics based on ethnicity).

differences between religions, castes and regions allow niche construction, some of them with very special supportive environments. A proportionally very small, but still large, cognitive elite is selected by achievement-based tests:

Their [Indian Institutes of Technology] greatest strength is that they administer one of the world's most ruthlessly competitive entrance exams. Three hundred thousand people take it, five thousand are admitted – an acceptance rate of 1.7 percent ... The people who make the mark are the best and brightest out of one billion. (Zakaria, 2011, pp. 205–206)

However, the old caste system and newer affirmative action undermine meritoric principles and motivation (Sowell, 2004). A small well-educated elite, traditionally the Brahmin, Parsis and Jains, a rising middle class and a small IT workforce shape the modern identity, but a very large fraction of the society lags behind.

*Southeast Asia and the Pacific Region*     In this region can be observed impressive cultural achievement, e.g. the temple complex of Angkor Wat; the rice terraces in the Philippines, Vietnam and Bali; ritual dances and beautiful pagodas in many countries. The region has benefitted from the northern East Asian countries and India. Religions and technological developments were adopted. Today, religious practice is characterised by concrete forms and contents mixed with animism and by Islam. Chinese minorities, if not suppressed, constitute the elite in economy and higher education (Chua, 2003; Sowell, 2004). This corresponds to differences in ability levels of around 16 IQ points (IQ 101 vs. IQ 85). Today, international companies manufacture textiles, shoes and high-tech products. The Pacific Islanders are famous for their navigation skills.

*East Asia*     East Asia encompasses China (and smaller countries up to Singapore settled by the Chinese), Japan and Korea.[85] This region usually achieves the worldwide best student test results. Reports on invested time on education support the good test results: even afternoons, evenings, Sundays and holidays are dedicated to learning. But reports also hint at some overachievement in tests, especially after considering that participation in international student assessment surveys is seen as a kind of national competition. Nevertheless, more 'private' IQ assessments came to similar high results and corroborate the pattern. Until around the fifteenth century, China was leading in science and technological innovation (Needham, 1982) as

---

[85] General remark: regional classification is not fixed; different authors, theoretical orientations (e.g. geography vs. culture) and purposes lead to somewhat differing classifications. For instance, Vietnam is a borderline case.

indicated by the invention of the wheelbarrow, horse collar, crossbow, compass, porcelain, sluice, paper, printing (in a simple form using woodblock) and gunpowder. China was also leading in cleanliness and hygiene. Globally, China had the largest cities and the highest population density calling for an efficient political and social organisation, especially for a systematic control of violence (Clark, 2007; Murray, 2003, p. 41). Officials were selected according to merit, not to ideological criteria. In global comparison, Confucius (551–479 BCE) is the most rational among the founders of religion. His doctrine emphasises education and learning.

However, compared to Europe, since around the fifteenth century there have also been clear indicators of delay: no continuing development of science, of science using mathematics; no development of theoretical systems; until the nineteenth century no interest in other cultures; intellectual and economic isolation. Today China is catching up in science; nevertheless, until now the scientific achievements of East Asian countries have not kept up with their high cognitive potential (Kura, te Nijenhuis & Dutton, 2015). East Asian nations do not fulfil, e.g. in Nobel Prizes, what can be expected from their cognitive levels.

Instead, what many scientists outside China experience of modern Chinese 'science', nearly daily observable, prevailingly consists of emails with 'invitations' to simulated 'scientific conferences', 'journals' and 'books', all with larger fees to pay. For example, the author, as a psychologist, was 'invited' to chair a session on gynaecology at a medical conference in Dalian. The author has never received a reasonable science-related email from China, but during the writing of this book about 2,000 invitations to such conferences and journals (e.g. today, 10 minutes ago, 18-03-2017).[86] These are fakes, actually no fraud, a simulation of science, using the usual surface indicators of science to make profit. But even this bogus science is an indicator of a comparatively high cognitive level: it is not stealing, it is not robbery, it is high level simulation. If anything, it remotely resembles corruption; here, in low corruption, China lags far behind at rank 82 (for comparison Scandinavia ranks from 1 to 10, the West 1 to 30).

Another discrepancy to the worldwide leading cognitive ability level is the prevalence of Traditional Chinese Medicine:

Chinese view of traditional medicine today is basically the same as it has been for thousands of years; most believe it has value. The number of people opposed to its use, mostly scientists and other intellectuals, is small – probably less than ten percent of the total population. (Lee & Kun, 2014, p. 24)

---

[86] The situation is different for Hong Kong, Singapore, Taiwan, Korea and Japan.

There is no evidence that, for instance, the taking of tiger bones, turtle meat or herbs has any positive effect – even worse, due to contamination these medicines are definitely unhealthy and, additionally, they destroy nature. Some methods of physiotherapy and some herbs have shown a positive effect in experiments. However, these are lucky strikes. The entire concept of Traditional Chinese Medicine is based on analogical thinking, like there are fundamental energies in nature that are mirrored in the body (Qi, Yin and Yang, Wood, Fire, Earth, Metal, Water). Diseases are caused by disharmony or ancestors etc. Feng shui is another example of traditional and still-practised irrationality.

It would be possible to reply that also in other countries and cultures alternative medicine is used, e.g. in the United States and Britain by around 20 to 50 per cent (Barnes et al., 2004; Thomas et al., 2001). However, the comparison is skewed because therapies such as massage, practices such as meditation or praying either show positive effects or are not used as a kind of medical therapy (but for wellbeing) in the intention of the users. And more fundamentally, the benchmark for the smartest cannot be harebrained people from all over the world but reason and epistemic rationality.

Similarly to at the individual level, the Natascha Kampusch case contradicts many well-founded theories (see Section 3.4.8), East Asian test results contradict important theories on causes and consequences of cognitive ability: in school, there is no use of 'modern' instructional methods, but simply an increase of instruction and private learning time up to an unbelievable extent; authoritarian education prevails; there seems to be no intelligence-rationality nexus (see above) and no intelligence-ethics nexus in the form of democracy, rule of law and human rights (see Sections 7.1, 10.3.2). The answer to this objection is fourfold:

(1) Yes, the objections are correct. But other important fields underscore the impact of high cognitive ability: rapid technological and economic catch up, strong economic growth, a successful high-tech industry, space travel, electronics. Japan came four decades earlier than China; today it is a technology leader. Singapore and Korea have leading or at least advanced positions in similar fields.

(2) Yes; however, in social sciences we have no deterministic laws. There are always some unsystematic deviations.

(3) Yes, there is a time lag in important political and cultural domains. The lag could be based on culture, on more or less accidental historical factors or on (yet unknown) genetic factors. Nevertheless, let us wait. Time will bring change and cognitive ability will show its general effects.

(4) Yes, there is a systematic deviation from theory showing the limits of the given theory, making qualifications and amendments necessary.

Intelligence and knowledge may form *encapsulated islands of competence* not leading to a general attitude of epistemic rationality (cf. Germany and its inclination to intellectual and political follies). Two related factors contribute to this problem: (a) A too strong and too general *conformism*: East Asia is not only behind in science, but also in arts and music. Let us compare to the Caribbean: continuously, new styles of music and dance are developed, such as Calypso, Reggae, Ska, Son, Mambo, Salsa, Merengue and Bachata. Some see the East Asian problem in low openness to experience, a personality trait related to a culture of conformism. Internationally compared, openness is lower than in Latin America (1), the West (2) or Africa (3) (Lynn, 2007; Schmitt et al., 2007). Conformism as control of behaviour is in a densely populated premodern world surely beneficial. If the rules and leaders are at least somewhat smart and beneficial, conformism will lead with higher probability to good outcomes than deviation. If they are not smart nor beneficial, conformism may lead to the opposite including death. In the South Korean ferry accident of April 2014, students, being about 17 years old, remained in a capsizing ship under deck, this for half an hour, because the ship's captain and crew had told them. These were students with the highest intelligence levels in the world at an age of their highest cognitive and physical fitness. Only those who did not follow survived.

East Asia generally is too much a culture of (conformist) hard work and too little a culture of (independent) thinking. Thinking necessarily will lead at some point to deviance, but hard work by itself will not. The ultimate orientation for thinking is reason. In East Asia as ultimate orientation, agreement dominates, agreement with others and tradition. Tradition can be fulfilled by hard work, not by thinking, which always will lead to some critique of tradition. Reason itself is defined by abstract and general and never finally settable rules. Reason and thinking imply openness in their higher levels. Tradition implies having a final fixed point and an authoritative person or institution defining what is according to tradition and what is not. The occidental orientation towards truth and not towards agreement allowed individuals to question the given conditions, pushing the present state forward.[87] The new is developed by *questioning* the given, by *deviation*.

The fundamental contribution of those who were responsible for this revolution was not in methodological refinement or in a substantial perfection of the instruments of observation, but rather in a reformulation of problems constituting the object of scientific study. The revolution in mechanics was not the fruit of discovering new

---

[87] E.g. 'Non sub homine sed sub Deo et lege.' (Not under man, but under God and the law.) Ascribed to Henry de Bracton (1210–1268).

answers to the classical questions about motion, but resulted from the discovery of new questions, which permitted to formulate the problems in a different manner. (Piaget & Garcia, 1989/1983, p. 248)

The conformism-vs.-thinking-problem is linked to (b) the role of *intellectuals*. There were and are too few questioning and at least partly rationally answering intellectuals. No Bruno, Rousseau, Darwin, Nietzsche or Freud.[88]

One quote, the third sentence of Rousseau's Confessions, can illustrate it:

'I am made unlike any one I have ever met; I will even venture to say that I am like no one in the whole world. I may be no better, but at least I am different.' (Rousseau, 1953/ 1782, Book I, p. 17)

This has the consequence that a pure intelligence theory (in its Piagetian, psychometric or further forms), in which intelligence necessarily leads to ground-breaking intellectual achievement (among few), to epistemic rationality and ethically improved attitudes and behaviour, is too narrow, both for individuals as well as for societies and cultures. Of course, intelligence is still a supportive factor, but further factors need to be taken into account: a rational and liberal burgher culture; thinking abilities are embedded in such a cultural web, supported by it and furthering it. Analysing quantitative data alone will not help to understand why high cognitive ability does not always lead to the fulfilment of its promises.

*What Does That Tell Us?*   Persons who may perceive the descriptions as being one-sided and especially too critical towards developing countries should only look at the migration streams, from Africa and the Middle East to Western, Central and Northern Europe, from Latin America, Africa and Asia to North America and Trans-Tasman. Politically sensible scientific questions are easily answered in a global way by foot-voting of millions of people. Of course, nowhere an optimal social-cultural state of wellbeing is reached. But in current and recent Scandinavia the conditions seem to be the best of all present and past existing worlds.

The general pattern of observations fits to the general pattern of statistical test results. However, there is also considerable heterogeneity. And this is usually hidden in pure mean results – but observable in ability gaps between the 5 per cent and 95 per cent thresholds.

And there are important systematic deviations for East Asia and especially China: high and steadily high cognitive ability results on the one hand, and in

---

[88] The pattern is even broader as having brave and critical but smart and at least partly rational intellectuals is related to the existence of individual, but clever, heroes (e.g. Odysseus). This may be specific for the history of the West, not only beginning with the Renaissance and Enlightenment (Duchesne, 2011).

recent centuries low scientific and intellectual achievements, widespread belief and practise of magical thinking and low rule of law, democracy and liberty levels on the other.

Intelligence only increases the probability of certain outcomes. Effects need some time as individuals and countries develop; present states could be transitory. Scientific achievements may come, similarly a more rational way of thinking. Finally, a pure cognitive theory needs to be complemented by a broader theory including culture. Culture can be changed, but patterns are relatively robust. And culture influences not only the conditions relevant for cognitive development but also the possibilities of its expression, e.g. as exceptional intellectual achievement.

This *exercise in qualitative data* also shows the *problems and limits* of a qualitative approach. Politically, some may *perceive descriptions more than numbers as disparaging*. These could be answered: what is nasty, the description or the content? If the content is disparaging then in a scientific book that needs to be orientated towards truth the description has to veridically reflect this. Thus critics have to prove that the content is wrongly described: statements were either wrong as wrong facts (e.g. 'in Brazil the sun rises in the evening'), or wrong as being not representative (e.g. 'it's raining in the Emirates') or not correctly reflecting an international pattern (e.g. 'it's cold in Canada and it's colder than in Greenland'). Until such wrongness is proven any reproach is epistemically useless.

Somewhat related to political concerns is the phenomenon that *people perceive numbers as more persuasive*. Many simply do not understand statistics and are simply intimidated by numbers, models and the like. By contrast, an episode can always be answered by everyone with a contrary one. A typical objection could be to mention any tomfoolery as highly diagnostic and debunking information, e.g. 'In fact, Muslim sailors reached the American continent 314 years before Columbus, in 1178.'[89] Dealing with possible wrongness, there is a *problem of representativity of indicators and observations*.

A further problem and uncircumventable scientific task is to *evaluate criteria according to their meaningfulness and validity for cognitive ability* (see also Section 4.4.1). Cognitive test items themselves are the best investigated ones. Also convincing are all verbal and numerical products and results of problem solving and thinking. Technological mastery is also an appropriate criterion, less so order, income and wealth – the influence of further factors become stronger and stronger and phenomena less cognitive. A table with numbers reflecting closeness to the construct and degree of manifestation of a

---

[89] According to the Guardian the Turkish president, Recep Tayyip Erdogan (November 2014, www.theguardian.com/world/2014/nov/16/muslims-discovered-america-erdogan-christopher-columbus).

certain nation at a certain epoch could give more systemised information. Further qualitative studies could increase samples by (a) asking different experts to do literature surveys for cognitive indicators across times and nations, (b) by instructing several trained scientists to sample experience regarding cognitive achievement, e.g. speaking with people and analysing statements for argumentation, substantiation and rationality. Rationality items developed by Stanovich et al. (2016) could be used as an orientation. In a mixed-method approach the obtained results can be verbally integrated, statistically quantified and summarising means presented.

Summarising, *paper-and-pencil tests remain indispensable*, either as *classical psychometric intelligence tests used in local surveys* or as well-established *student assessment tests applied in large-scale studies managed by international organisations*; qualitative data add further evidence; their use should be improved compared to this first exercise.

*Can We Praise or Blame Nations for Cognitive Ability?*     Finally, can we praise or blame nations for cognitive ability? No, we *cannot* praise or blame nations for the cognitive ability of their average citizens, for the level of their society and eminent intellectuals. They depend on difficult to modify environmental conditions and probably also on genetic factors. Of course, they can be changed. But any intervention needs time. For the current status the generations living today and leaders have only a minor liability. They benefit or suffer from the past.

Nevertheless, current generations and leaders *should* be made responsible for all that is and what will come: believing in the malleability of humans, societies and cultures will support any endeavour to improve them.

No, we cannot praise or blame nations for cognitive ability, but we should.

# 5    Why Some Are Richer, Freer and More Democratic

In this chapter, common theories are introduced to explain differences between nations in wellbeing and their development. Internal vs. external and idealistic vs. materialistic approaches are distinguished. Economic freedom, quality of institutions, geographic and dependency theories are outlined. Finally, path analyses are suggested for modelling the interplay of proximal and distal factors.

As described in Chapters 1, 2 and 4, there are tremendous differences in living conditions between nations and across time. Some are rich and others poor and in some countries people live much longer and more peacefully than in others. Even height differences are large, ranging from around 1.55 m in Central America, South and Southeast Asia to around 1.75 m in Scandinavia. In some countries, people enjoy human rights, rule of law and liberty; in others they live in fear. Why is that? That is the million-dollar question frequently asked by scholars and laypersons.

## 5.1    Internal vs. External and Idealistic vs. Materialistic Paradigms

Let us start with a simplifying model: internal and external factors and an idealistic or materialistic perspective can be distinguished (see Table 5.1). A prominent *internal-idealistic* approach is to explain national differences by culture (e.g. Harrison, 2006; Sombart, 1998/1913; Weber, 2001/1905) or to explain historical developments by changes in culture (McCloskey, 2016). The main idea is that ideas, whether religious, ideological, political or psychological, guide the behaviour of individuals and societies, including institutions, economy and politics, resulting in wealth, liberty or rule of law.

The opposite model is the *external-materialistic* approach exemplified by natural resources (e.g. Diamond, 1997). Countries such as the small oil Emirates are rich because they have large, internationally needed natural resources and a small population. An *internal-materialistic* approach is exemplified by the genetic position (e.g. Lynn & Vanhanen, 2012). Genes, differently distributed across peoples, shape behaviour and this behaviour shapes

Table 5.1 *Paradigms for national differences in wellbeing*

| | | Agent | |
|---|---|---|---|
| | | *Idealistic* | *Materialistic* |
| **Locality** | *Internal* | Culture | Genetics |
| | *External* | Conversion by others | Natural resources |

*Notes*: For 'internal' also the term 'endogenous' can be used, for 'external' the term 'exogenous'.

outcomes at the individual and national levels. Finally, *external-idealistic* factors are, for instance, cultural patterns acquired from others as adopted institutions from former colonial powers (e.g. Feyrer & Sacerdote, 2009).

The scheme does not deal with *influenceability*. Internal factors seem to be more easily modifiable than external factors; however, that is not true, as the stability of cultural differences across centuries and of peoples of the same culture in different countries show (e.g. China and the Chinese). Natural resources can be used up quickly (e.g. timber in Spain, gold in Peru or phosphate in Nauru), lose or increase their worth (e.g. honey in the nineteenth century vs. rare earth elements nowadays) and their worth depends on the ability to obtain and manage their economic benefits (e.g. oil in Norway vs. Nigeria).

An important aspect is *connectedness*: factors are not isolated; they are connected. Institutions (best assigned to internal-idealistic) can be changed by external factors such as the influence of other countries and commodities and their effects. Especially, they influence how commodities can be used and their impact on wealth. Cultural and genetic factors are related: certain traditions enforce consanguineous marriages which themselves undermine modern political institutions such as democracy, meritocracy and rule of law (e.g. Woodley & Bell, 2013).

Within the four categories, factors are also related. Worldviews have an impact on economic systems, e.g. Protestantism on economic freedom, one of the most important single factors for growth and wealth. The quality and functionality of political, legal and economic institutions depend on culture; e.g. the Protestant focus on conscience, internal control and on generalisable ethical norms made Protestantism a positive determinant.[1] Economic freedom may influence individual attitudes and culture towards meritoric principles.

Factors are not only related; they form a *causal flow system*: There are *proximal* and *specific* factors, such as behaviour of workers (e.g. punctuality, conscientiousness), established laws (e.g. protection of property) and

---

[1] The percentage of Protestants in a society is positively correlated with trust in society ($r = .54$, $N = 115$). Sources: Data for religions see Table 10.11; trust from World Values Survey (WVS) around 2005 (Díez-Medrano, 2014).

institutions (e.g. administrative courts), which are dependent on *distal* and *global* factors such as culture, history and even genes. Whereas the first are tangible, the latter are more difficult to measure. For the first, research is relatively easy, but for the latter it is challenging.

However, only giving narrow answers leads to undercomplexity. Proximity and distality are relative units; technological progress is more distal than transport infrastructure. Why was there more technological progress in England than in Russia and why not two centuries earlier? One distal answer is given by Margaret Jacob (2014): in Britain, a scientific culture emerged which was based on education in mathematics and Newtonian science. This culture institutionalised itself throughout schools and universities and by private tutors and in private study. Science was not only taught, but acquired as a style of thinking. It became a powerful application for tinkerers outside the university. Science was not an alien stock of information, but something that could be used and improved.

But why did a small, yet still large enough group of British inventors, engineers and entrepreneurs behave like this and were at least able to understand and apply science?

## 5.2    Traditional Explanations

There is a huge amount of research on causes of wealth and its growth and on wellbeing development of societies. Statistical approaches can be distinguished from historical ones.[2] Statistical growth research as exemplified by Xavier Sala-i-Martin (1997, and with colleagues 2004) found the following factors: investments, economic freedom, rule of law and education are the most important positive determinants; cultural (fractions of religions), geographic (distance from equator, certain regions) and political variables (peace) were also relevant. Additionally, the achieved level of wealth is negatively relevant for growth – the economies of poor countries grow faster than the economies of rich countries ('advantages of backwardness' or statistically expressed 'beta-convergence'). Poorer, more backward economies can learn from richer, more forward ones.

However, the theoretical and empirical dependence between the determinants was not considered in this study.[3] The approach is a merely descriptive one. Why are there more or less investments in a country? Why is there more

---

[2] Exemplary authors for the statistical approach are Xavier Sala-i-Martin and Robert Barro, and for the historical approach David Landes and Gregory Clark.

[3] Additionally, in Sala-i-Martin's papers the dependent variable (growth? interval? source?) was not always described and standardised coefficients were missing, making comparisons across determinants difficult.

or less freedom, rule of law or education? Historically transient factors such as the demographic dividend (percentually large workforce and few dependents) in China from 1980 to 2030 are not considered.

A totally different approach is the historical one of David Landes (1972/ 1969, 1998). The development paths of single countries and regions were described and compared across centuries. Determinants of wealth may change with history and local conditions, e.g. water, timber and coal were important in the past, and later oil and technological progress became so. Culture and climate, and especially economic systems and institutions, are important determinants. However, there is no clear elaborated theory. Depending on time and country, different factors are stressed.

Clear positions can be found in the following paradigms: economic freedom, quality of institutions (both internal), geography and dependency (both external materialistic).

### 5.2.1   Economic Freedom (Capitalism)

Adam Smith (1982/1776) is the pioneer of economic freedom research. He saw four factors as the major causes of wealth: specialisation (the division of labour), economic freedom (competition), market size and trade. *Specialisation* (or division of labour) means that individuals and companies focus on single products, leading to a cheaper and larger amount of selected goods with high quality. *Economic freedom* stands for free economic decisions, such as in production, prices and trade, stimulating production and quality. *Market size* and *trade* reduce costs and increase the amount and variety of goods.

*Economic freedom* can be seen as the background factor of all four: the possibility to offer and choose jobs and goods, to trade, low taxes and tariffs and private property within a legal frame automatically lead to specialisation, larger markets and more trade. Economic freedom also means rule of law – no use of force, no fraud and no theft. The term *'capitalism'* describes the same concept as economic freedom but with a stronger focus on competition and private property. The 'invisible hand' of the market means that the efforts of individuals and companies to maximise their private gains are beneficial for the entire society.[4] Factors of production are allocated in an optimal way, demands are satisfied in an optimal way and the price is the indicator of shortage and stimulus for production.[5]

---

[4] Adam Smith's *Inquiry into the Nature and Causes of the Wealth of Nations* deals with further issues, e.g. commodities, infrastructure, prices, money and burgher ethics.

[5] Adam Smith (1723–1790) as a scientist and 'moral philosopher' was intellectually an unpretentious person guided by common sense. E.g. his aim was only 'to give at least a probable answer to each of those questions' (1982/1776, p. 588).

Later authors such as Mises (1996/1927), Hayek (2011/1960), Friedman (1962), Hoppe (2001) and Weede (2011) stressed the general positive social and political effects of a free market economy and society: trade produces peace; markets make people more rational and ethical; markets themselves, before any redistribution, are orientated towards the needs of customers and are therefore social.

The evidence for the positive effects of economic freedom on wealth is overwhelming: economic freedom and production per capita (GDP/c) are positively correlated ($r = .60$-$.70$, $N = 160$–$180^6$). Political experiments in formerly united societies underscore the causal impact: South Korea is much richer than North Korea ($20,469 vs. $1,416) and former West Germany was much richer than East Germany (GDP/c in US $ around 23,530 vs. 9,100).[7] Economic freedom is also positively correlated with political liberty, rule of law, democracy, psychological wellbeing, trust, peace, low crime rates and gender equality. Cross-sectionally and longitudinally, economic freedom shows positive effects on wealth and its development (Rindermann, 2008a, 2012).[8] Finally, economic freedom increases the effects of cognitive ability on economic outcomes, especially via larger intellectual classes' effects on innovation and competitiveness in free economies (Rindermann & Coyle, 2014).[9]

However, that is not the whole picture.[10] In empirical studies, cognitive ability and not economic freedom is the more relevant factor. Adopted from others, e.g. from former colonial powers, not only self-developed economic systems and the necessary political, legal and administrative institutions have a positive impact on economy (e.g. Feyrer & Sacerdote, 2009). But they need to be understood, accepted, valued and practised. To be a successful market player it is required to be a *rational actor*: to appropriately assess one's own competences and needs and those of others, to appropriately assess the quality of products and competences of others, to take responsibility for one's actions and their outcomes. The rational and autonomous citizen is the prerequisite for the success of freedom, whether it be economic or political.

---

[6] Sources for economic freedom: Fraser index (Gwartney, Lawson & Hall, 2013), Heritage index (Miller, Holmes & Feulner, 2013) and Sala-i-Martin (1997); for GDP and GNI, Maddison, Penn and HDR (see Table 1.1).

[7] Source for within-Korea comparison: Maddison; for Germany: http://de.statista.com/statistik/daten/ studie/249689/umfrage/vergleich-von-west-und-ostdeutschland-vor-der-wiedervereinigung.

[8] Economic freedom correlates strongest with rule of law (at $r = .78$; $N = 153$), lowest with *low* murder rates (at $r = .20$; $N = 167$). In between are: political liberty: $r = .65$; $N = 183$; democracy: $r = .61$; $N = 181$; wellbeing: $r = .58$; $N = 149$; trust: $r = .34$; $N = 115$; peace: $r = .28$; $N = 163$; gender equality: $r = .37$; $N = 135$. Longitudinal effects on wealth controlled for cognitive ability: $\beta_{EF \rightarrow GDP} = .23/.10/.15/.00$, on average $\beta_{EF \rightarrow GDP} = .16$. Sources see Chapter 2.4.

[9] Also, there are larger effects of average cognitive ability in freer economies; see Zajenkowski, Stolarski & Meisenberg (2013) or Hanushek & Woessmann (2015a, p. 58f.).

[10] 'Das Wahre ist das Ganze.' ('The truth is the whole.'; Hegel, 1999/1807, p. 19).

At least partly, Smith and others have committed the complimentary error that others are similar to themselves. But cultures and peoples differ in the shaping of the anthropological conditions for economic action. Smith himself has hinted at it on the very first page of his *Inquiry into the Nature and Causes of the Wealth of Nations*:

This proportion must in every nation be regulated by two different circumstances; first, by the skill, dexterity, and judgment with which its labour is generally applied; and, secondly, by the proportion between the number of those who are employed in useful labour, and that of those who are not so employed. (Smith, 1982/1776, p. 4)

'Skill, dexterity, and judgment' are paraphrases of competence and rationality. So ability, including cognitive ability, was seen by the Nestor of economic research as the fundamental requirement for a successful economy.

A second qualification is necessary for *government interventions*, which are usually negatively estimated in economic freedom approaches. As the examples of Japan and Singapore have shown, competent government interventions could have a benign effect on economic development. And government effectiveness correlates stronger with GDP/c than economic freedom ($r = .85$ vs. $.66$, $N = 155$ same countries).[11]

### 5.2.2 Quality of Institutions

Quality of institutions – in a broader sense also including infrastructure – is related to economic freedom (North, 1990; 'open access orders'; North et al., 2009). Therefore, attributes such as property rights, rule of law and (low) taxation are indicators of both economic freedom and institutional quality. By comparison, quality of institutions stresses the *active* role of a state, whereas economic freedom focuses on a night-watchman state securing Smiths invisible hand of the market. Empirical studies show a strong and positive effect of institutions on wealth (Acemoglu & Robinson, 2012). Variables such as rule of law, low corruption and government effectiveness are positively correlated with wealth ($r = .70$ to $.85$, $N = 160$ to $189$).[12]

Institutions, their development and quality are not only the responsibility of the state, but also of companies and general society. For example, low corruption, crime detection and functionality of administration depend on the actions of all three mentioned. Even more fundamentally, attributes of people enable the development and functionality of institutions; especially relevant is cognitive ability (using education as proxy: Glaeser et al., 2004).

[11] Data around year 2010, government effectiveness from Kaufmann et al. (2010, 2012 update); GDP per capita from Maddison; economic freedom see Chapter 2.4.
[12] Data around year 2010: rule of law and government effectiveness from Kaufmann et al. (2010, 2012 update); corruption from Transparency International (2012); GDP/c from Maddison, Penn and HDR.

### 5.2.3   Geography

Geography comprises long- to short-term conditions of climate, location and natural resources. Natural resources cover organic and inorganic resources. Best-known for this position is Jared Diamond (1997): his central position is that all peoples are equal in endowed abilities and attitudes and that the huge wealth and accomplishment differences observable today can be explained by decidedly external-materialistic differences in geography, climate and natural resources, which led to economic differences. His central premise is best summarised in this sentence: 'The reasons had nothing to do with differences in the peoples themselves.'[13]

According to Diamond, around 10,000 BCE all peoples lived at a similar level of development. But then those regions that had environmental advantages advanced. These were regions with more, easier and more productive to domesticate plants and animals – especially in the Fertile Crescent. And those regions had an advantage which had better possibilities of travel, trade and expansion across similar climates: the east-west axis in Eurasia contrary to the unfavourable north-south axis across different climatic zones in Africa and America. This led to higher wealth and population density, finally resulting in complex states and cities in which ideas could spread more easily, including technology development and military equipment. Infectious diseases and evolutionary adaptations to them spread too.

Maybe Diamond's model is correct. *But what has that got to do with wealth today?* Since the Stone Age and the first domestications and civilisations enough time has gone by. Today with the help of modern technology, every region in the world has access to all kinds of food, commodities and information. Why should anything that happened 200 or 2,000 or 12,000 years ago have any enduring impact? This past is theoretically irrelevant for modern economy, unless ... unless the past has shaped the competences and attitudes of peoples and individuals of today. And this mechanism has to be *cultural* or *genetic* or *both*!

Of course, if a present-day nation possesses a lot of in-demand resources and has a small population, this nation and its average inhabitant are likely to do well in terms of wealth. These circumstances exist for the small Emirates,

---

[13] www.jareddiamond.org. Diamond's work suffers from strong political considerations (see Section 14.2). A scientific book cannot be begun with a political premise; if so, it is not a scientific work.

Additionally, Jared Diamond's book shares with David Landes' work one common strength and problem: both are well-written narrative books; however, they lack systematic numerical data and analysis. Of course, records of historical data and their interpretation are part of science as a cognitive enterprise based on epistemic rationality, but numerical data and mathematical-statistical analyses enable a gain in objectivity and precision.

somewhat less for Saudi Arabia and Norway and less still for Iran, Russia and Nigeria – the latter three nations' population sizes are too large for gaining high per capita incomes through commodities. However, as the cases of Spain and Portugal (gold and other precious metals from America) and of Nauru (phosphate) have shown, there were no positive sustainable effects of resources. To the contrary: the mid- and long-term effects were even negative, because the resource extraction was accompanied by an effect of deindustrialisation. This problem was therefore called 'Spanish' (gold extraction) and 'Dutch disease' (gas extraction). This effect can be explained (more proximally) by economic and (more distally) by cultural-attitudinal influences:

According to the *economic explanation* (Corden & Neary, 1982), large natural resource exports will raise the value of a nation's currency. This rise will make exports of other goods more expensive and the import of other countries' goods cheaper. Apart from produced raw materials, refined goods such as textiles, machines and consumer goods are traded. Because manufacturing sector products will become relatively more expensive the country's own industry will decline, but the other countries' industries will flourish. And this will have long-term effects on production and probably on human capital development.

A *cultural-attitudinal explanation* was given by Landes (1998). In abbreviated form – abundance makes idle, whereas necessity begets ingenuity, diligence and competence:

Spain, in other words, became (or stayed) poor because it had too much money. The nations that did the work learned and kept good habits, while seeking new ways to do the job faster and better. The Spanish, on the other hand, indulged their penchant for status, leisure, and enjoyment – what Carlo Cipolla calls 'the prevalent *hidalgo* mentality.' . . .

By the time the great bullion inflow had ended in the mid-seventeenth century, the Spanish crown was deep in debt, with bankruptcies in 1557, 1575, and 1597. The country entered upon a long decline. Reading this story, one might draw a moral: Easy money is bad for you. It represents short-run gain that will be paid for in immediate distortions and later regrets. (Landes, 1998, p. 173)

Nothing so concentrates the mind as lack of money. (Landes, 1998, p. 363)

In modernity, geographic advantages such as pleasant climate, proximity to markets and abundant resources become less important. We have heating and air conditioning, mosquito nets, good transport infrastructure and human capital. Cases such as Switzerland, Iceland, Singapore and Utah exemplify it.

### 5.2.4   Dependency

The power of nations is unequally distributed. According to Kurian (2001, p. 66f., based on Ray Cline's World Power Assessment around 1999), the

United States is the most powerful country, followed by Russia and Brazil. Of the 35 countries mentioned, Iraq, Syria and Iran are the least powerful ones. Power depends on population size, production, military and political endeavours based on history and culture. More developed First World countries are more powerful than less developed Third World countries. Greater power enables stronger influence on the 'terms of trade', contracts and regulations. Whether this is good or bad and for whom, is an open question. Readers may ponder whether it would be better for, e.g. East and Southeast Asian countries and even for the Chinese people themselves if China had more power than the United States. Similarly, it could be asked whether it would be good for Africans if the power structures between the West and Africa were reversed. Research has provided evidence for positive effects of the West: Feyrer and Sacerdote (2009, p. 245) found for 81 Islands including those inhabited by Africans a 'strong connection between modern income and years of colonization' – they explain it by reference to the effects of established institutions.[14]

Dependency theory assumes that economic asymmetries are based at least partly on power asymmetries.[15] Power asymmetries stabilise economic asymmetries, which again reinforce power asymmetries. External rather than internal factors are seen as decisive for underdevelopment. Richer core countries ('metropolis') profit from the underdevelopment of the periphery ('satellite'). The wealth of the rich is supported by the poverty of the others. The idea is somewhat based on the epoch of colonialism. Here the colonies, so the approach goes, were forced to only deliver raw materials for the colonial powers, which forced the colonies to buy their refined goods. After decolonisation, the pattern remained or even became worse because multinational corporations and elites within the former colonies started to participate in exploitation and because the terms of trade deteriorated: developing countries receive fewer refined goods for their commodities compared to the past.

---

[14] To avoid any possible misunderstanding, it should be underlined that the Western world has not always treated others within and outside its hemisphere in an ethically appropriate way. Persons on slave ships, in Hiroshima and Dresden in 1945, in My Lai in 1968 or Algerians in 1961 in Paris would certainly agree. If the Third Reich is included in the West, then Auschwitz from 1940 to 1945 is the most salient negative case. All these occurrences were opposed to the (by origin occidental) idea of human rights. Theoretically more fundamental is a critique on immanent Western developments, e.g. if the initiated modernisation is ecologically, socially and culturally sustainable, or an aesthetical critique of modernity. This critique is also a result of modernisation – self-reflection and self-critique are distinguishing attributes of Western culture rooted in Protestant-Christian ideas.

[15] Exponents of dependency and related theories are, for instance, André Gunder Frank (1967), Fernando Henrique Cardoso (Cardoso & Faletto, 1979) and Immanuel Wallerstein (2004). Dependency theory has a more cautious scientific and a less cautious political-media branch.

Of course, the rich countries are only rich because there are poor countries! *Richness is a relative term and without less rich ones the rich would neither be nor feel rich.* Taking a historical perspective, today around 99 per cent of all people are much richer than people were 1,000 or 10,000 years ago. On average, we live longer, are healthier, more children survive, and we have access to modern technology and information. We live today in the best of all until-now-existing worlds, and this is due to inventiveness and progress in technology, organisation and lived values (e.g. McCloskey, 2010).

In which region did this progress start? For instance, the development of antibiotics (Fleming, British-Scottish), the separation of powers (England and France) and human rights (modern concept based on antique, Christian, Renaissance and Enlightenment ethics)? Additionally, there are pull-factors caused by the existence of more developed nations: the so called 'advantages of backwardness': less developed countries can adopt innovations from more developed countries. Adoption is easier, quicker and cheaper than initial invention. Trade with developed nations is more lucrative for developed countries than trade with less developed ones; e.g. the trade between Germany and Japan is larger than the trade between Germany and all of sub-Saharan Africa.[16]

Any predatory capitalism, theft and seizures had and have no long-term wealth effects for the agents, e.g. Spain (robberies in America, see above), Belgium (exploitation in the Congo ended in debts), or Russia, Poland and Czechoslovakia (annexation politics after Second World War). The Germans that were expropriated and expelled were richer a decade later than the former expropriators.[17]

Colonial powers did not produce goods in colonies but rather in the motherland because production in developed countries was cheaper and resulted in higher quality products sought after by consumers. The British did not produce textiles in India because they wanted to exploit India but because it was cheaper to transport cotton from India to Britain, pay higher wages to British workers and ship the textiles back than to produce in India! As the economist Gregory Clark has described:

Indian mills by comparison were undisciplined. This lack of discipline and high absenteeism continued at least into the 1960s. ... A substantial fraction of workers were absent on any given day, and those at work were often able to come and go from the mill at their pleasure to eat or to smoke. ... The mill yards would have eating places, barbers, drink shops, and other facilities to serve the workers taking a break. Some mothers

---

[16] Germany sold products worth 17 billion Euro to Japan in 2012 and bought 22 billion US Dollars' worth (source: ahk.de). Germany sold products worth 14 billion Euro to sub-Saharan Africa in 2012 and bought 13 billion Euros' worth (source: www.gtai.de).

[17] This is, of course, only true for the average and the pains and grief of the individual victims were dreadful.

allegedly brought their children with them to the mills. . . . One manager even stated that the typical worker 'washes, bathes, washes his clothes, smokes, shaves, sleeps, has his food, and is surrounded as a rule by his relations.' . . . Customs [. . .] allowed workers to read newspapers inside departments, [. . .] to sleep inside departments, and [to keep] children within the departments. By the mid-nineteenth century in England no textile mill would have allowed any of these practices. (Clark, 2007, p. 363f.)

Dependency theories cannot explain the rise of East Asian countries. And of course, they need to explain *why* there is asymmetric power. That asymmetric power boosts international differences should not be neglected. At the same time, developing countries can learn from more developed ones and benefit from their technological, social and cultural progress.

Finally, it is dysfunctional to politically or ethically criticise external conditions. As David Landes (1998, p. 328) has mentioned:

*Dependentista* arguments have flourished in Latin America. They have also traveled well, resonating after World War II with the economic plight and political awareness of newly liberated colonies. Cynics might even say that dependency doctrines have been Latin America's most successful export. Meanwhile they are bad for effort and morale. By fostering a morbid propensity to find fault with everyone but oneself, they promote economic impotence. *Even if they were true, it would be better to stow them.*

## 5.3   Interplay of Proximal and Distal Factors

All the given approaches did not model the interdependence between factors. But the factors are conceptually related (e.g. economic freedom and rule of law), historically linked (e.g. Protestantism and rule of law), empirically correlated (e.g. latitude and wealth) and causally determined (e.g. cognitive competence and productivity). They form a connected net. There are more general, distal, abstract factors and more specific, proximal, concrete factors (e.g. culture vs. tariffs).

Therefore, simple correlational or regressional methods are not satisfactory. But they gave first hints towards important factors. Mere historical approaches are also unsatisfactory. They do not adequately weight the importance of factors compared to others. However, they have theoretical strengths. They explain why and how certain factors work and they can elucidate single developments. Experiments are only possible for small-scale theories being tested in controlled laboratory environments.

The best solution is to develop theoretically based path models. They depict causal dependence among determinants, describe importance relative to other factors, and include indirect effects of determinants by influencing others leading to an impact on final criteria. If data are given, reciprocal effects can be estimated, e.g. of competence on wealth and of wealth on competence. Historical processes can be modelled and quantitatively assessed. Finally, effects found in natural experiments can be controlled for further factors.

# 6    History, Culture and the Burgher-Civic World

The broad field of culture will be defined and structured. World-view is the core of culture. Culture has a strong impact on the development of economy and politics and especially on education and competence. The central concept of 'burgher-civic' culture and its influence on societal wellbeing will be described. Finally, modernisation is understood as the result of reciprocal effects between culture, education, competence, society, institutions and economy best visualised as a spiral.

## 6.1    Worldview as the Core of Culture

What is culture? Culture is a worldview ('Weltanschauung') that *describes* nature, humans, society and a spiritual world and the relationship of humans towards them. Additionally, culture *prescribes* values for individuals, groups and entire nations, guiding their way of thinking and living. Finally, culture *shapes* via influencing thinking and behaviour the physical, social and mental environment and the life of individuals and groups. Culture as 'cultures' in the plural stands for distinctive characteristics including differences across time. What in a more everyday use of the term is seen as culture, e.g. eating and clothing habits, artefacts, works of art, architecture, literature and music, are the more tangible and easier to observe manifestations of culture, but they do not constitute the core of culture. In the core are the descriptive, normative and shaping worldviews.

Why are worldviews in the core? Styles in artefacts and clothing habits, in architecture and arts may quickly and entirely vary across time, e.g. in nineteenth-century Europe and at the end of the twentieth century or in Japan at the beginning and end of the nineteenth century or in China in the twentieth century. Eating habits largely differ and are more robust, but eating pizza or horsemeat, pork or beef, dog meat or mutton has hardly any impact on other spheres of life and society. By contrast, assumptions on the relationship between the individual, family and society or on education, conduct and aims of life are more stable and have an enduring and, on other aspects of life and society, spreading impact. Of course, they are subject to alteration too, but, for example, individualism was more stressed in Europe than in Asia in the past as well as is in the present.[1] The distinctive esteem of education held by Protestantism is still observable in international and, within Central Europe, regional comparisons (Weber, 2001/1905; Becker & Woessmann, 2009; Steppan, 2010).

### 6.1.1  Misunderstandings, Development and Components

Unfortunately, culture is frequently used as a diffuse and global category, as a hollow word and empty phrase, sometimes like a kind of devotional literature to avoid scrutiny in research. In this form, the concept of culture is neither informative nor useful. We need concrete assumptions on working factors and their effects.

Of course, culture is not monolithic. In societies there are subgroups with different convictions and habits, e.g. in Great Britain there are, among others, the English and the Scots. And cultures develop in history depending on the general causes which create culture and cultural differences. Environmental and genetic, social and, especially, cognitive and culture-inherent factors becoming a process with their own internal dynamics change cultures: For instance, where production and reproduction depend on co-operation more strongly, a stronger expression of collectivism is expected (e.g. rice vs. wheat farming; Talhelm et al., 2014). A diversified political organisation in secular and spiritual powers, in countries and cities, in local authorities and a weaker centre, stimulates liberal, meritoric and individualistic orientations (Weede, 2014). Smart people will develop more cognitively demanding and rational worldviews (Oesterdiekhoff, 2012c). A religion that stresses education, individual examination and thinking inherently has the tendency towards further subgroup formation and questioning of religious foundations (Albert, 1985/1968). Examples and neighbours influence culture.

Culture as a mental world comprises (more) transcendent religion and (more) immanent worldviews, philosophy, science, language, the arts and everyday life orientations and behaviour styles. Culture corresponds to instrumental and functional attributes of societies such as the economy, law, state, technology, health system and military. And culture corresponds to social traditions such as customs and habits, codes of conduct and fashion. Culture is reflected in persons and societies, in values and artefacts, in competences

---

[1] Philosophers standing, in their lifestyle and philosophy, for individualism, e.g. Jean-Jacques Rousseau, Max Stirner, Henry David Thoreau, Friedrich Nietzsche, Søren Kierkegaard, Ayn Rand. Current data for individualism, e.g. China 20 vs. USA 91, Japan 46 vs. Germany 67, India 48 vs. UK 89. Retrieved 21 June 2014 from the Geert Hofstede Centre Internet page, scale 0–100 with 50 as a midlevel (http://geert-hofstede.com).

and attitudes, in preferences and actions. Culture is transmitted and picked up, developed and at least partly acquired from others. Cognitive competence, intelligence and knowledge, transform culture. But they do not work independently from handed-down worldviews and given social environments and their modelled culture. Religion as a descriptive and normative worldview shaping individuals and institutions is an important part of culture.

## 6.2　　Religion, Thinking and Society

Religion is related to the holy and transcendent, and comprises at its core belief in the numinous: something not in the material world. Religions give sense and therefore orientation and guidance. So on the one hand, religions are about everything but this world. On the other hand, they are very much about it. Religions cover transcendental and secular contents, are blended with tradition and are subject to historical development in contents, their interpretation and practice.

There is not always a clear separation between religions and non-religious worldviews and ethics – for some Buddhists, Buddhism is a philosophy. Confucianism has only a few transcendental contents; it is as much or little a religion as the Nicomachean Ethics of Aristotle. Subsuming them all under the concept 'Weltanschauung' renders such differences less relevant. Both religions and non-religious worldviews, provide sense and order, give reasons for goals and provide orientation in everyday thinking and life.

Religions usually began with a founder such as Confucius, Buddha, Jesus or Muhammad, a historical person having created a certain doctrine and having found followers who sent out the message into the world. With the passage of time, the doctrine was interpreted by scholars, partially systematized and developed further, e.g. in Christianity by Augustine, Thomas Aquinas and Martin Luther. Religion shapes the spirit of a time but is not independent from it. Religion is an evolving idea in time.

Religion has an effect by its (1) *original message*, by the (2) *role model function of its founder*, by the (3) *revised doctrine and its transformed understanding* and by its (4) *lived practice*.

The lived practice depends on the original message and is an empirical proof of its ideas, but it also depends on the behaviour of the founder, on revisions of the doctrine and its transformed understanding and, of course, on further cultural, historical, sociological and psychological factors, including intelligence.

For this study, the real world impact of religions on thinking and behaviour of people and the forming of society and culture is relevant, rather than the core of religion, belief in God and the holy. Especially relevant is religions' *impact on cognitive ability* and its development; and religions' *impact, independent from cognitive ability, on economic productivity* and *on develop-ing and supporting the modern burgher world.*

Religious convictions are not directly relevant for cognitive ability, but indirectly and mediated via their attitudes towards learning and 'Bildung' (intellectual-ethical education), thinking, diligence and achievement and the forming of them at the level of individuals, families, institutions and society. They have an impact on personality and behaviour and via this on economy, e.g. via discipline, ambition, integrity and trustworthiness. They influence ability, personality, behaviour and general orientations relevant for rule of law, liberty and meritocracy. For example, liberty is not possible without self-discipline and the ability for autonomy. Do different religions have a different effect? How do the different effects evolve? What are the causes and how do they work?[2]

All religions initially are rather critical towards thinking. Salvation cannot be found via thinking, but via belief, meditation, a guided study of selected holy texts, charity or other works, sometimes including war, or a divine grace. Prophets and saints proclaim in a divine mission the holy truth which has to be indisputably accepted. All of this is not favourable for cognitive development, economic productivity, the forming of a burgher world and modernisation.

However, intended or not, some religions more than others have supported *cognitive education* by reading and understanding holy texts.[3] Similarly, intended or not, some religions more than others have supported *intellectual individualization* by the development of a personal, rather than mediated by institutions or priests, direct relationship to the numinous. This relationship is not only reached by worship or submission and by following given rules, but also by personally *understanding* the numinous. Unintentionally, some reli-gions became pathfinders for the development of thinking and of thinking for secular purposes, of the *burgher world* and of modernity.

Additionally, monastic cultures of reading, writing, discussing and arguing, constituted in the past, existed as the intellectual-cultural basis of a country, preserved its heritage, protected it in times of foreign domination and were intellectual centres of resistance, e.g. the Rila Monastery in Bulgaria, San Juan de la Peña in Spain, Arkadi in Creta and monasteries in Tibet. Monks

---

[2] These ideas of research go back to the works of Max Weber and Werner Sombart. Both worked at the beginning of the twentieth century on the relevance of religion for the forming of everyday life, institutions and society. Later on, materialistic and socio-structural thought styles became dominant. Contributions of Samuel Huntington and Lawrence Harrison have led in recent decades to a rediscovery of the relevance of religion.

[3] When speaking about education, most of the time we use the term in a narrower meaning of cognitive education. Education in its broader meaning includes interests and self-regulation, motivation and conduct. Every child was and is educated, even as regards education for slavery work, but not in the sense of a cognitive-intellectual education.

instructed others in reading, writing and mathematics. Monasteries were also founders of schools for layman and children.[4] Monks exercised argumentation and thinking in coherence of premise and conclusion. They translated, saved and read philosophical and scientific literature (e.g. Mont Saint-Michel; Gouguenheim, 2008). However, intellectual analysis, questions and answers, were constrained and questions were often only seen as a preparation for the preexisting answers.[5] What counted as argument was guided by tradition and holy texts.

Notwithstanding, the reading of texts was learnt and practiced, the understanding of texts having different semantic levels, rather than just memorizing the obvious content. Things are not only practical things, but have a meaning to be hermeneutically analysed, such as texts, graphs, concepts, art, music and architecture. All this was a complex and enduring cognitive training. Such activity was cognitively more demanding and stimulating than any other behaviour in premodernity such as herding, planting or repetitive craftsmanship. Intellectually, the world was perceived as something that could be understood by a coherent use of faith and thinking.

Certain religions constituted an influential driving force for modernization, weakening in this process their original message and strength. Biographically, it is best exemplified by the many scientists and intellectuals born in parsonages in nineteenth-century Germany (see Section 10.8.3). There is an inherent tension between religion and rationality, between revelation and thinking, between the doctrine, the result of thinking of others, and one's own thinking.[6] Thinking creates a dynamic that is barely controllable. However, even weakening religions still have an impact today on individual lives, society and culture, including those of non-religious people. They have a mediated effect from having changed customs, attitudes, institutions and worldviews.

### 6.2.1    One Example: Anshu Jain and Jainism

Let us look at one marginal example of a tiny and rarely known religion in India. Max Weber is, for some, an old and outdated scholar. He has written on religions in India but never went there. He did not understand the local

---

[4] Many Catholic orders saw their main purpose in education (Societas Iesu, Salesians of Don Bosco, Ursulines, Sacré-Cœur).

[5] A good example of this thinking, questioning and argumentation is the work of Thomas Aquinas, *Summa Theologica*; starting with a question (quaestio), then objections (objectiones), then confrontation with statements from the bible and by saints (sed contra) and finally finding an own answer (respondeo). However, he rather asks questions in a rhetorical way, like a teacher knowing the answer before asking the pupils.

[6] A similar tension exists between epistemic rationality and political-ideological orientations or between epistemic rationality and science as a mere routine job following given procedures. Arguing, proving and reasoning cannot be avoided.

languages. Limited in several aspects, was it possible for him to gain any insight into the attributes and effects of religions? And have the conditions and beliefs not 'radically' changed since then?

In Germany, we have a strange occurrence: the largest, most important and internationally best known German bank, a bulwark of national identity, was headed by an Indian from 2012 to 2015, Anshu Jain, who could not even speak German. There was no other German company and no known local branch bank led by a foreigner. Furthermore, India is known for receiving development aid, extensive poverty and, compared to Western countries, high levels of corruption, plus relatively low average cognitive ability – and a person from such a country with this reputation was entrusted with heading the largest German bank?[7] That seems to be less likely than Arnold Schwarzenegger becoming president of the United States.

Who is Anshu Jain? He was also considerably young (born 1963). At the age of 49, he was nominated as chairman at the Deutsche Bank. Anshu Jain belongs to the Jains as people and Jainism as a religion. This is a tiny and rarely known religion in India. Despite constituting such a small culture or weltanschauung, Max Weber also covered it in his research on religions and their social impact.

In one chapter, Max Weber (1958/1921, p. 193ff.) described Jainism as a 'specifically merchant sect', having 'a positive relationship of a confession to economic motivation which is otherwise quite foreign in Hinduism' and showing an effect on efficiency in organising life (p. 193). Weber explicitly compared them to Jews, who had and still have a leading role in the world of finance. According to Weber, Jains treat knowledge as the greatest good ('knowledge is the supreme', p. 195). To have knowledge it is necessary to acquire it, and this is only possible by learning and facilitated by higher intelligence, diligence and self-discipline. Jainism is characterised by a very strict ethic. Everything that could kill an animal is prohibited. Thus any occupation related to agriculture would be impossible.

People must not lie, not steal nor misappropriate the property of others (p. 200). This is nothing special, but is taken more seriously in Jainism, making Jains more trustworthy – an especially desirable characteristic in banking and financial operations. Absolute honesty in business was demanded; any dishonest economic activity such as contraband, bribery and forgery was strictly forbidden.

---

[7] Among 178 countries with data on freedom from corruption, India is at position 88, between Albania and Jamaica. At the top are Denmark, New Zealand and Singapore. Among the top ten countries are eight traditionally Protestant countries. Germany is at rank 15. Among the last ten countries are animist, Muslim and mixed animist-Muslim countries (Equatorial Guinea, Burundi, Chad, Sudan, Turkmenistan, Uzbekistan, Iraq, Afghanistan, Burma, Somalia). Source: Transparency International, www.transparency.org/cpi2010/results.

Jains believed in absolute honesty in business life, all deception was prohibited, including especially all dishonest gain through smuggling, bribery; and any sort of disreputable financial practice ... The honesty of the Jain trader was famous. Their wealth was also famous; formerly it has been maintained that more than half the trade of India passed through their hands. (Weber, 1958/1921, p. 200)

Jains should not be rich; joy at wealth was reprehensible. They should use their wealth for charity. But similar to Puritans, the acquisition of wealth was not prohibited. Having more meant one could spend more for charity, leading via social signalling to higher reputation. However, there is some inconsistency, as in other religions.

Jainism supported *cognitive development* by regarding knowledge as the highest good and by valuing behaviour relevant to knowledge acquisition. Jainism supported important traits and attitudes for *economic productivity*, favouring work in offices, integrity, honesty and efficiency. These abilities and attitudes also further the *burgher world and modernisation*, e.g. the rule of law, democracy and equality. This does not mean that all Jains are smart, honest and become heads of banks, but it means that Jains – due to their worldview and how it translates into ability and behaviour – relative to members of other religions tend towards this direction. No more but also no less.[8]

The *experimentum crucis* turned out in favour of religion as an enduring factor relevant to the development of human capital and economic success and in favour of Max Weber, supporting his 100-year-old studies as a reliable source on religion. Of course, *one case* and *one rather small religion* are not enough for building the fundamental basis for a cognitive capital and modernisation theory but they give hints that 'Weltanschauung', ideologies and worldviews, mental factors, are relevant in the real and present world. What have been found in single historical and in-depth qualitative analyses should be proved in statistical analyses at the cross-country level.

Religion is important for understanding why nations developed differently in cognitive, economic, social, political and cultural aspects. Religion is especially relevant because different religions differently facilitated or impeded the emergence of conditions relevant for modernisation in cognitive, behavioural, economic, political and cultural realms: the burgher-civic world.

---

[8] Additional and broader (but less illustrative) support could provide statistics on Jains compared to other religions in India. According to the 2001 Indian census and compared to other religions, Jains had 'the highest literacy rate' (94.1 per cent; source: Government of India, http://pib.nic.in/newsite/erelease.aspx?relid=3724). Other reports indicate high income (indirectly by high taxes or jobs in the financial world). Higher wealth also led in the past to more surviving offspring.

## 6.3 The Burgher-Civic World

The concept of a burgher-civic worldview was first explicitly described by Leon Battista Alberti (1969/1441). Roots of this thinking can be traced back to Thomas Aquinas and Aristotle. Philosophers and intellectuals such as John Locke (*Two Treatises of Government*), Benjamin Franklin (*Autobiography*), Georg Wilhelm Friedrich Hegel (*Elements of the Philosophy of Right*) or John Stuart Mill (*On Liberty*) are later forerunners. However, it would be wrong to assume that the burgher world is an intellectual-theoretical phenomenon. Usually it even has no name – e.g. Alberti only described but did not name it. And who has heard of Alberti?[9] The burgher world is an amalgamation of successful practice with theoretical-normative particles, but it is not an abstract intellectual concept. It was furthered by certain motives and values that facilitated thinking, individualism and achievement. It initially developed in cities and their merchant milieus and then spread within societies – see Werner Sombart's decisive work '*Bourgeois*', in English '*The Quintessence of Capitalism: A Study of the History and Psychology of the Modern Business Man*' (Sombart, 1998/1913). The occurrence of certain aspects and the general development of this worldview depend on country, culture and time.

'Burgher', 'middle class', 'bourgeois', 'civic' or 'civil' attributes, the terms can be used interchangeably, comprise at their core certain lifestyles, personality traits, forms of society and worldviews:

- *Appreciation, education and use of thinking, knowledge and rationality* (practical use of thinking for problem-solving, planning and calculation, only marginally for free reflection).
- *Diligence* (achievement motivation and behaviour).
- *Order* (predictability; reliability; fair-mindedness; emotional regulation, temperance, couth and moderateness, discipline and self-discipline; long-term marriage and familial stability; rule of law in politics).
- *Meritoric orientations* (acknowledgement of and gratification derived from accomplishment; merit-based criteria used in the distribution of jobs, income, and reputation; use of achievement measurement).[10]
- *Beneficial, efficient, thrifty use of resources* (in terms of time, raw materials and people).

---

[9] Even Deirdre McCloskey, who wrote thousands of pages on bourgeois culture, does not cite, and therefore seems not to know, Alberti's pioneering work.

[10] The term 'meritoric' is used, rather than 'meritocratic', to stress the meaning 'gains by competence and achievement' and not 'reign of the best'. 'Meritoric' is not equal to 'just'. 'Meritoric' means honouring and rewarding competence and achievement, but this does not only belong to factors influenceable by an individual. Genes play a part, chance too, and society differently honours comparable achievement, e.g. being an excellent tennis player has a totally different impact on one's life outcome than being an excellent table tennis player.

- *Rule of law* (law-abiding by individuals and institutions; human rights and property rights; related to order at the individual level).
- *Functional government* (effective government and administration orientated towards pragmatism and legal and ethical norms).
- *Balanced autonomy and freedom* (self-responsibility in terms of the individual, family, economy and society, which must sustain themselves, balanced between the individual, family and society).
- *Realism and pragmatism* (realistic orientation in the world and in life; no extremism in thinking and life; common sense, adaptability, functionality, compromise, prudence, foresight).
- *Burgher worldviews* ('*Weltanschauung*' or orientations that contain the aforementioned attributes as norms and descriptions; rationality, liberty, equality, moderateness, functionality, efficiency, order, meritocracy, responsibility, autonomy).[11]

In Section 4.4 ('Everyday Life Evidence and Sediments'), we presented a longer quote from Alberti on well-structured and efficient use of time that gives a typical example of a burgher-civic worldview and lifestyle. Two further illustrations of thinking, autonomy, realism, modesty and honesty:

I have tried all my life to know things by experience, and not to count much on what others have said. I know what I know more from the actual truth of it than from anyone's persuading me. If one of those people who spend all day reading says to me, 'this is how it is', I believe him only if I see a reason for believing it. I like a reason which amounts to a clear demonstration rather than an argument which forces me to admit a point. If another, an uneducated person, gives me the same reason for the same thing, I will believe him without his citing authorities, just as much as I would the man who gives me evidence from a book. I assume the writer of a book was only a man like myself. (Alberti, Book III, p. 171)

Be honest, fair, and friendly with everyone who comes in, with strangers no less than with friends. Be truthful and precise at all times. Beware that no one ever, through your

---

[11] Related models were used to explain development in the twentieth century, e.g. by the sociologist Mariano Grondona (2000). Cultural factors supporting development are, e.g. 'competition', 'value of work', 'questioning mind', 'utility', 'rationality' and 'lesser virtues': 'Advanced societies esteem a series of lesser virtues that are often irrelevant in traditional cultures: a job well done, tidiness, courtesy, punctuality. These contribute both to efficiency and harmony in human relations' (p. 51).

Deirdre McCloskey (2006) gave an alternative overview on burgher-civic virtues. However, her '*bourgeois virtues*' stress Christian ('faith, hope, love') and heroic hunter-warrior virtues ('courage') too much. Regarding 'prudence' (prudence and practical use of thinking; a concept being important also for Adam Smith, 2004/1759, p. 248) and 'temperance' (moderateness) we came to similar conclusions, and regarding 'justice' if merit-based criteria and equality are stressed. The entire range of core burgher values such as order, diligence, functionality, efficiency, meritocracy, pragmatism, rationality, freedom, autonomy and responsibility is not mentioned.

roughness or malice, leaves your shop feeling cheated or discontented. ... I should command them also to sell nothing at an extra high price. Whether confronted by a creditor or a debtor, they would be told always to remember to be fair and square with everyone. They must not be proud or spiteful or negligent or quarrelsome, and above all they must be most diligent in keeping records. (Alberti, Book III, p. 196)

A final example, indicating internal steering, family values, efficient-thrifty use of resources and intelligent-rational orientations is given by David Landes, the famous economic historian, describing his own thoughts after buying an expensive watch in Paris:

I didn't sleep that night. Not for pleasure at my acquisition but for guilt at spending so much. On myself, no less. Was this reasonable behavior for the father of a family? The next morning I did what I should have done before I bought the watch: I went comparison shopping. (Landes, 1983, p. XII)

Why is the burgher-civic world important for understanding cognitive capitalism, economic development and the development of wealth differences? Because it represents and shapes the orientations, norms, competences and behaviour patterns essentially important for creating the peoples, institutions, norms and customs relevant for the modern economy. Without the appreciation, education and use of thinking, knowledge and rationality, without diligence, order, meritoric orientations, the beneficial-efficient-thrifty use of resources, the rule of law, a functional government, autonomy and freedom, realism and pragmatism, and without all of them reinforcing and stabilising burgher worldviews, there is no durable modern society and economy and no self-produced wealth.

## 6.4   Reciprocal Causality Leading to Modernisation

The fundamental thesis is that at the beginning of an enduring development stands an impetus given by a worldview. A worldview and its changes are evoked by single intellectuals. Its dissemination is advanced by natural and societal conditions. Development interacts between worldviews, attitudes, lived practice, intelligence and knowledge and their transfer in families and schools, institutions and society. These factors and units of development influence each other and push themselves forward with mutual impact. Development creates development. Development continues independently from its initial impetus and motives. Small triggers can have huge effects over the course of centuries. Development is based on former development and transforms its own fundamentals. Development becomes a process with its own internal dynamics (see Figure 6.1).

This development is a process of modernisation usually going forward, sometimes being interrupted, sometimes going backward for a while, having

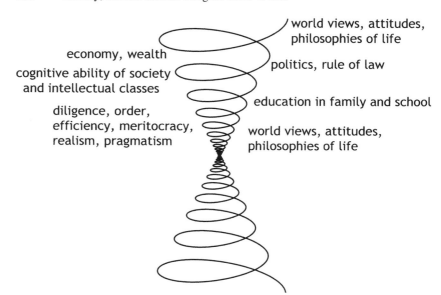

economy, wealth
cognitive ability of society
and intellectual classes
    diligence, order,
    efficiency, meritocracy,
    realism, pragmatism

world views, attitudes,
philosophies of life

politics, rule of law

education in family and school

world views, attitudes,
philosophies of life

Figure 6.1 Macrosocial process of development including worldview, society
and the individual

in the past a strong internal dynamism pushing the development ahead.
Modernisation includes individuals and society, thinking and behaviour, technology and culture:

- *Thinking*: literacy, intelligence, knowledge, formal-abstract thinking;
- *Personality*: self-control, moderation, autonomy, self-discipline, peacefulness, diligence;
- *Technology*: mastery of nature, production and competent use of complex
  technologies as in information technology, biotechnology, logistics,
  medicine;
- *Economy*: differentiation of labour, mastery of technological, organisational
  and administrative complexity, economic growth;
- *Society*: differentiation, individualization, independence, smaller and
  nuclear families, equal rights, civil non-violent conflict regulation;
- *Politics*: rule of law, freedom, democracy;
- *Culture and worldview*: universalism, enlightenment, human rights,
  rationality.

These are no independent factors. Modern technology emerged from a certain
cognitive, societal and cultural background, supported by free markets and

property rights (e.g. Jacob, 2014; Mokyr, 2016; Oesterdiekhoff, 2014a). Without this background, modern technology can only be adopted, understood and applied to a certain degree. Historically, individual maturation and societal civilisation went hand in hand, for personality and manners as differentiation and pacification (Elias, 2000/1939), for intelligence and scientific knowledge as decentration and increase (Oesterdiekhoff, 2012c), for economy and culture as growth and sophistication. These psychogenetic and sociogenetic developments are interdependent.[12] It is no coincidence that attributes of the burgher-civic world resemble the ones of modernisation.

What has that got to do with cognitive ability? Is it not rather uncommon to relate intelligence and knowledge to factors belonging to worldview, society and politics? The key assumption is that burgher worldviews, burgher society and burgher personality traits (favoured by certain religions) stimulate cognitive development. They stimulate it by influencing individual and institutional decisions in lifestyle, education and politics, e.g. stressing reading, diligence and discipline, linking competence and effort to success in the educational system and society. This enhanced cognitive ability again has an effect on individual and macro-social characteristics. This constitutes a spiral-shaped, reciprocal causal process at the macro-social level. Therefore, cognitive ability is as much a cause of favourable societal development as it is an indicator of such an outcome.

Intelligence is not an isolated, purely individual, and only understandable at the individual level, phenomenon. Cognitive ability and at its centre intelligence, the ability to think, are incorporated in a certain social, economic, cultural and ideological milieu; they depend on it and they create this milieu. Cognitive ability is furthered by such societies, cultures and worldviews, which can establish competence, achievement and orientation in thinking as values and practice.

Intelligence is a changing entity interacting across time with culture. The development of psyche and environment are interwoven; intelligence impacts the whole and is affected by the physical, social and mental environment.

Finally, intelligence not only works by changing and selecting the environment. It has an impact on its own. With better understanding and increasing knowledge, a historical rise of intelligence was launched. Thinking impacts thinking. Higher cognitive ability makes mistakes, contradictions and weaknesses in one's own thinking better observable and by this means and a propensity for consistency it stimulates its own improvement. Cognitive development becomes a process with its own dynamics that can only be stopped by serious interference or an objectively given limit.

---

[12] 'Pychogenetic': psyche in development, according to Piaget, Elias and Oesterdiekhoff; 'sociogenetic': society in development, according to Elias and Oesterdiekhoff.
   On possible differences between the burgher world and modernisation see Chapter 12.

# 7 Why Cognitive Factors Are Important: A Theory of Cognitive Capitalism

The modern economy is based on the cognitive resources of its labour force from all workers up to a few top developers of new ideas and technology. Cognitive ability drives the functionality of institutions and their development. Individual, aggregated and genuine higher level effects are distinguished.

> But if they don't rouse themselves and learn how to think,
> the best irrigation systems in the world won't
> do them any good. (Bertolt Brecht,
> *Life of Galileo*, 1939/2007)

## 7.1 General Cognitive Ability Effects

As alluded to by Brecht's famous play *Galileo*, technology does not help people unless they 'learn how to think', how to use and – in modernity even more importantly – how to improve it and reflect on it: Cognitive factors are important for economy, society and culture. But what are 'cognitive factors'? The usual term 'cognitive ability' (synonymous with 'cognitive competence') covers the ability to think (intelligence), knowledge (the asset of true and relevant knowledge) and the intelligent use of this knowledge. A broader concept of 'intelligence' also includes knowledge aspects ('crystallised intelligence') (see Chapter 3).

Cognitive ability is an important psychological construct: it enhances the individual's understanding of concepts and causal relationships; it increases insight, foresight and rationality – φρόνησις (phronesis, prudence), the Aristotelian term meaning a circumspect and thoughtful way of life in a rational manner. Cognitive ability leads to *proximal consequences*, such as higher quality of work and more reasonable decisions in everyday life. Higher cognitive ability also improves individuals' access to better environments and enables individuals, institutions, societies and cultures to improve the quality of the available environments. Cognitive ability also brings about *distal consequences*, such as greater wealth and health; a more democratic society; political and economic freedom; a more complex culture; and longitudinally, by reverse effects of these environmental factors, enhanced intelligence. Intelligence begets intelligence.

In statistical analyses of *job performance*, cognitive ability shows within different countries the highest predictive validity (between $r/\beta = .25$ and $.80$; see Section 3.1). In more complex jobs, its predictive validity is higher than in less complex ones. Cognitive ability is relevant for the *economic realm*, making action more efficient and innovative, more 'zweckrational', literally 'goal rational', more rational in an instrumental, target-oriented manner. Cognitive job requirements are easier and better to solve with higher intelligence.

In addition, cognitive ability has a more general effect on the *conduct of life*; it has an instrumental effect and emancipatory, ethical, reflective, epistemic-rational and cultural effects. Persons with higher intelligence are better able to solve *everyday life complex problems* as measured by *realistic scenarios* ($r = .43$; Stadler et al., 2015). In road traffic, persons with higher intelligence have intersection *accidents* less frequently ($r = -.17$; Smith & Kirkham, 1982). Why 'intersection accidents'? Driving through intersections is a more difficult cognitive task compared to intersection-free roads. According to the same source, smarter persons also less frequently violate speed limits ($r = -.18$). As a result, persons with higher intelligence less frequently die due to traffic accidents ($r = -.14$; O'Toole & Stankov, 1992).

People who were more intelligent at age 11 *lived longer* ($r = .18$; Whalley & Deary, 2001). There are cognitive reasons directly relevant for this positive effect such as insight and health literacy leading to healthier behaviour, e.g. concerning drugs and substances (stopping smoking, drinking less alcohol), nutrition (choosing better food quality and quantity), physical activity (doing sports), coping with sickness (managing diabetes, hypertension) and traffic (making fewer mistakes; Cunha et al., 2006; Goldman & Smith, 2002; Gottfredson, 2004a, 2004b).

However, some qualifications have to be mentioned:

(1) Several correlations are, with $r < .20$, rather small. Therefore, their predictive validity and explanatory power are limited. Also, conceding that the predictive validity of IQ is higher than that of parental SES, the effect is small. Many other factors, including intelligence of others and chance, also contribute.

(2) The causal link from intelligence to healthy behaviour and health outcome has to be carefully proved. Maybe intelligent people live a healthier life due to cultural lifestyle, rather than intelligence: boozing, smoking and gluttony until becoming drunken, not smelling good and becoming overweight – perhaps, simply, people in certain circles do not do that (Fussell, 1983). Lifestyle, general health, status and cognitive factors are correlated.

(3) Intelligence helps to improve one's environment, through one's or others' choices and through modifying it. There is an environment-mediated effect on health.

(4) Intelligence is also a general indicator of health ('system integrity'), which itself leads to a longer and healthier life.

Thus there is a stronger causal impact of cognitive ability on job performance than on health.

However, there are further positive cognitive effects such as on *ethical behaviour* and *law-abidingness*, both are, along with efficiency, crucial features of the burgher world (Chapter 6). Cognitive ability and moral judgement correlate with $r = .62$; if age is partialled out, the correlation is still at $r = .50$ (Krebs & Gillmore, 1982).[1] Cognitive and moral development are structurally equivalent; in both a well-founded, reasonable structure is acquired. As Jean Piaget (1948/1932, p. 404) has stated:

Parallelism exists between moral and intellectual development: . . . Logic is the morality of thought just as morality is the logic of action.

The most relevant link between them is the ability of role-taking, putting oneself into the position of others, taking their spatial point of view (see three mountains task, Figure 3.2) as well as understanding their feelings, emotions and conflicts, furthered by cognitive development and supporting moral development. Of course, not only is abstract moral development important but also realised behaviour. Information on this can be taken from experiments and from real-world behaviour such as studies of crime.

McNamee (1977) compared stages of moral development (according to Kohlberg) and helping behaviour in an experiment. More persons at a higher moral level helped a person in need of help by giving an advice ($r = .63$) or by personal assistance ($r = .60$). Similarly, Kohlberg (1984, p. 70, p. 546) found that in Milgram's (fictitious) torture experiment fewer persons at a higher moral development level followed an order to torture a person. In Milgram's experiment on obedience, participants were asked to treat another person with electric shocks in order to improve their learning; at the highest stage only 13 per cent followed this order vs. 75 per cent of participants at lower moral development stages.

Correlations between intelligence, measured by different tests, and various real world crimes, both collected in different studies and published by different authors, are around $r = -.23$.[2] The negative correlation is *not* due to an inability to conceal one's perpetration ('dumb-ones-get-caught'), because the pattern found by using official statistics can be also detected by using self-reports. The correlation also remains within social status groups and families, thus

---

[1]    The cognitive ability correlation in the Krebs & Gillmore study (1982, p. 880f.) is the average of the cognitive development ($r = .50$) and IQ correlation ($r = .73$) with moral development. $N = 51$ children from age 5 to 14.

[2]    Results on the relationship between cognitive ability and crime: $r = -.23$, Cunha et al., 2006, p. 751, reanalysis; $r = -.21$, Herrnstein & Murray, 1994, pp. 247–248; $r = -.27$, Hirschi & Hindelang, 1977, p. 575; $r = -.21$, Steinberg et al., 1994, p. 761. Cunha et al. and Herrnstein & Murray presented percentages; correlations were calculated by the author.

eliminating social status differences (Ellis & Walsh, 2003). However, it is clear, if the possibilities to reach an aim by regular means are blocked, whether because of classism and racism or because of low ability and dysfunctional personality, persons are more inclined to choose other paths such as theft or fraud. And general life frustration due to failure may lead to irrational and dysfunctional violence.

A negative relationship between intelligence and, generally speaking, 'non-order' could be found for a wider array of *'non-burgher behaviours'*, as described by Halpern et al. (2000, p. 214):

There is a generic inverse relationship between intelligence and rule breaking that has been observed across a wide spectrum of behaviors. For example, intelligence is negatively correlated with acquiescence, crime, delinquency, truancy, and out-of-wedlock births, and conversely is positively correlated with moral reasoning and development, and social skills.

The empirical correlation between intelligence and out-of-wedlock births is at $r=-.27$ (Herrnstein & Murray, 1994, pp. 180f.) and with teen births at $r=-.24$ (Cunha et al., 2006, p. 751).[3] These results are corroborated by a positive effect of preschool education on intelligence, law-abidingness and within-wedlock births, and they are backed up by results on the aggregated level for the UK.[4]

Persons with higher intelligence are more *interested in politics*, and they are better informed and more engaged, e.g. in participation in elections and signing petitions ($r=.09$ to .14; Deary et al., 2008), all citizen behaviour. Regarding political direction (left or right), results are inconsistent. Stankov (2009) found a negative relationship for the United States between cognitive ability and conservatism ($r=-.35$). The pattern is backed by research from Kanazawa (2012), who documented that liberals (left) in the United States are smarter than conservatives (up to eight-points difference). Generally, smarter persons tend to be less radical, less racist, *more liberal* and *more democratic*. More recent studies show a centrist trend, e.g. in Brazil, persons with higher intelligence tend to have centre and centre-right positions (IQ 103 vs. IQ 94–99 for the left or far right; Rindermann, Flores-Mendoza & Woodley, 2012). Taking the largest parties, in British elections voters for the

---

[3] Giving birth to a child is generally a positive life event and for various reasons, including ultimate evolutionary ones, it is positively appraisable. However, out-of-wedlock and teenage birth is risky for the development of the child, mother and father, and it is a non-burgher behaviour.

[4] Effects of preschool education, preschoolers vs. control: at age 5 IQ 95 vs. 83, no conviction until age 19, 69 per cent vs. 49 per cent (of course, still much too high), within- (vs. out-of-)wedlock births at age 27, 43 per cent vs. 17 per cent (Barnett, 1985, p. 335; see also: www.highscope.org/Content.asp?ContentId=232). At the aggregated (regional) level in the UK between intelligence and single-parent households $r=-.42$ resp. $r=-.50$ (Carl, 2016a, his table 1).

Conservatives had a small lead compared to the ones for Labour (IQ 103 vs. 102; Deary et al., 2008), but Centrist Liberal Democrats reached an IQ of 108.[5] In the United States, Republican supporters showed around three points higher IQs than supporters of the Democrats (Carl, 2014).[6]

Cognitive ability also enhances preference for *economic freedom* such as support for policies associated with limited government and meritoric principles in the economy ($r = .09$; Caplan & Miller, 2010), both of which are classical burgher orientations.

Individual and school class intelligence have a positive effect on *learning* and *instruction*: Smarter students understand more difficult subjects and learn faster (Helmke & Schrader, 2007); in classes with a higher cognitive ability level, instruction is given at a higher quality level. Instruction is faster and more complex and instruction and learning are less impeded by discipline problems and nerd harassment (Rindermann, 2007b). The ability level of one's peers and class has a positive effect on cognitive development (Dar & Resh, 1986; Sacerdote, 2011). Intelligence changes one's own behaviour, improves the environment and is supportive for the social environment. Intelligence of others makes intelligent.

## 7.2    Higher Level Effects

School class effects lead to higher level effects: *individual* effects can be distinguished from effects at higher, more global, abstract levels as at the level of an *institution, society* and *culture*. Higher level effects could be simple *aggregated effects* – the same pattern emerges for families, school classes, neighbourhoods, districts, cities, regions, states, ethnicities, races, countries and cultures.

For instance, intelligence and crime negatively correlate within populations at the level of individuals, but also at the level of counties within the United States, of regions within Italy, of states within Germany and at the level of countries in international comparisons.[7] Usually, due to higher reliability, the correlations at aggregated levels are higher. The size of correlations is also more variable, with $r = -.23$ to $-.85$: a smaller number of units (e.g. maximally

---

[5] Voters of smaller parties not in the parliament showed higher or lower intelligence compared to the average. Different scientific positions towards the intelligence-politics-relationship are discussed by Solon (2014).

[6] Conservatism (studies of Stankov, Kanazawa) is not identical with being Republican (study of Carl).

[7] Correlations between intelligence and crime: at the level of individuals $r = -.23$ (see above); US counties $r = -.53$ (Beaver & Wright, 2011, p. 24); Italian regions $r = -.85$ (homicides; Templer, 2013, p. 47); German states ('Länder') $r = -.59$ (around 2005, own calculation); countries $r = -.23$ (homicides; Rindermann, 2008a, p. 136).

20 regions in Italy or 16 states in Germany instead of thousands of individuals) leads to 'bouncing' coefficients across samples, i.e. some coefficients are very large or low or even change their algebraic sign.[8]

Higher level effects could also be genuine *group, institutional, societal* and *cultural* effects. These are all those that can only work at these levels, either as individuals' or aggregated individuals' effects on groups and institutions or as interaction effects between groups, institutions, macrosocial phenomena and culture (Jones, 2016).

Examples: according to Simonton (1984, p. 10), among political leaders intelligence and morality are positively correlated ($r = .23$). This is insofar as 'individual' as politicians are also individuals, but their behaviour has a direct effect on the shape and quality of politics.[9] The ability level of individuals and groups influences the *quality of institutions* and they again have an impact on individual and group development, for example via instructional quality of teachers (Chetty et al., 2011; Rindermann, 2007b).

This could be extended from classes and schools to administrative bodies, companies, politics, countries and cultures. Economies and societies at a higher ability level are more likely to develop new and complex technology and to faster absorb innovation from other countries (Jones, 2012). Intelligence reduces corruption (Potrafke, 2012). More intelligent people also prefer pro-market policies (Caplan & Miller, 2010), having a positive impact on economic growth. Cognitive ability levels of societies (averages and intellectual class levels) indirectly support wealth through government effectiveness, innovation, competitiveness, economic freedom and productivity (Rindermann, Kodila-Tedika & Christainsen, 2015).

A concrete example is Singapore's long-term Prime Minister Lee Kuan Yew (1923–2015). He studied at the London School of Economics and at Cambridge and finished his studies with exceptional 'Double Starred First Class Honours'. He governed Singapore from 1959 to 1990 and served as minister from 1990 to 2004. Singapore has reached second place in government effectiveness (2009–2011) after Finland and followed by other Scandinavian countries – Singapore seems to have one of the best governments in the world. In patents per capita (1991–2007), Singapore has reached first place. Of course, Singapore was and still is no standard-bearer of liberty and democracy.

---

[8] The ecological fallacy problem (correlations cannot be logically inferred across levels) has to be considered, see Chapter 9.

[9] Morality was rated on the basis of personality descriptions provided by biographers. The ratings correlate at $r = .64–.69$ with other independently carried out ratings (Simonton, 1984, p. 8). A correlation of $r = .23$ between intelligence and morality of political leaders allows many exceptions, e.g. Stalin was the best student of his class and he was interested in books and reading, but he was also the second worst dictator of history (using death toll as criterion for political performance).

But Lee stands out due to his exceptional success for Singapore in growth, modernisation, technology and, for several years, also in science (up to now in instrumental, economically productive science, in 'zweckrational' STEM, including biotechnology). Lee, apparently, was also the only politician who read and used the results of intelligence research. In speeches he cited Thomas Bouchard and Richard Lynn (Chan & Chee, 1984) and he was the only statesman who saw that national cognitive enhancement not only needs an improvement in the environment such as in education, but also in demographic policies, because parents transfer cognitive ability to their children by creating a stimulating environment (especially by education and modelling) and by transmission of their genes.

Negative examples of political leaders are better known, ranging from Adolf Hitler to Joseph Stalin, from Pol Pot to Mao Zedong, from Idi Amin to Saddam Hussein. They also show the *limits* of an individual politicians' intelligence approach for explaining political outcomes. Usually, all politicians have, compared to their society, an above average cognitive ability level, including dictators. Gustave M. Gilbert (1947, p. 31), a US-American psychologist with an Austrian-Jewish background, tested 21 political and military leaders of the former National Socialist Germany (e.g. Göring, Speer, Keitel, Jodl) after the end of the Second World War. They achieved an average high IQ of 128 points.[10] Thus, for ethics and political rationality not only intelligence but also further factors are important. Additionally, as is true for all other factor-outcome-relationships, interactions, retroaction effects and chance factors are relevant. Prussia survived the Seven Years' War because the Empress of Russia, Elizabeth, an enemy of Prussia, died and her successor, Peter III, was a friend of Prussia and ended the war between the two countries.

Cognitive ability is *differently important* at *different times* for producing wealth. In the premodern epochs tasks in production and society were less cognitively complex and less knowledge loaded. Farmers, for instance, only had a few options; most things were largely determined by tradition and custom, including sale, distribution and storage. Barley was cultivated because

---

[10] An IQ of 128 points seems to be too high for political leaders in general and National Socialist leaders in particular. In fact, the majority of political leaders come from the better educated and higher intelligent strata of society, but usually, political leaders do not form the intellectual elite. One reason is that many tasks of leading are not cognitively difficult, e.g. representing, opening new buildings, receiving congratulations. The other reason is that such tasks and the continuous communication with all sorts of people attract fewer persons with intellectual interests. In our international study on estimating politicians' intelligence using educational degrees we came, e.g. for the UK to an average leaders' IQ of 116, in the United States of 122, in Germany of 126 (for 1990 to 2009; Rindermann et al., 2009, table 1). National Socialism was critical towards education; Hitler had not studied and Hermann Göring (but according to Gilbert IQ 138) had not finished his studies. Probably, the norms used by Gilbert were outdated; that is, they were too easy due to the FLynn-effect leading to overrated IQs.

the farmer's father did it, as did the neighbour and everyone else, and if there was any change, it was done for the same reasons. Today, selection of plants, their cultivation, fertilisation, harvest and sale are a kind of science and management process. The success of a farmer differs depending on the ability to manage information regarding modern technology, organisation, markets and subsidies.

Epochs of large and continuing growth supported by intelligence leading to innovation and rationalisation started and continued in different regions at different moments in history: in the West 1820–1973 (especially 1950–1973); in the East later, in Japan from around 1870 to 1973, in the four Asian tiger countries of Hong Kong, Singapore, South Korea and Taiwan from around 1960 to 1997, in China from 1980 until around 2020. Again, cognitive ability is not the only factor. Onset and timing cannot be explained by intelligence.

### 7.2.1   Society and Culture: Music as an Example

Cognitive ability has also a *broader political, societal and cultural impact* at the macrosocial level. It shapes worldviews. For example, Stankov (2009, p. 300) presented that intelligence and conservatism are correlated at the cross-country level with $r = -.73$. Smarter people are less traditional and more modern. Convergingly, smarter people are also less religious ($r = -.60$; Lynn et al., 2009, p. 13). Indirectly, these characteristics have an economic impact, via peace, freedom and rationality, on productivity and its beneficial framework conditions. Cognitive capitalism is not only an economic system, but a culture.

A rather remote but illuminating field is the *preference for and production of certain music*. Satoshi Kanazawa presented (2012, pp. 141–155) an interesting theory under the title 'Why more intelligent people like classical music'. He began by observing that persons from groups who excel in cognitive realms, from tests to top real world achievement, Jews and East Asians, are also outstandingly represented among classical musicians. Then he reviewed large surveys from the United States that showed that persons who like classical music have, with 107 points, a higher IQ than persons who dislike classical music, with 93 points (p. 151), a difference of about one standard deviation. In a British survey, persons who listen to classical music achieved an IQ of 107, whereas ones who do not listen have an IQ of 100 (p. 152).

The classic music-IQ pattern is clear and empirically robust, but according to Kanazawa less so the interpretation. Classical music is cognitively more *complex* than pop music, as far as the number of chords, tones, instruments, their relationships, melodic structure and general length are concerned. However, because there are no general complexity assessments of music and because persons who like complex classical music also like less complex reggae music, Kanazawa favoured a 'novelty' approach: classical music as instrumental music compared to vocal music is evolutionarily newer, and everything that is evolutionarily new is a cognitive challenge preferred by smarter persons.

An unambiguous example for the complexity theory is the *Vuvuzela*: a monotonic instrument that gives only one sound, one tone, only varying in volume, usually played extremely loud. A scientist of the psychology of music, Reinhard Kopiez, analysed the Vuvuzela and the music of sport fans which can be produced using it in 2010:

Those fan groups reach 'high-school diploma' level who coordinatedly sing melodies and show a feeling for rhythm. On the other hand are those fans using primary, unspoilt reactions like clapping and making noise, representing the lowest school qualification. I classify the Vuvuzela as being at the cradle of any fan culture. Belonging there are all noisemakers such as signal-horns and shouting. The Vuvuzela is no more than such a noisemaker. With Vuvuzelas no elaborate interplay is possible. There is only an uncoordinated hooting at diverse pitch levels which sounds as if a pianist has pressed all piano keys at the same time. The Vuvuzela is really just what we call in the psychology of music a distractor, an interfering signal. The vividness of fan culture, carried by melodies, by texts related to the game, its current situations and footballers, is killed by the Vuvuzela.[11]

According to Kopiez, the Vuvuzela represents a low complexity instrument and a low complexity practice of music. Essentially, it stands for the preference for noise instead of melody and it also destroys, by its noise and loudness, more sublime forms of music produced by others. It fits to an evolutionary theory of novelty and even better to a *complexity theory*. Finally, it is also backed by the cultural development theory from Charles Murray (2003, p. 211), stating that the invention of polyphony is a meta-invention comparable to the linear perspective, to logic, ethics and the scientific method. From a cognitive perspective, the Vuvuzela as monophony represents a less advanced level of cultural development.

The Vuvuzela (Zulu language) in its current form was invented in the 1990s in South Africa. Of course, there are many precursors in various cultures, but it was only widely used in football games in South Africa, especially at the 2009 Confederations Cup and the 2010 World Cup. However, is there any evidence for a cognitive interpretation? For this proof, a correspondence to objective cognitive ability test measures is necessary. In international student assessment studies, e.g. in TIMSS 2003 Mathematics 8th grade, organised by the International Association for the Evaluation of Educational Achievement (IEA), South African students had a result of 264 SASQ points (Mullis et al.,

---

[11] Translated from German and shortened by the author (HR).

2004, p. 34). This is more than two standard deviations ($SD = 100$) below an international benchmark of 500 SASQ points: directly transformed representing an IQ of 65. Considering more studies, such as psychometric intelligence tests for children, students, young adults and adults, the results in South Africa were, with an average IQ of 69 to 70, only somewhat better.

The average cognitive level of a society, be it low, average or high, is mirrored in cultural products: here for illustration, preference and production of certain forms of music. This was an example of everyday culture. The cognitive aspect is even more obvious for explicit cognitive tasks such as technological innovation, literary and artistic works, scientific discoveries and philosophical reflection. However, for these the impact of intellectual classes is crucial, leading to the next chapter.

# 8 The Impact of Cognitive-Intellectual Classes

The cognitive ability level of intellectual classes, frequently termed 'elites', is crucial for technological development and more generally for the governance, maintenance, wellbeing and development of a society.

## 8.1 General Cognitive and Specific Intellectual Class Effects

Studies at the level of individuals, classes, regions and nations have shown that cognitive ability is positively correlated with positive occurrences in educational institutions, in work and in everyday life.[1] Longitudinal studies controlling retroactive effects and cross-sectional studies controlling other determinants such as liberty or wealth have shown that cognitive ability positively influences outcomes across the mentioned realms. This can be explained by the improved ability to process information, to use knowledge, to learn (to acquire new knowledge), to understand and to solve problems. Higher cognitive ability stands for quantitatively extended (more information), qualitatively improved (less mistakes, better structured, more approximating truth and functionality) and usually faster cognitive processing.

This causal effect due to *cognitive improvement* has to be complemented by a positive impact of ability on socially introduced *selection processes*, e.g. only those who were successful in a cognitively demanding educational system can become engineers and construct bridges. If the environmental selection processes are competence-based, this institutional process itself is intelligent, because it ensures environmental quality and because it longitudinally enhances cognitive ability.

---

[1] The pattern of positive correlations includes *personality*, e.g. openness (especially for educational subjects including interest and motivation; $r = .33$, Ackerman & Heggestad, 1997), lower aggression ($r = -.19$; Ackerman & Heggestad, 1997) and lower anxiety and neuroticism ($r = -.15$; Ackerman & Heggestad, 1997). Theoretically, a broader transformation effect in direction of moderateness, self-control, prudence and φρόνησις (phronesis) is assumed, a development from a more childlike to a more mature personality similar to the Norbert Elias approach (Oesterdiekhoff, 2012c).

But that is not all. Intelligence is widely distributed; it has a broad range. At the macrosocial level, the *upper tail* in intelligence seems to be especially important. With rising cognitive demands in everyday life, in economy, law, organisation, administration, technology, science and culture, the relevance of the upper tail is growing even more.

The terms used for this 'elite' group vary with author and paradigm: *high ability groups* or *gifted* (both terms are traditionally used in high ability research), *intellectual classes* (macrosocial intelligence research; Rindermann et al., 2009), *creative classes* (economics; Florida, 2002), *smart fractions* (intelligence research; La Griffe du Lion, 2002), *rocket scientists* (economics; Hanushek & Woessmann, 2008), *global performers* or the *team in the tail*, who can 'compete internationally' and 'perform at a globally competitive level' (economics; Pritchett & Viarengo, 2009). All these terms stand for a high achieving group with positively valued accomplishments. From their high achievement we infer high competence. This is plausible because modern societies are at least partially meritoric and because the essential tasks they are coping with are cognitively complex ones.[2] Therefore, we should use a term such as 'cognitive' or 'intellectual'.

Rocket scientists, inventors and intellectuals are essentially important for scientific, technological and cultural progress; they have changed the world (Murray, 2003). But their ideas would not have spread missing a broader high achieving group of 'normal' scientists, engineers, professionals, academics and entrepreneurs and a whole beneficial cultural milieu. Additionally, data from cognitive ability studies deliver information on a broader top group, the lower bound of the top 5 per cent, the 95th percentile ability level.

The terms 'group', 'fraction' or 'class' denote rather similar meanings; the term 'class' slightly stresses that they form a somewhat distinct group. The idea of 'distinct' is visible in different phenomena: in daily interaction, this group has less contact with cognitively average and, especially, below average people. Many of them even have no children. In daily activity they prefer cognitively stimulating tasks and communication, e.g. they avoid watching ordinary TV programmes. Their lifestyle directs them to more complex environments. Especially in meritoric societies with a high educational level, they overwhelmingly stem from cognitively above average parents and neighbourhoods.

Such *intellectual classes* can be estimated using tests in two different ways: by the *size* of higher ability groups, e.g. the share above SASQ$\geq$600,

---

[2] If job assignment were to be random or only by affiliation, race, sex or class, not correlated to ability, and if tasks did not include cognitive demands, we could not infer from achievement or job performance to competence. Of course, education and experience on the job modify abilities, but this would be a consequence of a non-meritoric assignment in such a case.

equivalent to an IQ equal to or above 115 points, as presented by Hanushek and Woessmann (2009) or by the *ability level* of a top group, e.g. the level of the brightest 5 per cent as proposed by Rindermann, Sailer and Thompson (2009).[3] Both operationalisations not only cover a small elite, but also a broader spectrum of cognitive workers including teachers, engineers, entrepreneurs, physicians, lawyers, normal scientists, managers, accountants and politicians, working in the areas of education, innovation, economy, administration and politics.

The impact of intellectual classes in the *economy* works via technological innovation and management of complexity in companies and administration. Contrary to other forms of 'capital' there seems to be no diminishing returns from cognitive ability: the higher the ability level and the more persons at high levels, even at the highest ability levels, the better (Robertson, Smeets, Lubinski & Benbow, 2010; Wai, 2013). On the one hand, this is the consequence of competition. The fastest will always win the hundred metres, but everybody who can walk will reach the finishing line. On the other hand, and this is theoretically more important, there are tasks different to the hundred metres that necessarily require high to the highest ability to successfully cope with, such as, for instance, developing new software.

The effect for *society* and *culture* goes beyond mere instrumental usefulness, but includes it: intellectual classes create scientific and intellectual progress. Enlightenment, the development of thinking in the direction of rationality, meaning being orientated towards logic, empiricism and arguments, away from traditionalism, 'bookishness' (what is written in holy books is true and nothing else), hierarchism and collectivism, guided by formal epistemic and argumentative rules, paved the way for technological development. Both enlightenment and technological development are essentially cognitive accomplishments (Jacob, 2014; Mokyr, 2016; Oesterdiekhoff, 2013). An inventor such as James Watt was both an engineer and scientist, reading, understanding and applying the then current mathematics and natural sciences. British schools taught Newton's physics and mechanics, which formed, along with practical experience, trial and error and fiddling, the basis for the development of technology.

## 8.2    Pilots, Airlines and Accidents

The relevant intellectual class group is wider, as mentioned, and comprises well-educated, high achieving persons in schools, universities, companies, administration and politics. In quite normal job performance, intellectual

---

[3] More precisely, the intellectual classes' level is the ability level at the 95th percentile rank, meaning the lower cognitive ability threshold of the top 5 per cent group.

classes' cognitive ability is crucial: sometimes a matter of life and death. A good example is the work of *pilots*. And one of the best examples of competence and its consequences is the pilot Chesley Sullenberger.[4]

### 8.2.1   Chesley Sullenberger and US Airways Flight 1549

Chesley Sullenberger was a US Airways pilot educated by the US Air Force, who moved to civil aviation. He was born in 1951; his father was a dentist and his mother a teacher. His paternal lineage goes back to Swiss immigrants in the eighteenth century. Reports mentioned that as a student he was tested in the 99th percentile in academic categories (equivalent to IQ 135). His IQ should have been high enough to become a member of Mensa International, a high IQ society. He graduated close to the top of his class. Sullenberger has a Bachelor of Science, a Master in Industrial Psychology and a Master in Public Administration. He acquired his psychology Master from Purdue University, ranked among the top 100 universities of the world.[5] All information hints to above average ability. However, for pilots this is nothing special; they are selected for academic achievement and cognitive ability, and additionally for health and personality traits such as reliability, conscientiousness, robustness, reasonableness and ethical orientations. Nevertheless, his test results indicate not only a high cognitive ability level, but also an above average level for a pilot. Apart from being a pilot he worked as an instructor, in accident investigation, in safety programmes and pilot unions etc., also indicating above average competence and commitment among pilots.

In 2009, he was the pilot of US Airways Flight 1549 from New York to Carolina. After taking off, the plane hit a large flock of birds, disabling both engines. Sullenberger discussed with air traffic control the possibilities of landing at the next airport, which became unfeasible. He decided to make an unpowered emergency ditching in the Hudson river. This was not part of any pilot training and is very dangerous due to the resistance of turbines in the water. During landing he slowed down the plane by first touching the water with the tail of the aircraft and then landed on the river. All passengers and all crew members, altogether 155 persons, survived. After landing on the river and before he left, as last person, the plane, he checked the plane for any still-remaining passengers.[6]

---

[4] Sources: Various English and German newspapers and Internet pages.

[5] Purdue University in rankings: according to Times Higher Education around the year 2010 at rank 60 to 110; to QS World University at around rank 90; to Shanghai Ranking at rank 50 to 70 (see Section 4.4.2).

[6] A similar example is the pilot performance of Qantas Flight 32 in Singapore 2010, landing a heavily damaged aircraft safely. 'Their crew performance, communications, leadership, teamwork, workload management, situation awareness, problem solving and decision making

The incident became well-known as the 'Miracle on the Hudson'. As always, chance played a role: a river was near, no ships were on the river during landing but they were near enough to rescue the passengers and crew. However, without the pilot's competence any survival would have been impossible. Cognitive ability *increases the chances* of acquiring specific competences such as flying an aeroplane and behaving in a complex situation in a reasonable, goal-reaching way.

### 8.2.2    Contrasting Examples: Costa Concordia and Ramstein

In contrast, Francesco Schettino, captain of the *Costa Concordia*, who in 2012 drove his ship onto rocks off the Isola del Giglio, which caused its sinking and the death of 32 passengers, is reported to have left the ship during its evacuation (description follows different media reports, e.g. BBC and Time). At the beginning of the sinking, the crew gave misinformation to the passengers to stay in the ship, as there would be only a short power failure, which was not true. The Costa Concordia example is not only illuminating in comparison to the US Airways Flight 1549 because it demonstrates the relevance of the competence of leading persons usually belonging to the intellectual class, but because it again illustrates that competence and ethical behaviour are related.[7]

But is there any evidence for a correspondence to a not high enough cognitive ability level? Francesco Schettino stems from Campania, Southern Italy. This region achieved an average IQ of 90 in PISA studies (transformed from SASQ), which is around ten points below Northern Italy and the Western mean score (Lynn, 2010, p. 94; based on OECD, 2007, pp. 250, 304, 308). Of course, as for pilots, ships' captains also belong to the higher cognitive strata of society. But educational and selecting institutions have to take persons from the given ability pool applying for professional training and a job. If the average is lower, it becomes more difficult to keep a minimum competence threshold as necessary for the demands of the job. Therefore, professionals from lower and higher competence regions also usually differ in their competence according to the general level of their social environment. Additionally, institutions and their staff depend in their functionality on the given societal ability level.

Finally, if notable ability differences between groups exist such as between Italians from Northern and Southern Italy, competence-based selection may be

---

resulted in no injuries to the 450 passengers and crew. QF32 will remain as one of the finest examples of airmanship in the history of aviation.' (Edwards, 2013, pp. 17–18) The average cognitive ability level in Australia is IQ 99, of intellectual classes IQ 121.

[7] In February 2015, Schettino was sentenced to 16-years' imprisonment: ten years for manslaughter, five years for causing the shipwreck and one year for abandoning passengers (www.bbc.com/news/world-europe-31430998).

impaired by political considerations, as practised in many countries and called 'balanced application of criteria for personnel selection' or 'affirmative action' etc. (Sowell, 2004). Such non-competence-based regulations are immunised by political and ostensibly ethical arguments against criticism.

This does not deny the possibility of geniuses stemming from relatively low ability strata; Schettino could be one of them, but the probability for such a case is very low.[8] There is no personal evidence for Schettino having above average ability; at least he succeeded in his given social environment in becoming a captain.

A similar, even more harmful incident, was the *Ramstein air show disaster* in 1988 at the US Ramstein Air Base in Germany. The Italian Air Force display team, Frecce Tricolori, put on an air show leading to an accident with three casualties among the Italian pilots and 67 casualties among the spectators and local ground staff. The investigation has revealed that pilot Lieutenant Colonel Ivo Nutarelli, during performance of a 'pierced heart' air figure, arrived too early and was flying at too low an altitude and therefore collided with another aircraft, hitting a third aircraft. They all crashed, into other aircraft, air show staff and the audience on the ground.

Nutarelli (1950–1988) hails from Sicily. This region achieved an average IQ of 89 in PISA studies (transformed from student assessment scale), which is around 11 points below Northern Italy and the Western mean (Lynn, 2010, p. 94; based on OECD, 2007, pp. 250, 304, 308). All the qualifications mentioned above have to be applied again; there is no information on test or school achievement results for Ivo Nutarelli; inferring from group averages to individuals is a rough method; there can be single positive or negative exceptions, but the given information hints more towards a relatively low, or at least not high enough, cognitive ability level increasing the risks for making errors on the job, especially in cognitively complex tasks. Readers who may perceive an association between accidents and average country ability levels as being unfavourable and stereotyping may reflect about whether they would accept such an association if instead of individuals and countries, abstract entities and relations were used: for instance, showing an association between single items of a class and the class average. Logically, it is the same. Name is but sound and smoke.[9]

Both accidents could have not only been prevented by avoiding mistakes by the *responsible captains* but also by *better management* and the use of *technological progress*. For instance, ship routes can be controlled by GPS in a headquarters. In Ramstein, there were several additional serious

---

[8] On inference from higher order categories to single cases as from groups to individuals see Section 9.4. What in such a situation can be done better – see Chapter 14.

[9] Additionally, at the individual data level using a representative sample and statistical analyses: intelligence and *accidents* negatively correlate with $r = -.17$ (Smith & Kirkham, 1982).

shortcomings in managing the accident, in treating the injured and in transporting them to hospitals. Air shows can be forbidden. The incidence led to several reforms in disaster management. Finally, in the future, manned aircraft can be replaced by drones less prone to mistakes.

### 8.2.3    Airline Safety in Statistical Cross-Country Comparisons

Qualitative data have their strengths and weaknesses (Section 4.4). Illustrative case studies need to be complemented by systematically compiled broad data sources, preferably collected by other researchers or research organisations, and statistical analyses based upon them. Such analyses on technology mastery can be applied at the cross-country level: airline safety (see Tables 4.6 and 4.7 and here Table 8.1) correlates with average cognitive ability at $r = .53$, in direct comparison of mean level, 05th%-rank and 95th%-rank the correlations are $r_M = .50$, $r_{05\%} = .45$ and $r_{95\%} = .57$. This means that cross-country differences in the *intellectual classes' level* ($r_{95\%} = .57$) can statistically *better explain* cross-country differences in *airline safety* than differences in the mean level ($r_M = .50$) and much better than differences in the low ability groups' level ($r_{05\%} = .45$). This empirically backs the relevance of intellectual classes and their cognitive

Table 8.1 *Correlations between cognitive ability estimates and technological safety measures*

|  | Airline safety 2009–2010 (AERO) | Road traffic safety 2010 (WHO) | Occupational safety 1998, 2001/3 (Hämäläinen) | Technological safety 1998–2010 |
|---|---|---|---|---|
| **CA corrected (max 194)** | .53 (.53) | .51 (.64) | .71 (.72) | .71 (.73) [.30] |
| **SAS mean corr (max 98)** | .50 (.54) | .61 (.63) | .71 (.73) | .70 (.73) [.31] |
| **SAS 95% corr (max 98)** | .57 (.62) | .64 (.66) | .74 (.76) | .75 (.79) [.39] |
| **SAS 05% corr (max 98)** | .45 (.48) | .56 (.57) | .67 (.69) | .65 (.67) [.22] |
| **N max** | 37 | 182 | 192 | 194 |

*Notes*: The three SAS measures, mean, top ability level (95% threshold, intellectual classes) and low ability level (5% threshold) for each single variable in the same country sample. In parentheses comparison for the same country sample in all variables, $N = 34$. In the last column in brackets [ ] GDP/c partialled out. Airline safety, source AERO: Aero International (Wolf, 2010, 2011; see chapter 4); Road traffic safety as (low) road traffic death rate: estimated road traffic death rate per 100,000 population (WHO, 2013, pp. 244–251); Occupational safety by (low) accident rate: average of years 1998, 2001 and 2003, fatality and occupational accident rate per 100,000 workers averaged (Hämäläinen et al., 2009, p. 134); Technological safety: average of the former three measures (Cronbach-$\alpha = .85$).

ability level – not only for the ability level of pilots, but also of airline leaders, engineers, flight controllers, administrators and politicians setting the framework conditions for airlines and securing the technological and organisational basis of airports, aeroplanes and the entire surrounding infrastructure.

Similarly to low accident rates in air traffic, low road traffic death rates and low occupational accident rates are positively correlated to cognitive ability (on average at $r = .71$; see Table 8.1). The intellectual classes pattern is stable across road and occupational safety: correlations with the 95th%-level are always higher than correlations with the average or the 5th%-level. But the pattern is more accentuated for airline safety: here, comparing the same country sample (correlations in parentheses) the difference ($\Delta$) between the 95th%-level and average is larger (airline $r_\Delta = .08$ vs. road $r_\Delta = .03$ and occupation $r_\Delta = .03$), as is the difference between the 95th%- and the 5th%-level ($r_\Delta = .14$ vs. .09 and .07). We interpret this as a consequence of the higher cognitive complexity level of steering an aeroplane and related activities, from air-traffic control to maintenance, compared to driving a car or working in industry. Nearly everybody can become a car, truck and bus driver and worker in at least slightly dangerous jobs such as in the chemical and mining industries but not everybody can become an airline pilot. What is comparable, is the similar influence of politicians setting the legal, executive and control frame, and the influence of entrepreneurs, administrators and engineers.

Considering GDP per capita – partialling out produced income for the correlations between cognitive ability and technological safety – leads to lower correlations. The idea behind this is that in richer countries more means will lead to more safety, e.g. by having more money to buy better technology and spare parts. Of course, partialling out produced income overcontrols wealth effects on technological safety because produced income also depends on cognitive ability. However, the correlations remain, and the intellectual classes pattern in particular becomes more pronounced: the difference between the 95th %-level ($r_{95\%} = .39$) and the 5th%-level ($r_{05\%} = .22$) is, with $r_\Delta = .17$ ($N = 89$), the largest. The cognitive ability level of intellectual classes is important for safety in using machines and for managing technological complexity.

### 8.2.4    Accidents, Ruling Classes and Airlines in Turkey

In the international airline safety list, Turkish airlines are ranked at number 33 of 37. In the same country sample in road traffic safety, Turkey reached number 23, in occupational safety, number 30.[10] News programmes in Europe

---

[10] The more countries from the developing world are added, from Africa, South Asia and Latin America, the better is the relative Turkish position in the entire country sample. Airline safety ranks were only given for a smaller country sample, which focuses on developed countries.

repeatedly report bus accidents.[11] Tourists give accounts of brake failures, speeding and organisational problems. The worst mining accident in the twenty-first century happened in Turkey; in May 2014 in Soma, 301 persons died. Reports mentioned that miners, two to three weeks before the fire in the mine which caused the catastrophe, communicated that they dug out 'hot coal', meaning that they detected an underground fire. For around 800 miners there was only one rescue room that held no more than ten persons. This all hints at deficits in technology and workforce management, in control and legislation. Additionally, according to reports during a visit to Soma, a leading politician kicked at a protester laying on the ground and being held by two police men.[12] The then Prime Minister himself, several times since 2002 elected by the Turkish people, is said by reports to have 'offended' another local protester by calling him 'Israeli sperm' and slapped him.[13]

The average cognitive ability level in Turkey is 87 (compared to Greenwich IQ 100) and of the intellectual class 103 (compared to Greenwich IQ 121). While the difference for the average is 13 points (100 vs. 87), the difference for the intellectual class is 18 points (121 vs. 103). There is a larger deficit at the top level than for the societal average. The same pattern was found in international comparisons using systematically collected data and statistics to analyse them (Table 8.1). Of course, cognitive ability is not the only factor for successful handling of technology; also relevant are values, attitudes and personality and a general culture of attention and circumspection. And having more wealth makes it easier to spend money on safety. But intelligence affects everything.

*Birgenair Crash* The cognitive ability component becomes more obvious in detailed accident analyses, as here in the example of an air crash. *Birgenair* was a Turkish airline (1988–1996) and in the 1990s it was used by the Turkish holiday company Öger Tours.[14] Birgenair transported tourists from

---

[11] Bus accidents, e.g. 21 fatalities, January 2014 (www.bz-berlin.de/welt/21-tote-bei-schwerem-busunglueck-in-der-tuerkei); 11 killed, December 2013 (www.hurriyetdailynews.com/at-least-11-university-students-killed-in-bus-crash-in-turkey.aspx?PageID=238&NID=59942&NewsCa tID=341). Of course, smaller accidents abroad do not reach international news (sensation report bias); however, the mentioned statistics back an impression of a higher-than-average (Greenwich standard) road traffic death rate.

[12] www.theguardian.com/world/2014/may/24/turkish-pm-aide-sacked-kicking-protester-mining-disaster.

[13] www.aydinlikdaily.com/Detail/PM-Erdo%C4%9Fan-Why-Are-You-Running-Away-Israeli-Sperm!/3242.

[14] Sources: Report by JACDEC (Jet Airliner Crash Data Evaluation Centre, http://archive-de.com/page/145213/2012-07-17/http://www.jacdec.de/media/books/sample1.htm), official report by the Dominican Authorities (www.fss.aero/accident-reports/dvdfiles/DO/1996-02-06-DO.pdf, www.rvs.uni-bielefeld.de/publications/Incidents/DOCS/ComAndRep/PuertoPlata/bericht.

Europe to the Caribbean and back. In February 1996, Birgenair should have transported tourists home from the Dominican Republic.

According to reports, the initially designated aeroplane from the airline ALAS Nacionales, an airline belonging to Birgenair, had a defect. Thus it was substituted for a Birgenair aeroplane which had been standing unused for 20 days at Puerto Plata airport in Dominican Republic. During parking, the air speed indicators (ASI, pitot tube) have to be covered; this seems to have been forgotten in February 1996. Probably during this idle time, one ASI got dirty; it is assumed this was the result of a wasp building its nest in the tube. Before starting the ASIs were not checked, or at least the soiling was not detected.

During take-off the captain noticed that his ASI did not work correctly. But he did not abort the take-off. The co-pilot mentioned that his ASI was working properly. Later the captain thought that his ASI was also functioning correctly. The aircraft had three air speed indicators, but the captain's did not work correctly. After taking off, they switched on the autopilot. The autopilot only used information from the captain's ASI. Then the engine-indicating and crew-alerting system (EICAS) gave warnings indicating that the plane had too much speed. This information was based on the defective ASI of the captain that was automatically used by the autopilot. The ASI indicated a high speed that was practically impossible for a full Boeing 757 aircraft during climbing. On the other hand, the ASI of the co-pilot showed a much lower speed, most probably the correct one, which appeared to the captain as being too low.

According to the JACDEC report, the pilots wanted to change the ASI used by the autopilot from the captain's one to the co-pilot's. This is possible by manual operation. However, because both pilots pushed their button to change the autopilot at the same time, the captain's ASI was still used by the autopilot. The pilots did not notice. Then warnings started sounding, indicating that the plane was flying much too slowly: the so-called stick-shaker stall alert. This is a kind of last warning before an air crash. Information was contradictory; one system gave information on overspeed, and the other on underspeed. The autopilot was switched off, but the captain did not give the necessary power to both engines and did not alter the angle of attack of the wings and the inclination of the plane. The co-pilots, being lower in the hierarchy, did not correct the captain. Finally, the aeroplane rotated and crashed into the ocean. All 13 crew members and 176 passengers died.

According to the official report by the Dominican Authorities, the pilots were confused and overstrained by contradictory information given by their instruments:

html); we mainly follow here the JACDEC report. Translations by the author with the help of other Internet sources, including Wikipedia.

The probable cause of the accident was the crew's failure [in Spanish: falta] to recognise [reconocer] the activation of the stick shaker as a warning of imminent entrance to the stall, and the failure [falla] of the crew to execute the procedures for recovery from the onset of loss of control. Before the warning from the stick shaker the erroneous speed display and the warning of overspeed contributed to the confusion [confusión] of the crew. (p. 22, original in Spanish)

The report (p. 23) lists additional factors that contributed to the accident:

- Discipline of the crew. Use of the cockpit resource management. Basic abilities of flying an aeroplane [capacidad básica de aviacion].
- Low knowledge [Poco conocimiento] of the aeroplane and its instruments.
- Insufficient maintenance of the aeroplane during its stay at the airport in Puerto Plata. Missing control of the air speed indicator before starting.
- Insufficient training of pilots by Birgenair.
- Insufficient information in the Boeing operation manual about such cases.[15]

Summarising, there is more than one single cause for this accident and the death of nearly 200 people. It started with *technological problems* (e.g. simply use more ASIs and automatically correct single outliers, install an automatic closing system during parking, install an automatic test system before taking off); it continued with local *maintenance failures* at the airport in the Dominican Republic, continued in a *wrong decision of the pilots* during take-off (noticing the failure of the main speed measure but not cancelling the take-off) and culminated in *several serious errors in processing contradictory information* by the captain and his co-pilots. In standard conditions, even beginners can fly an aeroplane; it is only under challenging conditions that the differences in competence become obvious. And not all problems can be solved by technology because technology sometimes creates new, previously non-existing challenges.

The crew problem was not any lack of experience. The captain, 62 years old, as the official report mentions, in many countries too old for flying an airliner, had 24,750 hours of flying experience. The other pilots (51 and 34 years old) had 15,000 and 3,500 flight hours. It was not a problem due to lack of experience but due to lack of ability, lack of ability in information processing ('failure to recognise'), usually called intelligence. As previously mentioned, the average cognitive ability level in Turkey is 87 (compared to Greenwich IQ 100) and of the intellectual class 103 (compared to Greenwich IQ 121). While the difference for the average is 13 points, it is 18 points for the intellectual class.[16] There is a

---

[15] The case of conflicting information on speed was better described in operation manuals written by US airlines using this Boeing aircraft. However, in such a stress situation under time constraint it is hardly possible to use.

[16] The aeroplane maintenance failure at the airport in the Dominican Republic also contributed to the accident. The average cognitive ability level in the Dominican Republic is 78 (compared to Greenwich IQ 100). The Dominican Republic first participated in student assessment studies

larger lag at the upper level than for the average. There is no test information on the individual cognitive ability levels of the pilots but all given information about the case indicates that it was not high enough.

And this lag may not only manifest itself in the behaviour of the pilots of one single aeroplane. It is corroborated by statistics and further examples. Statistics: (1) Surveys report general lower airline safety. (2) There are higher rates in traffic and occupational death surveys. Further examples: (3) In 2009 Turkish Airlines Flight 1951 crashed during landing at Amsterdam: one radar altimeter did not work correctly, all other instruments worked correctly, but the autothrottle was based on the dysfunctional radar altimeter, causing airspeed to be too slow, resulting in the air crash. In fact, the pilots had recognised the discrepancy between different instruments, the defectiveness of the radar altimeter and the too slow airspeed and consequently tried to increase the speed, but they did not realise for some time that the autothrottle was based on the dysfunctional radar altimeter, cancelling all their manual speed corrections – too late, they deactivated the autothrottle. The aircraft crashed and all pilots died. The case is very similar to the 13 years older Birgenair crash.

(4) Due to safety defects, the Turkish airline Onur Air was banned in 2005 by several European authorities.[17] (5) As 'revenge' Turkey banned German airlines. To feel offended and ban safe airlines in one's own country – is this the rational answer to safety problems provided by government officials? Rather, the government officials and aviation authorities should have been grateful, because foreign authorities took on the job the local authorities should have, in which they had failed. Finally, the foreign authorities protected not only Turkish crew members but also the Turkish people because airlines usually transport more nationals of their home country than foreigners. (6) Due to technological deficits in 2005, a Fly Air (a Turkish airline) plane was forbidden to take off from Paris. The Belgian pilot, who, due to technological defects, made an unscheduled landing in Paris, was reported to have been fired by the airline.[18] This means that the airline management had little regard for the safety of its plane, cargo, crew and passengers. (7) In 1997, the Turkish airline Holiday Air was banned from landing in Germany.[19] (8) In July 2014, a Turkish F-16 fighter in an air-show in Lincolnshire, England, flew

in PISA 2015 (not considered in our data base). Taking PISA 2015, the intellectual class' level is 470 SASQ, some way below the norm of average students in developed countries (500 SASQ). Transformed to the IQ scale, the intellectual class' level is between IQ 95 and 96; corrected for youth not at school and adapted to UK natives' Greenwich scale it is IQ 93. This level of an intellectual class is too low for solving complex cognitive tasks.

[17] May 2005 (according to www.spiegel.de/reise/aktuell/sicherheitsmaengel-luftfahrtamt-verbietet-onur-air-die-landung-a-356001.html), by German and Dutch authorities.

[18] August 2005, Source: www.n-tv.de/panorama/Pilot-fristlos-entlassen-article157280.html.

[19] February 1997, Source: www.focus.de/kultur/leben/birgenair-unglueck-exoten-unter-druck_aid_164316.html.

approximately 1 to 4 meters over the heads of spectators.[20] One tiny deviation with his joystick and he and many others would have been killed.

What about air crashes by other airlines in countries with on average higher cognitive means, including their intellectual classes? For instance, the Air France air crash in 2009 in the South Atlantic, which was also due to problems with the air speed indicators? Intelligence only increases the *chances* of success, of mastering a challenging situation. It only reduces the *probability* of mistakes, but does not entirely eliminate them. And, of course, it should not be neglected that a larger airline with many more flights, planes and pilots, a longer history and more traffic will statistically have more accidents in absolute terms than a smaller airline.

And what about the Germanwings Flight crash in March 2015? It was *deliberately* caused by the German co-pilot, Andreas Lubitz, and therefore it is not an example of competence problems. Nevertheless, it shows German institutional and cultural problems ('data protection') in dealing with pilot health and safety. In Sweden, pilot health information is delivered to the civil aviation authority. Additionally, in the United States a pilot was not allowed to be alone in the cockpit.

Finally, from a cognitive perspective there is empirically well-backed reason to hope: as for other emerging countries, there is a relatively strong increase of intelligence across generations, for Turkey of about 3.52 IQ points per decade (Rindermann, Schott & Baumeister, 2013). This will raise the mastery of complexity across different domains.

---

[20] July 2014, www.ibtimes.co.in/watch-f-16-fighter-jet-almost-hits-crowds-waddington-air-show-video-603834.

Methods and peculiarities of cross-country human capital research
are described, and solutions for problems are offered: in general,
a scientific approach guided by epistemic rationality is suggested;
more specifically, measurement and comparability problems are
discussed; causality, correlation and path analysis; relations
between individuals and categories at different levels (including
ecological fallacy and conclusions from groups to individuals and
from individuals to groups).

It would be ridiculous to claim that research on cross-country differences, and
particularly on cross-country differences in wealth and cognitive ability, is
neither difficult nor contentious. For instance, research is complicated by
obvious measurement problems and the complexity of causal networks.
But research is also compounded by a less obvious influence of interests,
ideology and ideals and by the impact of researchers' or recipients' social-
cultural background. They all seriously interfere with developing a clear and
realistic view and understanding of international differences.

## 9.1    An Epistemic Rationality Approach to Research

To begin with the obvious: methods need to be adapted to the questions and
features of a research field. Different methods coming from different paradigms should be used and compared in their suitability and outcomes. But that
is not enough. Broadly speaking, research has to be based on the same
principles as thinking. Research is the application of thinking and its principles
in a more systematised and institutionalised way. The development of principles of thinking (or cognition or cognisance) is interwoven with philosophical epistemology and cognitive development theory. *Epistemology* is
concerned with the possibilities of cognition and the rules that have to be
followed to come to true, relevant and new knowledge. *Cognitive development
theory* deals with the individual development of cognition as the ability to
think and understand. In the Piagetian approach the formal operational stage of
abstract, logical and decentred thinking is set as the objective for this

development. This way of rational thinking is not only the objective of cognitive development, but it is also the normative principle of epistemology and it is the precondition for science in general.

Bringing them together, epistemology and cognitive development theory, we suggest to use them as the normative background for research and to term this perspective the 'epistemic rationality approach'. *Epistemic rationality* describes a truth- and search for knowledge-orientated attitude in thinking guided by logicality, empiricity and argumentativity. It starts with an orientation in thinking (Kant, 1996/1786). That is to say, the willingness and ability to align one's thinking to truth; to direct it towards correctness, justification and argumentation; an attitude to admit objective problems for one's own thinking and to consider them as problems that are solvable by thinking; to avoid solving problems by intuition, tradition, majority opinion, zeitgeist, compulsion or violence[1]; to choose an attitude based on arguments in interaction with oneself, with others and problems; to accept only logic, empirical evidence and good reasons; not to accept persuasion by others, reputation or power or other criteria not based on arguments; to use in epistemic communication an appropriately precise and comprehensible language, including the language of mathematics.

This also includes trying to rationally reconstruct the statements of others. The ideas of others are apprehended in a productive way as valuable ideas for epistemic purposes. Truth is in single statements, not in the characteristics of the proponents of statements (even where they are empirically correlated). Statements in their logical, empirical and argumentative substance are important, not what a person as an individual thinks or has mentioned at other places. Theories are developed based on observations and thinking, and observations and thinking serve as criteria of theories. Inductive and deductive reasoning work together.

Epistemic rationality can be also used as the landmark for navigating through scientific thunderstorms: science sometimes creates tensions between research findings and society. It becomes quite difficult to overcome the dominance of the political within research. Epistemic-scientific principles can be in conflict with, in their frame, legitimate economic, cultural and ideological interests, usually represented by the political class, media, church or intellectuals. However, in hotly debated areas of research, fundamental principles of scientific thinking should be maintained. Here, too, the aim is to find knowledge: true and new knowledge. Scientists write for a rational

---

[1] Kant (1996/1786, p. 16): 'Freedom in thinking signifies the subjection of reason to no laws except those, which it gives itself.' 'Thinking for oneself means seeking the supreme touchstone of truth in oneself (i.e. in one's own reason); and the maxim of always thinking for oneself is enlightenment' (p. 18).

reader who can be convinced (a willingness and an ability) through argumentation using logic, empirical facts and systematic reasoning. Freedom of research and respect for others in their scientific endeavour are helpful for the scientific community to progress in this direction (e.g. Mill, 2015/1859; Flynn, 2007a).

Other orientations, which may be legitimate in their fields, can be empirically relevant as catalysers or obstacles, but not for science as an endeavour to pursue truth. In science, from an epistemic view, only the truth or falseness of statements matter and an angel's truth is as true as a devil's truth. It is irrelevant if a statement is blue or red, progressive or conservative, up or down, right or left, politically correct or not, morally superior or not, published here or there, welcomed and repeated by the right or wrong people.[2] Of importance is if it is correctly describing the world and explaining it, and secondly, if it is new and helpful for the development of inspiring theoretical approaches. Statements, developed by Marxists, burghers or reactionists, men or women, Christians or atheists, Westerners or marginalised, of people we like or not, can be true. If Hitler (or Stalin, Mao, Idi Amin, Saddam Hussein) would have said on Friday 'tomorrow is Saturday', this is more true than if Jesus (or Marx, Buddha, Nobel laureates) would have said on Friday 'tomorrow is Thursday'.

Not all those acting and arguing in science and in the media dealing with science have always observed such principles. Some participants of past conflicts have suffered from offensive treatment, including violent attacks. However, intellectual conflicts are not new in the history of thought, as the fate of scholars like Thomas Aquinas, Galilei, Spinoza and Darwin showed. From today's perspective many past disputes sound quite ridiculous and their formerly not questionable 'arguments' are today scientifically and ethically disapproved. But those conflicts have been important in developing in the long run a climate of legitimate argumentation and thinking. The frequently difficult process of enlightenment would have not been strengthened if people shied away from such conflicts.

Today, due to its increased 'embeddedness' in society, research on disputed subjects is becoming even more difficult. The influence of media, political interest groups, politics and economic pressures is stronger than around one century ago. It becomes difficult to imagine an independent person such as Max Weber for today's science. A scientific orientation needs not only to be established in society, but in science and among scientists themselves,

---

[2] LePan (1989, p. 151): 'The union of natural and supernatural often tends to assume a moral dimension where causal thought is concerned.' Lacking the differentiation between questions of truth and moral is, according to the Piagetian approach, an indicator of a not completely finished cognitive development.

in *science as institutions* (universities, journals, publishers) and in *science as individual researchers*.

An obvious problem of an epistemic rationality approach is that it does not provide researchers with an operating manual describing in detail what to do. But researchers cannot delegate their task to deal with questions of how to do research. Research only implementing given standards is less science than a routine carried out in a quasi-authoritarian manner. A further problem is that many people in scientific institutions, including those in leading positions, are strongly interested in non-scientific aims. They are occupied with keeping things running; papers and presentations have to be produced, funds raised, success of oneself and one's staff to be promoted. Success in these measures is more important than any reflective approach towards science. Not uncommonly, practised science lacks a scientific orientation.

The aim of research cannot be to repeat the zeitgeist. Science is not the Vuvuzela of currently dominating views. But science also does not have the task of provoking these views. It simply pursues epistemic aims, whether there is an overlap with the zeitgeist or not. This includes overlaps with what is known as 'Mokita' or 'stereotypes.' 'Mokita', or the 'Elephant in the room', is the term for a truth that everybody knows but no one expresses and all agree about not expressing. Statements that are known as 'stereotypes' or 'prejudices' are usually considered to be essentially wrong; however, they can also be true and empirically they are among the most correct existing statements (Ashton & Esses, 1999; Jussim, 2012, his tables 17-1 to 17-3): according to self-assessment and measured objective data and including meta-analyses, the average correlation between stereotypes and criteria as group averages is about $r = .81$! This correlation is much higher than the average effects and replication rates of studies in social psychology. And it is of similar size to the correlation between two measures of an identical construct at the country level – of GDP Maddison and Penn with $r = .87$ (see Section 1.3.1).

Beyond this, it should be noted that dealing with normative scientific concepts and a communication of them carries the risk that such concepts are used as a kind of monstrance substituting good practice with a signalling of scientific integrity to others. Hence and as always, a careful check of the practice is inevitable.

*In concreto*, applied to problems of research on international cognitive ability differences, scientists have to deal with different paradigms. The main division is the genetic-evolutionary versus environmental one. Within the environmental one, theories of culture, wealth, health, politics, dependency, geography, modernisation and education can be distinguished. Some proponents of them have missionary zeal and not so tolerant attitudes. There are subtle rules depending on paradigm, e.g. about whom to refer to or not, which source to use or not or which term to drop or not. Even broader, general political climates in science may bias research and its perception: according to Duarte et al. (2015), in psychology a left-leaning majority tends to avoid positions which are perceived as not being left-leaning. Sometimes, other positions are even suppressed by illegitimate means, in other fields usually known as 'discrimination'. Finally, dealing with cognitive ability and religious convictions may interfere with collective identities. Research coming to unfavourable results for a certain group or any research revealing differences between nations could be perceived as being offensive or at least inappropriate. Differences between countries and cultures ought to be silently overlooked; they should be denied without denying them.

## 9.2　Measurement Problems

Can we compare cognitive ability, education, wealth, institutional quality or religious affiliation and their measures across countries? Does not the meaning of indicators change with culture and society? These are serious questions. For instance, production statistics do not sufficiently cover black market activity and this leads to an underestimation of income and wealth. The size of black market activity and, consequently, the underestimation of wealth differ across countries. And underestimated wealth goes along in such countries, particularly developing countries, with lower test experience, resulting in an overestimation of the international wealth-intelligence correlation.

The consequence cannot be to bury one's head in the sand but to improve the given indicators, to use different estimates of a construct and to combine them in a more reliable and valid measure (see Chapters 1 to 4 and especially Section 4.3). E.g. GDP can be compared with alternative wealth and wellbeing indicators such as height and longevity; psychometric IQ measures can be compared with student assessment tests, cognitive achievement in everyday life or the amount of education.

But quality differences between variables should not be neglected. Not all variables are equally deficient: results of achievement tests are better comparable than information on educational degrees or outcomes of rating scales. Student assessment studies are based on larger samples than psychometric intelligence test studies; however, they only use data relating to students and need to be corrected to be informative for the entire age cohort and to allow conclusions on society. Quantitative data should be complemented by qualitative information, e.g. test results should be backed up by information on historical accomplishments – which could be quantified too (e.g. Chapter 4). Critics should suggest improvements, not just express their discomfort. Critique has to be used productively to improve research.

## 9.3     Causal Assumptions

The causal question is the crucial issue. Either starting from a theory, research tries to check this theory (e.g. cognitive human capital raises productivity, leading to production, income and wealth) or starting from an observed relationship, research tries to explain this relationship (as of intelligence and wealth at the international level). Usually, in research, theories are tested with experiments. But this common path is not possible to choose either at the international or at the historical level: experiments are not feasible at the international level. And even a theory confirmed by an experiment does not necessarily explain why aspects of societies are associated. A theory helps to understand a relationship between variables and it supports the development of interventions. But the corroboration of a theory by an experiment gives only a provisional answer. Whether the appropriate specific conditions are present has to be checked. And it is unlikely that there is only one causal path explaining a correlation between two variables (see Figure 9.1). If, e.g., economic freedom stimulates wealth, cognitive ability may stimulate wealth too and cognitive ability may also stand behind economic freedom.

Variable A (e.g. intelligence) may influence variable B (e.g. wealth) or B may influence A or A and B may reciprocally influence each other (first row of Figure 9.1 from left to right). Or a background variable C (religion) may affect both variables A (intelligence) and B (wealth). Or a background variable C (religion) may influence intelligence (A) and wealth (B) but intelligence (A), depending on religion (C), also affects wealth (B). This could be the

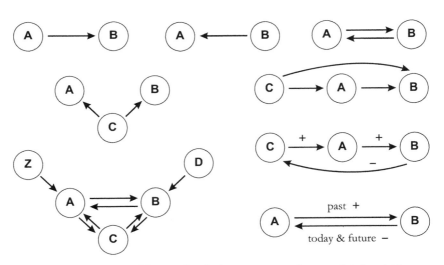

Figure 9.1 Possible causal paths between two and more related variables

case, e.g., for Protestantism or Confucianism stimulating education, achievement motivation and discipline (second row). To complicate things, there can
be a negative reverse effect, as wealth may reduce religiosity and its possible
positive effect on intelligence (third row). Or three variables reciprocally
influence each other (e.g. education C, cognitive ability A and wealth B) and
cognitive ability additionally depends on genes (Z) and wealth also on mineral
resources (D; Figure 9.1 last row on the left). Finally, effects that were positive
in the past can become inverted to negative ones in the present: Protestant
religiosity (A) has increased education in the past (B) and education reduces
Protestant religiosity today.

One solution to prove causal relationships between two variables independent of other factors is the use of *partial correlations*: Statistically, in partial
correlations the covariance of interested (two) variables is corrected for the
covariance with other (third) variables, e.g. the covariance of education and
intelligence is corrected for the covariance with wealth, an analysis dubbed
'wealth is partialled out'. The bivariate correlation $r = .74$ becomes the partial
correlation $r_p = .61$ ($N = 181$). However, if the partialled out variable (here
wealth) depends on one or both of the two interested variables (here education
and intelligence) the partial correlation underestimates the true correlation
between those variables (here between education and intelligence). For this
reason, another method, known as *path analysis*, a method considering the
dependency between variables, is preferable (see Figure 9.2).

As shown in Figure 9.2 cognitive ability has a stronger direct impact
on wealth (wealth indicated by income) than education has on wealth
($\beta_{CA \to GNI} = .47$ vs. $\beta_{Ed \to GNI} = .20$, $N = 181$ countries). However, that cannot
be the ultimate answer:

- Educational differences between countries are possibly less valid measures
  (underestimating education's impact);
- education also has an indirect effect in this model ($.74 \times .47 = .35$, total
  effect: $\beta_{EdLtot \to GNI} = .54$);

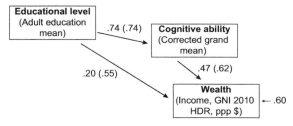

Figure 9.2 Path analysis with adult educational level, cognitive ability and
wealth ($N = 181$), standardised path coefficients, correlations in parentheses,
unexplained variance on the right

- cognitive ability also has an impact on education that is not possible to investigate in a cross-sectional model as presented in Figure 9.2; the model is therefore somewhat faulty, or at least the model is insufficiently complex;
- wealth also has reverse effects on education and on cognitive ability that are not investigable in cross-sectional models.

Single path models have opportunities, but also limits, which should not be forgotten. Only a combination of different methods – here of longitudinal and cross-sectional models – can lead to a more accurate answer.

It is frequently missed that in bivariate cross-sectional and longitudinal correlations between two variables such as between IQ and GDP, empirical interactions between these variables are included: the IQ of measurement point 1 includes former GDP influence on IQ and the GDP of measurement point 1 includes former IQ influence. Nevertheless, cross-lagged effects within longitudinal studies (e.g. Figures 10.1 and 10.2) can be a good estimate of the true effect, because under and overestimations are probably equal: there is an underestimation because only changes between measurement points 1 and 2 are analysed, not the development of GDP; there is an overestimation because past effects of the other variable are included in the effect on changes, the current effect of IQ on GDP also includes the past positive influence of GDP on IQ. There is no single appropriate method.

Finally, path analyses with current data analyse the relations between current variances. Often a historical development process is then inferred from present and twentieth-century phenomena. To back such conclusions, data from former epochs are needed. And historical analyses should complement statistical approaches.[3]

## 9.4    Relationship between Individuals and Higher Order Categories (Levels)

One frequently mentioned objection to country analyses is that any *inference across categories* (also called levels) is regarded as being impossible and ethically questionable. Criticised inferences are inferences from higher order to lower order categories, such as from countries or regions to individuals, or from lower order categories to higher order ones, such as from individuals to

---

[3] Complementing historical analyses are, for instance, from Clark (2007), Jacob (2014), Landes (1998), LePan, (1989), Mokyr (2016), Nelson (1974), Oesterdiekhoff (2014a,b), Sombart (1998/1913), Weber (2007/1923) and Weede (2012).

Table 9.1 *Correlations between variables at different data levels*

| Variable ↓           Level → | Individual level | Cross-country level |
|---|---|---|
| Psychometric IQ and student assessment | .65 | .85 (.86 corrected) |
| Cognitive ability and education | .68-.96 | .74 |
| Cognitive ability and income/wealth | .25 (.35 corr.), .35 | .62 |
| Cognitive ability and democracy | .24 | .47 |
| Cognitive ability and brain size | .31-.40 | .70-.77 |
| Cognitive ability and religion (C-M-contr.) | .28 | .28 |
| Interest and competence | .20 | -.77 |
| Homework and competence | .18 | -.18 |

*Notes*: IQ and student assessment: CogAT with PISA manifest (see Chapter 3; there are further correlations reported between .50 and .83), cross-country own calculations with Lynn & Vanhanen 2012 data and averages of student assessment studies, uncorrected $N = 89$, corrected $N = 108$, same correlations for the same countries of $N = 89$; education: amount/length, individual correlation from Ceci (1991), cross-country own calculations, corrected $N = 192$; wealth, individual level income in Germany (meta-analysis; Kramer, 2009) or Britain (Irwing & Lynn, 2006), internationally GNI 2010 HDR ($N = 183$), corrected grand mean of student assessment and psychometric intelligence-studies; democracy: individual level political involvement (Deary et al, 2008), cross-country ($N = 187$) see Section 10.3.2; brain size: see Section 10.7.2; religion (Christian-Muslim-contrast, Christians coded as 1), individually average from three studies in Graz with $N = 257$ students (see Section 10.8.4), internationally $N = 199$ countries; interest: interest and science competence, $N = 398,570$ students or $N = 55$ countries (PISA 2006; Täht et al., 2014, table 2, p. 265); homework: see Section 10.5.2.

countries. Usually, this problem is termed *'ecological fallacy'*.[4] There is no logical inference between different category levels but there is a *plausible inference*: the directions of relationships are usually identical; the correlations are typically only larger at the higher level (see Table 9.1).

In Table 9.1, individual and cross-country correlations are compared. It is obvious that correlations are usually similar, but somewhat higher at the aggregated data level. But there are also two correlations with changing signs: for interest and competence and homework and competence. Personality ratings – including attitudes and preferences – suffer from frames of reference effects (Schmitt et al., 2007, p. 206). Homework at the individual level represents diligence, and at the country level the outsourcing of learning from the school to the student and family. So answer patterns and changes of meanings of variables alter correlations. As mentioned, there is no compelling inference across data levels. At best, they are tentative and plausible.

[4] The ecological fallacy problem – relations including causes being valid at the individual level cannot be transferred to the level between groups – was addressed by different researchers; especially relevant for cognitive ability are the contributions of Richard Lewontin (1970) and Ned Block (1995).

But why are the correlations at the cross-national level usually higher? Aggregated data are more *reliable*; additionally, *multiplicative positive interactions between individual and macro-social determinants over time* increase correlations, e.g. between intelligence and quality of educational systems or between intelligence, production and wealth.[5] Individuals create institutions stabilising patterns in societies and increasing them across generations. Thus, even slight psychological differences between initially similar peoples may create ample and long-term stable national differences (e.g. Wade, 2014, p. 244).

The second feature of the category objection is an assumed missing *relationship between an individual and group assignment*. E.g. Frank is male and young. Even if crime or maths ability are above average for young males compared to older males or females we cannot infer from his group affiliation (youth, male) to his individual behaviour. Such group-based conclusions to individuals are frequently politically and ethically criticised as 'racism' even if 'race' is not an issue. The same answer applies for this objection as for the ecological fallacy problem: there is *no logically compelling inference* from the category to the case or from the case to the category, but an *inference is plausible*. Groups are composed of individuals and thus across all members of a group (vs. members of other groups) a positive correlation between individual trait and average group trait exists. The condition is that group assignment is not at random, e.g. being a member of a football team is determined by self- and external selection based on competence in football and being a member of a certain team changes the ability to play football via training, team influence and common experiences. Thus we can conclude from membership of the FC Barcelona football team that the individual FC Barcelona football player is a better footballer than the individual Malmö FF footballer.

Empirically this is given, e.g. for individual students and classes: individual student and class average ability levels correlate with $r = .37$ to $.44$ (Rindermann & Heller, 2005, figure 2). What does this correlation mean? The correlation is between Cohen's thresholds for a 'medium' ($r = .30$) or 'large' ($r = .50$) effect. Smarter students usually attend smarter classes and in smarter classes, on average, are smarter students. We can reasonably infer from an individual's ability level to a class' ability level and from a class' ability level to an individual's ability level. However, whenever possible we should avoid decisions on individuals only based on higher order category data: the correlation is not $r = 1$ and it is actually far away from $r = 1$; it would be *unfair*

---

[5] The higher reliability of aggregated data has, for example, the consequence that the fate of individual smokers is hard to predict, but the average fate of cigarette smokers can be predicted with accuracy. See also Jones' 'Hive mind' (Jones, 2016) or Wade (2014, pp. 122ff.) on 'Societies and institutions'.

(many individuals are over- or underestimated), *not meritoric* – decisions would not be based on individual behaviour in the long run, thus not supporting individual effort – and for an institutional selection process, *not informative enough*. Football clubs choose individual footballers according to their individual ability not due to their membership of another team, even if they are correlated. Finally, averages do not imply that any given individual will be average (Hallpike, 1980, p. 58; LePan, 1989, p. 43). Usually, there are substantial overlaps and within-group heterogeneities.

But all those arguments do not make group membership irrelevant. Group membership is informative. The philosopher Neven Sesardic:

> If it [the statement that people should be treated as individuals] is understood as saying that it is a fallacy to use the information about an individual's group membership to infer something about that individual, the statement is simply wrong. Exactly the opposite is true: it is a fallacy not to take this information into account ... If scholars wear their scientific hats when denying or disregarding this fact, I am afraid that rather than convincing the public they will more probably damage the credibility of science ... Of course, if we knew *everything* about a particular individual, then the information about groups to which that individual belongs would fade into irrelevance. An omniscient god would have no use for Bayes' theorem. We mortals, however, often have to deal with people about whom we know relatively little, and in these situations relying on prior probabilities from group data is *epistemically reasonable*. (Sesardic, 2005, pp. 217ff.)[6]

A similar position is taken by the psychologist Lee Jussim that is known as the '*Stereotype Rationality Hypothesis*':

> It is rational and reasonable to use stereotypes in the complete absence of individuating information, when the individuating information is perceived to be useless, and when individuating information is either scarce or ambiguous. (Jussim, 2012, pp. 380f.)

And a category or concept (stereotype is a category applied for social objects as groups and individuals) based on aggregated information, say based on the experience ('social reality') of many different and not completely dependent situations and persons, is more reliable and valid than the information gained by a single person. Less intelligent or left-wing persons are less accurate in their use of social concepts either due to a wrong use of accurate concepts, the use of wrong concepts or due to the denial and disuse of accurate social concepts (egalitarian ideology; Jussim, 2012, pp. 332, 398).

As mentioned by Sesardic and by Jussim, if we would have perfect information on an individual any inference from a higher order category would be unnecessary. However, because we do not have perfect information and we do not know for certain whether we have perfect information, inferences are

---

[6] Sesardic (2005, pp. 217–224) also gave a mathematical-statistical justification.

epistemically rational. Everybody is doing this in everyday life, and if not he or she will have to quickly face serious negative consequences. Correspondingly, inferences from individual experiences to higher order categories are also rational; this includes gender, ethnicity, nationality and culture. Both inferences reflect simple inductive and deductive concept formation as described by Jean Piaget as being indicative for the third cognitive development stage of concrete operations, beginning at age seven. Categorisation is the basis of thinking. Therefore, categorisation must not be avoided; but correcting too broad and too narrow generalisations and reducing illogical or uninformed empirical inferences is necessary. Errors cannot be completely avoided, only reduced. Arguing against the use of empirically informed and logically constructed and appropriately applied concepts means arguing against rational thinking at all.

Of course, (a) the smaller a group and the more specific a categorisation, (b) the larger the differences between groups and (c) the more homogenous groups are – and in the above mentioned Rindermann and Heller (2005) study students were assigned by ability to different tracks – the higher is the individual-group-correlation and the more reliable and valid are inferences across data levels, from individuals to groups and from groups to individuals. Actually, modern student assessment studies use correlations, categorisations and probabilities for estimating competences. Higher correlations increase probabilities and make categorisations more reliable. The more variables are given, which at least somewhat correlate with a criterion, the higher are the probabilities and the more reliable are categorisations. PISA, TIMSS and PIRLS do not apply complete test booklets but only excerpts (multiple matrix sampling). E.g. in PISA 2006, there were booklets only covering science tasks or only science and mathematics tasks. However, each student received results for reading, mathematics and science. The missing data were estimated by using other data and knowing the correlations between the variables of ability, personality, gender, family, class, school or country.[7] The given uncertainty, regardless of whether the variable was actually measured or not, is displayed by presenting five plausible values, there is not one single result for each scale. The five plausible values of one competence measure of one individual differ; the more they differ, the less reliable the measurement was, leading for only estimated variables to larger differences among the five plausible values.

PISA, TIMSS and PIRLS do not have the aim of measuring an individual's ability or motivation. Decisions on students' school career were not made, nor was any information provided for consultation. Only a measurement for

---

[7] The student assessment studies did not publish their formula, variables and weights for estimating data. E.g. PISA 2000 only mentioned the general procedure and two variables among others (gender and occupational socio-economic index; Adams & Wu, 2002, p. 107).

groups was intended, e.g. for French students at age 15 or male immigrants attending Gymnasium in Bavaria, a state in Germany. However, category-based data can also reasonably be used for individual probability or risk decisions: who should be controlled less or more at the security check in airports? Dragnet policing, advertisement, marketing research or decisions on production volume are based on such information. Google, Amazon and Facebook are quite successful at using such sophisticated algorithms. People having shown interest in cat litter and cat food probably have a cat, like cats, are White but are not Nobel laureates.[8] Implicitly, we all use such information in dealing with other persons, e.g. we use sex and age as information to guide with whom we meet and where and at what time.

Nevertheless, even if category-based inferences are reliable and valid, the limits should be kept in mind. There are no $r = 1$ correlations. Smart persons and sophisticated estimation processes take this into account. For instance, even if average ability levels for immigrants from Middle East countries are low – there are many intelligent immigrants, well-known scientists, competent professionals and reliable workers. There are dull Finnish students and impulsive Japanese. There are Muslims who drink wine and eat pork. However, for each exception, and the more extreme the exception is, there have to be more typical cases. The larger the differences, the more typical or offsetting cases have to exist to compensate for outliers: for every dull Finnish student many very smart ones are necessary, and for every genius among groups with average low ability many even more low ability persons have to exist to come to the known mean results.

As far as we have broader statistical data based on larger samples of individuals and situations, examples of individuals are not essential for international analyses. They only illustrate abstract relationships and causal impacts; for instance, what does it mean for airlines and passengers to have a smart intellectual class in a country (Chapter 8).

---

[8]  www.gallup.com/poll/102952/companionship-love-animals-drive-pet-ownership.aspx.

# 10 Causes of National and Historical Differences in Cognitive Ability – and Reciprocal Effects

> This chapter describes and discusses causes for national and historical differences in cognitive ability, covering wealth, health, politics, modernity, education, geography and climate, evolutionary-genetic dispositions and finally culture, including worldviews and religion. It analyses direct and indirect, reverse (of ability) and reciprocal effects. Cognitive ability depends on the described factors but also amplifies their effects and shapes them.

The outcomes of international comparative student assessment studies led to a broad consensus that students of different countries have different 'literacy', 'proficiency' or 'skill' levels. Empirical analyses showed that they are highly stable across scales, grades, measurement points and study approaches (see Chapter 4). These results – precisely the cross-country differences – also highly correlate with results of psychometric intelligence test surveys and with results of adult literacy studies (see Figure 4.2, Section 4.3). Correlational studies at the *individual* level performed by different authors using different tests corroborated a pattern of homogenous ability differences across scales and tests. Finally, theoretical analyses of tasks, task demands and cognitive processes during task processing showed a large overlap of different scales of the same tests and different test approaches. This altogether not only allows, but enforces recognising test survey differences as *cognitive ability differences between nations*. Furthermore, large differences can be observed not only *across countries* but also *across time* within countries – the latter standing for the 'FLynn effect', the secular rise of cognitive ability.

These differences are not trivial. According to cognitive human capital theory they generate technological, economic, health, political and cultural differences. Through cultural-institutional dynamics they lead to national wellbeing differences. Higher ability levels lead to societal conditions that are preferred by the majority of people and that are justifiable by arguments, by referring to norms as wellbeing, life, health, liberty, autonomy and enlightenment.

But *why* do nations and people differ in the important characteristic of cognitive ability? Speculations can be quickly proposed, but are hypotheses backed by empirical evidence? And if we have found an effective determinant, how important is it in the context of other, frequently related factors? One confirmed factor will not be the single one explanatory factor for all country differences across regions and time. Stressing one factor and neglecting others may be motivated by ideology. From an epistemic view, a narrow one-factor view is insufficient:

'Das Wahre ist das Ganze.' – 'The truth is the whole.' (Hegel, 1999/1807, p. 19)

It is correct to claim that tigers have two legs, but in total they have four. It is correct to claim that birds have two legs, but birds have four limbs and the distinction for birds is that they have two wings. Knowledge gaps can be filled by more research and broader inquiry. But the omission of information with the aim of diverting perception from other relevant determinants is either unconscious delusion or conscious fraud. Either way, both are not compatible with epistemic rationality.

The main causes discussed in research and frequently in a wider interested academic public are wealth, health, politics, modernity, education, geography, genes and culture. Let us take a look in detail at those.

## 10.1   Wealth

There are large wealth differences across time and nations. What is more obvious than first looking at wealth as a causal factor for national cognitive ability differences?[1] However, money just by itself will not make people smart, only expediently spent money. What means 'expediently spent'? It means here that money is spent for the improvement of human development. Thus spending money for expensive holidays in the Caribbean or a cruise, for a Porsche or brand-name clothing, a Rolex or an iPhone, attending the Georgia Aquarium or Disneyland will not boost intelligence nor relevant knowledge. Even spending on private schools – depending on country and local conditions – does not convincingly cause cognitive achievement gains![2]

Money spent on certain deficiency conditions for remedying them can have large positive impacts on cognitive ability. Some examples for effects via health improvement:

- The *price of infant formula* in a poor country such as the Philippines shows a negative effect on intelligence. Lowering infant formula costs

---

[1] E.g. Christainsen (2013) with analysis of reverse causality.

[2] E.g. for the UK according to a study by Bond & Saunders (1999, p. 235), the achievement effect of attending a private school is only $\beta = .07$ or even negative. More robust positive effects are found in the United States for lower achieving or lower ability students, especially due to uncompromising education for discipline in private schools (Neal, 2009). Generally, private school students achieve better results in ability tests, but usually they are not better due to better school quality but due to selection by students, their parents and the school.

by 50 per cent increased children's intelligence six to eight years later by 4.4 IQ points (Glewwe & King, 2001, p. 97).

- *Deworming drugs* in Africa improved pupils' health and as a result their school attendance rates by 25 per cent (Glewwe & Kremer, 2006, p. 980f., 983f.; Miguel & Kremer, 2004, p. 160). Because instruction increases cognitive ability, IQ effects are probable. The treatment costs only $3.50 per year.
- Similarly, improving *water infrastructure* in developing countries leads to higher school attendance rates (Koolwal & Walle, 2010).
- Adding *meat* to school meals in Kenya improved intelligence measured by Raven's Matrices (because of proteins, trace elements and vitamins, about 3 IQ; Whaley et al., 2003).

It becomes obvious that positive wealth effects are overlapping with positive health and education effects. Wealth works through improving health and through making children, adolescents and adults physiologically better prepared for learning.[3] And of course, there can be reverse effects: smarter peoples, politicians and officials as well as parents and adults, will modify their environment in the direction of beneficial effects.

At the international level the correlations between cognitive ability and wealth indicators are high (see Table 10.1). They are considerably higher for the Maddison data than for Penn or Human Development data (Chapter 1). The reasons for this are unknown. The correlations with logged data are higher than for data in 'natural' currency units. The differences among the four wealth indicators become smaller using logged data. Using the logarithm emphasises wealth differences among the poorer countries. Wealth increases for the poor have a stronger impact on the quality of life relevant for cognitive development. Another systematic pattern is that there are higher correlations with ability levels of intellectual classes (95 per cent level) compared to the means and especially the low ability group level (5 per cent). This is also plausible, since intellectual classes are crucial for innovation, production and the development of societies (see Chapter 8).

But what influences what?

Longitudinal studies at the level of countries can disentangle IQ-wealth correlations by distinguishing cognitive ability from wealth effects.[4] So far it has been shown analysing cross-lagged effects in longitudinal studies that the

---

[3] Health also includes psychological health. Experimental studies by Mani et al. (2013) show for adults that cognitive poverty stress leads to a temporary intelligence decline as measured by the Ravens of about 13 IQ points. However, as they have also shown, these declines were situation-specific (under hard economic threats, not under weak economic threats) and they could be recovered within weeks (e.g. for farmers after a successful harvest).

[4] On 'wealth effects': this is a smaller inexactness in the use of terms. In the narrower sense GDP per capita stands for measured economic production per year, not wealth. But production leads to wealth and there is no argument why production other than via wealth should increase cognitive ability. GDP is used here as an independent (1970) and dependent (2010) variable: as an

Table 10.1 *Correlations between wealth and cognitive ability indicators*

| | CA (corrected) | SAS M (corrected, all) | SAS M (uncorrected., PTP) | SAS 95% (uncorrected, high ability) | SAS 05% (uncorrected, low ability) |
|---|---|---|---|---|---|
| **GDP 2010 Maddison (production)** | .76 | .77 | .74 | .77 | .71 |
| **(logged)** | (.82) | (.78) | (.76) | (.79) | (.73) |
| **GDP 2010 Penn (production)** | .55 | .47 | .43 | .48 | .39 |
| **(logged)** | (.73) | (.68) | (.66) | (.70) | (.62) |
| **GNI 2010 HDR (income)** | .62 | .55 | .51 | .55 | .47 |
| **(logged)** | (.74) | (.68) | (.66) | (.70) | (.62) |
| **Credit Suisse 2010 (assets)** | .60 | .59 | .57 | .60 | .54 |
| **(logged)** | (.75) | (.69) | (.66) | (.69) | (.63) |

*Notes*: CA (corrected): average of student assessment and psychometric intelligence studies, corrected (see appendix), $N = 161–188$; SAS M (corr., all): mean of student assessment studies including local studies in developing countries and older studies until 1990, corrected for grade, age and school attendance rates, $N = 101–106$; SAS M (uncorrected, PTP): only mean of higher quality SAS studies PISA, TIMSS and PIRLS 1995–2012, uncorrected, $N = 92–97$; SAS 95% (uncorrected, high ability): top ability level (intellectual classes) at $95^{th}$ percentile, based on PISA, TIMSS and PIRLS 1995–2012, uncorrected, $N = 92–97$; SAS 5% (uncorrected, low ability): low ability level at $5^{th}$ percentile, based on PISA, TIMSS and PIRLS 1995–2012, uncorrected, $N = 92–97$; wealth indicators in currency units or using the logarithm ('logged'; see Tables 1.1 and 1.4).

impact of cognitive ability on produced wealth is slightly larger than the impact of given wealth on cognitive ability. In such studies cognitive ability was measured by student achievement in the late 1960s and early 1970s vs. 1995 to 2007 and wealth by GDP per capita in 1960s and 1970 vs. 1998 to 2000. As control variables economic freedom, democracy, rule of law or political liberty were considered. Across those six analyses the impact of cognitive ability on wealth was $\beta_{CA \rightarrow GDP} = .27$ and the impact of wealth on ability $\beta_{GDP \rightarrow CA} = .24$ ($N = 17$ countries, mean of six analyses in Rindermann, 2008a, 2008b, 2012). Including newer data, the effect sizes are $\beta_{CA \rightarrow GDP} = .27$ vs. $\beta_{GDP \rightarrow CA} = .25$ ($N = 17$, seven analyses).

The difference in effect sizes was more accentuated using years of education as proxy for cognitive ability and having a larger country sample of 79 to 94 countries: $\beta_{Ed \rightarrow GDP} = .37$ vs. $\beta_{GDP \rightarrow Ed} = .04$ (mean of five analyses from the

independent one GDP reflects wealth effects on freedom and human capital, as a dependent one it reflects production being influenced by freedom and human capital.

same papers). There is a positive effect of wealth on national intelligence development as measured by tests but the cognitive human capital (CHC, ability and education averaged) effect on wealth production is larger (averaging both, ability and education studies: $\beta_{CHC \rightarrow GDP}$ = .32 vs. $\beta_{GDP \rightarrow CHC}$ = .14). But a negation of a positive wealth effect would be wrong.

The pattern will become more obvious in more detailed analyses. First, we use newer data and distinguish between *wealth as measured by GDP in currency units* and *GDP in logged units* (see Figure 10.1). Logging means taking the logarithm of GDP and stressing differences in the poorer realm (see also Section 1.1). For our purpose, to understand wealth effects on cognitive development, this makes sense, because more wealth for the rich will not have such an impact in improving the relevant conditions for development compared to improvements for the poor – the additional iPad is irrelevant for thinking, but meat for the malnourished is crucial.

Figure 10.1 shows the analyses for using either GDP-raw in currency units (above) or GDP-logged (below).[5] Corroborating the old results, for producing wealth, in both analyses cognitive human capital is more important than economic freedom ($\beta_{CHC70 \rightarrow GDPr10}$ = .31 vs. $\beta_{EF70 \rightarrow GDPr10}$ = .19, $\beta_{CHC70 \rightarrow GDPl10}$ = .19 vs. $\beta_{EF70 \rightarrow GDPl10}$ = .11).[6] Even more than before, economic freedom is strongly supported by cognitive factors ($\beta_{CHC70 \rightarrow EF10}$ = .83 and $\beta_{CHC70 \rightarrow EF10}$ = .62), but economic freedom has also a positive impact on cognitive human capital ($\beta_{EF70 \rightarrow CHC10}$ = .14 and $\beta_{EF70 \rightarrow CHC10}$ = .12). This is probably due to meritoric stimulation.

And similarly to the older GDP-raw results, the cognitive effect on wealth is larger than the one from wealth to cognitive human capital: $\beta_{CHC70 \rightarrow GDPr10}$ = .31 vs. $\beta_{GDPr70 \rightarrow CHC10}$ = .05. However, for GDP-logged, the opposite is true, a larger wealth than a cognitive effect: $\beta_{CHC70 \rightarrow GDPl10}$ = .19 vs. $\beta_{GDPl70 \rightarrow}$

---

[5] Data sources: Two indicators of *cognitive human capital*, either years of school education ($N$ = 47) or cognitive ability tests (student assessment test results, $N$ = 17). *Years of school education* 1970 is the 'average schooling years in the total population over age 25' according to Barro and Lee (2000), same as in Rindermann (2008a). Years of school education 2010 from HDR 2010 (UNDP, 2010, pp. 143–147). *Student assessment results* from 1964 to 1972 collected by Lee and Barro (1997). For around 2010 newer studies from TIMSS 1994 to PISA 2012 (majority of studies between 1999 and 2011). Economic freedom 1970 from Gwartney et al. (2013, pp. 17–20, chain-linked, Madagascar was added and adapted from unchain-linked data). *Economic freedom* 2010 is a combination of the Fraser index (Gwartney et al., 2013) and Heritage index (Miller et al., 2013). GDP raw or logged 1970 and around 2010 from Maddison in 1990 international \$ (Maddison, 2008; 2010 from Bolt & van Zanden, 2013). 'Maddison-original' only provides data for 2008, not 2010, 'Maddison-successors' Bolt & van Zanden also for 2010, but for fewer countries ($N_{2008}$ = 159, $N_{2008}$ = 117). Therefore, we combined the 2008-scale adapted to the 2010-scale. Due to rounding errors in Figure 10.1 $R^2 = \Sigma r\beta$ and unexplained variance at the right do not always exactly add up to 1.

[6] The higher relevance of ability than of economic freedom is corroborated by analyses from Hanushek & Woessmann (2015a, p. 56) using growth as the dependent variable.

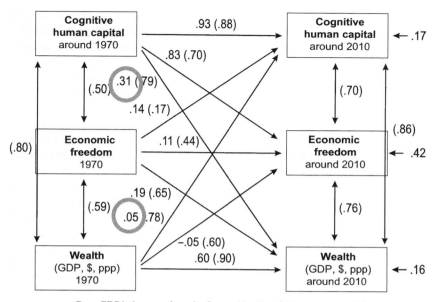

Raw-GDP/c (averaged results form a $N=47$ and 17 country sample)

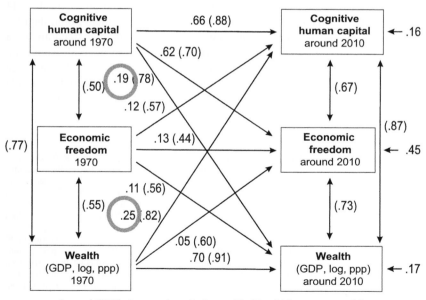

Logged-GDP/c (averaged results form a $N=47$ and 17 country sample)

Figure 10.1 Cross-lagged effects; stronger cognitive effect in the raw-GDP analysis; stronger wealth effect in the log-GDP analysis (standardised path coefficients; correlations in parentheses; unexplained variance on the right)

CHC10 = .25. Following the idea that taking the logarithm stresses wealth differences in the poorer realm, the larger log-wealth effect stresses the *importance of wealth increases for cognitive development in poorer countries*, whereas the larger cognitive effect for raw-wealth stresses the *importance of cognitive ability in rich and complex modernity*: rich countries are rich because they are smart and poor countries are not smart because they are poor (see Figure 10.3).

This pattern can be checked by separate analyses for richer and poorer countries. For the cognitive ability country sample of 17 countries, a subdivision in richer and poorer countries is not sensible, but it is for the large years of education sample covering 88 countries (figure 4 in Rindermann, 2008a). Using median split the longitudinal cognitive human capital effect on wealth produced annually per capita was somewhat higher for richer countries (richer: $\beta_{\text{Ed} \rightarrow \text{GDP}}$ = .41, $N$ = 44; poorer: $\beta_{\text{Ed} \rightarrow \text{GDP}}$ = .35, $N$ = 44). The reciprocal effect of wealth on cognitive human capital is considerably larger in poorer countries: in richer: $\beta_{\text{GDP} \rightarrow \text{Ed}}$ = .04, $N$ = 44; in poorer: $\beta_{\text{GDP} \rightarrow \text{Ed}}$ = .18, $N$ = 44. Using newer data for 2010 and a smaller country sample the pattern was corroborated: there is a stronger GDP effect in poorer countries on cognitive human capital: richer 24 nations: $\beta_{\text{GDP} \rightarrow \text{Ed}}$ = −.03; poorer 24 nations: $\beta_{\text{GDP} \rightarrow \text{Ed}}$ = .20.[7]

In Figure 10.2 we present the average of both analyses combined, the 44 + 44 and 24 + 24 country samples with, at the second measurement point, data for 2000 or 2010 and for the first measurement point economic freedom for a broader interval representing 1970s freedom or a narrower interval. Above are the results for the richer country sample, below for the poorer. The average wealth effect on cognitive human capital is much smaller in the richer sample ($\beta_{\text{GDP} \rightarrow \text{Ed}}$ = .01) than in the poorer country sample ($\beta_{\text{GDP} \rightarrow \text{Ed}}$ = .19).

---

[7] In the newer data set we have restricted the first measurement point for economic freedom ('n' standing for narrow). In the former data set we used a longer time period for the first measurement point until the early 1980s. $N$ = 48, split $N$ = 24 and $N$ = 24 ('b' standing for broad). Data sources, 88 (44/44) country sample from Rindermann (2008a, figure 4) – see there. Data sources, 48 (24/24) country sample: 1970 the 'average schooling years in the total population over age 25' according to Barro and Lee (2000), same as in Rindermann (2008a). Economic freedom from Gwartney et al. (2013, pp. 17–20, chain-linked, Madagascar was added and adapted from not chain-linked). GDP 1970 logged from Penn World Table Version 7.1 (PPP Converted GDP Per Capita, Laspeyres, derived from growth rates of c, g, i, at 2005 constant prices, unit: 2005 International dollar per person; Heston et al., 2012). Years of school education 2010 from HDR 2010 (UNDP, 2010, pp. 143–147), economic freedom and GDP 2010 from the same sources as 2010. Due to rounding errors in Figure 10.2, $R^2 = \Sigma r\beta$ and unexplained variance on the right do not always exactly add to 1.

It should not go unmentioned that the 'years of education' indicator for cognitive human capital (cognitive ability) is not a perfect one and prone to ceiling effects, especially for smarter groups.

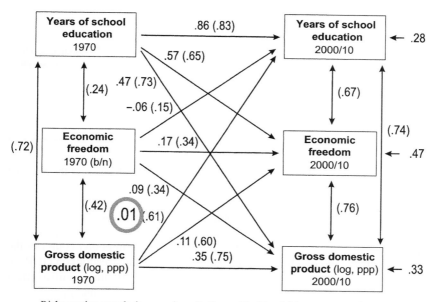

Richer nation sample (averaged results form a *N* = 44 and 24 country sample)

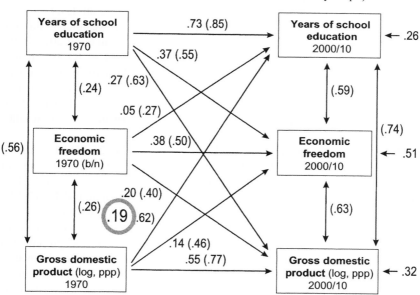

Poorer nation sample (averaged results form a *N* = 44 and 24 country sample)

Figure 10.2 Cross-lagged effects; stronger wealth effect on cognitive capital in the poorer country sample (standardised path coefficients; correlations in parentheses; unexplained variance on the right)

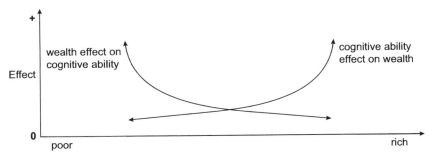

Figure 10.3 Wealth is relevant for the cognitive development of the poor and cognitive ability is relevant for the wealth development of the rich

The second important result is that again the cognitive human capital effect is larger in richer countries than in poorer ones (richer: $\beta_{Ed \to GDP}$ = .47; poorer: $\beta_{Ed \to GDP}$ = .27; Figures 10.2 and 10.3). While in poorer countries the positive effects of cognitive human capital and economic freedom on GDP are comparable (poorer: $\beta_{Ed \to GDP}$ = .27 and $\beta_{EF \to GDP}$ = .20), the cognitive effect is much larger in wealthy countries (richer: $\beta_{Ed \to GDP}$ = .47 and $\beta_{EF \to GDP}$ = .09). *As economies modernise, cognitive abilities grow in importance.*

Further evidence for low wealth effects from a certain wealth level upwards is given by countries that benefited from passively gained wealth, e.g. through oil resources in the Arab world: for instance, oil-rich Kuwait (GNI 2010 HDR: $55,719) reached only an average cognitive ability level of IQ 79 (student assessment studies SAS: 69 IQ points). Compared to Western countries (GNI: $36,643) of around IQ 98 (SAS: 99 IQ) and even poor countries such as Morocco (GNI: $4,628, IQ 76, SAS: 63 IQ) and Iran (GNI: $11,764, IQ 85, SAS: 81 IQ), the Kuwait result is too low for confirmation of the wealth-hypothesis.

The same is true for wealthy Saudi Arabia (GNI: $24,726, IQ 81, SAS: 77 IQ) and Bahrain (GNI: $26,664, IQ 86, SAS: 85 IQ). Their results are not notably superior to those from poor Tunisia (GNI: $7,979, IQ 91, SAS: 82 IQ), Palestine (GNI: no information, IQ 83, SAS: 77 IQ), Lebanon (GNI: $13,475, IQ 83, SAS: 78 IQ) and Jordan (GNI: $5,956, IQ 87, SAS: 85 IQ).

Pupils in the richest countries of the world have lower or similar cognitive ability results compared to pupils from a similar cultural background and comparable economic system but poorer economy because of the absence of extensive mineral resources relative to a small population. This does not mean that financial means are totally unimportant. They have to be invested in the proper way. This includes ensuring health and education.

In summary, there is no consistent positive effect of wealth on cognitive human capital in richer countries, but there is in poorer countries.

This suggests that *wealth effects on cognitive ability peter out*; that general stimulation effects by economic-technological modernity on cognitive ability are less relevant compared to basic health effects. We want to look over these now in more detail.

## 10.2 Health

### 10.2.1 Parasites, Nutrition and Hygiene

We have just mentioned basic health conditions: nutrition and parasite control have positive effects on individual cognitive development. There is an important cross-country study showing high negative correlations between parasite load and cognitive ability ($r = -.76$ to $r = -.82$; Eppig et al., 2010). The cause for this negative relationship is seen within the individual body and here in the competition for relevant nutrients between fighting off infectious diseases versus neurological maturation and brainwork.

Of course, cross-country studies cannot prove processes at the level of individuals and even within them. However, the biological theory is convincing and it is backed by a study with children in Brazil (Jardin-Botelho et al., 2008): after correcting for further background factors, especially parental SES, having hookworms and roundworms decreased cognitive ability as measured by various scales at $d = 0.38$ (5.72 IQ); losses are especially large in Raven's intelligence test ($d = 0.54$, 8.03 IQ). Physiologically, the negative effect may be due to a more enduring negative impact on neurological maturation or a more temporary impeding of cognitive processing, especially concentration. But continuing impairment of processing will also lead to a delay in cognitive development, with long-term effects on cumulative knowledge acquisition.

Finally, there is experimental evidence for a positive cognitive ability effect of deworming: treated children compared to non-treated (placebo) children in Indonesia gained more in Raven's intelligence test (Hadidjaja et al., 1998).[8] The treatment effect for children was roughly +8 IQ – an important increase.

More hygiene in food production and in dealing with water, accompanied by the use of conveniences (water closet) and the practice of hand washing would not only preserve against worm infection but also more broadly against diarrhoea. Additionally, mosquito nets protect against malaria and dengue. For all these cases, the behaviour of the social environment is crucial: individual malfunctions in a healthy environment, healthy either due to favourable

---

[8] The authors (Hadidjaja et al., 1998) did not present IQs, *d*s or standard deviations. Thus effect sizes cannot be taken from the article. But it was possible to recalculate them by using Raven's CPM manual and the raw scores.

natural conditions or prudent behaviour, entail less serious consequences. In the opposite case, even the merest mistake can be lethal.

All interventions mentioned in this section are far from expensive. Deworming is extraordinarily cost-effective at only $3.50 of an additional year of schooling as outcome (Glewwe & Kremer, 2006, p. 983). Maybe that is astonishing, but there is no lack of money hindering improvement. There is a deficit in reasonable distribution of money. A study conducted in Uganda by Reinikka and Svensson (2004) revealed that in the 1990s only 13 per cent of government grants intended for schools and education were actually received by the schools. There are misallocations of resources, corruption and personal enrichment, which are negatively related via average and intellectual classes' cognitive ability level to institutional quality, especially supervisory bodies in the police, administration, judiciary and the media (Section 10.3). Ethical and cultural norms have an additional impact (Section 10.8).

Obstetrics, inoculation, nutrition and the general health system also contribute to health. Nutrition implies not only having enough to eat but also having a healthy diet. Some, also in wealthy nations, suffer from so-called hidden hunger: they eat enough calories, but take low quality food lacking micronutrients such as vitamins (e.g. vitamin A, Bs, C) and trace elements (zinc, iron, iodine) leading to stunting. An enrichment of food by meat, milk, fish, eggs, fruits and vegetables is necessary in such cases.

For health, a basic wealth level is necessary, which today for the vast majority of nations and people is provided. Many of the very poor countries receive international help. Nowadays, cultural and cognitive factors – the other way around – are more important for explaining international health differences. This is especially revealing for the case of AIDS.

### 10.2.2    AIDS as an Example: Effects and Causes

HIV infection rates and wealth are negatively correlated at the international level (around $r = -.24$; see below). And it is intuitively convincing that poverty is not helpful in the treatment of an infection which needs a high-cost pharmaceutical treatment. No treatment leads to higher virus loads, facilitating the transmission of the virus by sex and during pregnancy and birth. Finally, other untreated sexually transmitted diseases (STDs) also facilitate HIV transmission. What is therefore more obvious than to place a responsibility on poverty for AIDS as by Thabo Mbeki (Nattrass, 2012)? Another frequently mentioned thesis is that *discrimination* fosters the spread of HIV; discrimination of homosexual people, of persons infected with HIV or of AIDS patients. One indicator for this is gender equality (Hausmann et al., 2011). However, this indicator does not, as expected, negatively correlate with HIV infection rates; depending on country samples the correlations are around zero ($r = \pm.06$).

Another indicator for (low) discrimination is *political modernity*. This measure is a composite of democracy, rule of law and liberty.[9] As expected, political modernity correlates negatively with HIV rates (around $r = -.17$).

Nevertheless, as discussed in Chapter 7, cognitive factors may also play a role. *Cognitive ability* helps one to conduct a more healthy lifestyle, e.g. by anticipating and preventing dangerous situations through insight, setting proper priorities and, if someone is sick, by better treatment adherence and disease management. Further indirect effects may be selection of better environments (social environments, social climbing by educational titles in richer and therefore healthier environments), general lifestyle differences independent of intelligence and general health (IQ as an indicator of it).

Several researchers have described how cognitive ability – or indirectly its proxy education – has positive impacts on *infection preventing behaviour* as well as on *infection and disease management*. For instance, in Zambia, Fylkesnes et al. (2001, pp. 909, 914) described the positive influence of education on promoting cautious sexual behaviour:

The dominant pattern was decline [of HIV prevalence in Zambia] in the higher educational groups and no change or rising rates among groups with lower education ... Condom use was strongly associated with educational status at both time points ... Taking men aged 20-29 years as an illustration, the likelihood of [condom] 'use last time you had sex' was 29% in the group with less than 8 years of schooling versus 69% among those with 10 or more years of school attendance.

De Walque (2004) emphasised for Uganda the importance of education and cognitive abilities for understanding AIDS-related information, responding to this information by avoiding risky sexual behaviour, and generally a greater appreciation of burgher values in life:

More educated individuals are more likely to have visited an AIDS counseling center and to have obtained the results from an HIV-test ... They are also more likely to start their sexual life at a later age ... In addition, for females, the number of partners is negatively associated with schooling. (p. 16f.) These findings reveal that educated individuals have been more responsive to the HIV/AIDS information campaigns. The analysis of sexual behavior reinforces that conclusion: condom use is associated positively with schooling levels. (p. 1)

But the question still remains: being confronted with a deadly, but easily avoided infection – why did so many people not change their behaviour towards more caution and prudence? A more fundamental answer could be based on Piagetian cognitive psychology (Oesterdiekhoff & Rindermann, 2007): the main argument is that *people at the level of preoperational thinking*

---

[9] Democracy, rule of law and political liberty: data description see Section 2.4. The average has a reliability of Cronbach-$\alpha$ = .88.

*deal in a prerational, magical and delusional style with reality* including sexuality and health. So it was and possibly is still common for sexual stimulation and increase of fertility among several peoples in the region of the Rift Valley ('Great Lakes' in Africa) to use blood of male and female monkeys, e.g. by injecting blood in the thigh or pubis of men and women. Others put the meat of wild animals in the vagina as a magic ritual (Kashamura, 1973, p. 135f.). The circumcision of girls increases later infection risks; men believe that intercourse with a virgin cures AIDS (Grill, 2005, p. 303); people believe that AIDS is transmitted and curable by supernatural powers (e.g. about one third of all people in Zambia; Grill, 2005, p. 302), especially by witchcraft (Caldwell, 2002; Signer, 2004, p. 249); to speak about AIDS, to inform and warn, may attract the disease and is therefore avoided; women have to be 'cleaned' with the husband's sperm or even other men's before marriage, during pregnancy and after the death of a husband and sometimes babies are rubbed in with sperm (called 'Fisi' or 'Cleansing'; Benning, 2007; Grill, 2005, p. 302f.).

Even some leading African politicians and intellectuals have irrational convictions and publicly communicated them. According to Nicoli Nattrass (2012), the former South African president Thabo Mbeki denied or did not understand the role of HIV for the development of AIDS – he stressed that HIV is not the cause of AIDS. Political leaders preferred to ignore reality by saying that AIDS was not a problem and was not transmitted by unprotected sex. Leaders believe in 'Voodoo-science' (Grill, 2005, p. 305f.) and invent conspiracy theories, for instance AIDS was a fabrication or an invention by the West/CIA etc. to kill black people (Nattrass, 2012).[10] In 2001, the South African health minister and physician Manto Tshabalala-Msimang declared that modern medication against AIDS is not necessary; therefore, offers of free medication to prevent transmission of HIV from the mother to the unborn baby were refused; the government seemed to be indifferent to the welfare of its citizens (Nattrass, 2012). Even South African politicians like Peter Mokaba who died from AIDS denied the existence of HIV (source: Grill, 2005, p. 313). Following the BBC (see Section 4.4.3), Jacob Zuma, the president of South

---

[10] If we follow for a moment this blaming pattern of thinking, a kind of opposite statement would be more true: AIDS was not 'created by Whites to kill Blacks', but 'has emerged among Blacks and killed Blacks and everybody else including Whites'. AIDS came from sub-Saharan Africa and spread all over the world. For example, many Cambodians died from AIDS introduced by UN-troops from Africa. The advanced technological and economic state of the Occident led to 'advantages of backwardness' for other regions, whose progress and economic growth are supported by adopted Western technology and institutions. In the case of AIDS, they can use education and medicine developed in the West to fight AIDS. But the 'advantage of backwardness' can be used only where the social, cultural and cognitive prerequisites for their use are given. In the case of AIDS, 'Western' knowledge can be put to use only where at-risk people and their politicians are prepared to understand the issues.

Africa, was accused of rape and said taking a shower after sex with an HIV-infected woman protected him against HIV-transmission; therefore, he would not need an HIV-test. Wangari Maathai, the winner of the Nobel Peace Prize, is reported to have said that AIDS was invented in Western laboratories to kill black people ('biological warfare'; source: Nattrass, 2012, p. 1). In Nigeria, radical Protestant churches, supported by parts of the Nigerian film industry, disseminated the conviction that praying cures AIDS. The former President of Gambia (1994-2017), Yahya Jammeh, believed AIDS can be cured by personally developed ointments of natural herbs; a United Nations official who questioned this treatment was later expelled. And even when modern treatment is used, the effect of the medicine is attributed to its magic properties (Signer, 2004, p. 10).[11]

The common cause of irrationality – denying of research results, belief in magical convictions and conspiracy theories – is low cognitive development. This does not necessarily mean that the politicians who raised these irrational ideas have preoperational cognitive development levels and IQs at around 60 to 80. Most probably, they have at least average cognitive ability. But they developed and communicated their ideas within a social environment of low ability that appreciated such ideas, did not criticise them or even supported them.

All this together (a) helped to transmit the virus from monkey to man, (b) helped to transmit the virus from adult person to person, (c) helped to transmit the virus from adults to children and youth, (d) increased the virus load in infected persons, leading to higher risk of transmission in unprotected sex and earlier death.

The strongest support for the education-intelligence-thesis of health in AIDS (if already being infected) comes from a study from Goldman and Smith (2002). They investigated the relationship between education (years of schooling), intelligence (knowledge-loaded WAIS), wealth, health behaviour and health in two samples of persons in the United States afflicted with either HIV or diabetes. The health of persons with higher treatment compliance

---

[11] According to Nicoli Nattrass (2012, p. 45) in South Africa around 16 per cent of Blacks believe in conspiracy theories ('AIDS was invented to kill Black people' or 'AIDS was created by scientists in America'), Whites and others at around 1 per cent. Nattrass (2012, p. 12ff.) also reported results from US surveys showing that in the United States persons with African background more frequently (around 20 to 60 per cent) believe in AIDS conspiracy theories (e.g. 'The AIDS virus was deliberately created to infect black people.') than persons with European background. Usually, the majority rejected such theories. On belief in conspiracy theories in the United States see also Crocker et al. (1999) or Gordon (1997). According to Nattrass (2012), AIDS conspiracy theories were first developed by 'mad' right-wing Whites in the United States, e.g. William Cooper. They are also common among 'mad' left-wing politicians, e.g. Manto Tshabalala-Msimang or Peter Mokaba, but not among centrist politicians. Attributing 'mad' was based on statements and behaviour within and outside the AIDS field.

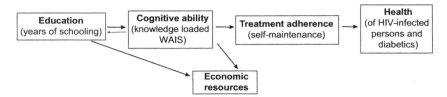

Figure 10.4 Influence of education and cognitive ability on health behaviour resulting in health of HIV-infected persons and diabetics (following Goldman & Smith, 2002)

improved (or more slowly deteriorated) compared to persons with lower compliance. Treatment adherence depended on education, but this direct impact vanished when intelligence was controlled (Figure 10.4): According to Goldman and Smith, it is not treatment, but treatment adherence that was the crucial variable for health and treatment adherence depending on 'the individual's ability for higher-level reasoning'. (p. 10933).

Summarising the evidence from the individual level, it is expectable that cognitive ability and HIV infection rates are negatively related at the cross-country level. In former analyses, the correlation between national HIV rates and cognitive ability levels was $r = -.48$ (Rindermann, 2008a; Rindermann & Meisenberg, 2009). In the current data set the correlation is $r = -.41$ ($N = 145$, for around 2010 $r = -.37$, $N = 145$). Excluding sub-Saharan Africa, the correlation is $r = -.30$ ($N = 100$, for around 2010 $r = -.17$, $N = 100$). Compared to wealth, gender equality and political modernity ($r_{GNI/GDP} = -.24$, $r_{GendE} = \pm.06$, $r_{PolMod} = -.17$) the negative correlations – higher IQ and lower HIV rate – are higher.

Using a path analysis which shows relative, direct and indirect effects, the pattern becomes clearer. 'Relative effects' means that the relationship between two variables is calculated in the context of other factors, leading to less biased and purer effects; 'direct effects' are relationships between two variables without further variables in between; 'indirect effects' are relationships between two variables mediated by another one or more. Such a path analysis does make sense when a causal mechanism is assumed to be standing behind relative, direct and indirect effects. For this assumption of a causal mechanism a causal theory is necessary and it should be backed by experimental studies, longitudinal cross-lagged studies and natural-experiment studies controlling the impact of further important factors. The results of such a natural experiment, a cross-sectional study controlling the impact of further important factors are presented in Figure 10.5.

Educational differences between countries correspond to cognitive ability differences ($\beta/r = .80$). In this model, we assume a unidirectional educational

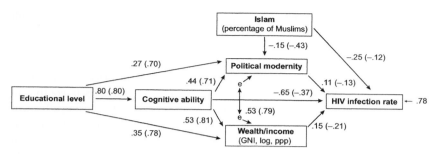

Figure 10.5 Education, cognitive ability, political modernity, economic
wealth, percentage of Muslims and HIV-infection rate (standardised path
coefficients, correlations in parentheses, unexplained variance on the right),
$N = 143$ to 146 nations[12]

effect on cognitive ability; in individual and historical development the relationship is more reciprocal – education furthers intelligence and smarter
individuals and nations select and create educational environments (see
Section 10.5). Further factors behind them such as culture and genes are not
considered. Compared to education cognitive ability has a stronger impact
on political modernity ($\beta_{Ed \rightarrow PolMod} = .27$ vs. $\beta_{CA \rightarrow PolMod} = .44$) and wealth
($\beta_{Ed \rightarrow GNI} = .35$ vs. $\beta_{CA \rightarrow GNI} = .53$). Islam – indicated by percentage of
Muslims – has a (smaller) negative impact on political modernity ($\beta_{Islam \rightarrow PolMod} = -.15$). Its negative impact is presumably underestimated because its
possible indirect impact via education and cognitive ability is not integrated
in the model. What is more important in a model explaining international
differences in HIV infection rates is Islam's reducing impact on HIV: $\beta_{Islam \rightarrow HIV} = -.25$. Cognitive ability has a very strong negative impact ($\beta_{CA \rightarrow HIV} = -.65$). Theoretically most interesting are the *positive* effects of wealth ($\beta_{GNI \rightarrow HIV} = .15$) and political modernity ($\beta_{PolMod \rightarrow HIV} = .11$) on HIV. In the context
of cognitive ability (and less important of religion) they do not have,

---

[12] The fit of the model presented in Figure 10.5 is very good with $CFI = 1$ (Comparative Fit Index,
range 0-1, good is $\geq.95$) and $SRMR = .01$ (Standardised Root Mean Square Residual, range 0-1,
good is $\leq.08/.05$). Good fit means that the model can render the empirically given relationships
between variables, if no paths are missing and not too many (unnecessary) paths are placed
between variables. All data sources have been described previously except for percentage of
Muslims (mainly CIA World Factbook; see Rindermann & Meisenberg, 2009). 'e' in the model
stands for 'error' or rest, not explained variance. A correlation is placed between the errors of
modernity and GNI (bivariate correlation of the variables: $r = .79$, bivariate correlation of the
errors: $r = .53$). This means that both variables, modernity and wealth, share more, are closer
and are more empirically related than their common predictors, cognitive ability and education,
can explain. E.g. because a further common factor is missing in the model such as economic
freedom, or because they influence each other (modernity furthers wealth; wealth furthers
modernity).

as assumed, a decreasing effect on HIV, but an increasing effect: wealth and modernisation increase AIDS!

But why? And what does the change of signs mean in these variables, and the larger beta-coefficient than correlation between cognitive ability and HIV infection rates? Technically, they are called 'suppressor effects' – in mathematical expression $\beta \times r < 0$ (change of signs) or $|\beta| > |r|$ (larger beta-coefficient than correlation). Theoretically, it means that the true HIV-increasing effects of modernisation and wealth are masked by their dependence on cognitive ability. Cognitive ability stimulates both modernisation and economic productivity but reduces HIV rates. Therefore, modernisation and HIV as well as wealth and HIV are negatively correlated ($r = -.13$ and $-.21$). But their own pure impact, corrected for cognitive ability (in this model by using these variables as simultaneous predictors), is an increasing one. Why? Modernisation relaxes constraints on sexual behaviour, including on homosexuality, facilitating the spread of sexually transmitted diseases. Such an interpretation is supported by the HIV-reducing impact of Islam – standing for strong constraints on sexual behaviour.[13] And wealth leads to higher mobility, increasing the possibilities of less constrained contacts.

However, the increasing effects of modernisation and wealth are not very large ($\beta_{PolMod \rightarrow HIV} = .11$, $\beta_{GNI \rightarrow HIV} = .15$): weaker constraints on sexual behaviour are also given in more traditional contexts such as in sub-Saharan Africa. Many have more than one wife or husband in loose relationships ('sugar daddies', 'lovers', 'outside wife'; Benning, 2007; Caldwell, 2002, p. 179ff.; Signer, 2004; Standing, 1992, p. 479). Prostitution is a further risk (Wellings et al., 2006, p. 1715).[14] And AIDS treatment needs costly medication.[15]

---

[13] Islam sets strong constraints on sexual behaviour. Taking for granted that the numbers are correct, constraints have a reducing impact on STDs. It cannot be excluded that in Muslim countries due to stigmatisation the HIV rates are somewhat underestimated. Showing a reducing impact on HIV does not mean to ethically value the way that in Muslim countries 'constraints on sexual behaviour' are set (women's rights, treatment of men and women with same-sex preferences).

[14] According to Standing (1992, p. 477), men in Kenya treated for STDs reportedly had 'an average of 17 sexual partners in the previous year'.

[15] Some numbers. Canada, 2011: HIV/AIDS is costing Canadians $1.3 million per each new diagnosis of HIV (www.cdnaids.ca/cost-of-hiv). In Germany just the medication per year is €20,000 (www.derwesten.de/gesundheit/hiv-therapien-kosten-jaehrlich-mehr-als-eine-milli arde-euro-id7344629.html). Hecht et al. (2010) expect costs for developing countries until 2031 ranging from US$397 to $722 billion. Because intellectual property (patent rights) is less respected by developing countries and because of discounts, the medication is much cheaper than in developed countries. Medication is indirectly subsidised by insurance holders (workers, companies) and the taxpayers in developed countries.

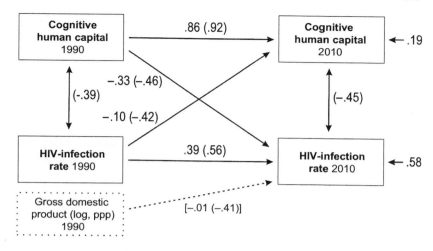

Figure 10.6 Cross-lagged effects; stronger reducing cognitive effect on HIV than of HIV on cognitive human capital, average of $N = 47$ (student assessment studies) and $N = 96$ (years of education) nations

But this analysis (Figure 9.5) gives only results of a cross-sectional study. Longitudinal studies could better prove causal effects. For this purpose, we used two measurement points of cognitive human capital (earlier and later student assessment studies, years of schooling, around 1990 and 2010) and HIV-infection rates (earliest measurement point 1990 and 2010) for 47 or 96 countries and averaged their results; in a further analysis we added 1990 wealth (Figure 10.6).

First of all, cognitive human capital (indicated by student assessment tests and education) is always negatively related to HIV rates.[16] Longitudinally, cognitive ability more strongly reduces HIV rates than HIV rates reduce cognitive ability ($\beta_{CHC90 \rightarrow HIV10} = -.33$ vs. $\beta_{HIV90 \rightarrow CHC10} = -.10$).

---

[16] Results in detail for Figure 10.6: CHC and HIV 1990, $r_{1990} = -.39$, $r_{CA90} = -.56$, $r_{Ed90} = -.22$; CHC and HIV 2010, $r_{2010} = -.45$, $r_{CA10} = -.75$, $r_{Ed10} = -.15$. $\beta_{CHC90 \rightarrow HIV10} = -.33$, $\beta_{CA90 \rightarrow HIV10} = -.57$, $\beta_{Ed90 \rightarrow HIV10} = -.09$; $\beta_{HIV90 \rightarrow CHC10} = -.10$, $\beta_{HIV90 \rightarrow CA10} = -.20$, $\beta_{HIV90 \rightarrow EdC10} = .01$. $\beta_{GDP90 \rightarrow HIV10} = -.10$ ($N = 43$), $\beta_{GDP90 \rightarrow HIV10} = .09$ ($N = 90$). Analyses using Penn data show more extreme results (higher minus and plus) leading to the same zero average effect.

Data: *HIV* from UNAIDS (2013, electronic data set), precisely 1990 and 2010. *Years at school* from Barro and Lee (2000) and HDR 2010 (UNDP, 2010), precisely 1990 and 2010. 'Precisely' means their reported years. *Cognitive ability 1990* from student assessment studies TIMSS 1994/95; if no data given from IEA Reading measured 1991 (Elley, 1992) and IAEP-II mathematics and science 1991; if still no data were given from old student assessment studies from 1964 to 1972 collected by Lee and Barro (1997). *Cognitive ability 2010* from TIMSS and PIRLS 2011 and PISA 2009 and 2012, all corrected society estimates. GDP 1990 from Maddison (2008).

The pattern of effects is more marked for ability test results than for educational measures. This is reasonable: thinking ability is the crucial variable, not years spent in school. Additionally, tests measure national differences more reliably and validly. If the wealth indicator GDP/c 1990 is added there is no HIV-reducing effect from wealth, corroborating the results from the cross-sectional study in Figure 10.5.

The *negative* (but small) *longitudinal effect of HIV on cognitive ability* is not astonishing, as it was reported for Africa that at the beginning well-educated persons, including teachers leading to teacher shortage, died from AIDS. Without teachers, and more generally, without role modelling intellectuals and academics, the cognitive development of the youth of a country suffers.

The results of studies at the individual and cross-country levels underscore that *AIDS*, in particular, *is a behavioural disease, caused by behaviour and avoidable by behaviour*. And risk vs. health behaviour depends, not only, but crucially, on *cognitive ability*. Reciprocal effects are also negative, impeding cognitive development across decades. Intelligence and health form a positive spiral, low intelligence and AIDS a vicious circle. In every individual case *chance* factors are also relevant. The transmission risk in male-female sexual intercourse is only around 1:1,200.[17] But one unlucky time can be enough.

## 10.3    Politics

Why may politics influence cognitive development? Political conditions, actively created or passively experienced, shape the physical, social, educational and institutional frame, impeding or stimulating cognitive development.

### 10.3.1   Peace

A fundamental condition is *peace*. War, depending on its severity and outcome, leads to a shortage of means, to famines, lower economic growth, lack of teachers, reduced education, psychological stress, loss of fathers, frequently to destruction of houses, schools and means of transportation, sometimes to suppression, torture, expulsion and loss of one's language and culture. Not every war is equal. The experiences, for instance, were different for Vietnamese and Americans, Poles and French, Germans and British, Russians and Austrians, Arabians and Israelis, Japanese and Australians. The long-term consequences of avoiding war or giving up autonomy could be even worse compared to the short-term consequences of a successful military conflict.

---

[17] Transmission risk depends on forms of sexual intercourse and skin health. Numbers e.g. here: Public Health Agency of Canada, February 2013, www.phac-aspc.gc.ca/aids-sida/publication/ hivtr-rtvih-eng.php.

Empirical evidence shows that during more severe wars intelligence declines. According to Raven (2000, p. 5), the SPM norms obtained in UK 1943-1944 were two raw score points lower than the ones from 1938, corresponding to around −4 IQ in the mean ability range. DeGroot (1951) reported an intelligence decline for the Netherlands during the Second World War and National Socialist-German occupation, from IQ 101.5 to 97.7, again about −4 IQ. In several Western countries the speed of the FLynn effect (see Section 4.1) declined during the Second World War (*dec* = 7.20 before and *dec* = 2.10 IQ points during, about −5 IQ; Pietschnig & Voracek, 2015, p. 285). During war, children are frequently separated from their parents. Pesonen et al. (2011) found a decline of around −3 IQ for such Finnish children separated during the Second World War. For countries such as Poland or Russia, and especially for Jews who survived, a greater loss is expectable, but data are not present. Finally, long-term negative effects are to be expected, because more likely the average and better educated and able men were recruited and therefore had a higher mortality risk, with consequences for the environmental and genetic conditions of the next generation.[18]

Using different data sets, war and cognitive ability are negatively correlated, around $r = -.13$ to $-.37$, on average $r = -.24$.[19] Partialling out GDP as indicator of wealth leads to lower correlations at around $r_p = -.06$. The pattern in a scatterplot reveals that all countries with a very high level of destructive wars in the last 50 years have a low average IQ (<IQ 75, Afghanistan, Somalia, Liberia, Haiti), but among countries at peace are countries with high and low IQs (e.g. Bahamas with 81 or Botswana with 73 versus China and Finland with 101). This points out that war is a detrimental factor for cognitive ability, but peace does not automatically lead to high IQ nor low IQ necessarily to war.

While war depends and interacts with outside conditions, *revolutions*, *revolts* and *coups* depend on internal ones.[20] Therefore, they as a summary variable 'uprising' correlate higher than war with cognitive ability, on average $r = -.39$. Partialling out GDP reduces but does not eliminate the negative correlation ($r_p = -.20$). Looking at the scatterplot shows that among politically

---

[18] According to Whalley & Deary (2001, p. 1, 4): 'Men who died during active service in the Second World War had a relatively high IQ. ... Men with high IQ were more likely to die in active service in the Second World War.'

[19] Information on wars was taken from Sala-i-Martin (1960–85; Sala-i-Martin, 1997; based on Barro & Lee, 1993) and Marshall (1946–2012; Marshall, 2013). The author (HR) has also made an estimation based on these sources and an additional rating of the negative impacts of war (1960–2000). E.g. the United States has been involved in many wars, but all since the Civil War (1861–1865) were outside their territory with no destruction in their own country. Haiti was not involved in any foreign war, but its society and infrastructure have been destroyed due to continuous civil wars (plus effects of the 2010 earthquake).

[20] Data for revolutions and military coups between 1960 and 1984 come from Sala-i-Martin (Sala-i-Martin, 1997; based on Barro & Lee, 1993).

stable countries the entire range of cognitive ability levels could be found (e.g. Saint Lucia and Malawi with IQs around 60 and Japan and Singapore with around 104). But at the higher levels of revolutions and revolts there are only countries with IQs lower than 90. The higher negative correlation of uprising with IQ than of war with IQ indicates that uprising depends more strongly on internal country factors or that it deteriorates more the conditions supportive for national cognitive development.

Because at the zero revolution level all cognitive levels are observable, but at the higher revolution level only lower IQs, similar to war, the opposite direction, a negative effect from revolutions to lower IQ, is more convincing. An example may illustrate this: whereas slow runners can be found among people with ideal and excess weight there are no fast overweight runners because fast running is seriously impeded by weight.

### 10.3.2  Rule of Law, Political Liberty and Democracy

War and suppression are often intertwined. The Soviet Union, National Socialist Germany, China, Cambodia, Vietnam and many Latin-American, Arabian and African countries in the past and many in the present not only suffered from war, including civil war, but also from suppression. Suppressive, illiberal and undemocratic countries are more frequently enmeshed in wars and revolutions.

The political situation in a country depends more on internal factors and has more impact on society than an external war. Thus *rule of law*, *political liberty* and *democracy* should be more highly and positively correlated with cognitive ability than peace ($r = .24$). The long-term correlations are $r_{RoL} = .63$ ($N = 153$), $r_{PL} = .41$ ($N = 193$) and $r_{Demo} = .55$ ($N = 187$).[21]

For all three variables it is true that measures covering longer periods correlate more highly with cognitive ability estimates than around 2010 measures (on average: $r_{long} = .53$, $r_{ar10} = .47$). Variables based on longer periods more reliably measure country phenomena. A longer period also better covers the relevant conditions for cognitive development: past deficits in political conditions can have long-lasting effects.

---

[21] The pattern that liberty is less correlated with intelligence than law and democracy repeats itself in a same country sample for all three variables ($r_{RoL} = .63$, $r_{PL} = .55$, $r_{Demo} = .63$, $N = 152$). Longer periods, rule of law: 1970–2011, political liberty: 1972–2012, democracy: 1950–2012. Around 2010: 2007–2011. Sources, rule of law: Gwartney et al. (2013), political liberty: Freedom House (2013), democracy: average of Vanhanen & Åbo Akademi (2013) and Marshall et al. (2013). For rule of law we can use two sources, Gwartney et al. (2013) or Kaufmann et al. (2010). The Gwartney data go back until 1970 (Kaufmann only until 1996), but the Kaufmann data cover, with $N = 200$, more countries (Gwartney only $N = 153$). Both indicators correlate with $r = .87$ to .89. In the same country samples the Kaufmann data correlate around .10 higher with cognitive ability. We have used the Gwartney data covering a longer period.

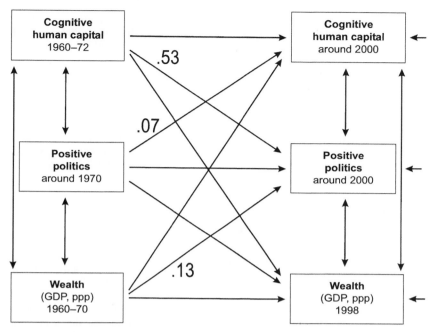

Figure 10.7 Main results from cross-lagged analyses with rule of law; political liberty and democracy and cognitive capital controlled for wealth; average of six analyses with $N = 17$ (student assessment studies) and $N = 79–94$ (years of education) nations; stronger cognitive effect on politics than of wealth on politics or of politics on cognitive capital; original results in Rindermann (2008b, fig. 2–7)

But, cross-sectional bivariate analyses cannot clarify whether A influences B or B influences A (Chapter 9). For this purpose we need longitudinal studies controlling further important variables, especially wealth. Longitudinal analyses comparing cross-lagged effects controlled for GDP showed stronger effects of cognitive capital on politics than vice versa (Rindermann, 2008b).

We have averaged the main results and present them in Figure 10.7: cognitive capital, indicated either by student assessment studies (cognitive ability) in smaller country samples or by years of education in larger country samples, has a strong positive impact on the development of positively valued political conditions (rule of law, political liberty and democracy; $\beta_{CA70 \rightarrow Pol00} = .53$). Political conditions have a minor positive impact on cognitive ability ($\beta_{Pol70 \rightarrow CA00} = .07$). Annually produced and given wealth also has a smaller positive impact on politics ($\beta_{GDP70 \rightarrow Pol00} = .13$). The message is clear: the positive effect of cognitive ability is responsible for the positive correlations between

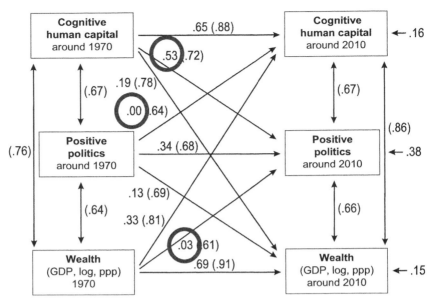

Figure 10.8 Results from cross-lagged analyses with rule of law, political liberty and democracy and cognitive capital controlled for wealth; average of six analyses with $N = 17–18$ (student assessment studies) and $N = 44–92$ (years of education) nations; stronger cognitive effect on politics than of wealth on politics or of politics on cognitive capital

cognitive ability and politics. Theoretically, such results are backed by a cognitive-historical development approach:

> The intellect conceptualised and described democracy and rule of law long before their historical realisation. These institutions are not the 'unplanned result of intentional actions', not the result of a 'situational logic' as simple sociological doctrines may have suggested. Thus, the idea existed before its materialisation, the plan before its institutionalisation. (Oesterdiekhoff, 2013, p. 471)[22]

Are these results corroborated by newer data? We applied here the same method, longitudinal analyses, and looked at the cross-lagged effects between indicators of cognitive human capital (student assessment studies or years of education) and political conditions (rule of law, political liberty and democracy) controlled for wealth (here logged GDP; Figure 10.8).[23]

---

[22] Quote translated by the author (GWO). For individual level explanations of positive intelligence effects on politics see Chapter 7.

[23] Data sources: *Cognitive human capital*: (a) Student assessment results as cognitive ability estimates from 1964 to 1972 collected by Lee and Barro (1997). For around 2010 newer studies

According to the newer results from around 1970 to 2010 again past cognitive ability has the strongest effect on positively evaluated political conditions ($\beta_{CA70 \rightarrow Pol10} = .53$; Figure 10.8). The result is robust. Political conditions have no impact on cognitive ability ($\beta_{Pol70 \rightarrow CA10} = .00$). The former small effect of .07 was reduced to .00. Wealth has a very small positive impact on politics ($\beta_{GDP70 \rightarrow Pol10} = .03$). Despite using a different time interval (around 1970 to 2000 vs. to 2010), a more focused period for rule of law (nearer to 1970, less countries) and a different averaging method (arithmetically vs. via Fisher $z$-transformation) the pattern is very robust.

At a closer look, among the three political variables again *rule of law* showed the largest positive effect on cognitive ability ($\beta_{RoL70 \rightarrow CA00} = .14$ and $\beta_{RoL70 \rightarrow CA10} = .14$). Apart from the focus on politics, an important deviation of this new analysis is the now stronger wealth effect on cognitive ability with $\beta_{GDP70 \rightarrow CA10} = .33$ versus old $\beta_{GDP70 \rightarrow CA00} = .15$. In the present and past analyses the effect on test results ($\beta_{GDP70 \rightarrow SAS10} = .45$ and $\beta_{GDP70 \rightarrow SAS00} = .28$) was larger than on educational measures ($\beta_{GDP70 \rightarrow Ed10} = .20$ and $\beta_{GDP70 \rightarrow Ed00} = .02$). This all hints that cognitive ability development (indicated by student test performance), more than education development (indicated by years at school), depends on wealth.

But why is the wealth effect now larger? We used logged GDP this time, but in the 2008a analysis non-logged GDP. In the 2012 paper with an interval similar to the old one, the effects of logged GDP were also higher, but only somewhat ($\beta_{GDPraw70 \rightarrow CA00} = .08$, $\beta_{GDPlog70 \rightarrow CA00} = .14$). Using logged GDP also led to a smaller decline of the cognitive ability effect on wealth ($\beta_{CA70 \rightarrow GDPraw00} = .35$, $\beta_{CA70 \rightarrow GDPlog00} = .31$). This again indicates that wealth increases in the lower range (stressed by logarithm) are more relevant for cognitive ability than wealth increases in the higher range (more stressed by raw GDP). The same was demonstrated in Figures 10.1 to 10.3.

Increases in cognitive ability help more to become richer at the upper wealth levels (stressed by GDP raw) than in the lower wealth levels (stressed by GDP

from TIMSS 1994 to PISA 2012 (majority of studies between 1999 and 2011). b) Education as years of school education 1970 is the 'average schooling years in the total population over age 25' according to Barro and Lee (2000), same as in Rindermann (2008b). Years of school education 2010 from HDR 2010 (UNDP, 2010, pp. 143–147).

*Politics*: rule of law: Gwartney et al. (2013; covering a longer period than Kaufmann et al.), political liberty: Freedom House (2013), democracy: average of Vanhanen & Åbo Akademi (2013) and Marshall et al. (2013).

*Wealth*: GDP 1970 logged and around 2010 from Maddison in 1990 international $ (Maddison, 2008; 2010 from Bolt & van Zanden, 2013). 'Maddison-original' only provides data for 2008, not 2010, 'Maddison-successors' Bolt & van Zanden also for 2010, but for fewer countries ($N_{2008} = 159$, $N_{2008} = 117$). Therefore, we combined both; the 2008-scale was adapted to the 2010-scale.

Due to rounding errors in Figure 10.8, $R^2 = \Sigma r\beta$ and unexplained variance at the right not always exactly add to 1. Averaging via Fisher z-transformation.

log) – again, the same was demonstrated in Figures 10.1 to 10.3. *Wealth is relevant for the cognitive development of the poor and cognitive ability is relevant for the wealth development of the rich.*

However, we should not overlook the limits of the method. Only changes are analysed. And only *changes* in a *certain period.* Specific historical developments may depend more on local factors as on the influence of unique politicians or the discovery of mineral resources. Measurement problems leading to low correlations between different GDP measures are probably also true for older student assessment studies, decreasing their impact. International data sets usually do not include extremely negative cases of political conditions because in such countries no data are measurable, at least not in a reliable and valid way. We simply do not have measures for Germans', Poles' and, especially, Jews' cognitive ability level before and after National Socialism, Afghans' before and after Taliban rule or Arabs' and Africans' before and after the rule of Muslim fundamentalists (e.g. in Syria, Iraq and Nigeria). We can, for example for Afghanistan, only indirectly infer, e.g. by the positive effects of a primary school programme on pupils (girls $d = 1.28$, boys $d = 1.24$, both equivalent to 19 IQ; Burde & Linden, 2013). Because during the Taliban's rule not all youth missed school the effects can be somewhat smaller, but because the Taliban had further negative effects on other important conditions of cognitive development such as nutrition, health care and psychological stress, the effects can be also somewhat larger. Due to missing data for such countries and epochs the global zero effect of political conditions is less astonishing.

Nevertheless, *rule of law* shows a robust positive impact on given student assessment results as a measure of cognitive ability, robust across differently precise 1970 measurements, across different periods, country samples and student assessment combinations.[24] Rule of law supports meritoric principles. In a predictable social world, problems can be solved and aims be reached by effort, by the use of intelligence and good formal qualifications, rather than by coercion, family connections and bribery. By favouring *meritocracy* throughout society, and this includes the educational system, rule of law tends to support the development of cognitive abilities. Under such circumstances learning is a good investment, increasing cognitive ability.[25]

### 10.3.3    Meritoric Orientation and Management

Twice we have speculated that the positive effects of political conditions operate via meritoric orientation and management: the impact of economic

---

[24]    Effects on student assessment results: $\beta_{RoL70 \rightarrow SAS00} = .24$ and $\beta_{RoL70 \rightarrow SAS10} = .22$. The positive effects on length of education are negligible: $\beta_{RoL70 \rightarrow Ed00} = .03$ and $\beta_{RoL70 \rightarrow Ed10} = .06$.

[25]    The cultural theory proposed here (a predictable, orderly world furthers cognitive development) resembles an evolutionary *r/K*-theory according to which a stable environment selects for more investment in fewer offspring, including more investment in intelligence (see Section 10.7.1).

freedom and of rule of law could be explained by their stimulation of endeavour and investment in education and thinking (Sections 10.1 and 10.3.2). Success is obtained by achievement, not by knowing the right people, by bribery, class, party, ideology, race or family affiliations. Of course, there is no perfect meritocracy, but a larger meritoric shaping should support cognitive development.

We have three indicators of meritoric principles:

(1) Evans and Rauch (1999) developed, based on expert evaluations, a 'Weberianness' indicator for the years 1993–1996 in 35 'semi-industrialised' and poorer countries. There, whether higher officials in bureaucracy are selected via examinations and whether there are prospects for promotion and competitive salary was rated. The country with the highest value in Weberianness was Singapore followed by other small East Asian countries (South Korea, Taiwan and Hong Kong). The last countries were Latin American, Arabian and sub-Saharan African countries.

(2) Strenze (2013) proposed the variable *allocation of talent*. It covers effects of ability and education on wages, effects of ability on occupation, use of ability tests in recruitment and effects of occupational complexity on occupational wages in a country. The different variables are based on data, e.g. from the OECD, and were combined in one score (Cronbach-$\alpha$ around=.55). This score is given for 91 countries.

Both different approaches found positive effects of meritoric principles on economic growth, this for different country and time samples. But what about effects on cognitive development? Unfortunately, in both sources data are not given for different decades, and the Evans and Rauch data cover only a small country sample. Last but worst: both negatively correlate in a common 26-country sample ($r = -.41$)! However, we have a further rating variable, meritoric achievement orientation:

(3) *Meritoric achievement orientation* represents work ethic, internalisation and practice of achievement as a regulatory instance and aim in a society. Endeavour, competence and accomplishment are valued. By their means persons reach success. Society distributes wealth, recognition and status according to endeavour, competence and accomplishment and not according to kinship, religious convictions, status, membership in a party or military, ethnicity or race. This orientation was assessed by four scientists and academics for $N = 186$ countries.[26]

---

[26] Four scientists and academics: all with a PhD; they have studied psychology, medicine, history and philosophy; age 37 to 60 years; all men; German and Turkish origin; one Protestant, two Catholics, one Muslim; together with knowledge of twelve languages; experiences of working abroad including developing countries; assessed for the period 1990s to 2004; Cronbach-$\alpha$ = .92.

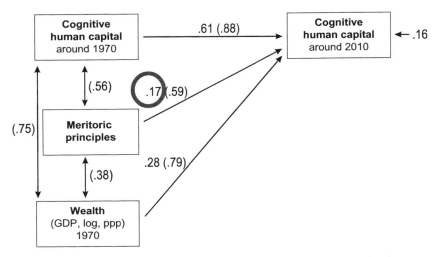

Figure 10.9 Effects of meritoric principles on cognitive capital development controlled for past ability and annual GDP/c, average of five analyses with $N = 17–18$ (student assessment studies) and $N = 30–93$ (years of education) nations

Weberianness and talent allocation correlate with meritoric achievement orientation at $r_{W-M} = .67$ ($N = 35$) and $r_{T-M} = .34$ ($N = 90$). All three positively correlate with economic freedom (mean $r = .47$) and rule of law (mean $r = .50$), thus a mediating effect via meritoric principles is backed by empirical results (law → meritocracy → intelligence).[27]

We can use them to look, in 'half' cross-lagged analyses, for effects of meritoric principles controlled for past cognitive human capital and wealth on present-day cognitive human capital. This was done by using student assessment results and education (together standing for cognitive human capital) and the three variables of meritoric principles. Finally, the results were averaged.[28]

Figure 10.9 shows the results. Meritoric principles have a positive impact on national cognitive development between the 1970s and around 2010: $\beta_{Merit \to CA10} = .17$. The size of this effect is independent from the chosen

The survey was organised in 2004 by the author (Rindermann). Correlations with ability and modernity measures are presented in Table 10.3.

[27] Correlations with economic freedom: $r_{W-EF} = .47$ ($N = 35$), $r_{T-EF} = .35$ ($N = 89$), $r_{M\ -EF} = .58$ ($N = 179$), correlations with rule law: $r_{W-RL} = .56$ ($N = 35$), $r_{T-RL} = .23$ ($N = 85$), $r_{M-RL} = .71$ ($N = 151$).

[28] Student assessment results and education from around the 1970s and 2010 as mentioned in all prior analyses; GDP logged from Maddison 1970; the three described meritoric principle variables. An analysis for student assessment results and Evans-Rauch's Weberianness was not possible ($N = 4$). For the other analyses $N = 17$ and 18 (SAS) or $N = 30$, 69 and 93.

meritoric principles and cognitive ability variable and from country sample size.[29] Stressing and enabling success via effort, education and accomplishment stimulates national cognitive ability development.

### 10.3.4 Fragmentation of Power

Regarding the European rise in the last millennium, a frequently mentioned theory stresses the benign effects of *fragmentation of power* (e.g. Weede, 2012): except for the Roman Empire, there was never a force strong enough to rule the entire continent of Europe. There was always competition between different countries, between Spain and Portugal, Spain and Britain, Spain and the Netherlands, Britain and France, France and Germany, and so on. Additionally, state and church, state and cities, different churches and different cities shared political power. This fragmentation stimulated *competition*, frequently including wars, but also led to innovation and learning from the rival. And it was possible for intellectuals to emigrate to the rivals, thus increasing political liberty, e.g. Descartes between France and the Netherlands, Voltaire between France, England and Prussia, Hobbes between England and France or Schiller within Germany between different principalities. Smarter religious and ethnic minorities, such as the Huguenots (from France to Germany) and the Jews (from Iberia to Venice, Flanders, Germany, Eastern Europe and Ottoman Empire) could maintain their way of thinking and living. The Genoese Christopher Columbus smartly used the rivalry between Portugal, Spain and France to obtain means for his intended circumnavigation of the globe, resulting in the discovery of America. Artists such as Michelangelo and Leonardo acted similarly. Entrepreneurs, as in the case of present-day US IT companies, could avoid taxes and in the past also confiscations.

This all means increased *economic* and *political liberty*, *rule of law* and *meritoric principles*. However, competition also existed in fragmented India, in minor form for one to two centuries also in Japan (around 1400–1600) and in all premodern regions of the world. Thus fragmentation and competition as themselves cannot be crucial. But what is unique for Europe, the Southern, Western, Middle and Northern parts of Europe, is the important role of *independent cities*, starting with Ancient Greece and continuing via Rome, having its peak in the Middle Ages in Northern Italy, in Benelux and Germany

---

[29] For Evans' Weberianness: $\beta_{EvWeb \to CA10} = .19$; for Stenze's allocation of talent: $\beta_{StAoT \to CA10} = .16$; for Rindermann's meritoric achievement orientation: $\beta_{RiMaO \to CA10} = .19$. For student assessments: $\beta_{Merit \to SAS10} = .18$ (average of $N = 17$ and 18); for years at school: $\beta_{Merit \to EdS10} = .17$ (average of $N = 30$, 69 and 93). The positive effects of meritoric principles are also supported (but weaker) if returns to skills (higher income for those with higher cognitive competences) are used as a more narrow measure of meritocracy provided by Hanushek et al. (2015), on average $\beta_{RtS \to CA10} = .08$ ($N = 11$ and 19 countries).

(and somewhat less so in France and England). Here a *city culture* developed, an independent burgher society, being the initial milieu for modernity.

An impressive example is the medieval contest for the largest and most beautiful church in town, as between Pisa and Florence, Siena and Florence, and especially, leading to the first modern architecture, in France between cities for the Gothic cathedral aspiring to the most height and light.

### 10.3.5   Demographics: Migration

In a broader sense, nearly all national differences are connected to demographic differences. For example, the British settled either 10,000 kilometres to the West or around the globe even farther to the Southeast resulting in more or less the same average IQs: the United Kingdom has an average of 100 IQ points, the United States 99, Canada 102, Australia 99 and New Zealand 100.[30] Or for another nation but the same attribute, for the Chinese: the Chinese in China have an IQ of around 100, in Hong Kong of 103, in Macau of 96, in Taiwan of 103 and in Singapore of 105.[31] There are some differences, but they are not larger like typical within-country regional differences. The US-American blogger Steve Sailer (2007) succinctly summed up the demographic approach for the outstanding model Finland:

'The most important reason why Finland is so Finlandy is because it is full of Finns.'

However, that is no explanation. We need to know *why* Finns and others have their distinguishable characteristics, which, with a pinch of salt, they take wherever they go. It could be habits rooted in institutions fixed by tradition, history and culture or it could be genes, working through habits on institutions, tradition and culture.

The same theoretically empty variable as demographics is *migration*: migration itself has only a passing effect on cognitive development. In particular, language differences create educational difficulties. But they could be solved within one generation.[32] If migrants and natives in the same society with the same schools and stimulation constantly differ in abilities, this has to do with the same general background factors as sketched a paragraph ago for demographics: culture or genes.

What can be analysed are the differences between natives and immigrants, the impact of immigration on cognitive competence development of nations

---

[30] Data from Table A.2, natives corrected.

[31] In Singapore, inhabitants come from China (78 per cent), but larger minorities also from Malaysia (11 per cent) and India (9 per cent).

[32] Differences could be enlarged and consolidated by caste-like social systems. Depending on country pairs, different people may immigrate, e.g. the smarter strata from India and Iran to the United States (Feliciano, 2005).

and whether there are factors that can explain native-migrant differences (Rindermann & Thompson, 2016). What should not be overlooked is that the concept of 'immigrant' is less clear than usually assumed. Studies organised by the IEA, TIMSS and PIRLS, use a wider definition of being a migrant: students with one immigrant parent and one native parent are categorised as having an immigrant background, whereas in the OECD-organised PISA they are categorised as native students. Consequently, in TIMSS and PIRLS more students (having 50 per cent native and immigrant ancestry) are classified as immigrants *and* the gaps between natives and immigrants are smaller. Usually, third generation immigrants are categorised as natives – the more such natives with immigration background in a country, the more an ability gap, if present, is concealed. In Table 10.2, averages, differences and migration gains are listed for regions and selected countries (in the Appendix in Table A.2 for $N$ = 93 nations).

Immigration gains or losses for receiving countries depend on two variables: on native-migrant differences and on the immigrant proportion (for percentages see Table A.3). The larger the gap and the larger the immigrant proportion the larger is the positive or negative effect of the IQs of migrants on a country's average IQ. Looking first at regional data, immigration *gains* are given for the Middle East, Central-South Asia and Trans-Tasman. All regional mean gains are below <+0.20 IQ points. Within the Middle East, these gains are the largest for countries with oil-based economies such as the Emirates (gain +7.42 IQ) and Qatar (+4.21 IQ). The average ability level is remarkably lifted by immigrants. However, Middle East countries are highly heterogeneous; Egypt, for instance, faces losses (–1.81 IQ).

In all other regions there are *losses*, the largest in Central Europe with –2.10 IQ points, less in Western Europe (–0.83). The largest losses are found here for Luxembourg (–3.37 IQ), Switzerland (–2.19 IQ), Liechtenstein (–1.96 IQ), Germany (–1.59 IQ) and Belgium (–1.54 IQ). North America loses –0.56 IQ. For the West in general, the immigration-based losses run up to –0.91 IQ points. In these numbers, *emigration*-based gains (emigration of lower ability groups) and losses (emigration of higher ability groups) are not considered.

Interestingly, for sub-Saharan Africa, already at a low level, immigration losses are also observed (–1.12 IQ points). But we have here only data for three from around 50 countries (for Botswana, Ghana and South Africa).

Summarising, immigration leads in the West to decreasing IQs. According to the cognitive human capital theory, a negative impact for society could only be avoided if immigrants catch up through generations. The other strategy would be trying to adopt the indirectly ability-based immigration strategies of countries such as Australia and Singapore, which, already at high levels, attract and admit well-educated and cognitively competent immigrants with their families (see Chapter 14).

Table 10.2 *Cognitive ability averages, natives and migrants and gains (or losses) for receiving countries*

|  | CA totc | SAS-IQc | Nat-IQc | Mig-IQc | N-M-Diff | Migr-gain |
|---|---|---|---|---|---|---|
| **Africa (sub-Sahara)** | 69.19 | 66.97 | 59.45 | 50.88 | +8.57 | −1.12 |
| South Africa | 70 | 59 | 61 | 51 | +10.50 | −1.90 |
| **N-Africa M-East (ArabM)** | 84.24 | 78.80 | 78.64 | 75.58 | +3.06 | +0.16 |
| Egypt | 84 | 80 | 82 | 70 | +11.60 | −1.81 |
| **America (North)** | 99.45 | 99.80 | 100.36 | 97.61 | +2.75 | −0.56 |
| USA | 98 | 98 | 99 | 95 | +4.11 | −0.82 |
| **America (Latin)** | 79.32 | 76.14 | 78.73 | 73.10 | +5.63 | −0.39 |
| Mexico | 86 | 81 | 81 | 73 | +8.20 | −0.39 |
| **Asia (Central-South)** | 79.41 | 76.06 | 79.50 | 80.88 | −1.38 | +0.10 |
| India | 78 | 69 | − | − | − | − |
| **East Asia** | 99.43 | 99.43 | 102.18 | 95.73 | +6.45 | −0.20 |
| China | 101 | 99 | 100 | 90 | +9.66 | −0.38 |
| **Southeast Asia, Pacific** | 85.16 | 86.50 | 89.97 | 82.73 | +7.25 | −0.22 |
| Philippines | 80 | 70 | − | − | − | − |
| **Australia-NZ (English)** | 99.06 | 99.34 | 99.30 | 99.26 | +0.04 | +0.04 |
| New Zealand | 99 | 99 | 100 | 99 | +0.91 | −0.22 |
| **Western Europe** | 98.83 | 99.20 | 100.03 | 95.20 | +4.84 | −0.83 |
| United Kingdom | 100 | 100 | 100 | 97 | +3.06 | −0.40 |
| **Scandinavia** | 97.06 | 98.80 | 99.49 | 92.39 | +7.10 | −0.69 |
| Norway | 98 | 97 | 97 | 91 | +5.68 | −0.54 |
| **Central Europe** | 98.85 | 98.58 | 100.69 | 93.46 | +7.23 | −2.10 |
| Germany | 99 | 99 | 100 | 92 | +8.26 | −1.59 |
| **Eastern Europe** | 95.54 | 94.57 | 94.81 | 90.05 | +4.75 | −0.24 |
| Russia | 97 | 97 | 97 | 95 | +2.63 | −0.32 |
| **Southern Europe** | 92.61 | 90.40 | 90.69 | 87.01 | +3.68 | −0.30 |
| Italy | 98 | 97 | 98 | 92 | +5.99 | −0.52 |

*Notes:* Data for natives and immigrants from student assessment studies PISA, TIMSS and PIRLS; in SAS-IQc for countries without data from the large three added from older or local student assessment studies (therefore native and immigrant means may differ from this general mean; also more countries are covered in these means than in native and immigrant means); CA totalc also includes psychometric intelligence test studies; all results corrected, corrections do not influence native-migrant differences nor gains; CA totc: average of all cognitive ability studies; SAS-IQc: average of student assessment studies; Nat-IQc: mean of natives; Mig-IQc: mean of migrants; N-M-Diff: native-migrant differences; Migr-gain: gains or losses through immigration for receiving country's competence mean; for United Kingdom the exact country averages in CA totc and SAS-IQc are 99.60, for natives 100.00, for immigrants 96.94. Kenya was substituted by South Africa (data given in SAS). Further countries see Table A.2 and see information in appendix.

## 10.4 Modernity and Modernisation

Modernisation plays, according to James Flynn, the central role in causing the twentieth century's IQ increase. People acquired the ability to think more abstractly and at the same time the general conditions of life improved, resulting in higher intelligence (Flynn, 2012a; Neisser, 1998). On the other hand, modernisation depends on cognitive ability and is not possible without reaching the formal operational stage of thinking (Oesterdiekhoff, 2007–2014).

Modernity and modernisation are frequently used as global concepts. We defined and distinguished three aspects and measured them with ratings:

(1) *Technological modernity*: societies use and produce technically modern things and processes; they have, use and produce modern cars, sky-scrapers, mobile phones, computers, functioning water supply, heating and/or air conditioning, electricity, Internet, TV and means of transport (road, railway, shipping and air traffic). We assessed this by using the same four-scientist sample as for meritoric achievement orientation (Section 10.3.3; here Cronbach-$\alpha$ = .94).[33]

(2) *Societal-cultural-political modernity*: societies value and practice human rights, democracy and democratic attitudes, justice, women's equality, peace and peaceful coexistence, press freedom, religious freedom, free-dom of opinion, equality before the law, fair treatment of foreigners, preference and acceptance of modern art. This was assessed by the four-scientist sample (Section 10.3.3; here Cronbach-$\alpha$ = .93).

(3) *Cognitive-intellectual modernity*: autonomous and universal-ethical think-ing, rule of law and autonomous art are, according to Max Weber and Jürgen Habermas (1984/1981, pp. 159ff.), indicators of rationalisation ('Vernunft', 'Rationalisierung'). Rationalisation is a process leading to cognitive-intellectual modernity. There is an overlap between the concepts of intelligence (especially in the conceptualisation of Piaget), rationality and cognitive-intellectual modernity. They all describe a positive influence on societal-cultural-political and technological modernisation. We tried to measure cognitive-intellectual modernity with '*rationality*' standing for empirical orientation, reflection and seeking reliable information, includ-ing their use for problem-solving; interest in appropriate solutions and trying to understand problems, means, perspectives and aims; consider-ation of alternatives and consultation of experts without blindfold following them; no orientation in illogical, empirically disproved and implausible sources (such as astrology, witchcraft, delusional ideologies,

---

[33] A simple indicator could be the ability to produce warm water in houses and hotels at a constant usable temperature at different levels of consumption.

Table 10.3 *Correlations of modernity ratings and estimates (and meritoric principles)*

| | Tech Mod | Soc Mod | Cog Mod | CAch Mod | Tech Safe | Pol Mod | CA corr | SAS mean corr | SAS 95% corr | SAS 05% corr |
|---|---|---|---|---|---|---|---|---|---|---|
| **Technological modernity** | 1 | .91 | .92 | .85 | .77 | .68 | .78 | .67 | .71 | .65 |
| **Societal-cultural-political modernity** | .91 | 1 | .95 | .86 | .80 | .80 | .77 | .74 | .76 | .73 |
| **Cognitive modernity (Rationality)** | .92 | .95 | 1 | .87 | .79 | .69 | .82 | .79 | .80 | .79 |
| **Meritoric achievement orientation** | .89 | .92 | .96 | .86 | .75 | .68 | .83 | .81 | .82 | .81 |
| **N** | 187 | 187 | 187 | 186 | 186 | 186 | 186 | 96 | 96 | 96 |

*Notes*: Tech Mod: technological modernity; Soc Mod: societal-cultural-political modernity; Cog Mod: cognitive-intellectual modernity (rationality; all three rated); CAch Mod: cognitive high achievement in science and technology in modernity from Table 4.6 (patents, high tech exports, airline safety, innovation, science Nobel, high cites, top universities); Tech Safe: technological safety, an average of airline safety, road traffic safety and occupational safety (see Chapter 8 and Table 8.1); Pol Mod: political modernity, an average of rule of law, political liberty and democracy (see Section 10.2.1); CA corr: cognitive ability average corrected; analysis for these four variables done in the same country sample of 186 countries; three SAS (student assessment test) measures mean, top ability level (95 per cent, intellectual classes) and low ability level (5 per cent), corrected.

mere opinions, traditional conventions or prevalent convictions and world-views merely based on authority or majority). This was assessed by the four-scientist sample (Section 10.3.3; here Cronbach-$\alpha$ = .92).[34]

All three measures highly correlate (on average $r$ = .93; see Table 10.3). There is a generalisation effect, usually known as the 'halo effect', on the part of the raters and the rating process leading to more global ratings. However, measured indicators of modernisation from other sources (see Table 10.2, cognitive high achievement, technological safety and political modernity) also highly

---

[34] Rationality is here less an individual than a societal-cultural trait. Habermas (1984/1981, p. 43): 'And in the sociocultural conditions for such a conduct of life there is reflected perhaps the rationality of a lifeworld shared not only by individuals but by collectives as well.'

correlate at $r = .70$. There is a strong common cultural-societal process across different fields of modernisation.

The three modernity ratings highly correlate with measured indicators of technological, societal and cognitive modernity. In detail, technological modernity with cognitive high achievement in science and technology: $r = .85$ and with technological safety $r = .77$; societal-cultural-political modernity with political modernity $r = .80$; cognitive modernity (rationality) with cognitive ability $r = .82$ (Table 10.3). The correlations are not specific; for example, the technological modernity rating does not correlate higher with the technological safety measure and societal not higher with societal and cognitive not higher with cognitive. There is a too-strong G *factor* of modernisation along with a halo effect in ratings. However, the level of intellectual classes correlates more highly with all modernity indicators; especially for technological modernity, an intellectual elite is a prerequisite ($r_{95\%} = .71$ vs. $r_M = .67$ and $r_{05\%} = .65$).

This leads to the important question – what causes what? According to our past considerations in Chapters 7 and 8, cognitive ability fosters technological, societal-political and cultural modernisation. But are there not positive reverse effects on cognitive ability? James Flynn (2012a, p. 15) referred to this reverse effect:

The ultimate cause of IQ gains is the Industrial Revolution. The intermediate causes are probably its social consequences, such as more formal schooling, more cognitively demanding jobs, cognitively challenging leisure, a better ratio of adults to children, richer interaction between parent and child.

That is to say that modernity works via the improvement of conditions relevant for cognitive development such as education, cognitive complexity in everyday life and stimulation in families. Cognitive stimulation via technological complexity (mobiles, smart phones, Internet, computer, car operation, TV and machine operation, all at the job and at home) and via improved social contact such as parenting styles, more and higher quality verbal input, argumentation and justification furthers cognitive development.

Unfortunately, as for meritoric principles, we do not have longitudinal data. And we have only ratings. Finally, in the estimated period from the 1990s to the first years of the 2000s, all cognitive effects on modernisation that emerged later than around 1970 may be integrated into the effects from modernisation to cognitive ability. So the results should be interpreted cautiously. In Figure 10.10 the results of a cross-lagged analysis are presented.

There is a positive impact of modernity on national cognitive development across time: $\beta_{Mod \rightarrow CHC10} = .21$. This effect is independent from controlled wealth effects and from chosen cognitive human capital and modernity indicators.[35]

---

[35] Six analyses: technological, societal-cultural-political and cognitive modernity on student assessment result development (each $N = 18$) or on years of education development (each $N = 93$). Cognitive human capital (ability) indicators, student assessment tests: $\beta_{Mod \rightarrow SAS10} =$

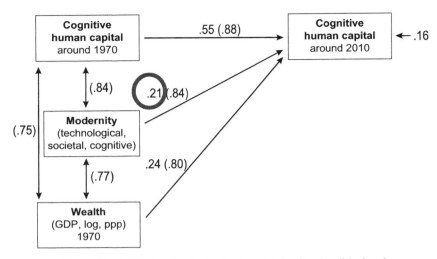

Figure 10.10 Effects of technological, societal-cultural-political and cognitive-intellectual modernity on cognitive capital development controlled for former cognitive capital and GDP; average of six analyses with $N = 18$ (student assessment studies) and $N = 93$ (years of education) nations

### 10.4.1   When Did Modernisation Begin? The Transition of the Thirteenth Century

Concluding that there are positive effects of modernisation and assuming that across centuries even such tiny improvements as a half IQ point per century would count, when in history did modernisation start? There was a first blossom of cognitive modernisation in *Ancient Greece*, which spread during the Roman Empire up to North Africa, the Near East and Britain. But as far as can be discerned, it did not lead to a broad cognitive progress within society.

The second phase of modernisation is said to begin at the latest with *industrialisation*, usually linked to the invention of the first effective steam engine by James Watt in around 1770 in Britain. In economic history, the beginning of the 'Great Divergence', the rise of the West and its relative enrichment compared to its own past and compared to other regions of the world, is usually dated in the late eighteenth to the nineteenth century. However, before industrialisation started there was the pioneer intellectual movement of the *Enlightenment*, with philosophers and scientists such as Descartes, Newton and Locke preparing the cognitive ground for technological

.20, $N = 18$; years of education: $\beta_{\text{Mod} \rightarrow \text{YoE10}} = .21$, $N = 93$. Modernity indicators, technological modernity: $\beta_{\text{tMod} \rightarrow \text{CHC10}} = .20$; societal-cultural-political modernity: $\beta_{\text{sMod} \rightarrow \text{CHC10}} = .21$; cognitive modernity: $\beta_{\text{cMod} \rightarrow \text{CHC10}} = .22$.

modernisation. And, of course, before the era of Enlightenment came the *Renaissance*, *Humanism* and *Protestantism*, with their important contributions to progress in intellectual, cultural and technological modernisation.

Finally, the Middle Ages were less dark than frequently described. Emperors such as Charlemagne or later Frederick II supported education and science. But the Carolingian Renaissance occurred in a social environment that was not mature enough for consecutive development. We see the very beginning of the present modernisation process, a process that has continued for centuries – occasionally being interrupted in certain regions and for limited periods – *in the thirteenth century*. What happened in this era of awakening?[36]

- *Thomas Aquinas* (1225–1274) developed the practice of critique, doubt and *argumentation*. He appreciated and practised the use of *reason* (however, not in a perfect form). This was embedded in scholastic philosophy and accompanied before, during and after by other intellectuals such as Anselm of Canterbury (1033–1109), Abelard (1079–1142), Albertus Magnus (1193–1280), Duns Scotus (1266–1308), William of Ockham (1288–1347), Dante Alighieri (1265–1321) and later Petrarch (1304–1374).[37] Trial by ordeal began to be discouraged by thinkers and smarter rulers. Empirical methods were developed (Roger Bacon, 1220–1292). An 'arithmetical' mentality emerged including prudence and planning.
- *Spiritual reform movements* within religion such as Catharism, preceded by Cluniac Reforms (in the tenth century) and Cistercians (in the eleventh century), followed in the sixteenth century by Protestantism.
- In education, *foundation of universities*: Bologna, Paris, Oxford and more in Italy, Germany, France, Britain and Spain, preceded by cathedral and monastic schools. Advancement in education through success in examinations (similar to China), reign of meritoric principles.
- Development of *inquisitiveness* and *science* as exemplified by Frederick II (1194–1250) conducting experiments, writing a book on falconry, arguing against superstition: 'Our purpose is to set forth the things that are, as they are.' ('Manifestare ea, quae sunt, sicut sunt.') Natural sciences were rediscovered as astronomy (Campanus of Novara, 1220–1296), anatomy

---

[36] This overview is based on works of Benjamin Nelson (1974), David Landes (1983, 1998), Don LePan (1989), Werner Sombart (1998/1913), Jacob Burckhardt (1990/1860), Gregory Clark (2007), Jacques Le Goff (1993/1957) and Sylvain Gouguenheim (2008).

[37] Dante Alighieri, Divina Commedia, Paradiso, Canto IV, lines 130-133:

'Therefore, our doubting blossoms like a shoot out from the root of truth; this natural urge spurs us toward the peak, from height to height.'

Petrarch is the first person who climbed a mountain for the observation of nature, its enjoyment and reflection including himself.

(Mondino de Liuzzi, 1270–1326) and physics (e.g. magnetism, Petrus Peregrinus, ca. 1240–end of thirteenth century; e.g. optics, Witelo, 1230–1280/1314).

- Commencement of *rule of law* (Magna Carta Libertatum, 1225 in Britain).
- In *agriculture*: development of the three-field system, use of yokes (invented in China) and horses.
- *Technological progress* such as invention, improvement and spread of wind and watermills, shipbuilding, navigation, energy production, compass (invented in China), buttons for cloth, spinning wheel (from Arabia), mechanical clocks, spectacles, firearms (from China), later, in 1453, movable-type printing (precursors in China).
- *Economical developments* in trade, finance and monetary economy, taxing and accounting leading to double-entry bookkeeping.
- Spread of understanding of time, velocity and acceleration, of time-measurement and of *time-based co-ordination*, leading to acceleration of work (see Alberti's book on conduct of life).
- *Discoveries*: Marco Polo's travel to China and India, later followed by the Portuguese and Spanish to India and America.
- Development of *independent cities* and the *burgher society* with its first perfect exemplification in the fifteenth century, Leon Battista Alberti.
- *Gothic style*, with its *aspiration to height and light*, blossomed in the thirteenth century. It presents progress in architecture, applied mathematics and statics. Culturally, it stands for competition, dynamism and strive for *progress*.[38]

Benjamin Nelson summarised the onset of modernity in a few words:

'From the sociological side, the 12th and 13th centuries were the seedbed of the modern European society. It was exactly the differentiation into kingdoms, principalities, cities, estates (*stände*), professions, universities and so on which helps us understand the extraordinary pulse-beat of the developments of the 12th and 13th centuries.' (Nelson, 1974, p. 459 [VII])

In the thirteenth century a process of cultural, cognitive and technological modernisation began that led to a first culmination in the Renaissance and Reformation and later resulted in the Enlightenment, industrialisation and an increase of wellbeing for nearly all people around the world. This historical

---

[38] Max Weber (2001/1905, p. 15): 'In architecture, pointed arches have been used elsewhere as a means of decoration, in antiquity and in Asia; presumably the combination of pointed arch and cross-arched vault was not unknown in the Orient. But the rational use of the Gothic vault as a means of distributing pressure and of roofing spaces of all forms, and above all as the constructive principle of great monumental buildings and the foundation of a style extending to sculpture and painting, such as that created by our Middle Ages, does not occur elsewhere.'

process was not free of inconsistencies and interruptions, but was strong and persistent enough to recover again and again.

Why was the onset of modernisation not located in China, India or Arabia? Were these cultures not comparable or even ahead 750 years ago? Yes, there had been leads in important fields, such as in China in certain technology products (e.g. compass), in Arabia (e.g. sugar) and in India (sophisticated arts and food). However, these were isolated and non-dynamic proceedings. In these cultures a long-term process leading to the Enlightenment, the Industrial Revolution, rule of law and human rights did not emerge. China has had the largest chances due to its own prior developments. Arabia has had great possibilities due to its intermediate position between Europe, India and China. The question is why China, India and Arabia did not follow the path to full modernisation based on their own internal development? We will try to answer this in the coming chapters. Benjamin Nelson outlines a first answer – abstract universalities, a distinctive feature of thinking:

The universalities of Greek philosophy and science, the universalities of Roman law and political theory, were an enduring heritage which recurrently entered into new fusions in the Western world. The 12th and 13th centuries built upon these universalities, both in Greek science and Roman law and were thus committed to structures of consciousness different in critical respects from those which had prevailed in China, in India, in Islam, among the Hebrews, etc. (Nelson, 1974, p. 469 [XII])])

## 10.5   Education

The amount of school education is a frequently used proxy for cognitive ability. Education furthers cognitive development and is itself supported by cognitive ability. Unsurprisingly, education highly correlates with cognitive ability (see Table 10.4). Altogether, the correlations are independent from used measures, whether the amount of education is more broadly or narrowly measured, whether psychometric intelligence or student assessment tests are applied.

Undoubtedly, the amount of education of a population and a nation's cognitive ability level are highly correlated. This is even more remarkable as the educational variables cover past experiences of adults and the student assessment tests abilities of present children. The mean of all bivariate correlations presented in Table 10.4 is $r = .73$. The best guess seems to be at $r = .76$ – the average correlation in the largest, less range-restricted sample shown in the first column. The correlations are reduced by partialling out wealth, but they remain high at about $r_p = .60$ (raw wealth-GNI partialled out) or $r_p = .45$ (logged wealth-GNI partialled out).

Why is this correlation so high? Education furthers thinking and knowledge; smarter nations further education, e.g. because education supports

Table 10.4 *Correlation between cognitive ability and educational variables*

| | CA corrected | Psychometric IQ (Lynn & Vanhanen) | SAS corr. (all) | SAS corr. (higher quality) |
|---|---|---|---|---|
| **Education (average)** | .74 (.61/.42) | .72 (.58/.39) | .75 (.64/.50) | .75 (.66/.52) |
| **Years at school 2010** | .77 (.65/.48) | .74 (.60/.42) | .68 (.53/.34) | .68 (.55/.36) |
| N | 192/172 | 192/172 | 106/103 | 97/94 |

*Notes*: CA corrected: corrected average of student assessment and psychometric intelligence studies; Psychometric IQ: Lynn and Vanhanen's intelligence test collection; SAS corr. (all): average of student assessment studies including local studies in developing countries and older studies until 1990, corrected for grade, age and school attendance; SAS corr. (higher quality): only average of TIMSS, PISA and PIRLS, corrected; Education (average): educational level of society, average of (a) literacy, percentage of adults with ability to read and write a simple sentence (Kurian, 2001, pp. 349–350), (b) percentage of persons between 12 and 19 years old 1960–1985 (today adults) having graduated from secondary school (Mankiw et al., 1992) and (c) mean of years of schooling of persons 25 years old or older for 1990, 1995 and 2000 (Barro & Lee, 2000), Cronbach-$\alpha$=.93; Years at school 2010: expected years of schooling (from HDR; UNDP, 2010); in parentheses partial correlation for wealth taken out (GNI 2010 HDR raw/logged).

occupational qualification and personality development (here, for the sake of argument, no cognitive effects); there are reciprocal effects, education furthers intelligence and intelligent nations therefore extend education; there are common background factors, such as culture, stimulating both sending youth to school and thinking.[39]

### 10.5.1   Reciprocity between Education and Ability

To prove the direction of causation, longitudinal studies analysing cross-lagged effects are the best choice (see Figure 10.11). Different measurement points were chosen. This enables dealing with the high correlations between education and ability and a risk of unstable patterns. In the upper part, developments from 1970 to 1990 ($N$ = 19 nations) and from 1990 to 2010 ($N$ = 45) are presented. In the first period, only cognitive ability has a positive effect; in the second, the effect of education is larger. In the longest period, from 1970 to 2010, both effects are positive and considerably high ($\beta_{CA70 \rightarrow Ed10} = .25$, $\beta_{Ed70 \rightarrow CA10} = .16$).

[39] Behind each single factor, education or intelligence, may stand further factors such as culture or evolution. They are not considered here because these further factors would work via education on intelligence or via intelligence on education, e.g. Protestantism via attending school on intelligence or evolution via intelligence on education. At the within society level it is sometimes suggested that educational institutions only select and signal competence by their high demands to get through (Spence, 1973; Charlton, 2009; Miller, 2009). For the level of societies, this can be excluded because at this level competence signalling is useless.

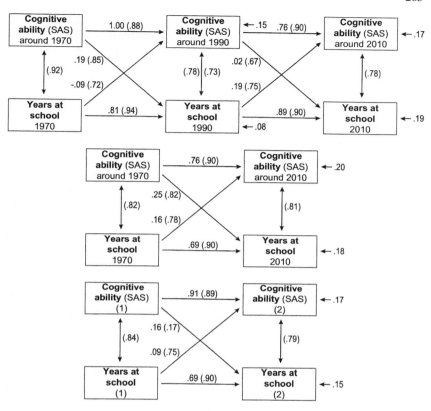

Figure 10.11 Cross-lagged effects between cognitive ability (as measured by student assessment tests, SAS) and education (years at school), 1970 to 1990: $N = 19$ nations, 1990 to 2010: $N = 45$, 1970 to 2010: $N = 18$; the last figure presents the average of the first three

Using the largest sample with 45 nations has brought the strongest education effect ($\beta_{CA90 \rightarrow Ed10} = .02$, $\beta_{Ed90 \rightarrow CA10} = .19$). In the final graph, which reports the average of all single period analyses, the cognitive ability effect is somewhat larger ($\beta_{CA1 \rightarrow Ed2} = .16$, $\beta_{Ed1 \rightarrow CA2} = .09$). A final conclusion regarding what effect is stronger is not possible. Both directions are relevant: education furthers ability as ability furthers education.

## 10.5.2   Educational Quality

At the individual level, educational effects on cognitive ability are well backed by an extensive amount of research (see Section 3.4.6). They can be grouped in four categories:

- *Time and extension*: More brings more. Going earlier and longer in life and sending larger proportions of a generation to school furthers intelligence and knowledge – at the individual level about 3 IQ points per year.[40] Increased learning time leads to more learning and more learning to more knowledge and improved thinking. More quantity of education stands for more quality of the entire educational system.
- *Ability level of social environment:* The average competence level of a class and school (classmates' cognitive ability level) leads, via better instruction, stimulation and modelling, to better and more learning and thus to higher ability. The same is true for teacher quality.
- *Structure, quality and achievement orientation*: This is a more heterogeneous category and includes discipline and class management (increases learning time); direct instruction (facilitating efficient knowledge delivery); structure and clarity (leading to efficient use of time and attentiveness); periodical tests (motivate and inform students, parents and teachers); central exams (define a minimum standard, signal achievement as being important, motivate to learn, improve discipline, more objective, reliable and valid information for students, parents, teachers, school administrations, receiving schools and employers); tracking (signals the importance of achievement, increases average class ability for the better students, supporting instruction and learning, better adaptation of instruction to the ability level of all students).
- *Single quality factors*: problem-based learning and teaching of thinking (not only rote learning); open questions for the entire class (stimulates attention); modern media and computer-assisted instruction (motivate, individualisation of learning, efficient use of attention, structure); modern individualised learning methods; school autonomy (decisions based on better access to local information); competition by private schools (competition leads to improvement).

Educational effects are larger on knowledge (crystallised intelligence) than on thinking ability (fluid intelligence). It is easier to deliver and acquire knowledge by teaching and learning than changing the more enduring but also more generalising intelligence. The factors work *compensatory*, that is, deficits in one environmental area can be compensated by advantages in others. Additionally, the effects are usually described as *linear for an average zone of factor intensity*: more education for people without any education has a huge effect; between 2 and 10 years of education the total outcome increases linearly

---

[40] Theoretically, more school education at a young age should have more positive effects than at an older age (i.e. a preschool year more than a university year); similarly, larger effects are expected at the lower cognitive ability level than at the higher. However, the findings are less clear.

and then the effects become smaller. Children having formal education for 24 hours each day will die. Of course, nobody will develop the idea of offering 24-hour instruction. But it means from a certain point onwards more does not bring more; it even harms! Finally, the educational factors can *influence each other* and may depend in their magnitude and in their size on effects of *background factors* such as family support, culture and genes.

What can be found at the level of national comparisons? We have chosen 24 theoretically and empirically important educational indicators and correlated them with the corrected cognitive ability average of student assessment and psychometric intelligence studies (correlations for $N_{max} = 192$ countries), the corrected average of all student assessment studies since the nineties ($N_{max} = 106$), the uncorrected average of all higher quality student assessment studies (PISA, TIMSS, PIRLS 1995-2012; $N_{max} = 97$), the uncorrected intellectual classes level ($N_{max} = 97$) and the uncorrected low ability level ($N_{max} = 97$). We have chosen different variables to test the robustness of relationships across different ability operationalisations and different country samples.[41] We added for comparison the correlation with wealth (GNI, $N_{max} = 181$) and finally partialled out wealth, modernity and the educational level of society (Table 10.5, last column). The idea is that education-ability correlations should be higher than education-wealth correlations and they should be still there after partialling out general indicators of national development. If not, education-ability correlations could only exist due to general background effects influencing education and ability.[42]

*Education Expenditures (Absolute, Relative, for Teachers)*   Education expenditures ($N_{max} = 116$) represent total spending per individual student and strongly depend on the general wealth level of a country. Accordingly, the correlation with GNI is very high at $r = .84$ and it is higher than all correlations with ability measures ($r$ between .53 and .63). The correlation with the general cognitive ability measure is higher than the ones with student assessment measures ($r = .63$ vs. .53 to .60). This is due to the larger, more heterogeneous country sample for this correlation, including more developing

---

[41] Because educational effects are analysed, corrections applied in order to generate population estimates, including youth not at school, are less appropriate. Corrected values are appropriate for studying cognitive human capital effects on society. However, because older and regional lower quality SAS studies frequently are based on unrepresentative samples, corrections could be seen as necessary. Whether corrected or uncorrected – there is no definite final answer. For checking the robustness of effects, different indicators and procedures were chosen.

[42] Partial correlations are only a rough method for checking for the influence of background effects. In so far as background factors depend on education and ability, partial correlations would overcorrect real correlations and erroneously reduce them (see Chapter 9). Path models are a better method.

Table 10.5 *Correlations between educational indicators and cognitive ability*

| | CA (corrected) | SAS M (corr., all) | SAS M (uncorr., PTP) | SAS 95% (uc., high ability) | SAS 05% (uc., low ability) | GNI 2010 HDR | SAS M P (uc., PTP, partialled) |
|---|---|---|---|---|---|---|---|
| Education expend. | .63 | .60 | .55 | .53 | .53 | .84 | .24 |
| Educ. exp. (rel GDP) | −.25 | −.02 | .08 | .09 | .06 | −.12 | − |
| Teacher salary (rel) | .32 | .30 | .36 | .32 | .38 | −.09 | − |
| Kindergarten (years) | .69 | .65 | .66 | .66 | .62 | .35 | .47 |
| Young enrolment | .05 | .04 | −.02 | .02 | −.07 | .32 | −.18 |
| Young in high grade | .32 | .33 | .24 | .27 | .20 | .32 | .06 |
| Amount of instruction | −.14 | −.16 | −.17 | −.15 | −.16 | .07 | .02 |
| Amount of education | .54 | .54 | .52 | .51 | .51 | .39 | .31 |
| Tracking young age | .28 | .28 | .32 | .35 | .26 | .22 | .34 |
| Share of migrants | .07 | .08 | .04 | .07 | .04 | .58 | .02 |
| Language identical | .30 | .30 | .30 | .26 | .32 | −.08 | .16 |
| Class size/teacher ratio | −.66 | −.61 | −.51 | −.50 | −.49 | −.52 | .02 |
| Repetition rate | −.26 | −.32 | −.30 | −.33 | −.27 | .00 | −.02 |
| Discipline | .49 | .50 | .53 | .52 | .51 | .16 | .48 |
| Direct instruction | .06 | .06 | .07 | .08 | .05 | −.06 | .23 |
| Achievement tests | .08 | .11 | .12 | .13 | .12 | .05 | −.01 |
| Central exams-tests | .11 | .16 | .17 | .20 | .18 | −.16 | .38 |
| School autonomy | .40 | .41 | .41 | .40 | .41 | .11 | .20 |
| Teacher quality | .49 | .51 | .50 | .54 | .46 | .26 | .26 |
| Private schools | .12 | .11 | .10 | .06 | .12 | .21 | .17 |
| Homework | −.18 | −.20 | −.19 | −.19 | −.17 | −.40 | .00 |
| School quality overall | .65 | .67 | .67 | .70 | .61 | .32 | .49 |
| Adult education mean | .74 | .75 | .73 | .76 | .68 | .55 | .56 |
| Number of books | .70 | .69 | .69 | .71 | .65 | .53 | .35 |
| Sch. quality + Adult | .78 | .81 | .79 | .82 | .73 | .39 | .57 |
| $N_{max}$ | 192 | 106 | 97 | 97 | 97 | 181 | 97 |

*Notes*: For cognitive ability estimates see also Table 10.1; GNI 2010 HDR: wealth indicator in 2008 ppp, US dollar per capita; SAS M P (uncorr., PTP, partialled): mean of higher quality SAS studies, partialling out wealth (GNI 2010 HDR), social-cultural modernity (democracy 1950-2012) and educational level of society (see Table 10.4); in the partial correlation between adult education and ability, educational level is not partialled out; Class size/p-teacher ratio: Class size/pupil-teacher ratio; Sch. quality + Adult ed.: multiple correlation of school quality and adult educational level of society, educational variables see text and in detail see Appendix.

countries ($N = 116$ vs. 81 and 73). In the same country sample of 73 countries, the difference between CA and SAS is only $r = .02$.

In addition, general cognitive ability and the first SAS mean are corrected. Correction slightly increases the correlation (from $r_{CAnc} = .62$ to $r_{CAc} = .63$, from $r_{SASnc} = .55$ to $r_{SASc} = .60$). All this points to an interpretation that absolute education expenditures represent the general wealth level of a society. More informative would be a look at expenditures relative to GDP – the next variable.

Education expenditures *relative* to GDP/c ($N_{max} = 127$) covers the total spending per student corrected for the general wealth level. The correlations with ability measures circle around zero. As found in studies by other authors, any effects of expenditures are only small or even zero (e.g. Hattie, 2009, p. 74). Hanushek, Peterson and Woessmann (2013, p. 98) summarized: 'On average, an additional $1,000 in per-pupil spending is associated with a trivial annual gain in achievement of 0.1 percent of a standard deviation.'

However, applying a plausibility check, this is a strange result. Education cannot work without adequate funding! This is especially clear for the lower end of education expenditures: blackboards, books, chairs, tables and a teacher salary being high enough to live on are just necessary. But money is frequently not spent in the right way to support learning, e.g. as described by Richard Nisbett (2009, p. 58) for the United States:

The classic case of this occurred in Kansas City, where judicial orders increased hugely the amount of money pumped into the schools. Olympic-size pools were built, state-of-the-art science labs were provided, and a computer was given to every student. The result: no improvement in scores. Money by itself does nothing to improve student performance, especially when administrators are incompetent and corrupt.

In developing countries, money designated for education is frequently spent for other purposes, e.g. according to Reinikka and Svensson (2004, p. 679):

According to official statistics, 20 percent of Uganda's total public expenditure was spent on education in the mid-1990s, most of it on primary education. One of the large public programs was a capitation grant to cover schools' nonwage expenditures. ... The survey data reveal that ... the schools, on average, received only 13 percent of the grants. Most schools received nothing. The bulk of the school grant was captured by local officials (and politicians).

Thus it is not money itself but *how* it is spent for education that is important.

*Teacher salary* relative to GDP per capita ($N_{max} = 40$) is a more specific and 'arrival' expenditure indicator: teacher salary means that education expenditures have been spent at least for one important field in education – salaries. High salaries attract more competent school graduates to study teaching and to become and remain a teacher (for different countries: Dolton & Marcenaro-Gutierrez, 2011; Nickell & Quintini, 2002). More competent teachers give better instruction, furthering students' abilities. Corresponding to this assumption the correlations with abilities are positive and robust ($r$ around .35). However, the sample is, with 40 countries and one source (PISA 2009), rather small. And there is one 'famous' exception: Finland's teacher have only a comparatively small salary but their school system can attract the most able school graduates to become teachers. This is explained by the high reputation of the teaching profession in Finland – a cultural attribute – attracting the best among the young generation (e.g. Simola, 2005). However, other leading nations in ability such as Hong Kong, Korea, China, Singapore and Switzerland pay relatively good salaries.

Finally, further data corroborate a positive effect of teacher salary: Dolton et al. (2014) presented data for 30 countries on teacher salaries compared (adjusted for purchasing power) to the benchmark, Finland. We divided a country's average teacher salary by Finland's benchmark and correlated it with the ability measures. The correlations are high (in the order of Table 10.5, $r = .70, .69, .68, .62, .66$, all $N = 30$) and robust after partialling out wealth, modernity and educational level ($r_p = .54, .60, .69, .53, .67$). Well-paid teachers seem to be more important for lower ability than for high ability groups ($r_{95\%} = .32$ vs. $r_{05\%} = .38$). Internationally, the positive effect of relative teacher salary on student competence is backed by analyses of Hanushek and Woessmann (2015a, p. 85).

*Preschool Education: Kindergarten Attendance*    Kindergarten represents the average years of institutional preschool education in age three to six, usually called 'kindergarten' ($N_{max} = 82$). As studies at the within-country level have shown, preschool education has positive long-term effects on school attendance, students' achievement and personality (see Section 3.4.6). Intelligence effects tend to peter out but school attendance, students' achievement and personality effects such as more discipline, all factors that support cognitive development, hint at indirect and probably more enduring effects on cognitive development.

Cross-country analyses reveal a high positive and robust pattern; correlations are high at around $r = .65$ to $.69$. However, could it not be that kindergarten attendance is merely another indicator of a country's modernisation as a *background factor*? In well-developed countries, it is simply conventional to send one's child to kindergarten. Additionally, in such countries women work and childminding is plainly inevitable. Because modernisation depends on cognitive ability, kindergarten attendance is also a distant dependent variable of ability – kindergarten attendance is also a *reverse effect* of ability.

However, the correlation of kindergarten attendance with cognitive ability is considerably higher than of kindergarten with wealth ($r \approx .65$ vs. $r_{GNI} = .35$) and robust against partialling out the societal development indicators wealth, modernity and educational level of adults ($r_p = .47$). Also considering gender equality in a partial correlation leaves a high correlation ($r_p = .56$).

Studies at the individual level corroborate positive long-term competence effects. Preschool education is an important explicative variable for understanding international ability differences.

*School Enrolment at a Young Age*  At the individual level, school attendance shows positive effects of about 3 IQ points per year (see Section 3.4.6): Children enrolled at a younger age in primary school show an advantage in intelligence, especially in more knowledge-loaded scales. Thus school enrolment at a young age ($N_{max} = 96$) should also show a positive effect in cross-country comparisons. Past research at this level revealed positive correlations with ability indicators; however, these were not robust in partial correlations and the correlation with wealth was higher (Rindermann & Ceci, 2009).

This 'negative trend' is continued in the newer and larger data set (Table 10.5): correlations wobble around zero and are higher to GNI. Ergo: cross-country differences in ability cannot be explained by school enrolment age. There seems to be an indispensable minimum maturity level for supportive effects of school education. Having said that, it should not be forgotten that we are speaking about the country level (ecological fallacy problem): for young children it is usually beneficial to go to school early. Further factors may mask a positive effect. For example, a high-quality preschool education received by nearly the entire age group may make early school enrolment unnecessary.

*Being in a High Grade at a Young Age*  Being younger than usual in a given grade in fourth and eighth grade level studies TIMSS and PIRLS or being in a high grade at age 15 in PISA are indicators of an efficient educational system ($N_{max} = 100$). Further, ability is an age-related construct in childhood: being able to solve cognitive tasks at an earlier age represents higher cognitive ability.

In our cross-country comparisons, the correlations with ability are stable and positive at around $r = .25$ to .33. Contrary to expectations, the correlation to wealth is of similar strength and after partialling out background factors the ability correlations are rather small with $r_p = .06$. Delaying education is not an indicator of an effective (leading to a high level of competences) nor an efficient (using time in a profitable way) educational system but the negative effects are not large.

*Amount of Instruction per Year*  At the within-country level the overwhelming evidence shows positive effects of instruction on cognitive ability (see Section 3.4.6). However, the global positive impression has to be specified: more instruction as years of education per life shows effects, but less is known on more instruction per year. We have cross-country data for the per year variable for $N_{max} = 96$ countries.

Different to previous analyses performed by me and others (e.g. Lavy, 2015) there is no positive effect of more teaching time per year; correlations are negative to zero. Using only the more reliable TIMSS and PIRLS data on instruction does not improve the results. A closer look at the data reveals that the group of countries with a large amount of instruction is very heterogeneous: there are the expected East Asian candidates, Singapore, Macau, China, Taiwan, Japan and Korea, but also Egypt, Costa Rica, Philippines, South Africa and Ghana. At the low amount of instruction end are developing countries from Latin America, Arabia and countries from Southeast Europe. But excluding Africa or only using First World countries does not result in a robust pattern of positive effects. Of course, we rely here as in all other variables on the validity of published data. But there is no evidence for the amount of instruction per year as an explaining variable of cross-country differences.

*Amount of Education*    Amount of education covers all received institutional education until around age 15 years, in many countries the end of compulsory education. Our summary variable ($N_{max} = 101$) consists of kindergarten attendance, being in a high grade at a young age, amount of instruction per year and attendance at additional schools ('cram schools') as is usual in East Asian countries.

Amount of education is positively and robustly correlated with cognitive abilities, higher with ability than with wealth and also correlated after partialling out background factors ($r \approx .52$ vs. $r_{GNI} = .39$, $r_p = .31$). The basic assumption that 'more brings more' is backed.

*Tracking at a Young Age*    Tracking is a contentious issue within educational science and educational politics. Therefore, we give more information on the state of research: Hanushek and Woessmann (2006) compared ability development between primary and secondary school across countries. In their study, early tracking had a negative impact on ability ('tendency for early tracking to reduce mean performance' p. C63) and increased educational inequality. But according to a within-country meta-analysis of Hattie (2009, pp. 74, 89ff., 99f.), the average impact of ability grouping is positive. Whereas the general effect is rather small ($d = 0.12$), the effect for gifted students is remarkable ($d = 0.30$). This is supported by a more recent study in Germany using a psychometric measure in an above average sample (CogAT-figural scale, a culture reduced scale of reasoning, $d = 0.48$ in three years or 2.40 IQ points per year; Becker, Lüdtke, Trautwein, Köller & Baumert, 2012).

Two more recent studies also show positive effects of early tracking: first, Koerselman (2013) found for the UK a general positive effect ($d = 0.10$) and for above average students again a larger one ($d = 0.17$) – about 1.50 to 2.55 IQ. Not every country in his sample showed effects, e.g. in Sweden the impact was at zero. Even more important, in a cross-country comparison the effects were larger with $d = 0.35$ or 5.25 IQ. Koerselman (2013, p. 149) summarised:

All in all, it is clear that there is a robust and strong gap in early test scores between early and late tracking countries.

Methodically, the best study is an experimental one on tracking in Kenya conducted by Duflo, Dupas and Kremer (2011): in school group A, 61 primary schools assigned their pupils randomly to one of two sections; in school group B, 60 schools assigned their pupils according to individual prior achievement measured by an exam either to higher or to lower ability classes. Which school practised which system – no tracking or ability tracking – was randomly selected. After 18 months the ability level was measured by an objective achievement test. The result was a positive tracking effect of $d = 0.18$ being robust across one year. The effect was similar for above and below average pupils, but a little higher for the above average ones ($d = 0.19$ vs. $d = 0.16$).

Summarising, there is a positive effect of tracking, but why? The first of two usually given answers is that above average students benefit from the *higher average ability level* in their class, enabling a faster, more demanding and inspiring instruction including more stimulation by their smarter classmates. However, this can only explain the effects for above average groups but not positive effects also found for below average groups – according to this theory, the effects for them should be negative. The other answer is that tracking leads to *more homogenous classes enabling teachers to provide better adapted instruction* for both the above and below average students in a class. The precondition here is that it is not homogeneity itself that leads to better ability development but rather teachers' adequate instructional reaction to this homogeneity.[43] Duflo et al.'s (2011) study indicated that weaker pupils, especially, gained in easier tasks, suggesting that teachers in ability-tracked classes focused more on basic competences, thus avoiding teaching over their pupils' heads. Additionally, they argued that teachers in tracking schools, especially in higher ability classes, were more likely to be present in class, increasing instructional and learning time for their pupils.

Koerselman (2013) referred to additional positive incentive effects working *before* tracking: students, parents and teachers try their best to learn and to

---

[43] Studies at the level of classes have usually shown that homogeneity itself has no or rather small positive effects on ability development (Dar & Resh, 1986; Hanushek et al, 2003; Rindermann, 2007b).

promote learning in order to reach the higher ability schools. This may explain the negative post-tracking effects found by Hanushek and Woessmann (2006).

Finally, the average output of an educational system can be much higher if the smarter students are put together: as shown for worker groups, the gains by ability grouping (compared to mixed grouping) in smart groups are much higher than the losses in non-smart groups (Jones, 2016, p. 141). The age cohort and, subsequently, society benefit much more from unhindered cognitive development among the intellectual classes.

Our own cross-national analyses show positive effects of tracking (Table 10.5, $N_{max} = 72$): the correlation is at $r_M = .30$ and higher for the top than for the low ability group ($r_{95\%} = .35$ vs. $r_{05\%} = .26$). The latter is in accordance with Hattie's meta-analysis findings of stronger effects for high ability students at the within-country level. The correlation with ability is higher than with wealth and is robust towards control of background factors ($r \approx .30$ vs. $r_{GNI} = .22$, $r_p = .34$).

PISA 2009 and PISA 2012 themselves reported their own tracking ages. Taking their variables the above results are supported for 2009 and 60 countries: $r = .19$ vs. $r_{GNI} = .17$, $r_p = .25$; and 2012 and also 60 countries: $r = .14$ vs. $r_{GNI} = .04$, $r_p = .27$. The positive findings are supported by data from other authors, by former studies of the same author, by studies at lower data levels including experiments and by theory. Tracking supports ability development and contributes to the explanation of cross-country differences.

*Share of Migrants*    The share of immigrants (percentage among students) is slightly positively correlated with ability scales ($N_{max} = 93$). However, the correlation with wealth is much higher ($r \approx .06$ vs. $r_{GNI} = .58$). This pattern hints that across countries it is not immigrants that are raising a nation's IQ but that immigrants are attracted by wealthy nations which have smart populations. This becomes much clearer when ability levels of native and immigrant students are compared (see Tables 10.2 and A.2, Section 10.3.5): here the average gain (or better loss) is −0.35 IQ points, strongly varying across countries from the Emirates with +7.42 to Luxembourg with −3.37 IQ points. Depending on natives' and immigrants' ability levels and their percentages the outcomes of immigration are different. The standard cross-country correlational procedure is inadequate here. And, of course, the category of immigrants within and across countries comprises very different groups with different impact.

*Languages Spoken at Home and in School Are Identical*    Similar to the proportion of migrants, the identity of languages spoken at home and in school ($N_{max} = 92$) itself is no quality indicator of educational systems but a social feature influencing instruction and its success. If languages are different and students have no good command over the school's language, instruction becomes more difficult and less effective. Why students do not have a good command over the school's language may have different reasons such as recent arrival from a country with a different language, cultural segregation, missing language courses or low cognitive ability. Cross-country correlations of language identity show a positive and robust pattern: higher with ability than with wealth and still recognisable after controlling background factors ($r \approx .30$ vs. $r_{GNI} = -.08$, $r_p = .16$).

The interpretation is less obvious. Theoretically, it is clear that without knowing the language of instruction well positive school effects and ability development are impeded. On the other hand, self-segregation and low ability hinder language acquisition.

*Class Size and Pupil-Per-Teacher Ratio*   Small classes and few pupils per teacher usually count as favourable conditions of instruction. Students are better observed, their personal strengths and weaknesses are known to the teacher, enabling him or her to tailor individual furtherance and instruction. Homework and examinations can be better controlled, class management is easier and more effective, contact is intensified and for all involved the instruction is less stressful. Thus a negative correlation between class size and abilities is expected ($N_{max} = 189$).

At the cross-country level, class size and ability are highly negatively correlated ($r = -.50$ to $-.66$). However, the correlation to wealth is similar ($r_{GNI} = -.52$) and after partialling out background factors the ability correlation is around zero and even slightly positive ($r_p = +.02$). Using only data based on PISA, TIMSS and PIRLS reveals a somewhat more robust negative pattern ($N = 94$, $r \approx -.50$ vs. $r_{GNI} = -.39$, $r_p = -.14$).

In spite of its theoretical plausibility, the pattern is less strong at the within-country resp. class level. In Hattie's (2009, pp. 74, 85ff.) meta-analysis the impact of large classes is negative, but not strongly ($d = -0.21$). Enlarging class size from 15 to 25 pupils has a negative impact of $d = -0.13$. An experimental study with younger pupils in the United States came to similar effects ($d = -0.22$, $r = -.11$ to $-.14$; Krueger, 1999).

Small positive effects of smaller classes are accompanied by increasing salary costs for more teachers and by decreasing selectivity in selection of teacher applicants, resulting in lower quality teachers. Thus, reducing class size is not the best idea. The better idea is to train teachers and prepare students to teach and learn in larger than optimal classes.

*Repetition Rates*   High repetition rates ($N_{max} = 68$) are not a sign of good school systems. Correlations are negative and higher than with wealth ($r \approx -.30$ vs. $r_{GNI} = .00$, $r_p = -.02$). However, partialling out background factors leads to a very small negative correlation. Repetition implies a delay in school career, which itself is no positive characteristic. It would be better to prevent achievement problems or to solve them with other means, e.g. by additional instruction. However, doing nothing and simple promotion to the next grade would be no solution.

*Discipline*    Discipline, regular school attendance, no tardiness or early going home, no disruption of class but following teachers' instructions, briefly, to behave well, is a characteristic of a good pupil and one of the aims of education ($N_{max}$ = 95). As everybody knows, at least outside East Asia, pupils do not always behave like this. But discipline furthers learning, simply because it increases time spent for teaching and learning. Reciprocally, cognitive development has a positive impact on moral and norm-orientated behaviour (see Chapter 7).

The correlations between discipline and ability measures are high and robust ($r \approx .50$ vs. $r_{GNI} = .16$, $r_p = .48$). They confirm previous results based on smaller samples and somewhat different indicators ($r \approx .41$; Rindermann & Ceci, 2009, p. 560). Studies at the level of classes support an interpretation of positive discipline effects on ability (for class management: $d = 0.52$; Hattie, 2009, p. 74, 102f.). Discipline is a crucial factor for understanding cross-country differences.

*Direct Instruction*    Direct instruction ($N_{max}$ = 80) – the teacher presents and explains the subject matter – is the classical teaching method. When thinking about school, people have this method in mind. Frequently, its description is extended by being well-structured and student-orientated and by being completed with periodical achievement controls. Alternative methods set against direct instruction emphasise self-directed learning, 'constructivist' teaching (students as active, self-directed learners), discovery learning or co-operative learning.

Empirical research at the class level has shown strong positive effects of direct instruction. In Hattie's (2009, p. 201, 204ff.) meta-analysis its effect is $d = 0.59$:

Results show that active and guided instruction is much more effective than unguided, facilitative instruction. (Hattie, 2009, p. 243)[44]

The same positive pattern can be found using international student assessment data (OECD, 2016b, p. 65):

---

[44] Gabriel Heller-Sahlgren (2015b, p. 66) goes even further by explaining Finland's good student assessment results by the application of traditional methods in instruction and the avoidance of 'harmful' methods: 'Progressive teaching methods appear harmful for cognitive achievement'.

In all but three education systems . . . using teacher-directed instruction more frequently is associated with higher science achievement, . . . Students in all countries also hold stronger epistemic beliefs, such as believing that scientific ideas change in light of new evidence, when their teachers used these strategies more frequently. A positive association is also observed between these teaching practices and students' expectations of pursuing science-related careers.

The average positive effect of 'teacher-directed instruction' is +28 SASQ points (in an IQ-scale 4.20 IQ points), on the other hand class debates (about −25 SASQ, equiv. 3.75 IQ) and students designing their own experiments (about −45 SASQ, equiv. 6.75 IQ) showed negative effects. However, the reception of studies on direct instruction is biased, as described by Hattie (2009, p. 258):

All but one program had close to zero effects (some had negative effects). Only Direct Instruction had positive effects on basic skills, on deeper comprehension measures, on social measures, and on affective measures. . . . Those in the Direct Instruction compared to peers not in this program were twice as likely to graduate from high school, had higher scores on reading ($d = 0.43$) and mathematics ($d = 0.28$). . . . The outcome of this study, however, was not to support more implementation of Direct Instruction but to spend more resources on the methods that did not work but were preferred by educators. . . . The romantic view of students discovering learning was more powerful than a method invented by a teacher that actually made a difference; a method that required an attention to detail, to deliberately changing behavior, and to teaching specific skills.

Our cross-country results hint at small but stable positive effects of direct instruction ($r \approx .07$ vs. $r_{GNI} = -.06$, $r_p = .23$). The correlation is higher than with wealth and increases after correction for background factors. This pattern indicates that direct instruction may be substituted by other positive working factors (see also Figure 10.13). All this together does not mean that teaching should only use direct instruction. Periods of structured knowledge transfer should be accompanied by the use of cognitively activating and self-directed learning phases and by exercise and practice.

*Achievement Tests*    The use of achievement tests covers the application of such tests and the use of their results for student selection or placement, frequently in combination with the use of grades. That means tests are not applied as a kind of PISA test but are used for decision-making. They give schools and teachers better information and signal all parties involved, students, parents, teachers, administrators and politicians, that achievement at school is relevant. This should stimulate motivation and learning and improve instruction (Crooks, 1988; $d = 0.34$, Hattie, 2009, p. 178; $d \approx 0.72$, Phelps, 2012). More or less this is also the argument for conducting student assessment studies such as PISA – better information for political decisions should improve educational systems.

We have data for $N_{max} = 88$ countries. However, the correlations are rather small. They are higher than with wealth but not robust against background factors ($r \approx .12$ vs. $r_{GNI} = .05$, $r_p = -.01$). So there is only some evidence for a positive effect.

*Central Exams and Tests*     Central exams should define a minimum standard, signal achievement as being important, improve discipline and their results inform students, parents, teachers and school administration, altogether leading to higher motivation, more learning and better achievement. Data are given for $N_{max} = 54$ countries.

The correlations are not high, but higher than with wealth ($r \approx .18$ vs. $r_{GNI} = -.16$, $r_p = .38$). A control for background factors substantially increases the correlation ($r = .17$ vs. $r_p = .38$). This positive pattern is backed by analyses of other authors in and across different countries, e.g. within Germany ($d = 0.12$; Jürges, Schneider & Büchel, 2005), Canada and the United States (Bishop, 1997, 2006; Fuchs & Woessmann, 2007) or in international comparison (Hanushek & Woessmann, 2015a, p. 84).

*School Autonomy*     The school autonomy concept is based on the liberal ideas of autonomy and subsidiarity (e.g. Hayek, 2011/1960): locally given information enables better decisions such as on teacher recruitment, spending and instruction. A precondition is an ability to make rational decisions. Economic researchers (e.g. Woessmann, 2001) using TIMSS data have found positive results. The same pattern resulted in our analysis ($N_{max} = 72$): the correlations with ability measures are rather high, larger than with wealth and robust against background factors ($r \approx .41$ vs. $r_{GNI} = .11$, $r_p = .20$).

*Teacher Quality and Competence*     Teacher quality is certainly an important variable. Teacher education revolves around the idea that it is possible to improve teacher quality by selection of the better applicants and by their education and that teacher attributes are important for school quality and students' development. Especially in Africa, low teacher quality impedes instruction, with detrimental effects on pupils (Woessmann, 2016). Using TIMSS 1995 Sandfur (2016) showed that teachers in Africa reach a competence level in mathematics comparable to students in eighth grade in Europe and East Asia. This is backed by Isaac Mbiti (2016, p. 116):

Data from a variety of settings suggest that teacher subject knowledge is quite limited. In Kenya, sixth grade math teachers scored about 50 percent on an externally administered grade appropriate math exam (. . .) About 40 percent of teachers in Kenya, 20 percent of teachers in Uganda, 5 percent of teachers in Senegal, and 1.2 percent of teachers in Tanzania had the minimum knowledge needed to be effective.

According to Hattie (2009, pp. 110f., 113ff.), teacher education and teacher subject matter knowledge have only small effects ($d = 0.11$ and $d = 0.09$). Other researchers come to somewhat more favourable, but not large, effects: E.g. Hanushek and Woessmann (2011, p. 115) found for PISA 2003 math +9.72 SASQ points for fully certified teachers (corresponding to 1.46 IQ or $d = 0.10$). Others used income as an indicator of competence and found positive effects (Dolton & Marcenaro-Gutierrez, 2011, pp. 35, 41: + \$5,000 led to $d = 0.26$). Here the effect is empirically not distinguishable from salary effects (see sub-section above).

We have information on teacher quality in our data that is based on teacher education for $N_{max} = 92$ countries. The correlations with ability results are high: higher than with wealth and robust against background factors ($r \approx .50$ vs. $r_{GNI} = .26$, $r_p = .26$). Teacher competence helps to explain cross-country differences in ability. Longitudinally, reciprocal effects are to be expected: teacher quality furthers ability and ability furthers teacher quality.

*Private Schools*   Private school percentage among schools or students is, similar to school autonomy, a favourite of the liberal-libertarian tradition. Private institutions compared to public ones are more efficient and usually achieve higher quality. What is nearly universally accepted for economic systems in general and for industry and the service sector in particular is less accepted for education. But among the ten most recognised universities of the world, according to the Times Higher Education World University Rankings 2013–2014, are six private universities.[45] Also the most recognised secondary schools are private ones, e.g. Eton, Harrow, Salem, Sankt Gallen, Miss Porter's School ... The economic explanation claims that competition, self-interest and local information lead to more motivation, better organisation, higher efficiency and better quality. This applies for the level of schools (private schools are better) as well as for the level of school systems (competition fosters quality).

Whether private schools actually offer higher quality and why – maybe private schools attract only the better students resulting in better school-leavers or their main quality feature is the higher ability level of their students, creating all the other advantages – has to be empirically researched. Following a comparative study in 22 countries by Dronkers and Robert (2008) private schools showed better results but solely due to their better students. And larger shares of private schools did not improve school systems:

---

[45] 1. Caltech, 2. Harvard, 4. Stanford, 5. MIT, 6. Princeton, 9. Chicago. The three British universities among the top ten (Oxford, Cambridge, Imperial College) have much more autonomy compared to other public universities in the world. Ranking from www.timeshighereducation.co.uk/world-university-rankings/2013-14/world-ranking.

We did not find any significant positive effect of the size of the private independent school sector on the reading score. (Dronkers & Robert, 2008, p. 574)

However, that is not all. As they and other authors have shown (Hanushek & Woessmann, 2011, pp. 150ff.), privately operated but publicly funded schools show an advantage: access is not limited due to parents' income and competition shows its positive effects, including spillover effects for public schools.

International comparisons (Table 10.5) for $N_{max} = 68$ countries reveal small positive effects ($r \approx .10$ vs. $r_{GNI} = .21$, $r_p = .17$). The correlation is robust towards control of background factors, but the correlation with wealth is higher. Maybe, the distinction between private operation and private funding, which is not reflected in our variable, is indeed important.

*Homework*    Homework increases learning time. Doing homework serves as exercise of the theoretically taught subject, as individual acquisition and analysis of the subject, it shows whether a student has understood the subject and, incidentally, doing homework has a pedagogical purpose: it supports acquiring a work ethic. In the United States, private Catholic schools give more homework and their students do more homework (about +1.7 hours per week; Coleman, Hoffer & Kilgore, 1982). This is seen as one factor contributing to Catholic schools' higher effectiveness. According to Hattie's meta-analysis (2009, pp. 201, 234ff.), homework has a positive impact on achievement at $d = 0.29$. In student assessment studies, doing homework and student achievement are positively associated (IAEP-1991, within countries; Lapointe et al., 1992a, pp. 50, 52, 70). However, the causal direction is not always clear: are schools good because they assign, monitor and control homework or are they good because their students do the requested homework?

In our cross-country sample ($N_{max} = 91$), amount of homework and abilities are *negatively* correlated ($r \approx -.19$ vs. $r_{GNI} = -.40$, $r_p = .00$)! By all accounts, homework is *no* indicator of an effective educational system. The results are corroborated by my older analyses with data on fewer countries ($N = 46$; Rindermann & Ceci, 2009, p. 560) and by a study of other authors at the cross-country level (Boe et al., 2001, pp. 17, 26, 39, 48). The macrosocial level result is contrary to the positive relationship between homework and achievement in within-country analyses.

Here we have an exemplary case for the '*ecological fallacy*' problem. Homework has a different meaning depending on the data level: At the *individual level*, the homework variable refers to the time spent on homework, which increases learning time, and it depends on the educational quality in families, on discipline and probably on unknown genetic factors. In contrast, at the *national level* and in comparison of educational systems, the same variable is a proxy for institutionalised (negative) educational quality: good school systems try to increase monitored learning time in school rather than delegate instruction and learning to the home and parents.

*Overall School-Education Quality*   Overall school-education quality bundles all those educational variables that have a theoretically convincing and empirically, on different levels, backed positive effect on students' cognitive competence development: preschool education (kindergarten attendance), swift uninterrupted educational course (being in high grades at a young age including no grade retention), early tracking, discipline, direct instruction, use of central exams and achievement tests, school autonomy, percentage of private schools and teacher quality ($N_{max}$ = 96).[46]

School-education quality is highly and robustly positively correlated with ability and less with wealth ($r \approx .67$ vs. $r_{GNI} = .32$, $r_p = .49$). That means that quality and ability are not another expression of wealth. Results from studies at the within-country level and theoretical considerations point to education on ability effects; however, positive reverse effects, especially at the level of nations, are not excludable, e.g. smarter citizens and politicians opt for kindergarten and discipline education. Additionally, educational variables can influence each other as kindergarten lays the ground for a swift educational career. Multivariate analyses at the cross-country level and case studies within countries have to analyse such interdependencies.

*Adult Education Mean (Educational Level of Society)*   The adult education mean, the educational level of society ($N_{max}$ = 192), is not a characteristic of a school system or of its students. It is the outcome of an educational system of a society. The correlations of adult education with students' abilities are extremely high and robust ($r \approx .73$ vs. $r_{GNI} = .55$, $r_p = .56$). The high correlations become more astonishing considering that different generations are compared – the information on adult education is somewhat outdated, based on generations and measurement points before 2000. So neither attributes of students nor of the educational system most highly correlate with children's IQ but rather the adults' educational level. This hints that general background factors – but not wealth – are crucial for the ability level and development of coming generations. For example, smarter adults – taking education as a proxy for intelligence and know-ledge – vote for smarter politicians, creating a more beneficial environment

---

[46] The overall school-education quality variable is the variable that most highly correlates at $r = .71$ ($r_p = .49$) among all chosen society variables (see Chapter 11) with 'educational efficiency' according to Dolton et al. (2014). This corroborates the validity of our school-education quality variable.

at home, at schools and in society. And in the long run a good school system leads to a high educational level of society.

*Number of Books at Home*    Finally, the number of books at home is also not a characteristic of an educational system but a general background variable standing for education and interest in intellectual topics. The number of books also highly correlates with students' ability levels ($N_{max} = 85$, $r \approx .69$ vs. $r_{GNI} = .52$, $r_p = .35$). High correlations are supported by studies of other authors at different levels, e.g. by Evans, Kelley, Sikora and Treiman (2010). Hanushek and Woessmann (2011, p. 117) summarised:

Books at home are the single most important predictor of student performance in most countries.

Again, general education and intellectual interests are more important than any other single indicator of schools. Books are an indicator of interests and intelligence, including their genetic portions; they stimulate reading and indicate further intellectual behaviours as attending museums. Reading them promotes knowledge acquisition and trains intelligence. Finally, at the within-country level, books help people to be perceived as being smart in social interactions.

*Multiple Correlation of Overall School Quality and Adult Educational Level of Society with National Ability Levels*    Both general indicators together show the highest correlations to ability measures ($R \approx .80$, $R_p = .57$) and to ability much higher than to wealth ($r_{GNI} = .39$). Statistically, it is not astonishing that both together correlate more highly with ability because the two predictors only correlate with $r = .60$ ($N = 94$). The high correlation of $R = .80$ means that educational quality and quantity can be used as proxies of ability. They cause ability, are caused by ability and both are caused by common background factors.

*Special Educational Effects for High and Low Ability Groups*    Intellectual classes are important for managing institutions and society and they are especially important for technological, scientific and cultural accomplishments (see Chapter 8). Therefore, any educational characteristic that is capable of explaining cross-country differences in high ability groups is relevant. Any improvement here could result in especially important outcomes.

Looking at Table 10.5 and the differences in correlations of educational characteristics with mean, top and low ability levels (uncorrected SAS M, SAS 95%, SAS 5%) shows that

- early tracking ($r_{95\%} = .35$ vs. $r_M = .32$ and $r_{05\%} = .26$),

- being in a high grade at a young age ($r_{95\%} = .27$ vs. $r_M = .24$ and $r_{05\%} = .20$),
- teacher quality ($r_{95\%} = .54$ vs. $r_M = .50$ and $r_{05\%} = .46$)
- and all general indicators (school quality, educational level, number of books, on average: $r_{95\%} = .72$ vs. $r_M = .70$ and $r_{05\%} = .65$)

are specifically relevant for *intellectual classes* and their cross-country ability differences. That early tracking supports the cognitive development of gifted students is well-known in research (in England: $d = 0.17$ for above average students, $d = 0.10$ for entire group, Koerselman, 2013; in a meta-analysis: $d = 0.30$ high ability vs. $d = 0.18$ middle ability and $d = 0.16$ low-ability students, Kulik & Kulik, 1992). Above average students benefit from an improved ability level in class and its indirect effects on stimulation, teachers and instruction. However, *all* ability groups show improvement by tracking, as demonstrated by studies within and across countries (see previous sub-sections). Considering being in a high grade at a young age, a faster school career ('acceleration') is a typical programme for supporting the gifted at the level of students, classes and schools. Enabling the smarter students a fast school career boosts their ability development. Why teacher quality and all general indicators correlate more highly with intellectual classes' level is less obvious. For instance, good teachers could be at least similarly important for weaker students – strong students should be better able to cope with bad environments, not weak students. Maybe there is a reverse effect; high levels of intellectual classes boost teacher quality.

*Low ability group levels* correlated relatively higher with language identity (same language at school and in family, $r_{05\%} = .32$ vs. $r_M = .30$ and $r_{95\%} = .26$), teacher salary ($r_{05\%} = .38$ vs. $r_M = .36$ and $r_{95\%} = .32$) and – counterintuitively – with private schools ($r_{05\%} = .12$ vs. $r_M = .10$ and $r_{95\%} = .06$). That language problems particularly impede immigrants who furthermore have low ability levels is not astonishing. If low ability students master the local language it helps them to follow the instruction – the smarter ones will learn it anyway. Teacher salary is an indirect indicator of teacher quality – weaker students may benefit more from environmental quality. However, teacher quality results are inconsistent. Usually, private schools are attended by above average and wealthier students. The pattern cannot be explained.

### 10.5.3 Summary on Educational Quality and Methodological Considerations

Which educational factors are relevant for explaining cross-country ability differences? Higher ability results can be found in countries with[47]

---

[47] Ordered by the correlation with uncorrected SAS-M and partial correlation. Language identity was not included because it is, in the narrower sense, not an attribute of an educational system.

- higher kindergarten attendance,
- more discipline,
- more education including kindergarten and being in high grades at a young age,
- higher teacher quality and teacher salary,
- earlier tracking,
- more school autonomy,
- central exams and tests,
- more direct instruction and
- more private schools.

The majority of results confirm older analyses based on smaller samples and somewhat different indicators (Rindermann & Ceci, 2009). New characteristics that have not previously been analysed are teacher quality and salary, school autonomy and private schools. Studies by other authors at different data levels and theoretical explanations support the patterns presented here. So ecological fallacy problems can be excluded.

The consequences of the *ecological fallacy* problem can be exemplified for the homework variable: depending on chosen data level the correlations go in different directions. Due to these opposite relationships, practical implications are different for the level of individuals and nations: parents should keep an eye on their children in order that they carefully do homework. Teachers should use or even increase homework, though there could be negative side effects on valuable leisure time activities of children. By contrast, politicians and educational policymakers should reduce homework by making homework superfluous through the extension of professionally monitored learning time in schools.

A second problem is the implied assumption that effects are *linear*: if standard correlations are used, linearity is implied. More brings more and is better. However, as for the use of tests and exams it is obvious that within time allocated for school and instruction an increase of tests and exams beyond a given point will be detrimental for ability development. The time necessary for instruction and learning would be lost to testing. For discipline, direct instruction and school autonomy there could be similar diminishing returns or even tipping points.

Empirically, a curvilinear relationship is corroborated for *discipline* (see Figure 10.12): there are countries with high discipline and low cognitive competence. The quadratic correlation is higher than the linear ($r_q = .66$ vs.

---

Weaker positive evidence is found for few class repetitions, but this characteristic is indirectly covered by being in high grades at a young age. Education expenditures – except for teacher salary – are more an indicator of a nation's wealth.

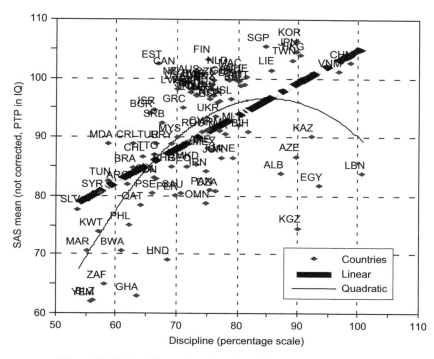

Figure 10.12 Discipline and students' cognitive competence for 93 countries, linear: $r = .53$, curvilinear-quadratic: $r = .66$

$r_1 = .53$). Too much stress on discipline, little freedom and only following the given rules may impair cognitive development. However, discipline is based on estimations given by students, teachers and directors. There could be biases by frames of reference in answering questionnaires. Additionally, all relatively high discipline and low ability cases are Muslim countries. Muslim countries are not only found at the top of discipline (Lebanon, Egypt, Kazakhstan, Kyrgyzstan, Azerbaijan and Albania) but also at the bottom (Morocco, Yemen, Kuwait, Syria and Tunisia).

For *direct instruction*, a curvilinear relationship is also observable (Figure 10.13): there are countries at the high cognitive competence level who apply a lot of direct instruction in teaching, all of them in East Asia (South Korea, Taiwan and Japan). And there are countries at a similar level which use it only rarely, all of them in the West (Iceland, New Zealand and Denmark). The corroborated positive effects of direct instruction at the class level can be substituted by general favourable background conditions of society or school system or by other similarly effective teaching methods in class.

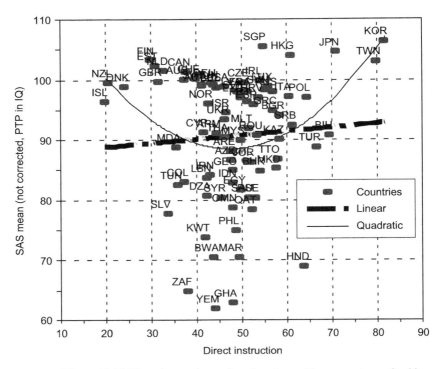

Figure 10.13 Direct instruction and students' cognitive competence for 80 countries; linear: $r = .07$; curvilinear-quadratic: $r = .34$

## 10.6    Geography and Climate

Among geography and climate theories, short- and long-term perspectives should be distinguished. According to the *short-term theory*, coolness has a freshening effect on the mind, while heat has a fatiguing impact. Montesquieu was the first to couch this in famous terms. Heat should make people lazy, resulting in lower intelligence in the tropics:

The heat of the climate can be so excessive that the body there will be absolutely without strength. So, prostration will pass even to the spirit; no curiosity, no noble enterprise, no generous sentiment; inclinations will all be passive there; laziness there will be happiness; most chastisements there will be less difficult to bear than the action of the soul, and servitude will be less intolerable than the strength of spirit necessary to guide one's own conduct. . . . [There is a] certain laziness of the spirit, naturally bound with that of the body, which makes that spirit incapable of any action, any effort. (Montesquieu, 1989/1748, pp. 234–235)

Although this might be intuitively convincing, several contradictions are to be addressed: civilisation emerged in hot regions, in Mesopotamia, Egypt and the Indus Valley; very smart people live near to the equator today, in Hong Kong, Singapore and Australia; and people in the tropics living in colder mountains are not smarter than their neighbours in the lowlands, e.g. in the Andes vs. coast and Amazonian regions, in Lesotho and Swaziland vs. South African surroundings; the same is true for the more southern and colder South Africa, where people achieve no better cognitive ability test results compared to more equatorial and tropical African countries.[48]

How can these critics be answered? Always there are exceptions. And the first advanced civilisations can be described as being 'advanced' only against the background of the development and population size at that time. The vast majority of their people could not read or write, preoperational thinking dominated up to their leading intellectuals and scientists (even true for more advanced Ancient Greece and Rome: Oesterdiekhoff, 2012c, Chapter 3). Today, on average smarter populations live more to the north.

There are no immediate or short-term effects of climate. People in the north migrating to the south or from the south migrating to the north usually remain as intelligent as they are in the regions where they come from. This evidence favours theories looking at *long-term* processes. Such a theory was first developed by the German philosopher Arthur Schopenhauer in 1851 (*Parerga and Paralipomena*, § 92):

Necessity is the mother of invention because those tribes that emigrated early to the north, and there gradually became white, had to develop all their intellectual powers and invent and perfect all the arts in their struggle with need, want, and misery, which in their many forms were brought about by the climate. This they had to do in order to make up for the scantiness of nature.[49]

Schopenhauer's theory assumes not only a *long-term development* but, unlike Montesquieu, it sees the driving force in the *scarcity and challenges of the northern climate*, not in fatigue due to heat. It is not the south that differs but the north. Finally, it was not personality but *intellect* that adapted.

A statistical proof of climate theories can be achieved by correlating latitude and longitude with national ability levels (see Table 10.6). Climate theories – not divided into short and long-term theories – would be supported by a pattern of positive correlations with latitude but zero correlations with longitude.

---

[48] Numbers, corrected cognitive ability results in IQ: Swaziland 74 and Lesotho 66 vs. South Africa 70 (no advantage of the higher and colder two countries). South Africa 70 vs. Nigeria 75, Ghana 64 and Kenya 74 (no advantage of colder South Africa). In the Andean mountains of Peru (cold) lower results are found than in Lima on the coast (hot), IQ 78 vs. 90 (Manrique-Millones et al., 2015).

[49] Translation was slightly adapted by me.

Table 10.6 *Correlations of geographical indicators and cognitive ability (compared with wealth)*

| | CA (corrected) | SAS M (corr., all) | SAS M (uncorr., PTP) | SAS 95% (uc., high ability) | SAS 05% (uc., low ability) | GNI 2010 HDR |
|---|---|---|---|---|---|---|
| **Latitude (+ & −)** | .53 (.39) | .51 | .44 | .39 | .45 | .40 (.11) |
| **Distance to equator** | .69 (.58) | .62 | .53 | .52 | .53 | .47 (.07) |
| **Longitude (+ & −)** | .17 (.20) | .29 | .24 | .26 | .22 | .02 (−.11) |
| **Distance to Greenwich line** | .15 (.26) | -.03 | .01 | .01 | .03 | −.09 (−.23) |

*Notes*: Cognitive ability variables see Table 10.5. Distance to equator: absolute latitude; Distance to Greenwich line: absolute longitude. In parentheses for cognitive ability (grand mean of student assessment and psychometric intelligence-studies) and GNI correlations partialled out GNI or cognitive ability. All geographical variables $N_{max} = 199$. Geographical indicators taken from Todd Stavish.[50]

Looking at empirical data (Table 10.6), cognitive ability correlates stronger with latitude than with longitude ($r = .53$ vs. $.17$). The theoretically most relevant correlation with distance to equator (absolute latitude as indicator for climate) is higher than with latitude ($r = .69$ vs. $.53$). The correlation with distance to equator is highly robust against partialling out wealth ($r_p = .58$). Using both indicators to predict cognitive ability only distance is relevant, not latitude ($\beta_{dte} = .67$ vs. $\beta_{lat} = .03$). Wealth only correlates with distance to equator and latitude ($r = .40$ and $.47$), not with longitude or distance to the Greenwich line (absolute longitude, $r = .02$ and $-.09$). Partialling out cognitive ability (see values in last column in parentheses), correlations of GNI with distance to equator and latitude wobble around $r = .00$. Summarised, distance to equator is the crucial geographical variable and only for intelligence, not for wealth, which (statistically) depends on intelligence, not on geography.

Positive latitude-ability correlations are also found for within-country differences, such as for Spain ($r = .77$; Lynn, 2012), Italy ($r = .96$; Lynn, 2010), United States ($r = .63$-$.78$; Pesta & Poznanski, 2014) and Vietnam ($r = .33$; Malloy, 2014), but not within Germany ($r = -.69$; own calculation).[51]

[50] Source for geographical indicators (Todd Stavish): https://opendata.socrata.com/dataset/Country-List-ISO-3166-Codes-Latitude-Longitude/mnkm-8ram.

[51] Pesta & Poznanski (2014, their tables 1 and 2) published solely information for the correlation between state level intelligence and temperature, $r = 1.75l$ to $1.53l$. Information for correlation with latitude was received by email from Bryan Pesta (25-10-2014).

More interesting than the pure empirical fact is the question of *why* there is a correlation between distance to equator and cognitive ability. Geography itself cannot have an impact. Only natural conditions caused by geography such as nutrition, climate and diseases could be relevant. Because after migration cognitive levels remain generally stable across geographic shifts these short- to mid-term factors cannot be decisive. Additionally, cognitive ability can change nutrition and the impact of climate (e.g. by air conditioning) and diseases (by medical development, hygiene, prevention and treatment). When there are no immediate and mid-term effects, only long-term effects can have an impact: and these work via culture and/or genes.

Geography is more than only latitude and longitude; for instance, it also includes distance to markets and prosperous regions, to harbours and having access to natural resources – all potentially influencing wealth and, indirectly, ability. But natural resources rents correlate negatively with cognitive ability $(r = -.17)$.[52] Having natural resources without other competitive production has a negative impact on cognitive ability or is a result of low cognitive ability – having no other competitive production. There is no striking positive effect of natural resources.

Other geography theories such as of Jared Diamond (1997) mention a more favourable east-west trade and migration route compared to the difficult south-north traffic across different climate zones or having tameable and domestic-able animals. As mentioned in Section 5.2.3, these theses are not convincing: Palestine is dryer than Haiti, southern California too. But they are richer. Why should the animals of Asia and Europe be more domesticable than those of Africa or America? And, even more importantly, there is no theory explaining why there should be persistent effects across centuries and millennia on cognitive ability.

Other hypotheses assume that living in the south, with its easier possibilities of surviving, would reduce motivation. An easier living creates an easygoing attitude. If birds fly into one's mouth ready roasted, this would not stimulate effort, learning and progress. Assuming that this theory is accurate, a mechanism is necessary which perpetuates its effects: culture or genes.

## 10.7   Evolution and Genes

On genes two answers are possible: a short or a longer, based on indirect evidence and theoretical-empirical considerations. The *short answer* is that because intelligence coding genes and differences in them are not known, at

---

[52] Total natural resources rents, calculated as the sum of oil rents, natural gas rents, coal rents, mineral rents and forest rents as a percentage of GDP from the World Bank (2011). Data come from the years 1995–2011 for $N = 195$ countries.

least not replicated and not their way of working via proteins, neurological structures and neurological processes on cognitive development resulting in substantial psychological intelligence differences, we cannot explain international differences in cognitive ability based on genes. 'A' cannot explain 'B' if we do not know 'A'. Over and done.

However, it is not so easy. It is a task of science to develop theories going beyond the current rock-solid body of knowledge. There is a huge body of *indirect evidence* that genes contribute to international intelligence differences. And there is tentative evidence for intelligence coding genes.

### 10.7.1   Indirect and Tentative Evidence on Genetic Determinants

*Stability of Group Differences across Regions and Time*    Ethnic groups usually have both cultural and biological markers, making them to distinguishable entities for laypeople in everyday life and for scientists analysing cultural and biological indicators. Differences between these groups are relatively stable across time and regions and minority-majority status. That does not mean that *ability levels*, which were subject to increase in the last centuries, the so called FLynn-effect, themselves are stable, *but rather patterns*, differences as relatively high or low outcomes. For instance, the Chinese consistently show high cognitive achievement, as majorities according to test results in China, Hong Kong, Macau, Taiwan and Singapore, and as minorities according to real-life indicators in Indonesia, Malaysia, Thailand, Canada, United States, Australia, Latin America and Europe.[53] Similar patterns can be observed for the Japanese, Koreans and Vietnamese or for the West-North-Middle-East Europeans in Europe and America, Australia, New Zealand and South Africa. Evidence is also given for Arabs, especially the Lebanese, as economically successful in West and East Africa.

Whilst these were examples of more comfortable to communicate 'positive' patterns ('positive' put in quotation marks, because any positive comparison needs a less positive benchmark), similar examples can be found for less comfortable to communicate 'negative' patterns ('negative' put in quotation marks, because any negative comparison needs a positive benchmark): people of sub-Saharan African origin show on average lower ability test results in Africa, North America, Latin America and Europe (Lynn, 2008, his chapters 2,

---

[53] Sources: Lynn (2008, his chapters 12, 13, 6, 3, 9, 5), Chua (2003), Sowell (2004). Data for minorities are frequently only given for 'East Asians' or 'Asians'. Because the Chinese are the largest group among East Asians and very likely make up the majority among immigrants from 'Asia' the data seem to be usuable. If 'Asians' also include many West Asians the results become less informative. Indicators of cognitive ability: test results, student achievement in schools, economic productivity and production, taxes, affirmative action against them (discrimination).

4, 5, 6, 7, 10, 13). The same is true for people from Latin America in the United States (NAEP test results; Rampey, Dion & Donahue, 2009). Finally, in PISA for various home and receiving countries, robust ability patterns can be found for students with migration background from Albania, Bosnia, China, Germany, Greece, the Netherlands, Turkey and Britain in different receiving countries (Levels et al., 2008). That is to say, emigrant students of one country (they or their parents emigrated) usually show results similar to their country of origin relatively independently from destination country.[54]

These patterns of the present time are roughly stable across centuries if compared to achievement indicators of the past (see Section 4.4.2 and Table 4.4). However, some exceptions have also to be mentioned: People from India and Iran in the Western world show much better cognitive achievement than expected from their home country averages. Migrations are differently selective regarding education and cognitive ability (Feliciano, 2005).[55]

Of course, all results deal with *averages*: *Individuals vary*, there are *overlapping distributions* and there are *within group heterogeneities*. And this all gives no decisive evidence for genetic factors, only that enduring factors have to be at work: They could stand for effects of culture, of genes or of both.

*Behavioural Genetics Explain Individual Differences with Genetic Factors* Twin, adoption and patchwork family studies undoubtedly show that individual differences in intelligence rely more on genetic factors ($h^2$ = .50–.80; Johnson, 2010) than on shared (common) family environmental factors. When we want to understand why some persons are smarter we have to look at their genes. This pattern includes all concepts related to intelligence and measurement approaches such as student achievement and grades (e.g. Plomin et al., 2013a). As if this were not enough, also personality

---

[54] A. The average correlation of six correlations in PISA results between the emigrants of the same country in different countries is $r = .69$. This means emigrants of one country in different countries have similar cognitive ability levels (e.g. emigrants of Albania in Austria, Greece and Switzerland). B. The correlation between countries' of origin and emigrants' average ability level (e.g. Albanians in Albania vs. Albanians in Austria, Greece and Switzerland) without three outliers is $r = .51$, with outliers $r = .23$ ($N = 35$). The outliers are India (emigration of a well-educated elite), South Africa (white flight to Australia and New Zealand) and Nigeria (special case of well-educated emigration to Ireland). For a small country sample of six countries we have both data for emigrants and immigrants: There is a closer relationship between home country's and emigrants' level ($\beta = .59$, $N = 6$) than between receiving country's and immigrants' level ($\beta = .34$, $N = 6$). C. For 16 emigration countries, emigrant averages (SASQ 489, $\approx$IQ 97) can be compared with country averages in PISA 2003 (SASQ 482, $\approx$IQ 96) (e.g. means of Albanians in Albania vs. Albanians in Austria, Greece and Switzerland). Accordingly, there is on average only a 1 IQ positive selection or modification effect. All reanalyses by HR. Finally Carabaña (2011, p. 213): 'Emigration hardly affects students' PISA scores, which remain at the level of the country of origin and do not come closer to the level of the destination country.'

[55] Reports also mention relatively positive patterns in the United States for Cubans and for Blacks from the Caribbean. Hard test evidence should corroborate it.

factors contributing to real world achievement and environmental conditions show substantial genetic impact (self-efficacy: $h^2$ = .40, personality: $h^2$ = .46, home environment: $h^2$ = .46, school environment: $h^2$ = .45; Krapohl et al., 2014).[56] All this has an effect on individual income and wealth.

What could be more appropriate than assuming that at other levels genetic factors are also important? However, a logical conclusion from individual to national differences is not possible (Lewontin, 1970, pp. 7f.): genetically identical populations having within high heritabilities of differences may largely differ in any outcome due to systematic differences in environmental conditions between these populations. For instance, the life expectancy of people in Bhutan today and one century ago or of Russian soldiers today and between 1941 and 1945 are totally different despite almost genetic identity. The same can be transferred to plants; the yield of crops in humid climate is larger than in a desert, or to intelligence, cognitive development under favourable conditions is better than under unfavourable ones.

All these objections are correct, but high heritabilities make it rather improbable that genes were not involved in group differences as in international ones (Jensen, 1970, pp. 21ff.; Sesardic, 2005, Chapter 4): E.g. Pygmy men are on average 140 to 150 cm tall, whereas men from Sudanese peoples reach 180 to 190 cm. Height shows a heritability of around $h^2$ = .80 (Johnson, 2010). This makes it probable that genes are also relevant for group differences in height. Finally, environment is nothing immutably external that has to be accepted by the people. As studies show, family and school quality have a strong genetic component ($h^2/A$ = .46 and .45 vs. $C$ = .11 and .09; Krapohl et al., 2014, Table S3). The environment outside an individual, a group or a species can be seen as the extended phenotype of genes, e.g. the environment shaped by beavers, the dam, the reservoir and the cut trees (Dawkins, 2008/1992).

*Genomewide Association Studies in the Search for Genes*     Genomewide association studies (GWAS) search for correlations between genes and human traits, here focused on cognitive ability. Up to now there are not really robust findings, for example correlations found in one sample and replicated in several others.

Some more recent evidence was summarised by Piffer (2013): gene variants COMT Val158Met and FNBP1L (SNP rs236330) are positively correlated

---

[56] $A$ (also $h^2$): the effect on individual differences due to additive genetic factors; heritability, the explained variance due to genetic factors. $C$: (also $c^2$) is the effect on individual differences due to common, shared family environment factors, e.g. parental education, wealth and interests, size of home, parenting styles, leisure activities, etc. $E$: (also $e^2$) is the effect on individual differences due to specific unknown environment factors or simply error. A, C and E give general information on explained variance, not on specific factors and how they work.

with intelligence at the individual level ($r \approx .25$ and $.12$). Allele frequencies of such genes could be used in country comparisons.

*Correspondence of Intelligence Coding Genes and Intelligence at the International Level*   The final aim of any genetic explanation of group differences is to apply genes that can explain intelligence at the individual level also to the group level. This was first done in a pioneering study published in *Anthropological Science* by the Italian researcher Davide Piffer (2013): he used the allele frequencies of COMT Val158Met and FNBP1L (rs236330), which at the individual level positively correlate with intelligence, to explain intelligence differences between different peoples. The COMT Val158Met, for which the individual level correlation is $r_{ind} \approx .25$, correlates at the group level to farming (agriculture vs. hunter-gatherer society, $r = .41$), latitude ($r = .55$) and, most importantly here, to intelligence ($r = .57$). FNBP1L (rs236330), the other gene positively correlated to intelligence at the individual level ($r \approx .12$), also correlates across groups with intelligence ($r = .81$). Corresponding individual and cross-national patterns are also given for APOE (SNP rs429358 e4) with negative correlations at both levels.

This is the first evidence for the explanatory power of genes at the group level. Nevertheless, further empirical support is needed from individual-level studies and it is necessary to detect the causal way via molecular, neurological and psychological processes. If this aim could be reached the genetic contribution is *directly* explained.

*Correspondence of General Genetic Markers and Intelligence at the International Level*   Another approach is to use general genetic markers and correlate them with international intelligence distributions. Genetic markers indicate evolutionary and current genetic differences; it is not known whether they do code intelligence. As mere correlations they are not so informative because they only show that differences between peoples in genes correlate with differences in intelligence. Their empirical relationship could be also due to associated common background factors such as culture or wealth. So, to be more informative, first a theory is needed connected to the observed genes, and second a control of competing environmental background factors.

Such an attempt was made using non-coding male Y-chromosome haplogroups for a European-Middle East sample by Rindermann, Woodley and Stratford (2012). Evolutionarily, the Y haplogroups used represent more recent cultural developments in the Mesolithic and Holocene (haplogroup set A) vs. older cultural progress (haplogroup set B).[57] In the analyses, the possible

---

[57] *More recent cultural progress in the Mesolithic and Holocene*: Gravettian culture, earliest works of figurative art, a proxy for advanced symbolic communication and abstract thinking;

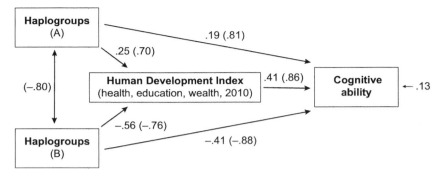

Figure 10.14 Prediction of cognitive ability by using two haplogroup sets as genetic markers of evolution and by a general development indicator of society (HDI) ($N = 47$ countries)[58]

genetic effects tagged by haplogroups on cognitive ability were controlled for the general development level of society (HDI 2010; see Figure 10.14). This control is theoretically an overinflated control because the control variable HDI also depends on cognitive ability: theoretically and empirically there are reciprocal effects between cognitive ability and HDI, usually with cognitive ability having a stronger effect on the level of a society's development than a society's development on cognitive ability (see Figures 10.1, 10.2, 10.6, 10.7, 10.8).

Haplogroup distributions (frequency of haplogroup set A in a country positively, of haplogroup set B negatively) as markers of evolution show strong effects on cognitive ability differences among nations, even controlled for general development ($\beta_{HsA \rightarrow IQ} = .19$ and $\beta_{HsB \rightarrow IQ} = -.41$; Figure 10.14). The effect is also found in within-country analyses in Italy ($r_{HsA\text{-}IQ} = .81$ and $r_{HsB\text{-}IQ} = -.61$) and Spain ($r_{HsA\text{-}IQ} = .68$ and $r_{HsB\text{-}IQ} = -.30$): for the same genetic markers the same pattern emerged. The effect of environmental or cultural background factors beyond HDI cannot be large because the Human Development Index is a very broad environmental measure.

Ertebølle, Funnelbeaker and Corded Ware culture, using pottery, agriculture, metallurgy, husbandry; finally, people lived among conditions of environmental harshness (i.e. winter cold) being evolutionarily demanding in terms of the need for heightened cognitive resources (e.g. farsightedness and planning).

*Older cultural progress*: Development of farming, rain-fed agriculture and semi-nomadic herders present in the Fertile Crescent and East Africa. Less severe environmental harshness except for aridity.

[58] Analysis presented in Figure 10.14: FIML, model is saturated, fit is perfect, standardised path coefficients, correlations in parentheses, error term as unexplained variance on the right.

*Correspondence of Proximity in Genes and Intelligence at the International Level (Genetic Distances)* A further approach using abstract genetic information is comparing the similarity of populations in genes and intelligence. If genetic proximity covaries with intelligence proximity, say, when genetically more similar people are also more similar in intelligence, this supports a genetic effect on intelligence differences between peoples. Genetic proximity means similarity in general genes not necessarily including intelligence-coding genes.

This approach was first developed by Becker and Rindermann (2014, 2016). Results of several studies on genetic distances (e.g. Cavalli-Sforza et al., 1994, pp. 75, 270) were compared with intelligence differences. Additionally, latitudinal and longitudinal distances and HDI were controlled (see Figure 10.15).[59]

Controlled for latitude, longitude and general social development (HDI) genetic proximity has a positive direct impact on cognitive similarity ($\beta_{\text{GenP} \rightarrow \text{CAP}} = .15$). Theoretically also very important is that among geographic factors latitudinal proximity has a positive impact on cognitive similarity ($\beta_{\text{LatP} \rightarrow \text{CAP}} = .29$, $r = .47$), whereas longitudinal proximity is not ($\beta_{\text{LatP} \rightarrow \text{CAP}} = -.24$, $r = .12$). This means that cognitive ability depends on the north-south gradient, not on the east-west gradient – exactly what is supposed

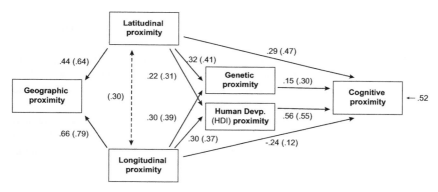

Figure 10.15 Prediction of proximity in cognitive ability by proximity in latitude, longitude, HDI and genes (*N*=67 correlations and 840 comparisons)[60]

---

[59] Correlations between distances are identical to correlations between proximities. In research 'distance' is used more frequently (e.g. Huckins et al., 2014, correlation between geographical and genetic distance $r = .68$). For easier understanding we used the term 'proximity'.

[60] CFI=.95, SRMR=.05 (both standing for good fit), standardised path coefficients, correlations in parentheses, error term as unexplained variance on the right.

by the evolutionary cold-winter-theory. Additionally, this contrasts the pattern for general social development (HDI): for HDI, longitudinal similarity is somewhat more relevant than latitudinal similarity and both effects are positive ($\beta_{\text{LonP} \to \text{HDI}}$ = .30, $\beta_{\text{LatP} \to \text{HDI}}$ = .22). The pattern suggests that the genetic and latitudinal effects are not proxies for further, not yet considered, environmental conditions.

Again, we have no single genes and nothing is known about the physiological path from genes via neurological structures and processes to thinking ability, but it is another indirect evidence for genetic effects at the international level.

*A Phenotypical Proxy for Evolution: Skin Lightness (Skin Colour)*    Skin lightness is usually termed 'skin colour'. However, colour is not measured, but reflectance. Additionally, colour is not the relevant aspect, but high or low melanisation. We do not use the term 'skin reflectance' because 'reflectance' is not the correct evolutionary association: skin did not become 'reflecting' as white to protect against sun but became more bright. Skin lost melanisation to enable more vitamin D synthesis in regions with less sunlight. Compared to the term 'skin brightness' 'skin lightness' carries less associations and is therefore used. Nevertheless, the skin variable and its relation to evolution, but also to history, could be distressing for science. The variable is used here as a further indicator for evolution and, of course, a control of social and environmental factors is necessary.

Skin lightness *cannot* have a causal effect on cognitive ability; the possible vitamin D or cancer protection effects are too small or come too late in life. The effects can be only *associative*, either by 'pleiotropy' or by other gene connections that emerged during evolution:

Pleiotropy means that genes have broad, at least at a first glance, unrelated effects.[61] In the case of pigmentation, these genes may also contribute to cognitive ability (Jensen, 2006b). However, until now molecular genetic

---

[61] Ducrest, Keller and Roulin (2008) described pleiotropy for the melanocortin system and behaviour: within different species, e.g. lions, barn owls and reptiles, the darker individuals were more aggressive, sexually active and resistant to stress. Intelligence was not included in the study. In a taming experiment, tamed foxes became not only more docile after ten generations but also lighter coloured (Trut, 1999). For humans, there are findings in the same direction: according to studies in the United States and Germany, children, even 14-month-old infants, with less pigmentation measured in the hair or iris showed more behavioural inhibition, representing more anxiety and shyness, e.g. $d$ = 1.55 between light blond and dark brown hair colour; this is a very large effect (Moehler et al., 2006). Theories see a connection between climate, intensity of sunlight, environmental harshness, necessity of a male provider and behaviour: women and children have a lower probability of surviving in colder climates without a male provider, resulting during evolution in more prudent, less aggressive, more cautious and more fearful men and more monogamous men and women (Roth, 2014/2010, p. 149).

evidence is lacking. In the second genetic perspective, skin lightness is seen as an indicator of evolutionary history, similar to haplogroups or genetic proximity.

Within societies in the sixteenth to twentieth centuries, skin lightness was associated with different treatment of people: Africans were enslaved, there were apartheid and physical and psychological maltreatment of African people. Skin lightness is internationally connected to history as colonialism and slavery. So skin lightness could also be a proxy for environmental factors, within and across countries. A biological explanation could be only conceivable as a net effect corrected for the most important remaining effects of history on intelligence, measured for example by the Human Development Index (HDI).

There are two (resp. three) measures for skin lightness at the international level, from Jablonski and Chaplin (2000, pp. 74f.) and Templer and Arikawa (2006, pp. 124f.); the latter is based on Biasutti (1967, p. 224). The three lightness indicators correlate with each other at $r = .91$ to $.98$ ($N = 43$–$129$). Because the Templer measure is based on Biasutti and because Biasutti covers more countries than Templer (129 vs. 193 countries) we combined Jablonski with Biasutti for an average measure.[62] The different surveys come to very similar results for overlapping country samples.

Correlations between skin lightness and cognitive ability are very high (see Table 10.7). The Templer and Arikawa variable correlates somewhat higher than the Jablonski one with ability ($r_{JC} = .82$ vs. $r_{TA} = .90$). Their country sample is larger and more heterogeneous than Jablonski's ($N_{JC} = 48$ vs. $N_{TA} = 123$). Reduced to the same country sample the correlations become more similar ($r_{JC} = .82$, $r_{TA} = .88$, $r_{Bi} = .87$, $N = 43$).

The high correlations are exceptional. At the international level skin lightness is the *highest correlating single variable* with cognitive ability. For comparison, GDP correlates with $r = .55$–$.82$ (see Table 10.1), adult education mean with $r = .74$, school quality with $r = .65$, adult education and school quality together (multiple correlation) with $R = .78$ (CA-M, or $.79$ SAS-M).

Backing this, in a multiple regression analysis using absolute latitude ($\beta_{LatA \rightarrow CA} = -.11$), school quality ($\beta_{SQ \rightarrow CA} = .35$) and adult educational level ($\beta_{AdE \rightarrow CA} = .20$) as further controls, skin lightness was the most important variable ($\beta_{SL \rightarrow CA} = .57$) to predict cognitive ability at the

---

[62] Jablonski and Chaplin, as well as Templer and Arikawa, used data sets published by other researchers. The standard procedure is to measure skin lightness with a reflectometer at a place where sun exposure can have no effect (at the upper inner arm site). All data sets focus on indigenous human populations. In order to estimate the current averages for Australia, New Zealand, America and Singapore, corrections are necessary, made by the author (HR). Higher numbers stand for lighter skin (brighter, more reflectance, less melanin). The Biasutti data were additionally corrected for population density of different parts of a country. Some minor imprecision is possible due to missing country borders in the Biasutti map. Jablonski and Biasutti combined Cronbach-$\alpha = .96$ ($r = .92$, $N = 48$).

Table 10.7 *Correlations of skin lightness and cognitive ability and GNI*

| | CA (corrected) | SAS M (corr., all) | SAS M (uncorr., PTP) | SAS 95% (uc., high ability) | SAS 05% (uc., low ability) | GNI 2010 HDR |
|---|---|---|---|---|---|---|
| **Jablonski & Chaplin, ad. (lat./educ. partialled out)** | .82 (.64) (.62) | .58 | .69 | .66 | .69 | .68 (.56) (.50) |
| **Templer & Arikawa (lat./ educ. partialled out)** | .90 (.87) (.82) | .81 | .79 | .78 | .76 | .54 (.31) (.20) |
| **Biasutti, adapted (lat./educ. partialled out)** | .87 (.74) (.80) | .76 | .74 | .70 | .75 | .50 (.26) (.19) |
| **Skin lightness average (lat./ educ. partialled out)** | .87 (.74) (.80) | .74 | .74 | .69 | .74 | .50 (.25) (.18) |
| **Skin lightness average excluding sub-S-Africa** | .76 | .71 | .68 | .64 | .69 | .34 |

*Notes*: Cognitive ability variables see Table 10.5. Data see text and footnote. 'Ad.' or 'adapted' means replacement migration was considered. Numbers of countries: $N_{maxJC} = 48$, $N_{maxTA} = 129$, $N_{maxB} = 188$, $N_{maxA} = 188$ or $N_{maxNAf} = 145$ countries. In parentheses partial correlations, first distance to equator (absolute latitude) partialled out, second school quality mean and adult education mean partialled out.

cross-country level ($N = 93$). In comparison with HDI, skin lightness has a larger impact ($\beta_{HDI \to CA} = .43$, $\beta_{SL \to CA} = .53$, $N = 161$). Finally, excluding sub-Saharan African countries still results in a high correlation ($r = .75$, $N = 145$; Table 10.7). Skin lightness is at the macro-social level the highest and most robust correlating single variable with cognitive ability.

Templer and Arikawa (2006, p. 123) reported a correlation of $r = |.92|$ (skin lightness with older Lynn & Vanhanen IQ data). Meisenberg (2009, p. 525) found a standardised regression coefficient of $\beta = .79$ on intelligence (compared of $\beta = .16$ of education).[63] The results are robust across different studies, authors and data sources.

---

[63] Meisenberg (2009, p, 522) used data from Jablonski & Chaplin (2000), with missing data extrapolated under the assumption of clinal variation.

Nonetheless, Templer and Arikawa were criticised in a paper 'Sorry, Wrong Numbers' by Hunt and Sternberg (2006, p. 132, 136) for low data quality and possible stereotype effects in calculating numbers for skin lightness:

> The 'skin color' referred to in the paper is the skin color that graduate students who had not visited the relevant countries, and, for all we know, had no relevant knowledge whatsoever of those countries, think is predominant in each country! If Templer and Arikawa's paper had been entitled 'IQ is correlated with graduate students' stereotypes of skin color across nations,' we might not have objected so vehemently as we do here (although we would like to see a rather larger and more diverse sample of graduate students). The paper would then become a paper about stereotypes rather than bio- logical variables. In fact, that is what we think it is. . . .
> We maintain that the Templer and Arikawa paper is an almost prototypical example of such bad research. To summarize, these are our observations: Their measure of 'skin color' is in fact a measure of social stereotypes about skin color. Social stereotypes and IQ scores may or may not be correlated. If they are the explanation certainly is not biological.

Templer and Arikawa (2006, p. 122) had described their procedure to come to national skin lightness numbers based on a map published by Biasutti (1967, p. 224, Tavola VI):

> The source contains a map of the world with eight categories of skin color ranging from 1 (very light) to 8 (very dark). Because the map does not delineate the various countries of the world, three graduate students who were unaware of the purpose of our study independently determined the predominant skin color for each of the 129 countries. The word predominant was used because some countries had more than one skin color. The product-moment correlation coefficients between raters were 0.95, 0.95, and 0.93, suggesting very little subjectivity. For each country, the mean of the three skin color ratings was used.

So, who is right? Can there be any influence of stereotypes on assigning numbers to countries based on shadings in a map? Is this a plausible suspicion? The mentioned accusations of Hunt and Sternberg are based on nothing more than subjective speculations. Instead of 'sternberging' other researchers, i.e. to make moral reproaches against other research ('stereotype') in an unethical way, the scientifically correct way would have been to either compare the Biasutti source with other sources or to remeasure the skin lightness map and to recalculate the analyses.[64] The comparisons presented here with the Jablonski and Chaplin data ($r = .91$, $N = 43$) and the original Biasutti data ($r = .98$, $N = 129$) suggest that the numbers of Templer and Arikawa are

---

[64] Using the Templer–Arikawa data and the original Biasutti 'data' (there are no data, but a map containing hatchings without borders that need to be assigned to current countries, done by a university student), the correlation is $r = .983$ ($N = 129$); Biasutti corrected for population density and migration the correlation is $r = .982$ ($N = 129$). The correlations are so similar because Templer and Arikawa left out all countries with replacement migration for which correction is necessary.

correct. Of course, the best would be to collect newer data on skin lightness in large and representative samples as done for ability by the student assessment studies. Why are they not doing this? A rhetorical question.

A theoretically more challenging objection is the comparatively rather small correlation of $r = .20$ between skin lightness and intelligence at the *individual within-country level*, reported by Jensen (2006b, p. 130) based on an older meta-analysis from the early 1970s. The much higher correlation at the cross-country level needs an explanation going further than possible individual level genetic and environmental factors. One explanation is a methodological phenomenon: the higher reliability of country averages. Another possibility is a reference to reciprocal effects between genes, culture and physical environment relevant for cognitive development, e.g. small genetic effects are amplified by culture (such as rationality) and environment (such as impact of parents, teachers, peers and the health system), a 'hive mind effect'. Finally, newer studies at the individual level are necessary, checking the relationship between skin lightness and intelligence and the possible biological and environmental roots of that correlation. For Argentina they are similarly low as previously reported ($r = .16/.20$; Kirkegaard & Fuerst, 2017).

*Expert Opinions*    Expert opinions cannot substitute empirical research but they give a further clue what is plausible resp. seen as plausible. In particular, anonymous surveys can be revealing in a controversial area such as explaining national differences in abilities. According to an expert survey with 71 cognitive ability researchers (Rindermann, Becker & Coyle, 2016), 17 to 20 per cent of international IQ differences are attributed to genetic effects. According to experts, it was the second most important determinant and only surpassed by a summed education factor.

Such a view seems to be indirectly supported by a wider range of scientists, as half-humorously but also half-sincerely concluded by James Flynn:

The collapse of the Ice Ages hypothesis does not, of course, settle the debate about whether there are racial differences for genes for intelligence. If universities have their way, the necessary research will never be done. They fund the most mundane research projects, but never seem to have funds to test for genetic differences between races. I tell US academics I can only assume that they believe that racial IQ differences have a genetic component, and fear what they might find. (Flynn, 2012a, p. 36)

As indicated by Flynn, only empirical research can give the final answer.

### 10.7.2    Evolutionary Theories and Indicators

Correlations between variables are one aspect. But theory is needed to give them a meaning. There are more global and more specific evolutionary theories explaining cognitive differences between populations.

*Cold-Winter Theory: Out of the Cold Emerges Intelligence*   According to the cold-winter theory, cold winters in colder climates represent a more severe challenge for survival than seasonal changes in warmer climates. And – added by the author – those challenges are better manageable with higher intelligence. The selection pressure on cognitive abilities was stronger, leading in the long run to higher intelligence. What could have been the cognitive demands? Keeping warm was crucial, especially for children, e.g. by finding shelters, constructing houses, heating with fire, making and using cloth. Other tasks were to build up stocks for the winter and to hunt big animals in open grasslands (this was also a challenge in warmer climates). Domestication of animals is one important kind of stockpiling. Stockpiling of food was necessary to survive the winter and was also possible in colder climates. Stockpiling needs foresight, delayed gratification and self-control, additionally the development of the idea of property and its protection. This theory was developed by different authors such as Richard Lynn (1987, 2006), Edward Miller (1991), Michael Hart (2007) and Philippe Rushton (1997/1995, p. 228f.).

The evolutionary cold-winter theory can be easily combined with a cultural theory as proposed by Lawrence Harrison (2006, p. 3):[65]

'That colder climates forced humans to plan ahead to get through the winter, while humans in tropical zones had no such problem, must surely be relevant in explaining why most poor countries are found in the tropical zones; and it may also be relevant in explaining why the warmer portions of some countries – for example, the south of Italy, the south of Spain, the south of the United States – are poorer than the colder portions.

Evolutionary-genetic explanations would be backed if there is evidence for a cognitive lead among people of colder climates in prehistoric times. Is there any evidence for such an assumption? It can be found in the origin of figurative art in Europe (around 33,000 BC; Conard, 2003), in realistic skilful cave painting (cave Chauvet and others: ca. 33,000 BC), in the invention of religion (around the same time; Renfrew, 2008) and in the complexity of developed tools in the Pleistocene (Foley, 1987):[66]

High-latitude populations have more tool types, and these tools are themselves more complex, made up of more components. ... Although there is a general and global technological development during the Pleistocene, it is in the high latitudes that it is most marked; in parts of the tropics the artefacts remained simple. ... Expansion to high latitudes thus exposed hominids to new selective pressures, the solution to which lay in

---

[65] Cultural theorists usually oppose genetic theories.

[66] Cave painting: recently dated cave art from Sulawesi (Indonesia) seems to be older (around 33,000 to 37,000 years BCE) than cave art in Southern France (Chauvet around 30,000 to 33,000 years BCE); however, Chauvet cave paintings are much more realistic and elaborate and cover more diverse species.

technological dependence. This dependence in turn was likely to have promoted general cognitive skills. (Foley, 1987, p. 269)

Additionally, in prehistory the colder South-African regions were leading within Africa in the development of artefacts (Conard, 2008).

A frequently used indicator for the evolution of thinking is brain size. Brain size and intelligence are related, across species, in human evolution, in behavioural genetics, historically, cross-nationally and finally at the individual level:

- *Across species*: within birds, species with bigger brains are more innovative regarding feeding ($r = .72$; Sol et al., 2005).
- *In human evolution*: increase of brain size in evolution ($r = .95$; Henneberg & de Miguel, 2004, p. 27).
- *Genetically*: genetic correlation of $r = .25$ between intracranial volume and intelligence or of $r = .44$ with education ($N = 36035$ to $111114$; Hagenaars et al., 2016).
- *Historically*: in the twentieth century, head and brain sizes increased and similarly average intelligence of each generation (Lynn, 1990).
- *Cross-nationally* ($N = 164$): using data from Beals et al. (1984) cranial capacity and intelligence correlate at $r = .77$.[67]
- *Individually*: $r = .24$ to $r = .40$ ($r = .56$, Deary et al., 2007; meta-analyses at $r = .24$ to $r = .40$, Gignac & Bates, 2017; McDaniel, 2005; Pietschnig et al., 2015; Rushton & Ankney, 2009).

Similarly to intelligence, individual brain size differences are highly heritable ($h^2 = .90$; Payton, 2009). Backing up the cold-winter-theory, cranial capacity is cross-nationally correlated at $r = .70$ with latitude.[68] The positive correlation between absolute latitude and cranial capacity can also be found among past hominids ($r = .52$; Henneberg & de Miguel, 2004, p. 28).

Results for current populations are presented in Table 10.8. Data are taken from the study of Beals, Smith and Dodd published in 1984 in *Current Anthropology*. Their data are based on 122 native populations (e.g. for America American Natives), results for men and women were averaged. Beals et al. assigned the data to seven size categories. They are presented in a map containing hatching. We used the present countries and the current populations: for instance, the territory of Russia is marked by four different categories of cranial capacity. However, the majority of people live in the western parts. Thus the values for the western parts were weighted more for the Russian average. Another example: in Australia today, Aborigines are a small minority.

---

[67] Meisenberg, personal communication, 25. November 2014.
[68] Meisenberg, personal communication, 25. November 2014. For birds and their brain-climate-relationship see Roth & Pravosudov (2009) and Roth et al. (2010).

Table 10.8 *Correlations (in parentheses corrected for latitude or education) between brain size (cranial capacity) and cognitive ability and GNI*

| | CA (corrected) | SAS M (corr., all) | SAS M (uncorr., PTP) | SAS 95% (uc., high ability) | SAS 05% (uc., low ability) | GNI 2010 HDR |
|---|---|---|---|---|---|---|
| **Cranial capacity, Beals, Meisenberg smoothed** | .73 (.50) (.54) | .59 (.32) (.27) | .56 (.33) (.22) | .52 (.28) (.11) | .56 (.34) (.26) | .45 (.22) (.22) |
| **Cranial capacity, Beals, own not smoothed** | .58 (.35) (.47) | .52 (.29) (.37) | .51 (.32) (.35) | .46 (.26) (.26) | .52 (.33) (.36) | .34 (.13) (.20) |
| **Cranial capacity, Beals, GM & own combined** | .68 (.46) (.53) | .58 (.33) (.33) | .56 (.36) (.30) | .52 (.29) (.20) | .57 (.37) (.34) | .42 (.19) (.22) |
| **C. capacity/height, Beals, Meisenberg smoothed** | .67 (.59) (.53) | .42 (.23) (.04) | .44 (.28) (.10) | .38 (.21)(-.04) | .47 (.33) (.19) | .30 (.13) (.01) |

*Notes:* Cognitive ability variables see Table 10.5; all cranial capacity data are based on a collection of Beals et al. (1984, p. 304, figure 3), all for modern populations; Meisenberg (GM) smoothed-graduated results ($N$ = 191, 108, 99, 99, 180); own assignments not smoothed ($N$ = 180, 102, 93, 93, 169); both combined ($N$ = 193, 108, 99, 99, 182); cranial capacity related to height represents the relative brain size, data also delivered by Meisenberg ($N$ = 188, 108, 99, 99, 177); in parentheses first distance to equator (absolute latitude) partialled out, second school quality mean and adult education mean partialled out.

Thus the cranial capacity values were estimated from Britain and other origin countries of current Australians.

Table 10.8 shows high and robust correlations between estimated brain size and cognitive ability measures. The correlations with student assessments are lower than with general IQ and lower than reported by Meisenberg because for general cognitive ability a larger country sample with information on more developing countries can be used (larger variation).[69] The correlations are not totally robust against partialling out latitude or education, but they still remain. Of course, by partialling out latitude or education the associations are over-corrected because according to evolutionary theories the correlation between latitude and cranial capacity is not accidental and education depends at least partly on cognitive ability.

The correlations are discernibly higher for cognitive ability than for wealth. This supports a theory that brain size increases cognitive ability.[70] The correlations for relative brain size are somewhat smaller, especially for the level of intellectual classes. Because Meisenberg's graduated smoothing is slightly speculative we use results based more on the published data taken from Beal's map.[71] It should be kept in mind that this measure is more *cautious* and conservative, resulting in lower correlations.

If all regions settled by Europeans after 1500 are excluded and for which we have imputed the data – America and Trans-Tasman – the results remain stable, e.g. for our own data based on Beals' cranial capacity variable, the correlation with cognitive ability changes from $r = .578$ ($N = 180$) to $r = .587$ ($N = 143$), partialling out latitude from $r = .354$ ($N = 177$) to $r = .335$ ($N = 140$), partialling out adults' and children's education from $r = .470$ ($N = 88$) to $r = .377$ ($N = 71$). Some go up, others down, but the positive associations remain.

Brain size, in some degree, depends on current environmental quality – there was a 'brain size FLynn effect' in the twentieth century (around $d \approx 0.20$ in 10 years; Lynn, 1990, p. 274; Miller & Corsellis, 1977). Therefore, brain size is not only a causal variable for cognitive ability (at the individual level $r = .40$; Gignac & Bates, 2017) but also an outcome variable and hence no purely evolutionary indicator.

Finally, there is evidence from research on further species by research groups independent from the evolutionary-psychological approach on humans:

---

[69] Interestingly, all correlations with the low ability threshold are higher than with the intellectual classes' level or the country mean. The higher correlations with intellectual classes found in other variables are not a mere higher reliability effect of the intellectual class variable.

[70] In the same country samples ('GM' standing for Gerhard Meisenberg data, 'Own' for data based on Beal's map taken by us, 'Both' both combined, 'CCr' relative to height: $r_{GM-CA} = .71$ vs. $r_{GM-GNI} = .45$, $r_{Own-CA} = .57$ vs. $r_{Own-GNI} = .36$, $r_{Both-CA} = .67$ vs. $r_{Both-GNI} = .42$, $r_{CCr-CA} = .67$ vs. $r_{CCr-GNI} = .30$, $N = 164$.

[71] Thanks to David Becker for performing this task.

the chickadee (*Poecile atricapillus*) is a small North American bird. Chickadees living in colder climates such as Alaska have bigger brains and are smarter than birds of the same species living in warmer climates such as Kansas. These differences are very probably genetic, as in the study birds from both populations were raised in and had experienced identical environmental conditions from ten days of age. This is explained by the challenges of a harsh environment in a cold climate – smarter birds better solve food problems that are crucial for survival and reproduction (Roth & Pravosudov, 2009; Roth et al., 2010).

So the cold-winter theory is far from 'collapsing' (Flynn, 2012a), there is strong evolutionary and neurological evidence across species. However, the cold-winter theory can be called into question by showing cognitive demands outside the cold regions, e.g. big-game hunting in Africa – Pygmies hunt elephants – or navigation across the Pacific by Polynesian people. Survival in the desert and balancing water consumption with route distances and cruising speed are also cognitive demands.

In summary, there is a lot of evidence for a long-term higher intelligence in colder regions but the theory is not free of objections.

r/K-*Theory*    The r/K-theory, developed by MacArthur and Wilson (1967), describes reproductive strategies adapted to different environmental conditions. Species and subspecies, as well as individuals, differ in these strategies. Under conditions of less stable and less predictable environments or in less crowded, newly settled, more open environments, an r-strategy (fast rate) leads to higher reproductive success and is therefore more frequent. Here organisms produce a large number of offspring, become fertile at a young age, have a low probability of survival to adulthood, have a short generation time and show low investment in offspring. In contrast, in more stable and predictable environments or if living close to the carrying capacity of an environment, a K-strategy (capacity, in German *Kapazität*) is more advantageous: a small number of offspring is produced, organisms have a late maturity onset, they live longer and have a long generation time and show high parental investment in offspring.[72]

Species differ in their relative inclination towards r- or K-strategies. Generally, smaller and evolutionary older subspecies, species, genera, families, orders, classes etc. relatively follow r-strategies more, while bigger and evolutionary younger subspecies, species, genera, families, orders, classes etc. follow K-strategies. Examples are insects vs. mammals, rabbits vs. whales, prosimians vs. hominidae.

---

[72] r/K-theory is part of the broader life history theory dealing with reproduction, investment and limited resources.

The British-Canadian psychologist Philippe Rushton (1985, 1997) applied this theory to human evolution and within present humans to race-based subgroups. Humans, compared to other species, follow $K$-strategy. However, within humans, relatively more $r$- vs. $K$-strategists could be distinguished, according to class but also according to a subspecific evolutionary classification for humans usually called 'races'.[73] Here marked differences are observed for rate of maturation, age of first sexual activity, time spacing between births, number of offspring, parental investment, infant mortality and longevity, all of which is known from $r/K$-theory. Rushton added previously less-studied characteristics such as two-egg twinning ($r$-strategy), activity level and aggressivity ($r$), rule-following and law-abidingness ($K$-strategy), and brain size and intelligence ($K$). People of sub-Saharan descent are more developed in motor skills at a younger age than people of European and especially East Asian descent. An African-European-Eastasian pattern can be found for skeletal development, sexuality, impulsivity and aggressivity. The pattern is inverted (East Asians, Europeans, Africans) for cautiousness, marital stability, brain size and intelligence (Rushton, 1997, Table 1.1).

Readers who have not previously known this theory may imagine the reaction of colleagues at universities, especially in the social sciences, and of prevailing media. Similar to Darwin's evolutionary theory and its adaptation to humans it provoked opposition but different to the nineteenth century less by the conservative, right-dogmatic church but by the progressive, left-dogmatic zeitgeist, including attempts to dismiss Rushton from his job, reprimand by leading politicians and violent attacks by left-wing activists. Darwin himself did not suffer from violent attacks, indicating a more liberal atmosphere in the nineteenth century than a century later.

However, the application of the evolutionary $r/K$-theory on humans is empirically backed by a vast amount of single studies. A scientific critique needs to focus on the evolutionary paradigm: first, it is not clear why for Africans the environment should have been more unstable and unpredictable than for Europeans to Indians and East Asians. Second, while for Africans (Blacks, 'Negroids') the pattern is applied for the entire group of sub-Saharan African people, it is less applicable for the entire group of Europeans to Indians ('Caucasians'). Here we have extreme differences such as between Northwest central Europeans and Arabs, European Jews and Roma (gypsies), Europeans and Indians. The same heterogeneity can be found for 'Mongoloids', between East Asians and American Indians or East Asians and Southeast Asians.

Additionally, history shows large differences in the $r/K$-continuum. So the strategy is maybe less genetically fixed than environmentally influenced.

---

[73] Not relevant here but important for humans as well as animals: males are relatively more $r$-strategists compared to females who are more $K$-strategists.

However, showing further important determinants does not refute a theory; it only adds additional factors. Natural environment was becoming much less important for humans than manmade environment. Here, the stability vs. instability dichotomy is boosted by culture, institutions and politics. Finally, the r/K-theory is compatible with the cold-winter theory, but they are not internally coherently connected; that is, the cold-winter theory cannot be deduced from the r/K-theory or vice versa. Cold winters are not more predictable than a usually stable tropical climate without or with seasonal changes of pluvial and dry periods.

*Novel Challenges and the Evolution of Intelligence*  According to the evolutionarily novelty theory from Satoshi Kanazawa (2004, 2012), new environmental challenges stimulate cognitive evolution. Cold winters are an example of such new challenges that are more successfully manageable with higher intelligence. Droughts, finding water, protection against wild animals, making fire, hunting, collecting food, detecting enemies and forming alliances are, according to Kanazawa, not new challenges, but planning ahead for surviving winter, storing food, domesticating animals, developing and undertaking agriculture including irrigation and anything abstract such as in modern schools, technology, organisation and society.[74]

Critically, it can be argued, similarly to the cold-winter theory, that there are new cognitive-environmental challenges that were successfully solved in the past by peoples with not so high intelligence, e.g. navigation in the Pacific, irrigation farming, development and use of calendars and astronomy in ancient Mesopotamia and Egypt. FLynn effects may alter current international intelligence differences and undermine their validity for backing the theory (see also Wicherts et al., 2010b).

*High Cognitive Ability Level of Jews and Genetic Theories*  Jews, especially European Ashkenazi Jews, have achieved a tremendous amount of intellectual and scientific accomplishment in the last two centuries.[75] This raises the question of why they have achieved such accomplishment. Because intelligence is necessary for high intellectual achievement and because Jews on average show higher intelligence than Gentiles (with an IQ of around 110 in the West about 10 IQ points higher than Gentiles; Lynn, 2011, pp. 275ff.), an explanation by a 'higher intelligence leads to better achievement in highly complex cognitive domains theory' is convincing.

---

[74] The author (HR) somewhat adapted the examples.
[75] Sources describing high Jewish achievement in the sciences, technology, literature, arts and chess, e.g. www.jinfo.org, Lynn (2011), Nisbett (2009) or Van Den Haag (1969).

This leads to the next question: why do Jews have an elevated intelligence level? Hank Pellissier (2013) and Richard Lynn (2011, chapter 20) have given overviews on theories ranging from environmental to cultural and historical-cultural-genetic interaction paradigms. The most important theories are sketchily described:

- *Education, especially for reading*: Jews were and are highly motivated for literacy education, due to internal reasons: to be able to read the Tanakh and Talmud, to understand a difficult religion. This religious motivation was extended in recent centuries to secular academic subjects. And due to external reasons: environmental pressures led to a selection for complex jobs better mastered with higher education. This tradition is maintained as an environmental effect on intelligence until today or has had a genetic effect by selection of the smarter persons (more surviving children). This theory cannot only explain an elevated cognitive ability level but also the, for Jews, more frequent tilt towards verbal ability (vs. visuospatial ability): reading was trained and selected.
- *Persecution and discrimination* for millennia has had two effects: the smarter people had higher chances of survival, by detecting threats and reacting to them, e.g. flight or ransom (Jews were usually too outnumbered to fight). Less convinced, less resistant and lower rank Jews within their community left Jewry (if this was an option of rescue; it was not during the Nazi period). This led to an environmentally-culturally educed genetic effect regarding intelligence, cautiousness, fortitude and motivation (e.g. Botticini & Eckstein, 2012; Murray, 2007).
- Explicit or implicit *exclusion from ordinary jobs* in the last 1,000 years in Europe led to a requirement to work in the remaining, on average cognitively more demanding, jobs such as merchants, tax collectors, bankers and from the nineteenth century on as academics. Under such conditions, smarter persons were more successful leading to higher wealth and in past centuries to larger families with higher survival probability of children until adulthood resulting in an environmentally-culturally educed genetic improvement effect regarding intelligence (e.g. Cochran et al., 2006; Cochran & Harpending, 2009).
- *Bottleneck hypothesis*: Jews lived in reproductive isolation chosen by themselves and reinforced by the social environment within a rather small group. Hence any accidental mutation had a good chance to spread (e.g. Carmi et al., 2014). A past accidental mutation led to high intelligence and a higher probability for certain neurological diseases.
- *Babylonian exile* (sixth century BCE): Jews were forced to leave Israel. The smarter, more convinced and successful ones remained as Jews (e.g. Murray, 2007).

- *Difficult religion*: to be a Jew means to practice a cognitively complicated religion with a compulsory exercise to read the Tanakh and Talmud. Without literacy, persons cannot be good Jews. Today, this is nothing unusual, but 500, 1,000 or 2,000 years ago it was. The smarter ones had higher chances to remain as Jews and the more wealthy ones had the means to educate their children to become literate (Murray, 2007).
- *Preference of the rich for the educated*: richer Jews preferred well-educated sons-in-law for their daughters. Even poor scholars had a good chance. Education indirectly has had an evolutionary advantage (MacDonald, 2002/1994; Nisbett, 2009).
- *Rabbis having their own children*: unlike Catholic priests, Jewish priests, in both groups for centuries constituting the major part of the intellectual elite, had their own children, spreading genes supportive for education, literacy and intelligence in a population.
- *Genetic contribution of Gentiles:* when, unofficially or officially, Jews had children together with Gentiles the rather smarter persons among Gentiles were part of this relationship. Because many of these children were officially Jews this genetically improved the basis for intelligence. Around 50 per cent of the genetic heritage of European Jews is of European origin (Carmi et al., 2014).

All these conditions more apply for European Jews (Ashkenazi) than for Southeast European (Sephardi), Oriental (Mizrahi) and Ethiopian Jews. However, it is difficult to decide which of the mentioned theories can better explain the elevation of Jewish intelligence. Several or all of the mentioned factors may be relevant but in different times and for different subgroups of Jews.

Why at all assume any genetic factor for the high intelligence and cognitive achievement of Jews? First of all, high heritability of individual differences and all the other supportive evidence for genetic factors generally hint at a genetic contribution (see Section 3.4.3). Specific evidence comes from the stability of Jewish–Gentile differences across different countries and cultures. And within Israel the three to four different Jewish groups show the same pattern, as known from their results in their former countries of origin, in spite of living in a totally different and more friendly social environment within one country and the same culture: Ashkenazi Jews show an average IQ of around 105–110 IQ points, Oriental Jews of around 90–95 and Ethiopian Jews of around 70 (Lynn, 2011, his chapter chapter 11). The mentioned environment-culture-genetic interaction theories are theoretically plausible. The Cochran et al. theory is further backed by evidence showing relations to special diseases which are the result of homozygotic endowments having positive effects on intelligence as heterozygotic ones. Finally, there is a high prevalence of myopia among Jews (double to fourfold; Lynn, 2011, p. 324f.; Storfer, 1999). On the individual level, myopia is correlated to intelligence and has a genetic factor.

Why not assume only environmental factors? One researcher, the sociologist Paul Burstein mentioned:

> There are three major reputable social-scientific explanations of why Jews do so well. (I emphasize 'reputable' and 'social-scientific' to exclude genetic explanations and those proposed by anti-Semites.) (Burstein, 2007, p. 214)

Burstein published this statement in a serious scientific journal and certainly took his judgement seriously – that 'reputation' of theories and political ascriptions support epistemic endeavours for truth. But, statements can be true or wrong independent of their reputational side effects and political associations.

A stronger critical argument is that intelligence, whether it be genetic or environmental, cannot completely explain the achievement gap between Jews and Gentiles – the achievement gap is larger than the intelligence gap.[76] There have to be further motivational or environmental reception factors. Or the measured IQ difference underestimates the real ability difference – a phenomenon also found for other ethnic comparisons: the tested IQ of higher ability groups is underestimated compared to their real-world achievement; the tested IQ of lower ability groups is overestimated (e.g. Farron, 2010; Davis et al., 2013).[77] Additionally, Jewish eminence is a rather new, historically and locally restricted phenomenon of the nineteenth and twentieth century up to the present: *a certain open and modern cultural environment enabled this high achievement.* There have to be further factors that contributed to the achievement level of Jews in modernity.

### Gregory Clark's Theory on Evolution of a Human Capital

*Personality*    The economist Gregory Clark published in 2007 a theory that tried to explain the onset and success of the Industrial Revolution in England by a preceding several-century-long process of the 'Survival of the

---

[76] Assuming an IQ-difference of 10 IQ points (IQ 100 and 110) this would lead at a threshold of IQ 130 (giftedness threshold) to a ratio of 1:3.98. That means that among Jews there would be nearly four times more persons than among gentiles with an IQ equal to or above 130 points. At a threshold of IQ 140 (good for exceptional achievement) the ratio would be 1: 5.94, at IQ 150 1:9.24. Given odds ratios (always considering the different population sizes) for academic professions (1:4) and enrolment at universities approximately represent this ability gap. But among elite university faculty and top achievement groups such as Nobel Prize and Fields Medal winners the empirical gap is larger than expected based on the intelligence gap (empirically, depending on country, time and domain, around 1:10 to 1:40; Lynn, 2011, pp. 342ff.). The analyses are based on the assumption of equal normal distributions and $SD = 15$.

[77] Davis et al. (2013, their table 3, p. 597) listed an overestimation of student achievement in studying medicine for African Americans (3.13 per cent) and Hispanics (2.20 per cent) and an underestimation for Whites (–0.50 per cent).

Richest': richer and middle-class persons had, from medieval times until the nineteenth century, more children surviving to adulthood than poorer persons. Belonging to a class was not only dependent on one's parents' class but also on one's own behaviour. Because the social positions for the richer and middle-class persons were limited, many of their children moved downward, taking positions of the formerly poorer groups. By this process, the prevailing attitudes and habits within successful strata of society diffused to lower classes. These attitudes and habits include predictability, conscientiousness, discipline, peaceableness, delay of gratification and industry. They all lead and historically led to a rise in human capital useful for more efficient production of goods and more generally for a more rational and efficient organisation of economy and society. It might be objected that the developing unit could also have been mere culture but Clark's analysis shows that the genetic endowment of people could have changed too, resulting in a 'human capital personality'.

Clark never explicitly dealt with cognitive ability, only indirectly ('more literate, and more thoughtful society'; Clark, 2007, p. 183f.), but the entire upward human capital trend is correlated with cognitive ability. Additional historical evidence from England points in that direction (Stone, 1964): condemned men, e.g. for larceny, survived if they could demonstrate that they were able to read the Bible. Clever persons with foresight may have started to learn reading and educated and intelligent people have survived and had more children. However, and the careful reader may have noticed it, if thefts survive this may be at odds with other aspects of burgher personality such as conscientiousness. Even more important is that Clark's analyses have plausibly demonstrated that human populations within around 500 years can genetically change to an extent that is important for society and economy even without any influence of immigration.

However, it is – like for Cochran et al. for Jews – only a case study. It did not ask and cannot answer why the Industrial Revolution was very successful somewhat later in Central Europe and Scandinavia. And it does not explain why centuries ago other regions and people such as in Northern Italy, the Netherlands and France had been economically and culturally advanced and had produced important economic and cultural achievement.

Clark gave no compelling evidence for the genetic mechanism itself (Boberg-Fazlic, Sharp & Weisdorf, 2011) and genes for the mentioned personality human capital attributes are missing. However, he gave a historical description of such a possible process.

### 10.7.3   Recent Evolution among Humans: Evolutionary Acceleration?

Conventional approaches in anthropology assumed that human evolution with the appearance of *Homo sapiens* came to an end 200,000 to 100,000 years ago, at least since modern humans left Africa around 50,000 years BCE. For instance, the Harvard palaeontologist Stephen Jay Gould mentioned:

There's been no biological change in humans in 40,000 or 50,000 years. Everything we call culture and civilisation we've built with the same body and brain. (Gould, 2000, p. 19)

Of course, this cannot be true. Evolution never stops. Evolution may alter its pace and direction, but not its continuation. And this includes humans. At first glance this becomes obvious in looking at gene frequencies: in 1492 there were no genes of Europeans in America, Australia or New Zealand, but now the genetic heritage of the majority of people is made up of them. Increases can be also observed for sub-Saharan African, Chinese and Indian genetic heritages.

It could be objected that only genetic markers moved but not the genes for relevant physical or psychological traits. But that objection is not correct: American natives had weaker resistance against several lethal infectious diseases such as influenza, measles and chickenpox. Entire populations disappeared due to infections. What is more serious than decisions of life or death?

Evolutionary scientists around Gregory Cochran and Henry Harpending (Cochran, Hardy & Harpending, 2006; Cochran & Harpending, 2009; Hawks, Wang, Cochran, Harpending & Moyzis, 2007) reversed the traditional belief of finished evolution into a theory of *accelerated evolution*: because humans had radically changed their environment and lifestyle in the Neolithic Revolution, from hunter-gathering to animal husbandry and agriculture, evolution became faster than before. New environmental challenges and harsh selection pressures led to different survival and fertility rates, creating rapid genetic changes. Additionally, larger populations enabled more mutations to emerge, among them some beneficial ones, which spread later on (e.g. Woodley et al., 2014). Thus, so the assumption goes, there has been an accelerated evolutionary process for 10,000 years.

Examples of such changes are the mentioned *resistance against infectious diseases*, which developed more frequently in densely living populations enabled by animal husbandry and agriculture. In addition, living together with livestock meant having a further potential source of dangerous infectious diseases such as influenza. A second example, an adaptation to keeping cattle, is the development of *lactose tolerance* resp. *lactase persistence* around 8,000 years ago. Lactase persistence made it possible to digest cow milk, an important source of proteins, fats, carbohydrates (different sugars including lactose), vitamins and trace elements. People able to digest cow milk had a clear survival and fertility advantage. Other examples, even 'obvious' ones, are *skin lightness* (skin colour), an adaptation to regions with less sunlight – the reception of UVB radiation is necessary for synthesizing vitamin D in the skin[78] and adaptations in *systems of respiration and circulation* for living in highlands such as the Himalayas, Andes and Ethiopia. Because humans did not settle earlier than around 14,000 years ago in America and about 11,000 years in the Andes, the evolutionary adaptation must have happened in the last millennia.

For human capital research selection processes or simple accidental genetic changes due to mutation, gene drift and bottleneck effects are important, probably having led to changes in *personality, cognitive ability* and *behaviour*. Some examples for such theories:

- Sedentism, agriculture, densification and urbanisation had a general burgher personality effect, such as being able to wait for later but greater rewards (delayed gratification, e.g. saving, storing), care and respect for property, reduced aggressivity and pacification and foresight and industry ('bourgeois values'; Cochran & Harpending, 2009, pp. 113ff.). Persons having this personality pattern in the aforementioned environmental-cultural conditions were more successful, had more surviving offspring and their genes spread in the population. And there was enough time for evolution, for instance a gene with a six per cent selective advantage doubles its frequency within 300 years (Cochran & Harpending, 2009, p. 122).
- According to Clark (2007), England's early and epoch-making way to industrial revolution was facilitated by an evolutionary process starting in the Middle Ages leading to more predictability, conscientiousness, discipline, peaceableness, delay of gratification and industry.
- This theory can be broadened (to all of Western Europe) and deepened (i.e., grounded in a specific cultural pattern) by appeal to the *Western European marriage pattern* (Hajnal, 1965). It was socially prescribed that an individual (especially a man) could only marry if he could make a living for himself, a spouse and their children – i.e. if he had achieved a certain position within society, e.g. possessing a farm, being a master craftsman, or practising as a professional. This led to late marriage, high rates of childlessness (of about a half of a cohort) and large investments in education. Going further than Hajnal himself, it arguably also enhanced delay of gratification, self-control (especially of sexuality), conscientiousness, frugality, industry and ability. The causes of this marriage pattern can be traced to Roman, Germanic and Christian traditions, to the interests of the church and to the interests of landlords and guilds. Its impact via both culture and evolution, via both personality and ability, laid the foundation for burgher society, for industrialisation and for the socio-political ascent of the West.

---

[78] Some researchers assume further evolutionary pressures on skin lightness such as sexual selection (Darwin, 1871) or pleiotropy (Jensen, 2006b).

Former centuries' age at first marriage and today's IQs correlate at $r = .55$, with today's GDPs at $r = .77$ (data of mostly European countries from Hajnal, 1965, and Dennison & Ogilvie, 2014). The pattern is confirmed by within-country differences in Italy and Spain, with older marriage ages and higher psychometric IQ and PISA test results in the north as well as higher GDPs per capita.

- The high intelligence at an average of around 110 IQ points of Ashkenazi Jews is based on a 1,000-years-old selection process enforced by environmental conditions set by Jewish culture and by gentiles (by Cochran et al., 2006, 2009).

- Rural Chinese people lived for generations under dense and poor conditions (many died due to diseases or periodic famines) *and* in an at least partially meritoric, achievement-based society. These were selective pressures leading to endurance, industry, adaptability, cooperativity, and higher cognitive ability ('high intelligence, sharp business sense, extremely hard work, and great diligence'; Unz, 1981, p. 6), resulting in higher offspring rates and the past centuries' success of Chinese people (Unz, 1981, 2013).

- Following Frost (2010), Roman institutions controlling behaviour, as by central authority, courts, guards and military, led to a monopolisation of violence, resulting in the Pax Romana. The powerful state punished males for internal violence (in premodern societies male violence has a positive fertility effect; Chagnon, 1977) and had in the long run a culturally and genetically pacifying impact on Romans, a pacification according to standards of a usually violent premodern world. For Europe, this trend was interrupted between the fifth and eleventh centuries. But from the eleventh to the nineteenth century, strong states backed by supportive worldviews of the church and philosophers conducted a war against murder and crime. About 0.5 to 2 per cent of all men were removed from each generation through court-ordered executions or imprisonment, leading in the long run to a genetic pacification. Accordingly, murder rates declined from between 20 and 40 to between 0.5 and 1 homicides per 100,000 (Frost & Harpending, 2015). Of course, past justice was far from being impartial and perfect but effective enough for causing such a development.

These plausible theories are backed by a cross-environmental stability of attributes, e.g. the Chinese were and are successful in different minority or majority societies, cultures and epochs. But all these theories also suffer from a lack of knowledge of genes and of the paths from genes to behaviour. The genetic explanations cannot be confirmed before such genes are found and the way that they cause psychological traits and differences in them. Due to principal problems of historical theories, no historical explanation can be backed unequivocally by empirical evidence. What past challenge caused elephants to become so big or why was the Roman Empire declining? There will never be only one answer. Theories can be backed but no explanation for a single historical process, be it cultural, genetic or otherwise, can indubitably rule out all other explanations.

### 10.7.4 *Consanguineous Marriages and the Genetic Effects of Culture*

Genetic effects were traditionally seen as 'old' and purely 'biological' ones. But modern evolutionary approaches of Cochran and others have shown that, rather, recent environmental and cultural changes in ways of life, production and consumption can have a crucial impact on human evolution. So the genetic heritage is *not only a cause* but *also a consequence*: lifestyle and culture are not only influenced by genes but they influence genes too! This is especially true for the effect of consanguineous marriages having a negative outcome on health and cognitive ability of the subsequent generation due to creating homozygotes for autosomal recessive genetic disorders.

Children from cousin–cousin pairs have on average a –3 IQ point cognitive reduction (Jensen, 1983; Woodley, 2009). According to a meta-analysis of Jan te Nijenhuis (2010) with 6,429 persons, including uncle–niece pairs and repeated inbreeding across several generations, the consanguinity effect is around –6 IQ points.[79]

Consanguineous marriages such as cousin–cousin or uncle–niece relationships are dependent on culture: according to Catholic Canon Law (Codex Iuris Canonici, § 1091), marriages between cousins from first to third degree are not allowed.[80] Even more important than formal law may be the customs influenced by law – usually you do not marry your cousin, 'you just don't do that!' Among the European aristocracy this rule was not always followed, with terrible health consequences for some male children – in the case of haemophilia, minor lesions led to endless bleedings and sometimes to death (e.g. Alexei Nikolaevich, Tsarevich of Russia, 1904–1918). The Spanish Habsburgs, which repeatedly practised inbreeding, became extinct: the last king, Charles II of Spain (1661–1700), called 'the Bewitched', was mentally and physically disabled and infertile.

---

[79] Negative effects of consanguineous marriages on intelligence largely vary from study to study. A recent study found an astonishingly high effect of –24 IQ (Muslim populations of Jammu in India; Fareed & Afzal, 2014). Others refer to examples as the Rothschild family, for whom a cognitive decline is not known. Negative effects depend on having autosomal recessive genetic disorders. In cases not having those, negative effects of consanguineous marriages are not existent. Not yet mentioned: there seems to be a curvilinear relationship between an inbreeding-outbreeding continuum and fertility, as modest kinship at the level of third and fourth cousins increases fertility (Icelandic population; Helgason et al., 2008).

[80] The medieval scholar and Doctor of the Church Thomas Aquinas (1225–1274) proscribed consanguineous marriages (Supplementum Tertiæ Partis, Questio 54).

In Arabian, Muslim and African countries, consanguineous marriages are more common (around 30 to 40 per cent; see Table 10.9 and Tadmouri et al., 2009; Woodley, 2009). The percentage of Muslims and consanguinity rate are very highly correlated ($r = .80$, $r_p = .81$), the percentage of Catholics and consanguinity highly negatively ($r = -.60$, $r_p = -.59$). Within European countries consanguinity rates mainly depend on immigrant populations and their cultural background. E.g. in United Kingdom, at least 55 per cent of British Pakistanis are married to cousins; their children account for only 3 per cent of all

Table 10.9 *Percentages of consanguinity and correlations*

| | | Consanguinity | | Correlations with ability and GNI | |
|---|---|---|---|---|---|
| **Africa (sub-Sahara)** | | 37.50 | | **CA** (corrected) | −.60 (−.60) |
| | Nigeria | | 51.20 | **SAS M** (corr., all) | −.49 (−.44) |
| **North-Africa M-East** | | 29.24 | | **SAS M** (uncorr., PTP) | −.53 (−.49) |
| | Egypt | | 23.89 | **SAS 95%** (uc., high) | −.50 (−.45) |
| **America (North, English)** | | 0.71 | | **SAS 05%** (uc., low) | −.56 (−.52) |
| | USA | | 0.17 | **GNI 2010 HDR** | −.23 (+.22) |
| **America (Latin, Central-South)** | | 2.35 | | *Notes: N* between 77 and 59 | |
| | Mexico | | 1.07 | (in parentheses GNI partialled out, | |
| **Asia (Central-South)** | | 30.44 | | for GNI cognitive ability removed) | |
| | India | | 21.90 | **Correlations with religions (%)** | |
| **East Asia** | | 2.08 | | Animism | .18 (.09) |
| | China | | 2.09 | Judaism | −.10 (−.09) |
| **Southeast Asia, Pacific** | | 6.91 | | Christianity | −.70 (−.68) |
| | Philippines | | 0.34 | Catholicism | −.60 (−.59) |
| **Australia-NZ (English)** | | 0.27 | | Orthodoxy | −.01 (−.02) |
| | Australia | | 0.27 | Protestantism | −.34 (−.30) |
| **Western Europe** | | 0.46 | | Islam | .80 (.81) |
| | United Kingdom | | 0.26 | Hinduism | .04 (.02) |
| **Scandinavia** | | 0.55 | | Buddhism | −.11 (−.14) |
| | Norway | | 0.62 | Confucianism (E-A) | −.18 (−.14) |
| **Central Europe** | | – | | Weighted religions | −.83 (−.84) |
| | Netherlands | | 0.16 | *Notes:* On religions see Table 10.11, | |
| **Eastern Europe** | | 0.14 | | *N*=77 ("()"=GNI partialled out) | |
| | Slovakia | | 0.17 | | |
| **Southern Europe** | | 4.79 | | | |
| | Italy | | 0.41 | | |

*Notes:* Data for consanguinity from Woodley (2009) and supplemented by Tadmouri et al. (2009); both correlate with $r = .87$ ($N = 15$). Their common most important source is Bittles (2001). Country examples without data were substituted for countries from the same region (Nigeria, Australia, Slovakia) or neighbouring countries (the Netherlands); correlation with cognitive ability is exactly $r = -.599$, the partial correlation $r_p = -.596$.

births but about a third of all British children with genetic disorders belong to them (Rowlatt, 2005).

Rates of consanguineous marriages are clearly negatively correlated to national cognitive ability levels with $r = -.60$ (see Table 10.9). A causal relationship is corroborated by a fourfold correlational pattern: first, negative correlations with cognitive ability are higher than with wealth (ability $r = -.49$ to $-.60$ vs. GNI $-.23$). Second, negative correlations with cognitive ability remain to be substantial after partialling out wealth (reduction maximally $|.05|$). Third, partialling out cognitive ability between the negative correlation of consanguinity and GNI does not only reduce the correlation between consanguinity and GNI but turns it into positive! That means the negative correlation between consanguinity and wealth could be entirely traced back to their common relationship to intelligence. Fourth, the negative relationship between consanguinity and cognitive ability is the largest for the low cognitive ability group (5 per cent-threshold: $r_{05\%} = -.56$ vs. $r_M = -.53$ vs. $r_{95\%} = -.50$ for the three comparable CA variables). The cognitive elites' IQ is less impeded by consanguineous marriages than that of the less educated, more traditionally living low ability groups. The size and pattern of correlations strongly back a cultural-genetic interpretation of international differences, but, of course, consanguineous marriages cannot explain all variation in international cognitive ability. E.g. this factor cannot be successfully used for within European or for West-East comparisons.

Indirectly, the entire pattern lends support to a more general genetic perspective on international cognitive ability differences: the genetic perspective seems to be important. This view is backed by correlations between genetic factors (Table 10.10).

Consanguinity also has broader implications; it has a *negative impact on democracy* (Woodley & Bell, 2013): according to the theory, consanguineous marriages lead to high levels of within-kinship genetic similarity that discourage within-nation cooperation outside kinship groupings and that encourage resource predation as an inclusive fitness-enhancing behaviour by members of kinship networks. Additionally, consanguineous marriages restrict gene flow, leading to stronger within-family collectivism inimical to the recognition of individual and formal rights. Individualism and universalism, which are connected and depend on each other, cannot develop in consanguineous societies. Backing this theory, there is a strong negative correlation between consanguinity and democracy ($r = -.70$, $N = 74$) being robust against partialling out GNI ($r_p = -.67$) and being robust against partialling out cognitive ability ($r_p = -.58$).

Whether consanguineous marriages have a cross-generational long-term negative impact on third generation children even if the second generation (impeded by consanguinity) itself has married a non-related person is less clear. At least, indirect individual-psychological and macrosocial-cultural effects of grandparental consanguinity are at work, such as by having a

Table 10.10 *Correlations among three genetic indicators*

|  |  | Skin lightness | Cranial capacity | Consanguinity | CA (corrected) |
|---|---|---|---|---|---|
| **Skin lightness,** | r ($r_p$) | 1 | .61 (.57) | −.60 | .87 (.83) |
| **mean** | N | | (179) | (75) | (179) |
| **Cranial capacity** | r ($r_p$) | .61 (.57) | 1 (179) | −.21 | .58 (.47) |
| | N | (179) | | (75) | (179) |
| **Consanguinity** | r ($r_p$) | −.60 (−56) | −.21 (−.14) | 1 | −.62 (−.60) |
| | N | (75) | (75) | | (75) |
| **G factor** | r ($r_p$) | .90 (.88) | .90 (.89) | − | .81 (.74) |
| **evolution** | N | (179) | (179) | | (179) |
| **G factor genes** | r ($r_p$) | .91 (.90) | .70 (.71) | −.77 (−.76) | .77 (.75) |
| | N | (75) | (75) | (75) | (75) |

*Notes*: First line correlations and in parentheses partial correlations (GNI per capita partialled out). Skin lightness (Biasutti–Jablonski-mean) and cranial capacity (own assignment) in the same country samples of 179 nations. G factor evolution: evolutionary factors skin lightness and cranial capacity. G factor genes: also including non-consanguinity, which is a genetic factor, but not unambiguously an evolutionary factor (largely depending on culture).

handicapped model parent with a lower than average intelligence and living in a society with less democracy and rule of law.

The three genetic factors are robustly related at the international level: the two evolutionary indicators skin lightness and cranial capacity are correlated with $r = .61$ ($N = 179$; Table 10.10). When income is partialled out the correlation is still $r_p = .57$. A *G fact*or of evolution or of genetic effects (the last with consanguinity) highly correlates with cognitive ability ($r = .81$ or .77); the correlations remain high in different country samples ($N = 179$ or 75) and if income per capita is partialled out ($r_p = .74$ or .75). Even if one variable were to be wrongly measured genetic effects on cross-country differences in cognitive ability would remain.

### 10.7.5   The 'Race' Issue (Biological Categorisation within Species)

*Dealing with the Race Issue?*   The race issue, the biological categorisation within *one* species, here *Homo sapiens*, is perceived in science and politics as a contentious issue. Is it relevant scientifically and for the understanding of international differences in ability and wealth?

An answer regarding the relevance of genetic factors could be very quick: because there are large genetic differences *within races*, such as between Roma (Gypsies) and Scandinavians, and even *within single distinct peoples*, such as between European (Ashkenazi) and Middle East (Mizrahim) Jews or between Italians of the North and the South, which are all associated with intelligence, any genetic theory on international differences in intelligence does not need a within-species biological categorisation, whether it is biologically appropriate or not.

The above-mentioned differences independent of within-species categories were presented by the two most prominent race researchers in psychology, Philippe Rushton and Richard Lynn. Rushton has shown stable intelligence differences *between different races*, such as between Americans of European and of sub-Saharan African ancestry at 15 IQ points (IQ 100 and IQ 85; Rushton, 1997/1995), but also *within one race*, such as within 'Caucasians' between non-Romani (Gadje) and Romani (Gypsies), the difference is here around 20 to 40 points (Rushton et al., 2007; Cvorovic, 2014, p. 153ff.). Lynn has demonstrated that *within one race*, such as within 'Mongolians' between Chinese, Mongols and Tibetans, the difference is around 6 to 14 points (Lynn & Vanhanen, 2012, pp. 21ff.), and *within one nation* the difference is similarly high; the IQ of Italians in the north is around 10 IQ points higher than the one of Italians in the South (Lynn, 2010; Piffer & Lynn, 2014).

So any biological subspecies categorisation seems to be unnecessary. Additionally, any reference to the race issue attracts ideologically and politically biased attention and constricts the perspective from the whole issue – why is cognitive human capital relevant for wealth? How can we explain differences? What will the future be and what could be done – to one aspect.[81] Is it not strategically, for the success of the entire enterprise of cognitive capital research, more prudent not to mention any evolutionary categorisation and especially not the term 'race'?

No.

For two reasons.

There can be no serious research on international cognitive ability differences without dealing with the race issue. It is the oldest and, in the public, most controversial approach to explaining group differences in intelligence, in which international differences form a part. So it has to be addressed. Research neglecting it is politically biased research.

This leads to the second reason: *science has to be always a process of enlightenment*. Science is based on enlightenment; historically, culturally and intellectually, science and enlightenment are intertwined. There is no good science without enlightenment and enlightenment without science is empty. Science produces enlightenment, by producing knowledge and giving an example of enlightenment in practice. Yes, a huge project, but not less. Epistemic aims and intellectual integrity (*Redlichkeit*) are more important than

---

[81] See the descriptions of his experiences with reactions after writing an article on the evolutionary history of humans by Armand Leroi (2005, pp. 5f.), e.g. 'The Insane who believed that I am racist. They condemned or praised me according to taste.'

strategic aims.[82] Avoiding intellectual mistakes is more important than avoiding attacks or appreciation by ideologically orientated people and times. We try to be *sub specie aeternitatis* correct and not according to any passing sentiment.

*Biological-Evolutionary Arguments*    The main problem with any biological categorisation is that distinct interpreted categories are given to the continuous process of evolution. Speciation is a slow and, in its beginning, hardly observable process. Tiny genetic-phenotypic changes first lead to different subspecies, then to species, genera, families etc. Somewhere in this continuum a demarcation criterion has to be placed. The variability and similarity that all individuals both distinguish and connect have to be put in a reasonable system. Thus, there will never be the one and only solution. Categorisation systems are more or less appropriate – how many colours exist, what is a bush and what a tree, how many planets are orbiting the sun?

Biological categories and nomenclatures change with respect to the current state of knowledge. Even a changing political climate may have an impact. It is taken for granted that animals have distinct races but for around four decades this has not been the case for humans: 'There are no human races, my dog though, I consider to be a Border Collie'. The author himself has been interested in animals since childhood and especially in terrapins, colourful pond turtles living in freshwater. When he acquired in the late 1970s his first baby terrapin, a red-eared slider, its scientific name was Chrysemys scripta elegans. Becoming bigger it received a new name, Pseudemys scripta elegans. And, after around 20 years, when it died, it was officially named Trachemys scripta elegans. In biology, there are not only renamings for given species and subspecies, but also splittings of species in new subspecies or even species. There is a trend of *taxonomic inflation of species among animals*, e.g. among the (great) apes: formerly, three species were accepted, but today there are two orangutan species (Sumatran orangutan, Bornean orangutan, since 1996, Bornean orangutan with three subspecies), two chimpanzee species (bonobo, common chimpanzee with four subspecies) and two gorilla species (Western gorilla with two subspecies and Eastern gorilla with two subspecies).[83] According to newer behavioural and genetic studies, Orcas should be also split into different species and subspecies. Similar developments have occurred for elephants, imperial eagles and thousands of reptile, amphibian and insect species.

---

[82] '*Redlichkeit*' is a term coined by Karl Jaspers (1883–1969), a philosopher and psychologist.
[83] Humans can be added as further ape species (Hominidae).

The opposite trend has happened for humans, a deflation of subspecies, from formerly three 'races' to today only one species. Critics of polytypic human models are e.g. Gould (2000), Hochman (2013) or UNESCO (1969/1950). Their main arguments against within-human categorisation are:

- 'Race', even if phenotypically observable, is only 'skin deep', and has no further physical-biological or psychological meaning.
- Distributions of morphologic and genetic attributes are continuous.
- Humans share most genes.
- The genetic variation within races is larger than between races.
- The number of 'races' is not clearly defined.[84]

Thus, why not revise taxonomic categorisations? With increasing knowledge, especially due to improved genetic methods and more sophisticated categorisation schemes, species could be reorganised. If the *same criteria* are applied to all living beings this would be good science!

This would start with using the same terms for the same phenomena. If within a species subspecies can be distinguished they should be called 'subspecies' for all species and not something else for certain ones. So within humans the term 'race' should not be used, but equally 'subspecies'.[85] As Charles Darwin has mentioned:

The term 'sub-species' might be used with propriety. But from long habit the term 'race' will perhaps always be employed. The choice of terms is only so far important in that it is highly desirable to use, as far as that may be possible, the same terms for the same degrees of difference. (Darwin, 1871, p. 227f.)

And what are the criteria for a differentiation in subspecies? Species are defined as groups of individuals that can have fertile offspring.[86] Subspecies are groups of individuals that can have fertile offspring together (identical to species) and which form a recognisable (and genetically transmitted) pheno-typical and genotypical pattern distinguishable from other recognisable patterns within a species.[87] The ornithologist Dean Amadon (1949) suggested for

---

[84] See also Sesardic (2010, 2013) for a review of the arguments. However, frequently no argumentation is used: an example from Elizabeth Chin (2013): 'The American Anthropological Association in its statement on race, specifically rejects the genetic validity of the idea of race, period.'

[85] See also Rescher's (1988, p. 16) criteria for rationality: 'Rationality demands: consistency (avoid self-contradiction), uniformity (treat like cases alike), coherence (make sure that your commitments hang together), simplicity (avoid needless complications), economy (be efficient).' The criteria of epistemic rationality overlap with the ones of Piaget for formal operational thinking.

[86] Individuals which can have fertile offspring together: except for the problem of consanguinity leading to inbreeding depression. Definition is simplified here, frequently a recognisable phenotypical pattern and no crossbreeding in nature are added.

[87] Frequently added are geographic or evolutionary history criteria – however, they are not essential. Different subspecies may live in the same region or not (e.g. Corvus corone corone and Corvus corone cornix); the past is frequently unknown.

this purpose the quantitatively precise 'seventy-five percent rule for subspecies': 75 per cent of individuals in a population A should be separable by the similar pattern from all members (+99 per cent) of another population B.

Is there any evidence similar to animal categorisation that supports a differentiation in subspecies among current humans?

- Within humans, systematic phenotypical patterns can be described (e.g. Baker, 1974) and recognised by persons (scientists, laypeople including children and authorities) and this is much easier for humans than for subspecies of other species (e.g. of chimps; Woodley, 2010).[88]
- Self-identification of race is correct (error rate at 0.14 per cent; Tang et al., 2005).
- Phenotypical (seen from the outside or inside as skeleton) and genotypical attributes are measurable. They are correlated and together (the more attributes the better) they enable a reliable identification of evolutionary affiliation. Using two attributes the classifications are at around 80 per cent correct, using more than ten attributes more than 95 per cent of all classifications are correct (Edwards, 2003; Ousley et al., 2009; Sesardic, 2010).
- Morphological differences between human subspecies are larger than between ape subspecies, sometimes reaching the typical level of species differentiation among animals (Woodley, 2010).
- Genetic differences among humans exhibiting well-defined subspecies are larger than genetic differences among animal species (Woodley, 2010; Wright, 1978).
- Worldwide dissemination of humans across different climates make the evolution of different subspecies more probable (but not cogent).
- Criteria of evolutionary history and genetic as well as morphological and linguistic patterns fit together (Andreasen, 2004; Cavalli-Sforza, 1997). The fit of these features allows a genealogical tree to be drawn (see Figure 10.16).

Based on this evidence and a comparison to criteria successfully applied to animals, among humans several evolutionarily developed subspecific patterns can be distinguished. In biology, they are named subspecies, among humans more frequently 'races', 'varieties', 'breeds', 'populations', 'genetic clusters', 'ancestry' or 'ancestral histories'. The usual objections, continuity, common share of the majority of genes, within subspecies variation and difficult to determine number of 'races', are all true but irrelevant because these aspects

---

[88] Wright (1978, p. 439): 'It does not require a trained anthropologist to classify an array of Englishmen, West Africans, and Chinese with 100% accuracy by features, skin color, and type of hair in spite of so much variability within each of these groups that every individual can easily be distinguished from every other.'

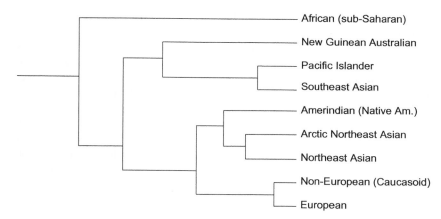

Figure 10.16 Cladistic model of the evolution of (larger) human populations following Andreasen (2004, her figure 2, adapted)

are not constitutive for refuting a subspecific categorisation and are also found for animal subspecies.

Of course, as for other species, individuals with mixed background are difficult to categorise – they simply do not belong to one category, but to several ones! This dissolves subspecific categories to often more appropriate continuous qualifications such as e.g. 40 per cent White-European, 40 per cent Black and 20 per cent American-Indian.

*Explanatory Value of the Subspecies Concept and Its Limits*   The categorisation of species in different subspecies does not mean that there have to be relevant differences in behaviour. We do not assume that the Siberian tiger is smarter than the Sumatran tiger; the Siberian tiger is only bigger and better adapted to the cold. Categorisations themselves do not evoke psychologically relevant characteristics, but genes and environment. Categorisations do not explain; they only systematise. To find and describe substantial and stable differences between subspecies does not explain these differences. Race is no explanatory variable, but evolution. Evolutionary theories and the detection of genetic-neurological-psychological pathways are necessary.

Thus the entire race issue is less scientifically relevant. But it is relevant as an *indicator of epistemic rationality of a person and scientist, of a scientific field* and *an intellectual climate.* Denying the subspecies concept without denying it for other species and without comparing the applied criteria for its refutation or acceptance with the ones applied for other living beings certainly fails in epistemic rationality. The race issue is the litmus test of scientific attitude.

Coming back to its usefulness for human capital research, a finer distinction than in subspecies is frequently more meaningful, such as among Italians between the North and South. However, finer distinctions and further factors do not refute broader distinctions and the effects of other factors. Depending on research question, subspecies remains a relevant concept. For instance, Beaver et al. (2014) found for the US National Longitudinal Study of Adolescent Health (Add Health) that attributes of adoptive parents such as education and parenting styles showed only modest and frequently unstable effects on children's intelligence, e.g. parental education with $\beta = |.14|$. But African ancestry of the child showed a larger and more robust effect with $\beta = |.20|$. Still, for most societies and analyses at the level of nations finer distinctions will be more revealing. Theoretically, the focus on the last 40,000 to 10,000 years will be more explanatory than on the 60,000 years before (see Section 10.7.3).

### 10.7.6    Summary on Evolutionary Explanations

What can be learnt from the described evolutionary approaches? At first glance, there is an open question: All genetic explanations suffer from hard and replicated evidence on cognitive ability coding genes and their biological mechanism. The world is explained with a postulate. But the theoretical argument and indirect empirical evidence are broad and convincing.

To work with an empirically not yet successfully proven theory is not rare in research; it stimulates empirical research. One example is the theory of relativity: this theory postulated many empirical phenomena, which were not successfully proved until decades or even a century later.

So what we have learnt about a possible genetic impact on international cognitive ability differences? First and foremost, there is no genetically based psychological uniformity of humankind. Of course, there are common attributes such as love and aggression, human intelligence compared to animals, development of ethical reasoning and helpfulness, but large differences between people and stable patterns are observable. Their relative robustness across countries and time hint at a genetic influence. Behavioural genetics have shown a strong heritability of individual differences. Genomewide association studies have detected the first candidate genes coding intelligence and differences in intelligence at the individual as well as at the cross-country level. Differences in cognitive ability vary with genetic markers representing a different evolutionary history. Genetically more similar nations are also more similar in intelligence, even if further factors are controlled. Morphological features and indicators of evolution (cranial capacity, skin lightness) highly correlate with results in international intelligence and student assessment studies. Bigger brains lead to higher intelligence. Evolutionary theories explain the development of differences between peoples in psychological traits. There is evidence for recently accelerated evolution among humans. Deleterious effects of consanguineous marriages underscore the importance of genetic factors for cognitive ability at the level of individuals and nations and also show that genetic effects depend on culture. Current humans can be distinguished in different evolutionary branches that are usually named 'subspecies' for other living beings. The total evidence indicates that recent evolution, in the last 20,000 to 100 years, is more important for current human macrosocial differences than former evolution.

Finally, all assumptions that genetic theories are pure genetic theories are wrong: *all genetic theories are in the long run environmental theories* – environmental pressures resulted via selection in genetic and physical changes.[89]

## 10.8   Culture and Worldviews

Culture is a *worldview* ('Weltanschauung') that (1) *describes* the external and internal, natural and social, corporeal and mental world, that (2) *prescribes* values and that (3) via describing and prescribing *shapes* the world. Worldviews constitute the core of cultures (see Chapter 6). Worldviews form a relatively stable perspective of describing and prescribing the world, leading to a modification of this world. *Religions* are worldviews: the oldest and, due to their long-term impacts, the most important ones. In modernity, they are supplemented by *secular worldviews* dealing more explicitly with politics. Such secular worldviews are prominent for the left, such as communism, socialism or a more general left-wing programme. They are also available for the right, such as fascism or national socialism. Political liberalism (Locke, Mill) and economic liberalism (Mises, Hayek) or a more diffuse concept of modernisation are less salient worldviews.

The major religions are all more than one thousand years old. They have a long-term effect across centuries. They have an enduring impact on contemporary societies, including on people who are not religious at all. To analyse the effects of religion, four influences have to be distinguished: religions take effect via

- the original message (the initial holy text),
- the exemplary figure of the religious founder and his role model,
- the interpreted and revised doctrine and its changed understanding across time and
- the lived practice in present time.

---

[89] Chance factors, that via mutation are essential in evolution, are weeded out by environmental selection.

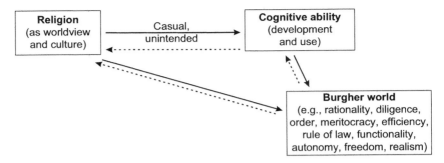

Figure 10.17 Theoretical model for effects of religion on cognitive ability and the development and preservation of a burgher world

For our study, the religious content as a holy text is less important than the content's *unintended consequences for shaping cognitive ability*, its development and use, and its *unintended consequences for shaping society in the direction of a burgher world* (see Figure 10.17). Culture is, compared to the other factors initially discussed, a much more generally working *background* factor, similar to evolution.

In presenting such a model two questions immediately arise: first, where do the specific attributes of religions come from which apparently impact cognitive ability and shape the world? And second, does religion really matter?

Attributes of religions (original message, founder, interpreted doctrine, practice) at the beginning depend on very accidental local conditions, narratives and personality attributes of the founders. But there were so many prophets and religious trends that only those that met the historically and socially given expectations spread. So religions in the early stages depend on acceptance but the more successful they become the more they shape the expectations and become a self-fulfilling need producer: they shape motifs and then fulfil them. They create questions and give answers to them. They originate a perspective and reinforce it by obviousness.

Older culturally, historically, geographically and genetically determined conditions have impacts but they become modified by religion. And, of course, religion as a worldview is not an eternal unchanged unity. As the model in Figure 10.17 implies, cognitive ability, current society and practice can have a back effect on religion (see concept of spiral-shaped developments in Figure 3.6). For instance, Protestantism initiated via education a development towards higher literacy and intelligence, via conscience towards individualism, conscientiousness and 'Redlichkeit' (honesty) and via education and 'sola scriptura' towards rationality, but all together these consequences of Protestantism have an undermining effect on religiosity.

Worldviews and religions matter; ideas change people. Three examples illustrate this: one for the past, two for the present: Angus Maddison, from whom we have the data for past production and wealth levels, described a huge gap between Protestant and Catholic countries on the American continent, for the United States and Canada compared to Mexico:

> The British colonies had a better educated population, greater intellectual freedom and social mobility. Education was secular with emphasis on pragmatic skills and Yankee ingenuity of which Ben Franklin was the prototype. The 13 British colonies had nine universities in 1776 for 2.5 million people. New Spain, with 5 million, had only two universities in Mexico City and Guadalajara, which concentrated on theology and law. Throughout the colonial period the Inquisition kept a tight censorship and suppressed heterodox thinking. (Maddison, 2001, p. 108)

Maddison's view is backed by the nearly two centuries older seminal study of Alexis de Tocqueville on 'Democracy in America'. Religion was supportive for the development of liberty, democracy and rule of law in North America:

> They brought to the New World a Christianity that I cannot portray better than by calling it democratic and republican: This will singularly favor the establishment of the republic and of democracy in public affairs. From the onset, politics and religion found themselves in accord, and they have not ceased to be so since. (Tocqueville, 2010/1835, Vol. II, part ii, chapter 10, p. 467).

Coming back to education, the second example deals with current youth in Germany being Christians or Muslims: According to a study by the Criminological Research Institute of Lower Saxony, higher religiosity among Muslim youth corresponds to lower education, while among Christian youth (Germans or immigrants as well) higher religiosity corresponds to higher education (Baier et al., 2010, pp. 90f.). For violence, the religious effect is reversed: more religious Christian immigrants are less violent while more religious Muslim immigrants are more violent (Baier et al., 2010, pp. 117f.).

The third example deals with Communism versus capitalism. According to a meta-analysis of Schwekendiek and Pak (2009), South Korean children are about 6 to 8 cm taller than their North Korean peers. A similar pattern was found for the former East and West Germany, with around one to two cm favouring West Germans (Komlos & Kriwy, 2003). The influence of political worldviews goes *indirectly* through producing economic wealth (nutrition, health) to height.

Granted, there may be differences in any behavioural or physical aspect between worldviews and religions and their followers, but how do we know that religion causes these differences? E.g. between Mexico and the United States and Canada there is also a difference in latitude – why not attribute all differences between these nations to latitude? Or Muslim youth may have more violent parents depending on their education and socio-economic status.

To address these objections we need a theory and detailed description of possible effects of each single religion. And we need to specify theoretically and by empirical research the net effect of other factors. These possible *effects of religions on cognitive ability and the shaping of the burgher world* are now described. Religions are roughly ordered along historical development and regions.

### 10.8.1   Animism

Animism is the initial human religion. Animism prevailed in the past in all regions and cultures. Specific founders are not known. Spiritual powers are seen as the hidden forces that influence nature and humans. Via magic practice humans can influence the physical and spiritual world. Psychologically, human thinking patterns, especially self-centred wishful thinking ones, are projected in the outside world.

For Jean Piaget (e.g. 2001/1947), Animism is a cognitive phenomenon indicative of the preoperational stage of cognitive development. Piagetian Animism comprises self-centred *anthropomorphic thinking* (nature and its elements are seen as being persons with their own intentions), *confusion of inside and outside* (own intentions are seen as intentions of others), *artificialism* (the world is made by humans or by human-similar beings as anthropomorphously imagined gods), *finalism* (the world is made to fulfil a purpose; there is no chance), *naive realism* (what a person perceives including dreams is real), *conceptual realism* (no distinction between signs, a symbol or word and objects, e.g. speaking about something may create it), *similarity* (superficially similar things are treated as identical things, e.g. the rhinoceros horn supports virility) and *magical causality* (there is a spiritual-psychic relationship between objects and beings which is influenceable by spiritual-psychic actions). This theoretical concept is well corroborated by extensive empirical research on cognitive development, behaviour and thinking of peoples all over the world in the past and present (e.g. Lévy-Bruhl, 1923/1922; Hallpike, 1980; LePan, 1989; Oesterdiekhoff, 2007ff.).

There are three main objections, first that animistic thinking is more a kind of folklore, second that Animism is a Western concept wrongly describing the thinking prevalent in other cultures and third that Animism is a result of (low) cognitive ability and not a factor influencing cognitive development.

(1) *Folklore*? Animistic beliefs do not just result in seemingly unproblematic irrationalities, like believing that God can put money in one's purse (present among urban middle-class people in Nigeria; Rindermann et al., 2014, p. 26), but they create angst and mental immaturity, leading to wrong and frequently harmful decisions in everyday life: for example, in dealing with the HIV risk and AIDS, in road behaviour and religious cults (Voodoo) (Dagona, 1994; Oesterdiekhoff & Rindermann, 2007); Animistic beliefs

induce cruelty against humans, including children, e.g. female genital mutilation, homicide of children whose teeth come in the 'wrong' order, burying of twins alive (Lévy-Bruhl, 1923/1922); Animistic beliefs cause false accusations of being witches against average adults and children or different-looking persons such as albinos, resulting in expulsions or killing.[90]

(2) *Wrong Western concept?* It is true that the concept of Animism was developed by scientists in the West such as Lucien Lévy-Bruhl and Jean Piaget. It would be also possible to defame it as a 'Jewish' concept (Lévy-Bruhl was a Jew and Judaism was opposed to magic; Deuteronomy 18:10-11[91]). But does 'Western' also mean wrong? Is the number 'zero' wrong for Europe because it was invented in India? The origin of a concept does not give any answer about its veridicality. However, it could be still 'wrong'. Extensive ethnological and historical research (Lévy-Bruhl, Hallpike, LePan, Oesterdiekhoff), casual observations of travellers and journalists (e.g. by Luisa Falkenhayn; Rindermann, Falkenhayn & Baumeister, 2014; Grill, 2005)[92] and studies on cognitive development (Piaget) strongly corroborate the concept.

(3) *Intelligence → Animism and not vice versa?* There is no dissent in research or among intellectuals regarding a correspondence of low intelligence and Animism.[93] Theory explains and empirical data show that low cognitive development leads to animistic thinking (Piaget, Hallpike, Oesterdiekhoff). But is there any theory and evidence that, conversely, Animism impedes cognitive development? Theoretically, according to Georg Wilhelm Friedrich Hegel, animistic thinking, in his view exemplified by superstition within the Catholic Church, favours concretism and authoritarianism impeding own thinking:

The ecclesiastical piety of the period displays the very essence of superstition – the fettering of the mind to a sensuous object, a mere Thing – in the most various forms – slavish deference to Authority; for Spirit, having renounced its proper nature in its most essential quality [having sacrificed its characteristic liberty to a mere sensuous object], has lost its Freedom, and is held in adamantine bondage to what is alien to itself. (Hegel, 2001/1837, p. 432)

---

[90] On witchcraft accusations, search for 'Return to Africa's Witch Children' or 'Nigeria's Child Witch Scandal: Children Killed as Witches' on YouTube (be careful, terrifying content).

[91] Deuteronomy 18:10–11: 'Let no one be found among you who sacrifices their son or daughter in the fire, who practices divination or sorcery, interprets omens, engages in witchcraft, or casts spells, or who is a medium or spiritist or who consults the dead.' Cf. Landes (1972/1969, p. 21): 'One finds a strong tendency in the Judaic tradition to eliminate magic and superstition as a senseless degradation of faith.' Cf. Max Weber (2007/1923, chapter 4, § 9, p. 360).

[92] Many reports are hard to believe but search on the Internet, e.g. for 'children' and 'witchcraft'.

[93] Theodor W. Adorno, in *Minima Moralia* (2006/1951, 151:VI): 'The occult is the metaphysics of knuckleheads.'

Or according to Lawrence Harrison, Animism, exemplified by Voodoo in Haiti, discourages thinking and rationality and in a broader sense the development of an autonomous person and burgher:

Voodoo discourages initiative, rationality, achievement, education. . . . Not only does Voodoo nurture irrationality; it also nurtures a sense of impotence and fatalism and discourages the entrepreneurial vocation. . . . I believe that Voodoo has made a major contribution to the sociopolitical pathology, including poverty and extremely low levels of trust, that has plagued Haiti's history. (Harrison, 2006, p. 30, p. 87)

Insofar as magic is perceived as a method to find truth, it is a short cut that helps to avoid strenuous rational thinking and a critical proof of empirical hypotheses. Animism as concretism, authoritarianism and traditionalism is hostile towards thinking. It does not support education and the development of thinking ability. It joins canonical knowledge to power and violence. It interdicts any questioning. One's own reading and own and rational thinking are not only unnecessary but dangerous. There was no development of institutions for formal education.

It could be objected that animistic doctrines frequently are very complex constructions of the world (as documented e.g. by Evans-Pritchard, 1976/ 1937, or Griaule, 1965/1948). But they lack rational systematisation, open critique and empirical proof. Content does not represent information, but myth (e.g. Signer, 2004, p. 20). Animism does not support thinking and its progress, only memorisation.

### 10.8.2   Judaism

The exceptional cognitive achievement of Jews is beyond question. There are long lists of outstanding scientists and accomplishments in various intellectual realms such as in chess, literature, music and cinema.[94] Jews are overrepresented in any high cognitive achievement domain, including student and faculty body at well-recognised universities. The average measured IQ of Western Jews, the Ashkenazim, is around 110 points. This striking intellectual excellence gave rise to cultural causal theories:

In traditional Judaism, self-reading of the Torah and Talmud was highly appreciated and practised (Botticini & Eckstein, 2012; Murray, 2007). Education was also highly regarded in the marriage market. Religious intellectuals were the leaders of the community.

Since the eighteenth century and the European Enlightenment and liberalisation the educational focus was even more stressed and redirected to secular aims: education and own thinking were seen as legitimate ways out of

---

[94] E.g. www.jinfo.org, Lynn (2011). See also Sections 4.4.3 and 10.7.2.

self-marginalisation and discrimination (Lipset & Raab, 1995; Nisbett, 2009).[95] Cognitive ability was not only perceived as a functional instrument but also as a self-liberating process leading to *intellectual and ethical rationality*:

The enormous emphasis on learning, intellectuality, articulateness, and argument – even argumentativeness – is characteristic of Jews. (Van Den Haag, 1969, pp. 18f.)

The European history of ideas is not conceivable without the contribution of Jewish, frequently Jewish-German, intellectuals.[96]

However, the entire picture is not as uniform as portrayed here. Traditional Judaism favoured reading and knowledge of holy texts but was critical towards independent thinking. Well-known is the example of Baruch Spinoza, who was exiled from the Jewish community of Amsterdam because of his divergent ideas. The traditional Jewish belief is highly dogmatic and exclusive.[97] In the old books (Leviticus, Numbers, Deuteronomy, Joshua etc.), stoning is recommended against deviationists.[98] Jewish ethics was not universalistic (double standard, dualism; Sombart, 1998/1913, pp. 265f.; Weber, 1952/1919, pp. 343ff.). A double standard in ethics means that other people have been treated differently, usually worse than one's own people. This impedes ethics, rationality and the development of the rule of law.[99] According to a meta-analysis, religiosity and universalism are among Jews still, but only slightly, negatively correlated ($r = -.18$; Saroglou, Delpierre & Dernelle, 2004).[100]

---

[95] According to Max Weber (2001/1905, chapter 1, footnote 8, p. 189), the population in Baden (South-West-Germany) was composed in 1895 by 37.0 per cent Protestants, 61.3 per cent Catholics and 1.5 per cent Jews. However, the most selective school, the Gymnasium, was attended by 48 per cent Protestants (1:1.30), 42 per cent Catholics (1:0.69) and 10 per cent Jews (1:6.67).

[96] Some names: Karl Marx, Heinrich Heine, Edmund Husserl, Georg Simmel, Hermann Cohen, Franz Kafka, Sigmund Freud, Albert Einstein, Walter Benjamin, Karl Mannheim, Ernst Cassirer, Franz Boas, Martin Buber, Wilhelm Reich, Max Horkheimer, Theodor Wiesengrund Adorno, Norbert Elias, Ernst Bloch, Herbert Marcuse, Leo Strauss, Hannah Arendt, Ludwig von Mises, Karl Popper, Ludwig Wittgenstein, Friedensreich Hundertwasser, Joseph Weizenbaum, Carl Djerassi, Walter Laqueur.

[97] Van Den Haag (1969, p. 25f.): 'No people is more parochial and discriminatory in its feelings and attitudes than the Jewish people. The temper is dogmatic. ... Even Jewish liberals are dogmatically tolerant (and quite intolerant of those who are not, or who tolerate different things). How else could they have survived with their Jewish identity intact?'

[98] E.g. Deuteronomy 21:18-21: 'If a man have a stubborn and rebellious son ... And all the men of his city shall stone him to death with stones: so shalt thou put away the evil from the midst of thee; and all Israel shall hear, and fear.' However, later Rabbinic reinterpretation made it nearly impossible to impose a death penalty on somebody; it had not been practised for millennia (Cohn et al., 2007).

[99] Van Den Haag (1969, p. 30): 'Judaism has essentially remained a tribal religion.'

[100] For Muslims, the negative correlation between religiosity and universalism is stronger ($r = -.40$).

Unlike the majority of other religions, religion and nation are linked.[101] The average IQ in Israel is only 95.

But are these critical aspects related to intelligence or, more precisely, do they have a negative effect on education, thinking and intelligence? Universalism is according to Piaget and Kohlberg an indicator of the highest cognitive and the highest ethical development stage.[102] Traditionalism impedes education towards comprehension and independent thinking. Non-universalistic ethics may impair development towards universalistic epistemic rationality. However, empirical studies on negative effects for intelligence are not known.

Obviously, the Jewish intellectual rise occurred in a historical stage of detachment from traditional religiosity without losing its contact to religion. This historical process of secularisation was indirectly suggested to Judaism by the surrounding occidental culture based on Greek-Roman-Germanic and Christian (Catholic and especially Protestant) roots, leading to the burgher world and Enlightenment. Similarly to the Christian religion, and especially similarly to Protestantism, Judaism is today threatened by dissolution.

### 10.8.3   Christianity

For Christianity, it is important to come back to the differentiation of the beginning: it is necessary to distinguish between the effects of (1) the *original message*, (2) the *religious founder*, (3) the *revised doctrine and its changed understanding across time* and (4) the *lived practice* in the present age. Among Christianity there are three major branches (Catholicism, Orthodoxy, Protestantism), which can not only be distinguished in religious doctrines but also in cultural development, including educational practices and average cognitive ability levels of their members. If anything, these differences cannot be traced back to the Bible or Jesus but to later developed differences in (3) the understanding of the doctrine and (4) the lived practice.

Taking the original message of the New Testament, Christianity is very sceptical if not disapproving of education and intellectuality, with education understood as cognitive-intellectual 'Bildung'.[103] There are many polemics of

---

[101] E.g. apostle Paul, Galatians 3:26-28: 'So in Christ Jesus you are all children of God through faith, for all of you who were baptised into Christ have clothed yourselves with Christ. There is neither Jew nor Gentile, neither slave nor free, nor is there male and female, for you are all one in Christ Jesus.'

[102] Universalism as a utopian concept can modify reality in the direction it implies – that all humans are equal. However, taken as a descriptive concept (empirically and truly describing reality) it is wrong. Finally, universalism can be functionally problematic as a false concept overburdening people and undermining the basics of individuals, families, societies and cultures.

[103] Weber, 1958/1921, p. 371 (footnote 1), in German original: 'Gerade der Gegensatz gegen jedes vornehme Intellektuellentum [war ihm, dem alten Christentum] das grundlegend

Jesus against the scribes, against well-educated, knowledgeable, reputable, somewhat older and burgher-conservative men.[104] Jesus' approach towards truth is based on having direct access to eternal truth and God. Jesus has this exceptional access not via arguments but as son of God, at least as a prophet. The scribes have had an access to truth only via texts, their reading and interpretation. According to original Christianity being unsmart and uneducated is no barrier to Heaven. By contrast, believing, including the absurd, is the way to understanding the truth and to salvation.[105] Rationality is further undermined by reports of miracles. Good Christians have faith in miracles.

Additionally, taking a broader perspective on supporting a sustainable burgher society, the anti-family lifestyle of Jesus – being himself unmarried and having no children – the removal of men out of their families to become disciples and their end as victims by crucifixion and martyrdom is at odds with an enduring, exemplary and realisable way of life.

However, even in the initial Christian message there are elements supportive for a development towards rationality, modernity and burgher society: the New Testament is given in *internal pluralism*: the holy message is presented in four varying versions (four gospels), containing many open parables and accompanied by letters from the apostles. Additionally, there are obvious contradictions between the Old and New Testament. The truth in the Bible is not directly given in each sentence but needs to be *interpreted* and weighted. Further, Old or New Testament are *too long to be learnt by heart*. Memorising the Bible cannot be the way to its truth.[106] Christianity is based on *universalism* and generally on an *ethical standard* positively judged by a human rights

---

Wichtige.' Translated by HR: 'Opposition to genteel intellectuality was fundamentally important to the latter [the early Christianity].'

[104] Some quotes: 'But woe unto you, scribes and Pharisees, hypocrites! because ye shut the kingdom of heaven against men: for ye enter not in yourselves, neither suffer ye them that are entering in to enter. Woe unto you, scribes and Pharisees, hypocrites! for ye devour widows' houses, even while for a pretence ye make long prayers: therefore ye shall receive greater condemnation.' (Matthew 23:13-14) 'For it is written, I will destroy the wisdom of the wise, and will bring to nothing the understanding of the prudent. Where is the wise? where is the scribe? where is the disputer of this world? hath not God made foolish the wisdom of this world? For after that in the wisdom of God the world by wisdom knew not God, it pleased God by the foolishness of preaching to save them that believe.' (Paul 1 Corinthians 1:19-21)

[105] 'Blessed are the poor in spirit: for theirs is the kingdom of heaven.' (Matthew 5:3); 'Knowledge inflates with pride, but love builds up.' Paul (1 Corinthians 8:1); 'sancta simplicitas', Jerome (Hieronymus 347–419); 'credo quia absurdum', Tertullian (ca. 155-220); 'credo ut intelligam', Anselm of Canterbury (1033–1109).

[106] Against memorising the Bible, e.g. the clergyman Henri-Marie Boudon (1624–1702) (Groethuysen, 1968/1927). Later the opposition towards memorising was repeated in enlightenment and neohumanism (Kant, W. v. Humboldt). General opposition towards memorising can be found until today, e.g. in constructivist learning theories or in the theoretical background of the literacy approach applied by PISA.

approach (Mark 12:31): 'You shall love your neighbour as yourself.' And even more radical (Matthew 5:44-45):

Love your enemies and pray for those who persecute you, so that you may be sons of your Father who is in heaven. For he makes his sun rise on the evil and on the good, and sends rain on the just and on the unjust.

The woman has to be treated like the man, the stranger as the friend, the excluded as the included.[107] Peace and restraint, care and love, honesty and equality are highly regarded.[108] This ethical universalism can have a positive impact on cognitive development because the structures of ethical universalism and epistemic rationality are similar.[109] Fundamental for Christianity is the *opposition of world and norm, might and moral*, the *given being of the world and the truth*. Jesus himself was always critical towards political power and ruling classes. Persons in disputes, especially in a minority position, can refer in argumentation to an abstract and general rule. The given state of the world can be criticised on ethical grounds; natural law and truth are valid for all, including the rulers and the dominated. Critique not only includes critique of others but also of oneself by oneself; conscience and penance are essential ideas. This opens space for liberty and separation, for self-regulation and autonomy.

*Catholicism*     Catholicism is an amalgamation of original Christianity with Greek and Roman ideas and their continuous development under local conditions, especially in the European-Romance-Germanic culture. The most important person for the development towards rationalisation and modernisation is Thomas Aquinas. But at first the church father Augustine and other older developments have to be mentioned:

---

[107]  E.g. Christians from Europe fought for the rights of Indians (Bartolomé de Las Casas), for the abolition of slavery of Africans (Blacks) and Quakers supported Jews in the Nazi era. Of course, there are many opposing examples, but war, violence, exploitation and suppression are the standard in history, and explicit resistance against them is the remarkable exception.

Benjamin Nelson (1974, p. 465): 'The hallmark of the West in the twelfth and thirteenth centuries is the crystallization of orientations and institutions which simultaneously rest upon the two-fold commitment to the *concrete individual person* and *objective universal*. The main notion on which the institutions are reared is that individuated persons are the bearers of rights and rationalized universals become the focal points of governing norms. ... Faith pursuing understanding of itself and its new contents, elaborates structures of rationality.'

[108]  One example: In Christian iconography, apostle Paul is depicted with a sword in his hands (e.g. Saint Paul Outside the Walls, Rome). But this sword does not stand for fighting or killing others but for Paul being killed by others with the sword. On Christian universalism, e.g. Meyer, Boli & Thomas (1987, p. 28): 'The key fact is that the spread of Christianity meant the spread of universalist ideology as such – it became not only common but natural to develop theories and ideologies of sweeping, all-encompassing scope.'

[109]  See Piaget or Kohlberg. On the relevance of Christianity for universalism and of universalism for modernity, Jürgen Habermas (Mendieta & Habermas, 1999).

*Augustine* (354–430) was highly contradictory in his views towards education, thinking and epistemic rationality. This contrariness is exemplary for original Christianity. Being himself a well-educated scholar he polemicised in his Confessions against epistemic curiosity and defamed it as *cupiditas* of eyes and mind, as greed for the new and a pathological curiosity for knowledge. Faith and love are more important than knowledge and wit. Naïveté is a way to truth; knowledge and searching for knowledge block this way.[110] The Bible is the authority.

However, he also objected to magic and sorcery overcoming Animism.[111] His fight against rhetoric as a part of education was – similar to Plato – also a struggle for the primacy of the content against the form: it is not the beauty of expression that counts, but the semantic content.[112] Truth is more important than convincing others and truth is also valid independently from consent. Rhetoric has a tendency towards intimidation and authority and distracts from the content. By contrast, argumentation is rational, supporting thinking, and is emancipatory. In this perspective, Augustinian truthfulness was a trailblazer for enlightenment.

The *monastery culture* maintained a culture of scripture in the early Middle Ages and preserved the knowledge of the Ancient World. The religious elite was educated in monastery schools. To become a priest set a high cognitive threshold because not only were reading and writing mandatory but also reading and writing in a foreign language. Several orders, such as the Benedictines, Jesuits or Salesians, later explicitly dealt with education and science. For the Benedictines, the second most important room in a monastery after the church was the library. Bishops argued against ordeals (Agobard, 769–840, Lyon). Others supported universities (cardinal Basilios Bessarion, Bologna). Catholic scholars such as Alcuin influenced, via convincing Charlemagne, education and culture; book writing, an improvement of scripture and the foundation of schools were stimulated. Beginning at this time, Mary's mother Anne and Mary are frequently depicted together with a book, Anne teaching Mary reading. In the Annunciation, angel Gabriel meets Mary while reading a book. Monogamy and Mariolatry brought more equality for women.[113] The Christian idea of humans being the image of God and having

---

[110] Augustine, (1991/400, IV, 16, V, 3, VI, 5). See also Paul 1 Corinthians 8:1: 'Knowledge inflates with pride, but love builds up.'
[111] Augustine (1991/400, X, 35, X, 42), also Civitate Dei, X, 11.
[112] Augustine, (1991/400, I, 18, V, 3, XII, 1). Plato: Gorgias 462Dff., Phaidon 91Aff.
[113] Women have had a more privileged position compared to other cultures, especially in the upper European classes: women were admired in courtly love (German 'Minne', French 'amour courtois') and in the 'Minnedienst', the homage rendered by a knight to his lady. Adelaide (931–999), the wife of emperor Otto (912–973), her second husband, was herself empress, owned land and monasteries, and governed the Holy Roman Empire in times without male sovereign. She could read, spoke several languages and was well educated ('gebildet'). This special European path was supported by Christianity, but not exclusively.

inalienable natural rights helped – relative to the Ancient World – to pacify and humanise society (Frost, 2010). Similarly, the idea of two kingdoms led to a differentiation between the religious (mental) and secular power. Catholic law was a codified law persons could appeal to. Later struggles for the of rule of law could refer to foundations in Catholic appreciation of natural law.

The thirteenth century, with the scholastic philosophy of reason of *Thomas Aquinas*, was the starting point for a long development towards enlightenment and rationality (e.g., Sombart, 1998/1913).[114] Thomas explicitly argued for the use of reason as a way to truth and God. He used an argumentative style in thinking, beginning with a question (*quaestio*), then rising objections (*objectiones*), then confrontation with statements from the bible and by saints (*sed contra*) and finally finding an own answer (*respondeo*). Of course, this was not a fully rational argumentation based on logic, evidence and real open questioning, but it was a step in this direction. A quotation underscores his rational approach:

A sin, in human acts, is that which is against the order of reason. (Second Part of the Second Part, Question 153, 2)

According to Thomas, wisdom comprises memory (memoria), intelligence (intelligentia), inventiveness, reasonable consideration, scholarship, foresight, prudence and cautiousness (Second Part of the Second Part, Questions 49, 53).

In one chapter (First Part of the Second Part, Question 6, Article 8), Thomas dealt with the relationship between knowledge and will. Intended ignorance (*ignorantia affectata*), i.e. knowledge that could be acquired but was intentionally avoided, is not excusable. *Who is able to know has to know!* Even a first glance at the contents of the *Summa Theologica* reveals Thomas' high appreciation of thinking; terms used are e.g. 'intellect', 'knowledge', 'intellectual powers', 'understanding', 'cause and effects', 'causality' or 'truth'.[115]

Thomas' thinking and speaking is fundamentally different from the one of the religious founder, Jesus, who proclaimed the truth via divine mission, being the son of God: "'But I say unto you . . .' (Matthew, 5:22). And Thomas was not alone in his striving for reasoning; the general stream of scholastics did so. To give some names: Anselm of Canterbury (1033–1109), Peter Abelard (1079–1142), Albertus Magnus (1193–1280), Duns Scotus (1266–1308), William of Ockham (1288–1347). There were institutionalised

---

[114] Werner Sombart (1998/1913) has written extensively on Thomas' positive relationship towards reason and thinking (in German 'Der Bourgeois'; in English '*The quintessence of capitalism* '). On argumentation of Thomas see also Jürgen Habermas (Mendieta & Habermas, 1999). According to Elizabeth H. Boyle and John W. Meyer (2002/1998, p. 68), Thomas Aquinas represents the 'celebration of reason'. Le Goff (1993/1957) underscored the relevance of scholastics for the occidental intellectual culture. About the relevance of Thomas and the Catholic Church for enlightenment see also Max Horkheimer (1997/1947).

[115] Source: www.newadvent.org/summa/index.html.

discussions (*'quodlibet'*) with certain argumentative rules (*'sic et non'*) on theological and other issues. It would be wrong to allege that their advocacy for thinking and epistemic rationality was free of inconsistencies, but the later occidental rationalisation process in thinking, ethics and education could be based on Christian-scholastic grounds.[116]

This tradition of education and the supportive but also *contradictory* attitude towards thinking and reason are still maintained to today. The Catholic Church directs schools and universities. Leading clergymen were intellectuals (e.g. Cardinal Ratzinger/Pope Benedict XVI). Modernity emerged in a Catholic country, in Italy. At the same time, 'heretics' were prosecuted. The formal procedure of inquisition was applied to intellectuals. Deviationists were executed. This was not only in contradiction to Jesus and his original message of love and peace but also in contradiction to epistemic rationality.

But what about the – religiously demanded – childlessness of the Catholic intellectual elites? Van Den Haag (1969, p. 15) very clearly described the problem:

Consider how many outstanding scholars (...) descended from married Protestant ministers or Jewish rabbis. Had they, too, been childless, the contributions of their proverbially numerous offspring would have been lost. The magnitude of the contributions of the non-Catholic clergy's actual offspring suggests the size of the loss society suffered because of the celibacy of the Catholic clergy in the many countries during which Catholicism dominated the Western world.

Even without adopting any genetic theory the negative socialisational consequences are obvious. Additionally, the Catholic Church has always known the truth for laymen. There is a paternalistic approach towards the world and thinking, being related to dogmatism: the world requires a paternalistic leadership by authority to come to the right view.

More general positive effects on a burgher world deal with *achievement ethics*: monks have to work, earn their own monastery's and order's life. *Time* was highly regulated and had to be used efficiently (e.g. Benedictines, Cistercians, the Dominican Domenico Cavalca 1270–1342; Le Goff, 1980; Landes, 2006, p. 9).[117] Monks largely lived in a highly self- and external-*disciplined* way.

*Orthodoxy* There is only a little analysis and research on Orthodox Christianity.[118] What is obvious is that in enlightenment, rule of law, economic

---

[116] Meyer & Jepperson (2000, p. 106): 'In effect, Christendom had some modest attainments as a missionary movement, but has achieved vastly greater hegemony in its transformation into science, law, and rationalized education.'

[117] Supported by Paul (2 Thessalonians 3:10): 'If any will not work, neither let him eat.'

[118] In the works of Max Weber and Werner Sombart nothing is written on Orthodox Christianity. Weber has written only some political-historical comments on Russia ('On the Situation of

and political freedom and cultural modernity, even in its fundamental form of non-serfdom, countries with an Orthodox tradition lagged and still lag behind compared to Catholic countries and especially compared to Protestant countries. However, in current education or cognitive ability estimates the differences are small.[119]

Similarly to Protestant churches, Orthodox churches are nationally organised, leading to a closer relation to the state, sometimes in subordination. There was no self-developed Reformation as in Protestant countries and no confrontation with Reformation as in Catholic countries and no confrontation with an autochthonously developed enlightenment or burgher culture as in the West. Orthodox churches are more conservative than Catholic and Protestant churches. Mysticism and spiritualism, liturgy and conformity to rites and rituals were more important in the Orthodoxy; there was less intellectual interpenetration and orientation towards reason:

The former [Orthodoxy] emphasized liturgy and conformity to rites and rituals, as its theologians fine-tuned existing dogma rather than addressing the meaning of Orthodoxy in the light of evolving intellectual thought. By contrast, Catholicism in the late Middle Ages produced outstanding theologians who further developed Christian dogma in the process of addressing the changing social realities of their time. (Pollis, 1993, p. 341f.)

Individualism as catalyser of cultural, political and economic modernisation was weak (Dinello, 1998; 'absence of individualization in Orthodoxy', Pollis, 1993, p. 344). Paternalistic-authoritarian structures remained stable in Orthodoxy, as described by Irakli Chkonia:

Submission to authority, discouragement of dissent and initiative, discouragement of innovation and social change, submissive collectivism rather than individualism, emphasis on ethnic cohesion rather than supranational relationships, isolationism and particularism, spiritual determinism and fatalism. (Chkonia, 2006, p. 354)

Similarly, Nikolas K. Gvosdev, but also including negative effects on thinking:

Highly centralized, vertical traditions of authority; a focus on the past as opposed to the future; an intellectual life characterized by irrationality and fatalism; and the suppression of individual initiative and achievement. (Gvosdev, 2006, p. 204)

However, the impact of Orthodox Christianity is far from unambiguous; for instance, Gvosdev also mentions positive attitudes towards rationality:

Bourgeois Democracy in Russia', 1906), in which he stressed that progress in Russia was positively influenced by the importation of ideas from the West.

[119] The results of traditionally Orthodox countries are only around 2 IQ below Catholic countries in a within First-Second-World comparison (IQ 94 vs. IQ 92); for all countries, including Africa, Latin America and Asia, Orthodox country averages are slightly better than those of Catholic countries (see Table 10.11).

Orthodox anthropology conceives of the human being as a creature possessing free will, personal autonomy, accountability, and the capacity for rational choice. (Gvosdev, 2006, p. 197)

Further positive aspects include the long tradition of scholastic and cultural work by congregations and monasteries. The nineteenth and twentieth centuries saw the development of an impressive intellectual culture in Eastern Europe, including dealing with Christian topics (e.g. Dostoyevsky, Tolstoy) and high-tech (spaceflight).

So why did they, and do they still, lag behind in modernisation? Because the original religious message and the founder are identical (Bible, Jesus) the reasons have to be found in later religious-cultural developments or in other factors beyond culture. This is further proof for the claim that it is important to distinguish between the original message and its development. Among causes frequently mentioned are the Mongol raids in the thirteenth to fifteenth centuries having destroyed an independent burgher-civic society and cultural endeavour. In the southern Orthodox regions, a similar effect can be attributed to the Ottomans. But in western parts of Europe there had been a war or plague more or less in every generation. In the Italian twelfth to sixteenth centuries – an age of cultural ascendancy – military conflicts were standard, similarly in ancient Greece. More important is that Orthodox churches and countries were lacking a cognitive elite of independent scholars transforming the initial message. This includes a large number of East European Jews living in very Orthodox and conservative ways until the nineteenth century. They gave no intellectual stimulation. There were no independent cities and there was only a weak burgher culture. There was no rivalry between church, state, congregations and local centres of accomplishment.

Finally, the question was put wrongly. It is not 'why did Orthodox regions lag?' that should be asked but 'why were Catholic and Protestant regions more forward?' Enlightenment, rule of law, liberty and democracy are anomalies, not the opposite. Russia was not backwards but the West was ahead and moved on from the global stasis of history. *Backwardness is normal; progress is exceptional.* That is the unique development and the intellectual challenge.

*Protestantism*   Protestantism is the first religion founded by a *university professor*, Dr Martin Luther (1483–1546). Luther was not only a theologian but also a philologist capable of reading and understanding several languages. Additionally, he is a *prototype of an intellectual*: strict orientation towards the word and rules (*sola scriptura*) and thinking (hermeneutics) going along with disregard of power, institutions and mere tradition. Any assurance is based on the fundaments of scripture, reading, thinking and the confidence of his own reasoning. Luther was not alone; he was surrounded and supported by exceptional intellectuals of his time, such as Philipp Melanchthon (1497–1560), a gifted theologian and humanist, Martin Bucer (1491–1551), theologian and university professor in Cambridge, or Sebastian Franck (1499–1543), theologian and author.

Within Protestantism there are different movements and churches. They all connect in the idea that a Christian has to interpret the Christian message individually, so as to conduct life in the correct way. A person has to *read* and *understand* the Bible personally and *apply* its message. For this purpose, *education* is necessary. The development towards an *autonomously thinking individual* is both a result of Protestantism and supportive for Protestantism. Over and above, the transformed religious message urged being *diligent*, *conscientious*, *orderly* and *achievement-oriented*, all supporting cognitive development, rationality and the rise of a burgher society. Autonomy and liberty are based on the *ability of self-regulation. Bildung* helps to acquire them. E.g. Georg Wilhelm Friedrich Hegel:

This is the essence of the Reformation: Man is in his very nature destined to be free . . . Luther repudiated that authority [of the church], and set up in its stead the Bible and the testimony of the Human Spirit. (Hegel, 2001/1837, p. 436)

The third point of sanctity in the Catholic Church – blind obedience, was likewise denuded of its false pretensions . . . Man himself has a conscience; consequently the subjection required of him is a free allegiance. This involves the possibility of a development of Reason and Freedom, and of their introduction into human relations; and Reason and the Divine commands are now synonymous. The Rational no longer meets with contradiction on the part of the religious conscience; it is permitted to develop itself in its own sphere without disturbance, without being compelled to resort to force in defending itself against an adverse power. (Hegel, 2001/1837, p. 442)

Max Weber (2001/1905) and Werner Sombart (1998/1913) dealt a lot with the Protestant-Puritan idea of predestination, meaning that to be chosen by God is indicated by having success in everyday life. Although to be chosen or not is only decided by God and cannot be achieved by one's own endeavour, it should have stimulated Protestants to be achievement-oriented. Whether this is true or not, if we take only the reading motif leading to education as *Bildung* and all that is connected to it (diligence, discipline and self-discipline, order, individualism), it is enough to explain the, on average, higher educational and cognitive ability level of Protestants. Even a *hard work ethic* alone supports education, as it leads within an academic context to higher competences and in several cases to high accomplishment.[120]

---

[120] E.g. 'Idleness is indeed the nursery of sins', in the chapter 'Of Industry in General' (Isaac Barrow; 1630–1677, mathematician, teacher of Isaac Newton, 1642–1726). In the Ancient World (in Rome and Greece, somewhat still today in the Mediterranean world, in the Catholic, Orthodox and Muslim region) work was viewed as being dishonourable for a free man.

Moreover the repudiation of work no longer earned the reputation of sanctity; it was acknowledged to be more commendable for men to rise from a state of dependence by activity, intelligence, and industry, and make themselves independent. It is more consonant with justice that he who has money should spend it even in luxuries, than that he should give it away to idlers and beggars ... Industry, crafts and trades now have their moral validity recognized. (Hegel, 1999/1821, p. 442)

Over and above, a hard work ethic supports success in any job domain, leading to higher economic productivity and wealth. Education, cognitive ability, hard work ethic, strictness in education, frugality, integrity, trustworthiness, moderateness, rationality and discipline were all initially religious virtues but as a consequence made possible a development towards Capitalism or, on a broader interpretation, the burgher society and modernity (Sombart, 1998/1913; Weber, 2001/1905). This view is supported by the historian Margaret Jacob, who sees the important rout of British industrialisation in religious motives that were applied for secular aims:

James Watt, who invented the modern steam engine, brought to his workshop his religiously inspired habits of disciplined work and the profit motive. (Jacob, 1997, p. 3)

They needed to assimilate applied scientific knowledge along with business skills and the Protestant values of disciplined labor and probity. (Jacob, 1997, p. 114)

Protestants needed to *learn to read* because every Christian has to read and understand the holy message. There should be no mediation between Christian and God by an institution or a third person. Requiring a personal relationship to God and having an own conscience based on individual reading of the scripture implies not only having the possibility and capability of literacy but also of *freedom*.[121] It is not possible to demand personal faith and individual understanding of the Bible without allowing others also the same right to their own understanding. The same is true for thinking: it is not possible to demand thinking for oneself without allowing it for others.

Education is based on the demand of *autonomy of a person*. Autonomy (intertwined with individualism) again is the individual aspect of cultural and social *liberty*. Autonomy is not given without liberty and liberty not without autonomy. Autonomy again is individually based on the ability of self-regulation and *self-control*. Life and conduct do not depend on an external authority, but on internal control. For this, *self-discipline* is necessary. *Discipline, order, systematology, obligation* and *duty* mean in Protestantism to practise a godly lifestyle. Finally, there is a tightening of traditional Christian

---

[121] E.g. Luther's treatise from 1520 'De libertate christiana ('On the Freedom of a Christian' or 'A Treatise on Christian Liberty').

ethics, especially in the treatment of others: it is a *non-dualistic ethic*; all persons have to be treated equally:

> In the writings of the Quakers and Baptists ... we find jubilation over the fact that the Godless deposit or invest their money not with their own ilk but with the pious brethren, whose notorious honesty and reliability appear as more valuable than a security; they also note that the clientele of their retail stores is growing since the Godless know that even their children and servants will be charged nothing but the fixed and fair price and will receive only priceworthy goods. (Weber, 1978/1922, pp. 1205f.)

This all should have a *positive impact on education and cognitive ability*, on developing *rationality and epistemic rationality*, including philosophy and science, and on *developing a burgher world*: rule of law and interpersonal trust, political and economic liberty, democracy and equality, industry and wealth, progress and care for others, functionality of institutions and economic productivity.

## Research on Effects of Protestantism

Several sociologists, including Weber, Sombart and Durkheim, observed the strong emphasis of Protestants on education. Emile Durkheim estimated it as being the basis for scientific research and critique.

> 'The desire for learning must be stronger among Protestants than among Catholics.' 'The taste for free inquiry can be aroused only if accompanied by that for learning.' (Durkheim, 1951/1897, p. 162)

Max Weber (2001/1905, chapter 1, footnote 8, p. 189) mentioned a higher educational level of Protestant students in *Germany* (see sub-section on Judaism). This is supported at the German regional level – regions with higher percentages of Protestants had a higher educational level on average in the nineteenth century and were economically better developed, leading to higher wealth (Becker & Woessmann, 2009). Becker and Woessmann (2007, p. 29) even showed that Catholics in predominantly Protestant counties in Germany had a higher literacy level than in predominantly Catholic counties – they profited in their educational level from Protestants. And reading not only meant reading, but 'reading, understanding, and knowing the Word, including its exegetical comprehension' (Becker & Woessmann, 2009, p. 542).

Further support is given from different authors for different countries and historical epochs:

*United States, nineteenth century*; Protestantism generally supported education, also among slaves:

> The U.S. may have been more inclined to invest in public education because of the religious views that were more prevalent in the English colonies. Proponents of the idea that religious faith was an important, if not critical, element of the early history ...

typically cite the example of seventeenth-century New England, where the organization of primary schools was often rationalized as necessary for ensuring that all members of the population were able to read the Bible. (Black & Sokoloff, 2006, p. 74)

For many slaves, the economic returns may have been secondary to the religious returns associated with the ability to read the Bible. (Collins & Margo, 2006, p. 118)

*Switzerland, around year 2000*: Students applying to study medicine from predominantly Protestant cantons achieved better results in the cognitive selection test than students from predominantly Catholic cantons (average IQs 100.46 IQ vs. 98.56 IQ; Steppan, 2010).

*Netherlands, around year 1960*: Protestants achieved higher IQs in the GIT (Groningen Intelligentie Test) than Catholics (average IQs 101.16 IQ vs. 97.95 IQ; Steppan, 2010).

*Europe, first decade of the twenty-first century*: Within Europe, predominantly Protestant countries achieved higher averages in student assessment and psychometric IQ tests than Catholic countries ($d = 0.52$, equivalent IQ 100 and 92 or SASQ 500 and 448; Steppan, 2010).

*Internationally, recent decades*: A higher proportion of Protestants in a country is positively correlated with education and cognitive ability of its adults and students (Table 10.11, $r = .19$-.40). The number of books at home, in particular, is highly correlated with Protestant shares ($r = .60$-.62).

*United States, twentieth century*: According to Zuckerman (1996/1977), compared to their population share (66 per cent vs. 25 per cent) many more US Protestants (72 per cent) than Catholics (1 per cent) are among Nobel Prize winners (see also Merton, 1936).

*United States, twentieth century*: Members of the big Protestant churches have a higher average IQ (107–113) than Catholics (IQ 107) (Nyborg, 2009).[122]

Two final remarks: of course, a mixed genetic-cultural impact cannot be excluded. Similarly to the Jews, the religious elites had their own families and children in social and genetic exchange with other leading groups (e.g. merchants). A vast amount of important intellectuals descended from parsonages.[123]

---

[122] Nyborg (2009) chose for better comparability only Whites. Different religions compared, the typical pattern emerged (Jews at 112, Protestant Christians at 109, Catholic Christians at 107, Muslims at 105). Atheists and Agnostics at IQ 110. However, members of more dogmatic Protestant churches such as Holiness or Pentecostal showed lower IQs (around 103).

[123] Examples for intellectuals being descended from parsonages in German-speaking countries: Georg Philipp Telemann (composer, 1681–1767), Johann Christoph Gottsched (author, 1700–1766), Leonhard Euler (mathematician, 1707–1783), Gotthold Ephraim Lessing (author, 1729–1781), Christoph Martin Wieland (author, 1733–1813), Matthias Claudius (author, 1740–1815), Georg Christoph Lichtenberg (mathematician, physicist and author, 1742–1799), brothers August Wilhelm and Friedrich Schlegel (philologists and philosophers, 1767–1845, 1772–1829), Friedrich Schleiermacher (theologian and scholar, 1768–1834), Gustav Fechner (psychophysics,

Of course, it is not baptism itself that has had any positive effect on education, cognitive ability and technological, economic, political and cultural modernisation. Only certain forms of Protestantism have a positive impact via their impact on conducting one's life. Very different to the classical form is post-modern Protestantism, e.g. in Germany and Sweden or Pentecostal churches in developing countries of Africa and South America.

## Secularisation and Protestant Dissolution

Today in many traditional Protestant countries there is a tendency towards petering out of Protestantism and its behavioural impacts, ending in self-dissolution and a calm egalitarian social-humanitarian worldview. For Eric Kaufmann (2004), dissolution in a general egalitarian-humanitarian orientation is a logical possibility of the Protestant doctrine. Some examples from Germany:

In Wittenberg, the Martin-Luther house is usually empty; there are no or only a few visitors.[124] Regular Sunday church services in Sachsen-Anhalt, the homeland of Luther, are attended by around 15 persons (*Aschersleben*).[125] Churches built for hundreds of worshippers are only occupied in one corner. Pastors and their religious messages are characterised by a zeitgeist-left-wing worldviewand not conversely: E.g. a pastor of Martin Luther's Wittenberg church, Friedrich Schorlemmer, is a member of the Social Democratic Party (SPD), as are the former and present presidents of the German Protestant church, Wolfgang Huber and Heinrich Bedford-Strohm.[126] Leading SPD and Green party members work in and for the church.[127] In 2013, Irmgard Schwaetzer (left-wing member of liberal FDP) was voted as the president of the Protestant lay organisation EKD. She is twice divorced and has no children. She won the election against Dr Günther Beckstein (member of right-wing Christian Social Union, CSU), who is married and has three children. Beckstein has also fallen into disrepute because he has called for more piety in the Protestant church.

---

1801–1887), Friedrich Nietzsche (philosopher, 1844–1900), Albert Schweitzer (physician and theologian, 1875–1965), Carl Gustav Jung (psychiatrist, 1875–1961), Hermann Hesse (author, 1877–1962), Gottfried Benn (author, 1886–1956), Karl Barth (theologian, 1886–1968), Paul Tillich (theologian, 1886–1965).

Some examples for other countries: Pierre Bayle (French Enlightenment philosopher, 1647–1706), Jane Austen (British author, 1775–1817), Ralph Waldo Emerson (American author, 1803–1882), Vincent van Gogh (Dutch artist, 1853–1890), Alfred North Whitehead (British mathematician and philosopher, 1861–1947), Martin Luther King (US pastor and civil rights activist, 1929–1968), Margaret Thatcher (British stateswoman, 1925–2013, father lay preacher).

[124] February 2011, during two hours on Sunday, four other visitors; the majority of visitors were Catholics.

[125] Sunday morning, July 2014.

[126] Prof Dr Wolfgang Huber, SPD, former president of the German Protestant church, is the son of Prof Dr Ernst Rudolf Huber, former NSDAP member and important NSDAP jurist. Zeitgeist is adaptive.

[127] Manfred Stolpe, Steffen Reiche, Johannes Rau, Reinhard Höppner, Katrin Göring-Eckardt.

Irmgard Schwaetzer was preceded by the Green party politician Katrin Göring-Eckardt, who is a university drop-out having separated herself from her husband, a priest, and being now the partner of another divorced priest. The church favours degendered toilets, gay marriage, Muslim immigration and leniency towards criminals. An edition of the Bible is rewritten in gender-sensible language. Strict rules for behaviour are given up and replaced by soft and lax orientations, e.g. the former president of the German Protestant church, Margot Käßmann, is divorced and was caught drink-driving and crossing red traffic lights. Today, among leading church lay persons, Catholics have more children and higher education than Protestants.[128] But it would be wrong to claim that the dissolution has only affected Protestantism – it is just that dissolution is stronger within conventional Protestantism than in other Christian denominations.

Why has this development happened? Religion and epistemic rationality inherently are at odds. A religion furthering epistemic rationality up to its intrinsic end will end in self-dissolution. It always needs a further element based on revelation. The original idea of predestination – that election to salvation is identifiable by success having stimulated education and achievement to reach this success but one's own endeavour cannot lead to salvation – is quite absurd. Once understood and this understanding is enabled by education, intelligence and rationality, the suspense is gone. Based on some of its own premises, but neglecting others, Protestantism runs inevitably into aporias. Leniency, humanitarianism and charity without strictness, requirement of autonomy and expectation of a personality similar to the benefactor will lead to overload and dissolution of leniency, humanitarianism and charity. Individualism and freedom without strong and strict ethical orientations end in *anything goes*.

### The Development of a Protestant Student Dorm in Heidelberg

A final example may illustrate the general trend: the author studied in the late 1980s and early 1990s in Heidelberg and lived there in a Protestant *student* dorm. The dorm was established in 1914 by a Protestant teacher and was dedicated by him to support 'Protestant philologists and theologians'. The 'condition of admission was that students practised a religious moral and ecclesiastical attitude'. This should lead to a 'familiar and Christian atmosphere'. In its beginning it was a 'real community on conscious-evangelic ground'; there were daily devotions in the morning and evening.[129]

---

[128] Protestant lay organisation EKD, Catholic lay organisation ZDK. From 1972–2010. 25 per cent of EKD presidents have had a PhD, but 75 per cent of Catholic ZDK presidents. No Protestant EKD presidents were university professors, but 50 per cent of ZDK presidents were. EKD presidents had on average 2.7 children, ZDK presidents 3.5 children.

[129] Translated by the author, sources:
   www.keller-thoma.de/wohnheimsgeschichte.pdf, p. 5, p. 19.
   www.keller-thoma.de/hausgeschichte_auflage_1.pdf, p. 11.

However, this was all given up in the late 1960s and early 1970s. Not only Protestant theologians or not only Protestant students or not only Christian students or not only students with a moral attitude could live there, but any university student. There was no requirement on any Christian-religious confession. Students were admitted according to criteria of need and diversity, nationally and internationally.

One consequence was that the old system based on voluntary student services for the dormitory lost support and needed to be transformed to a token system. Anyone who participated in voluntary work could reside in the cheap student dorm for longer (cheap due to the initial donation of the founder and the support of the church), being surrounded by the expensive housing market of Heidelberg. Token economies work everywhere, even including higher animals, but they are not all based on Protestantism, which is based on internal principles, conviction, faith and sense of duty.

Another consequence were problems with the accessible dormitory telephone: there was a regular telephone for all residents. There was no barrier; everybody could use the phone and make calls to all parts of the world. There was a counter and a paper-pencil notebook in which callers have to note the counter reading before and after their call, the used units, the date and time and their name. However, frequently callers 'forgot' to note units, or even entire notebooks with all noted calls disappeared – they were stolen. In response, the administration of the dorm made appeals to all residents to write down their units and simultaneously the price per unit was raised to cover the unpaid costs. So the honest callers paid for the dishonest ones. Because the units became so expensive more and more payers started to use the public phone boxes outside the dormitory (in the 1980s and early 1990s mobiles were not common and too expensive; smart phones did not exist). Finally, a coin-box telephone was installed inside the dormitory. A system based on trust and conscientiousness only works with people who are trustworthy and conscientious and who are bound to the worldview behind these attitudes. Because all were admitted, the internal institutions had to be adapted. The former internal behavioural control did not work anymore, and was replaced by external control in the form of a machine. With the outside world entering the institution, so did the same controls that worked on the outside.

However, the administration of the Protestant student dorm did not only violate the wish of the founder of the dorm by admitting students not studying Protestant theology (to become a pastor or religious education teacher) and by admitting even non-Protestant and non-Christian students, but the administration also refused to perceive what happened inside the dorm due to its own politics. To perceive and understand what happened would have meant needing to change their optimistic-egalitarian conception of humanity. They would consider a modification to a more realistic conception of humans as a non-Christian, non-humanitarian, prejudiced and 'bad' and thus 'wrong' perspective.

They not only eliminated the old Protestant dorm by their politics but also introduced a distorted view on humans and reality, excluding other views as being morally secondary and by this stabilised their cognitive-institutional system. Only the final economic pressures led to a correction of their administrative behaviour, ending in a conventional-realistic solution, but not in a 'familiar and Christian atmosphere'.

### 10.8.4   Islam

*Education and Cognitive Autonomy*   In the Koran (Quran), a frequently cited Sura regarding education exists:

Read, and your Lord is the most generous, who taught by the pen, taught man what he did not know. (Sura 94, 3-5).[130]

This is much more supportive for education, knowledge acquisition and thinking than anything taught by Jesus with his well-known polemics against the scribes or, more generally, taught by Judaism with its initial parable of the negative effects of eating from the tree of the knowledge.[131] Additionally, Islam follows a strong anti-magic approach and bans pictures supporting abstract thinking.

However, this is not the full story. A closer look is necessary (a) for understanding the *meaning of the term 'read'*, (b) *what else is said in the Koran*, (c) *what else is said and done by the religious founder*, Muhammad, and (d) what since then has occurred as *interpreted and revised doctrine and its changing understanding across time* and *lived practice*. Indirect effects of religious messages on ability, e.g. via shaping personality and behaviour, have to be included. To substantiate any conclusion, a broad collection of quotes and ample empirical evidence are necessary.

Let us start with the Sura 94, 3–5 cited at the beginning. 'Read' is here better interpreted as 'recite', meaning saying by heart, declaiming and repeating:

Recite in the name of your Lord who created ... (Sura 96, 1)

Reading in this context does not refer to literacy or understanding but to repeating of a given message with a voice. Accordingly, learning Arabic and the content of the Koran in Koran schools is practised as rote learning of the given single truth without autonomous thinking and questioning (Uslucan,

---

[130] http://al-quran.info/#96:3.
[131] 'But from the tree of the knowledge of good and evil you shall not eat, for in the day that you eat from it you will surely die.' (Genesis 2:17)

2007). This is different to the practice of reading, understanding and discussing holy texts in other religions. It is also different to the concept of literacy as intended by PISA. In line with this, 'Hafiz' are highly respected persons who are able to completely memorise the Koran. The Koran is usually recited in sprechgesang, a recitative following traditional rules of intonation. The Koran is not interpreted.

Non-Arabic Muslim children learn to read the Koran in their religious education, but this learning amounts to nothing more than reading and does not cover understanding and interpretation. They were taught a word-for-word reproduction of Koran suras, the phonetically correct reproduction is the aim. From the perspective of learning and education theory this way of learning is a very superficial, failure-prone and for everyday life problems not serviceable method. There is no deep learning, no independent cognitive elaboration and semantic penetration of content. ... Rote learning and word-for-word knowledge of Koran suras is a requirement of religious practice, intellectual investigation is secondary. According to the self-understanding of Islam humans are not entitled to question and personally interpret Allah and its word, the Koran. (Uslucan, 2007, p. 3; translated by the author)

The Koran is the verbatim word of God transmitted by his final prophet Muhammad. It is a holy text and the relationship between God and person and Koran and person is a decidedly *authoritarian, commanding* one. Convergently, 'Islam' means 'devotion' but also 'subjugation' and 'submission to God'; 'Mosque' means 'to bow down in prayer':

O you who have believed, obey Allah and obey the Messenger and those in authority among you. And if you disagree over anything, refer it to Allah and the Messenger, if you should believe in Allah and the Last Day. That is the best [way] and best in result. (Sura 4:59)

This authoritarian, not discursive and not deliberated aspect is characteristic for Koran and distinguishes it from other religions, especially from Protestantism. Muslims shall not discuss the content of the Koran.

Allah Knows, while you know not. (Sura 2:216)

And when you see those who engage in discourse concerning Our verses, then turn away from them until they enter into another conversion. (Sura 6:68)

The only statement of the [true] believers when they are called to Allah and His Messenger to judge between them is that they say, 'We hear and we obey.' (Sura 24:51)

Additionally, Arabic was seen as a sacral language dedicated to the Koran, to religion and worship, resulting in an opposition to writing and printing (Diner, 2009/2005). This forms one part of a more general 'Muslim hostility to learning' (Landes, 1998, p. 54). As late as 1729, the first book was printed in Arabic. There was and is (in more radical movements of Islam) opposition against education for girls. All this has implications until today: according to the Arab Human Development Report 'curricula taught in Arab countries seem to encourage submission, obedience, subordination and compliance' (UNDP, 2003, p. 53). In families, the most widespread style of child rearing is an authoritarian mode affecting by 'suppressing questioning, exploration and initiative' children's thinking and its development (UNDP, 2003, p. 3).

As shown in Table 10.11, Islam and number of books at home are negatively correlated (correlations at around $r = -.50$); in predominantly Muslim countries families have on average only 32 books at home, but in predominantly Christian countries 73 books, in Jewish 87 and Protestant 113. However, at the individual and at the national level number of books are important family characteristics as the measure is correlated to children's intelligence ($r_{ind} = .25$, Section 3.4.5; $r_{nat} = .70$, Table 10.5). This indicates an indirect negative impact of Islam on cognitive ability.

Additionally, book production and book reception are very poor and focused on religion:

In 1991, Arab countries produced 6,500 books compared to 102,000 books in North America, and 42,000 in Latin America and the Caribbean. Book production, including literary production, in Arab countries is evidently far from vigorous in comparison to the size of the population and with other countries. . . . In general, Arab book production centres mainly on religious topics and less on other fields such as literature, art and the social sciences. . . . Would literate Arab citizens who can afford to buy some books for themselves and their families purchase literature to read in their leisure time? There are no accurate statistics on the types of books preferred by Arab readers, but according to many publishers and observers, the bestsellers at the Cairo International Book Fair are religious books, followed by books categorised as educational. This observation reflects on the educational process itself. Issues such as the almost total absence of reading classes in schools, apparently the result of 'not having enough time to teach the basic curricula', and neglect of the modern Arab literary heritage should give knowledge advocates food for thought. (UNDP, 2003, pp. 77f.).

Finally, Arabic language itself is an obstacle: many terms comprising science and modern lifestyle are missing. Usually, Arabic script does not use vowels, making reading complicated. A word has to be known before it is possible to read it.[132]

> *Impact on Political Environment: Human Rights, Rule of Law, Gender Equality, Liberty and Peaceableness*   The Koran gives advice on how

---

[132] However, the same problem of difficult readability is given for Hebrew and Chinese without having noticeable negative consequences. In particular variants of Arabic script, vowels are added.

to treat people in many places. There are very positive Suras from a human rights perspective:

If you should raise your hand against me to kill me – I shall not raise my hand against you to kill you. (Sura 5:28)

We decreed upon the Children of Israel that whoever kills a soul unless for a soul or for corruption [done] in the land – it is as if he had slain mankind entirely. And whoever saves one – it is as if he had saved mankind entirely. (Sura 5:32)

Ethically praiseworthy, but the message of Sura 5:32 is addressed to Jews ('Children of Israel') and the very next verse (Sura 5:33) addressed to Muslims deals with the crucifixion of enemies of Muslims and the cutting of hands and feet:

Indeed, the penalty for those who wage war against Allah and His Messenger and strive upon earth [to cause] corruption is none but that they be killed or crucified or that their hands and feet be cut off from opposite sides or that they be exiled from the land. (Sura 5:33)

This is not only contradictory but one such single sentence shatters all other positive ones: a person who has killed in his life only once – he is a killer. And this is not the only outlier sentence. The Koran deals in too many places with *suppressive and violent treatment of people*, including Muslim women, Arabs that are not Muslims, and generally of members of other religions. Some quotes from the Koran:

- On *women*: 'Men are in charge of women by [right of] what Allah has given one over the other and what they spend [for maintenance] from their wealth. So righteous women are devoutly obedient, guarding in [the husband's] absence what Allah would have them guard. But those [wives] from whom you fear arrogance – [first] advise them; [then if they persist], forsake them in bed; and [finally], strike them. But if they obey you [once more], seek no means against them. Indeed, Allah is ever Exalted and Grand.' (Sura 4:34)
- On the *treatment of disbelievers*: 'And when the sacred months have passed, then kill the polytheists wherever you find them and capture them and besiege them and sit in wait for them at every place of ambush.' (Sura 9:5) 'Wherever you may be, death will overtake you, even if you should be within towers of lofty construction.' (Sura 4:78) 'And kill them wherever you overtake them and expel them from wherever they have expelled you, and fitnah [apostasy] is worse than killing. And do not fight them at al-Masjid al-Haram until they fight you there. But if they fight you, then kill them. Such is the recompense of the disbelievers.' (Sura 2:191) 'So when you meet those who disbelieve [in battle], strike [their] necks [meaning behead them] until, when you have inflicted slaughter upon them, then secure their bonds, and either [confer] favor afterwards or ransom [them] until the war lays down its burdens. That [is the command].' (Sura 47:4)

- *Ethical dualism*: 'Muhammad is the Messenger of Allah; and those with him are forceful against the disbelievers, merciful among themselves.' (Sura 48:29)
- On *Jews*: 'O People of the Scripture: ... Say, "Shall I inform you of [what is] worse than that as penalty from Allah? [It is that of] those whom Allah has cursed and with whom He became angry and made of them apes and pigs and slaves of Taghut."' (Sura 5:59-60)
- *Robber economy*: 'Allah has promised you much booty that you will take [in the future] and has hastened for you this [victory] and withheld the hands of people from you – that it may be a sign for the believers and [that] He may guide you to a straight path.' (Sura 48:20)

While early Christianity is also full of violence, it is violence suffered by martyrs (e.g. Jesus, Peter, Paul, Catherine of Alexandria); Islam's original message and role model of the religious founder favours the active practice of violence.[133] This also includes cruel punishments such as stoning, recommended by the founder (Hadith), killing, such as beheading of prisoners of war (Jews of Banu Qurayza) or of a poet (Kab ibn al-Ashraf), enslavement (wives and children of Banu Qurayza Jews were sold as slaves), approval of 'marrying' women captured in war and of behaviour that today is called by law as illegal.[134]

### The Indirect Significance of Violence for Cognitive Ability, Burgher Society and Modernisation

But does violence have any impact? Is it not 'merely' an ethical problem? No, a modern burgher-civic society is built upon the rule of law, upon peace, economic and political liberty and upon democratic participation of autonomous individuals having equal rights. Respect for human rights is fundamental. Political structure is built on violence control and the way it is done is indicative of the historical development status of a society (North, Wallis & Weingast, 2009). At the behavioural level, higher impulse control is an indicator of the civilisation process (Elias, 2000/1939). Both the

---

[133] The violence aspect was noticed early on, e.g. by Enlightenment philosophers Voltaire (his drama from 1736 'Fanaticism, or Mahomet the Prophet') or Montesquieu, e.g. in the The Spirit of the Laws: 'It is a misfortune for human nature when religion is given by a conqueror. The Mohammedan religion, which speaks only with a sword, continues to act on men with the destructive spirit that founded it.' (1989/1748, p. 462)

[134] Aisha, married by Muhammad at six years of age, consummated at age nine.
Sources Hadith, e.g. Sahih al-Bukhari, 7:63:196, Volume 7, Book 63, Number 196, 'The Prophet then said (to his companions), "Go and stone him to death."' Muhammad ordered the stoning of an adulterous woman (but not of the man; Hadith 885, Book 50, Vol. 3), while Jesus – against the old Jewish law – using a smart rhetorical question ('Let any one of you who is without sin be the first to throw a stone at her') saved the life of a woman condemned to death by stoning (John 8:3–11).

institutional-political and the psychological-sociological approach estimate control of violence as indicative of modernisation.

Empirically, at the international level cognitive ability and murder rates are correlated at $r = -.48$ (Section 4.4.2), at the individual level intelligence and crime at $r = -.23$ (Section 7.1). From the perspective of a cognitive human capital approach any relationship between cognitive ability and violence poses a 'theoretical question': does violence negatively affect cognitive development at the individual and societal level or is it a consequence of low cognitive development as postulated by the Piagetian approach? Or are there any background factors influencing both, e.g. religion or local culture? E.g. Arabian culture may influence behaviour, contents of the Koran and an education-ability pattern.

A positive description of violence clearly has a *modelling effect*, leading to an imitation of behaviour. The Koran itself explicitly stresses the *modelling effect* of Muhammad (Sura 33:21):

The Messenger of Allah is an excellent pattern for anyone.

Violence is an *obstacle* for social and cultural *modernisation*. In the past and present, students and teachers were killed in schools for being non-believers, members of another or opposing groups or simply because they are learning and studying something seen as being un-Islamic. E.g. in the 2004 Beslan school siege (Russia) about 350 children and adults were killed, in the 2014 Peshawar school massacre (Pakistan) about 150 children and adults, in the 2015 Garissa University College attack (Kenya) about 150 Christian students and teachers and in Nigeria the Islamic terrorist group Boko Haram (meaning 'books are forbidden' or 'education is a sin') continuously attacks schools, students and teachers.

### The Broader View: Relationship Between Religion, Ethics, Personality, Behaviour and Ability

Even more importantly, there are *broad indirect effects* such as increasing fear, weakening educational-meritoric principles, an impediment of institutions (of schools, universities, research and libraries) which support cognitive development, and a strengthening of life goals opposed to reading, learning, working and thinking.

Empirical studies have shown that violence has *negative effects on short- and long-term cognitive development, resulting in lower IQs*: according to Delaney-Black et al. (2002) an exposure to violence (e.g. 'I have seen somebody get stabbed'; 'Grown-ups in my home hit each other') leads after controlling for confounders to a decrement in cognitive ability of $-7$ to $-10$ IQ points. A twin study controlling for genetic effects documented that domestic violence has a negative environmental effect on intelligence

($\beta = -.19$; Koenen et al., 2003). The more violence, the more severe were the effects up to $-8$ IQ points (see Sections 3.4.5 and 3.4.6). Finally, in a series of natural experiment designs, Patrick Sharkey and colleagues found that the smaller the local and temporal distances to experienced violence were (i.e. 1,000 vs. 2,500 feet; some days vs. some weeks), the more serious were the effects of violence on cognitive functioning and measured intelligence (Sharkey, 2010; Sharkey et al., 2012). *Peace makes smart, violence dumb!*

The lack of equal rights for women in Islam also results in a lower educational level of women and this leads to lower educational competence of mothers, which is unhelpful for their children: 'Uneducated women are transmitters of orthodoxy to their children.' (Harrison, 2013, p. 129).[135] Additionally, violence and submission are both *indicators* of an authoritarian, unfree attitude antagonistic to thinking. The Koran contains all knowledge – further individual thinking or institutional research are not needed. As two scholars described:

For centuries it [Islam] had held back the development of independent thought through subjecting people to religious dogma and rigid behavioural standards. (Luria, 1976/ 1974, p. 14)

Muslim doctors were rereading the selfsame books and turning in hopeless circles. ... The quest for truth is cleansing and invigorating, it keeps the mind alert and keen. On the contrary, the fear of novelty weakens the mind, and sterilizes it. If one be afraid to think for oneself, one soon becomes unable to think at all. (Sarton, 1956, p. 321)

Hard evidence for religious effects could provide a sample equal in other aspects such as language and ethnicity but differing in religion. The example of Roma in Serbia fits this pattern. Among them, Muslim Roma compared to Roma with Orthodox Christian faith generally show a more premodern and less development-supporting lifestyle: Muslim Roma have less school education ($M = 5.4$ vs. 7.3 years, $d = 1.17$); their children are breastfed for shorter periods (Cvorovic, 2014, pp. 111ff.). Girls marry at a younger age; the payment of a bride price is customary; marriages are usually arranged; Muslim Roma have more children and higher infant mortality. Sixty-two per cent of Muslim Roma have lost a child but the figure is 38 per cent for Orthodox Roma. In a common regression with parental education and income, religion was the most important predictor for infant mortality (pp. 114–117).

---

[135] Reverse effects cannot be excluded for a link between Islam and cognitive ability: Templer (2010) speculated that persons with lower intelligence may be more attracted to a religion characterised by authoritarian teaching, rote memorisation, simplicity of dogma and a high degree of certainty than to a religion with more abstract principles and critical thinking. This is in line with the general view that intelligence has an effect on religion (for United States: Nyborg, 2009; from the Piagetian approach e.g. Oesterdiekhoff, 2007).

At the cross-country level, Islam and political indicators seen as positive and modern are negatively correlated, such as rule of law, democracy, political freedom and low-corruption (around $r = -.43$; Table 10.12). Islam and enlightenment ($r = -.16$) and Islam and education and cognitive ability are also negatively correlated (around $r = -.42$; Table 10.11). In a wider range, indicators representing social and political functionality are similarly negatively correlated with Islam (trust, economic freedom, government effectiveness, around $r = -.21$; Table 10.12). The Turkish-American economist Timur Kuran has described such institutional problems:

It bears emphasizing that organizational capacity affected both technological creativity and the ability to exploit foreign technologies. Just as Middle Eastern schooling patterns affected the region's scientific and technological progress, so its organization of production shaped incentives for technological change and intellectual activity generally. Hence, the region's organizational history is among the factors responsible for its current knowledge deficit. (Kuran, 2012, p. 16)

Islam is a total institution not distinguishing between power and religion (Lewis, 2010). Muhammad was not only a religious founder, but also a military leader. Monasteries as largely independent spiritual-intellectual centres were not developed. However, a pure institutional perspective is too narrow. As the intellectual, education researcher and Marxist Hartmut Krauss described with Voltarian stridency, the message of *Islam* itself affects economy, culture and thinking:

The Islam superiority complex and the resulting will to dominate promote an orientation towards a kleptocratic-parasitical robbery, looting and tribute-blackmail economy instead of a productive-creative business activity and culture of knowledge guided by reason. I.e. the normative canon of Islam is focused on the fixation of an aristocratic-clientelistic sovereign culture with its characteristic premodern-medieval relationship of dependency, distribution principles, enrichment methods, moral concepts and code of honour. (Krauss, 2014)[136]

Coming back to the violence impact, is there any evidence for *modelling effects* by religion? Before showing empirical evidence it has to be stressed that violence is a rare phenomenon, an exception in everybody's life. Usually, the majority of all people across all countries do not use violence and do not appreciate it. But a worldview, an ideology or religion can prepare the ground for an inclination towards a certain behaviour. Is there such evidence?

- *Terror groups* in different parts of the world explicitly refer to Islam such as the Taliban (Afghanistan, Pakistan), Al-Shabaab (Somalia), Boko Haram (Nigeria), Al-Qaeda (initially Arabian countries), ISIS (or IS, Iraq and Syria), al-Nusra (Syria), Abu Sayyaf (Philippines), Caucasus Emirate

---

[136] Translation approved by the author (H. Krauss).

(North Caucasus) and Uyghur terror groups (China). Within Western countries, the higher the percentage of Muslims, the higher is the rate of Islamist terrorism ($r = .59$; Carl, 2016b).

- *Single terrorists* explicitly refer to Islam as Adebolajo and Adebowale (Nigerian-British Muslims, murder of a British man in London, 2013), Alexandre Dhaussy (knife attack against a French man in Paris, 2013), Ismaaiyl Brinsley (murder of two men in New York, 2014) or the Charlie Hebdo shooters (murder of 17 persons in Paris, 2015).

- *States* explicitly based on Islam suppress their own people, violate human rights and use cruel punishments (e.g. Islamic Republic of Iran, Saudi Arabia, Hamas' Gaza Strip).

- *States* explicitly based on Islam are more militarised and more involved in military conflicts and wars. E.g. Huntington (1996, p. 258):

  'The Muslim propensity toward violent conflict . . . The average force ratios and military effort ratios of Muslim countries were roughly twice those of Christian countries . . . Muslim states also have had a high propensity to resort to violence in international crises, employing it to resolve 76 crises out of a total of 142 in which they were involved between 1928 and 1979. . . . When they did use violence, Muslim states used high-intensity violence . . . While Muslim states resorted to violence in 53.5 percent, violence was used by the United Kingdom in only 11.5 percent, by the United States in 17.9 percent, and by the Soviet Union in 28.5 percent of the crises in which they were involved.'

- After criticism of Islam *outrages* explicitly based on religion led to deaths. For instance, the Jyllands-Posten Muhammad cartoons in 2005 resulted in around 300 deaths, and the Regensburg lecture of Pope Benedict XVI 2006 on 'Faith, reason and university' citing a critical comment on Muhammad led to mass protests, riots, attacks on Christians and murder of a nun.

- *Members of other religions*, especially Jews (e.g. Toulouse and Montauban shootings in France 2012 or the torture to death of Ilan Halimi, Paris 2006; e.g. Roth, 2014/2010, p. 410), but also Yazidis and Middle Eastern Christians and even members of other Islamic branches (Sunni vs. Shia) are suppressed, attacked and killed due to belonging to a different religion.

- *Women* in Muslim countries: in many Muslim countries *female circumcision* is practised (e.g. in Egypt, Sudan, Iraq, Somalia and Mali). *Acid violence* against women is more prevalent in Muslim countries (e.g. Pakistan, Bangladesh), but of course is forbidden by law. The more related the country is to Islam, the *fewer rights* women have (e.g. divorce, polygyny, marrying a non-Muslim, testimony, driving cars, having passport).[137]

---

[137] On Women in Islam, e.g. www.clarionproject.org/understanding-islamism/womens-rights-under-sharia. Female circumcision or genital mutilation (FGM) is positively correlated in a cross-country comparison with Islam (share of Muslims of a country, $r = .51$, $N = 29$ countries

- Not based on religious content itself, but related, is *low impulse control* leading to higher violence among Muslims with no instrumentally rational effect.[138] One example is violence in football games;[139] another is fights and attacks due to trivial causes with serious negative consequences not only for the attacked person but for the attacker too.[140] The relation to religion is indirect and is obtained via a promotion of an ideal of masculinity based on pride and physical force which supports the use of violence, via modelling violence itself and via less education towards self-control.

- Low impulse control in an extreme and rare manifestation covers *pathological violence* against one's own wife, own children or relatives.[141] Modelling violence and a similar male role model promote violence. Rare as violence is,

with UNICEF data, http://data.unicef.org/resources/fgmc-country-profiles), but negatively with Christianity ($r = -.42$, $N = 29$). Astonishingly, FGM is also negatively correlated with Animism ($r = -.46$, $N = 29$). Adding cognitive ability in a regression, religion and especially the Christian-Muslim-contrast (subtracted shares) remains much more important for explaining country differences in female genital mutilation ($\beta_{ChMu \to FGM} = -.52$, $\beta_{CA \to FGM} = -.11$, $N = 29$). Within countries with FGM more Muslim women suffer from FGM (56 per cent) than Animist women (35 per cent) or Christian women (32 per cent). It is not Animism that is decisive for genital mutilation, it is Muslim culture. FGM is itself not recommended in the Koran, but in a Hadith (Sunan Abu Dawood, 41:5251). FGM has been declining in recent decades. Religious authorities and governments have started to ban it.

[138] Within-country data on offenders usually lack information on religion. There is indirect evidence (given by country of origin, reported in more official news or less official blogs, indicated by asked religious support in prisons). Media, if religious or ethnic background is given, frequently call such cases 'isolated incidents' or explain them by 'mental disorder' not related to religion or culture.

[139] On football player violence there are no statistics, but frequent reports in the news, e.g. in Germany in amateur leagues against other players or referees, including aggravated battery (e.g. www.faz.net/aktuell/sport/fussball/probleme-im-amateufussball-gewaltexzess-in-altenessen-13184830.html, 2014), in the Netherlands (e.g. www.focus.de/sport/fussball/brutalitaet-im-amateur-fussball-bvb-boss-watzke-klagt-die-gesellschaft-verroht_aid_876463.html, 2012), of pro footballers in Turkey (e.g. www.spiegel.de/sport/fussball/0,1518,385444,00.html, 2005). Most famous is the tantrum of Zinedine Zidane in the 2006 World Cup Final, his last game as professional, headbutting a player from the other team. He was forced to leave the playing field and his team lost the game. His own general comment is reported as (following https://en.wikipedia.org/wiki/Zinedine_Zidane): 'My passion, temper and blood made me react.'

[140] Outside sports, dysfunctional violence, e.g. trampling to death of a person who wanted to settle a conflict (www.spiegel.de/panorama/gesellschaft/pruegelattacke-in-kirchweye-angeklagter-zu-haftstrafte-verurteilt-a-955845.html, 2013).

[141] 'Pathological violence' as well as 'violence due to low impulse control' are no clear categories (and there are no statistics for such cases). Some Islamic terror attacks were categorised as attacks of mentally ill people (e.g. France 2014, http://abcnews.go.com/International/wire Story/french-police-raise-security-weekend-attacks-27758432).
Others killed their own family members due to 'religious mania', e.g. an Afghani dentist cut his children's throats (Germany 2014, www.welt.de/print/die_welt/hamburg/art icle124213261/Familiendrama-Vater-toetet-seine-beiden-Kinder.html), an Iraqi father threw his children out of the window (Germany 2014, www.bild.de/news/inland/familiendrama/familien-drama-in-treuchtlingen-35155688.bild.html), a man beheaded his wife and shouted 'Allahu Akbar Sheytan' (Germany 2014, www.welt.de/vermischtes/weltgeschehen/art icle106415264/Auf-der-Dachterrasse-enthauptete-Orhan-S-seine-Frau.html),    a    nanny

it is a manifestation, in an extreme form, of an existing cultural tendency. (Regarding an objection that this can be found also in other groups see below.)

- *Rape* is not allowed in Islam, but the fewer rights of women, the emphasis of women's protection as part of a family and a kind of property of the father or husband and not as a person herself, and the emphasis of external, not internal, control, all together facilitate rape of unprotected women in situations such as during war, when not escorted or having another religion.[142]

- Also related is general *violence and crime.* According to Moore (2008) in Europe Muslims are highly overrepresented among prisoners (in France 60 per cent of the inmates but only 12 per cent of the country's population, 1:5, in Belgium 1:8, in The Netherlands 1:4 and in Britain 1:4).[143] In the Scandinavian countries Denmark and Norway as well as in the Netherlands and Germany crime can be predicted by religion of the country of origin: Islam has an increasing impact.[144]

beheaded a child (Russia 2016, www.mirror.co.uk/news/world-news/moscow-child-beheading-son-nanny-7497955).

[142] Examples: IS and Yazidi girls in Iraq 2014f. (e.g. www.dw.de/amnesty-international-report-yazidi-women-and-girls-face-islamic-state-sexual-violence/a-18147468); Pakistani abuse of about 1,400 children in Rotherham (1997–2013, http://en.wikipedia.org/wiki/Rotherham_child_sexual_exploitation_scandal) and in Oxford (2006–2013, www.telegraph.co.uk/news/uknews/crime/10061217/Imams-promote-grooming-rings-Muslim-leader-claims.html), according to systematically collected empirical data 'Pakistani are the group with the most conservative gender values' (Koopmans, 2016, p. 203); Muslim men and a Jewish woman in Paris (2014, www.tlvfaces.com/paris-jewish-community-shock-rape-muslim-group-saying-jews); sexual harassment of women in Germany (https://en.wikipedia.org/wiki/New_Year's_Eve_sexual_assaults_in_Germany, www.welt.de/regionales/bayern/article153834677/Maed chen-im-Schwimmbad-sexuell-belaestigt.html).

[143] The high rate of Muslims among prisoners in France (Moore, 2008) is corroborated by a more recent report from 2014: www.lefigaro.fr/actualite-france/2014/10/22/01016-20141022ART FIG00314-un-rapport-explosif-sur-l-islam-radical-dans-les-prisons-francaises.php. For Belgium and the Netherlands, studies report an overrepresentation of about 1:10 and 1:3 (Open Society Institute, 2007a, 2007b).

[144] Prediction of immigrant crime in Scandinavian countries based on analyses of Kirkegaard (2014a, 2014b), on average home country Muslim percentage $r = .60$, $\beta = .37$, home country IQ $r = -.57$, $\beta = -.37$, home country GDP/c $r = -.43$, $\beta = -.28$. Because religion has an effect on cognitive ability and income a simultaneous regression analysis with religion, IQ and GDP underestimates the effect of religion: the indirect effects via IQ and GDP have to be added. A crime-increasing statistical effect of Islamic background is also found for the Netherlands (2015; $r = .24$); it is larger for men than for women ($r_M = .27$ vs. $r_W = .10$); it is the highest for young men between 18 and 24 years old ($r = .43$), higher for the second generation immigrants ($r_{2G} = .54$ vs. $r_{1G} = .12$) and increases if income is controlled ($r = .36$). Controlling for age and sex the effects are robust; in Denmark: home country Muslim percentage $r = .59$ ($r_c = .60$) and home country IQ $r = -.49$ ($r_c = -.47$); in Germany: home country Muslim percentage $r = .49$ ($r_c = .35$) and home country IQ $r = -.53$ ($r_c = -.46$; Kirkegaard & Becker, 2017). The crime effect is robust across countries and controls. (Note: Emil Kirkegaard is a young student of linguistics and researcher, born around 1990, who developed together with other scientists a new, peer-reviewed online publication platform. This is an example of citizen science not totally unusual in intelligence research. Intelligence research is attractive to intellectuals from outside the field

- Finally, *suppression* of citizens in Muslim countries which are not Islamic states but which are shaped by Muslim tradition. Human rights, political liberty and rule of law are reduced, e.g. women's rights, rights of religious or sexual minorities, of immigrant workers.[145]

Outcomes of belief systems can be found also in attitudes among immigrants from Muslim countries in Europe, e.g. '75% think there is only one interpretation of the Quran possible, which is binding for every Muslim, and 65 per cent say that religious rules are more important to them than the laws of the country in which they live' or '57 percent reject homosexual friends' (Koopmans, 2014, pp. 11, 16).

A subjugation relationship towards God, religious authoritarianism, ethical dualism, an inclination to violence as a means all impede development of a burgher society based on individual rights, civic autonomy and liberty. However, and this needs to be considered, government repression, strict law and lack of freedom may also be understood as an answer to a personality and behaviour pattern that is difficult to manage, less self-controlled and more prone to impulsivity and aggressivity and less orientated by ethical universalism. Liberty, rule of law and democracy are not only characteristics of political systems but also of peoples prepared for them. To be effective norms and institutions have to be adapted to the circumstances (North, Wallis & Weingast, 2009, pp. 264f.).

The majority of victims of violence by radical Muslims are Muslims themselves.[146] Culture, education, cognitive ability, general crime and specific Muslim violence are theoretically and empirically intertwined. For instance, according to the German intelligence service (Verfassungsschutz) ISIS combatants from Germany on average have no school qualifications (75 per cent), have no vocational training (94 per cent), have not studied (98 per cent), were not working (88 per cent, if working then in jobs in the low-pay sector) and many had a criminal past, usually because of violent offences (29 per cent).[147]

---

who pick up research questions that are not sufficiently studied by institutionalised science and frequently disregarded due to political reasons.)

[145] Human rights in Muslim countries: e.g. www.huffingtonpost.com/ida-lichter-md/united-nations-no-defende_b_4515337.html, www.washingtonpost.com/blogs/worldviews/wp/2014/02/24/here-are-the-10-countries-where-homosexuality-may-be-punished-by-death, www.jpost.com/International/Report-charting-persecution-of-Christians-worldwide-reveals-most-abuse-in-Muslim-countries-338682, www.economist.com/news/middle-east-and-africa/21583291-attempts-improve-lot-migrants-working-middle-east-are-unlikely.

[146] Examples of Muslim victims: Peshawar, December 2014, 132 pupils were killed by Islamists (Tehrik-i-Taliban); Algerian Civil War (1991–2001, Islamists against the state), around 50,000 to 150,000 deaths; civil wars in Somalia, Iraq, Syria, Libya; everyday violence against women, minorities and people who are different; migrant workers in Qatar.

[147] German intelligence report on ISIS combatants: 11.09.14, www.morgenpost.de/berlin/article132128684/Die-deutschen-IS-Kaempfer-sind-jung-maennlich-und-kriminell.html.

Islam also has genetic effects via supporting consanguineous marriages (see Section 10.7.1). Islam and consanguinity are very highly related across countries ($r = .80$, $r_p = .81$; Table 10.9). Within European countries, consanguinity rates mainly depend on Muslim background (Rowlatt, 2005). According to a meta-analysis, the negative effect on cognitive ability is around –6 IQ points (te Nijenhuis, 2010). Negative consanguinity effects also include impeding democracy (Woodley & Bell, 2013): intensified kinship ties as induced by consanguineous marriages hamper cooperation between non-related persons, a prerequisite for democracy, rule of law and liberty. The cost-benefit ratio becomes unfavourable for outside family cooperation.[148]

One objection is that some decades and centuries ago examples of nearly all those occurrences mentioned here were also found in European-Christian countries. The last two world wars are two of them. Yes, correct. But in the same time institutions were developed to promote human rights, to tame war, to give equal rights for men and women, to further liberty, rule of law and democracy. The values behind them were long ago established. Additionally, many demands for and positive descriptions of violence can be also found in other holy scriptures, especially in the Old Testament, e.g.: 'Do not spare them; put to death men and women, children and infants, cattle and sheep, camels and donkeys.' (1 Samuel 15:3) In analysing religion, not only the initial message and the role model of founders, but also the development of the religious message, its transformation by scholars and the lived practice have to be considered. *Violence is normal in human history; the opposite is exceptional* (e.g. Oesterdiekhoff, 2009a, 2014b; Pinker, 2011).

Finally, positive aspects of Islam can be strong discipline orientation in school. However, discipline needs to be directed towards educationally as well as ethically justifiable aims and it needs to be internalised. There are also clear signs of modernisation such as rising educational levels, especially among women and in Iran. There are important intellectuals criticising culture and working on its progress. Like everywhere, the majority of people want to live a peaceful and happy life. For instance, according to the Arab Youth Survey 2016 an overwhelming majority of young Arabs reject ISIS and its violent fundamentalism (ASDA'A, 2016).

*Cognitive Ability Studies: International Evidence* As documented in Table 10.11, percentage of Muslims and cognitive ability measures are negatively related (at around $r = -.42$). The pattern is robust across different measures (student assessment or psychometric IQ studies) and country

---

[148] Further (surely controversial) genetic hypotheses (Templer, 2010) deal with contributions of sub-Saharan Africans or a dysgenic decrease among the more educated Muslims because of employing birth control.

samples. The international outcomes are backed by within-country results: Dronkers et al. (2012) documented a 35 SASQ-gap (equivalent to 5 IQ points) for immigrants from Muslim countries. According to Dronkers and Velden (2013, pp. 91–94) the lag cannot be explained by characteristics of the school or of the educational system or of the attended curriculum nor by discrimination and negative selection of immigrants or by low SES but by a negative impact of Muslim culture:

It is the Islamic faith of individual immigrants that leads to a lower educational level. (Dronkers & Velden, 2013, p. 94).

Christian Arabs in Israel show an educational level corresponding to Oriental Jews which comprises 15 months more education than that of Muslim Arabs. The documented difference of 15 months, depending on transformation method, represents $d = 0.71$ or a 4 to 11 IQ points gap (Shavit, 1990). At the state level within India, percentage of Muslims and average cognitive ability are negatively correlated ($r = -.32$; Lynn & Yadav, 2015).

In a study in Austrian Graz with 139 fifth-graders, children of Protestant parents showed the highest IQ (108), followed by Catholic and Orthodox (around IQ 100) and by Muslim parents (IQ 90). Reducing confounding factors by only looking at children from former Yugoslavia ($N = 25$), the average for Catholic children was IQ 103, for Orthodox IQ 98 and for Muslim IQ 86 (Makotschnig, 2010). In a common regression with migration, education of parents and kindergarten attendance, religion was the variable which had the strongest impact on children's intelligence. In another sample from Graz with kindergarten children (4 to 7 years old, $N = 22$ children with information on religion), the difference between Muslim and Christian children was similar, 11 IQ points (Steinhauser, 2010). In a regression, religion showed, with $\beta = .24$, a weaker effect than parental education ($\beta = .32$) or migration background ($\beta = .26$). However, religion also has indirect effects via parental education. In a final Graz sample with 75 Muslim and 15 Catholic immigrants between age 10 and 15 years old the difference was 3 IQ points (Hofer et al., 2010). Summarising, the average mean difference for 137 children was 7 IQ points, equivalent to 100 and 93 IQ points. This corresponds to the international differences of around 8 to 11 IQ points (Table 10.11). The within-Austria difference is slightly smaller (7 vs. 8 to 11 IQ). If it is a true pattern, it is possibly due to a positive selection effect of immigration or due to better environmental conditions for cognitive development in Austria such as better health care, nutrition and education from kindergarten to university.

*Summary*    Based on content analyses and empirical data, Islam has a negative impact on cognitive ability and generally on the development of a burgher world and modernisation. The effects are broad, covering education in families and schools, institutions and culture, behaviour and personality, the economy and society. Between these individual and macro-social aspects a variety of reciprocal influences is working. The long and in-detailed description tried to specify it. However, the complexity of direct and indirect and reciprocal effects makes it difficult to precisely estimate the impact of single factors, e.g., of the violence effect. The description and analysis are based on many sources, on scientific studies and statistical data, on information from everyday life; they come from different empirical surveys and authors and from different countries and epochs. Different authors from the classical enlightenment (Voltaire) and Marxist philosophy and psychology (Krauss, Luria) to modern cross-cultural studies (Harrison, Huntington, Koopmans, United Nations Development Programme) and educational research (Dronkers) come to a similar assessment. Sceptics who are still not convinced should consider the recent migration waves: who is fleeing wherefrom where to? Millions of migrants vote with their feet.

The usually given excuses of 'isolated cases' or accidental coincidence are not convincing. Additionally, another frequently mentioned objection, that only Islamism is the problem and not Islam itself, is not substantive. Islamism is based on Islam and the ethical-educational-political phenomena sketched in this section are inherent to original Islam. Islamism is the exaggerated version of an existing idea. All presented empirical-statistical results are based on *average* Muslim samples, not on selected or extremist ones. But it is true that for cognitive ability and the 7 to 11 IQ point difference it is not possible to determine the exact numerical size of the effect, e.g. '5 of 7' or '7 of 11 IQ points' are due to culture. At the macrosocial level a degree of uncertainty always remains – and a future transformation of culture may improve the effects ('cultural change'; Harrison & Kagan, 2006).

### 10.8.5  Hinduism

Hinduism is an old, colourful, figural, concrete and various religion characteristic of India. Around 80 per cent of Indian people belong to Hinduism. It is polytheistic and there is no single religious founder, doctrine or holy book. Hinduism is an amalgam of national tradition, Animism, myths and religious beliefs. It is also a social doctrine arranging people in different castes. At the top are the Brahmins, a caste of scholars who traditionally have the mission in life to study and teach spiritual knowledge. They form a well-educated class but traditionally they were solely focused on religion, contemplative reflection and otherworld aims (Nirvana, escapism). In more modern orientations, the educational-cognitive ambition was also used for secular tasks such as becoming academics. People from this caste form an important part of the internationally well known 'high tech Indians'.

Central Hindu doctrines deal with rebirth and karma. Life is predetermined by karma and caste. Persons have to behave according to the rules of their caste. Who has behaved well will be reborn in a higher caste. Asceticism is a distinguished path to this aim. Traditionally, education is designated only for members of certain castes, especially Brahmins. There is no individual advancement possible in one's life due to education, learning or achievement. In reality, caste and life are determined by fathers' caste affiliation. In a person's life there is no liberty and individual merit. This all leads to high disparity in education and cognitive competences between a small but internationally competitive elite and a large premodern low ability class (e.g. Pritchett & Viarengo, 2009; Weede, 2010; Zakaria, 2011, pp. 205–206). Modern remedies – affirmative action – support lower castes but again do not foster meritoric principles (Sowell, 2004). Achievement motivation and efficiency among Indian workers were not high, making it more cost effective for the British to ship cotton from India to Great Britain, make cloth there and ship it back to India for sale (Clark, 2007, p. 363f.).

Summarising: Hinduism legitimates the stratification of society in a small intellectual elite and a lowly educated majority society in which persons are not able to rise by their own merit. This system is both religiously and sociologically cemented. With modernisation and Western influences of liberal, egalitarian and capitalist ideas, this cultural-religious system lost some of its impact. Still it neither fosters education nor parental, individual or national investment in cognitive development. It obstructs for the economy, society and culture – for society as a whole, not for the elite – development in technological, economic, intellectual or cultural fields. *Average* cognitive ability level is similar to Muslim countries; the *average* educational level is even lower (Table 10.11).[149]

### 10.8.6   Buddhism

Buddhism is based on the founder, Siddhartha Gautama Buddha (around 563 to 483 BC). Later, it split into different movements and schools that were in competition for the true doctrine. Some see Buddhism not as a religion but as a philosophy with a profound theory on psychology. One important doctrine, the *Kalama Sutta*, stresses not to follow what one hears, tradition, rumour, scripture, surmising, theory and other's opinion, even if profound, but only one's own experience. In Buddhism, education and knowledge are highly regarded. Buddhism as an institution comprises monasteries, schools and an educated religious elite. Order, discipline, self-control and a systematic

---

[149] On Jainism see Section 6.2.

lifestyle are trained in monasteries and schools. Many men attend monasteries in different phases of their life, especially in Thailand.

The term 'Buddha' itself means 'state of perfect enlightenment'. Siddhartha was no warrior; in art he is frequently depicted with rather female features. Siddhartha was son of a local king but, similarly to some Christian saints (e.g. Francis of Assisi), he chose voluntary poverty and a life devoted to religion, especially to meditation and teaching. Central doctrines are rebirth and its overcoming, including the overcoming of suffering and the refusal of the secular.[150] Life should be conducted in a decent style, not acting on impulses. Mindfulness and self-control are highly regarded. Serenity is an important aim.

Similarly to Brahmins in Hinduism, education and intellectual work were directed to contemplative reflection and otherworldly aims. Knowledge was gained by gnosis, in ascesis and meditation, not by empirical observation and rational thinking. Taught knowledge was focused on rituals and mysticism (Weber, 1958/1921). Knowledge was not proved in real world contexts but in spiritual experiences. Disputations followed ritualistic rules. Finally, Buddhism was mixed with local Animistic rites, most pronounced in Tibet, or with Confucianism as in China and Japan.

Positive effects of Buddhism on cognitive ability can proceed along three paths: First, by its *general appreciation of knowledge and learning;* second by its *emphasis on discipline, diligence, education and self-education* and third by its emphasis on *one's own experience.* These foster cognitive development and a peaceful, self-controlled and modest lifestyle all supporting economic productivity and a burgher society.

Share of Buddhists in a country positively correlates with cognitive ability averages. Country means are similar to Christian and Catholic countries (around IQ 89; Table 10.11).

### 10.8.7   Confucianism

Confucianism is not as focused on transcendence as other religions are. Confucianism is more an ethic and lifestyle, an ethical code. Its founder, Confucius, 551–479 BC, was a government official and minister. His biography is different to typical religious founders who were ascetics, saints or revolutionaries.

Confucianism emphasises *education, learning* and *hard work.* Children express gratitude to their parents by being hard working, disciplined and achievement-oriented. The required personal endeavour can lead to success.

---

[150] Weber (1958/1921, p. 333): 'Protection against the world and one's own acts, not in and through both.'

Success and status are modifiable goods accessible by individual work.[151] Confucius' analects start in the very first sentence with an emphasis on learning:

The Master said, 'Is it not pleasant to learn with a constant perseverance and application?' (I, 1.1)[152]

This learning should not be learning by heart and rote memorisation, but learning combined with thinking and understanding:

The Master said, 'Learning without thought is labour lost; thought without learning is perilous.' (Analects, II, 15)

Confucianism was an intellectual literary movement. (Spiegelberg, 1957, p. 315)

Carefully verified thinking, a feature of enlightenment, should guide one's judgement:

'There were four things from which the Master was entirely free. He had no foregone conclusions, no arbitrary predeterminations, no obstinacy, and no egoism.' (Analects, IX, 4)

However, the intellectual direction of impact is conservative: acquisition of given knowledge was important, but less so finding new knowledge; reproduction is stressed, not reflection; tradition, not critique; collectivist repetition, not individual discovery; discipline, not originality. There was neither appreciation of independent thinking nor of education as an intellectual aim for itself.

Confucianism, with its easy disdain for scientific research, which it disparaged as 'interventionist' and superficial, contributed its discouraging word. (Landes, 2006, p. 11)

Learning and thinking are means to solve given problems and to achieve success in one's life. Typical *burgher values* such as order, economy, modesty, farsightedness and self-control are stressed. Confucianism is a religion of officials and diplomats, an ethics of conformity and meritoric orientation. Parents and tradition are highly regarded, including ancestor worship.

There are no irrational elements such as belief in magic or life in the next world. There are no unattainable aims or self-destroying ethical standards. Confucianism is the doctrine of the mean. Confucianism is the prototypic *burgher ethic*. However, it is also without dynamism, individualism and ideas of liberty. Unlike Christianity, in which the existing needs to be adapted to the required, Confucianism calls for adaptation to the existing.

---

[151] In psychology, the *belief* in ability as a malleable and incremental characteristic has a positive effect on its development (Dweck, 2000).

[152] Source for analects: http://ctext.org/analects.

Confucianism stresses honesty, but not emancipation (Spiegelberg, 1957). It is more a *conservative* worldview and thus for progress dependent on the improvements achieved by others.

Confucius represented this trend to formalism. He laid down the rules, regulations, and procedures for a functioning bureaucratic state. (Spiegelberg, 1957, p. 315)

The virtue of Confucianism was the virtue of the party in power. It is the ethical system of the status quo. (Spiegelberg, 1957, p. 317)

Sociologically, the administrating class in China were the scribes, selected by written exams. Weber (1951/1920, p. 44) called it the 'influential aristocracy of education'. They were selected by a strong educational-meritocratic system:

For twelve centuries social rank in China has been determined more by qualification for office than by wealth. This qualification, in turn, has been determined by education, and especially by examinations. China has made literary education the yardstick of social prestige in the most exclusive fashion. ... Literati have been the bearers of progress toward a rational administration and of all 'intelligence'. (Weber, 1951/1920, p. 107)

Military virtues were secondary for social rise and success and any ideological radicalism was denied. No sacrifice, no madness, no struggle for ideology. In practice, Confucianism was blended with local and more transcendental cults such as Taoism (China), Shinto (Japan) and Buddhism (China, Japan, Vietnam).

East Asian nations and their students, as natives as well as immigrants, all over the world lead in intelligence and student assessment studies. The share of Confucians in a country is the religious variable that most highly and positively correlates with cognitive ability measures (about $r = .31$, Protestants: about $r = .30$; Table 10.11). Only choosing East Asian nations, the cognitive ability averages are at around IQ 102–105. However, scientific achievements and creativity estimates are rather low, lower than expected by the excellent cognitive ability level.[153]

### 10.8.8 Impact on Cognitive Development and Burgher World

Recapitulating, according to an analysis of content and practice three religions should have a clear positive impact on cognitive ability, thinking, meritocracy, the development of a burgher world and modernisation: Judaism, Christianity (especially Protestantism) and Confucianism. This impact works via shaping

---

[153] Using the standardised data for scientific-intellectual achievement from Tables 4.4 and 4.5, Confucianism shaped East Asia: eminent scientists only 88 (normed in comparison to the corrected total cognitive ability average, UK has 114). Science Nobel Prizes only 80 (identically normed, UK has 126).

Table 10.11 *Religions and ability and education*

| | CA (corrected) | SAS M (corr., all) | SAS M (uncorr., PTP) | SAS 95% (uc., high ability) | SAS 05% (uc., low ability) | Adult education | Books | GNI 2010 HDR |
|---|---|---|---|---|---|---|---|---|
| *Correlations with percentages of members in countries (in parentheses excluding developing countries)* | | | | | | | | |
| **Animism** | −.65 (−.38) | −.53 (−.26) | −.51 (−.22) | −.48 (−.21) | −.50 (−.20) | −.53 (−.08) | −.31 (−.15) | −.44 (−.07) |
| **Judaism** | .08 (.03) | .05 (.02) | .04 (.01) | .08 (.06) | −.01 (−.06) | .08 (.06) | .08 (.06) | .07 (.02) |
| **Christianity** | .26 (.31) | .22 (.32) | .25 (.33) | .25 (.34) | .24 (.30) | .46 (.44) | .39 (.39) | .21 (.06) |
| **Catholicism** | .15 (.17) | .02 (.14) | .09 (.16) | .06 (.15) | .09 (.16) | .23 (.02) | .04 (.06) | .17 (.14) |
| **Orthodoxy** | .22 (−.04) | .10 (−.13) | .05 (−.13) | .07 (−.10) | .02 (−.17) | .22 (.13) | .02 (−.12) | −.05 (−.37) |
| **Protestantism** | .19 (.23) | .35 (.40) | .32 (.37) | .31 (.36) | .32 (.37) | .33 (.48) | .60 (.62) | .27 (.30) |
| **Islam** | −.26 (−.63) | −.39 (−.68) | −.49 (−.71) | −.48 (−.70) | −.48 (−.67) | −.37 (−.55) | −.48 (−.53) | −.10 (−.13) |
| **Hinduism** | −.04 (.03) | −.13 (.00) | −.13 (−.04) | −.09 (.02) | −.18 (−.07) | −.09 (−.13) | −.02 (−.08) | −.09 (.28) |
| **Buddhism** | .15 (.21) | .14 (.14) | .19 (.18) | .15 (.14) | .24 (.21) | −.01 (−.06) | −.03 (.10) | −.08 (−.02) |
| **Confucianism** | .31 (.38) | .30 (.32) | .32 (.35) | .30 (.33) | .32 (.34) | .14 (.00) | .04 (−.02) | .19 (.12) |
| **Weighted religions** | .60 (.66) | .62 (.73) | .64 (.75) | .62 (.74) | .64 (.71) | .66 (.57) | .64 (.65) | .45 (.30) |
| **N** | 199 | 108 | 99 | 99 | 99 | 193 | 85 | 183 |
| *Traditionally a society shaping religion (means and number of countries)* | | | | | | | | |
| **Animism-Christ-** M | 74 | 67 | 70 | 97 | 47 | −3.79 | 23 | 5.669 |
| **Mix** N | (53) | (5) | (3) | (3) | (3) | (51) | (4) | (47) |
| **Animism-Islam-** M | 69 | 67 | 73 | 97 | 50 | −6.38 | 16 | 1.787 |
| **Mix** N | (17) | (4) | (3) | (3) | (3) | (17) | (2) | (16) |
| **Judaism** M | 95 | 93 | 94 | 118 | 67 | 0.00 | 87 | 27.831 |
| N | (1) | (1) | (1) | (1) | (1) | (1) | (1) | (1) |
| **Christianity** M | 90 | 89 | 93 | 114 | 71 | −1.17 | 73 | 20.258 |
| N | (75) | (64) | (58) | (58) | (58) | (74) | (50) | (71) |
| **Catholicism** M | 88 | 86 | 90 | 111 | 68 | −1.59 | 57 | 18.601 |
| N | (43) | (37) | (31) | (31) | (31) | (43) | (24) | (41) |
| **Protestantism** M | 98 | 99 | 100 | 119 | 78 | 0.61 | 113 | 34.207 |
| N | (14) | (13) | (13) | (13) | (13) | (14) | (13) | (13) |

| | | | | | | | | | |
|---|---|---|---|---|---|---|---|---|---|
| **Cath-Prot-Mix** | M | 95 | 99 | 100 | 119 | 77 | −0.55 | 87 | 37.579 |
| | N | (3) | (2) | (2) | (2) | (2) | (3) | (2) | (2) |
| **Orthodoxy** | M | 89 | 89 | 91 | 113 | 68 | −1.77 | 58 | 10.390 |
| | N | (15) | (12) | (12) | (12) | (12) | (14) | (11) | (15) |
| **Islam** | M | 82 | 79 | 82 | 104 | 60 | −3.57 | 32 | 15.259 |
| | N | (34) | (22) | (22) | (22) | (22) | (33) | (21) | (32) |
| **Hinduism** | M | 80 | 76 | 82 | 106 | 57 | −5.14 | – | 5.961 |
| | N | (3) | (2) | (2) | (2) | (2) | (3) | – | (3 |
| **Buddhism** | M | 86 | 87 | 93 | 112 | 74 | −3.81 | 17 | 3.862 |
| | N | (9) | (3) | (3) | (3) | (3) | (8) | (1) | (8) |
| **Confucianism-Buddhism** | M | 94 | 98 | 101 | 119 | 80 | −2.29 | 65 | 15.103 |
| | N | (17) | (10) | (10) | (10) | (10) | (16) | (7) | (13) |

*Notes*: Sources for religion: German Department for Foreign Affairs (www.auswaertiges-amt.de/www/de/laenderinfos), a country encyclopaedia ('Länderlexikon', Jahrbuch, 2004) and the CIA World Factbook; cognitive ability estimates see Table 10.1; Book: Number of books (approximately per family); GNI 2010 HDR: wealth indicator in 2008 ppp, US dollar per capita; Adult education: Adult education mean (UK $M = 0$, 'First World' $SD = 1$); Weighted religions: weighted for education, rationality, thinking and meritoric orientations (see text).

education, learning, rationality and everyday life in a favourable way relative to other religions. Catholicism, Orthodoxy and Buddhism should have less positive effects. Hinduism, Islam and Animism should have negative effects. The effects are not 'absolute', but 'relative' ones; compared to the aforementioned religions their effect is 'negative'. Conceptually, instead of 'positive' also 'stronger' and instead of 'negative' also 'weaker' are possible, mathematically expressed simply by adding a constant.

Effects are not only direct, but also indirect. Of course, any baptism alone or mere confession of faith do not create intelligence – only the active appreciation and practice of thinking, learning and education, usually unintended consequences of religion. Scholars such as Benjamin Nelson see the beginning of modernisation in the twelfth and thirteenth centuries in certain European regions. The amalgamation of an antique rationalisation process of Greeks and Romans (Athens-Rome-thesis) with a Christian rationalisation process of scholastic philosophy and Protestant reformation (Jerusalem-Aquino-Wittenberg-thesis) pushed development towards modernisation and its movements in specific epochs: Humanism, Reformation, Enlightenment, New-Humanism and Industrial Revolution. Additional cultural factors such as openness to foreign contributions, learning from accomplishments of others, integration of foreign and local advantages (of Arabic science, Indian mathematics, Germanic independence, Chinese inventions, American crop plants) and their advancement in interaction further contributed to this modernisation process.

Culture can be integrated in empirical-statistical analyses only when its impact is quantified. Based on the presented theoretical and historical analyses and similar ones such as from Lawrence Harrison (2013, pp. 16ff.), the impact on education, learning, rationality, thinking, meritoric orientations and the development of a burgher world and modernisation was mathematically estimated: Protestantism was assigned the weight +1, Judaism and Confucianism +0.8, Catholicism +0.5, Orthodoxy and Buddhism +0.2, other and not precisely given Christian groups +0.3, Hinduism and Islam –0.4 and Animism –1. Instead of negative values, the values could be also arranged between 0 and 1 or 0 and 2 or 1 and 2 etc. On the suggested scale from –1 to +1 the values and distances are easier to comprehend.[154]

Some further considerations:

A more sophisticated approach could assign different weights depending on epoch (especially relevant for Protestantism). Hinduism and Islam received the same weight. However, more impeding factors were listed for Islam than for Hinduism. But Hinduism established a class society seriously affecting

---

[154] A similar but qualitative approach was developed by Lawrence Harrison (2013, p. 16), who assessed religions according to the following criteria: 'Nurtures rationality, achievement; promotes material pursuits; focus on this world; pragmatism.'

achievement, education and learning. This single characteristic is important. On the other side, for the Brahmin, Hinduism has a positive effect on education and learning, but in the past not in secular fields. The assigned weights cannot be understood as final and are subject to discussion. Buddhism may deserve a higher weight, but theory and realisation of conditions for education, learning, rationality and thinking largely differ. Compared to the classical and critical work of Hegel and Weber the Catholic denomination achieved a higher weight. The positive attributes of Protestantism, its emphasis on education, liberty, autonomy and diligence, are all also given for Catholicism (Sombart), only weaker. Protestantism is the accentuation of a trend already previously existing in Catholicism.

Is the analysis maybe too critical or not critical enough? Too critical in describing negative aspects of religions and especially of Animism, Hinduism and Islam? Or not critical enough, as any religion is a violation of reason? Our aim is not to criticise religion but to research their possible effects on cognitive modernisation and development of a burgher world. This necessarily implies a comparative perspective in which some – if justified by the religious content and by empirical and statistical data – have a more positive or negative impact relative to other religions. The aim of a scientific study is doing science, not diplomacy.

In particular, the subject of Islam is perceived to be difficult to discuss; the problem was described by the philosopher Michael Walzer (2015):

One reason for this failure [to veridically understand, publicly describe and adequately react to Islam] is the terrible fear of being called 'Islamophobic.' Anti-Americanism and a radical version of cultural relativism also play an important part, but these are older pathologies. Here is something new: many leftists are so irrationally afraid of an irrational fear of Islam that they haven't been able to consider the very good reasons for fearing Islamist zealots – and so they have difficulty explaining what's going on in the world.

Science does not include pleasing nor offending others but finding a veridical description and developing an explanative theory in a clear language which, nevertheless – also depending on the attributes of a reader – may or wants to be perceived as pleasing or offensive. Science is built upon the utopian assumption of epistemic rationality on both sides, on the side of persons doing research as well as on the side of persons reading, understanding and thinking through research, its methods and results. But is the perspective not biased? If anything is wrong or biased – improvements are welcome. That is the way of improving thinking!

### 10.8.9   Empirical-Quantitative Findings

The measurement of religion and its effects is hampered by three factors: first and simply, religious affiliation is not always clear, especially not for Animism. For many countries, data are not precise, e.g. the CIA World Factbook lists for South Sudan only the information 'animist, Christian', but no percentages. For statistical analyses, more precise information has to be estimated; for

South Sudan, we estimated 80 per cent Animism and 20 per cent (general) Christian. Second, effects of religions need to be theoretically considered and then mathematically weighted as in this chapter above. Third, historical changes modify religious affiliation and religious effects. To address the last problem a second variable was used, the 'traditionally a society shaping religion'. Furthermore, effects of religions are long-term, conserved by institutions and cultural climates, both shaped by religions. For instance, the positive effects of Protestantism on trustworthiness are persistent until today in Scandinavian countries even if religious affiliation and belief have vastly declined.[155]

Table 10.11 (religions) presents correlations and means for cognitive ability measures, education, books and wealth, Table 10.12 for enlightenment, society and politics. Percentages of persons believing or belonging to Animism, Islam and Hinduism are negatively correlated with cognitive ability and education estimates; percentages of belonging to Christianity (especially Protestantism), Buddhism and Confucianism are positively correlated. Means for traditionally a society shaping religions emphasise the impact of religions. Correlations with Judaism are low – see the above discussion for Judaism and Israel (which is also only one country). Effects generally remain after controlling for wealth by partial correlations. It has to be considered that partialling out GNI overcontrols wealth effects because wealth production also depends on religion (e.g. Max Weber, Werner Sombart).

Animism and Islam are negatively correlated with enlightenment and development of society. Correlations for other Asian religions are around zero or slightly negative. Christianity, and here especially Protestantism, have a positive effect on enlightenment and on indicators of a positive development of society and politics (Table 10.12 and see theoretical analyses).

## 10.9    The Interplay of Determinants

We have discussed factors in this chapter for explaining cross-country and historical differences in cognitive ability that in research and public debate were

---

[155] Trust and trustworthiness (based on WVS, original scale, indexes over 100 correspond to countries where a majority of people trust others; Díez-Medrano, 2014): correlation of Protestantism with trust across 117 nations $r = .54$ (see also Table 10.12). The Scandinavian average for trust is internationally the highest with $M = 123$; the second highest region represents the former British colonies Australia and New Zealand with $M = 97$; international average is $M = 51$ ($SD = 28$) (see also Delhey & Newton, 2005). Religiosity in Scandinavia, 'Belief in God' (WVS, Inglehart, 1997): $M = 31$; only East Asia is lower ($M = 12$), international average is $M = 52$ ($SD = 27$).

Table 10.12 *Religions and enlightenment, society and politics*

| | Enlight. (Mokyr) | Trust (WVS) | Rule of law | Democracy | Political freedom | Economic freedom | Gov. effec. | Low corrp. |
|---|---|---|---|---|---|---|---|---|
| Correlations with percentages of members in countries | | | | | | | | |
| **Animism** | -.18 | -.30 | -.40 | -.27 | -.19 | -.38 | -.46 | -.36 |
| **Judaism** | -.01 | -.01 | .07 | .10 | .07 | .05 | .09 | .07 |
| **Christianity** | .23 | .07 | .38 | .60 | .61 | .28 | .38 | .36 |
| **Catholicism** | .10 | -.14 | .22 | .37 | .44 | .12 | .24 | .19 |
| **Orthodoxy** | -.08 | -.06 | -.04 | .14 | .01 | .04 | -.02 | -.08 |
| **Protestantism** | .38 | .54 | .44 | .42 | .42 | .32 | .40 | .52 |
| **Islam** | -.16 | -.16 | -.33 | -.51 | -.53 | -.16 | -.32 | -.33 |
| **Hinduism** | -.05 | -.06 | -.03 | .04 | .02 | -.01 | -.01 | -.04 |
| **Buddhism** | -.06 | .07 | -.06 | -.15 | -.21 | -.09 | -.03 | -.07 |
| **Confucianism (E-A)** | -.04 | .23 | .15 | .00 | -.02 | .13 | .18 | .17 |
| **Weighted religions** | .34 (.36) | .44 (.46) | .62 (.60) | .66 (.67) | .64 (.58) | .45 (.58) | .64 (.65) | .63 (.61) |
| $N_{max}$ | 186 | 117 | 198 | 189 | 194 | 180 | 198 | 183 |

*Notes:* Enlight.: Enlightenment Index eighteenth century from Joel Mokyr (2005), see Chapter 4 and Table 4.4; Trust: Interpersonal trust from World Values Survey (most recent data from 1995–2009); Rule of law: mean of 2009–2011, Kaufmann, Kraay & Mastruzzi (2010); Democracy: mean of 2007–2012, Vanhanen & Åbo Akademi (2013) and Marshall, Gurr & Jaggers (2013); Political freedom: mean of 2008–2012, $N = 196$, Freedom House (2013); Economic freedom: Economic freedom around 2010 based on Fraser (Gwartney et al., 2013) and Heritage index (Miller et al., 2013); Gov. effec.: Government effectiveness around year 2010, Kaufmann et al. (2010, 2012 update); Low corrp.: Low corruption, 2010–2012, Transparency International (2012); Weighted religions: see Table 10.11, in parentheses here correlations for the same country sample across all variables ($N = 111$).

mentioned, hypothesised and researched: (1) Wealth, (2) health, (3) politics, (4) modernisation, (5) education, (6) geography and climate, (7) evolution and genes, and (8) worldviews and culture with focus on religion. For every factor, we found empirical evidence, the theoretically weakest for geography and climate, the empirically and theoretically most robust for education.

These factors were analysed in detail and separately. However, the factors do not work independently, neither in historical development nor in presence: for example, genes may influence culture and culture again politics and they all together influence education and learning, leading to higher or lower individual cognitive ability, which in aggregated form results in large differences across nations. Culture can also have, via behaviour, an effect on genes, for instance by consanguineous marriages, by fertility patterns having a long-term effect on genes relevant for intelligence or by immigration and emigration. Cognitive ability changes culture regarding complexity, humanitarianism and modernisation. Education and ability transform culture.

What was first? Genes may work via shaping religion and religion has an effect on genes. Religion is certainly a switch but also an amplifier. Education drives modernisation. We need multivariate analyses modelling direct and indirect effects.

# 11 · Global Models for Education, Cognitive Capital, Production, Wealth and Wellbeing

> In this chapter models will be tested which combine background and specific factors and their interdependence. The models examine whether there is evidence for culture-education and evolution-education theories that explain cross-country differences in cognitive human capital leading to patterns in institutional quality, economic freedom, production and income finally resulting in differences in wealth, politics and wellbeing.

The wellbeing of nations does not depend on one single factor but on several. These factors are correlated and influence each other. Hence different possible causal factors and their interactions have to be combined. The factors stem from different, frequently competing, scientific paradigms developed in different fields of research, each with its own tradition of dominant questions, methods and perspectives. Among the vast amount of possible determinants only such were chosen for the combination into a global model that are theoretically and empirically backed (see Chapter 10). From the most important paradigms the following variables, being both factors and criteria, were taken:

- *Evolutionary paradigm*: There are no evolutionary theories on wealth, politics and wellbeing, but on ability and personality factors helping individuals to be more rational, moderate, self-controlled, innovative and productive, with the corresponding consequences for economy and society. The cross-nationally highest correlating evolutionary indicator was skin lightness; however, the theoretical support for a causal impact on ability or personality is weak and correlations at the individual level are low (not higher than $r = .20$). This also applies for the subspecies concept (races), which additionally is an imprecise categorisation. Assignment itself has no theoretical meaning. Haplogroups, like skin lightness and subspecies, are only indicators of the evolutionary past; haplogroups do not represent genes that code relevant traits. Consanguinity is a genetic factor; however, it is not an evolutionary factor: it largely depends on culture and was therefore not considered. By contrast, *brain size* (as measured by cranial capacity) is a theoretically and empirically supported causal factor at the individual level: larger brains represent increased numbers of neurones and connections, leading to higher intelligence. Assumptions and correlations are backed by evolutionary history (Sections 3.4.3 and 10.7.2, Table 9.1). Brain size has a causal meaning for intelligence and also serves as an evolutionary indicator. There are stable brain size differences, but there is also a secular rise in brain size (Section 4.1).

- *Cultural paradigm*: For education, learning, rationality, thinking, meritocracy, development of a burgher world and modernisation *weighted religions* were chosen as the second background factor (see Section 10.8 and therein 10.8.8). There is ample theoretical support and empirical evidence from the individual to the national level for a cultural impact on cognitive ability. Religious worldviews change behaviour and environment. However, modernisation and intelligence modify culture, and cultural factors can be influenced by evolutionary ones.

- *Educational paradigm*: Education is seen as the most important causal factor and the best proxy for cognitive ability and in a broader sense for human capital, including diligence, conscientiousness etc. Two educational indicators are used: *adult educational level* and *school quality* (see Sections 3.4.6 and 10.5). Education itself is influenced by background factors and by intelligence.

- *Cognitive ability paradigm*: Education cannot have a direct impact on wellbeing, but it can affect it by changing peoples' ability and personality. Among human capital, cognitive ability (intelligence, knowledge and its intelligent use) is crucial (see Chapters 7 and 8). *Average cognitive ability* of a society and *top ability level* (95 per cent-threshold, intellectual classes' level) are distinguished (theory of cognitive capitalism).

- *Political paradigm*: According to political theories, the quality of politics and institutions is crucial for production, wealth and wellbeing of nations (Section 5.2). We have chosen *government effectiveness*, *rule of law* and *economic freedom* as theoretically and empirically supported factors for production. They indirectly also measure democracy, liberty and meritoric principles. Political conditions are part of a broader wellbeing concept. They are not only economic means.

- *Economic paradigm*: Economic freedom is part of institutional-political theories. It is the most important theory within economics (Smith, Mises, Hayek, Friedman and others) and is very well backed by theory and research.

- *Economic criteria* production and wealth: While *economic production* covers annual production (per capita in across countries comparable units), *wealth* covers existing prosperity (see Chapter 1). Production is highly correlated with annual income but does not cover long-term assets such as housing. Production leads to income, and income permits the accumulation of wealth.[1]

---

[1] GDP: per capita logarithm, Maddison, around 2010; wealth: Credit Suisse, see Table 1.4. For the other variables, the aforementioned sources.

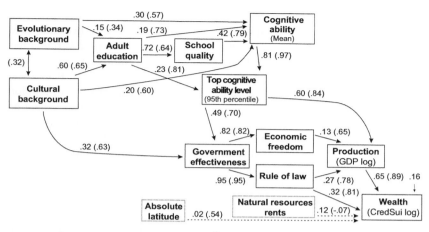

Figure 11.1 Global wealth model[2]

- *Wellbeing of nations*: Wellbeing covers economic wellbeing (production-GDP, income-GNI, assets), biological wellbeing (health: life expectancy), psychological wellbeing (life satisfaction, interpersonal trust), sociological wellbeing (low murder rate, peace, low corruption, low divorce rate) and political wellbeing (participation-democracy, political freedom, rule of law, gender equality) (see Section 2.4).

## 11.1   Economy: Produced Income (GDP) and the Wealth of Nations

In a cross-sectional path analysis for economic criteria, we have investigated the direct and indirect effects of background and more specific factors on wealth: of evolution, culture, education, cognitive ability, government effectiveness, economic freedom, rule of law and produced income (GDP) on Credit Suisse's asset indicator of wealth. As additional controls, latitude (distance to equator) and natural resources were considered (see Figure 11.1).

The two global background factors mainly relevant for cognitive ability differences are tested against each other. Cultural and evolutionary differences

[2] Data from around year 2010 (psychometric IQ and adult education around 1970–2010); *N* between 96 (school quality), 99 (top cognitive ability level) and up to 200 countries (cranial capacity/evolution, weighted religions/culture, cognitive ability, government effectiveness, production), FIML: full-information-maximum-likelihood, no listwise deletion of countries in the case of missing data, all observations used, *CFI* = .98, *SRMR* = .05, both standing for good fit of the model to the data (should be CFI≥.95 and SRMR≤.08). Standardised (comparable) path coefficients (beta, usually between –1, 0 and +1); correlations are in parentheses, error terms as not explained variance on the right.

are also tested as distal factors having indirect effects through educational and political factors on current national economic differences, here indicated by two wealth attributes, production and assets. *The cultural background* has a stronger impact on adult education than the *evolutionary background* ($\beta_{\text{Cul}\rightarrow\text{AdE}} = .60$, $r_{\text{Cul-AdE}} = .65$; $\beta_{\text{Evo}\rightarrow\text{AdE}} = .15$, $r_{\text{Evo-AdE}} = .34$). Reciprocal effects of education and intelligence on understanding and practice of religion may have boosted the cultural effect on education (reciprocal effects cannot be modelled in a cross-sectional design). However, there is strong theoretical support for an impact of religion on education (Section 10.8). Reverse effects of education and cognitive ability on evolution (cranial capacity) are rather small because at the individual level there is no support for such an effect; at the cross-country level indirect ability effects improving environmental conditions responsible for a secular rise in brain size need to be taken into account (see Section 4.1).

*Adult education* has a positive effect on *school quality* (better teachers and schools; $\beta_{\text{AdE}\rightarrow\text{SQ}} = .72$), but longitudinally both variables influence each other.[3] Adult education (directly $\beta_{\text{AdE}\rightarrow\text{CA}} = .19$, indirectly including the effect via school quality $\beta_{\text{AdE}\rightarrow\text{CA}} = .30$) and school quality ($\beta_{\text{SQ}\rightarrow\text{CA}} = .42$) have a strong impact on *cognitive ability* differences among nations.

The direct effect of the evolutionary background on national ability differences is larger than the direct effect of culture despite possible reverse effects of intelligence and knowledge on culture (direct: $\beta_{\text{Evo}\rightarrow\text{CA}} = .30$, $\beta_{\text{Cul}\rightarrow\text{CA}} = .20$). However, because of culture's larger indirect effects via education the total effect of culture on ability is larger than that of evolution (total: $\beta_{\text{Evotot}\rightarrow\text{CA}} = .37$, $\beta_{\text{Cultot}\rightarrow\text{CA}} = .50$).[4]

The bivariate correlations between evolutionary background (cranial capacity) and ability are slightly smaller ($r_{\text{Evo-CA}} = .57$ vs. $r_{\text{Cul-CA}} = .60$). There could be a reverse effect of cognitive ability on brain size and cranial capacity via improved environment (secular rise). However, a possible effect of

---

[3] There is a stronger path coefficient than correlation between adult education and school quality ($\beta_{\text{AdE}\rightarrow\text{SQ}} = .72$ vs. $r_{\text{AdE-SQ}} = .64$). Statistically, this cannot happen because no further factor in this model has an effect on school quality. This is a bug of the Mplus program; the difference between .72 and .64 should not be interpreted.

[4] If the cranial capacity variable is questioned, the theoretically less convincing skin lightness variable could be used. Using this variable would even increase the statistical effect of evolution ($\beta_{\text{EvoSL}\rightarrow\text{CA}} = .62$). Theoretically, there are no assumptions on reverse effects of society or ability on skin lightness. Alternatively, a $G$ factor of evolution (Table 10.10) also shows a larger effect ($\beta_{\text{EvoG}\rightarrow\text{CA}} = .35$) than the cranial capacity variable. The same is true for using the smoothed-graduated cranial capacity variable (see Table 10.8; in a path analysis: $\beta_{\text{EvoCC}\rightarrow\text{CA}} = .39$). Finally, using a path from evolution on culture would increase the total effect of evolution ($\beta_{\text{Evotot}\rightarrow\text{CA}} = .53$). As a result, the used cranial capacity variable ($\beta_{\text{EvoCC}\rightarrow\text{CA}} = .30$) and the chosen model give a cautious and conservative estimate of possible evolutionary effects. It should be interpreted as the *lowest bound* of evolutionary effects.

intelligence would be certainly larger on more malleable culture than on brain size. The problem can only be conclusively solved if intelligence-coding genes are used as an evolutionary causal factor; until now this has not been possible.

A similar pattern, a stronger total effect of culture, arises for *top cognitive ability level* ($\beta_{\text{Evotot}\rightarrow 95\%} = .33$, $\beta_{\text{Cultot}\rightarrow 95\%} = .54$, $r_{\text{Evo-95\%}} = .51$ vs. $r_{\text{Cul-95\%}} = .60$). Both factors, evolution and culture, are important, with a preponderance for culture. Top ability level is integrated in the model as a dependant of the average ability level of society ($\beta_{\text{CA}\rightarrow 95\%} = .81$) and of adult education ($\beta_{\text{AdE}\rightarrow 95\%} = .23$). Of course, longitudinally there are reciprocal effects between average and top ability level. But demographically, the average ability group is much larger; the majority of top ability people originate from broader strata of society.

Cognitive and cultural factors have an impact on institutions and society: *government effectiveness* depends on top ability level ($\beta_{95\%\rightarrow \text{Gov}} = .49$) and culture ($\beta_{\text{Cul}\rightarrow \text{Gov}} = .32$). Indirectly, government effectiveness also depends on the average cognitive level of society ($\beta_{\text{CAind}\rightarrow \text{Gov}} = .40$, $r_{\text{CA-Gov}} = .65$). Regarding the two background factors, culture has a stronger impact on politics ($\beta_{\text{Cultot}\rightarrow \text{Gov}} = .58$, $r_{\text{Cul-Gov}} = .63$ vs. $\beta_{\text{Evotot}\rightarrow \text{Gov}} = .16$, $r_{\text{Evo-Gov}} = .31$). This proceeds to a similar pattern for the further political-institutional and economic variables: Culture is more important than evolution (e.g. for wealth, $r_{\text{Cul-Wea}} = .61$ vs. $r_{\text{Evo-Wea}} = .40$). This neither means that evolutionary background has no effect nor that effects only happen via cognitive ability. Evolution also works on personality structures being more or less suitable for a burgher society such as peacefulness, moderateness, predictability and diligence (see in Section 10.7.3 the examples of Rome, China and England). Personality variables are not integrated in the model; their measurement at the international level suffers from problems of comparability (see Section 2.3.3). However, variables such as rule of law or education, democracy and freedom indirectly measure personality as discipline, self-control and moderateness: typical burgher attributes.

*Government effectiveness* is defined as the quality of public services, the quality of the civil service and the degree of its independence from political pressures, the quality of policy formulation and implementation, and the credibility of the government's commitment to such policies (see Sections 5.2.1 and 5.2.2). It is not identical with economic liberty nor with rule of law, but countries with better governments and administrations empirically are also economically more liberal ($\beta_{\text{Gov}\rightarrow \text{EF}} = .82$) and more constitutional ($\beta_{\text{Gov}\rightarrow \text{RoL}} = .95$). Reciprocal effects are not excluded, as more liberal, competitive and legally regulated economies will rub off on the quality of politics.

*Top ability level* is more highly correlated with all three political-institutional conditions than *average cognitive ability* ($r_{95\%} = .70$, $.51$, $.67$,

$r_{CA}$ = .65, .46, .61).[5] Both have similar positive effects but the effects of intellectual classes (top ability level) are always larger. Because both ability indicators are highly correlated, using them together as predictors in one model leads to large and implausible suppressor effects (e.g. for GDP 1.177 and −0.566). Thus we only used the top ability level. However, this does not mean that society's average ability level is not important − e.g. in our model the effects go indirectly.

*Economic freedom* and *rule of law* both have positive effects on annual production ($\beta_{EF \to GDP}$ = .13, $\beta_{RoL \to GDP}$ = .27), but the strongest effect is of *intellectual classes' ability level* ($\beta_{95\% \to GDP}$ = .60, $\beta_{95\%tot \to GDP}$ = .78). *Produced income* and *rule of law* both contribute to final *wealth* ($\beta_{GDP \to Wealth}$ = .65, $\beta_{RoL \to Wealth}$ = .32). Rule of law is not only necessary for the production of wealth but also for its maintenance.

What is the message of the model? Wealth positively depends on rule of law and economic liberty. Cognitive ability is crucial; less average cognitive ability than the level of the top ability group. These ability levels can be raised by education, depending on global background factors: on evolutionary and cultural forces.

However, is this the total truth? Reciprocal effects that were not covered were previously mentioned. Is there not only a positive correlation between evolutionary and cultural background, but also an effect? Culture has an effect on genes, as research on consanguinity shows. But consanguinity is not an evolutionary factor and thus was not considered here. Culture may indirectly increase brain volumes via education and wealth. Such increases in brain sizes would also not represent an evolutionary factor. Nevertheless, a change of international patterns due to past wealth differences is unlikely. There is older evidence on similar brain size patterns from the early nineteenth century before large wealth differences emerged (Section 4.3.).

And what about evolutionary factors changing culture? In a broader sense, there are certainly effects via personality (moderateness etc.). But brain size itself could work only indirectly via intelligence on culture. Such an indirect effect on culture is plausible. Thus presenting only a correlation ($r$ = .32) is a cautious way of dealing with the relationship between evolutionary and cultural factors.

And are there not further important, but until now not considered, determinants? Adding two control variables, *absolute latitude* and *natural resources rents* (see Section 10.6), the picture does not change: absolute latitude (distance to equator) is irrelevant for wealth ($\beta_{AL \to Wealth}$ = .02); natural resources rents have a minor positive impact ($\beta_{NRR \to Wealth}$ = .12). Natural resources rents

---

[5] In the same country sample ($N$ = 97), the pattern remains; correlations of top cognitive ability level with political conditions (government effectiveness, economic liberty, rule of law) are higher: $r_{95\%}$ = .72, .51, .70, $r_{CA}$ = .69, .47, .67.

additionally show an interesting suppressor effect: the correlation between natural resources and wealth is slightly negative ($r_{\text{NRR-Wealth}} = -.07$), while the effect is slightly positive ($\beta_{\text{NRR}\rightarrow\text{Wealth}} = .12$). This means that wealthy countries usually do not depend on natural resources; however, with production and rule of law subtracted they have a positive surplus. Natural resources are nice to have but not essential.

Astonishing for classical economics is the *rather low impact of economic freedom*; precisely: only a smaller share of international differences in GDP per capita is statistically explained by international differences in economic freedom. The pattern is not only found in a cross-sectional analysis as presented here (Figure 11.1) with $\beta_{\text{EF}\rightarrow\text{GDP}} = .13$ versus $\beta_{95\%\text{tot}\rightarrow\text{GDP}} = .78$. It is also found in longitudinal analyses (see Figures 10.1 to 10.2): Averaging all these four results, the mean economic freedom effect on GDP is only half the size of the cognitive human capital effect: $\beta_{\text{EF1}\rightarrow\text{GDP2}} = .15$ versus $\beta_{\text{CHC1}\rightarrow\text{GDP2}} = .31$. The pattern is always the same either choosing average cognitive ability, intellectual classes' level or top scientific-technological achievement (Rindermann, 2012): cognitive effects are more important.

The presented analysis deals with data from around the turn of the millennium to 2010. It statistically explains national differences in wealth. Together with theoretical assumptions and further analyses, insofar as possible partial correlations, controls and longitudinal analyses (see Chapter 10), its objective is to *causally explain the development of national differences in wealth*. Hence underlying historical differences and a development model are alluded to. Because reciprocal effects cannot be modelled with cross-sectional data, the unidirectional coefficients somewhat overestimate the effects of one variable on the other. E.g. between adult education and school quality, there is – interpreted as a causal development model – no '$\beta_{\text{AdE}\rightarrow\text{SQ}} = .72$' but there are (guessed) '$\beta_{\text{AdE1}\rightarrow\text{SQ2}} = .42$' and '$\beta_{\text{SQ1}\rightarrow\text{AdE2}} = .30$'. Adult education and school quality influence each other. This, taking in mind, the model is not wrong but a *simplification* of reality as all models necessarily are. And it is tentative or open to future challenges.

## 11.2   Politics: Democracy, Liberty, Rule of Law and Gender Equality

The wellbeing of nations is a broad concept and does not only cover economic production and prosperity but also political aspects such as rule of law, political liberty, democracy and gender equality (see Chapter 2). All these four variables stand for positively evaluated political conditions going along with political modernity (especially the aspect 'gender equality'; sources, see Section 2.4). They also indirectly cover human rights, treatment of minorities and peace. We performed a second path analysis with positive-modern politics as criterion (Figure 11.2).

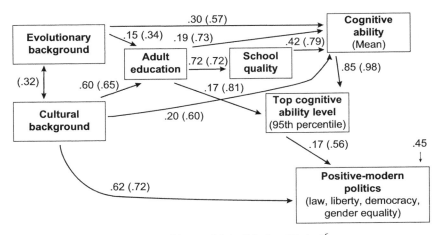

Figure 11.2 Global politics model (political wellbeing)[6]

For politics, the impact of culture is much stronger than for wealth ($\beta_{\text{Cultot}\to\text{Pol}}$ = .71, $r_{\text{Cul-Pol}}$ = .72 vs. $\beta_{\text{Cultot}\to\text{Wealth}}$ = .32, $r_{\text{Cul-Wealth}}$ = .61). The impact of the top ability level is considerably smaller ($\beta_{95\%\text{tot}\to\text{Pol}}$ = .17, $r_{95\%\text{-Pol}}$ = .56 vs. $\beta_{95\%\text{tot}\to\text{Wealth}}$ = .65, $r_{95\%\text{-Wealth}}$=.79). Also, the influence of evolutionary factors on politics is somewhat smaller ($\beta_{\text{Evotot}\to\text{Pol}}$ = .06, $r_{\text{Evo-Pol}}$ = .22 vs. $\beta_{\text{Evotot}\to\text{Wealth}}$ = .09, $r_{\text{Evo-Wealth}}$ = .40). However, the effect of evolutionary factors is certainly underrated: first, the 'older' evolutionary factors may have influenced the development of culture in history. We can assume a genetic effect on personality such as discipline and general predictability having a positive, but speculative, impact on institutional quality. Consequently, adding this path would largely increase the final impact of evolution on politics (without: $\beta_{\text{Evotot}\to\text{Pol}}$ = .06, with: $\beta_{\text{Evotot}\to\text{Pol}}$ = .29).

Finally, there is a characteristic pattern among the four political criteria: The more modern and left a political criterion (gender equality vs. rule of law) the stronger is the correlation with culture ($r_{\text{Cul-GE}}$ = .71 vs. $r_{\text{Cul-RoL}}$=.60, $N$ = 127) and the weaker with evolution ($r_{\text{Evo-GE}}$ = .19 vs. $r_{\text{Evol-RoL}}$=.33, $N$ = 127). Additionally, modern-left criteria are weaker correlated with top cognitive ability level ($r_{95\%\text{-GE}}$ = .51 vs. $r_{95\%\text{-RoL}}$ = .70, $N$ = 91). Political modernisation is furthered by cognitive ability, especially by the ability level of intellectual classes, but it largely depends on culture: on worldviews originated from religions. These factors together explain 55 per

[6] Data from around year 2010 (psychometric IQ and adult education around 1970–2010), $N$ between 96 (school quality), 99 (top cognitive ability level) and up to 200 countries (weighted religions, cognitive ability, politics), FIML, *CFI* = .95, *SRMR* = .06, standing for good fit.

cent of international differences in politics – a large amount for variables that are conceptually totally different!

Are the models also valid for the past? If the background factors 'evolution' and 'culture' are valid and reasonably stable across time, observable effects also have to exist for the past. Considering their long- and mid-term development and especially considering cross-national differences both factors should be 'reasonably stable': of course, development across centuries is possible, but national patterns should be stable ('relative stability'; see Section 3.3.1). However, because the formative cultural conditions present in the last few centuries did not exist around 2000 years ago and were considerably weaker 500 years ago (Protestantism evolved in the sixteenth century), effects of culture should be less pronounced in the more distant past.[7]

In Table 11.1, correlations for historical variables are presented. The two background factors 'evolution' and 'culture' are always positively correlated to technological-intellectual-scientific achievement, to production and democracy, and this is true from year 0 to the eighteenth century. In identical variables (technology 0 and 1500; GDP 1500, 1821 and 1913; democracy nineteenth century, first and second half of twentieth century), the correlations become higher with time. In particular, the correlations with the factor culture rise (+.44, +.58, for technology or GDP, identical country samples and variables), and they rise more than the correlations with evolution (+.11, +.18). The same could be observed for democracy (rises with time, culture: +.39; evolution: +.21).

All correlations support the background factors as being stable and differently variable: while the impact of evolutionary factors only slightly rises (on average: +.17) the impact of cultural factors became more and more important (+.47). Two processes are relevant: first, with modernisation and increasing complexity and institutionalisation cognitive and broader burgher human capital factors (self-control, discipline, predictability etc.) became more relevant for economy and society. Second and more important, culture changed; in particular, the development of Protestantism and burgher culture and their impact on surrounding milieus increased the impact of culture and cultural differences on technological-intellectual-scientific achievement, productivity and politics. They created a totally new, in human history, world of continuous technological progress, wealth, liberty and democracy.

A similar rising pattern can be noted for the impact of ability on technological-intellectual-scientific achievement (same variable Comin) and wealth

---

[7] We tried to present a path model; however, the statistical software (Mplus) could not calculate fit indices; the given correlations were strongly diverging from correlations calculated by SPSS; and correlations together with beta and errors did not result in the product sum 1. Hence we refrain from presenting a model.

Table 11.1 *Correlations between background compared to ability and historical indicators of intellectual achievement, wealth and democracy*

| | Technology 0 (Comin) | Technology +1500 (Comin) | Intellectual-scientific achievement | GDP 1500 Maddison (logged) | GDP 1821 Maddison (logged) | GDP 1913 Maddison (logged) |
|---|---|---|---|---|---|---|
| **Evolutionary** | .33 [.32] | .40 [.43] | .17 [.20] | .09 [.09] | .18 [.20] | .20 [.27] |
| **background** | (131) [112] | (118) [112] | (181) [112] | (32) [32] | (53) [32] | (64) [32] |
| **Cultural** | .12 [.18] | .56 [.62] | .37 [.46] | .13 [.13] | .52 [.51] | .61 [.71] |
| **background** | (134) [112] | (123) [112] | (197) [112] | (32) [32] | (55) [32] | (66) [32] |
| **Cognitive** | .36 [.49] | .82 [.78] | .40 [.42] | .26 [.26] | .53 [.55] | .52 [.70] |
| **ability m** | (134) [68] | (123) [68] | (196) [68] | (32) [31] | (55) [31] | (66) [31] |
| **Top (95%)** | .40 [.51] | .76 [.77] | .41 [.46] | .21 [.21] | .57 [.51] | .54 [.73] |
| **cognitive lv** | (78) [68] | (71) [68] | (99) [68] | (31) [31] | (49) [31] | (60) [31] |
| **Intellectual-** | | | | .20 [.20] | .71 [.67] | .67 [.68] |
| **scientific** | | | | (32) [32] | (55) [32] | (66) [32] |
| | **Democracy 19th century** | | **Democracy 1900–1949** | | **Democracy 1950–2012** | |
| **Evolutionary** | .08 [.08] | | .08 [.33] | | .20 [.29] | |
| **background** | (52) [52] | | (80) [52] | | (174) [52] | |
| **Cultural** | .29 [.28] | | .57 [.61] | | .68 [.67] | |
| **background** | (54) [52] | | (84) [52] | | (189) [52] | |
| **Cognitive** | .28 [.27] | | .55 [.53] | | .55 [.60] | |
| **ability m** | (54) [43] | | (84) [43] | | (187) [43] | |
| **Top (95%)** | .33 [.33] | | .57 [.55] | | .57 [.62] | |
| **cognitive lv** | (43) [43] | | (66) [43] | | (95) [43] | |

*Notes:* Evolutionary b.: Evolutionary background (cranial capacity, not smoothed-graduated; Section 10.7.2); Cultural backg.: Cultural background (weighted religions; Section 10.8.8); Technology: development and adoption of technology in 0 or 1500 according to Comin; Intellectual-scientific achievement: average of Eminent Scientists, Murray, −800 to 1950, and enlightenment index, Mokyr, eighteenth century, missing values set to 0, Cronbach-$\alpha$ = .69 (more information on these criteria in Section 4.4.2); democracy based on Polity and Vanhanen data, see Section 2.4; in second row number of countries, in brackets correlations and *N*s for same country samples (better to compare).

and the impact of intellectual-scientific achievement itself on wealth. With historical development, the correlations became higher (cognitive ability: +.29 and +.44; top level: +.26 and +.52; intellectual-scientific achievement: +.47; respectively in identical country samples and for technology or GDP). Finally, the correlations with democracy were also rising (cognitive ability: +.33; top level: +.29).[8]

---

[8] One objection is that correlations are only rising due to growing similarity of populations standing behind the variables. That is correct; therefore technology 0 is less comparable than technology 1500 with variables based on current populations, and GDP 1500 is less comparable than GDP

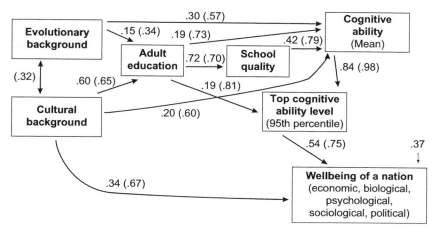

Figure 11.3 The wellbeing of nations and its determinants
Data from around years 1994–2012, *N* between 96 (school quality) and 99 (top ability group) and 192–199 (adult education, cranial capacity, religion, wellbeing) and 200 (cognitive ability mean), variable descriptions and sources see chapter 10.5.2 and appendix, FIML, *CFI* = .97, *SRMR* = .05, standing for good fit.

The results reveal that across centuries modernisation more and more depends on cognitive factors. *Modernity is a cognitive product.* Technological modernity, intellectual modernity, scientific modernity and political modernity are cognitive phenomena. And because the impact of cultural factors is also increasing, *modernisation is a cultural-cognitive process.*

## 11.3   Explaining National Wellbeing Differences between Countries

The most general criterion is the wellbeing of nations. It covers economic, biological, psychological, sociological and political wellbeing. Wellbeing is based on the following variables: production, income and assets (wealth); life expectancy (health); life satisfaction and trust; low murder rates, peace, low corruption, low divorce rates (security, peace and stability); and on democracy, liberty, rule of law and gender equality. Results of a path analysis checking the possible effects of causal determinants in a cross-sectional design are presented in Figure 11.3.

1821. But this is true for both background factors, evolution and culture, as well. We compare their different increases only for the same periods. And between the nineteenth, twentieth and the beginning of the twenty-first century the population changes are considerably smaller.

National wellbeing mainly depends on the cognitive ability level of a society – of its top ability group and behind it of a society's ability average. As more in-detail analyses have shown, intellectual classes have a crucial impact on innovation, on development of institutions and their maintenance (see Chapter 8). But the difference in correlations between average cognitive ability level of society and top ability group is not large ($r_{95\%\text{-}Wb} = .75$ vs. $r_{CA\text{-}Wb} = .71$, in a same country sample: $r_{95\%\text{-}Wb} = .74$ vs. $r_{CA\text{-}Wb} = .73$, $N = 99$). Society and cognitive elite both contribute to the wellbeing of nations. For instance, members of the intellectual classes develop institutions, and the entire society contributes to their function. The majority of intellectual class members come from the broad society. Both groups are essential and their levels are crucial. National wellbeing at low ability levels is not impossible but difficult to achieve.[9]

Comparing the two background factors, culture is more important than evolution ($r_{Cul\text{-}Wb} = .67$ vs. $r_{Evo\text{-}Wb} = .40$, in a same country sample: $r_{Cul\text{-}Wb} = .70$ vs. $r_{Evo\text{-}Wb} = .41$, $N = 179$).[10] Culture and evolution have an indirect impact via furthering education and ability, but culture also has a direct impact on national wellbeing ($\beta_{Cul \rightarrow Wb} = .34$). Culture is the important background factor for the success of nations but evolution is far from being irrelevant.

Differences in culture and in the ability level of intellectual classes (general society ability level, education, culture and evolution work behind them) explain 63 per cent of international differences in wellbeing. As for politics, this is an impressive result, because predictors and criteria are conceptually totally different variables.

## 11.4    The Impact of Education and School Education on Cognitive Ability

In the previous global models, education such as adult education and general school quality showed a strong impact on cognitive ability. Education at the individual and at the national level is highly correlated with ability. Theoretical considerations, as well as empirical studies, substantiate a causal impact on development of intelligence and knowledge (Sections 3.4.6 and 10.5). Additionally, education is seen as the most malleable and improvable factor by political decisions. But which educational factors have a strong impact

---

[9] The important role of cognitive ability for national wellbeing is corroborated by a study using another criterion of wellbeing (growth in life expectancy, leisure time, income equality), another type of analyses (regressions with robustness tests), presented by an economist (Hafer, 2017).

[10] This is also true if, instead of cranial capacity, skin lightness or a general factor of evolution are chosen ($r_{SL\text{-}Wb} = .64$, $r_{EvGF\text{-}Wb} = .59$).

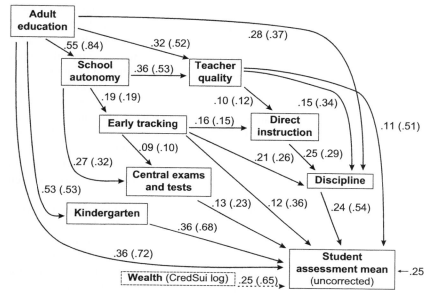

Figure 11.4 Model for education[11]

controlled for other educational factors and how do they work? Such direct and indirect effects were analysed in a further integrative model (Figure 11.4).

Uncorrected cognitive ability results of student assessment tests were taken as criteria. Student assessment results are more suitable as criteria: as youth and pupil measures they are closer to school conditions; results and factors are surveyed for the same countries and in the same period; the test scales (especially of TIMSS) are closer to curricula taught at school. However, the most distant variable of the model, measured in the past and valid for adults, the adult educational level (literacy rate, secondary school qualifications, schooling years at age 25) is the most predictive variable of students' cognitive ability ($\beta_{\text{AdE}\rightarrow\text{SAS}} = .36$, $r_{\text{AdE-SAS}} = .72$)!

The second most important factor is again not a student or school variable; it is kindergarten attendance ($\beta_{\text{Kiga}\rightarrow\text{SAS}} = .36$, $r_{\text{KigaE-SAS}} = .68$) depending, itself, on adult educational level ($\beta_{\text{AdE}\rightarrow\text{Kiga}} = .53$, $r_{\text{AdE-Kiga}} = .53$). Educational level also shows strong effects on school quality factors which explain cross-

[11] Data from around years 1994–2012, $N$ between 54 (central exams and tests), 106 (adult education) and 108 countries (student assessment mean), variable descriptions and sources see Section 10.5.2 and Appendix, FIML: full-information-maximum-likelihood, *CFI*=.99, *SRMR*=.07, standing for good fit. General background factors 'culture' and 'evolution' are not considered in the model of Figure 11.4, but are in the models of Figures 11.1 to 11.3.

country differences in students' cognitive ability such as school autonomy, teacher quality and discipline. Discipline is the variable with the third highest direct impact on ability ($\beta_{\text{Dis}\rightarrow\text{SAS}}$ = .24, $r_{\text{Dis-SAS}}$ = .54). It is the most important student and school variable for explaining cross-country differences in student cognitive ability. Teacher quality, early tracking and central exams show a weaker but still important impact (around $\beta$ = .12). School autonomy has indirect effects via teacher quality, central exams and early tracking ($\beta_{\text{SAtot}\rightarrow\text{SAS}}$ = .13). All educational variables together explain the large value of 75 per cent in international differences in student assessment tests. It should be kept in mind that educational variables are attributes of education, and cognitive competences are achievement data measured by tests – there is no overlap in measurement and this makes the size of the explained variance even more impressive.

As valid for all path models, the paths need a theoretical justification. Cross-sectional data cannot check reciprocal effects, e.g. adult education furthers kindergarten attendance and kindergarten attendance raises, in the long run, adult education. Additionally, the used variables are theoretically located at the individual, class, school and society level. But here we have data measured for all variables at society level compared across countries. Interpretations for other levels need empirical support from studies and theories at these levels. What is the theoretical background of the chosen paths?

- *Amount of education* is, at the individual level, the most important longitudinal environmental causal factor outside the family. Per attended year at school, intelligence increases at about 3 IQ points. However, here we have country data. We assume that better educated societies provide more supportive conditions for cognitive development, e.g. better parents (reading to the child, discipline education etc.) and institutions with higher quality (kindergarten, school autonomy, teacher quality). Indirectly, effects of evolutionary and cultural background factors are integrated, as are reverse effects.
- *Kindergarten* attendance is education that takes place in a sensible age period, raising intelligence, student achievement and personality attributes that are helpful for later schooling (Section 10.5). Aggregated effects are identical to individual effects.
- If *schools* are *autonomous* they want and can select their pupils (tracking). Both variables may also be indicators of more liberty in a school system. They are correlated with economic and political liberty.[12] Autonomous

---

[12] Correlations of school autonomy (SA) and early tracking (ET) with economic (EF) and political freedom (PF): $r_{\text{SA-EF}}$ = .30, $r_{\text{SA-PF}}$ = .23, $r_{\text{ET-EF}}$ = .18, $r_{\text{ET-PF}}$ = .22; on average $r$ = .23; whereas for the other educational variables in the model the correlations are $r$ = .15 on average.

schools can better select their teachers, leading to a general positive impact on teacher quality. Country effects are identical to school effects.

- In countries with better *teachers*, more active teaching methods are chosen in instruction and classes are better managed: There is more direct instruction and more discipline (see Section 10.5). All these conditions together result in more learning and higher student ability. Country effects are similar to class effects.

- Reasonable tracking, i.e. tracking based on ability, is based on the use of objective (central) tests.[13] Tests improve ability (motivation, objective benchmark, Section 10.5). *Early tracking, exams and tests, direct instruction* and *discipline* are all indicators of an achievement-oriented school system and a culture tending towards burgher, respectively burgher-conservative, values.[14] Early tracking and direct instruction also turn attention towards learning and achievement, leading to a positive effect on discipline. Tracking leads to a better match between instruction and student ability. Country effects are similar to school effects.

- *Discipline* increases learning time, raising cognitive ability. But cognitive ability also increases self-management: both are indicators of achievement orientation and burgher values. Country effects are similar to within-country effects.

If wealth (Credit Suisse wealth measure) is added to the model, its effect is, with $\beta_{\text{Wealth}\rightarrow\text{SAS}} = .25$, certainly not negligible. But the effects of adult education or kindergarten attendance are larger; the total education effect on students' ability is about three to four times larger than the wealth effect. Wealth differences are not decisive for understanding ability differences between nations.

## 11.5    Summary on National Wellbeing Differences

Today's national wealth and wellbeing differences are associated with the quality of political institutions, with the cognitive ability level of nations and therein especially with the level of their intellectual elites, with education and school quality and with global cultural and evolutionary background factors. Theoretical considerations, path models, historical observations and longitudinal analyses lead to the conclusion that wealth and wellbeing of nations are based on the interplay of long-term stable background factors with more

---

[13] It should be mentioned that the correlation between tracking and central exams and tests is astonishingly small with $r = .10$. This is critical because tracking is based in many countries on less reliable, fair and meritoric criteria.

[14] On average early tracking, exams, direct instruction and discipline are negatively correlated with an indicator of progressiveness, gender equality, $r = -.15$, whereas for the other educational variables the correlation with gender equality is positive, $r = +.43$.

variable specific factors: on the one hand culture and evolution and on the other education, cognitive ability and economic and political institutions.

While the relevance of education and cognitive factors for the development of economies, institutions and societies is not surprising and backed by theoretical considerations and a broad stream of research – it is also the background for all the many OECD PISA and IEA TIMSS and PIRLS surveys conducted in increasing country samples – the demonstration of the relevance of culture and evolution for the fate of nations is more startling, if not controversial. However, the relevance of long-term stable factors dealing with 'demography' was also shown by recent studies in economic research; some examples and quotes are presented here:

- Spolaore and Wacziarg (2013, p. 325) wrote in their article entitled 'How deep are the roots of economic development?': 'The evidence suggests that economic development is affected by traits that have been transmitted across generations over the very long run . . . biologically (via genetic or epigenetic transmission) and culturally (via behavioral or symbolic transmission).'
- Easterly and Levine (2012, p. 0): 'We find a remarkably strong impact of colonial European settlement on development. . . . One of our most surprising findings is the positive effect of even a small minority European population during the colonial period on per capita income today, contradicting traditional and recent views.'
- Chanda, Cook and Putterman (2014, p. 1): 'Using data on place of origin of today's country populations and the indicators of level of development in 1500 . . . we find persistence of fortune for people and their descendants.'
- Michalopoulos and Papaioannou (2011, p. 0): 'Our regression discontinuity estimates reveal that differences in countrywide institutional arrangements across the border do not explain differences in economic performance within ethnic groups. In contrast, we document a strong association between pre-colonial ethnic institutional traits and contemporary regional development.'

The specific contributions of our models are (1) to consider cognitive ability and especially the crucial ability level of intellectual classes, (2) to compare the impact of two background factors stemming from the rival paradigms 'evolution' and 'culture', (3) to use for evolution and culture specific variables with an explanative causal meaning (brain size for intelligence, and religion for the development of a burgher culture), (4) to analyse the interplay between different distal background and more proximal and easier to modify educational, political and economic variables, (5) to bring together psychological and institutional determinants, (6) to combine perspectives from different paradigms (psychology, education, economics, sociology, biology, political science, cultural research) and (7) to quantitatively estimate the direct and indirect effects of determinants using path models.

A cognitive human capital theory describing psychological (individual and aggregated persons' behaviour) and mediated (changing environments as society and institutions) effects on national development has to be completed by integrating background factors influencing conditions for cognitive development, supporting the practice of cognitive ability itself and establishing institutions relevant for societies' wellbeing. *Cognitive capitalism is a cultural-cognitive phenomenon.*

Global background factors are conceptualised as being longitudinally (in historical development) and cross-nationally (patterns and differences between nations) stable but not unchangeable: they are themselves shaped by environmental, cognitive, chance and internal developmental factors. For culture, the influence of intellectual classes is crucial. Intellectual classes themselves stem from broader spectra of society. There is a dynamic spiral-shaped process across time, including worldview and education, society and the individual, culture and intelligence, institutions and wealth.

# 12    Challenges of Future Development and First Predictions

Modernisation leads to rising complexity. Internal dynamics in the development of science, technology, culture and economy increase complexity. Cognitive ability both raises complexity and enables one to cope with complexity. Further future challenges include resource depletion, demographic change and rising inequality. They increase the difficulties and weaken the possibilities of managing future problems. Predictions for the twenty-first century are outlined.

In modernity, the wellbeing of a nation largely depends on progress in technology, organisation and knowledge, and this progress crucially depends on the ability level of society and its intellectual class. Wellbeing becomes cognitive wellbeing – wealth becomes high ability wealth. This is not only true for economic production and income, but also for science, technology and culture, which are all built upon the achievement of top ability groups. At the same time, modernisation processes lead to rising complexity in all fields: in research, in technology, in organisation, in finance, in politics, in management, in everyday life. Ability helps to cope with those challenges but at the same time ability also increases them.

## 12.1    Rising Complexity

*Technology: Photography, Heating Systems and the Space Shuttle as Examples*    An example covering a broad spectrum of technology is photography. Photography deals with mechanics, optics, electronics and information technology becoming more and more complicated. The first Nikon camera that the author owned, the Nikon FG from 1982, had, including its lens, 13 buttons and wheels. The D800 from 2012 has 34 mechanical controls, additionally six major electronic menu points with around 80 second-order menu points and many further third-order menu points and positions. And that is not the end. After taking a photo, the photographer has nearly endless possibilities in the photo editing software. The challenges for the photographer are obvious.

But not only *users*, also *companies* are increasingly challenged. Nikon and other manufacturers have serious problems in quality management. Nikon builds leading photographic products and their package of sensor quality and usability is the unmatched benchmark, but single shortcomings are obvious. For instance, reports and measurements showed that at the beginning of the production process the Nikon D800 autofocus sensors on the left side could not correctly focus lenses; another camera, the D600, produced dust or oil particles on its sensor; for the 300mm F4 PF VR lens at certain shutter speeds the image stabilisation did not work properly.[1]

Another example deals with *modern heating systems* that every current building in colder climates has: in a typical new single-family house, such a system works with at least three temperature sensors, one outside, one in each room and one for the water that transports the heat, and with at least two setpoints, one in each room and one variable setpoint for the heating system dealing with inputted changes from day to night and from weekday to vacation time. However, such systems frequently do not work as prescribed, do not achieve the required temperature and fitters do not understand them.

Technological products, production processes and their innovation become more and more demanding. Tiny faults can make a product nearly useless. Richard Feynman and the Rogers Commission described the weakness of a minute part of the space shuttle, an O-ring, being less resilient in cold weather as having led to the 1986 Space Shuttle Challenger disaster (Rogers Commission, 1986).

*Science*  Within science, previously gained knowledge and procedures such as statistical methods set the lower thresholds for new research. The more knowledge is given, the more difficult it becomes to find anything new and important. Admittedly, it is easy today to do routine science – it was never so easy to find data and use statistical software – but rates of innovation and patent rates per scientists are declining (Huebner, 2005; Strumsky, Lobo & Tainter, 2010). Scientists work on 'micro-innovations', which become less and less relevant. Such processes of facilitated routine production but more complicated major progress are prevalent in science, technology and economy and in society and culture. The low-hanging fruits of progress are all harvested (Cowen, 2011). To cope with the rising demands, higher cognitive ability is necessary, especially among innovators and developers, but also among the average workforce (Hunt, 1995). Not only does progress become more difficult but also the maintenance of the given complexity. This will lead in future

---

[1] D800 autofocus problem: Lukas (2012). D600 dust issue: www.lensrentals.com/blog/2012/10/d600-sensor-dust-issues. 300mm lens image stabilisation dysfunction: http://cameralabs.com/reviews/Nikon_Nikkor_AF-S_300mm_f4E_PF_ED_VR/index.shtml.

to a closer relationship between cognitive ability, growth and wealth (e.g. Hanushek & Woessmann, 2015a, p. 49).

However, these internal dynamics do not cover the entire process. They are accompanied by further compounding processes and by dysfunctional reactions that aggravate the problems: science as an institution is becoming more orientated towards derivative but simple to determine indicators of research. New and important truth is not crucial and is therefore not pursued, but the level of external funds and the number of publications and citations, both easy to measure, are valued. This insufficient attempt to reduce complexity comes along with a growing impact of various interests such as those representing society, lobbies, the economy and politics penetrating research, the consciousness of scientists and the organisation of science. Less complex and simple to handle political criteria and groupthink, frequently also called 'political correctness', replace genuine complex scientific orientations.[2] Reputation replaces truth.

*Economy*    Jobs become more demanding, and economic processes more complex. Following Autor and Price (2013), there is an increasing share of tasks in the US economy with non-routine analytical-cognitive and non-routine interpersonal demands, whereas tasks with routine cognitive and manual demands are decreasing. Different researchers have described a gap between the demand of the economy and the supply of the workforce and fear that this gap will rise in the future.[3] Because, compared to demand, there were too few well-educated (able) and too many less educated (less able) workers, the salaries for the first rose and for the last declined, leading to higher inequality in the United States (Autor, 2014; Dobbs et al., 2012, p. 7). The same diverging development using cognitive ability scores as indicators was described for 24 countries by the OECD (OECD, 2013b, p. 50): jobs requiring high cognitive ability are growing and the others are declining.

Based on such observations, Dobbs et al. (2012) predicted for 2020 a global shortage of around 40 million high-skill workers (13 per cent of demand) and a global surplus of around 93 million low-skill workers (10 per cent of demand).

However, the internal dynamics of modernisation towards complexity increase, leading to gaps between cognitive demands and supply, do not comprise all future challenges. There are further risks for future economic growth and the advancement or even preservation of national wellbeing. They include three different demographic changes; additionally resource reduction,

---

[2] In extreme cases, data are fabricated, e.g. by the social psychologist and zeitgeist trombonist Diederik Stapel, who faked that vegetarians are better people than the more selfish meat eaters, or data on stereotyping and discrimination.

[3] E.g. Autor & Price (2013); Dobbs et al. (2012); Hunt (1995); Strack et al. (2014).

climate change and rising within-country inequality, the last being related to the widening gap between demand and supply described in this section.

## 12.2  Demographic Changes

### 12.2.1  Ageing

Demographic ageing means that societies become older on average. There are more old and fewer young people. This development is supposed to have a threefold effect:

(1) People *live longer in periods of life in which they receive services and goods* produced by currently working generations. Life expectancy is increasing faster than health life expectancy (e.g. Murray et al., 2015). Average hours worked per person in society and during their lifetime will decrease (Gordon, 2016). Within the years of retirement, time in which care is needed will rise. Researchers assume that percentages of people with Alzheimer's disease will increase; a worldwide tripling is expected by 2050 (from 101 to 277 millions; Prince, Prina & Guerchet, 2013, p. 19). In 2010, ca. $604 billion US Dollar (448 billion Euros, 1 per cent of GDP) were spent on the care of Alzheimer patients; this will increase to 1,117 billion Dollar by 2030 (pp. 71, 78). General health care costs and economic transfers will make rising taxes and rising government spending ratios necessary, with their known detrimental consequences.[4]

(2) Ageing does not only increase dementia within retirees, but also *reduces total society intelligence*. Intelligence decreases with age, especially fluid intelligence, fast reasoning processes (see Section 3.4.1). This effect is frequently overlooked because in surveys the elderly are usually not taken into account. The same disregard applies to the rise of geriatric diseases being neglected for estimations of a society's happy life years.

(3) Similarly, *exceptional achievement and creativity decline* from around age 30 onward, resulting in a lower ingenuity level of the total workforce and society (see Section 3.4.1). Future nations will be less innovative.

Increasing longevity was no problem for the economy and society in the last century because life expectancy increases went along with better and longer healthy time during working age and because the increase in the percentage of retirees was compensated by higher employment rates, especially among

---

[4] Government spending ratio is a negative indicator of economic liberty. Longitudinally at the level of nations, high government spending ratios show a negative impact on cognitive ability ($\beta_{GSR67 \to CA10} = -.24$) and on GDP ($\beta_{GSR67 \to GDP10} = -.11$) ($N = 18$ countries between late 1960s and around 2010). See Rindermann (2008b).

women, and lower numbers of children. Nations became older while high-birth rate cohorts (baby boomers) with few children were working. Altogether, formed the demographic dividend. Employment growth was responsible in the last 50 years for +0.3% GDP growth per year, but for the future a negative employment trend is expected to be responsible for a GDP decline at –0.2% (Manyika et al., 2015).[5] Only faster productivity gains may compensate for coming demographic tailwinds. But there are more signs for slower rather than faster productivity increases in the near future.

### 12.2.2  Differential Fertility Effect: Lower Birth Rates among Higher Ability Adults

In modernity, better-educated adults have on average fewer children than less educated parents. For instance, in Great Britain adults with children had, in their own youth, a lower IQ at age eleven than those without children; the difference reaches on average –2.19 IQ points (men –1.84, women –2.54; Stumm et al., 2011). A similar pattern using different research approaches could be found for the United States: adults with an IQ below 85 have on average 2.50 children, with an IQ of 85 to 100 2.21 children, with an IQ 101 to 116 2.06, with an IQ 117 to 132 2.00 and above an IQ of 132 points only 1.98 children (Vining, 1995). The same is true if education is used as a proxy for ability (Loehlin, 1997): adults without High School Graduation have on average 2.69 children and the number of children decreases with higher education up to a Graduate or Master certificate with 1.31 children.

Other studies presented correlations: for the United States, the correlation between general intelligence and number of offspring is negative with $r = -.165$ (Reeve et al., 2013). Individuals with higher intelligence also delay marriage (intelligence $g$ and age at first offspring: $r=.120$, Reeve et al., 2013; at the aggregated level: $r = .996$, Herrnstein & Murray, 1994, p. 351f.). In another US data set a negative fertility-intelligence correlation is also found ($r = -.122$; Meisenberg, 2010). For Germany, $r = -.13$ could be observed.[6] All these studies used large public data sets such as Talent or NLSY, with up to several hundred thousand subjects.[7]

---

[5] Manyika et al. (2015, p. 5) distinguish between economic growth attributable to productivity growth (1.8 per cent per year) and employment growth (0.3 per cent), both together for the last 50 years per year and capita, resulted in an average 2.1 per cent growth rate.

[6] Germany, $r = -.13$: own calculation based on data from Statistisches Bundesamt (2010), for women born 1959–1963 and 1964–1968.

[7] Talent: longitudinal study of a nationally representative, stratified random sample of US high school students, begun in 1960. NLSY: National Longitudinal Survey of the Youth; representative US study of youth and its education, started in 1979.

Because parents' and children's intelligence are empirically positively correlated (observed $r = .43$, latent $r = .56$; Section 3.4.5), and because parents transmit their attributes to children via shaping a development environment and via genes, lower birth rates among the more intelligent adults *conclusively ceteris paribus* have to lead to a lower ability level of the next generation. The effects may be not as large as depicted by the 2006 science fiction comedy 'Idiocracy', but based on the well-corroborated, by theory and empirics, premises the effects compellingly have to be negative.

However, as we all know, this was not the situation in the twentieth century concerning intelligence tests used as indicators for cognitive ability: IQ scores were rising at about 2.80 IQ points per decade.[8] There was no *ceteris paribus*; other things were not equal. Environmental conditions improved to such an extent that any negative impact of differential fertility was compensated. There are forces working in different directions. Depending on which one is stronger the observable trend across generations will be negative or positive.

The differential fertility effect can be calculated using mathematical formulae. Usually, these formulae (resp. the theories behind them) assume only a genetic transmission and a genetic effect ('dysgenic').[9] The results per decade are around $dec = -0.2$ to $-0.7$ IQ points depending on assumptions such as regression of the next generation towards the mean of a population. Due to the assumption of normal distribution, the declining effects are larger for the top ability group: there are more average people and conditions for average manifestations are more frequent. Thus children of exceptional athletes are good sportspeople but usually not exceptional athletes. The same is true for children of exceptional artists or scientists. Do you know the sons of Albert Einstein? On the gravestone of Goethe's son was engraved: Goethe Filius without any name. The loss among high ability groups could be more than a third in 100 years:

"The proportion of highly gifted people with an IQ higher than 130 will decline by 11.5% in one generation and by 37.7% in one century." (Meisenberg, 2010, p. 228)

And, as is usually overlooked, environmental and cultural effects are integrated in a reciprocal relationship between ability and environment, leading to an *upward* or *downward spiral*:

---

[8] FLynn effect: $dec = 2.80$ IQ points in Western countries is a rather optimistic estimation based on a meta-analysis of Pietschnig & Voracek (2015). Somewhat weaker are the results showing $dec = 2.31$ presented by Trahan et al. (2014). See Section 4.1.

[9] From a strict evolutionary view, 'dysgenic' effects cannot exist because any gene that leads to more (itself fertile) offspring is a successful gene. To speak about 'dysgenic' effects an additional biological or normative theory is necessary to give reasons for why a certain attribute is more or less favourable for the organism or for a larger entity such as family, population and society.

Small reductions in the average intelligence of educational administrators will result in an increased probability that educational reforms will reduce rather than enhance students' intelligence, and thereby lead to even lower intelligence in the next generation of educational administrators and even greater deterioration of the educational system. (Meisenberg, 2010, p. 228)

A meta-analysis on past differential fertility studies covering $N = 202,924$ subjects and $k = 10$ studies resulted in an average effect of $dec=-0.39$ IQ points (Woodley, 2015).[10] In an informal meta-analysis (Rindermann & Thompson, 2011b), the average effect was $dec = -0.37$; the difference is only 0.02 IQ points compared to Woodley's more systematic meta-analysis. Predictions dealing with international development and fertility differences between nations come to around $dec = -0.26$ to $-1.34$ IQ points (Lynn & Harvey, 2008; Meisenberg, 2009).

These estimates suffer from five problems:

(1) Not only does genetic transmission lead to parent-children similarity, but broader *familial transmission*, including environment, does as well. Thus relying only on genetic effects will underestimate the effects of different reproductive rates (number of children).

(2) Not only is cognitive ability passed on to the next generation, but also *personality*, including attitudes. Personality contributes to human capital.

(3) The *generation span* varies. It varies between parents, being related to intelligence. As Reeve et al. (2013, p. 361) showed, smarter adults became parents later in life ($r = .120$), leading to a decreasing share of smart persons in society across generations (see also Herrnstein & Murray, 1994, p. 351f.; Section 13.2.4).

(4) For individuals, it is true that parents with more extreme attributes will have children with, on average, less extreme attributes. A mother having an IQ of 130 points most probably will have a child with a lower IQ and not with a higher one. A father with IQ 80 will more probably have a child with IQ 90 than 70. That is called '*regression towards the mean*' (e.g. Lynn, 1996). Conventional formulae incorporate this. However, at the level of society this is not tenable: if it were, a society would become totally homogenous in the long run. Additionally, there are different 'averages' to which groups in the long run tend.

[10] Independent from a differential fertility effect considered in this paragraph of demographic changes, there could be a further effect due to mutation accumulation described by Woodley (2015): parents become older and health systems better. Older parents transmit more mutations; purifying selection is reduced. This makes it possible that deleterious mutations accumulate across generations, more so than in the past. According to the analysis, this effect is $dec = -0.84$ IQ points, together with the differential fertility effect of $dec = -0.39$ results $dec = -1.23$. Finally, by adding migration effects, the three trends together would lead to totally $dec = -1.51$ IQ points in ten years. Of course, this is true only among *ceteris paribus* conditions.

(5) Finally, *hard test facts* do support an intelligence rise more than an intelligence decline. At least for the twentieth century, there is overwhelming evidence for a positive phenotypic development.

Mental speed indicators (Woodley et al., 2013), more recent intelligence test declines in several Western countries (Section 4.1), flat trends of top ability groups (in the last decades in US NAEP, $dec_{17y90\%} = 0.08$ for the most relevant 17-year-old age group; Rindermann & Thompson, 2013), the parallelism of genotypic intelligence (the genetic share of measured intelligence) and innovation rates across centuries (Woodley, 2012, see Figure 12.1), declines in complex working memory (digit span backward, a cognitive ability close to intelligence, about $dec = -0.16$ IQ; Woodley & Fernandes, 2015) and less frequent uses of difficult words (Woodley et al., 2015) give first hints corroborating a negative phenotypic trend. Possibly, research on intelligence declines is another case of science showing that theory (e.g. in astrophysics) can be a forerunner for discoveries previously seen as being impossible and nonexistent.

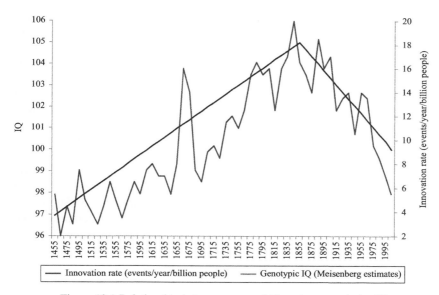

Figure 12.1 Relationship between assumed (linear) genotypic intelligence development and (zigzag) innovation over time ($r = .88$; Woodley, 2012, fig. 1)
Redrawn by David Becker with kind permission of the author, Michael Woodley.

The first four above-mentioned objections suggest larger differential fertility effects, and the last challenges any negative effect. However, only using logical reasoning based on the two statements that

(a) parents' and children's attributes are correlated and
(b) parents with better education and higher cognitive ability have fewer children and in older age,

there have to be negative intergenerational effects.
No doubt is possible.

### 12.2.3  Immigration

The leading countries in science and innovation in the past will not only grow old, but will also become more *diverse*. Diversity could mean growing creativity by bringing together new and different perspectives (Niebuhr, 2010). Nevertheless, it also means decreasing trust, which is negative for the economy and society (Section 2.4; Algan & Cahuc, 2014; Putnam, 2007). According to John Stuart Mill (1977/1861), ethnic and linguistic diversity are detrimental for freedom: 'Free institutions are next to impossible in a country made up of different nationalities'. (p. 547) It would be difficult to develop a common public and the relationship between the army and large fractions of the society resembles that of 'foreigners' being inclined to mistrust, suppression or opposition. Additionally, diversity combined with economic and cognitive differences is prone to cause 'group grievance', corruption and violence, all indicators of fragile and failed states (Fund for Peace, 2014).[11] Societies are more willing to redistribute wealth in more homogenous societies, less so in more diverse ones.[12] Diversity in groups and group achievement are not positively correlated, but the negative effect is small to negligible (ethnic diversity: $r = -.05$ and $r = -.004$, meta-analyses by Dijk et al., 2012; Schneid et al., 2014). By contrast in schools, ethnic diversity has a negative effect on natives' ability level with $-10$ SASQ (equiv. $-1.5$ IQ) and a strong negative effect on immigrants' ability development of around $-50$ SASQ points (equiv. $-7.5$ IQ) (Dronkers & Velden, 2013): diversity is certainly more detrimental for immigrants. Studies on institutional effects of ethnic diversity refer to lower primary school funding and worse school facilities (for Kenya: Miguel & Gugerty, 2005).

[11] Ethnic diversity and the fragile state index are correlated with $r = .42$ ($N = 152$; based on Meisenberg, 2007, and Fund for Peace, 2014). Similarly, Mauro (1995): he found a negative correlation of $r = -.41$ between ethnic diversity and political stability.
[12] Social welfare spending: gross public social expenditure in percentage of GDP according to OECD (2014a) and diversity measures (Alesina et al., 2003; Kurian, 2001; Meisenberg, 2007; Vanhanen, 2012) correlate at $r = -.18$ ($N = 33$ OECD countries).

Even more important than diversity effects are the effects of *ability levels of immigrants* (Section 10.3.5): except for small oil-based economies such as the Emirates and Qatar, and except for Australia and Singapore, countries lose average ability as a result of immigration. In Europe and North America the losses are prevailing.[13] They are still small, around 1 to 2 IQ points, and some of these losses will be caught up across generations. But they will lower the FLynn effect and the losses may rise with growing immigration from low-ability groups, enabling these groups to establish stable low-ability milieus.[14] The first adverse country level effects have been observed in Sweden, where the inflow of lower ability immigrants is one factor for understanding a trend of declining PISA results:

While scores among pupils with a Swedish background have declined by 22 points between 2000 and 2012, scores among pupils with an immigrant background have fallen by 39 points – and the performance gap between the two groups has grown from 36 points to 53 points. These are strong effects. In fact, the change in pupil demographics is the only factor that we know for sure has contributed to Sweden's falling scores. Furthermore, the full impact is probably somewhat larger. This is because immigration may also have lowered performance among pupils with a Swedish background, for instance through the redistribution of resources to immigrant pupils. ... So next time you read an article about declining Swedish scores and there's no mention of immigration, you know the journalist isn't doing his or her job properly – or is pursuing an ideological agenda. Or both. (Heller-Sahlgren, 2015a)

Economic effects of immigrants resemble the cognitive ability levels of their countries of origin; they are persistent and important: one higher immigrant homeland IQ point predicts 1 per cent higher immigrant wages (Jones & Schneider, 2010). According to Hanushek et al. (2013, p. 65f.), lifting the ability levels of Hispanic (and black) students and workers to that of Whites within two decades would result in a GDP gain for the United States of approximately $50 trillion in the twenty-first century. Low-ability immigration also slows down improvements in labour productivity (Kangasniemi et al., 2012).[15] Long-term analyses regarding different immigrant groups reveal a

---

[13] Nyborg (2012) predicted, based on past development, immigrant share prognosis, differential children rates and IQ levels, a declining average IQ for Denmark of around –6 IQ points in the twenty-first century. However, shrinking gaps between immigrants and natives due to rising immigrant ability levels (e.g. te Nijenhuis et al., 2004) were not integrated in the model.

[14] The results are based on representative student assessment samples and stand for long-term society effects. Those samples do not cover adult 'elite immigration' such as that of scientists and other in-demand professionals such as engineers, technicians and medical personnel. The United States (Wadhwa, 2012), Switzerland (Müller-Jentsch, 2008) and oil-producing countries have benefited from such elite immigration.

[15] However, low-ability immigration has a positive effect for low-ability native workers, pushing them to move into more complex and better paid occupations (Foged & Peri, 2015).

stable pattern and no gap closing (Salminen, 2015, pp. 13–15): For instance, for Finland immigrants from the Western world show from 1995 to 2011, a 26-year-interval, annual per capita net fiscal effects that fluctuate around zero, while for the same time the effects for immigrants from Somalia are between – 15,000 and –12,000 Euro and from the Middle East between –10,000 and – 9,000 Euro. These fiscal effects correlate with home country cognitive ability levels at $r = .86$ ($N = 11$). For a receiving society, immigrants from cognitively developed countries have on average a positive and stable effect.

Additionally, increasing immigration will lead to *more diverse ability levels and inequality* in society (Clark, 2014a). Probably, it is not ethnic diversity but rather ability heterogeneity along ethnic borders that is important, i.e. easy to observe ethnic differences in life outcomes due to ethnic ability differences. They will increase political pressures to implement anti-meritoric reforms. For instance, in universities ability-based admission standards will be substituted by political criteria; in the credit market economic criteria by eth(n)ical ones; in the economy and at schools objectively measured achievement by affirmative action and affirmative grading (Calomiris & Haber, 2013; Farron, 2010; Harber, 1998; Sander, 2004; Sowell, 2004). Such policies are detrimental for ability development, for achievement in education as well as in the economy: to obtain efficiency, productivity and quality in an economic system, in education and in general society, ability has to be allocated according to objective standards, the demand of the market and the job itself (e.g. Hunt, 1995, pp. 108ff.).[16]

Finally, immigration can have broader effects, not only on ability and its distribution, but, as hinted, also on the economy, politics and culture. There can be broad and spreading positive field effects, as observed in the past for science:

- *Jewish émigrés* from National Socialist Germany had an indirect positive impact on patent rates of native US inventors in the first half of the twentieth century – patent rates of native inventors increased in the émigré fields by 31 per cent and the effect was sustained across several decades (Moser et al., 2014).
- Huguenot *émigrés* from France to Germany in 1685 had a several centuries-long effect on the German *economy* (e.g., a regional 1.0 percentage point increase of Huguenots translated into 1.5 percentage point higher production

---

[16] Effects of meritoric orientations on ability development of nations: $\beta_{Merit \rightarrow CA10} = .17$ (see Section 10.3.3). The mentioned 'cures' could become more widespread (e.g., beginning with preferential admission for immigrants in the police force; Land Berlin, 2010; Sarrazin, 2014). Additionally, immigrants prefer parties that favour wealth distribution (for Denmark: Kirke-gaard & Tranberg, 2015), having via rising government spending ratios a negative impact on ability and economic growth.

in 1802; Hornung, 2014), on German *science* (e.g. the Humboldt brothers, Alexander the geographer and Wilhelm the philologist and education philosopher; Franz Karl Achard, inventor of the production of sugar from sugar beets; around 10 per cent of the members of the Prussian Academy of Sciences in the eighteenth century were Huguenots), on German *culture* (e.g., Theodor Fontane, novelist and poet; Anton Philipp Reclam, publisher and founder of the Reclam press) and on German *politics* (e.g., the de Maizière family, with several ministers and generals).

## 12.3   Resource Reduction

Since the famous report of the Club of Rome in the early seventies, sceptics referred to the limits of growth and wealth (Meadows et al., 1972). The report was based on highly plausible considerations: world population was and is still rising; peoples of all nations want to be rich like the West; the demand for natural resources rises due to population increase and international economic growth; but the earth and its resources are limited. A prominent example is the thesis of 'peak oil', the maximum of oil production. The demand for oil continues or becomes even larger but the natural mineral deposits are used up.

However, as it is easy to observe, there were no shortages of resources. In the last decade, there has been a boom in oil production fuelled by the discovery of new deposits and the development of new technologies of extraction (oil shale). The price for oil has been going down. There is no resource threat for international growth. There is only a problem of natural resources rents for countries producing oil in a traditional way.

Optimists like Goklany (2007, 'The improving state of the world') or Moore and Simon (2000, 'It's getting better all the time') have indeed predicted the development of such solutions: whenever humankind has to face a problem, new solutions will be found. Any shortage of raw materials can be managed by using the raw material *brainpower*:

The main fuel to speed the world's progress is our stock of knowledge, and the brake is our lack of imagination. The ultimate resource is people – skilled, spirited, and hopeful people – who will exert their wills and imaginations for their own benefit as well as in a spirit of faith and social concern. Inevitably they will benefit not only themselves but the poor and the rest of us as well. (Simon, 1996, p. XXXVIII)

However, the three demographic trends described in this section run in the opposite direction, favouring decreasing rather than increasing ability levels. And discovering and exploiting new sources, their more effective use and recycling of worn-out material will become more complex tasks than in the past.

### 12.4    Climate Change

Climate change is happening; average temperatures are rising. There are various objective indicators supporting a clear warming trend such as declining glaciers in the Alps and in the Himalayas, on Mount Kilimanjaro and at the poles; earlier spring migration dates of frogs and toads in the northern hemisphere; results of temperature measurements across decades. This warming trend most probably will continue in the coming decades.

The consequences for the economy and wealth are less obvious. A rising sea level is predicted, along with more extreme weather events such as more severe storms, droughts and rains. For GDP itself, the consequences may not be negative, as all catastrophes need a human answer and that will be reconstruction and improvement of protection. Any catastrophe, especially in saturated economies, will boost medium-term economic growth, as the construction of sea walls or dams will be required. While such an answer may be perceived as being cynical, it is simply the result of how Gross Domestic Product is defined. Therefore, we need alternative measures to determine wealth such as GNI, assets or life expectancy. In these variables, negative consequences of global warming will be observable. But negative consequences can be at least partly compensated by positive effects such as less need for winter heating, an ice-free Northeast Passage, larger agricultural productivity due to elevated carbon dioxide and expansion of fertile regions into the Sahara or the north of Russia and Canada. Effects largely vary across regions. Econometric predictions suggest a reduction in global GDP in the twenty-first century in the event of a 3°C warming of about one year of growth (1 to 3 per cent; Nordhaus, 2013). This means an annual loss of less than 0.05 per cent, which is negligible. Any change in cognitive human capital is much more important.

In the same way as rising complexity and the disappearance of easy to pick raw material, climate change is another challenge calling for higher cognitive resources.

### 12.5    Rising Inequality within Societies

While, internationally, nations become more similar, within-country heterogeneities are rising. For instance, countries become more alike in life expectancy (Figure 2.1), but within-country heterogeneities in incomes and wealth are growing. Rising within-country inequalities have been addressed by many different studies, e.g. in Lindsey's (2012) book *Human Capitalism: How Economic Growth Has Made Us Smarter – and More Unequal* or in Piketty's (2013) *Le Capital au XXIe Siècle.*

Piketty (2014/2013) claimed that inequality is rising because rates of return on capital have become greater than rates of economic growth. Other authors see the major reason for this trend in the rising wage premium for education and cognitive skills (e.g. Autor, 2014): in the United States, for example, between 1979 and 2002 the college-high school median annual earnings gap rose from $30,000 to $58,000 US (per household in constant 2012 dollars). The same pattern can be observed for many other countries (OECD, 2014b). Rising cognitive demands, a scarcity of well-educated and highly capable workers and imports from cheaper-producing countries in a globalised economy would lead to the observed gap increases.

Kirsch et al. (2007) offered similar interpretations: technological innovation and globalisation would lead to increasing economic returns to schooling and ability, resulting in wider gaps in employment opportunities and incomes. And they added further causes and related challenges: a population becoming older and more diverse by immigration, declining average ability levels, rising shares of people below the lowest ability thresholds and a growing disparity in ability. Bringing these trends together, they came to quite sceptic conclusions for future US development:

Unless we are willing to make substantial changes, the next generation of Americans, on average, will be less literate and have a harder time sustaining existing standards of living. (Kirsch et al., 2007, p. 10)

If we are unable to substantially close the existing skill gaps among racial/ethnic groups and substantially boost the literacy levels of the population as a whole, demographic forces will result in a U.S. population in 2030 with tens of millions of adults unable to meet the requirements of the new economy. Moreover, a substantial proportion of those adults will be members of disadvantaged minority groups who will likely consider themselves outside the economic mainstream. (Kirsch et al., 2007, p. 24)

Crudely speaking, as better-educated White non-Hispanics leave the workforce over the next two decades, increasingly their places will be filled by workers from minority groups with lower levels of education. (Kirsch et al., 2007, p. 22)

While declining ability is obviously negative, rising economic inequality itself does not have to be necessarily negative. Admittedly, economic studies showed a negative impact of inequality within the bottom half. This lowers economic growth because it leads to redistributive policies, higher taxes, rent seeking behaviour, risk of political instability and social unrest (Cingano, 2014). And observable wealth differences along ethnic lines will generate resentment. However, increasing economic returns to schooling and ability will encourage more investment in competence development, more investment of time, energy and money, resulting in a higher competence level – this is appreciated by individuals and society! Ethically, there is no problem if some become richer as long as their wealth is not built upon making others poorer than before (Mankiw, 2013). Having rich persons in a society can even be beneficial for others, as they stimulate progress by their consumption (Mises, 1996/1927; see Section 2.4).

Finally, richness buys much less advantage today than centuries ago. Technological progress levels out richness effects. For instance, the rich in the past had employees, couriers, horses and libraries. Today, nearly all in developed countries and every year more persons in developing countries have a washing machine, a hoover and a car. More and more have hot water, central heating, a lavatory and mobiles. People today consume fruits and vegetables in winter, and meat and milk in hot summer. More and more have access to public transport, modern medicine and the Internet, enabling access to millions of books and infinite information. While in the past, inventions needed centuries to spread from the rich to society at large, inventions need today only decades or even a few years. Glass windows needed 700 years from the Middle Ages to the nineteenth century to become common, electricity around 50 years from the late nineteenth century, telephones took 40 years in the twentieth century, radio and TV took 30 years, personal computers 20 years, mobiles ten years and in the last decades the Internet took around seven years.[17] In the near future we all will have our chauffeurs, the currently invented self-driving cars. And do you really need a yacht in Monaco?

*Growing Equality among Nations*     Internationally, development will lead to declining differences, resulting in more homogeneity. Currently poor countries have chances of catching up growth. The advantages of backwardness allow countries to benefit in a relatively simple way from the progress made by others that has been acquired in achieving more difficult to develop inventions. Basic medical support (vaccinations, hygiene, parasite control) is relatively cheap and simple and can be transferred to developing countries. Cheaper mobiles replace telephones or inoperative fixed line networks. Smart phones allow access to the Internet. There can be broad diffusion effects of development in competence, education, organisation and culture.

Africa will benefit from declining fertility rates and the demographic dividend. Richer but old nations may benefit by brain gain. But brain gain means for others a brain drain, especially for China, Vietnam and probably also Africa and the Arabian countries. If *'institution-builders'* are lost, crucial sectors of development suffer, such as in education and research, the health system, public administration and private entrepreneurship (Kapur & McHale, 2005).

---

[17] See Kurzweil's page 'The singularity is near', www.singularity.com/charts/page50.html.

## 12.6  Predictions in Research

### 12.6.1  Historico-Philosophical Ideas of Progress Versus Cyclic Theories of Rise and Fall

There is an old idea of progress: progress in technology, mastery and wealth, in thinking, ethics, culture and wellbeing. Prominent authors of this idea of progress are Marquis de Condorcet, Georg Wilhelm Friedrich Hegel, Auguste Comte, Karl Marx, James George Frazer and Norbert Elias. The two world wars and the two political ideologies, Communism and National Socialism, raised doubts whether there was really human progress. Nevertheless, not only did narrow economic production increase, but height and life expectancy did too, these being broader indicators of wealth. And at the same time, violence and homicide rates, both indicators of unethical behaviour, decreased (Pinker, 2011). There was a broad improvement trend across different fields, in science and technology, wealth and health, ethics and politics, in culture and thinking (Oesterdiekhoff, 2012–2014). Optimists such as Raymond Kurzweil or Julian Simon assume a continuation of this general positive trend, either permanently or ending in a final positive state of world society.

Others, pessimists, assume a less favourable or even negative trend. Empirical hints supporting such a view were documented above (rising complexity, demographic changes: ageing, adverse immigration, differential fertility, resource reduction, climate change, growing inequality). More philosophically, an *idea of progress* is contrasted with an *idea of cyclic movement*: cultures, societies and nations grow, reach a plateau and then decline. For everything there is a season. This process is caused either due to internal reasons similar to ageing, a law of life, of systems and history (cultural devitalisation), or due to more specific reasons such as elite corruption (reproduction not based on ability), demographic transition (dysgenic fertility) and the rise of non-meritoric worldviews, which may be interrelated (Spengler, 1991/1918; Toynbee, 1960/1934; Weiss, 2007).

In our focus will be national cognitive development and its effect on societies. Cognitive ability is crucial for the wellbeing of nations; it is not independent from evolutionary and cultural background factors and not independent from political, economic and institutional conditions, which are furthered by cognitive ability. Cognitive ability is the central moving force in this system of interwoven factors. Wealth development is one important criterion. Wealth is not the sole criterion of national wellbeing (Chapter 2), but wealth will become, in continuing modernisation processes, more and more connected to political and institutional conditions, and therefore a good indicator for national wellbeing. Growing complexity and the disappearance of easy to come by natural resources will lead to an increasing impact of cognitive human capital.

### 12.6.2    Keynes' Famous Prediction from 1930

John Maynard Keynes (1883–1946) made a famous prediction in 1930, namely, 'that the standard of life in progressive countries one hundred years hence will be between four and eight times as high as it is.' (Keynes, 2010/ 1930, p. 325f.)

Is there any possibility that Keynes' optimistic prediction will become real? We can check his prediction for the period from 1930 to 2010. Data come from Maddison's GDP pool for 50 countries in 1930. We can simply check, taking six times as the average of 'between four and eight times', if Keynes' prediction, not in 100 years, but already in 80 years up to 2010 has become real.

Table 12.1 shows that all regions and countries have increased their standard of living indicated by GDP in the last half century. Keynes predicted an average increase for 100 years of six times. This was even achieved within the shorter period of 80 years by 25 per cent of countries. So Keynes' prediction was even surpassed in some countries by reality. And this in spite of the ravages of the Second World War and Communism! Keynes' prediction for 100 years scaled down for 80 years (from on expected factor 6 times for 100 years to 4.8 times for 80 years) reveals that 42 per cent of all countries (he focused on 'progressive countries') achieved his wealth prediction.

The largest relative increases from 1930 to 2010 (factor 16.73) are observable for East Asia; the largest absolute increases occurred in North America ($22,204) and the Northwestern world ($19,528). Lagging behind in relative and absolute increases are sub-Saharan Africa (factor 2.42, $703), Latin America (3.99, $6,153) and Central-South Asia (4.46, $3,371).

While Keynes' prediction became by and large real, are there any factors that can explain the differences in growth between countries? Note, Keynes conditioned his prediction for 'progressive countries'. We have chosen for explanation the wealth determinants from the global path analysis in Figure 11.1 and correlated them with the absolute (difference) and relative (factor) increases between 1930 and 2010. Can they help to explain why some countries were more successful in the twentieth century and is there any relationship to Keynes' 'progressivity' assumption?

Except for natural resources rents all determinants are positively correlated with the past 80 years of economic growth. The variable that most highly correlates is cognitive ability as average or top ability level (mean $r = .64$ to $.78$) closely followed by government effectiveness (mean $r = .65$ to $.76$). Regarding the two background factors, evolution and culture are similarly important (mean $r_{Evo} = .47$-$.63$ and $r_{Cult} = .45$-$.62$). For absolute increases ('Difference 1930– 2010') all correlations are higher than for relative factor increases. Indirectly, this means that all factors are more explanatory for the richer countries since 1930. In comparison, poorer countries may benefit more from chance and

Table 12.1 *Wealth increases indicated by GDP/c ($) from 1930 onward*

| | | GDP 1930 Maddison | GDP 2010 Maddison | Growth rate per year 30–10 | GDP 2010 diff. in $ increase | GDP 2010 factor increase | GDP 2030 fact. incr. (estim.) |
|---|---|---|---|---|---|---|---|
| Africa (sub-Sahara) | | (671) | 1,373 | 0.84 | 703 | 2.42 | 3.03 |
| | Kenya | (488) | 1,141 | 1.07 | 653 | 2.34 | 2.92 |
| N-Africa M-East (ArM) | | 1,249 | 8,225 | 2.38 | 6,976 | 6.59 | 8.23 |
| | Turkey | 1,249 | 8,225 | 2.38 | 6,976 | 6.59 | 8.23 |
| America (North, Engl) | | 5,512 | 27,716 | 2.04 | 22,204 | 5.05 | 6.31 |
| | USA | 6,213 | 30,491 | 2.01 | 24,278 | 4.91 | 6.13 |
| America (Latin, C-S) | | 2,101 | 8,542 | 1.68 | 6,153 | 3.99 | 4.99 |
| | Mexico | 1,618 | 7,716 | 1.97 | 6,098 | 4.77 | 5.96 |
| Asia (Central-South) | | 996 | 4,336 | 1.88 | 3,371 | 4.44 | 5.55 |
| | India | 726 | 3,372 | 1.94 | 2,646 | 4.64 | 5.81 |
| East Asia | | 1,154 | 18,740 | 3.55 | 17,586 | 16.73 | 20.92 |
| | China | 568 | 8,032 | 3.37 | 7,464 | 14.14 | 17.68 |
| Southeast Asia, Pacific | | 1,386 | 5,947 | 1.69 | 4,560 | 4.17 | 5.21 |
| | Philippines | 1,382 | 3,024 | 0.98 | 1,642 | 2.19 | 2.74 |
| Australia-NZ (English) | | 4,834 | 22,235 | 1.91 | 17,401 | 4.62 | 5.78 |
| | New Zealand | 4,960 | 18,886 | 1.69 | 13,926 | 3.81 | 4.76 |
| Western Europe | | 4,690 | 23,025 | 2.04 | 18,335 | 5.16 | 6.44 |
| | United Kingdom | 5,441 | 23,777 | 1.86 | 18,336 | 4.37 | 5.46 |
| Scandinavia | | 3,985 | 25,024 | 2.36 | 21,039 | 6.68 | 8.35 |
| | Norway | 3,627 | 27,987 | 2.59 | 24,360 | 7.72 | 9.65 |
| Central Europe | | 4,602 | 23,263 | 2.08 | 18,662 | 5.31 | 6.64 |
| | Germany | 3,973 | 20,661 | 2.08 | 16,688 | 5.20 | 6.50 |
| Eastern Europe | | 1,965 | 9,157 | 1.95 | 7,192 | 4.82 | 6.03 |
| | Romania | 1,219 | 4,653 | 1.69 | 3,434 | 3.82 | 4.77 |
| Southern Europe | | 2,137 | 14,325 | 2.40 | 12,188 | 6.78 | 8.48 |
| | Italy | 2,918 | 18,520 | 2.34 | 15,602 | 6.35 | 7.93 |

*Notes:* Growth rate per year 30–10: average annual growth rate 1930–2010; GDP 2010 diff. in $ increase: difference between GDPs 2010 and 1930; GDP 2010 factor increase: GDP 2010 divided by 1930 (country samples of regions may differ between 2010 and 1930); GDP 2030 factor increase (estimated): linearly estimated 2030 factor increase based on the 1930–2010 increase; for sub-Saharan Africa 1930 data extrapolated from the 1950 to 2010 development; data for *N* = 65 countries (having data for 1930, in Africa extrapolated, Sudan as single outlier excluded), data for 2010 therefore not identical with Table 1.2 (based on different *N*); instead of Egypt and Russia (no data for 1930) Turkey and Romania taken as examples for the North-Africa-Middle-East and Eastern Europe regions.

Table 12.2 *Correlation of Figure 11.1 2010 wealth determinants with wealth increases from 1930–2010*

| | Background factors | | Education | | Cognitive ability | | Political-institutional factors | | | Controls | |
| | Evo factor | Cult factor | Educ adult | Schoo qual | CA total | 95%- IQ | Gov effect | Econ freed | Rule law | Abs latit | Nat ResR |
|---|---|---|---|---|---|---|---|---|---|---|---|
| **Difference 1930–2010** | .66 | .77 | .80 | .60 | .88 | .82 | .91 | .74 | .89 | .77 | –.28 |
| **Factor 1930–2010** | .60 | .40 | .40 | .57 | .60 | .46 | .45 | .33 | .41 | .33 | –.21 |
| **Mean (N = 45 to 66)** | .63 | .62 | .64 | .59 | .78 | .68 | .76 | .57 | .73 | .59 | –.25 |
| **Mean (N = 43)** | .47 | .45 | .53 | .54 | .64 | .65 | .65 | .42 | .62 | .43 | –.22 |

*Notes*: Means via Fisher z–transformation. Variables, see Figure 11.1 and Table 12.1, fourth and fifth result column; first two rows *N*s between 45 and 65, in the last row all *N* = 43 (better comparable).

external factors such as temporary resource discoveries, neighbour effects and development aid. Absolute latitude is correlated, but less than ability, education, background and politics.

It could be objected that the 2010 production and wealth levels are only the result of twentieth-century growth. Therefore, any stability 'across time' in correlations would not mean a lot. However, taking the 1930 GDPs (some of them are interpolated from 1950 GDPs) also shows high correlations for the most important variables: $r_{Evo} = .48$, $r_{Cult} = .69$, $r_{CA} = .69$, $r_{95\%} = .50$.[18]

We can summarise that the relevant factors for 2010 production and wealth differences are also valid for explaining wealth increases during the last century. *Cognitive ability, long-term background factors* and *political conditions* are stable and important explanative variables. Provided that they and cross-national differences in them are relatively stable they will also be *predictive for future development*. We tried a first attempt using a simple linear extrapolation from the past 80 years' GDP development to 2030 (last column of Table 12.1). Adding 20 years, approximately 40 per cent of all countries will reach Keynes' prediction, the majority will not. But among First World countries – if we take Keynes' vague term 'progressive countries' and replace it with another vague but more used one, 'First World' – about 70 per cent will reach Keynes' prediction. And such countries were more successful that were more 'progressive' i.e. having more supportive conditions in institutions, education, ability and culture.

### 12.6.3    Current Predictions from other Researchers

*Maddison's Optimistic 2030 Prediction*    Angus Maddison, the economist who provided estimates for past GDPs that are frequently used by us, also made predictions for the future. In 'The world economy in 2030' (2007, pp. 335ff.) he came to some quite positive forecasts: for the developed countries, economic growth will be at about the same rate as in 1990–2003. India will have the same 4.5 per cent a year per capita growth as China up to 2030. African countries will have a modest growth of 1 per cent a year to 2030. Generally, he expected a 2.25-fold increase in world GDP by 2030 (p. 347). Why he assumed the same economic growth rate for India as for China is puzzling. Growth was higher in China in the past (in China on average around 9 per cent vs. in India

---

[18] The multiple correlation using evolution, culture and average cognitive ability as predictors for predicting 1930 GDPs is $R = .73$ ($N = 62$) (excluding the estimated data for African countries: $R = .62$, $N = 44$), for the absolute difference 1930–2010 is $R = .89$ ($N = 62$) (excluding Africa $R = .85$, $N = 44$), for factor increase 1930–2010 is $R = .68$ ($N = 62$) (excluding Africa $R = .61$, $N = 44$). Excluding sub-Saharan African countries reduces variance, resulting in lower correlations, but the pattern remains: background factors and cognitive ability explain *across time* wealth differences between nations.

6 per cent in recent decades) and all national determinants, especially cognitive ability levels, favour higher growth in China.

*McKinsey's Hope*    Authors from McKinsey (Manyika et al., 2015, p. 7) expect a constant productivity growth of 1.8 per cent, similar to that which has been observable for the past 50 years. They give voice to a hope:

> Faster productivity gains can compensate for the waning of demographic tailwinds. To do so fully, productivity growth over the next 50 years would need to be 80 percent faster than the already high rate of the past 50 years. Productivity would need to accelerate by 22 percent to compensate for the shift in demographics on per capita income. In turn, productivity growth that is below its historical rate would mean even slower GDP and per capita income growth. (Manyika et al., 2015, p. 7)

As mentioned, they anticipate lower growth due to (less) rising employment per capita. But the average total 2.8 per cent observed growth in the last 50 years will (according to their scenario) only decrease to 2.3 per cent in the next 50 years. They hope productivity growth will increase. However, it is not clear on which grounds they base their optimism. It looks more like a postulation and an appeal to politicians to do something supportive as they suggested: 'deploy all available levers', more 'transparency and competition', 'incentivising innovation', 'mobilising labour', 'improve education and matching skills to jobs', 'opening up economies'. One third of the productivity potential depends on improvement of government policy (pp. 7, 83). Undoubtedly, Manyika et al. presented good ideas, but their successful implementation will depend on society and background factors.

*Hanushek and Colleagues: Apprehensions and Dizzying*

*Opportunities*    Hanushek, Peterson and Woessmann (2013) chose a quite alarming book title for their outlook – 'Endangering prosperity'. They focused on the example of the United States. Hypothetically, if the United States could improve their average cognitive ability level to that of Singapore, in 2093 the average GDP per capita in 2012 dollars, starting from around $50,000 in 2012, would be around $350,000, reaching the Canadian ability level would result in around $225,000, the German ability level around $190,000 and remaining unchanged in cognitive ability would result in $150,000 in 2012 (p. 61).[19] Any reform would need time for becoming effective: educational improvements need time to be implemented; the workforce is only gradually substituted by younger generations; and ability effects are slow but enduring, as by their realisation in new developed technologies.

---

[19] The numbers appear to be dizzyingly high but the projections are based on models of inflation-adjusted growth.

*Robert J. Gordon: Difficulties Are Coming*  Robert J. Gordon (2016) does not explicitly use cognitive human capital, though he considers related factors such as education and weakening innovation rates. His main statement is that the twentieth century economic growth of around 2 to 3 per cent was an exception of history. Future growth will become much more difficult. Former inventions had larger economic impact than more recent ones and further relevant technological advancement is becoming more complex and rare. Four headwinds, rising inequality, slower or no improvements in education, an ageing population and fiscal difficulties (rising debts, declining transfers per capita, rising taxes), will slow economic growth. For the United States he predicts average GDP growth of only 0.80 per cent in the comimg decades prior to 2040.

*Robert Fogel: The Rise of China*  Robert Fogel (2007) is quite optimistic regarding China's economic development: the average growth from 2000 to 2040 will be 8.21 per cent, leading to $85,000 GDP/c – more than twice the forecasted per-capita income of core Europe, with 40,000 GDP/c in 2040. For the United States he expects 2.90 per cent ($107,000), for Japan 1.48 per cent ($49,000) and for India 5.96 per cent ($24,000). However, the theoretical background of the estimates remains unclear – what were the assumptions and models? Without presenting such information they are mere speculations.

*Fernald and Jones: Research May Stimulate Future Growth*  In 'The Future of U.S. Economic Growth', Fernald and Jones (2014) stated that US long-term growth between 1870 and 2007 was 1.95 per cent per year. According to them, wealth and its growth depended in the past and will depend in future on invention of non-rival goods as new produced knowledge or institutions which are usable by all. Examples are the law, better organisation, patent-free products or the Internet. They assume that qualitative growth in human capital, indicated by rising educational attainment, and quantitative growth in human capital use, indicated by higher labour market participation, will in future be rather negligible, but further improvements by research and even higher rates of innovation are possible and this will be achieved by the quantitative gain of scientists: 'Though new ideas are harder to find, balanced growth can still occur because of exponential growth in the number of researchers.' (p. 46)

Internationally, research institutions and scientists will increase in number, especially due to more research in China and India. Ideas from new centres of research could and need to be implemented worldwide in the economy.

*Hart: Analysis of Past IQ Development*  Michael Hart (2007, p. 123ff.) was the first to analyse past cognitive ability development in different world regions. His estimates are based on a climatic model; the harshness of the

Table 12.3 *Hart's chronology of human intelligence and 2100 prediction*

|  | IQ 28000 BCE | IQ 8000 BCE | IQ 3000 BCE | IQ 2000 CE | IQ 2100 CE |
|---|---|---|---|---|---|
| **Africa (sub-Sahara)** | 70 | 70 | 70 | 70 | 70.00 |
| **N-Africa M-East (ArM)** | 76 | 81 | 84 | 87 | 87.05 |
| **America (North, Engl)** | – (81) | 91 (96) | 94 (91) | 101 | 101.05 |
| **America (Latin, C-S)** | – (81) | 90 (90) | 91 (89) | 94 | 94.04 |
| **Asia (Central-South)** | 71 | 71 | 82 | 84 | 84.10 |
| **East Asia** | 80 | 93 | 96 | 100 | 100.07 |
| **Southeast Asia, Pacific** | 71 | 71 | 85 | 88 | 88.13 |
| **Australia-NZ (English)** | 77 (81) | 82 (96) | 82 (91) | 101 | 101.05 |
| **Western Europe** | 81 | 96 | 91 | 101 | 101.05 |
| **Scandinavia** | 81 | 96 | 91 | 101 | 101.05 |
| **Central Europe** | 81 | 96 | 91 | 101 | 101.05 |
| **Eastern Europe** | 81 | 96 | 99 | 102 | 102.06 |
| **Southern Europe** | 81 | 92 | 88 | 99 | 99.06 |

*Notes*: Past cognitive ability levels based on Hart (2007, p. 124, his Table 17-1); in parentheses estimated for current populations (by HR, e.g. Australia based on Hart's Northern Europe); regions adapted to the classification used here; prediction for 2100 by HR based on (a) past 10,000 years development, double weighted, (b) past 30,000 years development, both averaged, assumption of linearity.

regions' environment (see Section 10.7.2, cold-winter-theory). Taking his estimates for past development, we made IQ predictions for the year 2100 (see Table 12.3).

Hart's time schedule covers long-term developments (in his original table until 60 kya). For this purpose, he considered long-term evolutionary factors for aboriginal populations, but not migration of the last few centuries and decades and not more current trends such as the FLynn effect or differential fertility. Unsurprisingly, a prediction for 2100 based on these long-term developments reveals nearly no changes compared to 2000 (see last column of Table 12.3). The assumptions are most likely too rough to predict national cognitive development for the future to 2100.

*Meisenberg: Economic Prediction Based on Dynamic*

*Processes*  Gerhard Meisenberg (2014, pp. 84ff.) developed a dynamic model: he distinguished between short-term (application of relationships in the recent past) versus long-term (recognising the dynamic process among factors) projections. Factors used are past growth and intelligence or past growth and intelligence combined with schooling. Regions are based on historical-cultural factors (such as Protestant vs. Catholic Europe, English, Ex-communist, Middle East, Latin America). Based on these assumptions, the

Table 12.4 *Average annual growth rates and achieved GDP 2050*

| | Average annual growth 1975–2011 | Average annual growth 2011–2050 | GDP 2050 ($ per capita) |
|---|---|---|---|
| **Africa (sub-Sahara)** | 0.13 | 0.75 | 2,568 |
| **N-Africa M-East (ArM)** | 1.87 | 1.26 | 10,016 |
| **America (North, Engl)** | 1.78 | 1.46 | 70,191 |
| **America (Latin, C-S)** | 1.34 | 1.16 | 16,020 |
| **Asia (Central-South)** | 3.69 | 1.54 | 11,028 |
| **East Asia** | 7.81 | 3.74 | 84,676 |
| **Southeast Asia, Pacific** | 3.69 | 1.54 | 11,028 |
| **Australia-NZ (English)** | 1.78 | 1.46 | 70,191 |
| **Western Europe** | 1.77 | 1.57 | 66,275 |
| **Scandinavia** | 1.77 | 1.57 | 66,275 |
| **Central Europe** | 1.67 | 1.58 | 57,051 |
| **Eastern Europe** | 2.16 | 1.96 | 28,779 |
| **Southern Europe** | 1.57 | 1.59 | 47,827 |

*Notes*: Predictions (versions 1 and 2 averaged) from Meisenberg (2014, pp. 85–87, his tables 4 and 5); regions adapted to the categorisation used here; growth in percentages.

predictions come to different average annual growth rates for different regions up to 2050 (see Table 12.4).

The highest annual economic growth rates are expected for East Asia with 3.74 per cent, the lowest for sub-Saharan Africa (0.75 per cent). Meisenberg's pattern is similar to the pattern based on an extrapolation of past growth according to Maddison data (Table 12.1). Hidden in aggregated regional predictions are some interesting single country forecasts, such as for South Africa, with a negative average annual growth until 2050 (–0.72 per cent), Singapore will be the richest country of the world in 2050, with $115,229 US dollar in 2011 units (for comparison, the United States is expected to be at $70,607, Germany: $64,141, China: $42,022, India: $5,830 and South Africa: $5,999).

Due to rising complexity, in the long run further economic growth will be enabled only by *rising* intelligence, not by stable high intelligence. But there are limits of cognitive growth and of cognitive convergence. Meisenberg assumes that developed and developing countries will become *more similar* in intelligence: in developed countries, twentieth-century gains are now decelerating due to anti-FLynn effects, whereas in emerging countries continued environmental improvements can achieve large intelligence gains in the present and the future. For the developing world, a *peak IQ* is expected for around the year 2075. However, despite narrowing gaps the cross-country IQ patterns will remain. The underlying assumption is that background factors will lead to different upper limits:

We do not know where the genetic limits of cognitive development are for different countries. If each nation has the same genetic capacity for higher intelligence, worldwide differences in intelligence and prosperity will diminish or disappear within two or three generations, much as the gaps between East Asian countries and the West have diminished or disappeared in the last two or three generations. However, there is no theoretical reason to expect equal potential for high intelligence in each nation, and no empirical evidence in its favor. (Meisenberg, 2014, p. 90)

It can be critically noted that the United States and Canada and especially Australia have different immigration policies and therefore should not be grouped in one English category. Diffusion effects of technology and organisation leading to 'beta-convergence', for example, catch-up growth by learning from the advancement of others, are missing.

### 12.6.4    Problems of Predictions

A rather simple problem of all future wellbeing and wealth predictions based on production and income is that GDP increases across time both overestimate and underestimate wealth increases: they *overestimate* wealth and wellbeing increases, because negative but not measured developments such as growing inequality and destruction of the natural environment are not covered (see Chapter 2). They also heavily *underestimate* wealth gains: the increased quality of goods is not covered because prices do not grow accordingly; additionally, increased health is not measured (e.g. Romer, 1990, p. 270).

Different factors work in different directions but influence each other. Internal technology-change and economy-change effects will lead to rising complexity, making further progress more difficult. Cognitive ability, although crucial for innovation, production, organisation and management in the economy as well as in politics and everyday life, is not the only relevant factor. Cognitive ability itself is furthered by supportive environmental conditions and especially depends on background factors, on culture and evolution. If the society is changed by replacement migration,[20] historically for instance in America, Australia, Singapore or Palestine, or gradually by different birth rates, historically for instance in Kosovo or South Africa, the background factors will change too, with corresponding changes in ability, politics, institutions, productivity and wealth.

Predictions cannot be based only on extrapolation of past development. The fundamental background factors, having shown their statistical validity by correlating with cognitive, technological, scientific, political, institutional and

---

[20] 'Replacement migration' is used by UN demographers to describe the amount of migration necessary to keep a population constant. However, in the narrow sense of the word it means replacing a population by another one.

economic variables today and in the past, and having shown their explanatory validity by theoretical argumentation, should be considered. What would have been predicted for Iran or Turkey in 1970 only based on twentieth-century development?

A good indicator for historical processes is a well-known and easy to observe outward but not superficial characteristic: the *wearing of headscarves by women*. It is an *indicator* for *political and cultural modernisation*, for *gender equality* and *liberty*. From 1936 to 1979 in Iran the headscarf (hijab) was banned by the government because of its incompatibility with modernisation of the country; since the Iranian Revolution it is a duty for women to wear it.[21] In Turkey, the headscarf was unofficially banned since around 1950 from the public sector such as in schools and administration, officially from 1982 to 2008. It was and is a constitutional principle of official Turk secularism. Turkey even had a woman as prime minister from 1993 to 1996. Tansu Çiller's election was not based on being a member of a dynasty. She was a university professor of economics. Photos showed her in the 1990s in a bikini at the beach. Since the 1990s there has been an Islamic revival. This is totally contrary to the twentieth-century trend and it was impossible to predict using only past trends. A similar development can be observed for other Muslim countries, e.g. for Egypt: since the 1950s the headscarf was rarely worn; a resurgence started in the 1970s and today about 90 per cent of women wear a headscarf; formerly, the headscarf was banned on TV, but since 2012 it has been permitted.

Any prediction only based on development until 1970 or 2000 would have foreseen a fast and continuing modernisation. Further examples: who would have predicted in 1980 the disintegration of the Soviet Union and Yugoslavia and the later wars between Orthodox, Catholic and Muslim peoples? Who would have predicted in 1990 the civil wars in Algeria, Iraq, Libya and Syria? Are Morocco, Jordan, Saudi Arabia and Oman different? What can be expected for them in the twenty-first century? For Singapore, France, Europe and the United States?

---

[21] For me, the most illustrative and vivid examples are photos published in 2017 (taken by Jila Dejam) of the inauguration of the Tehran Museum of Contemporary Art by Farah Pahlavi Diba in 1977 (source: www.spiegel.de/fotostrecke/ausstellung-in-teheran-1977-die-reichtuemer-der-kaiserin-fotostrecke-144957.html). There is not a single woman wearing the headscarf; all persons wear modern clothing, they behave in a modern way and a woman (being important because of her marriage to the Shah but with her own distinctive contribution) dominates the scene; it appears to be like the Guggenheim or Centre Pompidou. Two years later, the majority of the art collection disappeared into the vault. Farah Pahlavi also founded (in 1965) an 'Institute for the Intellectual Development of Children and Young Adults' – another hint that cognitive and cultural modernisation go hand in hand.

# 13    Models for Cognitive and Wealth Development in the Twenty-First Century

Based on assumptions for cognitive development at the level of nations, on past economic growth and on achieved wealth a theoretical model for cognitive and wealth development in the twenty-first century is described. Assumptions on future cognitive development include factors such as the FLynn effect; expansion and improvement of education; changes in demographics and differential birth rates; migration; general cultural and environmental changes. Economic growth and wealth models consider past growth, cognitive development, demographic change, achieved wealth (resp. advantages of backwardness), rising complexity, country risk factors and regional neighbour effects. Results for the year 2100 depending on the chosen models are presented.

Cognitive challenges will rise in the future but also the possibilities to cope with them. Technology, economy and everyday life become more complex but with complexity the average educational level will also rise. Depending on the level achieved and on demographic and environmental conditions, the past centuries' cognitive increases may continue, come to an end or may even change to a decline. At least in the near future, for economic development past growth will be the best predictor for coming growth. However, the further we go the less predictive will be an extrapolation of past development and the more important fundamental determinants of economic production and of the organisation of societies become, both influencing the wellbeing of nations. And those factors may change in the future.

To give an overview, our model for predicting future growth is based on these conditions:

(1) *Past growth.* The best predictor for the future is the past. Nations that are rich today will probably remain so. Nations who have shown high economic growth in recent decades have a higher probability to move on than nations with average or low growth rates. But the effects of inertia peter out and effects of basic causal determinants become stronger. An extrapolation of past growth is no explanatory variable; extrapolations are not based on determinants (only expectations of actors may work as

414

determinants). The extrapolation approach stands for the stability of unknown factors assumed to be robust for a couple of years.

(2) *Advantages of backwardness*. Less-developed countries can adopt progress in technology, organisation, education, science and culture from more-developed countries. Imitation is much easier than innovation, leading to a comparatively higher catch-up growth. Outcomes of competence, institutions, habits and production in the advanced countries (knowledge, technology, organisation, capital) diffuse to other countries. This includes cognitive ability, in which higher increases are expected at lower levels.

(3) *Cognitive ability*. Cognitive ability is the crucial force influencing political, social, technological, organisational and economic conditions at the level of nations, companies, institutions and individuals, leading to higher productivity, inventiveness, safety and regularity and, in the end, to higher wellbeing. Technological, social, scientific and cultural modernisation processes depend on cognitive ability.

(4) *Cognitive ability development*. Cognitive ability levels of nations are not fixed. In the past, average cognitive levels were rising (called FLynn effect), most probably due to environmental improvements. This trend may continue and training or neuro-enhancement may further support it, but, especially for developed nations, ceiling effects will limit further cognitive growth, and immigration of people at relatively lower cognitive ability levels and differential fertility may lead to a reversed FLynn effect, to a decline in cognitive ability.

(5) *Ageing societies*. Societies become older, implying higher social transfers, more expenses for health and care, less inventiveness and lower (fluid) cognitive ability. At the same time crime rates will go down with ageing.

(6) *Rising complexity*. Rising complexity will make average life more cognitively demanding and innovations more difficult, having a negative impact on growth.

(7) *Country risk*. Country risks cover political conditions influencing economy and wellbeing as (positively) democracy, freedom, rule of law and peace. Additionally, diversity is considered: diversity will grow with some positive impact on stimulating inventiveness but also with lower trust, more political fragility and, if diversity goes together with ability differences, with unfavourable countermeasures such as non-meritoric quota regulations.

Before constructing a more and more complex model step-by-step we start with a rather simplified model for cognitive development in the twenty-first century: based on a prediction of education rises we estimate ability rises resulting in higher economic production and wealth.

### 13.1    A First and Simple Model: Prediction of Rising Education Leading to Favourable Ability and GDP Development

The demographers Wolfgang Lutz, William Butz and Samir KC (2014) published estimates for the development of educational levels in the twenty-first century. As a measure they took the mean years of schooling for persons at age 25 or older. They presented estimates for the years 2010, 2020, 2030, 2040, 2050, 2075 and 2100. The sample covers 171 countries. Choosing their medium scenario (SSP2) that represents, from today's perspective, the most likely development, a remarkable increase in education until 2100 is expected (see Table 13.1, first two result columns).

For predicting future cognitive ability levels we started with running a regression using education 2010 as predictor for cognitive ability 2010. The result is that one more year of school education corresponds to +2.94 more IQ points.[1] The worldwide average of education in 2010 is 8.20 years, for 2100 13.03 years is predicted, an increase of nearly five years. The amount of education in 2010 corresponds to an average worldwide cognitive ability level of 83.47 IQ points, reaching 97.66 IQ in 2100, a rise of 14.19 IQ (*dec* = 1.58 IQ, based on 164 countries).

One IQ point in 2010 corresponds to a gain of $499 in GDP/c.[2] Starting from 2010 and an average at $8,464 (in 1990 International Geary-Khamis dollars), the average GDP reaches $20,490 in 2100, an increase of $12,027 or 242% (for 146 countries).[3] Both IQ and GDP results differentiated for regions are presented in Table 13.1. For more measurement points (in larger regions), the results are presented in Figures 13.1 (IQ) and 13.2 (GDP).

Based on education increases the estimated decadal IQ rises for the twenty-first century are, with a worldwide average of *dec* = 1.58 IQ points, noticeably smaller than in the twentieth century. In the last century in developed countries the FLynn effect was *dec* = 2.83 IQ. Even in Africa they would reach only *dec* = 2.23 IQ points in our century. For the United States, *dec* = 0.53 are estimated. This is somewhat larger than the increase calculated for 17-year-olds in NAEP between 1971 and 2008 (*dec* = 0.30) but very similar to a predicted rise in NAEP until 2060 (average of two scenarios: *dec* = 0.61;

---

[1] Regression equation: IQ10=59.38+2.94×Educ10; $r$ = .77 ($\beta$ = .77). A scatterplot gives no evidence for a curvilinear relationship. Data are given for 164 countries.

[2] Regression equation: GDP10=−33313.38+498.95×IQ10; $r$ = .76 ($\beta$ = .76; $N$ = 146). For calculations, we used the logarithm of GDP, finally converted back to $.

[3] Because in 2100 the worldwide average cognitive ability level is 14 IQ points higher than in 2010 the worldwide average GDP level should be about $7,000 higher. However, the increase is larger, on average $12,000. The log transformation leads to a closer relationship between cognitive ability and wealth ($r$ = .76 vs. .82).

Table 13.1 *Education, cognitive ability and GDP/c in 2010 and 2100*

| | | School y. 2010 | School y. 2100 | CA 2010 corrected | CA 2100 | IQ gain decade | GDP 2010 | GDP 2100 |
|---|---|---|---|---|---|---|---|---|
| **Africa (sub-Sahara)** | | 4.74 | 11.58 | 69.19 | 88.76 | 2.23 | 2,465 | 9,775 |
| | Kenya | 7.68 | 12.99 | 74.47 | 90.07 | 1.73 | 1,267 | 4,039 |
| **N-Africa M-East** | | 8.48 | 13.67 | 84.24 | 100.50 | 1.69 | 7,466 | 23,013 |
| | Egypt | 6.77 | 14.02 | 83.72 | 105.02 | 2.37 | 4,096 | 19,946 |
| **America (North, Engl)** | | 13.20 | 14.90 | 99.45 | 104.43 | 0.55 | 27,625 | 39,937 |
| | USA | 12.86 | 14.48 | 98.33 | 103.09 | 0.53 | 30,436 | 43,353 |
| **America (Latin, C-S)** | | 8.38 | 12.94 | 79.32 | 93.45 | 1.48 | 6,942 | 17,952 |
| | Mexico | 8.29 | 13.53 | 85.87 | 101.26 | 1.71 | 7,870 | 24,711 |
| **Asia (Central-South)** | | 6.87 | 12.26 | 79.41 | 95.89 | 1.76 | 3,720 | 9,894 |
| | India | 5.53 | 12.65 | 77.60 | 98.52 | 2.32 | 3,287 | 15,559 |
| **East Asia** | | 10.25 | 14.31 | 99.43 | 112.18 | 1.33 | 15,063 | 40,735 |
| | China | 7.36 | 12.19 | 100.77 | 115.01 | 1.58 | 7,424 | 21,407 |
| **Southeast Asia, Pacific** | | 7.91 | 12.70 | 85.16 | 99.79 | 1.40 | 7,870 | 19,608 |
| | Philippines | 9.27 | 15.57 | 99.06 | 90.46 | 1.12 | 3,089 | 6,533 |
| **Australia-NZ (English)** | | 12.44 | 15.63 | 99.17 | 108.42 | 1.04 | 21,875 | 44,920 |
| | New Zealand | 12.92 | 15.14 | 98.83 | 106.95 | 0.86 | 18,598 | 33,173 |
| **Western Europe** | | 11.18 | 15.14 | 99.60 | 110.44 | 1.29 | 23,458 | 56,065 |
| | United Kingdom | 10.44 | 15.05 | 97.06 | 113.14 | 1.50 | 23,496 | 64,294 |
| **Scandinavia** | | 12.73 | 15.72 | 98.85 | 105.99 | 0.79 | 24,952 | 39,673 |
| | Norway | 12.65 | 15.58 | 97.91 | 106.93 | 1.00 | 27,894 | 54,531 |
| **Central Europe** | | 12.40 | 15.15 | 98.82 | 106.79 | 0.90 | 23,048 | 38,666 |
| | Germany | 13.71 | 13.82 | 95.54 | 104.32 | 0.61 | 20,521 | 30,870 |
| **Eastern Europe** | | 11.28 | 12.73 | 97.26 | 102.99 | 0.83 | 10,489 | 18,091 |
| | Russia | 10.44 | 14.08 | 92.61 | 103.99 | 0.75 | 8,888 | 14,654 |
| **Southern Europe** | | 9.90 | 14.54 | 97.52 | 104.73 | 1.36 | 11,009 | 30,226 |
| | Italy | 9.81 | 14.54 | 97.52 | 111.42 | 1.54 | 19,021 | 53,429 |

*Notes*: School y. 2010, 2100: mean years of schooling, age 25+ (scenario SSP2), 2010 and estimated for 2100 by Lutz et al. (2014, pp. 682ff.); CA 2010 corrected: cognitive ability, grand mean of student assessment and psychometric intelligence studies, corrected, in IQ scale; CA 2100: cognitive ability calculated for 2100 based on estimated education; IQ gain decade: average IQ gain per decade from 2010 to 2100 based on education; GDP 2010: Maddison 2010 augmented by choosing additional data from 2008 for countries without data in 2010; GDP 2100: GDP estimated based on cognitive ability 2100; same lengths of education do not necessarily correspond to same ability levels, e.g. Scandinavia needed more years of education in 2010 for a lower ability level than Western Europe, Scandinavia is less effective – thus in 2100, 15.14 years of school education results for Western Europe in a higher cognitive ability level than for Scandinavia.

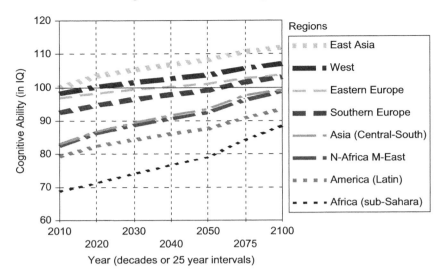

Figure 13.1 Education-based estimated cognitive ability development in the twenty-first century

Rindermann & Thompson, 2013; Rindermann & Pichelmann, 2015). Because it is not only school education that is relevant for cognitive ability but also nutrition, health and parental education and because in these fields improvements are expected, rises in developing countries could be higher, especially in the first decades of the twenty-first century.

According to the education-based model, international gaps in cognitive ability will decline, from a standard deviation of $SD = 11.86$ in 2010 to $SD = 9.37$ in 2100. The gap between the West and sub-Saharan Africa decreases from 29 to 19 IQ points. However, the gap between East Asia and the West nearly triples from 2 to 5 IQ points.

According to the cognitive capital theory and using the Lutz data, at the end of the twenty-first century all countries will have populations with more education, higher cognitive ability and higher economic production. East Asia will catch up with the West in wealth (see Figure 13.2). But according to the model, the gaps between the West (North-West-Central Europe, North America, Australia and New Zealand) and Southern and Eastern Europe will remain. The wealth gap between the West and sub-Saharan Africa will even increase from \$20,363 to \$32,945.

The presented model suffers, due to its simplicity, from several serious flaws: for wealth, there is no assumption of baseline economic growth. Only an increase in education and ability would lead to growth, which is too

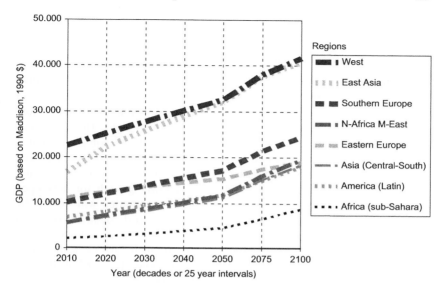

Figure 13.2 Estimated GDP/c development in the twenty-first century

pessimistic, as the currently reached ability level is high enough for further incremental productivity improvement. Advantages of backwardness are not considered, but they are important for Eastern Europe and the entire developing world. As mentioned previously, environmental conditions apart from education were not integrated. And some, at least from a today's perspective, highly implausible estimates such as higher IQ for Egypt than for the United States in 2100 (105 vs. 103 IQ points) question whether the 2010 cross-national education-IQ-correspondences can be directly transferred to future education-IQ-gains within countries. Maybe educational gains are hollow; they only increase the time spent at school without any remarkable improvement in ability. And years at school do not create the same outcomes in different countries. As the economist Eric Hanushek (2013, p. 206) has mentioned:

Using school attainment as a measure of human capital in an international setting presents huge difficulties. In comparing human capital across countries, it is necessary to assume that the schools across diverse countries are imparting the same amount of learning per year in all countries. In other words, a year of school in Japan has the same value in terms of skills as a year of school in South Africa. In general, this is implausible.

These all are crucial theoretical shortcomings. However, as a first approximation it helps to clarify the necessary adjustments and specifications.

## 13.2    Sophisticated Model for Ability Development

### 13.2.1    General Assumptions

For maintaining economic growth, societies do not need higher cognitive ability, but rather ability at a similar level as in the preceding decades and century, having led in the past to economic growth through innovation. Therefore, in comparable conditions growth should continue. However, conditions change: complexity in society, science and technology is rising, making further innovations more difficult. The low-hanging fruits have been picked long ago. Innovation-based growth will become more difficult, resulting, under *ceteris paribus* conditions, in lower growth for developed countries. By contrast, developing and emerging countries will benefit by adoption from the achieved progress in more developed countries. But with ongoing modernisation, cognitive abilities become not only more important for innovation but also for wealth production itself, including by adoption of technologies. Below certain societal ability thresholds (e.g. below IQs 85, 90 and 95) innovations cannot be successfully adopted.

Further obstacles deal with expected developments being difficult to handle such as climate change, reduction of resources (and their recycling, saving or replacement), ageing of workforces and societies, rising government spending ratios due to growing social transfers and public debt and hardly predictable in detail but generally expectable armed conflicts and civil unrest between and within nations. Who would have predicted in 1900 the First and Second World War and the genocides? Who in 1980 the end of the Eastern Bloc and of the Soviet Union? Who in the 1990s Islamist terror around the world? Who in 2010 the war in Ukraine?[4] While conflicts cannot be precisely predicted, they can be expected with differing likelihood for different countries, resulting in negative effects on conditions relevant for cognitive development, innovation and growth.

One certain improvement of the past was the increase in education and ability. As far as this process continues future challenges can be met by our descendants.

We assume that there will be an ongoing, but slower and less effective, improvement in environmental conditions relevant for cognitive development in developed countries and a stronger and more effective improvement in developing countries. However, positive historical processes will be also accompanied by negative ones. Further important factors will be immigration (and emigration), the attributes of immigrants and their development.

---

[4] Hints on these developments could be found in the work of Huntington (1996).

Additionally, differential birth rates and differential generation lengths have to be considered. Finally, ceiling effects for cognitive ability have to be taken into account.[5]

### 13.2.2  Continuing Environmental Improvements

The best predictor for the future is the past. The IQ improvements observable in the past, mainly based on improvements in environmental conditions relevant for cognitive development such as in nutrition, health, family and school education and based on general stimulation by technological and cultural modernisation, will at least continue for a while. It is the best starting point to assume a continuation of past processes, but it will fade out and continuation will be replaced by the outcomes of effective determinants and changes in them.

### 13.2.3  Migration Effects

Due to low birth rates, developed countries can benefit from immigration. These developed countries are also the countries with the highest cognitive ability levels. Using the data from Strack et al. (2014, p. 17), future labour shortage and today's cognitive ability levels are positively correlated, for 2020 $r = .51$ and 2030 $r = .41$. That means labour shortages will impede economic production in high-human-capital countries. Immigration is needed and it is also happening in the present.

But immigrants compared to native populations – especially long-term immigrants, as discernible by schoolchildren populations – have on average a lower ability level. For instance, Lanvin and Evans (2013, p. 18, their figure 1) described in their Global Talent Report an inflow of 'unskilled or low-skilled migrants' from North and sub-Saharan Africa and the Middle East to Europe. According to student assessment data (see Section 10.3.5), the West has lost in the past approximately 0.91 IQ points among its school population due to immigration.[6] This immigration loss is not a worldwide-valid pattern

---

[5] These ideas were first presented in 2011 at an ISIR conference in Cyprus (Rindermann & Thompson, 2011b). The analyses were rerun with modified and improved assumptions and with an entirely rewritten statistical program.

[6] This pattern is also found for adult data presented by PIAAC (OECD, 2013b, p. 171). The average competence difference between natives and immigrants in 21 nations is 33 SASQ points or 5 IQ points. Only in Slovakia was a positive pattern for immigrants observed. Because PIAAC does not present results for natives and immigrants themselves and also not independent from language (which is important for new adult immigrants), PIAAC results cannot be used for our calculations.

because oil-producing countries and Australia have made gains through immigration. Thus country-specific developments have to be considered.

*Migration-Ability Paradox*    But was the pattern correctly described? Is there not a 'brain drain' from developed countries? That is, cognitive elites are leaving and therefore they improve the levels in receiving countries? We have only few statistical data on emigrants' ability levels (e.g., because in Latin America the rewards for skill are higher than in the US the rather lower ability strata emigrate; Borjas, 2016, pp. 78ff.): There is more information on immigrants and here mainly on their children. However, there could be a *migration-ability paradox*: migration could lead in both countries to an IQ decline, in the emigration as well as the immigration country! If the above average cognitive strata in the emigration country emigrate, this lowers the ability level of the home society. But if the average ability gaps between the two countries are large, the above-average cognitive strata of the emigration countries would correspond to the below-average cognitive strata in the immigration countries. This is the case for sub-Saharan African countries, with an average cognitive ability level of 68 IQ and Western Europe of around 99 IQ points (see Table 10.2 and depiction in Figure 13.3). The fractions of (according to an international benchmark) real intellectual elites in emigrant countries are simply too small to be effective for raising immigrant country ability levels! The fractions of average emigrant groups, which compared to

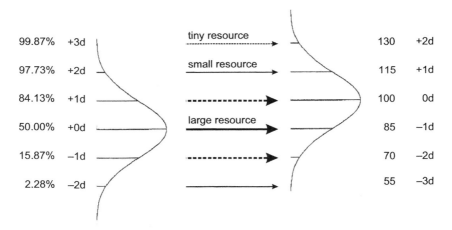

Figure 13.3 Migration-ability paradox exemplified for two countries with a *d* = 1 (15 IQ) gap (similar to United States and Mexico, France and Tunisia, UK and Trinidad, Germany and Turkey)

European natives have a low ability level, are much larger. Similar problems are observed for emigration from the Middle East to the West.

*Migration Predictions and Its Effects*    For the effect of immigration, it is not only mere immigration rates that count. The country of origin has to be considered, as well as immigrants' educational and ability level, immigration policies (selection and furtherance), birth rates and children's competence outcomes after leaving school. Not only cognitive ability levels of new adult immigrants, but also of their children and immigrant fertility differentials are important. Of course, immigrant shares also depend on native children rates. All this is best estimated by using the results of student assessment studies, their information on ability levels and percentages of native and immigrant students and by using their trends.

UN (2011) sources expect declining migration rates in the twenty-first century, similarly Lutz et al. (2014). For instance, while Lutz et al. expect for 2020 an average immigration rate per country and year of 38,000 persons (0.25 per cent of the receiving country's population), for 2080 33,000 persons (0.15 per cent) and for 2100 0 persons are expected.[7] But are declining migration rates plausible in times of globalisation and climate change? And what happened in the recent past and the present? However, because both sources do not assume a declining trend until 2070 the decline assumption is less important. More serious is that usually net migration rates are calculated (immigration minus emigration) for certain periods, not providing information on percentages of immigrants within a society. Additionally, many immigrants will leave the country after a while (return migration). So the numbers needed to be adjusted. Again, the past development in student assessment studies (1995–2009) seems to be a good source. But the number of students with immigration background is here underestimated because children of immigrants born in the country are categorised as natives.

Regarding ability development, a larger FLynn-effect for immigrants depending on their ability level compared to the FLynn-effect for natives is

---

[7] Numbers based on immigration estimation data (not migration net flow) were submitted by Jakob Eder (23. April 2015) from the Lutz research group at the Wittgenstein Centre for Demography and Global Human Capital in Vienna. Numbers for a period of five years were divided by five. All immigration projections do not include the most recent immigration waves 2014ff. from the Middle East and Africa to Europe, especially to Central Europe and Germany, Austria and Sweden. Due to their large numbers and comparatively low ability levels they will have a transformative effect for the young generation (e.g. Douthat, 2016). Including them would result in a larger declining effect in cognitive human capital. Further analyses have to consider these effects. First econometric studies on macroeconomic effects of refugee immigration predicted a loss in average productivity and production (GDP per capita about –2 per cent, varying with time horizon), in wage share (about –0.5 per cent) and an increase in unemployment (about +1 to 2 per cent; Weber & Weigand, 2016).

to be expected and was observed in the past (e.g. te Nijenhuis et al., 2004), similarly for Blacks and Hispanics in the United States (Rindermann & Thompson, 2013). However, the trend is not universal (e.g. not for immigrants with Muslim background in Germany or for immigrants in Sweden where the gap has widened; Heller-Sahlgren, 2015a, 2015c) and unstable (e.g. for Blacks and Hispanics in the United States).[8] Usually, native-immigrant gaps remain for generations (e.g. Borjas, 2001/1999).[9]

Not considered are effects of migrants on natives such as effects on instruction in school and teachers (Heller-Sahlgren, 2015a, 2015c), e.g. problems due to language differences and deriving from comprehension deficits or due to cultural differences, unfamiliarity with the practices of instruction and the demands of modern education and due to ability differences. Migrants will also have effects on migration such as chain immigration or long-term declining public social support and average per capita wealth in the receiving country, leading to higher or lower immigration.

Less important than usually assumed seem to be human capital losses by emigration for the sending countries. Emigrants can be bridge-builders between the country of origin and the country of immigration, stimulating trade, innovation and production in the country of origin. The brain drain has direct and indirect effects, increasing wealth and stimulating education:

Migrants may repatriate some of their earnings through remittances. Indeed, remittances constitute a more important source of capital to many countries than any form of foreign aid. The prospect of economic migration also creates positive incentive effects, such as higher levels of investment in education. (Bradford, 2013, p. 35)

### 13.2.4   Asymmetric Children Rates and Generation Lengths

As described in Section 12.2.2, better educated and more intelligent adults have on average fewer children (usually termed lower reproductive rates) and they have these fewer children later in their life. A meta-analysis on past differential fertility studies covering $N = 202,924$ subjects and $k = 10$ studies resulted in an average effect of $dec = -0.39$ IQ points (Woodley, 2015). The result of our own review of nine studies was at $dec = -0.37$ (Rindermann & Thompson, 2011b). These estimates are corroborated by a newer study with US data from Meisenberg and Woodley (2014), resulting in $dec = -0.31$.

---

[8]   Blacks are not immigrants but a group with a similar ability gap.
[9]   Taking data for the United States from Borjas across one generation, the educational differences between migrants of different origin remain moderately stable, from 1910 to 1940 $r = .53$, from 1940 to 1980 $r = .47$ and from 1910 to 1980 $r = .33$. Because in the past immigrants to the United States were indirectly selected for ability, the correlations may underestimate the current stabilities, especially in Europe.

However, all these studies did not consider differences in *generation span*. Generation span or generation length is the average age of adults when having their median child. If a group A of people has children at a younger age than another group B this leads across generations to a larger share of group A people in society. If generation span is correlated with cognitive ability differences, it is empirically (Herrnstein & Murray, 1994, p. 351f.; Reeve et al., 2013), the effect of asymmetric birth rates is largely increased from around $dec = -0.38$ to $dec = -0.87$ IQ (see results of an empirically based simulation study shown in Figures 13.4 and 13.5).[10]

For a simulation study to illustrate the effect we assumed the existence of three groups:

- Group A has on average 2.3 children, a generation span of 25 years, a life expectancy of 75 years, an average IQ of 80, initially representing 28 per cent of the population;
- Group B has on average 1.6 children, a generation span of 30 years, a life expectancy of 80 years, an average IQ of 100, initially representing 44 per cent of the population;
- Group C has on average 1.3 children, a generation span of 37 years, a life expectancy of 85 years, an average IQ of 120, initially representing 28 per cent of the population.

The numbers are orientated towards empirical data on IQ and children numbers in the United States of Loehlin (1997) with two modifications: the average IQ in the Loehlin sample was 108 (Whites) or 95 (Black); we used the society's grand mean of 100 and adapted the other two low and high IQ values to come to this average. Further, we reduced the children numbers from around 2.7 to 2.3, 1.9 to 1.6 and 1.4 to 1.3 – more typical children numbers today in developed countries.[11]

Further simplifying assumptions were no intermix and no influence across the groups and no regression towards a total society mean. The groups do not start arriving in a new society at age 20, but as entire populations in a given society covering the total age span.

Within around 40 years (about 1.6 generations of group A, but 1.3 generations of group B and 1.1 generations of group C), group A will form the largest group within society and after 150 years the other groups,

---

[10] In an alternative calculation made by an information scientist, the result was $dec = -0.59$ IQ. Different from the approach presented here, it was assumed to start on measurement point 0 with an entire new population being 0 years old (thus first offspring after 25 years). This slightly reduces and underestimates the effects.

[11] See also Coleman's assumptions for birth rates of different ethnic groups with different educational and ability levels (2010, pp. 450, 456).

Population development

Three groups (starting with 28%, 44%, 28%)

2.3/1.6/1.3 children, generation length 25/30/37 years, IQ 80/100/120

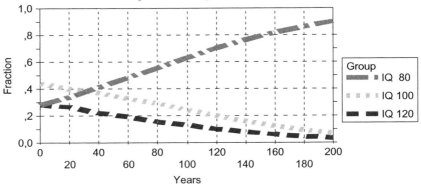

Figure 13.4 Simulation of combined fertility and generation length effects on population development

IQ-Level development (mean, at 95%, at 5%)

Three groups (starting with 28%, 44%, 28%)

2.3/1.6/1.3 children, generation length 25/30/37 years, IQ 80/100/120

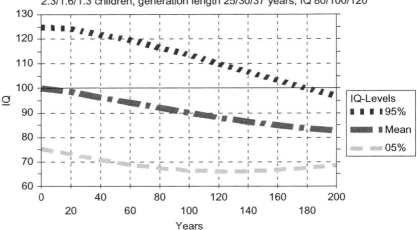

Figure 13.5 Simulation of combined fertility and generation span effects on cognitive ability development

previously representing 72 per cent of the population, will be minorities; after 200 years they together represent only 10 per cent of the population (Figure 13.4). This scenario would result in an intelligence decline of 17 IQ points in 200 years (Figure 13.5). The intellectual classes' ability level declines even more from 125 to 97 IQ, a decline of 28 IQ points among the cognitive elite. The loss for the lower ability group is, with 7 IQ points, the smallest. Finally, the lower fertility rates of the higher achieving groups B and C lead to a reduced standard deviation in the unchanged year 0 scale. Only a high level of homogamy (biologically: assortative mating) would prevent this (Woodley et al., 2017).

How we can come now to a usable number for estimating the effects of asymmetric birth rates? This estimate will be part of a more general model also including assumptions on probable ongoing environmental improvements working in a positive direction. We do not have information for differences between countries. We do not have assumptions for changing patterns in the twenty-first century. The meta-analytically found average effects of $dec = -0.37$ or $dec = -0.39$ IQ points (see previously) are certainly too low because they do not consider (a) effects of differences in *generation span* (totally $dec = -0.87$), (b) possible *mutation accumulation effects* ($dec = -0.84$, with fertility totally $dec = -1.23$; Woodley, 2015), (c) the additional effects of *environmental parental transfer*, also including attitudes and personality and (d) the supposed *interaction effects* between ability and environment (spiral).

While we know with certainty that an estimate of $dec = -0.38$ is too low, all information on higher effects is shaky: effects of mutation accumulation are a newly described phenomenon not yet corroborated by research of other authors;[12] generation span effects are based on a single simulation, deriving, however, from empirical data; environmental transfer and inter-action effects are not backed by numbers based on empirical studies. Considering all this we cautiously assume an effect of $dec = -0.57$, well below the upper bounds of $dec = -0.87$ and $dec = -1.23$ but well above $dec = -0.37$ and $dec = -0.39$ and still well below a simple average of these four numbers ($dec = -0.72$).[13]

---

[12] Negative mutation load effects of older parents on children's intelligence are also not robust (Arslan et al., 2014). In a personal communication with Michael Woodley (18 November 2015), he also stated that the mutation accumulation effects are smaller than previously assumed.

[13] −0.57 was chosen by a rough rule of thumb: below the average, above the underestimating results, roughly the average in between. The exact value is quite arbitrary; the range in between not. Because it is a constant, researchers with different assumptions can easily adjust the results. A study by Wang et al. (2016) published after developing our model supports the chosen number: the decadal decline in China based on fluid intelligence is $dec = -0.31$ and based on crystallised cognitive ability (education) $dec = -0.66$. Both scales arithmetically averaged results in $dec = -0.49$. This is still below our number of $dec = -0.57$, but Wang et al. did not consider differences in generation length.

### 13.2.5    Identical or Different Cognitive Ceilings: Train or Sailboat Model

FLynn effect predictions implicitly start with the assumption that there is no limit to development and that the speed and (infinite) finishing lines of cognitive rises caused by environmental improvements are the same for different peoples. The only difference is a time shift. We call this model the *train model*: All peoples are on the same train run by an external company, not by its passengers, reaching the same station; the passengers in the first carriage reach the first station only somewhat earlier. This is a *theory of common cognitive modernisation* without any selective constraints (see visualisation in Figure 13.6).

Figure 13.6 illustrates that achieved levels and expected increases are negatively correlated: the highest future increases are to be expected for today's lowest IQ groups (at IQ 60 and per decade about *dec* = +6.32), while above IQ 100 only *dec* = +0.46 can be hoped for. This can be backed by recent research showing larger FLynn effects in developing countries and declining First-Third World gaps in student assessment studies (e.g. Meisenberg & Woodley, 2013; Wongupparaj et al., 2015). Countries such as Brazil are catching up through reforms in their educational systems (Hanushek & Woessmann, 2015b, pp. 31ff.).

However, research showed ability differences being relatively stable across centuries (see Tables 4.4 to 4.6) and demonstrated the impact of

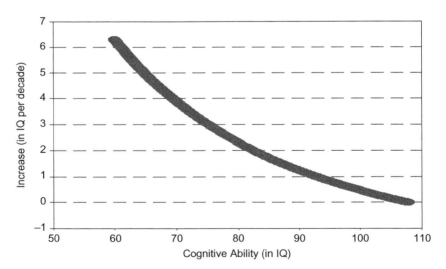

Figure 13.6 Train model of twenty-first-century cognitive ability development: larger increases at lower levels

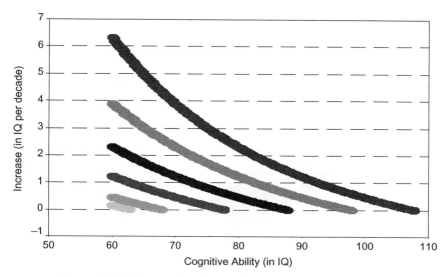

Figure 13.7 Sailboat model of twenty-first-century cognitive ability development

long-term determinants such as evolution and culture (see Sections 10.7, 10.8 and Chapter 11). This raises doubts if a common modernisation model is valid.[14] A simple clue is that the best predictor for the future is the past. The alternative to the train model is a *sailboat model*: different countries and peoples use self-constructed boats with differing speeds and differently qualified yachtsman navigating to different harbours (see visualisation in Figure 13.7).

Figure 13.7 illustrates for six different groups six different growth curves. For all groups, a positive development is expected, leading, however, to

---

[14] With focus on evolutionary grounds, a similar scepticism towards a train model was mentioned by the blogger Anatoly Karlin (2012). He assumed the following potential values in his categorisation of regions and countries: USA 100 IQ, China 108 IQ, India 92.5 IQ, Russia 100 IQ, Brazil 94 IQ, Germanic Europe 103 IQ, Med Europe 99 IQ, Turkey 96 IQ, Japan 105 IQ, Israel ? IQ, Australia 103 IQ, Canada 103 IQ. Anatoly Karlin is US-American with a Russian-Jewish background. Empirical data on possible convergence is given for Africa by the SACMEQ surveys 2000 and 2007. The economist Justin Sandefur (2016, p. 35) has analysed them and concluded: 'Is there evidence that African mathematics scores are converging to the international average? The answer is tentatively, no, or at best only slightly.' If we average Sandefur's score gains calculated by using three different methods, the annual mean gain is 0.80 SASQ (or 0.12 IQ points). For a gap of 200 to 300 SASQ (Sandefur, 2016) about 250 to 374 years of constant increases would be necessary to close the gap. For the estimated IQ gap of 30 points (Table 13.3), 249 years of annual 0.12 IQ point gains were necessary.

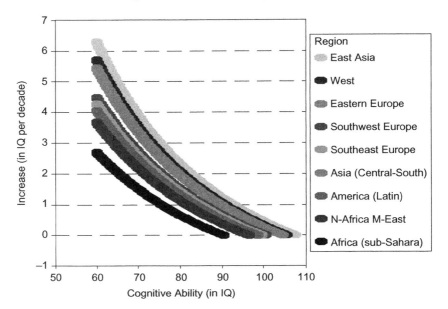

Figure 13.8 Same-boat-but-different-team model of twenty-first-century cognitive ability development

different finishing lines. E.g. if peoples of the upper-right group currently have an IQ at 60 points a large increase up to around IQ 108 is to be expected across decades. The progress from IQ 60 to 90 will be fast, but because increases per decade become smaller at higher levels the progress from IQ 90 to 108 will be slow. For the lower-left groups, the finishing lines are closer and their increases per decade are smaller.

While such a *theory of different cognitive modernisation* is backed by evidence on the stability of differences and the impact of long-term global determinants, it is questioned by larger FLynn effects in developing countries. Thus we choose a model considering both catch-up secular rises in ability and stable relative but developing absolute differences, a mix between the train and sailboat models, the *same-boat-but-different-team model* (see Figure 13.8). All teams use the same boats at the same time for the same route but have different crews.

Figure 13.7 illustrates for different regions different finishing lines and different increases per decade according to the same-boat-but-different-team model. For instance, for East Asia a ceiling point of IQ 108 is expected, but because East Asian nations are now near to their ceiling point, increases per decade possible due to environmental improvements will be small.

Table 13.2 *Cognitive ability and theoretical finishing lines*

| Region | Cognitive ability corrected 2010 | Possible finishing line '2200' | Development potential (maximum) | Expert rating '2100' |
|---|---|---|---|---|
| **Africa** (sub-Sahara) | 69 | 93 | +24 | +6.82 |
| **N-Africa M-East** | 83 | 97 | +14 | +3.62 |
| **America** (North, Engl) | 99 | 105 | +6 | −0.45/+2.07 |
| **America** (Latin, C-S) | 79 | 98 | +20 | +6.18 |
| **Asia** (Central-South) | 79 | 99 | +20 | +6.83 (India) |
| **East Asia** | 100 | 108 | +8 (+9) | +7.41 |
| **Southeast Asia, Pacific** | 85 | 98 | +13 | – |
| **Australia-NZ** (English) | 99 | 106 | +7 | +2.77 |
| **Western Europe** | 99 | 105 | +6 | +1.16 |
| **Scandinavia** | 97 | 106 | +9 | +1.55 |
| **Central Europe** | 99 | 105 | +6 | +1.16 |
| **Eastnorth Europe** | 97 | 105 | +9 | +2.72 |
| **Southwest Europe** | 96 | 103 | +7 | +0.34 |
| **Southeast Europe** | 91 | 101 | +10 | +0.34 |

*Notes*: Numbers due to uncertainty rounded (first three result columns); regions slightly modified, closer categorised due to culture; Eastnorth Europe, Southwest Europe and Southeast Europe with their noticeable ability differences are distinguished; East Asia includes Singapore; within-regional variations in obvious cases considered; East Asia precisely 104.5 (past and present losses due to elite emigration); North-Africa-Middle-East precisely 96.5; within North-America for Canada 106 as finishing line; within East Asia finishing line for Mongolia and Tibet 101; for Israel 103; for Vietnam 105; for Greenland 101; for Haiti 93 (as for Africa); for Albania and Kosovo 98 (Muslim countries); within-country differences are not considered (e.g. within Italy or Israel); experts were asked to distinguish between United States and Canada (regions here adapted).

On the other hand are African countries, with now very low levels and a far ceiling point of IQ 93. They can catch up at about 25 IQ points and their coming increases per decade will be large. At the end of this development of *similar-making cognitive modernisation* countries and cultures will become more similar but not identical.

In Table 13.2, we list present averages of cognitive ability tests for 14 regions, expected finishing lines at the end of an environmental FLynn effect (fictitiously 'year 2200'), the developmental potential (difference between now and 2200) and the gains expected by experts until the year 2100.[15]

[15] The expert survey was conducted in 2013, $N = 228$ participants, intelligence researchers and some educational scientists and biologists (81 per cent psychologists, 87 per cent PhD, 67 per cent tenured members of a university, average $h$-index in Scopus $h = 17$, 35 per cent from the United States). This question was answered by 58 experts (Rindermann, Coyle & Becker, 2013). The question addressed to the experts differed from the possible expected gains due to optimal environmental changes: the 'possible finishing line' deals with what is imaginable in

The fictitious developmental potential for the year 2200 is nearly four times larger than the as 'real' expected gains until 2100 ($M$ = 11.21 vs. 3.21 IQ points), but the patterns are correlated with $r$ = .74. Accordingly, our assumptions on the *pattern* of developmental potentials are supported by an expert view on realistic development.[16]

### 13.2.6  Intelligence of the Future – Results

*Asymmetric-Children-Rate-Generation-Length-Age Effects*    We assumed for all countries and all decades in twenty-first century a stable effect of asymmetric children rates, different generation spans and increasing mutation load with older age of parents at about $dec$ = $-0.57$. Across 90 years this effect will be $-5.13$ IQ. This may sound large but considering that the average FLynn effect in twentieth century was about $dec$ = $+2.31$ to $+2.83$ IQ points the asymmetry effect is about one third to a fifth ($dec$ = $-0.57$) and its negative consequences could be easily offset by environmental improvements – if they come. Also should be recognised that the $-5.13$ IQ decline does *not show the expected empirical trend but one factor of the three* contributing to the twenty-first century development: (1) Asymmetry effects, (2) migration effects, (3) continued FLynn effects based on environmental improvements.

The negative consequences of asymmetric birth rates and different generation spans (see second column of Table 13.3) seem to be too large. But the estimations are based on empirical studies and they will be at least partially offset by environmental improvements.

*Migration Effects Based on Changing Demographics*    For migration effects we have developed two models:

(1) Model 1 (*constant old immigrant SAS level*) is based on student assessment data (PISA, TIMSS, PIRLS) regarding native and migrant average cognitive abilities and regarding natives' and migrants' shares among students, on their past 10-year development and on information from the Lutz research group on immigration rates in the twenty-first century. The migrant share development in the twenty-first century is based more on the previous 10-years' development in student assessment data for

---

the best of all worlds, but the question for experts deals with what is to be expected in the real world considering further factors having an impact on development.

[16] The imaginable developmental potentials presented here are also higher than the Karlin's (2012b) estimated potential IQs. He has combined intrinsic potentials with expected demographic changes in his estimation and thus his estimates are more similar to the real-world expert survey ratings. Similarly, he expects better results for Canada than for the United States (experts: +2.07/−0.45, Karlin: 103/100).

Table 13.3 *Cognitive ability prediction 2100 (only based on assumptions on asymmetric fertility)*

| | CA corrected 2010 | | Asymmetry effect model 2100 | Difference 2100–2010 |
|---|---|---|---|---|
| **Africa (sub-Sahara)** | 69.19 | | 64 | –5.13 |
| Kenya | | 74.47 | 69 | –5.13 |
| **N-Africa M-East** | 83.28 | | 78 | –5.13 |
| Egypt | | 83.72 | 79 | –5.13 |
| **America (North, Engl)** | 99.45 | | 94 | –5.13 |
| USA | | 98.33 | 93 | –5.13 |
| **America (Latin, C-S)** | 79.32 | | 74 | –5.13 |
| Mexico | | 85.87 | 81 | –5.13 |
| **Asia (Central-South)** | 79.41 | | 74 | –5.13 |
| India | | 77.60 | 72 | –5.13 |
| **East Asia** | 99.99 | | 95 | –5.13 |
| China | | 100.77 | 96 | –5.13 |
| **Southeast Asia, Pacific** | 84.21 | | 79 | –5.13 |
| Philippines | | 80.38 | 75 | –5.13 |
| **Australia-NZ (English)** | 99.06 | | 94 | –5.13 |
| New Zealand | | 99.17 | 94 | –5.13 |
| **Western Europe** | 98.83 | | 94 | –5.13 |
| United Kingdom | | 99.60 | 94 | –5.13 |
| **Scandinavia** | 97.06 | | 92 | –5.13 |
| Norway | | 97.91 | 93 | –5.13 |
| **Central Europe** | 98.85 | | 94 | –5.13 |
| Germany | | 98.82 | 94 | –5.13 |
| **Eastnorth Europe** | 96.98 | | 92 | –5.13 |
| Russia | | 97.26 | 92 | –5.13 |
| **Southwest Europe** | 95.74 | | 91 | –5.13 |
| Italy | | 97.52 | 92 | –5.13 |
| **Southeast Europe** | 91.00 | | 86 | –5.13 |
| Greece | | 94.98 | 90 | –5.13 |

*Notes*: Regions closer categorised for culture (less for geography); asymmetry effect model 2100: results due to the asymmetry model for 2100 (asymmetric children rates, different generation spans, increasing mutation load with older age of parents); difference 2100–2010: difference between 2100 and 2010 (a constant, for all countries the assumption is the same).

more recent decades until 2040, in 2040 equally on SAS and Lutz data, then more strongly on Lutz data (results see Table 13.4 and Figure 13.9). Ability values are based on student assessment data and they are invariant, assuming no gap closing and the same ability level of new immigrants as for former immigrants (gap closing will be considered among FLynn effects, see Tables 13.5 to 13.7).

Table 13.4 *Cognitive ability prediction 2100 (only based on assumptions on migration), new immigrants with same or different ability levels*

| | CA corrected 2010 | Migrant effect m1 2100 | Diff. m1 2100–2010 | Migrants' share (%) 2010 | Migrants' share (%) 2100 | Migrant effect m2 2100 | Diff. m2 2100–2010 |
|---|---|---|---|---|---|---|---|
| **Africa (sub-Sahara)** | 69.19 | 68 | −1.56 | 14 | 30 | 68 | −1.56 |
| Kenya | 74.47 | 73 | −1.56 | – | – | 73 | −1.56 |
| **N-Africa M-East** | 83.28 | 82 | −0.87 | 18 | 45 | 82 | −0.87 |
| Egypt | 83.72 | 80 | −3.57 | 17 | 46 | 80 | −3.57 |
| **America (North)** | 99.45 | 98 | −0.97 | 26 | 59 | 97 | −2.43 |
| USA | 98.33 | 97 | −1.31 | 23 | 52 | 94 | −4.23 |
| **America (Latin, C-S)** | 79.32 | 79 | −0.80 | 10 | 26 | 79 | −0.80 |
| Mexico | 85.87 | 86 | −0.32 | 5 | 9 | 86 | −0.32 |
| **Asia (Central-South)** | 79.41 | 79 | −0.12 | 14 | 37 | 79 | −0.12 |
| India | 77.60 | 77 | −0.12 | – | – | 77 | −0.12 |
| **East Asia** | 99.99 | 99 | −0.67 | 23 | 42 | 99 | −0.67 |
| China | 100.77 | 100 | −1.19 | 4 | 16 | 100 | −1.19 |
| **Southeast Asia, Pacf.** | 84.21 | 84 | −0.63 | 4 | 10 | 84 | −0.63 |
| Philippines | 80.38 | 80 | −0.63 | – | – | 80 | −0.63 |
| **Australia-NZ** | 99.06 | 99 | −0.17 | 31 | 67 | 99 | −0.17 |
| New Zealand | 99.17 | 99 | −0.51 | 29 | 79 | 99 | −0.51 |
| **Western Europe** | 98.83 | 98 | −1.21 | 16 | 43 | 93 | −5.78 |
| United Kingdom | 99.60 | 99 | −0.67 | 15 | 35 | 95 | −4.65 |
| **Scandinavia** | 97.06 | 95 | −1.72 | 10 | 34 | 92 | −4.84 |
| Norway | 97.91 | 97 | −1.25 | 10 | 32 | 94 | −4.01 |
| **Central Europe** | 98.85 | 96 | −2.90 | 29 | 71 | 89 | −9.87 |
| Germany | 98.82 | 96 | −2.67 | 19 | 52 | 92 | −7.32 |

| | m1 2100 | m1 2010 | Diff. m1 2100–2010 | (%) 2010 | (%) 2100 | m2 2100 | Diff. m2 2100–2010 |
|---|---|---|---|---|---|---|---|
| **Eastnorth Europe** | 96.98 | 97 | −0.37 | 9 | 17 | 95 | −2.01 |
| Russia | 97.26 | 97 | −0.42 | 14 | 28 | 94 | −3.35 |
| **Southwest Europe** | 95.74 | 95 | −1.15 | 12 | 40 | 91 | −4.59 |
| Italy | 97.52 | 96 | −1.34 | 9 | 31 | 93 | −4.11 |
| **Southeast Europe** | 91.00 | 90 | −0.82 | 12 | 33 | 88 | −2.74 |
| Greece | 94.98 | 93 | −1.88 | 13 | 45 | 90 | −5.45 |

*Notes:* Migrant effect m1 2100: result due to changes in migrants' shares up to 2100; new immigrants have the *same ability level* as the old, model 1 (assumption of zero changes in the native-immigrant gaps); Diff. m1 2100–2010: difference between 2100 and 2010 due to the migration model 1; migrants' share (%) 2010: percentage of migrants in 2010 based on student assessment studies; migrants' share (%) 2100: estimation of the percentage of migrants in 2100 based on trends in student assessment studies and as reported by Jakob Eder (23. April 2015) from the Lutz research group at the Wittgenstein Centre for Demography and Global Human Capital in Vienna; m2 2100: result due to changes in migrants' shares up to 2100, *considering the ability level of new immigrants*, model 2; Diff. m2 2100-2010: difference between 2100 and 2010 due to the migration model 2.

435

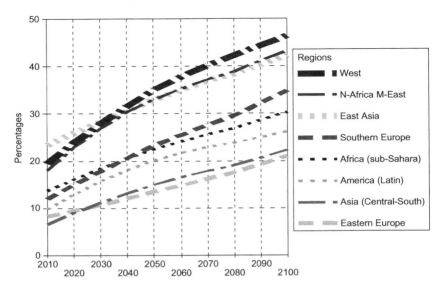

Figure 13.9 Estimated migrant share development in the twenty-first century

(2) Model 2 is identical to model 1 except for Europe and the United States, considering the probable *ability level of new immigrants*. The majority will most likely come, as in the past, from neighbouring regions, for Europe from Africa and the Middle East, for the United States from Latin America.[17] The ability level of their native populations should be considered for new immigration in the twenty-first century. The SAS immigrant level representing the old immigrants was used, fading out in the twenty-first century; the ability level of the neighbouring regions standing for new immigrants was increasingly used (in 2100 50–50). Two assumptions make the predictions more optimistic: we assumed that on average better educated and smarter persons emigrate (+5 IQ above average). Due to declining fertility rates, immigration from North Africa and the Middle East should decline; only sub-Saharan Africa with its still-high birth rates can expect larger immigration movements.[18] We averaged both regions but not stronger weighted sub-Saharan African countries. The assumed

---

[17] In recent decades for Europe, a large immigrant resource was Europe itself (from the East and South to Central, Northern and Western Europe). However, declining youth rates and rising wealth levels make similar large inflows in the rest of the twenty-first century unlikely.

[18] On immigration from sub-Saharan African countries, e.g. the demographers and migration researchers Abel & Sander (2014, p. 1522): 'Emigration from Africa will play a key role in shaping global migration patterns in the future.'

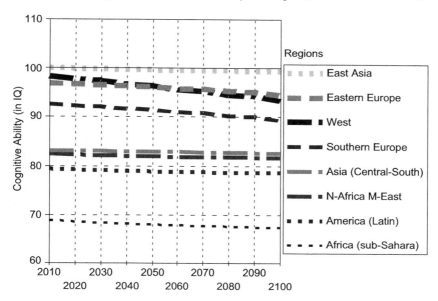

Figure 13.10 Estimated ability development in the twenty-first century based on migrant model 2

means are 83.73 IQ for Latin American immigrants in the United States and 74.02 IQ for African and Middle East immigrants in Europe (results see Table 13.4 and Figure 13.10). The means were held constant (for the final later model it was assumed that they rise).

Results of the two models not considering general fertility differences and FLynn effects can be found in Table 13.4.

The two models show important results: while an increase of the shares of given immigrants with their ability levels has only a minor decline as a consequence, for the entire West about −1.43 IQ points, the additional expected immigration with lower levels has much larger consequences, entirely at −5.01 IQ points. These are additionally −3.57 IQ; the size of this effect is more than double.

The largest declines are expected for Central Europe, for Liechtenstein and Luxembourg with −12 IQ points, for Switzerland, Austria and Germany between −10 and −7, for the Netherlands and Belgium between −7 and −6 IQ points. While some reader may remain sceptical, the OECD (2016a, p. 86) recently has published − not particularly highlighted − a similar result: the OECD research group compared trends in PISA before and after accounting for demographic changes. For instance, for Germany, the difference in the three-year trend in science was 2.58 SASQ − without demographic change, and this change is mainly due to immigration, the trend would have been 2.58 SASQ better in three years. Converted to a 10-year trend it represents a decline due to demographics of –8.59 SASQ and converted to IQ of –1.29 IQ points. From 2010 to 2100 – our chosen interval – it would lead to a decline of –11.59 IQ points. Compared with this, our value for Germany of –7.32 IQ points seems to be rather optimistic![19] An even much larger decline would result if a 2017 published study on fourth graders was utilised (Stanat et al., 2017, pp. 159, 176): Here an average decline of –16.33 SASQ was found between 2011 and 2016, which represents in an IQ scale for ten years $dec = $ –4.90 IQ points. Linearly transferred to 90 years (2010 to 2100) this would mean a decline of –44.10 IQ points! Of course, linear extrapolation is simplistic but it underscores that our predictions may be even too ambitious.

Model 2 was rather optimistically implemented, a plus 5 IQ assumption above regional averages and no major emigration from sub-Saharan Africa, although future population resources for immigration mainly come from Africa. And the models do not include effects of the large immigration waves 2014ff. to Europe, especially to Germany, Austria and Sweden. Because the majority of immigrants come from countries with on average low ability levels (in IQ between the averages of 83 for North-Africa-Middle-East and 69 for sub-Saharan Africa), the negative effects of immigration will be larger than estimated here. Only the 2015 immigration of around 1,200,000 persons to Germany would lead to a decline in Germany of around −0.31 IQ points. Supposing that the majority will stay, because immigrants are younger than natives, even without any further immigration their shares will increase and consequently the adverse ability effects across decades. A totally different development due to immigration is expected for some gulf countries: increases are estimated for countries as Qatar (+3) and Singapore (+1).

Without gap closing and without general FLynn effects the declines are remarkable. However, further improvements are expected, which will be integrated in the next models.

---

[19] The correlation between the OECD demographic (immigration) trend measure (based on PISA results from 2000 to 2015) and the here presented own immigration trend measure is $r = .61$ ($N = 66$ countries), averages for 10 years are $dec_{OECD} = -0.29$ and $dec_{Migr} = -0.21$ IQ points. Because the OECD measure only reflects past development and the own measure also considers assumptions on future development including some gap narrowing the two measures are not identical. However, a correlation of $r = .61$ and the similar averages underscore the plausibility of our prediction method. Further support comes from OECD's adult PISA (2016c): 25–34 olds compared to 55–65 year olds and corrected for psychological age-related development (unadjusted minus adjusted) show the best historical development in Singapore (followed by Korea) and the lowest in Germany (followed by other European countries and the US), the correlation with the PISA based trend is $r = .66$ and with our demographic trend measure $r = .38$. That means that the past 30-years adult cognitive ability trend (young and old adults compared, timescale from around 1975/85 to 2005/2015) is related to the trend among students (from around 2000 to 2015) and our prediction (2010 to 2100), backing the method.

### 13.2.7   FLynn Effects Based on Expected Environmental Improvements

We assume that the rise of cognitive ability will continue, but with lower speed for developed countries and with generally decreasing speed for all ('Same-boat-but-different-team model', see Figure 13.8). General environmental conditions from nutrition and the health system, including neuro-enhancement, to education and general stimulation by modernity, will contribute to rising cognitive ability. Additionally, we assume a reduction of the present native-immigrant differences of about one third, similar to the White-Black reduction in the twentieth century in the United States from around 15 to 10 IQ points (e.g. Rindermann & Thompson, 2013; for native-immigrant gaps e.g. te Nijenhuis et al., 2004). Tables 13.5 and 13.6 present data for countries with data on natives and immigrants ($N = 93$). In Table 13.5, the twenty-first-century prediction is based on the 2010 shares of natives and immigrants, which were seen as stable. Table 13.6 also considers the estimated changes in shares (see Table 13.4 and Figure 13.9).

For all countries and regions (see Table 13.5 and Figure 13.11), rises in intelligence during the twenty-first century are expected. The largest gains are estimated for sub-Saharan Africa (+26.26, $dec = 2.92$), the smallest for Central Europe (+4.04, $dec = 0.45$). No change in ranks is expected, e.g. the West passing East Asia. Gaps between developed and developing countries, the rich and poor and between different regions and cultures are decreasing. The model is quite optimistic but is no continuation of the past, where in the West and in East Asia much larger gains were observed. Present-day developed societies and their peoples have nearly reached their cognitive limits.

The first model (Table 13.5 and Figure 13.11) assumed no changes in shares of natives and immigrants during the twenty-first century, which is certainly wrong. The second model (Table 13.6) took account of such changes. Figure 13.12 shows the different cognitive outcomes for models without and with consideration of expected changes in immigrant shares – both including assumptions on reducing gaps from 2010 (observed gap '100 per cent') to 2100 (66 per cent of 2010).

The impact of immigrant share changes is smaller than expected, maximal (most positive) for Qatar with +2.02 IQ points and other oil-producing Arabian countries as well as for Singapore (+0.38 IQ points) and Australia (+0.13 IQ points). Most negative is the impact for African and Western countries, both due to large native-immigrant gaps. While for African countries the present data quality is shaky, for Western countries the data quality is much better and the prediction more trustworthy. Countries with large estimated losses are, for instance, Austria (−1.99 IQ points), Germany (−1.75 IQ points) and the United States (−0.79 IQ points). The recent migration waves were not included.

Table 13.5 *Cognitive ability prediction 2100 (based on assumptions on FLynn effect and no changes in migrant shares)*

| | Natives 2010 | Migrants 2010 | N-M-diff. 2010 | Natives 2100 | Migrants 2100 | N-M-diff. 2100 | Society mean 2010 | Society mean 2100 | Diff. 2100–2010 |
|---|---|---|---|---|---|---|---|---|---|
| **Africa (sub-Sah)** | 59.45 | 50.88 | 8.57 | 85 | 80 | 5.66 | 64.63 | 85 | 26.26 |
| South Africa | 61.18 | 50.68 | 10.50 | 86 | 79 | 6.93 | 59.27 | 84 | 25.08 |
| **N-Africa M-East** | 77.20 | 73.93 | 3.27 | 92 | 90 | 1.97 | 77.38 | 92 | 14.90 |
| Egypt | 82.07 | 70.47 | 11.60 | 94 | 86 | 7.66 | 80.26 | 93 | 12.47 |
| **America (North)** | 100.36 | 97.61 | 2.75 | 104 | 103 | 1.82 | 99.80 | 104 | 4.10 |
| USA | 99.10 | 94.99 | 4.11 | 104 | 101 | 2.72 | 98.28 | 103 | 4.77 |
| **America (Latin)** | 78.73 | 73.10 | 5.63 | 94 | 91 | 3.72 | 77.29 | 94 | 15.81 |
| Mexico | 81.23 | 73.02 | 8.20 | 95 | 90 | 5.42 | 80.84 | 95 | 13.86 |
| **Asia (Central-S.)** | 79.50 | 80.88 | −1.38 | 95 | 96 | −0.91 | 76.06 | 95 | 15.07 |
| Kazakhstan | 88.38 | 88.09 | .29 | 97 | 96 | .19 | 88.29 | 97 | 8.28 |
| **East Asia** | 102.57 | 97.21 | 5.36 | 107 | 103 | 3.54 | 100.15 | 107 | 4.24 |
| China | 99.52 | 89.86 | 9.66 | 106 | 100 | 6.38 | 99.14 | 106 | 6.69 |
| **Southeast Asia, Pac.** | 86.24 | 76.89 | 9.34 | 97 | 91 | 6.17 | 82.76 | 96 | 10.57 |
| Thailand | 87.05 | 79.31 | 7.74 | 96 | 90 | 5.11 | 86.82 | 95 | 8.55 |
| **Australia-NZ** | 99.30 | 99.26 | 0.04 | 104 | 104 | 0.03 | 99.34 | 104 | 5.14 |
| New Zealand | 99.52 | 98.60 | .91 | 105 | 104 | .60 | 99.30 | 104 | 5.06 |
| **Western Europe** | 100.03 | 95.20 | 4.84 | 104 | 101 | 3.19 | 99.20 | 103 | 4.12 |
| United Kingdom | 100.00 | 96.94 | 3.06 | 104 | 102 | 2.02 | 99.60 | 104 | 3.97 |
| **Scandinavia** | 99.49 | 92.39 | 7.10 | 105 | 100 | 4.67 | 98.80 | 104 | 5.26 |
| Norway | 97.16 | 91.48 | 5.68 | 104 | 100 | 3.75 | 96.62 | 104 | 6.99 |
| **Central Europe** | 100.69 | 93.46 | 7.23 | 104 | 99 | 4.77 | 98.58 | 103 | 4.05 |
| Germany | 100.28 | 92.02 | 8.26 | 104 | 98 | 5.45 | 98.69 | 103 | 4.18 |
| **Eastnorth Europe** | 97.15 | 92.40 | 4.76 | 103 | 100 | 3.14 | 96.86 | 103 | 5.76 |
| Russia | 97.41 | 94.78 | 2.63 | 103 | 101 | 1.74 | 97.08 | 103 | 5.57 |

| | | | | | | | | | |
|---|---|---|---|---|---|---|---|---|---|
| **Southwest Europe** | 95.15 | 91.32 | 3.83 | 101 | 99 | 2.53 | 94.77 | 101 | 6.18 |
| Italy | 97.83 | 91.84 | 5.99 | 102 | 98 | 3.96 | 97.31 | 101 | 4.18 |
| **Southeast Europe** | 88.52 | 84.98 | 3.53 | 98 | 96 | 2.13 | 88.36 | 98 | 9.83 |
| Greece | 95.86 | 89.97 | 5.89 | 100 | 96 | 3.89 | 95.11 | 99 | 4.24 |

*Notes:* Results only based on 93 nations with student assessment results; Kenya substituted by South Africa, India by Kazakhstan, Philippines by Thailand; differences are not identical with the differences of the presented means for 2010 and 2100 if the number of countries differ (e.g. for Africa); Natives 2010: based on average natives' IQ in student assessment studies ($N$ = 93); Migrants 2010: based on average immigrants' IQ in student assessment studies ($N$ = 93); N-M-diff. 2010: difference in 2010 between natives' and immigrants' average cognitive ability in IQ points; Natives 2100: estimated IQ of natives in 2100 only based on FLynn effect assumptions; Migrants 2100: estimated IQ of immigrants in 2100 only based on assumptions on FLynn effect and gap closing (minus a third); N-M-diff. 2100: estimated difference in 2100 between natives' and immigrants' average cognitive ability in IQ; Society mean 2010: based on average IQ in student assessment studies; Society mean 2100: for 2100 estimated average IQ; Diff. 2100–2010: FLynn effect and gap closing-based estimated gains until 2100.

441

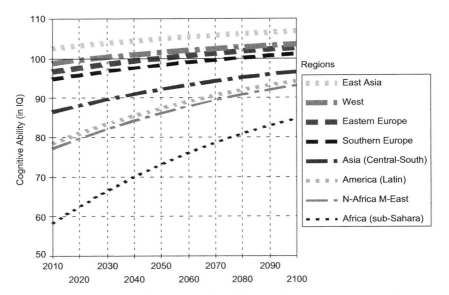

Figure 13.11 Estimated cognitive ability development in the twenty-first century based on FLynn effect and gap closing[20]

### 13.2.8    Combining Birth Rate, Migration and FLynn Effects

The final model combines

- effects of *asymmetric fertility* (asymmetric birth rates and generation spans and increasing mutation load with older age of parents, a constant of –0.57 per decade),
- of *migration* (model 2 with increasing immigrant shares and lower ability levels of new immigrants) and
- of further *environmental improvements* raising the intelligence of natives, of given immigrants (including reducing gaps between natives and immigrants by a steeper rise of immigrants' levels) and of incoming immigrants (including reducing gaps between inhabitants of receiving countries and new immigrants, steeper rise of new immigrants' levels).

The final model is not a simple summation of the former models because we assume gap closing also for new incoming immigrants and because we assume (smaller) positive feedback effects between rising levels of native, old and new

---

[20] There is a minor deviation between Table 13.5 (and Table 13.6) and Figure 13.11: in Figure 13.11, we used only those countries with data on natives and immigrants ($N = 93$) for 2010, in Tables 13.5 and 13.6 for 2010 all countries with results in PISA, TIMSS and PIRLS ($N = 99$).

Table 13.6 *Cognitive ability prediction 2100 (based on assumptions on FLynn effect and changes in migrant shares)*

| | Nativ. CA 2010 | Nati. % 2010 | Migr. CA 2010 | Migr. % 2010 | Nativ. CA 2100 | Nati. % 2100 | Migr. CA 2100 | Migr. % 2100 | Society CA 2010 | Society CA 2100 | Diff. 2100-2010 |
|---|---|---|---|---|---|---|---|---|---|---|---|
| **Africa (sub-Sah.)** | 59.45 | 86.29 | 50.88 | 13.71 | 85 | 70 | 80 | 30 | 64.63 | 84 | 25.31 |
| South Africa | 61.18 | 79.17 | 50.68 | 20.83 | 86 | 57 | 79 | 44 | 59.27 | 83 | 23.51 |
| **N-Africa M-East** | 77.20 | 81.51 | 73.93 | 18.49 | 92 | 55 | 90 | 45 | 77.38 | 92 | 14.39 |
| Egypt | 82.07 | 83.25 | 70.47 | 16.75 | 94 | 54 | 86 | 46 | 80.26 | 90 | 10.20 |
| **America (North)** | 100.36 | 73.90 | 97.61 | 26.10 | 104 | 41 | 103 | 59 | 99.80 | 103 | 3.53 |
| USA | 99.10 | 77.39 | 94.99 | 22.61 | 104 | 48 | 101 | 52 | 98.28 | 102 | 3.98 |
| **America (Latin)** | 78.73 | 90.22 | 73.10 | 9.78 | 94 | 74 | 91 | 26 | 77.29 | 94 | 15.29 |
| Mexico | 81.23 | 94.89 | 73.02 | 5.11 | 95 | 91 | 90 | 9 | 80.84 | 95 | 13.67 |
| **Asia (Central-S.)** | 79.50 | 86.12 | 80.88 | 13.88 | 95 | 63 | 96 | 37 | 76.06 | 95 | 14.97 |
| Kazakhstan | 88.38 | 81.72 | 88.09 | 18.28 | 97 | 30 | 96 | 70 | 88.29 | 96 | 8.18 |
| **East Asia** | 102.57 | 76.58 | 97.21 | 23.42 | 107 | 58 | 103 | 42 | 100.15 | 106 | 3.81 |
| China | 99.52 | 96.11 | 89.86 | 3.89 | 106 | 84 | 100 | 16 | 99.14 | 105 | 5.90 |
| **Southeast Asia, P** | 86.24 | 96.35 | 76.89 | 3.65 | 97 | 90 | 91 | 10 | 82.76 | 96 | 10.16 |
| Thailand | 87.05 | 96.96 | 79.31 | 3.04 | 96 | 89 | 90 | 11 | 86.82 | 95 | 8.14 |
| **Australia-NZ (E)** | 99.30 | 69.13 | 99.26 | 30.87 | 104 | 33 | 104 | 67 | 99.34 | 104 | 5.06 |
| New Zealand | 99.52 | 70.72 | 98.60 | 29.28 | 105 | 21 | 104 | 79 | 99.30 | 104 | 4.76 |
| **Western Europe** | 100.03 | 83.53 | 95.20 | 16.47 | 104 | 57 | 101 | 43 | 99.20 | 103 | 3.33 |
| United Kingdom | 100.00 | 85.22 | 96.94 | 14.78 | 104 | 65 | 102 | 35 | 99.60 | 103 | 3.56 |
| **Scandinavia** | 99.49 | 89.73 | 92.39 | 10.27 | 105 | 66 | 100 | 34 | 98.80 | 103 | 4.14 |
| Norway | 97.16 | 89.58 | 91.48 | 10.42 | 104 | 68 | 100 | 32 | 96.62 | 103 | 6.20 |
| **Central Europe** | 100.69 | 70.10 | 93.46 | 29.90 | 104 | 29 | 99 | 71 | 98.58 | 101 | 2.13 |
| Germany | 100.28 | 80.54 | 92.02 | 19.46 | 104 | 48 | 98 | 52 | 98.69 | 101 | 2.43 |
| **Eastnorth Eurp.** | 97.15 | 91.05 | 92.40 | 8.95 | 103 | 83 | 100 | 17 | 96.86 | 102 | 5.54 |
| Russia | 97.41 | 86.05 | 94.78 | 13.95 | 103 | 72 | 101 | 28 | 97.08 | 102 | 5.32 |
| **Southwest Eurp.** | 95.15 | 88.47 | 91.32 | 11.53 | 101 | 60 | 99 | 40 | 94.77 | 100 | 5.45 |
| Italy | 97.83 | 91.43 | 91.84 | 8.57 | 102 | 69 | 98 | 32 | 97.31 | 101 | 3.29 |
| **Southeast Eurp.** | 88.52 | 87.90 | 84.98 | 12.10 | 98 | 67 | 96 | 33 | 88.36 | 98 | 9.36 |
| Greece | 95.86 | 87.37 | 89.97 | 12.63 | 100 | 55 | 96 | 45 | 95.11 | 98 | 2.99 |

*Notes*: see Table 13.5; %: percentages of natives and immigrants, 2010 based on student assessment studies, 2100 estimated (see text for Model 1).

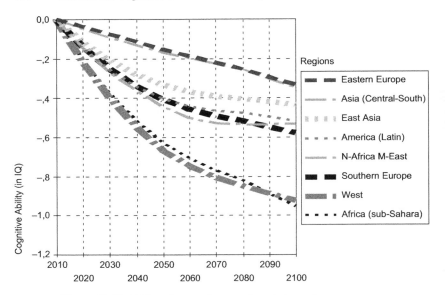

Figure 13.12 Ability changes due to migrant share changes

immigrants – instead of gap closing up to a difference of 66 per cent now to a difference of 60 per cent.

According to the most sophisticated model (Table 13.7 and Figure 13.13), considering asymmetric reproduction, migration and FLynn effects, IQ will rise in the twenty-first century every 10 years with a worldwide average of *dec* = 0.74 IQ points. This increase is smaller than that observed in the twentieth century in developed countries with around *dec* = 2.80, and this prediction is smaller than a prediction based on education (Table 13.1, Lutz data, *dec* = 1.58 IQ points). In Africa, the increases will be the largest; they would reach *dec* = 1.36 IQ points (education based: *dec* = 2.23 IQ points). For the United States *dec* = −0.28 are estimated (education based: *dec* = 0.53). This is somewhat lower than the increase calculated for 17-year-olds in NAEP between 1971 and 2008 (*dec* = 0.30) and lower than the predicted rise in NAEP until 2060 (*dec* = 0.61; Rindermann & Thompson, 2013; Rindermann & Pichelmann, 2015). While the NAEP prediction was based on the extrapolation of past development and on demographic predictions, the worldwide model is much more complex, considering asymmetric fertility and diminishing returns in environmental improvements.

Following the final integrative model, international gaps in cognitive ability will decline by a half, from a standard deviation of *SD* = 11.86 in 2010 to *SD* = 5.95 in 2100 (education based: to *SD* = 9.37). Developing countries will catch up; developed countries lose. The gap between the West and sub-Saharan Africa declines from 29 to 14 IQ points (education based: to 19 IQ).

Table 13.7 *Cognitive ability prediction 2100 (final integrative model)*

| | CA corrected 2010 | Cogn. ability 2100 | Asymmetry effect | Migration effect | Environ. improv. effect | Diff. 2100-2010 | IQ gain decade ('10–100) |
|---|---|---|---|---|---|---|---|
| **Africa (sub-Sahara)** | 69.19 | 81 | -5.13 | -1.56 | 18.92 | 12.23 | +1.36 |
| Kenya | 74.47 | 82 | -5.13 | -1.56 | 14.33 | 7.65 | +0.85 |
| **N-Africa M-East** | 83.28 | 92 | -5.13 | -0.87 | 14.36 | 8.34 | +0.93 |
| Egypt | 83.72 | 87 | -5.13 | -3.57 | 11.94 | 3.24 | +0.36 |
| **America (North, Engl)** | 99.45 | 97 | -5.13 | -1.50 | 4.24 | -2.38 | -0.26 |
| USA | 98.33 | 96 | -5.13 | -2.37 | 4.93 | -2.56 | -0.28 |
| **America (Latin, C-S)** | 79.32 | 89 | -5.13 | -0.80 | 15.73 | 9.81 | +1.09 |
| Mexico | 85.87 | 94 | -5.13 | -0.32 | 13.14 | 7.70 | +0.86 |
| **Asia (Central-South)** | 79.41 | 90 | -5.13 | -0.12 | 15.41 | 10.15 | +1.13 |
| India | 77.60 | 89 | -5.13 | -0.12 | 16.56 | 11.30 | +1.26 |
| **East Asia** | 99.99 | 99 | -5.13 | -0.67 | 5.19 | -0.60 | -0.07 |
| China | 100.77 | 101 | -5.13 | -1.19 | 6.71 | 0.39 | +0.04 |
| **Southeast Asia, Pacific** | 84.21 | 90 | -5.13 | -0.63 | 11.42 | 5.66 | +0.63 |
| Philippines | 80.38 | 88 | -5.13 | -0.63 | 13.63 | 7.87 | +0.87 |
| **Australia-NZ (English)** | 99.06 | 99 | -5.13 | -0.17 | 5.18 | -0.12 | -0.01 |
| New Zealand | 99.17 | 99 | -5.13 | -0.51 | 5.12 | -0.51 | -0.06 |
| **Western Europe** | 98.83 | 94 | -5.13 | -3.55 | 4.18 | -4.50 | -0.50 |
| United Kingdom | 99.60 | 96 | -5.13 | -2.84 | 4.05 | -3.93 | -0.44 |
| **Scandinavia** | 97.06 | 95 | -5.13 | -3.07 | 6.12 | -2.08 | -0.23 |
| Norway | 97.91 | 97 | -5.13 | -2.36 | 7.08 | -0.42 | -0.05 |
| **Central Europe** | 98.85 | 92 | -5.13 | -6.19 | 4.18 | -7.14 | -0.79 |
| Germany | 98.82 | 93 | -5.13 | -4.64 | 4.29 | -5.47 | -0.61 |
| **Eastnorth Europe** | 96.98 | 97 | -5.13 | -1.10 | 5.89 | -0.35 | -0.04 |
| Russia | 97.26 | 96 | -5.13 | -1.88 | 5.63 | -1.38 | -0.15 |
| **Southwest Europe** | 95.74 | 94 | -5.13 | -2.52 | 6.34 | -1.31 | -0.15 |
| Italy | 97.52 | 94 | -5.13 | -2.49 | 4.20 | -3.42 | -0.38 |
| **Southeast Europe** | 91.10 | 95 | -5.13 | -1.04 | 9.86 | 3.70 | +0.41 |
| Greece | 94.98 | 91 | -5.13 | -3.12 | 4.27 | -3.98 | -0.44 |

*Notes:* 2100-2010: difference between 2100 and 2010 (increases or decreases).

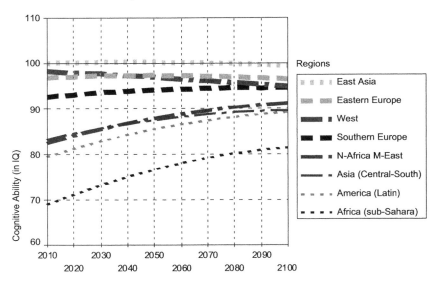

Figure 13.13 Final integrative model predictions for the twenty-first century

However, the gap between East Asia and the West doubles from 2 to 4 IQ points (education based: to 5 IQ).

Figure 13.13 illustrates that for East Asia and Eastern Europe nearly no changes are predicted, but the West will decline. Africa, Latin America, Asia and the Middle East will catch up but not reach the level of developed countries. Figure 13.14 shows that the positive FLynn effect due to assumed environmental improvements is expected to remain, but this FLynn effect is neutralized by the combined negative effects of migration and asymmetric birth rates.

The negative effects of migration are especially large for Central Europe (Figure 13.14, centre left), less so for the United States (centre right), approximately zero for Australia (bottom left) and positive for Qatar (bottom right). The predicted development for Central Europe is so critical that a tipping point may be reached, leading to negative interaction effects between demographic changes, asymmetric birth rates and ability-dependent deterioration of social and cultural environment affecting the development potential due to environmental improvement.

*Considering Population Sizes for Global Development*    The international mean calculated by weighting each country by one (as it is usual in international analyses) for 2010 is IQ 83 and for 2100 IQ 90. The predicted increase is about 7 IQ points or *dec* = 0.74 IQ points (gain per decade, 200 countries). For calculating an international mean, this seems to be a less reasonable

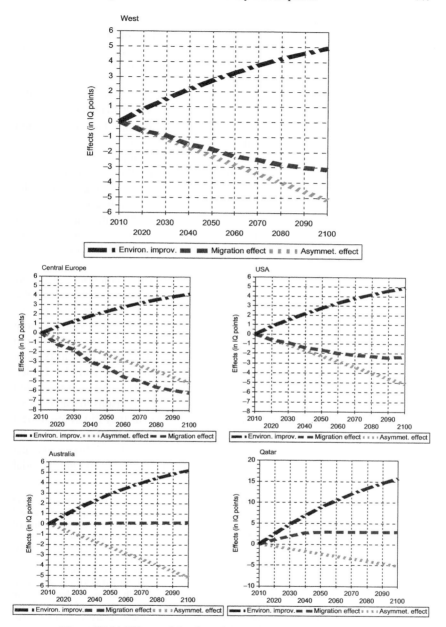

Figure 13.14 Effects of the three factors on cognitive development in the West in general, in selected regions and countries and in Qatar in the twenty-first century

approach because currently available data and projections assume a stronger increase of populations with relatively low cognitive development level.[21]

Using population sizes (from Lutz et al., 2014) of countries for weighting gives a different picture: The weighted average for 2010 is IQ 87 and for 2100 IQ 90. The increase is about 3 IQ points or $dec = 0.28$ IQ points. There is no remarkable difference for 2100; however, there is for 2010 – but why? We have only data for 166 countries from Lutz et al. (2014) and data from countries with lower ability levels are missing, in particular. For this restricted country sample, the increase is only $dec = 0.28$ IQ points.

Therefore, we additionally used population projection data from the UN covering 195 countries.[22] However, the result is robust: the average for 2010 is IQ 87 and for 2100 IQ 89. The increase is about 2 IQ points or $dec = 0.23$ IQ points. This means that in 2010 countries with relatively low cognitive ability levels have rather small populations but compared to 2010 their international share will increase in the twenty-first century, lowering the global positive cognitive development from $dec = 0.74$ to about $dec = 0.23$ IQ points.[23]

*Comparison with the 2011 Predictions* The predictions calculated in 2011 were based on the student assessment data available at that time ($N = 97$ countries).[24] A comparison of the outcomes of both models, of the 2011 and the present one, reveals that the present prediction is slightly more optimistic ($dec_{P18} = +0.41$ vs. $dec_{P11} = -0.03$, both $N = 97$), especially due to more optimistic assumptions for developing countries. But it is also more pessimistic for Central and Western Europe, Scandinavia and the United States. Here the student assessment studies and the Lutz data-based migration predictions lead to more declining predictions (see comparisons in Table 13.8).

The 2011 predictions were also more conservative, as they did not assume a strong narrowing of gaps and a change in ranks: Africa, the Middle East and Latin America were still far behind, the West still with higher ability levels than Eastern Europe. However, the correlation between the newer and older decadal

---

[21] E.g. the Pew Research Center (2015) assumes a strong rise of populations in sub-Saharan Africa and of Muslims (worldwide from 2010 23 per cent to 2050 30 per cent). Both a geographic and a cultural categorisation point at populations of comparatively lower ability and at less positive environmental conditions for cognitive development. However, larger FLynn effects are expected as well.

[22] Source: Population Division, UN Department of Economic and Social Affairs, World Population Prospects, The 2010 Revision, http://esa.un.org/unpd/wpp/index.htm.

[23] Meisenberg (2015b) calculated effects of population changes too but without considering positive FLynn effects. He came to a negative trend of $dec = -1.10$ IQ points for 2013–2043. If we want to compare our measures of international population change effects with the one of Meisenberg we need to subtract from our 'not considering population change effects' estimate of $dec = 0.74$ the 'considering population change estimate' of $dec = 0.23$ ($N = 195$) resulting in $dec = -0.51$ IQ points. This is around half of the $dec = -1.10$ population change effect reported by Meisenberg.

[24] Rindermann & Thompson (2011b) also used data from Hanushek & Woessmann (2009) for their cognitive ability measure, increasing their country sample.

Table 13.8 *Cognitive ability predictions (models 2018 and 2011 compared for 97 countries)*

| | Current (2018) model for 2100 | | | Former (2011) model for 2100 | | |
|---|---|---|---|---|---|---|
| | CA corrected 2010 | Cognitive ability 2100 | IQ gain decade ('10–100) | CA corrected 2010 | Cognitive ability 2100 | IQ gain decade ('10–100) |
| **Africa (sub-Sahara)** | 71.10 | 85 | 1.58 | 78.07 | 78 | 0.01 |
| Nigeria | 74.72 | 82 | 0.83 | 85.48 | 83 | −0.28 |
| **N-Africa M-East** | 83.11 | 92 | 0.99 | 81.30 | 83 | 0.24 |
| Egypt | 83.72 | 87 | 0.36 | 82.72 | 82 | −0.11 |
| **America (North, Engl)** | 99.45 | 97 | −0.26 | 100.45 | 99 | −0.20 |
| USA | 98.33 | 96 | −0.28 | 98.99 | 97 | −0.19 |
| **America (Latin, C-S)** | 83.76 | 93 | 1.06 | 80.55 | 83 | 0.29 |
| Mexico | 85.87 | 94 | 0.86 | 85.12 | 83 | −0.24 |
| **Asia (Central-South)** | 81.40 | 92 | 1.14 | 80.73 | 84 | 0.33 |
| India | 77.60 | 89 | 1.26 | 87.70 | 87 | −0.13 |
| **East Asia** | 101.17 | 100 | −0.12 | 102.81 | 101 | −0.23 |
| China | 100.77 | 101 | 0.04 | 104.11 | 102 | −0.28 |
| **Southeast Asia, Pacific** | 85.90 | 91 | 0.62 | 86.40 | 87 | 0.03 |
| Philippines | 80.38 | 88 | 0.87 | 75.59 | 81 | 0.65 |
| **Australia-NZ (English)** | 99.06 | 99 | −0.01 | 101.13 | 100 | −0.14 |
| New Zealand | 99.17 | 99 | −0.06 | 100.50 | 99 | −0.14 |
| **Western Europe** | 98.83 | 94 | −0.50 | 100.48 | 98 | −0.24 |
| United Kingdom | 99.60 | 96 | −0.44 | 100.00 | 99 | −0.15 |
| **Scandinavia** | 98.89 | 96 | −0.32 | 99.56 | 98 | −0.20 |
| Norway | 97.91 | 97 | −0.05 | 96.89 | 97 | −0.02 |
| **Central Europe** | 98.85 | 92 | −0.79 | 100.24 | 97 | −0.31 |
| Germany | 98.82 | 93 | −0.61 | 99.82 | 97 | −0.29 |
| **Eastnorth Europe** | 97.08 | 97 | −0.05 | 98.78 | 97 | −0.18 |
| Russia | 97.26 | 96 | −0.15 | 98.23 | 96 | −0.20 |
| **Southwest Europe** | 96.06 | 95 | −0.16 | 95.24 | 93 | −0.30 |
| Italy | 97.52 | 94 | −0.38 | 97.00 | 93 | −0.44 |
| **Southeast Europe** | 91.00 | 95 | 0.41 | 91.17 | 90 | −0.15 |
| Greece | 94.98 | 91 | −0.44 | 94.64 | 91 | −0.35 |
| **Average** | 90.18 | 94 | 0.41 | 90.43 | 90 | −0.03 |

*Notes:* N = 97 countries with student assessment data (therefore, deviations from Table 13.7); due to missing data, Kenya substituted by Nigeria; former model from Rindermann & Thompson (2011b).

449

developments is $r = .73$ ($N = 97$) and between the two final 2100 estimates $r = .61$ ($N = 97$). Different outcomes, although they are not huge, should remind the reader that predictions always depend on available data and assumptions.

## 13.3     Model for Wealth Development

### 13.3.1     Past Growth and Wealth

We start with the most simple model, taking past decades' growth and wealth indicated by GDP as predictors for near future growth and wealth development. We choose as the reference period 1970 to 2010, with stronger weight on more recent years.[25] Table 13.9 shows the results (result columns 2 and 3).

Generally, the predicted GDP levels for 2100, based on past growth, are very high – continuous compound interest leads to large long-term GDP outcomes. However, taking only past growth and wealth for predicting 2100's wealth reveals some strange results such as for Equatorial Guinea (GDP 2100 per capita of $852,403,311, 12.48 per cent growth rate) or Azerbaijan ($44,388,912, 9.98 per cent growth rate) being in 2100 the richest countries of the world. This is very unrealistic, because past development cannot be extrapolated in the future for such a long period. At the regional level similarly implausible outcomes are predicted: North-Africa-Middle-East will be the richest region of the world followed by East Asia and Central-South Asia. GDP levels for 2010 and 2100 are only correlated at $r = .14$. This is also unlikely. But can the present conditions constitute a trustworthy foundation for plausibility judgement?

### 13.3.2     Cognitive Determinants

Simple extrapolation of the past into the future is not enough. It is necessary to consider further factors for wealth predictions, especially cognitive factors being the most important ones for productivity and wealth and their development. As first source for cognitive factors we have the prediction of educational levels until 2100 by Lutz et al. (2014) presented in Table 13.1 (GDP level 2100 repeated in Table 13.9, fourth result column). This is contrasted by the GDP level predicted by using the 2100 cognitive ability level (from the last model presented in Table 13.7; GDP estimate in Table 13.9, last column).[26]

---

[25] Past decades' growth, stronger weight on more recent years: we took data from three sources, the World Bank ($N = 190$), Penn ($N = 189$) and Maddison ($N = 159$). We took their growth rates from 1970 to 2010 and averaged them using as numerical orientation the long-term source Maddison. 1970–2010 received the weight 1; 1980–2010 weight 2; 1990–2010 weight 3; 2000–2010 weight 6. All three sources, World Bank, Penn and Maddison together, resulted in information for $N = 196$ countries, Cronbach-$\alpha = .87$ (correlations are for identical measures quite low).

[26] Both cognitive capital measures use for prediction the competence growth compared to 2010, not the achieved level itself. Thus countries with relatively large competence increases gain more in GDP.

Table 13.9 *GDP per capita in 2010 and 2100 (different models)*

|  | GDP 2010 | Growth c per year | GDP pgr c 2100 | GDP Edu 2100 | GDP IQ raw 2100 |
|---|---|---|---|---|---|
| **Africa (sub-S.)** | 2,465 | 2.90 | 67,216 | 9,775 | 6,084 |
| Kenya | 1,267 | 2.35 | 10,209 | 4,039 | 2,237 |
| **N-Africa M-East** | 6,722 | 3.50 | 2,551,583 | 23,120 | 13,723 |
| Egypt | 4,096 | 4.03 | 143,635 | 19,946 | 5,211 |
| **America** | 27,625 | 2.08 | 175,166 | 39,937 | 23,111 |
| USA | 30,436 | 2.02 | 184,663 | 43,353 | 25,158 |
| **America** | 6,942 | 2.72 | 152,099 | 17,952 | 12,148 |
| Mexico | 7,870 | 1.90 | 42,993 | 24,711 | 13,946 |
| **Asia** | 3,720 | 5.01 | 810,665 | 9,894 | 7,159 |
| India | 3,287 | 5.73 | 493,397 | 15,559 | 7,616 |
| **East Asia** | 16,709 | 4.38 | 2,216,457 | 40,916 | 13,843 |
| China | 7,424 | 8.47 | 11,151,186 | 21,407 | 7,642 |
| **Southeast Asia, P** | 4,962 | 3.11 | 424,651 | 16,434 | 6,917 |
| Philippines | 3,089 | 2.95 | 42,427 | 6,533 | 5,546 |
| **Australia-NZ** | 21,875 | 2.50 | 210,727 | 44,920 | 21,787 |
| New Zealand | 18,598 | 2.29 | 142,245 | 33,173 | 17,905 |
| **Western Eur** | 23,458 | 2.27 | 202,310 | 56,065 | 16,836 |
| United Kingdom | 23,496 | 2.31 | 182,832 | 64,294 | 17,547 |
| **Scandinavia** | 24,952 | 2.11 | 182,863 | 39,673 | 20,041 |
| Norway | 27,894 | 2.43 | 241,855 | 54,531 | 27,041 |
| **Central Europe** | 23,048 | 2.36 | 130,553 | 38,666 | 14,370 |
| Germany | 20,521 | 1.81 | 102,734 | 30,870 | 13,661 |
| **Eastnorth Eur** | 12,121 | 3.65 | 470,393 | 20,007 | 11,567 |
| Russia | 8,888 | 3.36 | 173,936 | 14,654 | 8,021 |
| **Southwest Eur** | 15,182 | 2.47 | 91,062 | 46,341 | 12,461 |
| Italy | 19,021 | 1.34 | 62,958 | 53,429 | 14,753 |
| **Southeast Eur** | 8,447 | 3.62 | 447,118 | 16,549 | 10,962 |
| Greece | 15,397 | 2.58 | 153,049 | 38,947 | 11,453 |

*Notes*: GDP 2010: Maddison 2010 augmented by choosing additional data from 2008 for countries without data in 2010; Growth c per year: average past growth (1970–2010, more recent decades stronger weighted) assumed to continue until 2100, for the African average the outlier Equatorial Guinea was excluded; GDP pgr c 2100: GDP estimated on past growth extrapolated being continuous for the twenty-first century, outlier Equatorial Guinea excluded; GDP Edu 2100: estimated based on education-derived cognitive ability 2100 (see Section 13.1, Table 13.1; here in Table 13.9 categorisation closer to culture); GDP IQ raw 2100: GDP 2100 estimated based on IQ 2100 without any further assumptions such as of continuing economic growth; $N$ is slightly varying depending on available data (e.g. for Central Europe, $N$ = 3, 3, 5, 3, 3 or North-Africa-Middle-East, $N$ = 21, 18, 22, 21, 21).[27]

Both cognitive estimates, the first based on education, the second based on the last complex cognitive development model, do not assume any baseline

[27] GDPs and growth rates were calculated for each country and only then averaged for regions. Due to sometimes differing $N$s, averaged 2010 GDPs and averaged growth rates do not exactly lead to averaged 2100 GDPs. Additionally and more important, calculating growth rates and 2100 GDPs

economic growth between 2010 and 2100; they only predict GDP using cognitive human capital and 2010 GDP. The two outcomes are correlated with $r = .74$, with the 2010 level at $r = .88$ and $r = .73$, but not with the outcomes of continuous growth (third result column; $r = .00$, $r = .08$).

According to the continuous growth model, international differences extremely increase (from 2010 $SD = 7,997$ to $SD = 3,850,726!$); in the educational model they double ($SD = 16,473$) and in the cognitive model they slightly decrease ($SD = 7,264$).[28]

Without assuming any baseline growth the two provisional cognitive capital models are only informative regarding ranks of regions and nations. At the level of regions, there will be no inversion, the West and East Asia will remain the richest. However, these models are all *too simple*. Step by step we consider more factors and hope to come closer and closer to the real development.

### 13.3.3    Cognitive Determinants and Baseline Economic Growth

Up to now, we have not considered in the cognitive GDP model any baseline growth. But past and available cognitive human capital levels and further relevant conditions for economic growth are good enough for a continuation of growth. Baseline growth depending on cognitive ability level was hereafter integrated in two different ways: first, a stable cognitive ability level was assumed (Table 13.10, result columns 2 and 3), then a variable cognitive ability level (Table 13.10, result columns 4 and 5) based on the cognitive ability predictions presented in Table 13.7.[29] Both numbers

and then regional averaging is not mathematically equivalent to calculating regional 2100 GDPs and then calculating regional growth rates (the growth function is non-linear). The differences become larger with larger-within-regional heterogeneity. Because we always deal with single countries and then combine them to regions (for easier presentation) we prefer a single country approach and then later regional averaging for presentation. Regions are not economic entities.

[28] Standard deviations ($SD$) are based on countries as units and across all variables on the same country sample ($N = 145$).

[29] The IQ-growth-formula (1 IQ point increases annual growth by 0.054 per cent, 18.66 IQ points correspond to 1 per cent more growth) is based on long-term growth from 1950 to 2010 and from 1960 to 2010. Information derives from four sources: Penn, Maddison, Lynn & Vanhanen (2002), World Bank. World Bank data were only added for countries without data; they weakly correlated with the other sources (without: Cronbach-$\alpha = .95$, average $r = .84$; with Word Bank Cronbach-$\alpha = .93$, average $r = .63$). We took long-term growth (1960–2010 stronger weighted than the 1950–2010 period) because we try to predict long-term wealth development from 2010 to 2100. Compared to Hanushek & Woessmann (2015a, p. 40ff., 160), who calculated, for a 1 SD increase in ability, a 2 per cent increase in growth (equivalent to 15 IQ and 2 per cent or 1 IQ and 0.133 per cent), our findings are much smaller. If Hanushek & Woessmann's finding is more realistic we would underestimate the cognitive effects. Thus our approach is rather conservative. One simplification of our model is that we did not implement time lags (we have a mix of student and adult measures, but only adults work).

compared allow estimations of wealth effects due to changing cognitive ability levels.

The growth and GDP results of the two pure cognitive ability estimations are highly correlated (growth: $r = .98$, GDP: $r = .99$); with continuous growth the correlations are very low (growth: $r = .09$ and $.12$, GDP: $r = .03$ and $.04$). The richest regions are the West and East Asia, the richest countries smaller East Asian city states (Hong Kong and Singapore) followed by the United States and other East Asian countries and Northern and British-heritage countries.

Both models (Table 13.10, result columns 2–5) can be assessed as only provisional because simple continuous growth for short-term predictions and further factors such as demographic change (ageing), advantages of backwardness, rising complexity, risk factors and regional effects were not considered. The two last columns of Table 13.10 are a first step in this direction, as recent past growth (1970–2010, more recent decades stronger weighted) is combined with the variable cognitive ability model; for the nearer decades recent growth periods were more strongly weighted, and more so the cognitive model for farther decades in the twenty-first century.[30][31]

Its results are well-correlated with both single growth models ($r_{CGM} = .92$ and $r_{VCGM} = .51$) and the achieved GDP levels in 2010 ($r_{CGM} = .62$ and $r_{VCGM} = .68$). The richest region is East Asia followed with a huge gap by Western countries. The richest country will be Azerbaijan, an outlier, then Singapore, China and Hong Kong.

### 13.3.4   Including Further Factors

*Demographic Change (in Age Structure)*   Until now, the presented economic models have not considered demographic change. First to mention is the '*demographic dividend*' reducing the share of youth in society: fewer people depend on working people; less means have to be spent on upbringing and education; more women can work and more adults can work in more productive sectors of the economy. For example, in China, when the population dependency ratio fell by 1 per cent, economic growth rose by 0.115 per cent (Fang, 2009). But later on, one to three generations, the '*demographic burden*' will come with rising shares of retired people. According to Maestas et al. (2014) and for the United States, a 1 per cent increase in the fraction of the population ages 60+ decreases GDP per capita

---

[30] For calculating the IQ-growth-formula, long-term growth from 1950 to 2010 was used. For predicting growth in the future ('continuous growth') a more recent period was used (1970–2010).

[31] Weights: 2010–2020: 0.90 recent growth, 0.10 variable cognitive ability of this decade; 2020–2030: 0.78 and 0.22; 2030–2040: 0.66 and 0.34; 2040–2050: 0.54 and 0.46; 2050–2060: 0.42 and 0.58; 2060–2070: 0.30 and 0.70; 2070–2080: 0.18 and 0.82; 2080–2090: 0.06 and 0.94; 2090–2100: 0.01 and 0.99.

Table 13.10 *GDP/c in 2010 and 2100 (different cognitive models)*

| | GDP 2010 | Growth y constant Cog. Ab. | GDP 2100 cons. CA | Growth y variable Cog. Ab. | GDP 2100 vari. CA | Growth y cont + var CA | GDP 2100 ct +v CA |
|---|---|---|---|---|---|---|---|
| **Africa (sub-S.)** | 2,465 | 1.20 | 8,466 | 1.60 | 11,161 | 2.02 | 17,604 |
| Kenya | 1,267 | 1.49 | 4,785 | 1.75 | 6,012 | 1.92 | 6,997 |
| **N-Africa M-East** | 6,722 | 1.96 | 40,065 | 2.24 | 50,557 | 2.65 | 136,069 |
| Egypt | 4,096 | 1.98 | 23,982 | 2.08 | 26,148 | 2.88 | 52,610 |
| **America (North)** | 27,625 | 2.83 | 337,890 | 2.77 | 320,288 | 2.49 | 252,718 |
| USA | 30,436 | 2.77 | 354,670 | 2.69 | 332,958 | 2.43 | 265,029 |
| **America (Latin)** | 6,942 | 1.75 | 42,236 | 2.15 | 51,826 | 2.34 | 72,053 |
| Mexico | 7,870 | 2.10 | 51,001 | 2.36 | 64,182 | 2.08 | 50,200 |
| **Asia** | 3,720 | 1.75 | 20,821 | 2.10 | 26,067 | 3.21 | 87,775 |
| India | 3,287 | 1.66 | 14,402 | 2.03 | 19,972 | 3.48 | 71,456 |
| **East Asia** | 16,709 | 2.85 | 249,928 | 2.90 | 236,961 | 3.37 | 471,675 |
| China | 7,424 | 2.90 | 96,970 | 2.92 | 99,218 | 5.28 | 758,937 |
| **Southeast Asia, P** | 4,962 | 2.01 | 36,048 | 2.35 | 41,152 | 3.39 | 98,779 |
| Philippines | 3,089 | 1.80 | 15,445 | 2.07 | 19,590 | 2.36 | 25,286 |
| **Australia-NZ** | 21,875 | 2.81 | 263,583 | 2.82 | 268,012 | 2.68 | 240,524 |
| New Zealand | 18,598 | 2.81 | 225,375 | 2.82 | 226,424 | 2.59 | 186,102 |
| **Western Europe** | 23,458 | 2.79 | 280,387 | 2.67 | 252,413 | 2.55 | 231,973 |
| United Kingdom | 23,496 | 2.83 | 290,579 | 2.74 | 267,180 | 2.59 | 235,184 |
| **Scandinavia** | 24,952 | 2.70 | 299,661 | 2.72 | 278,901 | 2.53 | 238,130 |
| Norway | 27,894 | 2.74 | 318,666 | 2.75 | 319,322 | 2.61 | 284,693 |
| **Central Europe** | 23,048 | 2.79 | 279,444 | 2.63 | 239,037 | 2.39 | 194,386 |
| Germany | 20,521 | 2.79 | 244,717 | 2.64 | 215,008 | 2.34 | 165,022 |
| **Eastnorth Eur** | 12,121 | 2.69 | 135,451 | 2.71 | 135,104 | 3.11 | 206,892 |
| Russia | 8,888 | 2.71 | 98,506 | 2.69 | 96,793 | 2.99 | 125,758 |

| | | | | | | | |
|---|---|---|---|---|---|---|---|
| **Southwest Eur** | 15,182 | 2.63 | 163,501 | 2.62 | 154,639 | 2.37 | 124,054 |
| Italy | 19,021 | 2.72 | 213,386 | 2.64 | 198,214 | 2.12 | 125,424 |
| **Southeast Eur** | 8,447 | 2.37 | 72,969 | 2.50 | 78,891 | 2.95 | 130,624 |
| Greece | 15,397 | 2.59 | 153,267 | 2.48 | 139,432 | 2.57 | 150,773 |

*Notes:* Growth y constant Cog. Ab.: growth per year (every year the same) depending on cognitive ability assuming constant cognitive ability level (formula based on 1950–2010 growth); GDP 2100 cons. CA: GDP 2100 estimated based on growth with constant cognitive ability; Growth y variable Cog. Ab.: average IQ-dependent growth per year (varies across decades with IQ) assuming variable cognitive ability level (formula based on 1950–2010 growth, IQs from Table 13.7); GDP 2100 vari. CA: GDP 2100 estimated based on growth with variable cognitive ability; Growth y cont + var CA: average growth per year based on the model assuming continuous growth (1970–2010, Table 13.9, third result column, petering out across decades) and the model of variable cognitive ability and its dependent economic growth (Table 13.10, fourth result column, slowly increasing across decades); GDP 2100 ct+v CA: GDP 2100 estimated based on mixed model (continuous past growth + variable growth depending on variable IQ).

by 0.57 per cent. The mechanisms are mirrored but essentially the same as for the reduced youth effect: fewer people working but the same or more consuming are reducing the per capita production. However, effects are going further as older but still working people are less innovative (see Sections 3.4.1 and 12.2.1).[32] So demographic transition means that there is a passing historic window of opportunity with higher growth rates making way for lower growth rates. Some societies even will become old before being affluent.

Orientated to the presented numbers, we tried to modify the last combined model of continuous growth and variable cognitive ability (from Table 13.10, last two columns). In Table 13.11, the first result column represents (as always) the 2010 GDP level (based on Maddison 2010 and 2008 data), the second and third columns represent the effects based on the demographic dividend model (share of youth becoming smaller), the fourth and fifth columns represent the effects based on the demographic burden model (share of old adults becoming larger) and the final two columns represent the effects based on the general demographic model considering both the demographic dividend and burden. Within each column pair the estimated annual growth comes first and the estimated GDP 2100 level comes second.[33]

---

[32] Further associated factors deal with higher or lower savings and different productivity across periods of life.

[33] For the demographic dividend, we used the information provided by Fang (2009); we added onto the expected growth (estimated by the combined continuous and variable cognitive ability growth model) the effects of reduced youth rate based on UN (2011) sources for the development of the 0 to 19-year-old population. These numbers correlated across countries with Lutz et al. (2014) estimations by $r = .940$. Our UN data source gives information for more countries ($N = 185$ vs. 166); therefore, we used the UN data. This information (economic growth rises by 0.115 per cent when the population dependency ratio falls by 1 per cent) was used for modifying the annual growth rate. The Fang (2009) source is *not* optimal: (1) How it was calculated is not described. (2) It is only given for China. (3) Population dependency ratio may exceed the dependent youth also including the dependent pensioners. For future research, using a more sophisticated source is recommended.

For demographic burden we used the information provided by Maestas et al. (2014). The UN source used (share of 50 year and older) correlated with Lutz (share of 65 year and older) data by $r = .935$. We chose the younger cut-off age because from 50 years onward innovation (depending on field even at younger age) and productivity decline. However, the high correlation of $r = .935$ indicates that the specific cut-off age is less important. A 10 per cent increase in the fraction of the population ages 60+ decreases GDP per capita by 6.5 per cent. It was used for subtraction of each estimated decadal GDP. We raised the information given by the authors of 5.7 per cent to 6.5 per cent, reasons: (1) The Maestas et al. number is based on a within-US across states comparison. Within the United States, innovation declines due to older populations and workforces could be easily compensated by spill-offs from other states. But adopting innovations from other countries is less easy and if an entire generation is less innovative there will be no possibilities to absorb. (2) We subtract only every 10 years, thus compound interest (here growth) effects need to be considered. The Maestas source is also not optimal because it is only given for the United States.

Table 13.11 *GDP/c in 2010 and 2100 (different demographic models)*

| | GDP 2010 | Growth Youth– (d Divd.) | GDP 2100 Youth– | Growth Elderly+ (d Burd.) | GDP 2100 Elderly+ | Growth demogr. Change | GDP 2100 dem. Ch. |
|---|---|---|---|---|---|---|---|
| **Africa (sub-S.)** | 2,465 | 2.35 | 21,774 | 1.84 | 14,561 | 2.17 | 18,521 |
| Kenya | 1,267 | 2.24 | 9,340 | 1.75 | 6,023 | 2.07 | 8,039 |
| **N-Africa M-East** | 6,722 | 2.86 | 150,760 | 2.41 | 111,239 | 2.62 | 123,301 |
| Egypt | 4,096 | 3.14 | 66,317 | 2.65 | 43,230 | 2.92 | 54,493 |
| **America (North)** | 27,625 | 2.53 | 260,209 | 2.42 | 235,724 | 2.45 | 242,715 |
| USA | 30,436 | 2.48 | 276,383 | 2.36 | 247,453 | 2.40 | 258,054 |
| **America (Latin)** | 6,942 | 2.56 | 83,175 | 2.13 | 61,357 | 2.36 | 70,711 |
| Mexico | 7,870 | 2.32 | 61,824 | 1.85 | 41,102 | 2.09 | 50,619 |
| **Asia** | 3,720 | 3.46 | 102,904 | 3.00 | 75,036 | 3.25 | 87,747 |
| India | 3,287 | 3.73 | 89,019 | 3.26 | 59,128 | 3.52 | 73,660 |
| **East Asia** | 16,709 | 3.36 | 462,250 | 3.19 | 405,365 | 3.24 | 414,131 |
| China | 7,424 | 5.35 | 808,475 | 5.11 | 658,148 | 5.18 | 701,107 |
| **Southeast Asia, P** | 4,962 | 3.62 | 117,514 | 3.17 | 82,565 | 3.40 | 98,043 |
| Philippines | 3,089 | 2.67 | 33,075 | 2.14 | 20,844 | 2.45 | 27,264 |
| **Australia-NZ** | 21,875 | 2.74 | 251,589 | 2.59 | 220,996 | 2.64 | 231,163 |
| New Zealand | 18,598 | 2.66 | 196,875 | 2.50 | 171,003 | 2.56 | 180,902 |
| **Western Europe** | 23,458 | 2.57 | 237,417 | 2.48 | 216,977 | 2.50 | 221,973 |
| United Kingdom | 23,496 | 2.61 | 238,340 | 2.52 | 221,364 | 2.54 | 224,334 |
| **Scandinavia** | 24,952 | 2.54 | 241,971 | 2.47 | 226,722 | 2.49 | 230,350 |
| Norway | 27,894 | 2.65 | 293,461 | 2.54 | 266,902 | 2.58 | 275,122 |
| **Central Europe** | 23,048 | 2.37 | 191,714 | 2.33 | 183,507 | 2.31 | 180,935 |
| Germany | 20,521 | 2.30 | 158,457 | 2.31 | 159,938 | 2.26 | 153,576 |
| **Eastnorth Eur** | 12,121 | 3.08 | 202,409 | 3.05 | 196,197 | 3.02 | 191,935 |
| Russia | 8,888 | 2.95 | 122,093 | 2.93 | 119,078 | 2.89 | 115,609 |

Table 13.11 (cont.)

| | GDP 2010 | Growth Youth– (d Divd.) | GDP 2100 Youth– | Growth Elderly+ (d Burd.) | GDP 2100 Elderly+ | Growth demogr. Change | GDP 2100 dem. Ch. |
|---|---|---|---|---|---|---|---|
| **Southwest Eur** | 15,182 | 2.36 | 122,311 | 2.31 | 116,358 | 2.29 | 114,714 |
| Italy | 19,021 | 2.09 | 122,130 | 2.07 | 119,880 | 2.04 | 116,731 |
| **Southeast Eur** | 8,447 | 2.98 | 136,563 | 2.85 | 119,459 | 2.89 | 124,700 |
| Greece | 15,397 | 2.54 | 147,034 | 2.51 | 143,001 | 2.48 | 139,456 |

*Notes*: Growth Youth– (d Divd.): growth per year based on the last cognitive model of Table 13.10 additionally considering declining ('–') youth shares (demographic dividend); GDP 2100 Youth–: GDP 2100 estimated based on cognitive model and demographic dividend; Growth Elderly+ (d Burd.): growth per year based on the last cognitive model of Table 13.10 additionally considering growing ('+') shares of persons being 50 years and older (demographic burden); GDP 2100 Elderly+: GDP 2100 estimated based on cognitive model and demographic burden; Growth demogr. Change: growth per year based on the last cognitive model of Table 13.10 additionally considering both declining youth and growing elderly shares; GDP 2100 dem. Ch.: estimated based on cognitive model and demographic dividend and burden.

458

First, estimated 2100 GDP uncorrected (combined continuous and variable cognitive ability growth model, last column of Table 13.10) and 2100 GDP based on demographic dividend (third result column of Table 13.11) are compared: the comparison reveals the largest *demographic dividend* for Africa (+33 per cent), Central Asia (+25 per cent), Southeast Asia (+22 per cent) and Latin America (+22 per cent). Because Europe just has passed the demographic transition, current birth rates are below replacement level, but higher birth rates are expected for the twenty-first century, thus the demographic dividend will be negative (about −1 to −2 per cent).

Second, estimated 2100 GDP uncorrected (last column of Table 13.10) and 2100 GDP based on demographic burden (fifth result column of Table 13.11) are compared: North African and Middle East countries will suffer most from the *demographic burden* (in estimated GDP 2100: −19 per cent) followed by Southeast and Central Asia (both −17 per cent), Latin America (−16 per cent) and sub-Saharan Africa (−14 per cent). Western countries just having old populations now will also suffer but the least (around −4 to −6 per cent). So today's young countries will suffer most. The demographic dividend will phase out in the twenty-first century.

Third, estimated 2100 GDP uncorrected (last column of Table 13.10) and 2100 GDP based on demographic change (last column of Table 13.11) are compared: both demographic trends combined, sub-Saharan Africa profits the most by demographic change (for GDP 2100: +14 per cent). Western and Northern Europe countries and their former colonies suffer by around −4 per cent, South and East Europe and East Asian countries at −6 per cent to −7 per cent.

Single countries that are predicted to most benefit in economic growth by demographic change are Zimbabwe, Palestine and Ivory Coast (followed by further African and Middle East countries), countries that most suffer are the Emirates, Bahrain, Qatar, Spain, Kuwait and Southwest European, Central European and East Asian countries (Italy, Portugal, Hong Kong, Germany etc.). Effects on GDP reveal a similar pattern.

However, if considering demographic change there will be no long-term negative growth: in the past, long-term growth was always positive, even at lower IQ levels, except for specific local and decadal circumstances such as wars, the post-colonisation downturn in Africa or large increases of population with not equivalent economic growth.

The average predicted economic growth between 2010 and 2100 before the correction for demographic change was 2.56 per cent (2.5583 per cent), after 2.58 per cent (2.5831 per cent), the expected average GDP per capita in 2100 was before \$114,562, after \$108,668, all for the same country sample of 158 nations. There is no large change for the international average; some countries benefit, others not.

*Advantages of Backwardness*    Countries can benefit from technological, organisational, scientific and general cultural innovations and experiences of other nations. The economic growth effect of such benefits becomes larger with the *size of the developmental gap* between the less advanced and poorer countries and the more advanced and richer countries. This is called the 'advantages of backwardness', 'beta-convergence' or 'catch-up effect'. However, to benefit from the progress of others an *appropriate level of cognitive competence* is necessary. Thus we assume *a positive but cognitive-conditional effect of backwardness on growth*. Additionally and contrary to typical convictions, rich countries can also benefit by learning from others, including from poorer ones; more, the higher their adopting abilities are, i.e. the smarter they are.[34] Results can be found in Table 13.12, in the second and third result column.

Compared for the same countries, sub-Saharan African countries shall benefit the most in economic growth from the advantages of backwardness (about 24 per cent higher economic growth, from on average per year 2.17 per cent to 2.65 per cent). Also, other currently poorer regions benefit such as North Africa and the Middle East (19 per cent, predicted growth from 2.61 per cent to 3.01 per cent) and Latin America (18 per cent, from 2.36 per cent to 2.75 per cent). At least North America benefits (2 per cent, from 2.45 per cent to 2.50 per cent). In GDP, the largest relative benefits are seen for sub-Saharan Africa (+53 per cent, from predicted \$18,521 to \$26,228) and Central Asia (+52 per cent, from \$87,747 to \$109,745), the smallest relatively for North America (+5 per cent, from \$242,715 to \$254,696). But the absolute increases are still substantial in North America!

The single countries with the largest estimated benefits in growth are North Korea (+67 per cent), Palestine (+67 per cent), Zimbabwe (+54 per cent), Iraq (+39 per cent) and Eritrea (+39 per cent) – all countries with very detrimental political conditions today (first decades in 21st century) for their economy and

---

[34] Advantages of backwardness can have only a positive modifying effect on our growth estimates based on the variable cognitive model and demographic change. Thus all changes in economic growth compared to the cognitive-variable-demographic-change model are positive (higher growth). Across the twenty-first century this includes today's richest and most developed countries. We assume that with progress of time the importance of cognitive ability for the catch up process becomes more important. Additionally, we assumed that effects of advantages of backwardness will become larger in the twenty-first century, reason: for the nearer future, past growth is a good predictor, but the more time goes by theoretically founded economic factors such as cognitive human capital and advantages of backwardness gain in relevance. Additionally, proceeding globalisation makes adoption in the future easier. Mathematically, we formed rank orders for each decade according to GDP (based on former GDPs and growth rates corrected by advantages of backwardness) and the estimated ability of this decade; the poorer and smarter a country, the more it benefits, the richer and less smart, the less it benefits; across the decades, GDPs were less weighted (and indirectly cognitive ability higher) for the correction.

Table 13.12 *GDP per capita in 2010 and predicted for 2100 (modifying factors: advantages of backwardness, complexity burden, risk factors, regional umfeld-neighbourhood)*

| | GDP 2010 | Growth Advant. backw. | GDP 2100 Adv. bw. | Growth Complexity | GDP 2100 Complx. | Growth Risk factors | GDP 2100 Risk | Growth Regional effects (fi.) | GDP 2100 Regional (final es.) |
|---|---|---|---|---|---|---|---|---|---|
| **Africa (sub-S.)** | 1,968 | 2.65 | 26,228 | 1.70 | 7,912 | 1.45 | 6,439 | 1.56 | 6,342 |
| Kenya | 1,267 | 2.67 | 13,591 | 2.15 | 8,585 | 1.84 | 6,560 | 1.85 | 6,596 |
| **N-Africa M-East** | 6,722 | 3.01 | 145,642 | 1.66 | 28,701 | 1.43 | 23,295 | 1.43 | 21,048 |
| Egypt | 4,096 | 3.38 | 81,798 | 1.74 | 19,346 | 1.51 | 15,787 | 1.56 | 16,465 |
| **America (North)** | 27,625 | 2.50 | 254,696 | 1.88 | 151,350 | 1.69 | 127,168 | 1.76 | 133,229 |
| USA | 30,436 | 2.45 | 268,355 | 1.47 | 113,029 | 1.32 | 98,866 | 1.48 | 114,033 |
| **America (Latin)** | 6,942 | 2.75 | 90,338 | 1.51 | 25,633 | 1.36 | 22,842 | 1.83 | 29,516 |
| Mexico | 7,870 | 2.60 | 79,497 | 1.72 | 36,521 | 1.58 | 32,399 | 1.76 | 37,840 |
| **Asia** | 3,720 | 3.71 | 109,745 | 2.12 | 21,610 | 1.85 | 17,067 | 1.80 | 15,155 |
| India | 3,287 | 3.90 | 102,509 | 1.77 | 15,994 | 1.57 | 13,381 | 1.59 | 13,621 |
| **East Asia** | 15,968 | 3.56 | 435,449 | 3.42 | 362,178 | 3.11 | 267,428 | 3.58 | 263,750 |
| China | 7,424 | 5.27 | 753,783 | 4.88 | 542,408 | 4.44 | 369,824 | 4.38 | 351,886 |
| **Southeast Asia, P** | 4,962 | 3.86 | 138,782 | 2.59 | 57,433 | 2.28 | 40,343 | 2.37 | 44,077 |
| Philippines | 3,089 | 2.98 | 43,336 | 1.70 | 14,101 | 1.53 | 12,098 | 2.15 | 20,944 |
| **Australia-NZ** | 21,875 | 2.78 | 258,778 | 2.57 | 213,415 | 2.33 | 172,195 | 2.38 | 180,112 |
| New Zealand | 18,598 | 2.79 | 220,874 | 2.69 | 202,810 | 2.42 | 160,412 | 2.56 | 181,687 |
| **Western Europe** | 23,458 | 2.61 | 241,720 | 1.66 | 104,167 | 1.55 | 94,766 | 1.50 | 89,492 |
| United Kingdom | 23,496 | 2.60 | 236,897 | 1.99 | 138,771 | 1.86 | 122,876 | 1.68 | 105,363 |
| **Scandinavia** | 24,952 | 2.58 | 247,544 | 1.81 | 126,128 | 1.76 | 120,777 | 1.66 | 109,899 |
| Norway | 27,894 | 2.63 | 288,588 | 1.94 | 157,487 | 1.89 | 150,731 | 1.69 | 125,590 |
| **Central Europe** | 23,048 | 2.47 | 206,889 | 1.43 | 82,664 | 1.33 | 75,677 | 1.31 | 74,099 |
| Germany | 20,521 | 2.50 | 189,808 | 1.57 | 83,368 | 1.47 | 76,499 | 1.48 | 76,744 |
| **Eastnorth Eur** | 12,121 | 3.32 | 231,221 | 2.77 | 137,553 | 2.59 | 117,507 | 2.95 | 157,549 |
| Russia | 8,888 | 3.30 | 165,561 | 2.88 | 114,048 | 2.52 | 83,722 | 3.15 | 145,150 |

Table 13.12 (cont.)

| | GDP 2010 | Growth Advant. backw. | GDP 2100 Adv. bw. | Growth Complexity | GDP 2100 Complx. | Growth Risk factors | GDP 2100 Risk | Growth Regional effects (fi.) | GDP 2100 Regional (final es.) |
|---|---|---|---|---|---|---|---|---|---|
| **Southwest Eur** | 15,182 | 2.61 | 150,721 | 1.75 | 70,237 | 1.64 | 63,433 | 1.70 | 66,879 |
| Italy | 19,021 | 2.33 | 151,524 | 1.51 | 73,069 | 1.43 | 68,167 | 1.43 | 68,195 |
| **Southeast Eur** | 8,447 | 3.31 | 159,356 | 2.34 | 62,496 | 2.12 | 50,927 | 2.38 | 63,829 |
| Greece | 15,397 | 2.69 | 167,382 | 1.37 | 52,182 | 1.29 | 48,976 | 1.42 | 54,648 |
| **Average** | 7,941 | 2.97 | 129,272 | 1.94 | 58,463 | 1.73 | 47,843 | 1.89 | 51,823 |

*Notes:* GDP 2010: Maddison 2010 augmented by choosing additional data from 2008 for countries without data in 2010, only presented here for those countries with data in all columns; Growth Advant. backw.: estimated average growth per year 2010–2100 based on the last variable cognitive model of Table 13.10 considering both declining youth and growing elderly shares and corrected for advantages of backwardness; GDP 2100 Adv. bw.: estimated GDP 2100 based on variable cognitive model, demographics and advantages of backwardness; Growth Complexity: estimated average growth per year 2010–2100 based on variable cognitive model, demographics, advantages of backwardness and increasing complexity; GDP 2100 Complx.: estimated GDP 2100 based on variable cognitive model . . . and increasing complexity; Growth Risk factors: estimated average growth per year 2010–2100 based on variable cognitive model, demographics, advantages of backwardness, increasing complexity and risk factors; GDP 2100 Risk: estimated GDP 2100 based on variable cognitive model . . . and risk factors; Growth Regional effects: estimated average growth per year 2010–2100 based on variable cognitive model, demographics, advantages of backwardness, increasing complexity, risk factors and regional *umfeld* (neighbourhood) effect corrections; GDP 2100 Regional (final es.): estimated GDP 2100 based on variable cognitive model, demographics, advantages of backwardness, increasing complexity, risk factors and regional effect corrections; our final estimate; regional averages are based on countries as units; see also footnote for Table 13.9: mathematical regional averaging problem.

general wellbeing. It is assumed that they will learn and benefit from the example of more successful countries. Countries not or barely benefiting from advantages of backwardness are Trinidad (+0 per cent), Qatar (+0 per cent), Singapore (+0 per cent), Hong Kong (+0 per cent), South Korea (+0 per cent) and Azerbaijan (+1 per cent). These are all countries that are today relatively rich or relatively rich compared to their cognitive level and thus are expected to struggle in the twenty-first century at their high economic development levels. It will be difficult for them to further benefit from the progress of others.

The average predicted economic growth between 2010 and 2100 before the correction for advantages of backwardness was 2.58 per cent (2.5831 per cent), after 2.97 per cent (2.9714 per cent), the expected average GDP per capita in 2100 before \$108,668, after \$129,272 ($N$ = 158). There is a remarkable improvement.

*Growing Complexity and Higher Hanging Fruits*   The underlying assumption is that in the twenty-first century complexity increases – complexity in technology, financial sector, science and production – making further progress more difficult. This is especially true for countries at the *front line of modernisation and wealth*. While others benefit from the innovations achieved from the pioneers, the countries at the front line of modernisation have to struggle for any tiny progress which have to be achieved by themselves. And this is especially true for countries with populations at *lower human cognitive capital* levels: higher ability would help countries to cope with the cognitive challenges of complexity. We further assume that growing complexity will become a larger problem during the twenty-first century, including setting the threshold for economic growth higher and higher, even for backward countries. Where it was, for example, in the past enough to adopt the plough, it is today necessary to adopt rules of applying different fertilisers, when to buy and use it, what to produce for which market and when. Subsistence farming is still possible but does not lead to growing production and wealth.[35] Results are presented in Table 13.12 (fourth and fifth result column).

---

[35] Growing complexity can have only a negative-decreasing effect on our given growth estimates (based on the variable cognitive model, demographic change and advantages of backwardness). Mathematically, we formed rank orders for each decade according to GDP (based on former GDPs and growth rates corrected by increasing complexity) and the estimated ability of this decade; the richer and less smart a country, the more it suffers; across the decades GDPs as indicator for complexity were more weighted (and indirectly cognitive ability less) for the correction. Corrections become larger from decade to decade (reasons: growing complexity, past growth less predictive and past factors less relevant). The richer a country, the more economic growth depends on own innovation, not imitation, making any progress more and more dependent on cognitive capital, especially of intellectual classes (e.g. Vandenbussche et al., 2006).

The average predicted economic growth between 2010 and 2100 before the correction for complexity burden was 2.97 per cent (2.9714 per cent) and after 1.94 per cent (1.9447 per cent); the expected average GDP per capita in 2100 was before \$129,272 and after \$58,463 ($N$ = 158). There is an expected wealth 'reduction' by half – or better a slowing down of growth resulting in a GDP level of half the size than expected on the former model. The regions estimated suffering the most by complexity increase are Latin America (in growth: less –43 per cent, from 2.75 per cent to 1.51 per cent), North Africa and the Middle East (–43 per cent, from 3.01 per cent to 1.66 per cent) and Central Asia (–42 per cent, from 3.71 per cent to 2.12 per cent); least suffering is East Asia (–3 per cent, from 3.56 per cent to 3.42 per cent). Those countries are most suffering that achieved a relatively high economic level at a relatively low cognitive ability level. GDP-result patterns are similar; Central Asia (–71 per cent, from \$109,745 to \$21,610), North Africa and the Middle East (–64 per cent, from \$145,642 to \$28,701) and Latin America (–63 per cent, from \$90,338 to \$25,633) show the largest reductions.

At the country level, the largest declines in economic growth by complexity are predicted for Puerto Rico (–68 per cent), Mauritius (–66 per cent), Kuwait (–64 per cent) and Oman (–64 per cent); no declines are expected for Japan, Vietnam, Eritrea, Congo, Macedonia, Mongolia, Palestine, Zimbabwe and Ukraine.[36] Regarding GDP the largest retardations are observable for Azerbaijan (–93 per cent), Burma (–90 per cent), Qatar (–87 per cent), Angola (–86 per cent), Turkmenistan (–85 per cent) and India (–84 per cent). Given their current relatively good production level relative to other countries and their rather low cognitive human capital level, it is expected that they are challenged by the future obstacles of complexity.

*Country Risk Index*    Economic growth can be impeded by unfavourable political and sociological factors such as wars, low rule of law and high corruption, low political liberty and low democratisation. Inequality is a further risk factor. All these risk factors are increased by heterogeneity. According to research, heterogeneity has a negative impact on government quality, trust, public efficiency and further positively evaluated societal attributes.[37] For international data, heterogeneity-diversity positively correlates with income inequality $r$ = .36 ($N$ = 122), weakly with war $r$ = .07 ($N$ = 154), more with

---

[36] Of course, they, and all others, will suffer from reduced progress in countries at the front line of modernisation – fewer innovations to adopt. But our procedure based on ranks does not allow a comparison with an absolute benchmark. Further research should consider this; our model underestimates the negative complexity effects.

[37] See overviews, from an economic perspective: Alesina & Ferrara (2002); from a psychological perspective: Roth (2014/2010); from an evolutionary perspective: Salter (2007/2003).

corruption $r = .23$ ($N = 154$) and homicide $r = .43$ ($N = 156$); it negatively correlates with the positive factors economic freedom $r = -.20$ ($N = 153$), interpersonal trust $r = -.27$ ($N = 113$) and positive politics $r = -.25$ (rule of law, political liberty, democracy, additionally gender equality; $N = 145$).[38] According to Mauro (1995), ethnolinguistic fractionalisation is also negatively correlated to institutional efficiency ($r = -.38$), having an independent additional negative impact on growth.

We combined the given measures of heterogeneity and immigration – immigration will increase heterogeneity (see Section 13.2.3).[39] We do not have a country risk index predicting war and politics in the twenty-first century. We assume that past data will be the best predictor for the future. Income inequality is a risk factor for production and wealth (e.g. Cingano, 2014; Gordon, 2016), especially inequality along ethnic lines, also war and low levels of rule of law, freedom and democracy.[40] Those factors were predicted based on past measures of war and politics and on changing heterogeneity-diversity measures considering varying shares of persons with immigrant background.[41] Summarising, the risk factor contains constant

---

[38] Heterogeneity is measured by ethnic, religious and genetic heterogeneity resp. diversity (Meisenberg, 2007). Cronbach-$\alpha = .56$ ($N = 156$). Income inequality (Gini index) from Deininger and Squire (1996); war and positive politics (rule of law, political liberty and democracy) see Section 10.3; economic freedom from Fraser and Heritage index (see Section 5.1); corruption from Transparency International (see Table 10.12); homicide rates from UNODC (see Chapter 4); trust from WVS (see Chapter 10). All are long-term measures covering several decades. Partialling out GDP reveals an average correlation of $r_p = -.11$ (instead of $r = -.26$) between heterogeneity-diversity and positive attributes of society (income equality, peace, etc.); IQ reduces negative diversity effects. The pattern does not depend on the chosen diversity measure; it is similar for the heterogeneity measures from Kurian (2001, p. 56f., inverted 'ethnic homogeneity', average correlation $r = .25$), Alesina et al. (2003, "ethnic fractionalization" $r = -.31$) and Vanhanen (2012, heterogeneity $r = -.19$). Similar results were reported by Hadenius (1992, p. 115): e.g. ethnic-linguistic-religious fragmentation and democracy correlate with $r = -.23$. 'As has been evident, democracy is more likely to flourish in countries dominated by Christianity – and, in particular, by Protestantism – and where the population is relatively homogeneous and well-educated.' (Hadenius, 1992, p. 154) See also Collier (2013b). Finally, two new measured variables, honesty from Gächter and Schulz (2016) and time preference (delay of gratification) from Wang et al. (2016), show negative correlations with diversity measures; honesty: from $r = -.14$ (Meisenberg) to $-.43$ (Alesina; $N = 23$), time preference: from $r = -.28$ (Meisenberg) to $-.43$ (Alesina; $N = 51/52$). The pattern is robust across different variables and studies.

[39] Heterogeneity and immigrant share 2010 $r = .20$ ($N = 84$), Cronbach-$\alpha = .33$ ($N = 149$). Heterogeneity/immigrants (diversity) combined with war and (negative) politics results in Cronbach-$\alpha = .45$ ($N = 158$).

[40] See Section 10.3. Correlations in international data, heterogeneity and 2010 GDP: $r = -.28$ ($N = 148$); war and 2010 GDP: $r = -.35$ ($N = 155$); negative politics and 2010 GDP: $r = -.73$ ($N = 158$); heterogeneity and past growth 1950–2010 (sources World Bank, Maddison, Penn and Lynn and Vanhanen combined): $r = -.39$ ($N = 147$); war and past growth 1950–2010: $r = -.37$ ($N = 155$); negative politics and past growth 1950–2010: $r = -.40$ ($N = 156$). The correlation of heterogeneity including migrants with 2010 GDP becomes less negative ($r = -.21$, $N = 149$); the correlation with growth becomes more negative ($r = -.45$, $N = 147$).

[41] Risk factors can only have a negative impact.

measures of war and politics based on past and present data but variable measures of heterogeneity-diversity based on demographic predictions.

Maybe for some such a risk factor correction is too speculative. However, it is not reasonable to assume that countries with low democracy, rule of law and liberty levels will continue to exist in peace – see the examples of Libya and Syria. The situation in Saudi Arabia or North Korea will certainly differ in 90 years from the situation today. Within-country heterogeneity will increase the probability of redistributive policies (see Section 12.5) and also the risk of riots and civil unrest (see the mentioned sources and correlations). At the end of political transformations a more stable, free and productive society can emerge, as in Eastern Europe after the revolutions of 1989, or civil war, Islamist rulership and authoritarian systems as in many Arabian countries after the Arab Spring in 2010.

We have not considered further factors as government effectiveness nor the two global background factors evolution and culture. They all may have an impact on twenty-first-century development. However, they are related to our used risk factors anyway and theoretically depend on or cause them.

The risk correction has a reducing effect on economic growth; before, average growth was estimated at 1.94 per cent (1.9447 per cent), and including risk correction it is now 1.73 per cent (1.7263 per cent); in GDP, before it was $58,463 and is now $47,843 (all $N = 158$).[42] The regions with the largest risk-corrections for growth are sub-Saharan Africa (–15 per cent, from 1.70 per cent to 1.45 per cent), North Africa and the Middle East (–14 per cent, from 1.66 per cent to 1.43 per cent) and Central Asia (–13 per cent, from 2.12 per cent to 1.85 per cent); least suffering is Scandinavia (–3 per cent, from 1.81 per cent to 1.76 per cent). In GDP, the pattern is different: the largest predicted risk retardation is for East Asia (–23 per cent, from $362,178 to $267,428), then Southeast Asia (–23 per cent, from $57,433 to $40,343) and Central Asia (–21 per cent, from $21,610 to $17,067). At the country level, in growth the largest risk effects are estimated for Eritrea (–23 per cent), Chad (–22 per cent), Sudan (–21 per cent), Yemen (–21 per cent), Congo (–21 per cent) and Liberia (–21 per cent); the smallest negative impact is seen for Finland (–2 per cent), Norway (–3 per cent), Denmark (–3 per cent) and Sweden (–4 per cent).[43] In GDP, the largest reductions are expected for Vietnam (–39 per cent), Laos (–39 per cent) and Singapore (–36 per cent).

Why are growth and GDP losses different? GDP losses can only be large if there is large GDP. Minor changes in growth show larger effects in GDP at

---

[42] Averages are always based on countries and not weighted by population size.

[43] Last years' immigration movements were not considered which are especially relevant for Scandinavian countries.

higher GDP levels. And we have countries with higher country risks at high positive levels of other factors such as cognitive ability and advantages of backwardness, resulting in a larger harming effect. It is conceivable that the troubles for a poor country such as Eritrea will increase, but they will not result in large negative GDP effects because GDP is already very low.

*Regional Development Effects*   The final adjustment considers regional development effects, '*umfeldbedingungen*'. As in advantages of backwardness, the achieved level and the development of other countries influence the economic performance of a country. Unlike for advantages, the influence is regionalised – neighbourly conditions further or constrain a country's development.[44] Neighbouring countries influence each other by contact of their citizens and leaders, by trade and travel, by modelling, by migration, by spillovers of technological, political and cultural development, in bad cases by war and conquest, in better ones by cooperation.

This correction showed the most positive effects for Latin America, East Asia, Eastnorth Europe and Southeast Europe. At the level of countries the largest positive modifications for economic growth are found for Zimbabwe (+173 per cent, from 0.63 per cent to 1.73 per cent), Haiti (+133 per cent, from 1.16 per cent to 2.69 per cent), North Korea (+94 per cent, from 1.99 per cent to 3.86 per cent) and Palestine (+90 per cent, from 1.16 per cent to 2.21 per cent). The largest reductions are found for Mauritius (−53 per cent, from 0.93 per cent to 0.44 per cent), South Africa (−46 per cent, from 0.87 per cent to 0.47 per cent) and Namibia (−45 per cent, from 0.77 per cent to 0.42 per cent) and further African and Middle East countries as Botswana and Qatar. These are all countries relatively rich or poor compared to their neighbourhoods having an impact on their development.

---

[44] Regional effects can be positive or negative. Mathematically, we modified for each decade a country's estimated growth by 10 per cent of the expected regional mean growth based on the past calculations considering variable cognitive ability, demographic change, advantages of backwardness, complexity and risk factors. The next decade's growth is based on the achieved GDP considering all these six factors, including regional effects. We additionally corrected a country's GDP by adding or subtracting 10 per cent of a country's deviation from the regional mean. For 38 of 158 countries we integrated not only an effect of 'their' main region but also of other regions, e.g. for Australia and New Zealand 10 per cent of South East Asia and 10 per cent of East Asia, for Singapore 70 per cent of East Asia and 30 per cent of Southeast Asia, for Haiti 40 per cent of Latin America and 60 per cent of sub-Saharan Africa, for the Baltic countries 80 per cent of Eastnorth Europe and 20 per cent of Scandinavia, for Turkey 70 per cent of North Africa and the Middle East and 30 per cent of Southeast Europe, for France 70 per cent Western Europe and 30 per cent Southwest Europe etc. We considered not only geographic proximity but also cultural similarity. This, and the non-linearity of growth, also leads to changes in regional averages (without them, regional corrections should not change regional averages).

The largest GDP gains are found for North Korea (+416 per cent, from $8,320 to $42,928), Mongolia (+348 per cent, from $26,226 to $117,408) and Haiti (+288 per cent, from $2,808 to $10,897). The largest losses are found for Azerbaijan (–45 per cent, from $58,266 to $31,904), Kazakhstan (–44 per cent, from $45,999 to $25,887) and Qatar (–40 per cent, from $48,584 to $29,321), all today due to oil rich countries.

## 13.4     Wealth at the End of the Twenty-First Century

According to our final model, considering continuous past growth, growth depending on variable cognitive human capital (itself depending on environmental improvements, asymmetric fertility and immigration), demographic change (due to ageing etc.), advantages of backwardness, increasing complexity, risk factors and regional effect corrections, global wealth will increase in the twenty-first century. The region with the highest expected average GDP per capita (Table 13.12, last column; Figure 13.15) is East Asia ($263,750), followed by Trans-Tasman ($180,112), Eastnorth Europe ($157,549) and North America ($133,229). The poorest regions are sub-Saharan Africa ($6,342) and Central Asia ($15,155). However, all regions and countries gain in production and income, e.g. sub-Saharan Africa on average is expected to at least triple its wealth.

According to the predictions, Eastern Europe (due to Eastnorth Europe) will surpass the West around the year 2060. Like other predictions, this contradicts the present situation and also plausibility assumptions based on today's experiences. However, advantages of backwardness will ease economic development for Eastern Europe in the first half of the twenty-first century. Differences in cognitive development based on differences in demographics, having an impact on dealing with complexity and having an effect on risk factors, may change the ranks.

East Asia will surpass the West (North-West-Central Europe, North America, Trans-Tasman) around 2040; Eastern Europe will do so by around 2060. The gaps between these regions and developing and emerging countries will rise; Southern Europe will be in between. However, *all will become richer*, including Africa, which will by far surpass the poverty threshold of about 1 to 2 Dollars per day.[45]

At the country level, the richest nations will be Hong Kong ($361,583), China ($351,886), South Korea ($346,554), Singapore ($318,376) and Japan ($307,512). While East Asian countries are usually expected to be on the top based on their past productivity, growth, achievement motivation, discipline

---

[45] We have reported country averages. They do not preclude within-country inequality and temporary declines, e.g. during wars or natural disasters.

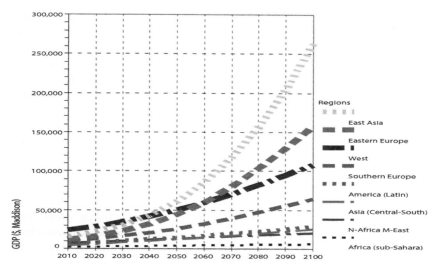

Figure 13.15 Predicted GDP per capita development in the twenty-first century

and cognitive ability level, the next coming country, Slovakia ($183,869), is rather astonishing. Advantages of backwardness, an estimated to maintain high cognitive ability level for Eastern Europe (Table 13.8) and low currently predictable risk factors come to this conclusion.[46] The countries predicted to be poorest are Zimbabwe ($4,297), Central African Republic ($4,647) and Liberia ($4,679), followed by other African countries. As is general for Africa, within-African differences (e.g. Zimbabwe vs. Benin or Congo vs. Togo) should be treated cautiously. Available data are not reliable enough and small favourable changes in environmental conditions at low developmental levels can have a huge positive effect.

Regarding growth, for Mongolia the highest growth is expected (5.13 per cent from 2010 to 2100), followed by China (4.38 per cent), Vietnam (4.35 per cent) and – usually not expected – Ukraine (4.05 per cent). Due to currently low wealth level, high and stable cognitive ability and positive regional effects, high growth rates are expected for Mongolia (assigned to East Asia, positive neighbour effects), Vietnam (current and predicted high cognitive ability level) and China (current and predicted high cognitive ability level, East Asia). But

---

[46] It should be stressed that for all countries, special local conditions were not considered such as natural resources or demographic changes independent from migration and ageing; for Slovakia especially relevant is the development of the Roma population.

Ukraine? The recent war was not considered by our international data sets. However, the applied models are the same: advantages of backwardness, good and expected stable cognitive ability level, low risk factors – as was assumed – and positive regional effects. From the present day perspective this view seems to be too optimistic but at least it casts a glance on what is possible.[47]

The highest long-term economic growth rates are expected for East Asia and Eastern Europe (see Table 13.12 and Figure 13.16). The lowest growth rates are expected for Namibia, Mauritius, South Africa, Kuwait, Gabon, The Emirates and other African and Middle East countries (all growth below 1 per cent). These are all countries that are currently rich compared to their neighbours but do not show a corresponding higher cognitive ability level, making it difficult for them to maintain their wealth. Additionally, there are risk factors which are obstructive for keeping up their advanced wealth levels.

The general growth trend across all regions is declining for the twenty-first century: challenges of complexity are rising and they are not accompanied by a similar cognitive rise or they are even accompanied by a loss, as in Western countries, those most advanced in the last centuries in technology, science, culture and thinking.

Although we have *not* used for predictions the two global background factors evolution and culture (see Chapters 10 and 11), they both positively correlate with predicted growth rates and resulting wealth levels in 2100 (see Table 13.13).

Generally, the correlations between *cognitive factors* and growth as well as its result, GDP, are higher than between global background factors and growth and GDP. That is not surprising because cognitive ability was used and not global background factors to estimate growth and GDP in the twenty-first century, including moderating the effects of advantages of backwardness and complexity increase. The correlations with cognitive ability are far below $r = 1$ because (a) further factors were considered and (b) more recent growth was used in a gradually reduced manner for the prediction of nearer decades.

However, the more factors were considered for growth and GDP predictions, the more similar become the correlations of background and cognitive factors with growth and GDP. Global background factors count in the future even if they are *not* considered in models. In particular, the *evolutionary background* factor is predictive for growth until the end of the twenty-first century (for growth: evolution $r = .39$, culture: $r = .26$; for GDP 2100: evolution $r = .54$, culture: $r = .59$). Again, this is astonishing because this factor was *not* used for predictions. Finally, migration will change the

---

[47] This prediction is in accordance with the view of Seymour Itzkoff, who expected for Eastern Europe around 2050 economic and cultural affluence (Itzkoff, 2003, pp. 101f.).

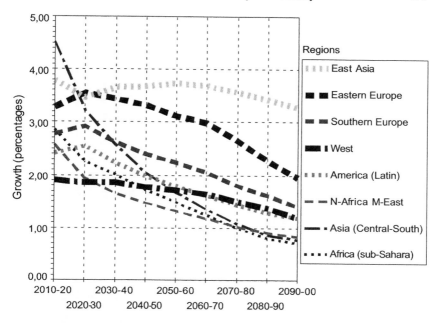

Figure 13.16 Predicted economic growth development in the
twenty-first century

informative value of this variable based on data of the twentieth century. If
the growth and wealth predictions are reasonably correct, the true correlations with evolutionary background have to be even higher! The same is
true for the *cultural background*, showing higher correlations when more
factors are considered.

The correlations with background factors only make sense if they have a causal
effect on economic development, indirect via shaping attitudes, abilities and
behaviour and via shaping institutions, the social, physical, political and cultural
environment in which economic actions take place. *Path dependence* may play a
minor role – who was rich in the past has an advantage for the future. However,
the factor advantages of backwardness underscore that countries lagging behind
have better growth chances. And even more important, cognitive ability and
wealth, especially wealth in modernity, are things that need to be gained in each
generation once again. Robust patterns across generations can only be given if
they are based on a transmission via relatively stable background factors.

From a human capital view, how could background factors work? The
possible cognitive mechanisms were described in detail: larger brains lead to
higher intelligence; a culture supportive for education, learning, rationality,

Table 13.13 *Correlations of background factors and cognitive ability with growth and production estimations in the twenty-first century*

| | Economic growth (past measured or estimated 2010–2100) | | | | | | Production-wealth (GDP/c) (2010 measured or estimated 2100) | | | | | |
|---|---|---|---|---|---|---|---|---|---|---|---|---|
| | 1950 to 2010 | var CA Dem | Adva of Back | Com-plexity | Risk | Region (all) | 2010 | var CA Dem | Adva of Back | Com-plexity | Risk | Region (all) |
| **Evolutionary background** | .29 | .18 | .14 | .35 | .40 | .39 | .40 | .37 | .39 | .47 | .49 | .54 |
| **Cultural background** | .37 | .13 | .02 | .19 | .27 | .26 | .68 | .37 | .40 | .47 | .53 | .59 |
| **Cognitive ability 2010** | .58 | .38 | .26 | .39 | .47 | .30 | .78 | .59 | .64 | .63 | .68 | .73 |
| **Cognitive ability 2100** | .55 | .42 | .32 | .43 | .49 | .35 | .67 | .57 | .62 | .62 | .66 | .71 |

*Notes:* Evolutionary background: indicated by cranial capacity (Section 10.7.2); Cultural background: indicated by weighted religions (Section 10.8.8); Cognitive ability 2010: cognitive ability measure based on student assessment and psychometric IQ tests (Section 4.2); Cognitive ability 2100: predicted by the variable cognitive model including demographics (Section 13.3.6, Table 13.7); Economic growth and GDP: 1950 to 2010: past growth based on World Bank, Penn, Maddison and Lynn and Vanhanen; var CA Dem: growth/GDP estimated based on the variable cognitive model plus demographic change; Adva of Back: based on variable cognitive model including demographics and advantages of backwardness; Complexity: based on cognitive . . ., advantages . . . and increasing complexity; Risk: based on cognitive . . ., advantages . . ., complexity and risk factors; Region (all): based on cognitive . . ., advantages . . ., complexity, risk and on regional *umfeld* (neighbourhood) effect corrections; *N*=156 (first column) or *N*=158 (all others).

thinking, meritocracy, burgher world and modernisation furthers cognitive development. The effects could be even broader, indirectly via the effects of intelligence and knowledge on attitudes and personality and directly via effects on attitudes and personality such as diligence, moderateness, trustworthiness and conscientiousness. Via such impact they will not only influence future productivity and wealth but also the future wellbeing of nations, the political development and institutional conditions being relevant for the life and happiness of millions of peoples.

*Limits of Our Approach and Method* While we have used only water and ordinary methods, others may come along and use fire and more sophisticated models. For instance, why did we correct regional deviations by 10 per cent and not by 9 or 11 per cent and why not different depending on a *country's population size*? Larger countries are less influenced by neighbours, smaller more. A large country such as India has a huge reservoir of talented people, probably compensating low ability population averages. All our "precise" numbers are somewhat arbitrary.

Missing are effects of level and size of *intellectual classes*. Such data are only given by student assessment studies, with few results for developing countries, especially for Africa. Those countries would have been all excluded if intellectual classes were used as additional factor. We dealt with immigration, but not with emigration. Thus, a possible loss of *institution-builders* is not integrated. The available data did not cover enough countries.

There are several estimates based on *plausibility* as the regional correction, but also by advantages of backwardness, complexity and risk factors. All these models are improvable by further research. The calculated cognitive ability predictions are based on a more solid information background. Their absolute numbers, including measures for today, are more reliable than GDP measures. Additional factors such as *natural resources* and within-country specific demographic trends can be integrated, also *interactions between factors*.

Especially difficult to handle are possible *black swan events* and *tipping points* in different directions, e.g. introduction of new technologies such as the smart phone, e.g. enabling farmers in developing countries to compare supply and demand, sudden migration waves or changes in immigration policies such as recently in Australia, Denmark and Hungary. Maybe potent neuro-enhancers with negligible side effects will be found. Nobody in 1900 expected the First and Second World War and the 1918 flu pandemic, nobody in 1930 the Holocaust, nobody in 1960 the coming climate change, nobody in 1980 the collapse of the Soviet Union, nobody in 1990 the Internet, Amazon and eBay, nobody in 2000 the Islamist attacks and movements, but surely similar events will come, positive and negative ones. The development of a country risk factor is a first step to model them.

A mathematical problem is averaging growth across countries for regions. For two countries, their 1 per cent and 3 per cent growth rates lead to better average outcomes (the better the longer the period) than two per cent for both of them. A multidisciplinary constituted research team should work on interactive development models. Finally, the meaning of future GDPs and GDP differences is opaque. What does it mean for the standard of living, for health and wellbeing, having an average GDP of around $200,000 in a country? Absolute numbers are less meaningful than cross-country patterns.

Finally, we have not dealt with different *scenarios*. While we have presented increasingly complex models considering more and more possible determinants, all those models have not distinguished between more optimistic or pessimistic or more or less probable developments. To do this will be the task of future research; the presented models here try to give a first analysis: what factors should be considered and what effects they may have for the future development of nations.

### 13.4.1   Comparisons with other Models

*Comparison with Own Estimations Done in 2011*   We undertook a first attempt at estimating future cognitive ability and GDP levels based on the cognitive capital theory of wealth in 2011. That estimation only used assumed cognitive ability levels and past growth (Rindermann & Thompson, 2011b). The starting value for GDP 2010 was based on data from the CIA and the IMF, which give considerably higher estimates than our Maddison data basis. The 2010 averages for a same country sample are $12,029 (Maddison) versus 20,434 (CIA and IMF; see Table 13.14). For instance, for the USA Maddison reports $30,436, but the CIA and IMF average is $47,057 (CIA: $47,284, IMF: $47,057) or for Norway $27,894 versus $55,271. This is not a new phenomenon (see Chapter 1). However, *this makes absolute numbers less meaningful; more important are country patterns.*

Our two different 2010 GDP/c measures correlate with $r = .75$ ($N = 88$); the international average is for the CIA-IMF measure about $8,000 or 70 per cent larger (calculated based on the averages). Comparing the growth estimates, the newer model is more pessimistic (1.90 per cent vs. 3.20 per cent per year), this is also true for the two more similar models without advantages, complexity, risk factor and regional corrections (2.74 per cent vs. 3.20 per cent per year, $N = 88$). This cannot be explained by a now lower estimated IQ for 2100 (for 2100, IQ 93.88 vs. 90.21; Table 13.8). The current and 2011 model growth estimates correlate with $r = .30$. That means there is a low coincidence in estimations of cross-country differences in growth.

However, the two 2100 GDP predictions correlate with $r = .83$ ($N = 88$); this correlation is higher than within the same sources across the twenty-first

Table 13.14 *Economic predictions (models 2018 and 2011 compared for 88 countries)*

| | Current model for 21st century (2018) | | | Former model for 21st century (2011) | | |
| --- | --- | --- | --- | --- | --- | --- |
| | GDP 2010 (Madd.) | Growth (final model) | GDP 2100 (final) | GDP 2010 (CIA-IMF) | Growth (2011 model) | GDP 2100 (2011 m) |
| **Africa (sub-Sahara)** | 3,000 | 1.10 | 6,979 | 5,497 | 4.73 | 167,824 |
| Nigeria | 1,840 | 1.52 | 7,178 | 2,126 | 4.79 | 143,907 |
| **N-Africa M-East** | 7,446 | 1.28 | 21,625 | 21,208 | 3.09 | 198,157 |
| Egypt | 4,096 | 1.56 | 16,465 | 5,992 | 4.03 | 209,935 |
| **America (North, Engl)** | 27,625 | 1.76 | 133,229 | 43,050 | 2.23 | 312,940 |
| USA | 30,436 | 1.48 | 114,033 | 47,057 | 2.11 | 307,191 |
| **America (Latin, C-S)** | 9,254 | 1.61 | 34,698 | 12,793 | 3.17 | 203,924 |
| Mexico | 7,870 | 1.76 | 37,840 | 13,830 | 2.98 | 194,459 |
| **Asia (Central-South)** | 5,836 | 1.50 | 18,975 | 5,813 | 4.31 | 187,415 |
| India | 3,287 | 1.59 | 13,621 | 3,085 | 4.75 | 200,239 |
| **East Asia** | 18,393 | 3.53 | 30,0553 | 29,325 | 3.22 | 349,460 |
| China | 7,424 | 4.38 | 351,886 | 7,174 | 4.34 | 329,653 |
| **Southeast Asia, Pacific** | 6,749 | 1.69 | 27457 | 7,614 | 3.93 | 205,978 |
| Philippines | 3,089 | 2.15 | 20,944 | 3,334 | 4.64 | 197,441 |
| **Australia-NZ (English)** | 21,875 | 2.38 | 180,112 | 33,706 | 2.66 | 352,107 |
| New Zealand | 18,598 | 2.56 | 181,687 | 27,198 | 2.87 | 345,647 |
| **Western Europe** | 23,458 | 1.50 | 89,492 | 36,596 | 2.32 | 289,655 |
| United Kingdom | 23,496 | 1.68 | 105,363 | 34,725 | 2.51 | 322,854 |
| **Scandinavia** | 24,952 | 1.66 | 109,899 | 41,112 | 2.18 | 282,118 |
| Norway | 27,894 | 1.69 | 125,590 | 55,271 | 1.75 | 262,552 |
| **Central Europe** | 23,048 | 1.31 | 74,099 | 39,120 | 2.22 | 283,224 |
| Germany | 20,521 | 1.48 | 76,744 | 35,682 | 2.36 | 291,712 |

Table 13.14 (cont.)

| | Current model for 21st century (2018) | | | Former model for 21st century (2011) | | |
|---|---|---|---|---|---|---|
| | GDP 2010 (Madd.) | Growth (final model) | GDP 2100 (final) | GDP 2010 (CIA-IMF) | Growth (2011 model) | GDP 2100 (2011 m) |
| **Eastnorth Europe** | 12,026 | 2.99 | 160,247 | 18,276 | 3.17 | 284,845 |
| Russia | 8,888 | 3.15 | 145,150 | 15,583 | 3.30 | 290,331 |
| **Southwest Europe** | 15,182 | 1.70 | 66,879 | 24,808 | 2.52 | 227,319 |
| Italy | 19,021 | 1.43 | 68,195 | 29,761 | 2.20 | 211,447 |
| **Southeast Europe** | 8,447 | 2.38 | 63,829 | 11,945 | 3.60 | 228,124 |
| Greece | 15,397 | 1.42 | 54,648 | 29,032 | 2.25 | 215,404 |
| **Average (SD)** | 12,029 (8,080) | 1.90 (0.88) | 80,186 (81,296) | 20,434 (17,622) | 3.20 (1.05) | 239,995 (61,233) |

*Notes*: N=88 countries with data from both studies (therefore deviations in regional averages from Table 13.12); due to missing data Kenya was substituted by Nigeria; GDP 2010 (CIA-IMF): based on CIA and IMF sources (www.cia.gov/library/publications/the-world-factbook, www.imf.org/external/pubs/ft/weo/2011/01/weodata/index.aspx); former model from Rindermann & Thompson (2011b).

century between 2010 and 2100 ($r = .528$, Madison based 2018 model; $r = .532$, CIA-IMF based 2011 model). The correlation between the two 2100 estimations ($r = .83$) is even higher than for the two 2010 reports of measured GDP ($r = .75$). This is especially remarkable, as for the current estimation process further factors were taken into account (demographic change, advantages of backwardness, complexity increase, risk factors, regional effects). And the 2100 GDP correlation between the different models ($r = .83$) is higher than the correlation between the current and 2011 predictions of cognitive ability ($r = .61$). All this means that our models seem to correct for peculiarities of GDP measures and model specifications. In particular, the cognitive factors will be relevant leading to a more and more cognitive-loaded economy and society. The wellbeing of nations, not only production and its growth, will be based on cognitive ability.

In the 2011 model the measured GDPs for 2010 and in particular the predicted GDPs for 2100 are considerably higher (international average 2100 $80,186 vs. former $239,995, a difference of 300 per cent). The international differences are now larger (current model 2100 $SD$ = $81,296; former model 2100 $SD$ = $61,233). As mentioned, in the newer model more factors were considered, especially the complexity burden, which reduces further growth (in this 88-country sample, on average about –$100,000). However, even comparing the two more similar approaches (cognitive change and past growth, for the current model also including demographic change) the newer model comes to a less optimistic estimate ($165,885 vs. $239,995). There are large differences in absolute numbers and absolute differences but not in patterns.

The present wealth estimates receive some support by the results of the older model: GDP estimates for 2100 are highly correlated, patterns are corroborated and the countries which are richer in the newer model were also so in the older model. Of course, a replication of results in different studies of one researcher cannot replace a comparison with alternative theoretical and methodological approaches of other researchers.

*Comparison with Results from other Researchers*   Currently, another twenty-first-century estimation using cognitive human capital is given by Hanushek et al. (2013), for the United States and until 2093. Meisenberg (2014) has given predictions using intelligence and schooling for selected countries until 2050. More theoretical approaches are collected in Palacios-Huerta (2013); Gordon (2016) focuses on the United States and Li et al. (2017) on China. A rough cognitive guess only for the United States in 2050 was presented by Roth (2014/2010, p. 471).

Hanushek and Woessmann (2015b) gave estimations for 76 countries and the year 2095, but only as relative education-based gains for growth and GDP, not as total growth and GDP estimates. A baseline growth of 1.5 per cent is taken for all countries. While the special approach is different, the basic background theory of the relevance of cognitive factors is the same, best condensed here (Hanushek & Woessmann, 2015a, p. 2):

Although many factors enter into a nation's economic growth, we conclude that the cognitive skills of the population are the most essential to long-run prosperity. These skills, which in the aggregate we call the 'knowledge capital' of a nation, explain in large part the differences in long-run growth we have seen around the world in the past half century.

Hanushek and Woessmann assume a basic growth (without reforms) in the twenty-first century of about 1.5 per cent for the United States, Japan and Germany (2015a, p. 170); our final average value for these three countries is more optimistic with 1.97 per cent. Li et al. (2017), considering education and further factors as demographic change and labour reallocation, predict for China until 2037 an average growth of about 3.0 per cent. Our estimate for China in the twenty-first century is, with 4.38 per cent, higher, especially for the first half with 6.13 per cent.

Meisenberg's (2014, his table 6; see also our Table 12.4) estimations for 67 countries in 2050 can be compared with our 2050 estimations.[48] For 62 common countries, the correlation between the results of his and our last and final models is $r = .92$; the GDP averages are similar at \$26,449 (our) and \$28,345 (his). For growth, the correlation is at $r = .69$; however, our growth estimates are higher (our: 2.50 per cent, his: 1.66 per cent, for the same 62 countries). Meisenberg's analysis, independently done, supports the one presented here: The GDP 2050 correlations ($r = .92$) are even higher than between published GDP measures for the year 2010 from different sources ($r = .75$, $N = 88$). As for the comparisons with our older 2011 estimation, correlations become higher with more corrections applied (from demographics to region), in GDP from $r = .80$ to $.92$, in growth from $r = .35$ to $.69$.

Roth assumed a loss in cognitive ability of about 3 IQ points in the United States by mid-century; by contrast, we predicted a loss of $-1.16$ IQ until 2050 and until 2100 of $-2.56$ IQ (Table 13.8). The difference between his and our more optimistic estimations is due to assuming further improvements, especially among groups currently being at lower ability levels (FLynn effect).

Finally, Fogel (2007) predicted for four exemplary countries (China, India, Japan, United States) for 2040 average per capita GDPs. Our forecasted growth rates are, with $r = .89$, very similar to his, also the 2040 income levels ($r = .86$). However, looking at means, Fogel's estimates are much more

---

[48] Meisenberg (2014) used two models, the first based on 2011 GDP and intelligence, the second on 2011 GDP, intelligence and average years of schooling of the adult population. Meisenberg's data were entered and analysed after finishing the first draft of this chapter (12 July 2015), meaning that our analyses were independently done and can be used for comparison.

optimistic; we expect for China in 2040 an average GDP/c of about $50,000, he predicts $85,000, we for India $8,000, he $24,000, we for Japan $40,060, he $49,000 and we for the United States $47,000, but he $107,000. Our average growth rates are 3.25 per cent, his 4.64 per cent. Fogel wrote his essay before the recession of 2007ff. However, economic crises are normal and have to be included. While there is a high level of agreement regarding ranks and differences between countries, estimations of levels seem to be much less consistent and probably less accurate.

Summarising, there is support from our older and other scientists' research. What will be true we cannot know now. But we can work on more sophisticated models. For an empirical proof we need to wait some time . . .

# 14    Summary, Comparisons and Suggestions

After summarising the results and comparing them with the major insights of other researchers, strategies of intervention for improving the development of cognitive human capital and the wellbeing of nations are presented. Mentioned are health policies; within and outside family educational policies; cognitive training; demographic and migration policies; institutional and political reforms and the development of culture.

We start with a summary of our approach and its results, compare them with major insights of other researchers and then develop, based on outcomes and feasibility, political and ethical considerations, suggestions how to positively influence the future development of societies. Whereas political and ethical perspectives in dealing with epistemic and scientific questions should be avoided – the production of truth matters, all other perspectives divert from this purpose – for practical interventions, the perspectives of ethics and politics including feasibility issues have to be considered.

One certainly odd, but problem-illustrating, example makes it clear: a problem of future societies will be their overageing. An 'effective' but ethically unjustifiable 'solution' would be 'socially compatible early passing', e.g. by encouraging chain-smoking from age 63 onwards or flying with Germanwings across the Alps and then (if still possible) above Eastern Ukraine to (if still possible) holidays in Syria, Iraq and Afghanistan. This 'intervention' may raise average per capita GDP among adults but it is obviously also in conflict with ethical principles!

However, is there any intervention without negative side effects? Every single intervention can have negatively evaluated political or ethical spillovers. Many negative side effects can be compensated by positive effects of further interventions. The entire programme needs to be balanced. For instance, the usually most popular expansion of school education will lead to higher costs for families, states and economies: children will need more support and will contribute less to households; schools will lack classrooms, teaching material and, especially, teachers, who all have to be trained and paid; youth will start work and contribute to government budgets at a higher age. If the state and the social security system need more means but receive fewer revenues, taxes and insurance premiums have to be raised. Tax increases will raise government spending ratios, having a negative impact on cognitive ability and GDP. However, at the same time, costs for crime will go down and in the long run GDP will rise.

This can be corroborated by empirical data: years of school education controlled for cognitive ability has a negative impact on GDP ($\beta_{ED60 \rightarrow GDP98} = -.22$, $r = .67$; Rindermann, 2008b, figure 9). This means that education controlled for (meaning without) cognitive effects is negative for the economy! Government spending ratio longitudinally shows negative impact on cognitive ability ($\beta_{GSR1967 \rightarrow CA2010} = -.24$) and GDP ($\beta_{GSR1967 \rightarrow GDP2010} = -.11$) (Section 12.2.1). Even the best advice will come with a price.

Or another example: the introduction of highly effective cognitive training programmes in school uses up time not spent on content-based instruction or free time. Only if learning e.g. in mathematics, languages or history would be improved so much that it compensates for those losses of instruction there would be no disadvantages. And, often overlooked, *higher cognitive ability itself can have side effects* such as a more difficult to manipulate citizenry – not always liked by rulers – and if not accompanied by a subtle attitudinal and ethical mentality it will not be appropriately used or may even be misused.[1] At least to a certain degree, ethics can be trained and changed too. But not all aporias can be solved. Mere intelligence is not all.

## 14.1   Summary on Results of This Study

There are large *economic production, income* and *wealth* differences across time and nations. While this is not at all astonishing nor new, it should be mentioned that today poor nations are even richer than rich nations were one century ago. Similar historical differences are observable in indicators of wider concepts of welfare representing *biological* and *psychological wellbeing* such as height and life expectancy. Additionally, today's wealth buys more health than it did in the past: people in developed countries at the beginning of the twentieth century with around $5,000 GDP per capita had a life expectancy of about 50 years, whereas at the end of the twentieth century people in developing countries with GDPs far below $5,000 live for 60+ years: more than 10 years longer. Furthermore, also *political characteristics* such as liberty, rule of law and democracy show large differences across time and nations. There is a general factor of *national wellbeing* that represents quality of living, development and modernisation in technological, economic, political, societal and cultural realms.

---

[1] Political and military leaders of National Socialist Germany (e.g. Göring, Speer, Keitel, Jodl) achieved an average IQ of 128 points in intelligence tests (Gilbert, 1947, p. 31).

Empirical research at the level of individuals and nations shows that cognitive ability is an important, and usually decisive, attribute of persons and nations, statistically *predicting* and theoretically *explaining* innovation, productivity, income and wealth differences and having a supportive impact on political and institutional criteria such as government effectiveness, rule of law, liberty and democracy.

Cognitive ability is defined as the *ability to think* (usually called intelligence) plus *knowledge* (the store of true and relevant knowledge) plus *the intelligent use of knowledge*. In different streams of research, different terms are used, 'cognitive ability', 'intelligence', 'skills', 'human capital', 'literacy' or 'cognitive competence', and different measurement approaches are applied: psychometric intelligence tests, Piagetian scenarios, student achievement tests, analyses of cognitive achievement in everyday life or proxies such as years of education and highest achieved academic degree. All present and past behaviour of individuals and social entities – of families, classes, schools, communities, ethnic groups, countries and cultures – dealing with *problem-solving*, *complexity* and *thinking* can be used as an indicator of cognitive ability. The main reason for cognitive ability's predictive value for an array of individual and collective life, economic, institutional, political, health and cultural criteria is that many challenges in the job as well as in everyday life include cognitive tasks, which are better solvable with cognitive ability.

Individual differences in cognitive ability are best explained by *genetic factors*, whereas *environmental factors* are more relevant for explaining national increases in intelligence (FLynn-effect). However, for both phenomena and in both explanations the exact determinants are uncertain: which genes and their neurobiological causal path to intelligence and which environmental factors have stimulated national intelligence to what degree – this is still unknown.

Relevant environmental factors range from basic physical-biological determinants such as nutrition and health to parenting styles, wealth, education and ability level of one's social environment (family, neighbourhood, school, country) and culture. Personal behaviour, decisions such as on smoking or not, on reading or not, and attitudes – the willingness to use one's cognitive ability and to orientate oneself in thinking – are moving forces.

*International differences* in intelligence and knowledge are very large, with up to 40 IQ or 300 student assessment test points, equivalent to around 13 years of learning at school. International patterns based on intelligence tests and student assessment tests are alike. These international differences are further corroborated by results of Piagetian tests, by observations of behaviour in everyday life, by accomplishments of intellectual classes in technology and science and by sediments of cultural achievement. The relationship between cognitive ability and extraordinary accomplishments is curvilinear, with higher ability the level of accomplishments rises even more. Current international differences between countries and historical differences within countries across time are similarly large. The cognitive *increases in the twentieth century* in developed countries are estimated at 2.83 IQ points per decade. Per century, if the trend was so long and constant, it would represent a rise of 28 IQ points.

These differences are not mere shallow test differences but according to the cognitive capital theory they are essential for *understanding historical and national differences in wealth, politics and culture*: The increases in cognitive ability stimulated social development and they themselves were positively influenced by their consequences, resulting in a reciprocal historical process – a *virtuous circle of cognitive-societal modernisation*. This development is psychologically driven by intelligence, sociologically supported by a culture akin to the burgher-civic world and pushed forward by intellectual classes.

But why did societies differ in the past – and why do they differ still today? Wealth, health and politics have some influence, but they themselves depend on cognitive ability. Education is a powerful determinant for improvement in thinking and knowledge that is effective for individuals as well as societies. But the factors capable of explaining stable differences, stable across territories and time and their changing environmental conditions, are the two background factors *evolution* and *culture*: they work via changing behaviour, values and thinking, via changing education in families and school, via influencing the quality and functionality of institutions and via supporting or impeding cognitive development of individuals, societies and cultures, all having an impact on production, income and wellbeing. Both also stabilise national patterns, which is very probably relevant for the future too. However, the large historical increases in cognitive ability, production, income and wellbeing also show that nations can progress.

*Future challenges* of societies and economies comprise rising *complexity* – every progress in technology, production or science becomes more difficult and everyday life becomes cognitively more complex, calling for higher cognitive ability. Additionally, *societies become older*, which goes along with declining average fluid intelligence and innovativeness, more health problems and fewer working people. *Immigration*, depending on who will come, can raise or reduce human capital levels. Western countries except for Australia lose cognitive human capital by immigration, and oil-rich gulf countries and even Singapore at its high level gain by immigration. Immigration will certainly raise diversity, which for many aspects such as trust, income distribution, crime, politics and growth does not have a positive impact. *Well-educated* and cognitively more able adults have relatively *fewer children*. Because families transmit ability and personality to the next generation, this asymmetry will be problematic for future generations. *Natural resources* are predicted to decline, *climate* to change, *inequality* to rise.

For *cognitive development in the twenty-first century* – the continuation of the FLynn effect or its reversal – several models were developed. The model considering the most factors – continuing environmental improvement, migration, asymmetric children rates – predicts a general international rise of *0.74 IQ points per decade*. This is positive but smaller than the around 3 IQ point increase per decade in the twentieth century in developed countries. In developing countries, the predicted gains will be larger, for example in Africa with 1.36 IQ points per decade. In *Western countries, the effect will be negative* with per decade –0.37 IQ points or in 90 years –3.33 IQ. Weighting for population size, the worldwide trend is still positive with 0.23 to 0.28 IQ point gains per decade. The worldwide outlook is sunny, but with some dark clouds: the most innovative countries in the past will descend in ability.

With ongoing technological modernisation the development of economic production will depend more and more on cognitive resources of a society. Because of the continuing upward cognitive trend and because in the past also at lower cognitive levels economic growth was possible, for the twenty-first century a continuation of economic growth is expected.

But further growth-modifying factors have to be considered: *demographic transition and change* (fewer youth and ageing societies), the *advantages of backwardness* (higher growth in poorer countries if they are able to catch up), *growing complexity* (problematic for all but especially for countries with lower ability levels and for those at the frontier of innovation), *political risks* (threats for political stability, security and economic development) and *regional effects* (influences of neighbouring countries and regions). Taking into account all these factors, an average annual worldwide growth rate of 1.89 per cent is predicted. East Asia will become the richest region, followed by (North-)Eastern Europe and the West. The world will increase sixfold its average wealth level as measured by GDP and all countries will surpass the poverty line. The wellbeing of nations will be improved. However, absolute values are much more difficult to predict than country patterns in growth, wealth and political conditions. Statements on levels are fraught with more uncertainty than statements on differences. Because the procedure and the considered factors are described, single assumptions can be easily changed by other researchers. The model should be understood as a first attempt.

In spite of several critical developments and rising challenges, the cognitive capital resources allow humankind to progress and at least maintain its achieved level of civilisation and culture. But progress will become slower and more incremental, sometimes interrupted by setbacks, but in the long run still continuing.

## 14.2    Comparison with Alternative and Complementary Approaches and Their Insights

This book is built upon the important works of many other researchers in different fields. We acknowledge their pioneering ideas, methods and insights, helping us – as we hope – to move even one step further. However, the work presented here also differs in essential aspects from former research. Our core message is that cognitive ability depending on culture and evolution influencing production, innovation and institutions has a crucial positive impact on national wellbeing comprising economic, health, psychological, sociological and political criteria. Within society, the impact of intellectual classes is crucial; they push forward technological, political and cultural innovation; within culture, the ethics and orientations of the burgher world create a spiral-shaped reciprocal development. We want to elaborate these results by recognising and comparing them with the perspective of others.

### 14.2.1    The Relevance of Enlightenment, Elites and Innovation (Margaret Jacob and Joel Mokyr)

Margaret Jacob (1997, 2014) and Joel Mokyr (2005, 2016) unify the perspective that intellectual-cultural factors were crucial for the British Industrial Revolution. In Britain, a scientific culture emerged in the seventeenth to eighteenth century. This culture was rooted in enlightenment and religiously inspired habits of disciplined work, the profit motive and probity. Psychologically, it is based on education in mathematics and Newtonian science. In this 'idealistic' approach, cultural and psychological factors are focused: enlightenment, orientations, style of thinking, education, behaviour. The rise of Great Britain was a cultural and cognitive accomplishment. There is some dispute whether theoretical science or practical tinkering were more relevant. From the perspective of a cognitive approach this distinction is less relevant: both science and tinkering depend on intelligence and knowledge.

There is no dissent between these results of a historical approach and our statistical analyses (e.g. Tables 4.4 and 4.5, Figures 11.1, 11.2 and Rindermann, 2012; Rindermann & Thompson, 2011a). However, Jacob's as well as Mokyr's scope is too much focused on a single country and epoch for understanding global development: why is Britain today still richer than e.g. Greece? The Industrial Revolution took place long ago. Why were and are Germany, Japan and Singapore also successful? Why can Peru or Zimbabwe not simply copy Britain's successful example? Both studies, of Margaret Jacob and Joel Mokyr, help us to understand modernisation, but they less help us to understand why there are still today so large differences and why the pattern is stable across time and geography.

### 14.2.2   Institutions: Economic Rights and Freedom (Douglass North, Daron Acemoglu)

The core idea of works of Douglass North and Daron Acemoglu together with John Wallis, Barry Weingast and James Robinson (North, 1990; North et al., 2009; Acemoglu & Robinson, 2012) is that institutions, e.g. the rule of law, property rights, economic freedom, administration, government effectiveness, are crucial for the success of nations both in economics and politics. Acemoglu and Robinson (2012) present persuasive examples for their comparison of successful inclusive (property rights, competition for all) and not successful extractive (exploitative, excluding) economic institutions, e.g. South versus North Korea or Nogales in the United States versus in Mexico. Stable patterns are explained by path dependence, the ultimate cause for them are historical contingencies. E.g. for the case of United States vs. Peru they state:

'History is key', a 'contingent outcome of several pivotal institutional developments during critical junctures' starting 'vicious and virtuous circles' being a 'contingent path of history' and generally: 'some luck is key'. (Acemoglu & Robinson, 2012, pp. 427, 432, 433, 436)

A theory of institutions can be traced back to Adam Smith and is akin to classical liberalism. Empirical studies show a positive and robust effect of institutions on wealth. In our model (Figure 11.1), rule of law has a positive effect on per capita production-income ($\beta_{\text{RoL}\rightarrow\text{GDP}} = .27$) and on longer-term wealth ($\beta_{\text{RoL}\rightarrow\text{Wealth}} = .32$); additionally, there is a positive effect of economic freedom on GDP ($\beta_{\text{EF}\rightarrow\text{GDP}} = .13$) and behind both of them, rule of law and economic freedom, stands government effectiveness ($\beta_{\text{Gov}\rightarrow\text{RoL}} = .95$, $\beta_{\text{Gov}\rightarrow\text{EF}} = .82$).

Yes, all is correct! *But why* do countries differ in their quality of institutions and why is it not possible, if they are 'contingent', to transfer institutions, e.g. from the United States to Mexico? Or from the West and East to Muslim countries, e.g. to Afghanistan, Iraq and Iran? The Persian Shah has tried it and many others in Muslim countries, e.g. Gamal Abdel Nasser in Egypt and Mohammed Najibullah in Afghanistan.

Even if institutions are transferred, frequently it is only their outer shell, but their meaning radically changes: institutions can be filled with anything, similar to shipping containers that can be filled with books or drugs. Havana has the same Capitol as Washington. The Paris-Dakar Rally is now held in South America and still bears its old name. In a mere institutional approach, important background factors are missing, as well as cognitive ability, which all make institutions work and give them their meaning. Democracy without conditions fulfilled in culture and cognitive ability hardly works (Figure 11.2). Of course, not only culture, genes or cognitive ability are important, but institutions too, as the examples of South versus North Korea and West versus East Germany clearly demonstrate. But all historical evidence underscores that institutions alone do not work.

Actually, the authors do not defend their theory against a cognitive human capital approach or against an evolution- or culture-background approach. They simply ignore them. However, the evidence for these complementing, if not rivalling, approaches is strong as shown by our own models (Figures 11.1 and 11.2): for instance, for the final criterion wealth, the cognitive ability effect is $\beta_{95\%tot \rightarrow Wealth} = .66$, while the combined effect of the institutional factors rule of law and economic freedom is $\beta_{Instot \rightarrow Wealth} = .58$ and for annually produced income the difference is even more pronounced: $\beta_{95\%tot \rightarrow GDP} = .78$ versus $\beta_{Instot \rightarrow GDP} = .40$. Support for competing approaches also comes from theories (Chapters 6 to 10) and from the work of others (e.g. Harrison, 2006; Landes, 1998; McCloskey, 2006). These quotes illustrate some:

The broader features of a population, rather than institutions only, might account for the pattern of persistence and change in the relative economic performance of countries through history. (Spolaore & Wacziarg, 2013, p. 335)

Human capital is a more fundamental channel of influence of precolonial conditions on modern development than is quality of institutions. (Chanda, Cook & Putterman, 2014, p. 1)

Europeans brought human capital and human capital creating institutions. (Easterly & Levine, 2012. p. 29)

*To ignore is no scientific attitude.* However, North, Wallis and Weingast notice after hundreds of pages that something important is missing in their theory:

The adoption of similar institutions in other societies later in the nineteenth century did not immediately foster transitions in those societies. For example, Latin American countries that adopted constitutions similar to the U.S. Constitution in the nineteenth century and the adoption of general incorporation laws elsewhere in Europe were insufficient in themselves to induce transitions. (North et al., 2009, p. 257)

Indeed, to the extent that these institutions are forced onto societies by international or domestic pressure but do not conform to existing beliefs about economic, political, social, and cultural systems, the new institutions are likely to work less well than the ones they replace. (p. 265)

The cultural environment – the political, economic, social context – fundamentally influences beliefs. (p. 262)

Yes, indeed! So their theory is far from being complete. At least culture is mentioned. But the concept of culture needs to be developed and explained.

### 14.2.3    Economic Freedom (Mises, Hayek, Friedman, Rothbard, Hoppe)

The economic freedom approach is the classical approach in economics. It is related to the institutional one, but is at the same time narrower and broader: more narrow, because quality aspects of institutions such as government effectiveness are not included. Broader, because economic freedom is related to the idea of general freedom being central for political and philosophical liberalism (Mill, 2015/1859; Mises, 1996/1927; Hayek, 2011/1960; Friedman, 1962; Rothbard, 2000; Hoppe, 2001). Economic freedom includes property rights and rule of law and as a consequence enables innovation (Schumpeterian creative destruction). Scepticism towards government intervention is widespread and is more than common in economics, e.g. regarding public education, police or taxes.

However, case studies such as on Japan, Taiwan, South Korea, Singapore or China show that low economic freedom (in their markets) combined with governmental interventions can be successful. Against this, authoritarian growth could be less sustainable and their model works only as long as America is free (Weede, 2008). And once China becomes a frontrunner it will have lower growth because for any progress at the forefront freedom is crucial.

Analysing worldwide development, the impact of economic freedom compared to that of cognitive ability is much lower: the pattern is found in different statistical analyses, cross-sectionally: $\beta_{EF \to GDP} = .13$ versus $\beta_{95\%tot \to GDP} = .78$ (Figure 11.1); longitudinally: $\beta_{EF1 \to GDP2} = .15$ versus $\beta_{CHC1 \to GDP2} = .31$ (Figures 10.1 to 10.2). The mean economic freedom effect on GDP is less than half the size of the cognitive human capital effect. However, economic freedom also has an indirect effect, as in freer societies the chances of cognitive ability having a positive impact are greater (Coyle, Rindermann & Hancock, 2016): economic freedom boosts cognitive effects on the economy.

Economic freedom makes a gain, of course, as the examples of Germany and Korea show. But once having left prison-like unfreedom, cognitive ability leading to innovation and improvement becomes crucial – even being enlarged by economic freedom! The same result can be found using a historical approach to economics:

Given innovation (which gives the most), the source of wealth is specialization and trade within a country, regardless of whether the country then sells snowmobiles to the Eskimos or TV sets to Nebraskans. . . .

'Macro inventions' in the making of cloth and surgeries and computers certainly do have the power to enrich us gigantically, trade not. Even the violent separation of East and West Germany had left on the table, to be seized on unification, 'only' a factor of, say, two or three. Not sixteen. (McCloskey, 2010, pp. 208, 212)

Economic freedom is important but cognitive ability is crucial. And all depend on background factors.

### 14.2.4 The Human Capital Approach within Economics (Eric Hanushek and Colleagues)

Eric Hanushek, frequently together with Ludger Wößmann (Woessmann), is the pioneer of the cognitive human capital approach within economics. As early as 2000 he used country data from TIMSS (Hanushek & Kimko, 2000) to statistically explain economic growth. One common theme of all his publications is that measures of 'school quality' (student assessment test results) are more informative and explanatory than measures of 'school quantity' (average years of schooling, percentage of adults with secondary school degrees).

A second thread (e.g. Hanushek & Woessmann, 2008) is the larger impact of intellectual classes measured by the percentage of pupils with ability levels higher than SASQ 600 (student assessment scale points, equivalent to IQ 115, casually called 'rocket scientists') on economic growth than the impact of average ability groups (percentage of pupils with ability levels higher than SASQ 400, equivalent to IQ 85). E.g. in Japan, the fraction above SASQ 600 is much larger than in Egypt and economic growth was larger in Japan too.

Finally, the research of Hanushek and Woessmann (e.g. 2006, 2011, 2015a, 2015b) deals with educational factors that may explain 'skill' differences between countries (of pupils aged between 9 and 16 years), e.g. teacher quality, private schools, central exams and tracking. Except for tracking, there are no discordances between their and my results. Hanushek and Woessmann (2006) come, using a different method, comparing fourth and eighth grade results, to the result that early tracking increases inequality and reduces performance. My own analyses with a larger country sample and controlling for background factors (Table 10.5) come to robust positive effects. The positive findings are supported by data of other authors, by using data from PISA, by studies at within-country data levels including experiments and by theory (see Section 10.5.2).

However, the tracking issue is a single discordance. Generally, there is an independent confirmation of my results,

(a) on the importance of cognitive effects on the economy,
(b) on the relevance of intellectual classes for the economy,
(c) on increasing effects of ability in free economies, and
(d) on many educational factors such as education expenditures (small or no effects), central exams and tests, school autonomy, teacher quality and private schools (all positive effects).

It is an independent confirmation because Hanushek and colleagues usually do not cite psychological research. Only once (Hanushek & Woessmann, 2011, p. 187ff.) did they mention psychometric intelligence research (Lynn & Vanhanen, 2002, 2006). But all psychological detail analyses are not cited, especially not all those analyses also using student assessment data such as by Richard Lynn, Gerhard Meisenberg or Heiner Rindermann. Hanushek and Woessmann use independently assembled sum values and different econometric methods, but come to similar results. We can only speculate why they do not cite and probably have not read the research of others. Maybe it is a general paradigm pattern not to roam around in foreign gardens. Maybe it is also shrewd not to mention the other fields, avoiding any associations with the frequently discredited intelligence research, a clever strategy to open the path of cognitive ability research into economics.

However, their own research has also not really been adopted in economics; it circulates in economics of education and in related fields but has not found its way into the centre of research into why nations differ in wealth (e.g. they are not at all mentioned in institutional or historical analyses). Nobody seems to be concerned about not knowing the central approach of cognitive human capital research for understanding international wellbeing differences. If allowed, a remark of Nietzsche can be eye-opening here:

Consider the cattle, grazing as they pass you by: they do not know what is meant by yesterday or today, they leap about, eat, rest, digest, leap about again, and so from morn till night and from day to day, fettered to the moment and its pleasure or displeasure, and thus neither melancholy nor bored. (Nietzsche, 1997/1874, p. 60)

The economist Deirdre McCloskey sees a general problem in low cooperation between different fields of science. Scientists should 'start reading each other's books' (McCloskey, 2010, p. 448). 'What prevents such scientific cooperation is sneering ignorance.' Such 'ignorance', as also observed for the institutional approach mentioned earlier, started, in her opinion, about 50 years ago:

'The turn to specialized illiteracy among economists, fortified by a scornful ignorance of history, philosophy, theology, and literature, happened in the 1960s and 1970s.' (McCloskey, 2010, p. 491)

Anyway, there are also some issues in the Hanushek approach that are somewhat problematic from a purely human capital research view:

- The used term is 'cognitive skill'. If this term is only meant as another, maybe easier to sell in economics, expression, then there is no problem. But if it is meant as a narrow ability, it is wrong (see Chapters 3 and 4). There is a propensity to *mask the generality and significance* of the cognitive ability concept, excluding the views of psychometric IQ, Piagetian and cross-cultural research done in psychology, sociology, philosophy, biology and anthropology.

- International differences are attributed to differences in education between countries. Education is certainly an important factor; however, all *background factors* are ignored such as culture and evolution (see Figures 11.1 and 11.2 and Chapters 6 to 14). Such associations may be a reason why OECD and standard educational research usually do not deal with the causes of national differences in PISA, TIMSS etc. (however, we are still happy that they provide interdisciplinary research with data). And societal factors such as rule of law or meritoric principles are also not studied (see Sections 10.3.2 and 10.3.3).
- *Intervening factors* are not analysed; there are no path models deploying direct and indirect effects of cognitive ability on institutions, innovation, production, income and wealth. Thus the causal effects of cognitive ability are not properly understood.
- The entire *network of reciprocal effects* between cognitive ability, education, society and culture is not modelled and caught. E.g. cognitive ability also has an effect on education and culture, leading in the long run to a positive spiral (Sections 3.4.2 and 6.4).

That said, the research of Hanushek and colleagues has an inestimably high value for the entire cognitive human capital approach. At the highest methodological levels and from the core of economic research the field is pushed forward.

### 14.2.5   Effects of Intelligence for the Economy (Garett Jones)

Similarly to Eric Hanushek, Garett Jones is a trailblazer for the cognitive human capital approach in economics (Jones, 2012, 2016; Jones & Schneider, 2006, 2010). Unlike Hanushek, he uses psychometric IQ test results; of course, he considers methodological weaknesses, e.g. by excluding countries with weak data. Additionally, institutional effects, social environment effects ('hive mind') and intervening effects such as via patience and cooperation are analysed. Especially important are the results showing that national ability levels due to improving institutional and economic environments have a larger impact on individual wealth than a person's own IQ. In his 2016 book '*Hive Mind* ', this is all done in convincing, and for the broader public understandable, language.

However, similarly to Eric Hanushek, an in-depth analysis of the causes of international differences is avoided. Both circumnavigate upsetting information. The *Hive Mind* book explicitly only deals with the consequences of cognitive ability for individuals and nations:

You might be wondering why some countries have higher average scores and others have lower average scores. That's an important question, but it's a question this book isn't designed to answer. This isn't a book about where a nation's IQ comes from, it's a book about where a nation's IQ takes it. (p. 11)

This is elegant and supports the reception of the approach. As long as researchers and readers know that further prolific research can be done this is an important step forward. Rome was not built in a day either.

### 14.2.6   The Climate Approach (Jared Diamond)

The core message of Jared Diamond's (1997, 2002; also see Section 5.2.3) work is that present and past wealth differences between nations are caused by differences in geography, climate and natural resources. In Europe and Asia, there were easier to domesticate and more nourishing plants and animals. Additionally, an east-west trade (Asia-Europe) is easier compared to a south-north trade across different climate zones (Africa, America). Peremptorily, Diamond denies any impact of peoples' attributes: 'The reasons had nothing to do with differences in the peoples themselves.'[2] All peoples are equal in abilities and attitudes.

However, this explanation is far from being convincing. Why should animals native to Asia and Europe be more domesticable than those of Africa or America? E.g. wild foxes can also be tamed (Trut, 1999) or elephants in India and even in Africa, as Hannibal has shown. Nourishing food grows on all continents. Nevertheless, let us assume Diamond's theory is correct: why should domesticable animals and cultivable plants still be relevant for today's wealth? Is it today important for Singapore? Finland? Afghanistan? Why should anything that took place hundreds or thousands of years ago have any enduring impact?

This past is irrelevant for today's economy, unless the past has shaped the competences and attitudes of present-day peoples. And such mechanisms would have to be related to *culture* or *genes* or *both*! But those mechanisms are beforehand denied by Diamond:

Why did history unfold differently in different continents? In case this question immediately makes you shudder at the thought that you are about to read a racist treatise, you aren't: as you will see, the answers to the question don't involve human racial differences at all. (Diamond, 1997, p. 9)

Any scientific book cannot be started with a political premise. Diamond's work suffers from a political mind-set from the outset. 'It is driven by ideology, not science.' (Wade, 2014, p. 222). It is a negative example of politically correct research being welcomed by the media. The only positive aspect it may have is to test epistemic rationality with a negative example. Of course, having natural resources that are needed today, such as fossil fuels, iron or rare earth elements, has a positive impact on a country's income and wealth (see Figure 11.1). However, resources' effects are with $\beta_{NRR \to Wealth} = .12$ much lower than those of cognitive

---

[2] www.jareddiamond.org.

ability ($\beta_{95\%tot \rightarrow Wealth}$ = .66) or of institutional factors ($\beta_{Instot \rightarrow Wealth}$ = .58). And they tend to fade out with time and maybe even have negative side effects on production and culture (Dutch disease, Section 5.2.3).

### 14.2.7   The Genetic-Economic Approach (Gregory Clark)

Gregory Clark's (2007) theory on evolution of a productive human capital personality was described in detail in Section 10.7.2. Thus here only some remarks are given. The essence of his theory is that in England from medieval times until the nineteenth century, successful and rich persons had more children, leading to a spread of attitudes and habits that make people successful, such as predictability, conscientiousness, discipline, peaceableness, delay of gratification and industry. The mechanism of this spread was in his view a genetic one but could have also been a result of culture or a combination of genes and culture.

Peculiarly, Clark never deals with the most important human capital trait: cognitive ability. This makes his theory relevant for a cognitive human capital theory only if differently interpreted: similarly to personality, this evolutionary process pushed cognitive ability.

A second problem is that like other theories (Cochran et al. for Jews, Frost for Europe, Hajnal for Western Europe, Unz for China) the scope of the theory is one nation or region, here England. However, the entire West, North and Central Europe and later Southern and Eastern Europe, and East Asia were economically and politically successful.

Finally, the genetic mechanism is not known – which genes coding what spread? In 2008, Clark presented a simulation study using data and plausible assumptions of his England book (heritability $h^2$ = .60, top quartile 3.2 children, the next quartile 2.4 children, the next 1.6 and the lowest 0.8) that demonstrates that evolution among humans can be fast: within one generation of 33 years the average of a trait is changed by 7 per cent (or about $d = 0.17$). Within five to six generations, or about 125 to 200 years, a trait can be changed by one standard deviation. This is enough for a considerable change of society. This can be used as a model for recent evolution of intelligence.

### 14.2.8   The Psychometric and Genetic-Psychological Approach at the International Level (Lynn & Vanhanen)

The psychologist Richard Lynn and the political scientist Tatu Vanhanen (2002, 2006, 2012) published a seminal series of books on international intelligence differences. Previously, it was standard to believe that all nations and countries have on average a similar cognitive ability level. From edition to edition results for more countries from psychometric IQ tests (e.g. the figural Ravens and CFT, the broader WISC or WAIS with verbal, numerical and figural scales) were presented. In the 2012 edition additional results from student assessment tests were used. In this last edition IQs of 136 countries were collected. The surveys themselves were done by other researchers; Lynn and Vanhanen collected the results, selected samples for quality and representivity and adapted results according to the FLynn effect.

From each edition to the next for fewer countries estimations by using results from neighbouring countries were necessary. The old estimates were not bad; the 2002 estimates correlate with the 2012 measured ones with $r = .92$ ($N = 48$). In new editions mistakes were corrected (e.g. for Equatorial Guinea). However, the lists are still not without error; e.g. Bosnia had a wrong sum value (instead of erroneous total IQ 83.2 the correct one was 93.1). Actually, there are some accuracy problems, but similar problems can be found in many fields (e.g., 'spreadsheet error of Reinhart & Rogoff'; generally: Panko, 1998).

A more serious objection is whether there are systematic errors, e.g. underestimating intelligence for Africa (Wicherts et al., 2010a, 2010b). However, the general trend of results is corroborated by student assessment data and qualitative observations (see Section 4.4.3). Regarding student assessment data, a newer calibration supports the reported psychometric IQ levels; African teachers have maths ability levels comparable to seventh or eighth graders in East Asia and Europe (Sandefur, 2016, his figure 6). Nevertheless, differences within Africa are probably less valid.

In the last update from 2012, the psychometric IQ test results were combined with results from student assessment surveys. The latter are provided for fewer countries and only for pupils, but if available, the samples were much larger. In our own analyses, psychometric and student assessment results correlate at $r = .85$ to $.86$ ($N = 89$ to 108; see Table 4.2). These correlations are nearly identical to correlations between different estimates for GDP/c (between Maddison's and Penn's $r = .87$, $N = 156$; see Section 1.3.1). But different from two GDPs that undoubtedly represent one single construct, psychometric IQ and student assessment tests are intended to measure different traits. Thus that high correlation particularly supports their validity.

Another critique concerns the analyses: all analyses presented by Lynn and Vanhanen are simple: many bivariate correlations, some regressions, pure Ockham's razor. Other researchers have applied more complex models. However, regarding their results on cognitive ability effects there is no dispute – all analyses of different researchers from different fields come to the conclusion that cognitive human capital is a major player in the economy.

This agreement is not given for the developed causal theory which is described in detail in Section 10.7.2. The core message is that, similarly to individual differences, international differences are mainly due to genetic causes; health (nutrition) as an environmental factor is also relevant. Genetic differences are theoretically explained by the cold-winter-theory, which can be combined with the *r/K*-theory (Rushton, 1985, 1997) and the evolutionarily novelty theory (Kanazawa, 2004, 2012): intelligence is a strategy to survive in difficult environments. Strengths and weaknesses of genetic explanations and empirical evidence were discussed in detail in Section 10.7.2. E.g. at present there is no certain evidence for intelligence-coding genes, and if such evidence does become available, information on their international distribution is necessary.

However, the in our study chosen measure 'brain size' (cranial capacity; Beals et al., 1984), an indicator for evolution and at the same time a well-established causal factor for cognitive ability, has shown robust positive effects on national ability levels (see Figure 11.1, Table 10.8). Proving that evolution shows a positive effect does not mean that further factors are not important; in our own analyses culture even showed a stronger total effect ($\beta_{\text{Evotot}\to\text{CA}} = .37$, $\beta_{\text{Cultot}\to\text{CA}} = .50$). Lynn and Vanhanen (2002, pp. 8f.) are sceptical regarding culture, discussing the works of Lawrence Harrison and David Landes. Their main critique is:

'The principal weakness of culture as an explanation of national differences in economic development is that it is hard or even impossible to measure and subject to rigorous testing.' (2002, p. 9)

Similar scepticism can be found in economics (see McCloskey, 2006, 2010, 2016). It is the task of research to solve the measurement problem (and not only for culture but also for genes).

### 14.2.9    The Economic History Approach (David Landes)

David Landes' main work, '*The Wealth and Poverty of Nations. Why Some are So Rich and Some So Poor*', from 1998, is a brilliantly written complex tome. But, unlike the works discussed earlier, e.g. of Acemoglu, Clark, Diamond, Jones or Lynn, Landes' book does not have a clear message. There is no single theory; it is more a ride of a *grand seigneur* across history, containing many inspiring insights. Being forced to summarise it, the main message is that internal factors of a nation are responsible for its success or failure, not external ones. As the ultimate internal factor Landes judges culture, e.g. work ethic as described by Max Weber:

If we learn anything from the history of economic development, it is that culture makes all the difference. (Here Max Weber was right on.) (Landes, 1998, p. 516)

The most important and crucial factor, as our study and the studies of others (Hanushek, Jones, Lynn) have shown, cognitive human capital (cognitive ability, intelligence), is not discussed, education is only marginally mentioned and genes or evolution not at all. Admittedly, the major works on these subjects were published after 1998, but as early as 1841 the economist Friedrich List underscored the relevance of intelligence:

Everywhere and at all times has the well-being of the nation been in equal proportion to the intelligence, morality, and industry of its citizens; according to these, wealth has accrued or been diminished. (List, 1909/1841, p. 87)

The human capital approach was later advanced by Walsh (1935), Mincer (1958), Schultz (1961), Becker (1993/1964) and Barro (1991). It should be also mentioned that due to a lack of numbers it is not possible to give a precise quantitative evaluation of the factors mentioned by Landes to explain wealth and poverty. Landes' work is great but lacks important determinants for understanding international and historical wellbeing differences. Backing his central thesis also in our own study culture is a very important background factor.

### 14.2.10  Culture (Lawrence Harrison)

Lawrence Harrison's works (2006, 2013; Harrison & Huntington, 2000; Harrison & Berger, 2006; Harrison & Kagan, 2006) have a clear twofold message: first, culture is responsible for wealth and wellbeing, and second, culture can be changed. What is meant by culture is elaborately described (e.g. Harrison, 2013, pp. 16–31). He distinguishes four main principles with 25 single aspects:

(1) *Worldview*, e.g. a *religion* that nurtures rationality, *time orientation* (planning ahead, punctuality) and *attitudes towards knowledge* (facts matter, search for practical and verifiable knowledge).
(2) *Values and virtues*: an *ethical code* that is rigorous within realistic norms, *appreciation of the lesser virtues* (a job well done, tidiness, courtesy) and *appreciation of education* (promoting or enabling autonomy, heterodoxy, dissent, creativity).
(3) *Economic behaviour*, e.g. *appreciation of work, frugality* and *advancement by merit*.
(4) *Social behaviour*, e.g. *reasonably law abiding, trust, elites are responsible to society, secularised church-state relations, gender equality* and *number of children* depend on the family's capacity to raise and educate them.

This resembles my list of the 'burgher world' (developed in 2004, first published in German in 2008; Rindermann, 2008c) and it resembles McCloskey's 'bourgeois virtues' (2006). Strangely, McCloskey's works are not mentioned. One reason may be that McCloskey's approach is a historical one – explaining the economic rise in the West from around 1600 to 1950. By contrast, Harrison pursues cross-cultural comparison inspired by his own experiences as a USAID officer in South America since 1961.

Harrison describes historical incidents, his own experiences and discusses the literature. Additionally, he has edited reports of experts on different cultures; however, as criticised by Lynn and Vanhanen, there are no numbers.

In the given form, the cultural approach cannot be used for statistical analyses. Based on my religion-related quantification of culture regarding the impact on education, learning, rationality, thinking, meritoric orientations and the development of a burgher world and modernisation and based on percentages of religions a value for culture was assigned to every country (see Section 10.8.8 and Table A.4). This variable 'cultural background' was very predictive for education ($\beta_{Cul \to AdE} = .60$); it also had a direct impact on cognitive ability ($\beta_{Cul \to CA} = .20$); the total effect on cognitive ability was larger than that of evolution (total: $\beta_{Evotot \to CA} = .37$, $\beta_{Cultot \to CA} = .50$) – as operationalized by cranial capacity (see Figure 11.1). Especially important was cultural background for politics (rule of law, political liberty, democracy and gender equality) with directly $\beta_{Cultot \to Pol} = .62$ and totally $\beta_{Cultot \to Pol} = .71$.

Lawrence Harrison, who died in 2015, would have been happy to see this. However, the quantification of culture as in my study is surely a weaker point of the book. Fortunately, the reviewers have not commented it ... Alternatively, it would be possible to rate single countries according to Harrison's criteria.

Harrison was always desperately anxious to state his politically progressive attitude, starting with a book title *'The Central Liberal Truth: How Politics Can Change a Culture and Save It from Itself'* and continuing by reporting 'I'm a lifelong Democrat' and 'an early and avid supporter of President Obama' (2013, p. 148). Many 'arguments' are introduced by what somebody from 'Harvard' said and of course, genes are dead certainly wrong:

It should be crystal clear from *The Central Liberal Truth* that the Culture Matters Research Project (CMRP) agenda is not conservative. I know of no one associated with the CMRP who believes in cultural determinism – that culture is immutable, perhaps even genetically rooted. All of us believe that culture is acquired, that it changes, ... (2013, p. 183)

No one at the symposium believed that culture is genetically determined. (Harrison & Kagan, 2006, p. XII)

Has anybody heard 'I know of no one who believes' as a scientifically valid argument? Science suffers from political pressure leading to internal constraints. Of course, it is also not necessary to shock people, but science has always to follow epistemic rationality.

### 14.2.11 The Burgher World as Bourgeois Dignity (Deirdre McCloskey)

Deirdre McCloskey studied the historical development of the West in a series of three books (2006, 2010, 2016): *The Bourgeois Virtues: Ethics for an Age of Commerce, Bourgeois Dignity: Why Economics Can't Explain the Modern World* and *Bourgeois Equality: How Ideas, Not Capital or Institutions, Enriched the World*. Like Harrison, culture is the moving force for McCloskey and, similarly to Clark, a set of burgher values and behaviour facilitated the Industrial Revolution in England. The initial spark was a change in worldview, a 'rhetorical revaluation' (McCloskey, 2010, p. 75) giving economic activity a higher value and people equal rights as well as liberty:

We are rich because of an ethical and rhetorical change. (2016, p. XI)

The original and sustaining causes of the modern world ... were ethical, not material. They were the widening adoption of two mere ideas, the new and liberal economic idea of liberty for ordinary people and the new and democratic social idea of dignity for them. (2016, p. XXXI)

It was ideas, not interests or institutions, that changed, suddenly, in Northwestern Europe. (2016, p. 511)

This change has created a thirtyfold increase in productivity and wealth since 1800. In an overview graph (2016, p. XXXVI), her causal path starts with reading and faith, then reformation, revolution, bourgeois revaluation, development in low science and technology, investment, higher education and high science, leading finally to 'the great enrichment'. Her cultural model resembles that of Harrison; however, she never mentions his works. My own model of the 'burgher world' is also supported by her historical analysis of 'bourgeois virtues'. In her view (as in my), people's attributes are decisive for the success of institutions:

In any case, an institution such as Acemoglu and Robinson think crucial – or a canal or school or coal mine that others think crucial – works well not merely because of good official rules of the game, what Samuelsonian economists call the 'incentives' or the 'budget lines.' An institution works, if it does, mainly because of the good ethics of its participants, intrinsic motivations powerfully reinforced by the ethical opinion people have about each other. (McCloskey, 2016, p. XXIIIf.)

So far, so good. But there are also important differences between her and my approaches:

(1) In her perspective of bourgeois virtues, the aspects of *discipline, order and tidiness, achievement and rationality* are undervalued compared to liberty. As the East Asian way but also British history show these were and are important traits for success. The same is true for instruction and job performance (Hattie, 2009; Sections 3.1 and 10.5.2).

(2) Her list of bourgeois virtues is rooted *too deeply* in *Christian virtues* ('faith, hope, love') and the contrasting *old heroic hunter and warrior 'courage'* and not enough in diligence, order, structure, realism, pragmatism, rationality and phronesis. Of course, citizens also love other persons but not due to bourgeois virtues.

(3) Deidre McCloskey is a real scholar, a person who reads, a 'femme de lettres'. However, in her entire series of books on bourgeois virtues, behaviour and

revaluation she never mentions the pioneering burgher book of Leon Battista Alberti (1441). Similarly missed is the historical and economic analysis of Werner Sombart (1998/1913), in German *Der Bourgeois*, in English *The Quintessence of Capitalism: A Study of the History and Psychology of the Modern Business Man*. It is rather strange to write thousands of pages and not to discuss the originals. As if somebody would write a book about liberty without mentioning John Stuart Mill or about the theory of relativity without describing Einstein's contribution. Admittedly, she refers, like Sombart, to Benjamin Franklin and, of course, the veridicality of her analysis does not depend on mentioning the pioneering work of others. But her skewed list of bourgeois virtues reflects the missing connaissance of Alberti and Sombart.

(4) Insofar as 'reading' is an ability, McCloskey's model (2016, p. XXXVI) is close to mine. But I assume her 'reading' means a habit and not a cognitive ability. She never mentions cognitive human capital, intelligence, cognitive ability or the like and their crucial effect on innovation, institutions and society.

All economists have realized since the 1870s that economics is something that happens between people's ears. (2010, p. 8)

How is it possible to state this and disregard intelligence? Likewise, it is not correct to claim:

Prudence is reasonably easy, and has always been widespread. (McCloskey, 2010, p. 393)

No, neither cognitive ability nor prudence were ever widespread (see Chapter 4 or the works of Hallpike, LePan, Lévy-Bruhl, Luria, Oesterdiekhoff). Rather, irrationality, from magic to trials by ordeal, was standard.

(5) McCloskey analysed the development within the West. It is no cross-cultural analysis. That may lead to an underestimation of the relevance of religion. Compared to her, Max Weber, Lawrence Harrison (and I) put more emphasis on religion.

(6) Every good science book is also a school in rational thinking. McCloskey intensively deals with alternative approaches (e.g. the effect of institutions). In chapter 31 of the 2010 book, she hinted on mathematical issues at Gregory Clark's theory. However, in the chapter before and at many other places there are political and ad hominem attacks. Here is a collection:

'Eugenicist' Gregory Clark (McCloskey, 2010, p. 48).

A pretty close approximation of crude British racism, however, has been asserted recently by the economic historian Gregory Clark, an old friend of mine, in his *A Farewell to Alms*, modestly subtitled *A Brief Economic History of the World*. (McCloskey, 2010, p. 266).

Crude, bold, racist, eugenicist, social Darwinism, right-wing policies, Überlegenheit, compulsory sterilization. (2010, terms in chapter 30)

Steven Pinker's equally eugenic theories (McCloskey, 2010, p. 271).

Race of *Übermenschen* living in an *Übergesellschaft* (McCloskey, 2010, p. 273).

Both are cultural chauvinists, Clark of England and Landes of Western and especially northern Europe. (McCloskey, 2010, p. 273).

Flood of scathing reviews of Clark's book by economists and economic historians (McCloskey, 2010, p. 273).

I am slightly disappointed; her work and intellectual approach are so convincing and then this flood of political and ad hominem attacks. This is no shining example of bourgeois virtues! And apart from stylistic questions looking at the epistemic-scientific aspect: let us assume researcher X and his statements were eugenicist, racist, bold and crude, respectively are perceived in today's political-cultural climate of Western universities as being eugenicist, racist, bold and crude: so what? Does it mean that a statement is wrong? Maybe nature is eugenicist?

(7) McCloskey definitely has not the faintest idea on genes.

Africa's genetic diversity – all the rest of us came from merely a thousand or so Africans, on account of the 'founder effect,' as the population geneticists call the falling away of lineages in small populations – implies that when over the next fifty years or so Africa acquires a European standard of living, it is going to dominate world culture, producing ten Mozarts and twenty Einsteins. (McCloskey, 2010, p. 437)

There is the wrong assertion that genetic diversity is crucial for human accomplishment. There is no behavioural or other human genetic study supporting this. Of course, consanguinity is harmful, but insofar as it is avoided there is no gain from diversity. Hybrid vigour is only relevant for the first filial generation of offspring. The exceptional accomplishment of genetically more homogenous Ashkenazi Jews is the best example (Cochran & Harpending, 2009). What only counts is having the right genes, e.g. against certain infectious diseases. Second, the assumption that wealth is a precondition for exceptional accomplishment is wrong. Mozart and Einstein were raised in above average conditions of their time, but Mozart frequently suffered from poverty, and of course, above average conditions of their time equate to as living conditions seen as unacceptable today. One single, but informative, measure: it is reported that Albert Einstein's height was only 1.75 m and Mozart's 1.63 m. The male averages today in Germany and Austria are 1.79m – height is a good indicator of long-term wealth (Chapter 2.1).

All these critical points do not weaken McCloskey's core message – the burgher world is an important psychological, societal and cultural precondition for a successful and modern society.

### 14.2.12   Interplay of Cognitive Psychogenesis and Sociogenesis (Georg Oesterdiekhoff)

Georg Oesterdiekhoff is a German sociologist who developed an ingenious theory based on the works of Norbert Elias, a German sociologist, and Jean Piaget, a French developmental psychologist. The core idea is that the historical development of psyche and society are entangled (Oesterdiekhoff, 2007–2014): *psychogenesis* (individual and historical development of thinking, behaviour and personality) and *sociogenesis* (historical development of institutions, of politics, the economy, of culture) influence each other. This model follows the idea of a civilisation process (Elias, 2000/1939), but unlike Elias' idea it was not mainly manners that developed, but the ability to think. The concept of intelligence follows the developmental and qualitative approach of Piaget (e.g. 2001/1947). Unlike Piaget, no psychological uniformity across time is assumed, but a variability according to environmental conditions; for recent centuries, an upward trend is observed.

Cognitive development in a historical scale can be compared to cognitive development in youth. Just as young children think in preoperational cognitive stages, the majority of adults in the Middle Ages thought in preoperational cognitive stages, and in cross-cultural comparison people of premodern societies usually think in a similar way. This can be proved by typical thinking patterns; the evidence is broad and strong (e.g. Animism; Hallpike, 1980; LePan, 1989; Lévy-Bruhl, 1923/1922; Luria, 1976/1974).

Cognitive ability has a transformative effect on society, on institutions, the law, development and respect for human rights, on production and the economy, on innovation, science, wealth, culture and philosophy. Piaget himself has performed a study on cognitive effects on science (Piaget & Garcia, 1989/ 1983). Habermas (1984/1981) – as one example of philosophers – has applied Piaget's theory to explain cognitive-instrumental, ethical-practical and aesthetical rationalisation processes of the West. Similarly, as in individual development morality depends on cognitive ability, in history rule of law depends on cognitive ability.

Society, culture and physical environment, e.g. via books, education and modernisation, have an effect on cognitive development.

Oesterdiekhoff has developed and empirically substantiated this theory in numerous German books and in several English journal articles. There is a close relation to the FLynn effect research; however, Oesterdiekhoff's approach is much broader, analysing historical cognitive development back to the ancient world (e.g. arena games in the Roman Empire; Oesterdiekhoff, 2009a) and premodern Indigenous people (e.g. Animism; Oesterdiekhoff, 2012b, 2012c). Unlike James Flynn, Oesterdiekhoff assumes no mere test result changes but substantive cognitive development. He follows a qualitative approach similar to Jean Piaget, not by doing experiments, but instead by analysing reports on behaviour and thinking or analysing artefacts (e.g. Section 4.4.3). The main thrust is on historical development but the approach is also usable for cross-cultural comparisons.

*Genetic explanations* are not chosen and are rejected; however, they can be added because they would not contradict the historical development theory: either as an evolution of cognitive ability in the last millennia (e.g. Clark, 2007; Cochran & Harpending, 2009; Frost, 2010; Unz, 1981; see Section 10.7.3) or as a further cause of cross-cultural differences. *Religion* or *worldview* are less seen as a cause or an obstacle for development (as by Harrison or me) but as a dependent variable and an indicator of cognitive development. *Numbers* are not presented, not for historical development and not for cross-cultural comparisons. However, it would be possible to estimate them based on cognitive analyses of everyday life and single cross-cultural studies, e.g. as percentages of adults at the concrete operational or formal operational stage, as mean ages achieving the formal operational stage or as transformed values into IQ (see Section 3.2.3).

The strength of this approach is deepening our understanding of cognitive ability and its consequences for everyday life, society and culture. Oesterdiekhoff has produced a sophisticated and unmatched scientific oeuvre with many links to the social sciences, humanities and philosophy. It can be combined with other approaches and it may serve as a global model.

Finally, it could be asked *why is this research not more well-known in the sciences or in the public*? First, the general political concerns may have an adverse impact. Assuming different cognitive levels for the past and present can find some acceptance (even among the left, see Habermas), but not assuming different cognitive levels for present-day cultures, at least not among the left or the 'sensitive'. E.g. Africans, Arabs or Inuit were on average less cognitively developed compared to Europeans, Japanese or Vietnamese.

Second, Oesterdiekhoff follows a classical scholarly approach, reading hundreds of books and thousands of single chapters and journal articles. He does not collect data (but neither do Hanushek, Woessmann, McCloskey, Landes etc.). Today's standard approach among scientists is to apply for grants, to do some research projects, to organise the staff, cooperate with similar scientists, write and read about 20 to 100 emails per day and ask and answer small questions. There is simply no time for reading thick books. Historical, cultural and philosophical knowledge is declining and intellectual dwarfism is spreading. Intellectual dwarfism combined with political opinionism do not create a favourable environment. Counterparts being able to discuss such research at an appropriate level are becoming rare.

Third, there are no numbers presented that are usable for statistical analyses prevailing in economics or psychology. Fourth, the major works were published in German; however, Piaget's, Hallpike's, LePan's and some works of Oesterdiekhoff were published in English. Fifth, it takes a little getting used to the peculiarities of the key player. Nietzsche (*Ecce homo*: 'Why I write such excellent books') was humble compared to him and Schopenhauer easy-going. However, unlike Kant, Hegel or Heidegger his works are readable.

### 14.2.13   Integrative Model: Evolution and Culture as Background Determinants, Cognitive Ability and Institutions as Crucial Intervening Factors and The Burgher World as the Societal and Ideological Frame, All Combined in a Reciprocal Network

Research can be linked to the many strengths of the aforementioned approaches: their theoretical developments, their collected data, their methods of analysis, their results. Our own core result is that cultural and evolutionary factors work via education, cognitive ability and intellectual classes on institutions, improving government effectiveness, economic freedom and rule of law, leading to higher productivity and income and finally to higher wealth. The same background factors of culture and evolution also work via education, cognitive ability and intellectual classes on a positive development of politics with rule of law, liberty, democracy and equality. Reciprocal effects across time may lead to an upward or downward trend. For the twenty-first century, a narrowing of gaps in ability and income is predicted (developing countries catch up), a further rise of East Asia and Eastern Europe and a decline for Central and Western Europe.

Quantitative methods, in particular, were used. Qualitative methods were supplementally applied. Path models checked dependencies controlled for further factors. Research, methods and results from different paradigms were considered. Questioning was not restricted by political criteria, but tried to follow epistemic rationality: the rules of logic, of empirical work and of argumentation.

Is it possible, based on the results of research, to develop suggestions for an improved future development?

## 14.3   What Can Be Done: Human Capital Policies and Burgher World

Cognitive ability is *embedded* in a network of behavioural, attitudinal, institutional, ethical and cultural attributes. Ability depends on those attributes and creates them. In particular, cultural orientations which create a more or less supportive environment for cognitive development in families, neighbourhoods, schools and institutions are crucial. Thus any single or technical reform as an improvement in instruction or the introduction of cognitive training may have some effect, but such effects will not be sustainable if the broader societal, political and cultural background is not modified too. Therefore, suggestions have to go beyond typical narrower reform ideas.

Additionally, do not the high correlations with evolutionary factors at the level of individuals as well as at the level of nations limit any change? Yes and no. It is true, they make changes in patterns rather improbable, but they do not obstruct large mean improvements as has been shown at the individual level by adoption and at the national level by FLynn effects.

As a consequence of the embeddedness of cognitive ability in a network of behavioural, attitudinal, institutional, ethical and cultural attributes best described by the concept of '*burgher-civic world*', this world should be promoted by a broader, sustainable long-term approach and this world in the long run would be promoted by successful cognitive enhancement programmes. It should be borne in mind that the last centuries' cognitive, technological, social and cultural modernisation processes were an extremely exceptional phenomenon of history. They can be maintained only under favourable circumstances. Human capital policy is broad and is more than mere IQ change.

Many reform programmes such as the No Child Left Behind Act in the United States are driven by huge optimism and a strategic overestimation of possible effects: *feasibility illusions* lead to unrealistic goals, ending in delusions and deceptions. Weaker groups, in particular, may feel forced to accomplish the prescribed goals by any means. 'Weaker groups' means groups with lower levels in student achievement, tests and general intelligence, frequently accompanied by lower compliance to burgher behaviour and burgher-civic norms.

One example is the *Atlanta Public Schools Cheating Scandal* in the first decade of the twenty-first century: for the local African American community – students as well as teachers and education administrators – the decreed standards were simply too high.[3] An *ethical-political zeitgeist pressure* to think all is changeable and that no specific limits exist left the persons involved, from the leading politicians to the teachers in the classroom, no other choice than to think and communicate in this way. However, while the politicians were celebrated for their encouraging and glorious plans, the local teachers, who were obligated to fulfil them and to communicate 'mission accomplished' and who had done it in the possible way, were punished. Within prevailing science, a public communication of any reference to background factors and

---

[3] Sources e.g. https://en.wikipedia.org/wiki/Atlanta_Public_Schools_cheating_scandal, https://en.wikipedia.org/wiki/Beverly_Hall, and further listed original sources there. 'An investigation by the Georgia Bureau of Investigation (GBI) released in July 2011 found that 44 out of 56 schools cheated ... 178 teachers and principals were found to have corrected answers entered by students.'

their limiting effects is seen as socially indecent. False consciousness is reinforced in a circle between society and science. Society selects and encourages the production of certain 'scientific' statements stabilising ideology and false consciousness (also see Section 4.4.3).

Another example demonstrating the limits is the *Perry Preschool Project*: in the scientific and broader public many positive results are communicated. Yes, there are, in fact, large positive impacts such as better student achievement, less crime, less necessity for income support, fewer out of wedlock births. However, a male arrest rate of 82 per cent at age 40 (vs. no preschool group: 95 per cent), a male violent crime rate of 51 per cent (vs. 62 per cent), a male property crime rate of 48 per cent (vs. 72 per cent), an average number of 32 months in prison for males (vs. 53), a high school graduation rate of 68 per cent (vs. 55 per cent) and a social services reception rate of 71 per cent (vs. 86 per cent) until age 40 in the successful programme group (Nores et al., 2005) are still shocking! A modern, peaceful, co-operative and civil society cannot be built on such a basis.

Programmes are successful – but only within given bounds.

### 14.3.1   Health

Bio-psychological health is the basic prerequisite for cognitive development and the preservation or even increase of an achieved level during adulthood. For children, *nothing more has to be done than every caring parent would do.* Because not every parent can do it, support, guidelines and control are necessary for a minority of not well cared for, neglected or maltreated children. There should be information campaigns on the negative effects of smoking and alcohol consumption during pregnancy for the child; additionally, it has to be outlawed. New-borns have to visit the doctor weekly, on an obligatory basis, infants every month, children twice a year, a whole-body examination with and without parents (to check for child abuse), inoculations have to be mandatory. Public programmes should promote breastfeeding; for others baby food should be given for free. Mothers should receive information on how to prepare food and how children have to be fed and educated. Parasite load has to be controlled. Health care for the pregnant and for children has to be free. This will all especially help disadvantaged children (disadvantaged due to different factors from nature to nurture).

Kindergarten and school should provide healthy food (with milk, fruits, vegetables, some meat) for free. In poor countries, this also increases school attendance, especially if pupils can take home food for their family. Medical care should be located in or near to schools. In the future, neuro-enhancement may be an effective additional tool, especially for the less advanced. While genetic improvement is up to now merely futuristic, harm for children caused by marriage among relatives can be avoided: Cousin-cousin and uncle-niece relations should be branded as outdated. Marriages among relatives should be prohibited and married relatives and their families excluded from immigration.

*Advantages*: health policies will show nearly no effects for those already observing all standard health guidelines, but large positive effects for everyone else. Health policies will reduce the handicaps of disadvantaged groups and contribute to gap narrowing. The vast majority of interventions will be cheap. Health policies can be introduced by politics.

*Disadvantages*: mandatory health policies will create some opposition among a small minority of semi-educated persons and among very religious or libertarian persons. There will be a minor loss of liberty for the majority in favour of a minority to be cared for. There will be some opposition against inoculations. The health topic is prone to ideology. Just as the use of seatbelts in rare cases will cause harm, some will suffer from inoculation. Information campaigns should support health regulations. The topic of marriage among relatives has a cultural aspect. But culture is nothing sacred and needs some change too (cf. Harrison, 2006). Health is too important to be excluded due to cultural sensitivity. Health policy has to quickly adopt new scientifically valid information.

*Summary*: health policies are cheap and effective and easy to change by governmental decisions and especially support disadvantaged children. Highly recommended!

### 14.3.2    Family Environment

The variable correlating highest with children's cognitive ability is parental education. Genetic and environmental effects are combined here. Nevertheless, there is clear evidence for environmental effects as children's intelligence increases through adoption. In detail, which parental factors are relevant and should be supported? Compared to health more can be done than fulfilling basic requirements: parents should form a stable couple and should be married. Parents should talk a lot with their child using understandable, but different, words in an appropriate long and complex sentence structure. Parents should read to the child. Books should be bought or lent and given to the child for reading. Authoritative parenting – structure and norms accompanied by warmth and support – helps children to develop. Public or private organisations can offer information campaigns on child education, a mandatory parent course or, for parents in need, consultation and training programmes (e.g. the parental training programme Triple P). Of course, child abuse has to be controlled. As cross-cultural studies show, strict and authoritarian education is less harmful than a permissive and neglectful one.

Certain leisure time activities from general health behaviour (sports) to intellectual stimulation support the development of interests and ability (e.g. attending museums).

*Choose Social Environment for Ability Level* Parents can create a supportive environment within their family and select a supportive one in their neighbourhood and in the schools their children attend. The intelligence of others makes people smart; their behaviour and values influence others. Thus a selection of residence according to the attributes of the people living there is important. For instance, the University of Michigan psychologist Richard Nisbett (2009, p. 183) recommended:

'Try to steer your child toward peers who will promote intellectual interests.'

Usually this happens incidentally, by coincidental similarities in interests, jobs, activities, habits and wealth. More difficult for politics is to care for an appropriate composition of milieus. Singapore established a quite successful quota system of ethnicities. Poorer and less-educated groups, in particular, would benefit from a quota system.

*Advantages*: all suggestions deal with behaviour that well-educated and caring parents show anyway and thus an implementation of those suggestions will show only small effects for their children. Campaigns will have more impact for children of disadvantaged families and thus reduce disparities. Suggestions are cheap and effective.

*Disadvantages*: mandatory requirements will create some opposition. Suggestions such as selection of a beneficial social environment exclude less supportive groups from their contact with more burgher-civic well-educated groups. Such suggestions are usually not publicly communicated. People simply behave so without making a fuss. However, the principal duty of parents is to care for their children and their development. But politics can support the development of less advantaged children through (sometimes mandatory) health and education policies.

*Summary*: individually effective and within all standard norms. Politically more difficult but recommended!

### 14.3.3 Formal Education

Formal education happens in the *classroom* by instruction (teaching, mainly cognitive) and education ('Erziehung', meaning behavioural, motivational and value-focused education) and is embedded in an *educational system* responsible, e.g., for the existence of central exams. Formal education has effects on cognitive ability, personality and attitudes and entails far-reaching consequences for economic performance, politics and national wellbeing. However, school education does not change rank differences between groups and individuals. Sometimes it reduces them.

The most important suggestions are briefly described.

*Longer and Higher Education for More People*    The amount of education – how long and how many of an age cohort attend school and the percentage of persons with secondary education – is the highest and most robust correlating educational variable with national ability. Individual level studies also show extremely high correlations between education and cognitive ability. As usual, bi-directional effects are shown; natural experiment and longitudinal designs show positive effects of education on ability. The consequence is clear: extend education! Longer education for more people leading to higher degrees. But education without effects, mainly cognitive ones, will not show positive consequences for society, but negative ones – it costs a lot and reduces the size of the workforce. Therefore, any reasonable educational extension has to be an extension of effective education.

More education during lifetime also means education at a younger age (preschool, see next point) and all-day schooling, which also reduces crime because youths are supervised in the afternoon (especially relevant for crime-prone groups; Blau & Currie, 2006). It means more teaching hours (note: internationally weak evidence) and also education for adults (yet no international evidence). Weaker students and students from families with lower educational levels, in particular, need more support from more school hours and additional lessons ('private coaching').

The argument is simple; more brings more, especially at a younger age. But it does not mean that all have to attend college and university; vocational training combined with general school education is also a very valuable education.

*Advantages*: education is effective and shows more than mere cognitive effects; it has a surplus for the economy, politics and society. To have knowledge and to be well-educated is an aim in itself.

*Disadvantages*: more education is costly and has diminishing returns. There is a reasonable upper limit. More education for weaker students together with stronger ones slows down the progress of the stronger ones (their ability level is crucial for society). Instruction, its aims and the exams can be too demanding, leading to anxiety, frustration and dropout or institutional fraud. Therefore, any additional education has to be adapted to given ability levels and streamed. Lifelong learning and vocational training are good examples.

*Summary*: costly extension of education is effective but has to be evaluated for its effects and has to be tailored to students' abilities and societies' needs. Recommended!

*Preschool Education*   Preschool education is the educational variable with the second highest correlation with national ability levels. Within-country studies with children from less-educated families and with average samples back positive preschool effects. In the long run, intelligence effects are fading out, but they are more than substituted by maintained positive effects on school career and general behaviour. There is no other suggestion possible as to recommend for all children education at an earlier age. It should be free of charge. It is especially important for children with special needs, e.g. for immigrants, if they do not know the language, for children with developmental problems, for children from families with low educational background. For these groups, preschool education should be compulsory from age two onwards.

*Advantages*: preschool education is highly effective and shows large returns on investment. It not only has cognitive effects but also a kind of broader 'burgher' effect: less crime, less living on welfare, fewer teenage pregnancies, less single motherhood, more homeownership etc. Additionally, both parents can work, which increases their and society's income. Parents' burden is lightened.

*Disadvantages*: early outside-family education (crèche) can accompany some negative side effects such as more behavioural problems. Smaller groups, training rules for behaviour in preschool and better qualification of kindergarten teachers can help here. Preschool education is costly – small groups are needed. Early childhood comes under state control with possibly intended political influence. Some parents want to educate their children only by themselves.

*Summary*: preschool education is highly effective, especially for disadvantaged children. Highly recommended!

### Discipline: Behavioural, Motivational and Value-Focused

*Education*   Discipline education as an achievement-oriented and value-based structure is important because it is supportive for teaching and its cognitive outcomes and because it has a broader positive personality effect. Self-regulation and self-discipline have to be learnt, also behaviour and values; interests and motivation should be stimulated. They all have to be orientated towards legitimate values.

What does this mean in detail? Rules have to be established, communicated and their fulfilment monitored, including applying appropriate consequences. Teachers should make yearly home visits: if necessary, e.g. in the case of truancy or classroom disturbance, more frequently. Teachers benefit from training in classroom management, parents in parenting, students in social behaviour. If problems cannot be solved in regular schools, special needs students have to attend special programmes, youth centres or educational correction centres. Schools and teachers and the general educational system need support from the law and courts, police and the judicial system and from a cultural climate of law-abidingness. Discipline education has broader effects and is connected to cultural values. As Carneiro and Heckman (2003, p. 147) wrote, discipline has a connection to 'middle-class values', what we coin as the burgher-civic world:

[A] more active social-policy approach would include mentoring programs and stricter enforcement of discipline in the schools ... Such interventions would benefit the child and the larger society but at the same time might conflict with widely held values of sanctity of the family for those families that undervalue self-discipline and motivation and resent the imposition of what are perceived as middle-class values on their children.

*Advantages*: discipline education is indispensable and effective. It not only helps the single student, but also peers, teachers and parents. It has not only cognitive but also broader personality effects.

*Disadvantages*: discipline can be misused for ethically unjustifiable aims and done in an unjustifiable way (e.g. in Nazi, Socialist and Islamist regimes). Discipline education can mean only submission. Discipline education has for many – more progressive persons – a negative flavour and may therefore evoke opposition. Public information campaigns on what discipline is and what it is not are necessary.

*Summary*: discipline education in an appropriate value-orientated way to focus on learning self-regulation and self-discipline is highly recommended!

### *Central and Objective Exams Covering Important Abilities and Contents at Appropriate Difficulty Levels*

There is overwhelming evidence for positive ability effects of central and objective exams – internationally, within the United States, in Canada and in Germany (Section 10.5.2). However, exams have to focus on relevant content and competences (not only memorising) and have to be at an appropriate difficulty level, increasing from easy to difficult tasks. The results of central exams have to be used in competence-based selection processes, and fraud has to be prevented. An example could be the CITO (Cito Eindtoets Basisonderwijs) in The Netherlands. Periodical objective achievement tests should prepare students and provide teachers with feedback.

*Advantages*: central exams are a cheap and effective method for stimulating learning. They not only change students' but also teachers' behaviour. In central exams, neither school type nor private or public, and not any school brand, count but individual competence. The system is highly fair.

*Disadvantages*: there are some negative side effects: central exams may support a costly test coaching industry. Students may learn and teachers may teach only for the exam. If exams do not cover important content, the learning process would not be reasonable. Because instruction and learning also depend on the quality of peers and teachers, school selection becomes more important. Social filtering may become more stressed. Form on the day becomes more important. This can be compensated by offering free preparation courses for all and by the possibility of repeating an exam. Groups with lower outcomes will oppose. They will make allegations of 'discrimination' by tests. However, all will be offered the chance to repeat an exam.

*Summary*: central exams organised in an appropriate way (covering important contents and abilities at appropriate difficulty levels, free preparation courses for all, repeatable, accessible for all students from all schools, free or at low prices) are cheap, fair and effective. Highly recommended!

*Competence-Based Open Tracking at a Young Age*   In international comparisons, school systems with earlier tracking show better achievement results than systems with late tracking (Section 10.5.2). Tracking should be competence-based on objective tests and not fix the achievable final degree, which should be determined by the result of open central exams. School attendance and school leaving certificates should be separated, as should teaching and competence measurement. There are different ways to come to identical school degrees. Individual achievement has to count, not school brand.

In a tracked school system, teaching is easier for instructors; weaker students are not overchallenged and stronger students are not unchallenged. Before tracking begins and before central exams students learn more, and teachers are motivated to instruct and support. Highly gifted, above average and motivated students, who are, as adults, relevant for innovation and management and who are especially important for the economy, politics, society, research and culture, learn more and develop better in a tracked school system.

*Advantages*: combined with central exams a tracked system is highly fair; it stimulates teaching and competence development. Self-esteem of weaker students is not damaged by comparison with better students. Tracking is especially important for the relevant group of above-average students. Tracking is supportive for the children of well-educated but not rich parents, for the smart among the poor. The rich could attend private schools anyway.

*Disadvantages*: weaker students do not have a model of stronger classmates. Schools with many low ability students may become problem schools. Politics dealing with housing and demographics can reduce the emergence of such problems. Early tracking could fix the achievable final degree at a too young age. Tracking and educational qualifications have to be separated. Social filtering is amplified; ability gaps increase. However, ability gaps due to larger increases of the more able students are ethically not problematic. By attending high ability schools the self-concept of the gifted can suffer. Groups with lower ability may oppose. Further support from health policies to preschool, discipline and cognitive training programmes are tailored for the competence development of weaker students.

*Summary*: early tracking is effective, but can have negative side effects. Therefore, early tracking has to be competence-based according to results in objective and central exams, should be formally independent from the achievable final degree and has to be flexible. Recommended and very important for the gifted!

*Direct Instruction*    Direct instruction is an effective teaching method. It should be combined with periods of self-directed and group learning.

*Advantages*: direct instruction delivers knowledge in a time-efficient way. It is especially helpful for weaker students.

*Disadvantages*: as a single method direct instruction does not sufficiently stimulate problem-solving, thinking and cooperation. Direct instruction should not be combined with an authoritarian attitude towards knowledge. Knowledge is something which needs individual thinking and verification.

*Summary*: direct instruction as a highly effective teaching method combined with other methods is recommended. For older and more competent students somewhat more time can be assigned to self- and group learning. Recommended!

*Teacher Quality*    Of course, better teachers are better teachers – but what are their attributes, how they can be found and trained? That is the main problem and all possible suggestions are not unequivocally supported by research. Basic conditions are good educational degrees (knowing the content a teacher should teach is certainly helpful), psychological health, a high intelligence level, social and emotional competence. Higher salary and reputation can attract persons with such attributes to become a teacher. Evaluations of teaching competence can be used. Teacher education has to focus on the mastery of the content, of teaching and of class management.

*Advantages*: teacher quality is essential and the focus on competence in teacher education and teacher selection is not costly.

*Disadvantages*: salary rises are costly and do not address the problem of existing weak teachers. Evaluation of teachers and dismissal of weaker ones create political problems and (understandably) conflicts with teacher unions (see, for example, Mexico). Teacher quality is difficult to measure. Merit-based systems may stimulate fraud. Countries may run out of qualified teachers and officials.

*Summary*: teacher quality is important but difficult to determine. The usual method is to look for good educational degrees of candidates; additionally, psychological health, cognitive ability, teaching abilities and social competence should be evaluated. Recommended.

*School Autonomy, Private School and Competition*   School autonomy in teacher selection, to a certain degree in curriculum and teaching material and combined with central exams and public funding, is effective. Additionally, it saves money. A private school is a form of school autonomy.

*Advantages*: school autonomy and private schools stimulate competition and quality.

*Disadvantages*: school autonomy can increase quality differences between schools and social stratification processes. A system is necessary to objectively measure and communicate school quality.

*Summary*: school autonomy combined with central exams and public funding is recommended.

*Intellectual Class Education*   Support for the development of 'talents' and 'the gifted', of 'highly able' students is essential for the development of a society. Pritchett and Viarengo (2009, p. 84) recommended for developing countries in particular the search for talents and better education of top performers:

'An effective development strategy would not simply raise the average schooling levels of the population, but would rather enhance the top.'

One method is competence-based early tracking (see earlier), others are acceleration, enrichment and mentoring (e.g. Hattie, 2009). Programmes should be addressed to both conventional above average students and the small minority of highly able students. Access should be based on objective test measures – to detect high potential and to avoid self-selection purely based on parental ambitions (albeit such ambitions are helpful).

*Advantages*: programmes are effective and the supported group is important. There are large returns on investment.

*Disadvantages*: in Western countries, there is some politically motivated opposition against programmes for the gifted ('elitist' etc.). Any additional offer costs money. Classes for the gifted are frequently small and expensive. The more selective the selection process and the programme the smaller is the potential group. Larger cities can better offer such programmes. According to the difference principle (Rawls, 1999/1971), such expenses are well justified because they indirectly – by societal effects – also benefit the less advantaged pupils.

*Summary*: intellectual class education comes in many variants. Programmes should be addressed to conventional above average and highly gifted students. For instance, early tracking, acceleration and enrichment show positive effects. Intellectual classes are crucial for the future of society and any developmental support for them shows large positive side effects for other groups. Highly recommended!

*Content and Thinking*   Special suggestions on content are not really backed by empirical research (e.g. 'mathematics being more stimulating than

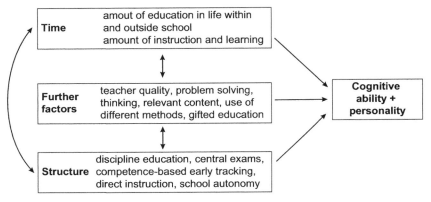

Figure 14.1 Summary on education

history'). Methods of instruction and testing especially relying on thinking, like problem-solving teaching and comprehensive learning, are somewhat effective, but there is no such evidence from international comparisons. Mere rote learning is less effective but not totally useless. The applicable instructional methods also depend on students' abilities. There is not one single good method. Content taught at school needs less a cognitive justification ('supports intelligence') than a justification based on value-orientated concepts ('Bildungstheorie'). E.g. receiving instruction in music and art or in history and geography is important in itself. Mathematics and language are important in themselves and functional for later success at a job and in life.

*Summary*: good teaching uses various methods from direct instruction to problem-solving. Content needs a value-orientated justification. Content is in itself important.

*Summary on School Education*    The two most important factors are invested *time in education and learning* from early childhood on and *achievement-oriented structure*, surrounded by further factors such as teacher quality, problem-solving and thinking in instruction and learning (Figure 14.1). They are interdependent, as discipline increases time on tasks, higher education increases teacher quality longitudinally in a society and relevant content tested in central exams shows positive effects on cognitive development and later institutional quality.

### 14.3.4  Cognitive Training

School education is already cognitive training. But special cognitive training programmes such as Klauer's reasoning training are shorter and very effective.

Because usually weaker students benefit more, training programmes help to reduce gaps. They show not only positive and lasting effects on IQ tests and intelligence but also on school achievement, attentional behaviour and language competences. Thinking makes smart!

*Advantages*: cognitive training programmes are cheap, short and effective.

*Disadvantages*: training programmes need time taken away from instruction in other subjects such as mathematics or history. However, a programme such as Klauer's only needs ten hours and shows transfer effects on academic learning. Trainers or teachers need to be educated in carrying out the training. Not all training programmes are equally effective.

*Summary*: cognitive training programmes are cheap and effective. Highly recommended!

### 14.3.5   Welfare Policies

Up to now we have focused on health and educational policies. Human capital, especially cognitive ability, is nurtured by these well-established means. Because ability and its development are embedded in a societal and cultural net we now broaden the perspective. The welfare system is relevant in different ways: it should ensure for disadvantaged persons, especially children, disadvantaged due to various causes from nature to nurture, society to culture, family to neighbourhoods, the possibility of *healthy development* and a *humane life*. It should support a *return to autonomous living* on one's own work and *resources. It should defend a peaceful and meritoric burgher-civic society.*

However, common welfare programmes show not only positive consequences. Welfare policies are usually not addressed to the typical citizen (who bear the costs). Functionality and progress of society, interests of typical citizens and interests of groups and persons, living on the work of others, have to be balanced. The possibility of living on welfare without one's own work can erode society and culture. For decades, welfare expenses have been continuously rising. They increase governmental spending ratios with all its negative effects on national cognitive development, economic growth and society.

To attain the positive aims of welfare policies, schools, youth welfare and health care have to be brought together (e.g. as in Finland). Welfare should be limited in time (e.g. Clinton's reforms in the United States) and in volume, also considering past achievement to society and include as a condition service in return. Obligations should be regular school attendance, acceptable achievement at schools and going to work. Generally, kindergarten and school attendance, health service and school lunch have to be free, as they are especially supportive for the poor.

*Advantages*: a specific form of binding, motivating and limited welfare policies supports healthy development, return to autonomous living and the maintenance of a meritoric burgher-civic society.

*Disadvantages*: welfare costs are very high. In Western societies, standard welfare policies frequently bolster the development of a stable underclass living across generations on welfare. Welfare attracts 'welfare migration'. Current welfare policies are not sustainable. Any reform or preservation of given policies will cause severe political and social problems (see e.g. Perkins, 2016), including possible conflicts with religious convictions.[4] What is to be done with persons not giving the appropriate services in return?

*Summary*: welfare policies for children are indispensable and have to be organised in an effective way. Meritoric reforms are indispensable and highly recommended.

### 14.3.6   Demographic Policies

Human capital, welfare and demographic policies are interlocked. Parents transmit abilities and attitudes to their children. Of course, there is no perfect correlation and also neighbourhoods, peers, schools, teachers, training programmes, society, people's own decisions and chance factors influence one's life. The more people within a country with average to high human capital, the wealthier the country will be, the easier will be progress in different fields, the lower will be the crime rates, the more equal and peaceful its society will be, the better will be the situation of the remaining poor. People benefit from the attributes of others in their family, neighbourhood and society. *Demography is destiny*.

Similar to climate policies, a value-oriented demographic policy implies having a long-term perspective. However, modern democracies are usually not oriented towards long-ranging aims. And even if they were, the success of demographic policies is not certain. A famous old example is the intention of emperor Augustus to increase marriages and birth rates among Roman citizens by the Lex Iulia et Papia and the Lex Papia Poppaea (18 BC and 9 AD). The reforms had only a few effects. Nevertheless, the modern state is implementing, by welfare policies, an 'effective' demographic policy through enabling the relatively poor and less educated to benefit from having more children. The old Western European marriage pattern (Hajnal, 1965), that only those have a family who can stand on their own two feet, was abolished.

What can politics do? One means is *family tax splitting* – the more children a family has, the lower will be their taxes. The richer (and indirectly the higher

---

[4] However, from the Pauline epistles, 'If anyone is not willing to work, let him not eat.' (2 Thessalonians 3,10)

the human capital), the more a family benefits from having more children. This would help to compensate the large opportunity costs, especially for well-educated women, of having a child or several children. Leon Battista Alberti recommended awarding *bequests only to those children who have their own children*. Such wills have to be allowed by the law. The welfare system should *focus less on the redistribution of income* but on *increasing support systems* such as the health system, schools including all-day care and food and training programmes. Crèche, kindergarten, full-time school and after-school care centres should offer the possibility of full-time child care, facilitating fathers and mothers to work. Additionally, some children are better educated by these institutions. Total welfare sums per family have to have an upper limit imposed (one-child policy for families living on the means of others); past contribution to society should be considered. *University students* having their own children should be supported. For instance, in the former GDR many university students had children because having children meant receiving benefits such as living in one's own apartment. After the German reunification these advantages were stopped and the number of children among students collapsed (Starke, 2007). Adults having children, especially women, should be supported in the job market (*affirmative action for parents*).

*Advantages*: explicit and implicit demographic policies are decisive for every society. Their effects will be huge on the wellbeing and future of societies.

*Disadvantages*: it is difficult to achieve intended demographic effects. There will be opposition from media and interest groups. Opponents will stress ideological conflicts. Proponents will be defamed. Politicians may be forced to rebrand aims and strategies. Family tax splitting reduces taxes. Children related tax benefits are higher for the rich – but for the poor there is institutional support and in the long run particularly the poor will benefit from demographic policy. It is not possible to beat demography. Demography cannot be escaped by ignoring it. Either the present policies will cause the predicted negative outcomes or changed policies will entail long-term positive consequences.

*Summary*: successful value-oriented demographic policies are difficult to implement but are vital to support a positive long-term development of society.

### 14.3.7   Immigration and Emigration

Immigration and emigration policies are one element of demographic policies. However, their effect is much more fast-acting and, depending on number, significantly larger. Within a few decades a society can be changed by immigration, as in the examples of the Americas, New Zealand and Palestine or currently cities in many Western European countries show (e.g. Birmingham, Brussels, banlieues of Paris or with other demographic background on Mediterranean coasts). Depending on country of origin, selection policies and the receiving country, there can be large ability gaps between different immigrant groups and between natives and immigrants (Section 10.3.5). Levels, Dronkers and Kraaykamp (2008, p. 850) summarised this pattern of results and connected it to a suggestion for immigration policy:

We have shown that the relatively good performance of immigrant children in Australia and New Zealand is attributable to their selective immigration laws. Our analyses thus indicate that selective immigration policies can elevate the general performance of immigrant children throughout the rest of the Western world.

Immigration policies, being explicit or implicit, are crucial. Certain immigrant groups, such as Huguenot émigrés in Prussia, Jewish scientists from National Socialist Germany in the United States or Western expats in Arabian Gulf countries had and have a clearly visible positive impact on their immigration country (Section 12.2.3).

However, in the majority of today's Western countries immigration policies lead to negative ability, income, employment and crime gaps and they do not support sustainable development.[5] While immigrants are highly rational in choosing wealthy welfare countries as destinations, immigration policies of receiving countries are highly irrational, not being based on competence and demand and on the wellbeing of their citizens.

Authors from different fields have provided various suggestions but all came to the same conclusion that the *receiving society should define who can come on what terms to benefit the receiving society*. For instance, the British economist and migration researcher Paul Collier from Oxford defined the following immigration policy criteria (Collier, 2013a, 2013b): qualification of immigrants, job market demand, cultural background (similarity to the receiving country) and need for protection. There is no human right to immigrate, but to control immigration.

The philosopher and ethicist Michael Walzer from Princeton argued that a receiving country has the right to choose immigrants, including refugees and their numbers according to its own criteria such as functional ones or for identity and culture ('collective right of admission and refusal'; Walzer, 1983, p. 44). Similarly, the aforementioned Paul Collier (2013b):

The control of immigration is a human right. ... The right to control immigration is asserted by all societies. You do not have the automatic right to move to Kuwait; nor do the Chinese have the automatic right to move to Angola.

---

[5] Native-immigrant gaps in ability, e.g. for Scandinavia 7 IQ, Central Europe 7 IQ (Table 10.2). No negative crime gap for the United States (e.g. Roth, 2014/2010, p. 360).

Also, according to George Borjas (2001/1999) from Harvard, immigration has to be oriented towards the wellbeing of the native population.[6] In the past, all successful immigrant countries controlled immigration: for instance, Prussia after the Thirty Years' War preferred skilled Huguenot workers; unskilled Huguenot workers were refused entry (Hornung, 2014, p. 91). Of course, past immigrants to the United States or within Europe received no social welfare benefits, no affirmative action, nothing; nonetheless, they were highly successful (e.g. Jews in Western Europe or the United States; Laqueur, 2007). Immigrants should be excluded from welfare or only granted limited access for several years after entry (see also Collier, 2013b).

Another suggestion using economic entry criteria is made by Carneiro and Heckman (2003, p. 203):

Only skilled immigrants are permitted to enter the country. One way to do this is to sell entry visas. This would screen out the unskilled.

However, while screening immigrants for wealth ('sell entry visas') or formal education (qualifications) is a practicable procedure, it is not the best and fairest one. The furiously debated Jason Richwine (2009, pp. 3, 19ff., 124ff.) has discussed in his Harvard dissertation such functional and ethical principles in dealing with immigration. According to him, it is ethically and functionally doubtful to select for race, ethnicity, group membership or citizenship (as usual in current policies); it is also problematic to select for educational qualifications – they are difficult to compare across countries. Following his argumentation, most fair and functional for immigrants and the receiving country would be to individually select for cognitive ability, measured by a culture-reduced test:

Attracting a different kind of immigrant – the poor with great potential. .... All people should be considered purely as individuals whenever possible. (Richwine, 2009, pp. 3, 21)

Immigration policies should not only consider the working immigrant, but also his or her relatives, as Paul Collier has stressed:

---

[6] Attentive readers will have noticed that I use here a kind of 'name-dropping', to mention 'reputable' institutions of researchers. This is contradicting the epistemic rationality approach described in Section 9.1 (names, origin etc. do not count). There are two reasons for this deviation: first, in this chapter we do not deal with research itself but with political suggestions. So it is less finding truth (for which any reference is only distracting) but trying to convince others that is important. Arguments are surrounded by indicators of reputation. Second, the suggestions presented here may be perceived as diverging from ordinary mentioned opinions that are frequently communicated by media and politicians. By showing that 'luminaries' from well-known research institutions have developed the suggestions presented here, timid persons may become somewhat more inclined to consider the *argument* itself – which, of course, here too only counts.

A particularly sensitive issue is the right to bring in a prospective spouse. Indigenous citizens have the right to bring in foreign spouses but it is viable as a right only because few indigenous citizens wish to use it. It may be unreasonable to extrapolate from the largely unexercised rights of the indigenous to infer a right that would be used very frequently by immigrants. A similarly contestable extrapolation to the rights of immigrants concerns social housing and related benefits. (Collier, 2013b)

Modern societies need *meritoric immigration policies*; they are especially important for poorer immigrants and the native poor because they compete for limited support. Competent immigrants would increase a society's income possible to spend for the poor; on the other hand, immigrants with low human capital will increase welfare costs and the competition for limited means. Quite good (but not ideal) benchmark countries in immigration policies are Canada and Australia.

Immigrants should be selected by *culture-reduced tests of abilities*. If admitted but having language deficits, *mandatory language classes* have to be offered for children and adults. If there are also broad cognitive deficits – but low human capital immigration should be avoided by smart immigration policies – additionally, *cognitive training* and *compulsory education from preschool age* on should be offered. The right to residency should be based on meritoric principles, on competence, employment, no need of social welfare and succeeded integration. Naturalisation should be offered only if these criteria are successfully met. *Cultural affinity* is a further important criterion (Collier, 2013a, 2013b). Culture is nothing superficial, only dealing with spaghetti versus chopsticks. Culture guides development, achievement, political orientations and life. Individual as well as societal cognitive human capital, success and wellbeing are highly correlated to culture (Section 10.8).

Illegal, costly or criminal persons have to *remigrate on their own costs* or – if not possible – are *relegated to a third country* (e.g. politics of Australia). Immigration decisions should not be irrevocable. And because the abilities, attitudes and behaviour of people in one's neighbourhood, in a class or school, in a company or in a country, have a huge impact on the life and success of others (Jones, 2016), those others in the receiving country (its citizens) have a right to be considered in such a decision process. Merit-based *emigration policies* include immigrants across generations (*remigration*) and may in certain cases also include natives; a policy successful in the past, e.g. for Great Britain. Incentives can be used here too. Depending on qualifications and ability levels, receiving countries can benefit. For many, this can be a second chance in their life; those who are successful can be offered the opportunity to reimmigrate. *Asylum can be admitted in third countries* receiving support by the international community, e.g. in the Middle East or North Africa such as in Egypt, Morocco and Lebanon. Based on qualification and demand and observable chances of integration refugees should be offered an opportunity to immigrate. Persons granted asylum have the right to work. An *active housing policy* such as in Singapore should aim at mixing and set *maximum limits of difficult to integrate groups.*

The Columbia jurist Anu Bradford (2013) made several in-detail suggestions: immigrants or their sponsors should *deposit $50,000 into a Migration Fund*. This privately managed fund should cover risks and costs of welfare, crime and repatriation. After a certain period, for instance after the possibility of naturalisation (based on meritoric principles), it can be paid back with interest to the migrant and sponsor or parts of it can be spent to cover education and human capital loss in the country of origin. In this way, the fund removes the concern that migrants impose a cost on the destination country:

The sponsors would also have an incentive to exercise care in screening foreign labor given the need to deposit the funds under the knowledge that the funds will only be returned if the migrant is successful. (Bradford, 2013, p. 53)

A productive migrant who voluntarily returns to the source country could also reclaim the deposited funds. Finally, this should *include family members*:

In principle, the Migration Fund could apply to family-sponsored migrants in the same way. Family members could follow the migrant as long as they have a sponsor that is willing to deposit the necessary funds or invest in a larger 'Family Migration Fund.' Most likely, the employer sponsor or the migrant himself would sponsor the migrant's immediate family who are thought to contribute most to the welfare of the primary migrant. (Bradford, 2013, p. 48)

Similar suggestions (price for entry, auctions to allocate entry permits) were proposed by Gary Becker (Nobel Prize Laureate in Economics), Richard Posner (Chief Judge of the United States Court of Appeals) and Julian Simon (Professor of Economics). The idea is that *markets*, including banks, sponsors and companies, would *allocate entry permits to those who derive the greatest utility from migrating and who are therefore willing to pay the highest price for the right to migrate*. Skilled, young, healthy and productive people can pay back entrance prices of around $50,000 within a few years. This includes political refugees. This procedure would also reduce large administration costs (Becker & Posner, 2009, pp. 38–42). Allen Posner additionally suggested using IQ tests (see also Richwine, 2009). Charity organisations can support immigrants and the immigration of the poor, thus unintended costs for society and the state will be reduced. Such a non-governmental approach promises to have fewer negative side effects than public migration policies usually have (e.g. in Europe).

There are many strategies to implement a better immigration policy – they can be combined and they need to be applied!

*Advantages*: even more than general demographic policy, immigration policy is necessary for a society's beneficial human capital development, with further effects on economy, political stability and wellbeing of a nation and its people.

*Disadvantages*: as with all political reforms, changes to immigration policy are difficult to get through. Conflicts based on general worldviews and ideology cannot be avoided. Unqualified immigrants and refugees are excluded from entry. However, international agreements and transfers can support third countries to help them.

*Summary*: effective strategies to improve immigration and immigration effects are known, many researchers have presented suggestions and several successful examples are given by different countries. Political decisions are necessary. As always, effects and side effects have to be evaluated and strategies and programmes tailored. In Western countries, reforms are *urgent* and *indispensable*!

### 14.3.8    Political and Institutional Reforms

As was previously shown (Chapters 7 to 11), cognitive ability is the most important attribute of human capital and it is crucial for the emergence, functionality and maintenance of beneficial institutions such as democracy, law, liberty, government effectiveness and economic freedom. However, why not directly improve institutions with fast effects on economy, politics and society?

One suggestion close to human capital policies is competence-based selection of persons working in administration and politics. The other suggestions are less spectacular or new such as control of corruption; moderately progressive tax rates; better statistics on achievement, crime risks, production, costs and benefits; more effective political decision structures; direct democracy, including on the most important issues such as taxes, spending and immigration; free market policy. Some have suggested a competence-based suffrage – however, even now, low-educated people participate less in elections. And in important political questions there seems to be a larger rationality problem among elites than among average citizens (e.g. on immigration in Western EU countries). Family size-based vote counts (in place of voting rights for children) are possible; politicians can be screened for having their own family and own children and living on their own means independent from the state (burgher-civic lifestyle). A leader such as Hitler would have been excluded by this procedure.

*Advantages*: institutional reforms have a fast-acting effect on the development of the economy and society.

*Disadvantages*: within a broader frame, different institutional structures come to similar outcomes (e.g. within Western countries, Switzerland vs. UK). Thus their reforms and particular design seem not to be crucial; more important are general background factors and cognitive ability.

*Summary*: institutional design is relevant, even if it depends on general background factors and cognitive ability. They work through the quality of institutions, and direct reforms will have impact.

*Crime and Reasonable Compliance with Norms*   Crime is lack of reasonable compliance with norms. Norms that are themselves justified have to be obeyed. Education and intelligence have positive effects on ethical behaviour, e.g. preschool education lowers (at least among problematic groups) crime in adulthood. Crime prevention resembles the strategies for improving discipline in school: teachers, classmates and the neighbourhood have to model compliance with norms. Rules have to be set and justified, their compliance reinforced and their violation punished. Reactions have to be fast, consequent and appropriate. For violent crime, much more severe sanctions are necessary than for other forms of crime. Age of criminal responsibility, in an *appropriate way*, should start at age 6, e.g. with extra exercise and penal labour, in more extreme cases and with increasing age including attendance centres. For adults, *forced emigration and remigration* are further options. There is no human right that others have to work and pay for people who are dangerous to them.[7] There is also no human right to live in a certain country. Early intervention such as by preschool education shows large returns on investment.

*Advantages*: security is crucial for wellbeing. Crime prevention as part of general enforcement of justified rules stabilises the burgher-civic world. Internal security is a fundamental aspect of a well-governed country.

*Disadvantages*: any crime treatment has side effects, e.g. imprisonment can have a negative modelling effect, convicts learn from others, punishment leads to negative feelings towards the authority, control reduces liberty and produces costs. Effective control in a society prone to crime is not possible in a radically liberal way. A night watchman state only works in strictly self-controlled groups such as the Protestant Amish or Hutterites, including their practice of expulsion.

*Summary*: the very first recommendation is early prevention of the development of criminal careers. The second is to take the corrective means in a fast, consequent and appropriate way. Highly recommended!

### 14.3.9  Culture

A modern and sustainable society is supported by the values of the burgher-civic world: by the appreciation, education and the use of thinking, of

---

[7] An example from France for criminals and supposed dangerous persons who need to be observed in their everyday life. Per observed person and day 20 to 30 police officers are necessary, including downtimes (recovery, holidays, sickness). Assuming cautiously a total salary cost of around 3,600 Euro per police officer, this would mean per observed person and month costs of around 90,000 Euro and per year of around 1 million Euro. The press chose an actual case: around 50,000 police officers are required to control all suspected Islamists in France. To pay these 50,000 police officers, around 2 billion Euro are calculated to be spent per year in France. (Sources: www.welt.de/politik/ausland/article143296144/Islamistische-Schlaefer-ueberfordern-Frankreich.html, www.welt.de/politik/deutschland/article136493969/Warum-sich-Terroristen-so-schwer-ueberwachen-lassen.html).

knowledge and of rationality; by diligence; by the respect for order; by meritoric orientations; by a beneficial, efficient and thrifty use of resources; by rule of law; by a functional government; by autonomy and freedom; by realism and pragmatism.

Norms are reinforced by following them, by successful models, by showing their advantages and their reasonable justification. Norms have to be embedded in a net of arguments. Norms are socially reinforced by trying to convince persons to follow them, by the exclusion of persons who constantly do not follow them and by the inclusion of new members in a group who want to follow them. Norms are supported both by their gradual adaptation and by the preservation of their core.

In the field of epistemic questions – the one issue science should work on and the crucially important aspect of science for culture and politics – the orientation on rationality and argumentation has to be strengthened. We need a new enlightenment – an enlightenment in the sense of a personal, cultural and institutional orientation.

# References

Abdallah, S., Michaelson, J., Shah, S., Stoll, L. & Marks, N. (2012). *Happy Planet Index: 2012 report*. London: New Economics Foundation (NEF).

Abel, G. J. & Sander, N. (2014). Quantifying global international migration flows. *Science, 343*, 1520–1522.

Acemoglu, D. & Robinson, J. A. (2012). *Why nations fail: The origins of power, prosperity, and poverty*. New York: Crown.

Ackerman, Ph. L. & Heggestad, E. D. (1997). Intelligence, personality, and interests: Evidence for overlapping traits. *Psychological Bulletin, 121*, 219–245.

Ackerman, Ph. L., Beier, M. E. & Boyle, M. O. (2005). Working memory and intelligence: The same or different constructs? *Psychological Bulletin, 131*, 30–60.

Adams, R. & Wu, M. (2002). *PISA 2000 technical report*. Paris: OECD.

Adorno, Th. W. (2006/1951). *Minima moralia*. London: Verso.

Albert, H. (1985/1968). *Treatise on critical reason*. Princeton, NJ: Princeton University Press.

Alberti, L. B. (1969/1441). *The family in Renaissance Florence. [I libri della famiglia.]* Columbia: University of South Carolina Press.

Alesina, A. & Ferrara, E. L. (2002). Who trusts others? *Journal of Public Economics, 85*, 207–234.

Alesina, A., Devleeschauwer, A., Easterly, W., Kurlat, S. & Wacziarg, R. (2003). Fractionalization. *Journal of Economic Growth, 8*, 155–194.

Algan, Y. & Cahuc, P. (2010). Inherited trust and growth. *American Economic Review, 100*, 2060–2092.

(2014). Trust, growth, and well-being. In Ph. Aghion & S. N. Durlauf (Eds.), *Handbook of economic growth* (Volume 2A, pp. 49–120). Amsterdam: Elsevier.

Altinok, N., Diebolt, C. & De Meulemeester, J.-L. (2013). *A new international database on education quality: 1965–2010*. Metz: Working Papers, Association Francaise de Cliometrie (AFC), No. 3. Retrieved from www.cliometrie.org/images/wp/AFC_WP_03-2013.pdf.

Amadon, D. (1949). The seventy-five percent rule for subspecies. *Condor, 51*, 250–258.

Andreasen, R. O. (2004). The cladistic race concept: A defense. *Biology and Philosophy, 19*, 425–442.

Anger, S. & Heineck, G. (2008). Do smart parents raise smart children? The intergenerational transmission of cognitive abilities. *Laser Discussion Papers, 23*. Retrieved from www.laser.uni-erlangen.de/papers/paper/71.pdf.

Armor, D. J. (2003). *Maximizing intelligence.* New Brunswick, NJ: Transaction Publishers.

Armstrong, E. L. & Woodley, M. A. (2014). The rule-dependence model explains the commonalities between the Flynn effect and IQ gains via retesting. *Learning and Individual Differences, 29,* 41–49.

Arslan, R. C., Penke, L., Johnson, W., Iacono, W. G. & McGue, M. (2014). The effect of paternal age on offspring intelligence and personality when controlling for parental trait levels. *PLoS One, 9,* e90097.

Arum, R. & Roksa, J. (2011). *Academically adrift: Limited learning on college campuses.* Chicago: University of Chicago Press.

ARWU (2010). *Academic ranking of world universities (Shanghai-ranking).* Institute of Higher Education of Shanghai Jiao Tong University. Retrieved from www.arwu.org/ARWUMethodology2010.jsp.

ASDA'A Burson-Marsteller (2016). *Inside the hearts and minds of Arab youth. Arab youth survey 2016.* Dubai: ASDA'A.

Ashton, M. C. & Esses, V. M. (1999). Stereotype accuracy: Estimating the academic performance of ethnic groups. *Personality and Social Psychology Bulletin, 25,* 225–236.

Augustine (1991/400). *Confessions. [Confessiones.]* Oxford: Oxford University Press.

Autor, D. H. (2014). Skills, education, and the rise of earnings inequality among the "other 99 percent". *Science, 344,* 843–851.

Autor, D. H. & Price, B. (2013). *The changing task composition of the US labor market: An update of Autor, Levy, and Murnane (2003).* Cambridge, MA: MIT, manuscript.

Baier, D., Pfeiffer, C., Rabold, S., Simonson, J. & Kappes, C. (2010). *Kinder und Jugendliche in Deutschland: Gewalterfahrungen, Integration, Medienkonsum. [Children and youth in Germany: Exposure to violence, integration, media consumption.]* Hannover: KFN, Report Nr. 109.

Baker, J. R. (1974). *Race.* Oxford: Oxford University Press.

Baltes, P. B. (1997). On the incomplete architecture of human ontogeny. *American Psychologist, 52,* 366–380.

Barnes, P. M., Powell-Griner, E., McFann, K., & Nahin, R. L. (2004). Complementary and alternative medicine use among adults: United States, 2002. *Advance Data, 343,* 1–19.

Barnett, W. S. (1985). Benefit-cost analysis of the Perry preschool program and its policy implications. *Educational Evaluation and Policy Analysis, 7,* 333–342.

Barro, R. J. (1991). Economic growth in a cross-section of countries. *Quarterly Journal of Economics, 106,* 407–443.

Barro, R. J. & Lee, J.-W. (1993). International comparisons of educational attainment. *Journal of Monetary Economics, 32,* 363–394.

  (2000). *Barro-Lee Data Set. International data on educational attainment: Updates and implications.* Boston: Harvard University. Retrieved November 18, 2004 from www2.cid.harvard.edu/ciddata/barrolee/readme.htm.

Barton, P. E., Coley, R. J. & Wenglinsky, H. (1998). *Order in the Classroom: Violence, discipline, and student achievement.* Princeton, NJ: ETS Policy Information Center Report.

Baumeister, A. E. E., Rindermann, H. & Barnett, W. S. (2014). Crèche attendance and children's intelligence and behavior development. *Learning and Individual Differences, 30,* 1–10.

Baumert, J., Klieme, E., Neubrand, M., Prenzel, M., Schiefele, U., Schneider, W., ... & Weiß, M. (Deutsches PISA-Konsortium) (Eds.). (2001). *Pisa 2000 im internationalen Vergleich. [PISA 2000.]* Opladen: Leske & Budrich.

Baumert, J. & Lehmann, R. (1997). *TIMSS.* Opladen: Leske & Budrich.

Beals, K. L., Smith, C. L. & Dodd, S. M. (1984). Brain size, cranial morphology, climate, and time machines. *Current Anthropology, 25,* 301–330.

Beaton, A. E., Mullis, I. V. S., Martin, M. O., Gonzalez, E. J., Kelly, D. L. & Smith, T. (1996a). *Mathematics achievement in the middle school years: IEA's Third International Mathematics and Science Study (TIMSS).* Chestnut Hill, MA: TIMSS Study Center.

Beaton, A. E., Martin, M. O., Mullis, I. V. S., Gonzalez, E. J., Smith, T. & Kelly, D. L. (1996b). *Science achievement in the middle school years.* Chestnut Hill, MA: TIMSS Study Center.

Beaver, K. M. & Wright, J. P. (2011). The association between county-level IQ and county-level crime rates. *Intelligence, 39,* 22–26.

Beaver, K. M., Schwartz, J. A., Al-Ghamdi, M. S., Kobeisy, A. N., Dunkel, C. S. & van der Linden, D. (2014). A closer look at the role of parenting-related influences on verbal intelligence over the life course: Results from an adoption-based research design. *Intelligence, 46,* 179–187.

Becker, D. & Rindermann, H. (2014). Genetic distances and IQ-differences: A cross-national study. Talk at 12. December 2014 at the 15th Conference of the International Society for Intelligence Research (ISIR) in Graz, Austria.

(2016). The relationship between cross-national genetic distances and IQ-differences. *Personality and Individual Differences, 98,* 300–310.

Becker, F. (1938). Die Intelligenzprüfung unter völkischem und typologischem Gesichtspunkt. [Intelligence measurement from a national and typological point of view.] *Zeitschrift für angewandte Psychologie und Charakterkunde, 55,* 15–111.

Becker, G. S. (1993/1964). *Human capital: A theoretical and empirical analysis with special reference to education.* Chicago: University of Chicago Press.

Becker, G. S. & Becker, G. (1998). *The economics of life.* New York: McGraw.

Becker, G. S. & Posner, R. A. (2009). *Uncommon sense: Economic insights, from marriage to terrorism.* Chicago: University of Chicago Press.

Becker, M., Lüdtke, O., Trautwein, U., Köller, O. & Baumert, J. (2012). The differential effects of school tracking on psychometric intelligence. *Journal of Educational Psychology, 104,* 682–699.

Becker, S. O. & Woessmann, L. (2007). Was Weber wrong? A human capital theory of Protestant economic history. *Cesifo Working Paper No. 1987.*

(2009). Was Weber wrong? A human capital theory of Protestant economic history. *Quarterly Journal of Economics, 124,* 531–596.

Belasen, A. R. & Hafer, R. W. (2012). Well-being and economic freedom: Evidence from the States. *Intelligence, 40,* 306–316.

Benning, M. (2007). "Lasst uns über Sex reden."[Let's talk about sex.] *Die Zeit, 38.* Retrieved September 28, 2007 from http://images.zeit.de/text/2007/38/M-Aids-Malawi.

Bertoni, M., Brunello, G. & Rocco, L. (2013). *Does mental productivity decline with age? Evidence from chess players.* Bonn: IZA DP No. 7311.

Biasutti, R. (1967). *Le razze e i popoli della terra.* [*Races and peoples of the earth.*] Turin: Union Tipografico-Editrice.

Bishop, J. H. (1997). The effect of national standards and curriculum-based exams on achievement. *American Economic Review, 87,* 260–264.

(2006). Drinking from the fountain of knowledge: Student incentive to study and learn. Externalities, information problems and peer pressure. In E. A. Hanushek & F. Welch (Eds.), *Handbook of the economics of education* (II, pp. 909–944). Amsterdam: North-Holland.

Bittles, A. H. (2001). *Consanguinity/endogamy resource.* Retrieved from www.consang.net.

Black, S. E. & Sokoloff, K. L. (2006). Long term trends in schooling: The rise and decline (?) of public education in the United States. In E. A. Hanushek & F. Welch (Eds.), *Handbook of the economics of education* (I, pp. 69–105). Amsterdam: North-Holland.

Blau, D. & Currie, J. (2006). Pre-school, day care, and after-school care: Who's minding the kids? In E. A. Hanushek & F. Welch (Eds.), *Handbook of the economics of education* (II, pp. 1163–1278). Amsterdam: North-Holland.

Blinkhorn, S. (1982). What skulduggery? *Nature, 296,* 506.

Block, N. (1995). How heritability misleads about race. *Cognition, 56,* 99–128.

Boberg-Fazlic, N., Sharp, P. & Weisdorf, J. (2011). Survival of the richest? Social status, fertility and social mobility in England 1541–1824. *European Review of Economic History, 15,* 365–392.

Boe, E., Barkanic, G., Shin, S., May, H., Leow, C. S., Singleton, J. C., Zeng, G. & Borouch, R. F. (2001). *Correlates of national differences in mathematics and science achievement: Evidence from TIMSS.* Philadelphia: University of Pennsylvania, Center for Research and Evaluation, Data Rep. No. 2001-DAR1.

Bolt, J. & van Zanden, J. L. (2013). *The first update of the Maddison Project. Re-estimating growth before 1820.* Groningen: Maddison-Project Working Paper WP-4. Data retrieved from www.ggdc.net/maddison/maddison-project/data/mpd_2013-01.xlsx.

Bond, R. & Saunders, P. (1999). Routes of success: Influences on the occupational attainment of young British males. *British Journal of Sociology, 50,* 217–249.

Borjas, G. J. (2001/1999). *Heaven's door: Immigration policy and the American economy.* Princeton, NJ: Princeton University Press.

(2016). *We wanted workers: Unraveling the immigration narrative.* New York: W. W. Norton.

Bos, W., Lankes, E.-M., Prenzel, M., Schwippert, K., Walther, G. & Valtin, R. (Eds.) (2003). *Erste Ergebnisse aus IGLU.* [*First results from PIRLS.*] Münster: Waxmann.

Botticini, M. & Eckstein, Z. (2012). *The chosen few. How education shaped Jewish history, 70-1492.* Princeton, Nj: Princeton University Press.

Bouchard, T. J. (2004). Genetic influence on human psychological traits. *Current Directions in Psychological Science, 13,* 148–151.

Bourdieu, P. (1993/1978). The racism of 'intelligence'. In P. Bourdieu (Ed.), *Sociology in question* (pp. 177–180). London: Sage.

(1988/1984). *Homo academicus.* Stanford, CA: Stanford University Press.

(2001). *Contre-feux.* Paris: Raisons d'Agir.

Boyle, E. H. & Meyer, J. W. (2002/1998). Modern law as secularized and global model. In Y. Dezalay & B. G. Garth (Eds.), *Global prescriptions* (pp. 65–95). Ann Arbor: University of Michigan Press.

Bradford, A. (2013). Sharing the risks and rewards of economic migration. *University of Chicago Law Review, 80*, 29–56.

Brecht, B. (2007/1939). *Life of Galileo.* Translation by Wolfgang Sauerlander & Ralph Manheim. Retrieved from http://buehnenkunst.ohost.de.

Brewers of Europe (2012). *Beer statistics 2012 edition.* Brussels: Brewers of Europe.

Brinch, Ch. N. & Galloway, T. A. (2012). Schooling in adolescence raises IQ scores. *Proceedings of the National Academy of Sciences (PNAS), 109*(2), 425–430.

Bronfenbrenner, U. & Ceci, S. J. (1994). Nature-nurture reconceptualized in developmental perspective: A bioecological model. *Psychological Review, 101*, 568–586.

Brophy, J. & Good, Th. L. (1986). Teacher behavior and student achievement. In M. C. Wittrock (Ed.), *Handbook of research on teaching* (pp. 328–375). New York: Macmillan.

Büeler, X. & Merki, K. M. (2003). Schulentwicklung in der Schweiz. In Ch. Burkard & G. Eikenbusch (Eds.), *Schulentwicklung international* (pp. 48–59). Hamburg: Bergmann.

Burckhardt, J. (1990/1860). *The civilization of the Renaissance in Italy.* [*Die Kultur der Renaissance in Italien.*] London: Penguin.

Burde, D. & Linden, L. L. (2013). Bringing education to Afghan girls: A randomized controlled trial of village-based schools. *American Economic Journal: Applied Economics, 5*, 27–40.

Burstein, P. (2007). Jewish educational and economic success in the United States: A search for explanations. *Sociological Perspectives, 50*, 209–228.

Cahill, M. B. (2005). Is the human development index redundant? *Eastern Economic Journal, 31*, 1–5.

Caldwell, J. C. (2002). The African AIDS epidemic: Reflections on a research program. *Journal of Population Research, 19*, 173–190.

Calomiris, Ch. W. & Haber, S. H. (2013). Why banking systems succeed – and fail. *Foreign Affairs*, November/December, 97–110.

Caplan, B. & Miller, S. C. (2010). Intelligence makes people think like economists: Evidence from the General Social Survey. *Intelligence, 38*, 636–647.

Carabaña, J. (2011). Why do the results of immigrant students depend so much on their country of origin and so little on their country of destination? In M. A. Pereyra, H.-G. Kotthoff & R. Cowen (Eds.), *Pisa under examination. Changing knowledge, changing tests, and changing schools.* (pp. 207–221). Rotterdam: Sense.

Cardoso, F. H. & Faletto, E. (1979). *Dependency and development in Latin America.* Berkeley: University of California Press.

Carl, N. (2014). Verbal intelligence is correlated with socially and economically liberal beliefs. *Intelligence, 44*, 142–148.

(2016a). IQ and socio-economic development across local authorities of the UK. *Intelligence, 55*, 90–94.

(2016b). An analysis of Islamist terrorism across western countries. *Open Quantitative Sociology and Political Science.* Retrieved from https://openpsych.net/paper/9.

Carmi, S., Hui, K. Y., Kochav, E., Liu, X., Xue, J., Grady, F., et al. (2014). Sequencing an Ashkenazi reference panel supports population-targeted personal genomics and illuminates Jewish and European origins. *Nature Communications*, *5*(4835), 1–9.

Carneiro, P. & Heckman, J. J. (2003). Human capital policy. In J. J. Heckman & A. B. Krueger (Eds.), *Inequality in America: What role for human capital policy?* (pp. 77–239). Cambridge, MA: MIT Press.

Carroll, J. B. (1993). *Human cognitive abilities. A survey of factor-analytic studies.* Cambridge: Cambridge University Press.

(1995). Reflections on Stephen Jay Gould's "The mismeasure of man" (1981): A retrospective review. *Intelligence*, *21*, 121–134.

Carter, S. C. (2000). *No excuses: Lessons from 21 high-performing, high-poverty schools.* Washington: Heritage Foundation.

Cattell, R. B. (1987/1971). *Intelligence: Its structure, growth and action.* Amsterdam: Elsevier.

Cavalli-Sforza, L. L. (1997). Genes, peoples, and languages. *Proceedings of the National Academy of Sciences (PNAS)*, *94*, 7719–7724.

Cavalli-Sforza, L. L., Menozzi, P. & Piazza, A. (1994). *The history and geography of human genes.* Princeton, NJ: Princeton University Press.

Ceci, S. J. (1991). How much does schooling influence general intelligence and its cognitive components? A reassessment of the evidence. *Developmental Psychology*, *27*, 703–722.

Chabris, C. F., Hebert, B. M., Benjamin, D. J., Beauchamp, J. P., Cesarini, D., van der Loos, M. J. H. M., ... & Laibson, D. (2012). Most reported genetic associations with general intelligence are probably false positives. *Psychological Science*, *23*, 1314–1323.

Chagnon, N. A. (1977). *Yanomamö. The fierce people.* New York: Holt.

Chan, Ch. K. & Chee, H. L. (1984). Singapore 1984: Breeding for Big Brother. In Ch. K. Chan & H. L. Chee (Eds.), *Designer genes: IQ, ideology and biology* (pp. 4–13). Kuala Lumpur: Selangor/Institute for Social Analysis (INSAN).

Chanda, A., Cook, C. J. & Putterman, L. (2014). Persistence of fortune: Accounting for population movements, There was no post-Columbian reversal. *American Economic Journal: Macroeconomics*, *6*, 1–28.

Charlton, B. G. (2009). Replacing education with psychometrics: How learning about IQ almost-completely changed my mind about education. *Medical Hypotheses*, *73*, 273–277.

Cheng, H. & Lynn, R. (2013). The adverse effect of Fluoride on children's intelligence: A systematic review. *Mankind Quarterly*, *LIII*, 306–347.

Chetty, R., Friedman, J. N., Hilger, N., Saez, E., Schanzenbach, D. & Yagan, D. (2011). How does your kindergarten classroom affect your earnings? *Quarterly Journal of Economics*, *126*, 1593–1660.

Chin, E. (2013). What Jason Richwine should have heard from his PhD committee. *Anthropology Now*. Retrieved from http://anthronow.com/online-articles/what-jason-richwine-should-have-heard-from-his-phd-committee.

Chinapah, V., H'ddigui, E. L. M., Kanjee, A., Falayajo, W., Fomba, C. O., Hamissou, O., Rafalimanana, A. & Byamugisha, A. (2000). *With Africa for Africa. Towards quality education for all. 1999 MLA project.* Pretoria: Human Sciences Research Council.

Chkonia, I. (2006). Timeless identity versus another final modernity: Identity master myth and social change in Georgia. In L. Harrison & P. L. Berger (Eds.), *Developing cultures: Case studies* (pp. 349–368). New York: Routledge.

Chomsky, N. (1999). *The fateful triangle: The United States, Israel, and the Palestinians.* Cambridge: South End.

Christainsen, G. B. (2013). IQ and the wealth of nations: How much reverse causality? *Intelligence, 41,* 688–698.

Chua, A. (2003). *World on fire.* New York: Doubleday.

  (2011). *Battle hymn of the tiger mother.* London: Bloomsbury.

Cingano, F. (2014). Trends in income inequality and its impact on economic growth. *OECD Social, Employment and Migration Working Papers, 163.*

Clark, G. (2007). *A farewell to alms. A brief economic history of the world.* Princeton, NJ: Princeton University Press.

  (2008). In defense of the Malthusian interpretation of history. *European Review of Economic History, 12,* 175–199.

  (2014a). The American dream is an illusion: Immigration and inequality. *Foreign Affairs, 26 August 2014.* Retrieved from www.foreignaffairs.com/node/139101.

  (2014b). *The son also rises: Surnames and the history of social mobility.* Princeton, NJ: Princeton University Press.

Cochran, G., Hardy, J. & Harpending, H. (2006). Natural history of Ashkenazi intelligence. *Journal of Biosocial Science, 38,* 659–693.

Cochran, G. & Harpending, H. (2009). *The 10.000 year explosion. How civilization accelerated human evolution.* New York: Basic Books.

Cohen, W. M. & Levinthal, D. A. (1990). Absorptive capacity: A new perspective on learning and innovation. *Administrative Science Quarterly, 35,* 128–152.

Cohn, H. H., Rabinowitz, L. I. & Elon, M. (2007). Capital punishment. In F. Skolnik & M. Berenbaum (Eds.), *Encyclopedia Judaica.* Detroit, MI: Gale. Retrieved from www.jewishvirtuallibrary.org/capital-punishment.

Cole, M. (1977). An ethnographic psychology of cognition. In P. N. Johnson-Laird & P. C. Wason (Eds.), *Thinking – Readings in cognitive science* (pp. 468–482). Cambridge: Cambridge University Press.

Cole, S. & Phelan, Th. (1999). The scientific productivity of nations. *Minerva, 37,* 1–23.

Coleman, D. (2010). Projections of the ethnic minority populations of the United Kingdom 2006–2056. *Population and Development Review, 36,* 441–486.

Coleman, J. S., Hoffer, Th. & Kilgore, S. (1982). *High school achievement. Public, Catholic, and private schools compared.* New York: Basic Books.

Collier, P. (2013a). *Exodus: How migration is changing our world.* New York: Oxford University Press.

  (2013b). How to have a sensible conversation about immigration. *New Statesman, 21 November 2013.* Retrieved from www.newstatesman.com/global-issues/2013/11/new-exodus.

Collins, W. J. & Margo, R. A. (2006). Historical perspectives on racial differences in schooling in the United States. In E. A. Hanushek & F. Welch (Eds.), *Handbook of the economics of education* (I, pp. 107–154). Amsterdam: North-Holland.

Comin, D. A., Easterly, W. & Gong, E. (2010). Was the wealth of nations determined in 1000 BC? *American Economic Journal: Macroeconomics, 2,* 65–97.

Conard, N. J. (2003). Palaeolithic ivory sculptures from southwestern Germany and the origins of figurative art. *Nature, 426,* 830–832.

(2008). A critical view of the evidence for a southern African origin of behavioural modernity. *South African Archaeological Society Goodwin Series, 10,* 175–179.

Conference des Ministres de l'Éducation des pays ayant le français en partage (2008). *Synthèse des résultats PASEC VII, VIII et IX.* Dakar. Retrieved from www.confemen.org/le-pasec/rapports-et-documents-pasec/synthese-des-resultats-pasec-vii-viii-et-ix.

Conway, A. R. A., Cowan, N., Bunting, M. F., Therriault, D. J. & Minkoff, S. R. (2002). A latent variable analysis of working memory capacity, short-term memory capacity, processing speed, and general f luid intelligence. *Intelligence, 30,* 163–183.

Corden, W. M. & Neary, J. P. (1982). Booming sector and de-industrialisation in a small open economy. *The Economic Journal, 92,* 825–848.

Costa, D. L. (2015). Health and the economy in the United States from 1750 to the present. *Journal of Economic Literature, 53,* 503–570.

Cotton, S. M., Kiely, P. M., Crewther, D. P., Thomson, B., Laycock, R. & Crewther, S. G. (2005). A normative and reliability study for the Raven's Coloured Progressive Matrices for primary school aged children from Victoria, Australia. *Personality and Individual Differences, 39,* 647–659.

Cowen, T. (2011). *The great stagnation.* New York: Dutton.

Coyle, Th., Johnson, W. & Rindermann, H. (2013, May 17). Open Letter – Letter of Protest on the comment of Robert Sternberg (2013) on Hunt (2012). *Perspectives on Psychological Science,* http://pps.sagepub.com/content/8/2/187.abstract/reply#sppps_el_84.

Coyle, Th. R., Rindermann, H. & Hancock, D. (2016). Cognitive capitalism: Economic freedom moderates the effects of intellectual and average classes on economic productivity. *Psychological Reports, 119,* 411–427.

Crafts, N. (2002). The Human Development Index, 1870–1999: Some revised estimates. *European Review of Economic History, 6,* 395–405.

Credit Suisse Research Institute (2013a). *Global wealth databook 2013.* Zurich: Credit Suisse.

(2013b). *Global wealth report 2013.* Zurich: Credit Suisse.

Crocker, J., Luhtanedn, R., Blaine, B. & Broadnax, B. E. (1999). Belief in US government conspiracies against blacks among black and white college students. *Personality and Social Psychology Bulletin, 25,* 941–953.

Crooks, T. J. (1988). The impact of classroom evaluation practices on students. *Review of Educational Research, 58,* 438–481.

Cunha, F., Heckman, J. J., Lochner, L. & Masterov, D. V. (2006). Interpreting the evidence on life cycle skill formation. In E. A. Hanushek & F. Welch (Eds.), *Handbook of the economics of education* (I, pp. 697–812). Amsterdam: North-Holland.

Cunningham, A. E. & Stanovich, K. E. (1998). What reading does for the mind. *American Educator, 22,* 8–15.

Cvorovic, J. (2014). *The Roma.* London: Ulster Institute for Social Research.

Dagona, Z. K. (1994). Substance use and road traffic accidents among Nigerian commercial motor cyclists. *Ife PsychologIA, 2,* 81–93.

Dar, Y. & Resh, N. (1986). Classroom intellectual composition and academic achievement. *American Educational Research Journal*, *23*, 357–374.

Darwin, Ch. (1871). *The descent of man, and selection in relation to sex*. London: John Murray.

Das, J. & Zajonc, T. (2010). India shining and Bharat drowning: Comparing two Indian states to the worldwide distribution in mathematics achievement. *Journal of Development Economics*, *92*, 175–187.

Davis, B. (1978). The moralistic fallacy. *Nature*, *272*, 390.

Davis, D., Dorsey, K., Franks, R., Sackett, P., Searcy, C. & Zhao, X. (2013). Do racial and ethnic group differences in performance on the MCAT exam reflect test bias? *Academic Medicine*, *88*, 593–602.

Davis, J. M., Searles, V. B., Anderson, N., Keeney, J., Raznahan, A., Horwood, L. J., Fergusson, D. M., Kennedy, M. A., Giedd, J. & Sikela, J. M. (2015). DUF1220 copy number is linearly associated with increased cognitive function as measured by total IQ and mathematical aptitude scores. *Human Genetics*, *134*, 67–75.

Dawkins, R. (2008/1982). *The extended phenotype. The long reach of the gene*. Oxford: Oxford University Press.

Deary, I. J., Batty, G. D. & Gale, C. R. (2008). Childhood intelligence predicts voter turnout, voting preferences, and political involvement in adulthood. *Intelligence*, *36*, 548–555.

Deary, I. J. (2012). Intelligence. *Annual Review of Psychology*, *63*, 453–482.

Deary, I. J., Whalley, L. J., Lemmon, H., Crawford, J. R. & Starr, J. M. (2000). The stability of individual differences in mental ability from childhood to old age. *Intelligence*, *28*, 49–55.

Deary, I. J., Taylor, M. D., Hart, C. l., Wilson, V. Davey Smith, G., Blane, D. & Starr, J. M. (2005). Intergenerational social mobility and mid-life status attainment. *Intelligence*, *33*, 455–472.

Deary, I. J., Ferguson, K. J., Bastin, M. E., Barrow, G. W. S., Reid, L. M., Seckl, J. R., Wardlaw, J. M. & Maclullich, A. M. J. (2007). Skull size and intelligence, and King Robert Bruce's IQ. *Intelligence*, *35*, 519–525.

DeGroot, A. D. (1951). War and the intelligence of youth. *Journal of Abnormal and Social Psychology*, *46*, 596–597.

Deininger, K. & Squire, L. (1996). *Measuring income inequality: A new database*. New York: www.worldbank.org/research/growth/dddeisqu.htm.

Delaney-Black, V., Covington, Ch., Ondersma, S. J., Nordstrom-Klee, B., Templin, Th., Ager, J., Janisse, J. & Sokol, R. J. (2002). Violence exposure, trauma, and IQ and/or reading deficits among urban children. *Archives of Pediatric and Adolescent Medicine*, *156*, 280–285.

Delhey, J. & Newton, K. (2005). Predicting cross-national levels of social trust: Global pattern or Nordic exceptionalism? *European Sociological Review*, *21*, 311–327.

Dennison, T. & Ogilvie, S. (2014). Does the European Marriage Pattern explain economic growth? *Journal of Economic History*, *74*, 651–693.

De Walque, D. (2004). *How does the impact of an HIV/AIDS information campaign vary with educational attainment? Evidence from rural Uganda*. Washington: World Bank.

Diamond, J. (1997). *Guns, germs, and steel: The fates of human societies*. New York: Norton.

(2002). Evolution, consequences and future of plant and animal domestication. *Nature, 418*, 700–707.

Díez-Medrano, J. (2014). *Interpersonal trust*. Madrid: WVS Archive. Retrieved from www.jdsurvey.net/jds/jdsurveyMaps.jsp?Idioma=I&SeccionTexto=0404& NOID=104

Dijk, H. v., Engen, M. L. v. & Knippenberg, D. v. (2012). Defying conventional wisdom: A meta-analytical examination of the differences between demographic and job-related diversity relationships with performance. *Organizational Behavior and Human Decision Processes, 119*, 38–53.

Dinello, N. (1998). Russian religious rejections of money and Homo Economicus. *Sociology of Religion, 59*, 45–64.

Diner, D. (2009/2005). *Lost in the sacred: Why the Muslim world stood still*. Princeton, NJ: Princeton University Press.

Ding, W. & Lehrer, S. F. (2007). Do peers affect student achievement in China's secondary schools? *Review of Economics and Statistics, 89*, 300–312.

Dobbs, R., Madgavkar, A., Barton, D., Labaye, E., Manyika, J., Roxburgh, C., Lund, S. & Madhav, S. (2012). *The world at work: Jobs, pay, and skills for 3.5 billion people*. New York: McKinsey.

Dobelli, R. (2013/2011). *The art of thinking clearly*. New York: Harper.

Döbert, H., Hörner, W., Kopp, B. v. & Mitter, W. (Eds.). (2004). *Die Schulsysteme Europas*. [*School systems of Europe.*] Baltmannsweiler: Schneider.

Dolton, P. & Marcenaro-Gutierrez, O. D. (2011). If you pay peanuts do you get monkeys? A cross country analysis of teacher pay and pupil performance. *Economic Policy, 26*, 5–55.

Dolton, P., Marcenaro-Gutiérrez, O. & Still, A. (2014). *The efficiency index. Which education systems deliver the best value for money?* London: GEMS Education Solutions.

Douthat, R. (2016). Germany on the brink. *New York Times, 9 January 2016*. Retrieved from www.nytimes.com/2016/01/10/opinion/sunday/germany-on-the-brink.html.

Dronkers, J. (2006). Ethnic riots in French banlieus. *The Tocqueville Review/La Revue Tocqueville, 27*, 61–76.

Dronkers, J. & Robert, P. (2008). Differences in scholastic achievement of public, private government-dependent, and private independent schools: A cross-national analysis. *Educational Policy, 22*, 541–577.

Dronkers, J. & Velden, R. v. d. (2013). Positive but also negative effects of ethnic diversity in schools on educational performance? In M. Windzio (Ed.), *Integration and inequality in educational institutions* (pp. 71–98). Dordrecht: Springer.

Dronkers, J., Velden, R. v. d. & Dunne, A. (2012). Why are migrant students better off in certain types of educational systems or schools than in others? *European Educational Research Journal, 11*, 11–44.

Duarte, J. L., Crawford, J. T., Stern, C., Haidt, J., Jussim, L. & Tetlock, P. E. (2015). Political diversity will improve social psychological science. *Behavioral and Brain Sciences, 38*, 1–13 & 45–58.

Duckworth, A. L. & Seligman, M. E. P. (2005). Self-discipline outdoes IQ in predicting academic performance of adolescents. *Psychological Science, 16*, 939–944.

Duchesne, R. (2011). *The uniqueness of Western civilization*. Leiden: Brill.

Ducrest, A.-L., Keller, L. & Roulin, A. (2008). Pleiotropy in the melanocortin system, coloration and behavioural syndromes. *Trends in Ecology and Evolution, 23*, 502–510.

Duflo, E., Dupas, P. & Kremer, M. (2011). Peer effects, teacher incentives, and the impact of tracking: Evidence from a randomized evaluation in Kenya. *American Economic Review, 101*, 1739–1774.

Dupuy, T. N. (1977). *A genius for war: The German army and general staff, 1807–1945*. Englewood Cliffs, NJ: Prentice-Hall.

Durkheim, E. (1951/1897). *Suicide*. Glencoe, NY: Free Press.

Dutta, S. & Lanvin, B. (2013). *The global innovation index 2013. The local dynamics of innovation*. Ithaca, NY: Cornell University, World Intellectual Property Organization (WIPO).

Dutta, S. & Mia, I. (2010). *Global information technology report 2009–2010. ICT for sustainability*. Geneva: World Economic Forum (WEF).

Dutton, E. & Lynn, R. (2013). A negative Flynn effect in Finland, 1997–2009. *Intelligence, 41*, 817–820.

Dutton, E., van der Linden, D. & Lynn, R. (2016). The negative Flynn Effect: A systematic literature review. *Intelligence, 59*, 163–169.

Dweck, C. S. (2000). *Self-theories: Their role in motivation, personality, and development*. Philadelphia, PA: Taylor & Francis.

Easterly, W. & Levine, R. (2012). The European origins of economic development. *MPRA Paper, 39413*.

ECB (European Central Bank) (2013). *The Eurosystem household finance and consumption survey. Results from the first wave*. Frankfurt: ECB. Retrieved from www.ecb.int/pub/pdf/other/ecbsp2en.pdf.

Edwards, A. W. F. (2003). Human genetic diversity: Lewontin's fallacy. *BioEssays, 25*, 798–801.

Edwards, C. (2013). *Airmanship*. Salisbury: Blacker.

Ehrenberg, R. & Brewer, D. (1994). Do school and teacher characteristics matter? Evidence from high school and beyond. *Economics of Education Review, 13*, 1–17.

Ehrenberg, R. G., Brewer, D. J., Gamoran, A. & Willms, D. J. (2001). Class size and student achievement. *Psychological Science in the Public Interest, 2*, 1–30.

Elias, N. (2000/1939). *The civilizing process: Sociogenetic and psychogenetic investigations*. Oxford: Blackwell.

Elley, W. B. (1992). *How in the world do students read?* The Hague: The International Association for the Evaluation of Educational Achievement (IEA).

Ellis, L. & Walsh, A. (2003). Crime, delinquency and intelligence: A review of the worldwide literature. In H. Nyborg (Ed.), *The scientific study of general intelligence. Tribute to Arthur R. Jensen* (pp. 343–365). Oxford: Pergamon.

Eppig, Ch., Fincher, C. L. & Thornhill, R. (2010). Parasite prevalence and the worldwide distribution of cognitive ability. *Proceedings of the Royal Society B, 277*, 3801–3808.

Ericsson, K. A., Krampe, R. T. & Tesch-Romer, C. (1993). The role of deliberate practice in the acquisition of expert performance. *Psychological Review, 100*, 363–406.

Evans, M. D. R., Kelley, J., Sikora, J. & Treiman, D. J. (2010). Family scholarly culture and educational success: Evidence from 27 nations. *Research in Social Stratification and Mobility, 28*, 171–197.

Evans, P. & Rauch, J. E. (1999). Bureaucracy and growth: A cross-national analysis of the effects of "Weberian" state structures on economic growth. *American Sociological Review*, *64*, 748–765.

Evans-Pritchard, E. E. (1976/1937). *Witchcraft, oracles and magic among the Azande*. Oxford: Oxford University Press.

Everett, D. (2008). *Don't sleep, there are snakes: Life and language in the Amazonian jungle*. New York: Vintage.

Eysenck, H. J. & Schoenthaler, S. J. (1997). Raising IQ level by vitamin and mineral supplementation. In R. J. Sternberg & E. L. Grigorenko (Eds.), *Intelligence, heredity and environment* (pp. 363–392). Cambridge: Cambridge University Press.

Fadera, H. (2010). President Jammeh discharges 41 HIV/AIDS treated patients. *The Daily Observer* (Banjul), *12 July 2010*. Retrieved from http://observer.gm/africa/gambia/article/president-jammeh-discharges-41-hivaids-treated-patients.

Falagas, M. E., Matthaiou, D. K., Rafailidis, P. I., Panos, G. & Pappas, G. (2008). Worldwide prevalence of head lice. *Emerging Infectious Diseases*, *14*, 1493–1494.

Falch, T. & Sandgren Massih, S. (2011). The effect of education on cognitive ability. *Economic Inquiry*, *49*, 838–856.

Fang, C. (2009). Future demographic dividend – tapping the source of China's economic growth. *China Economist*, *21*, 17–24.

Fareed, M. & Afzal, M. (2014). Estimating the inbreeding depression on cognitive behavior: A population based study of child cohort. *PLoS ONE*, *9*(10), e109585.

Farron, S. (2010). *The affirmative action hoax*. Quezon City: New Century Books.

Feliciano, C. (2005). Educational selectivity in US immigration: How do immigrants compare to those left behind? *Demography*, *42*, 131–152.

Fernald, J. G. & Jones, Ch. I. (2014). The future of U.S. economic growth. *American Economic Review*, *104*, 44–49.

Feyrer, J. & Sacerdote, B. (2009). Colonialism and modern income: Islands as natural experiments. *Review of Economics and Statistics*, *91*, 245–262.

Finkelstein, N. G. (2003/1995). *Image and reality of the Israel-Palestine conflict*. New York: Verso.

Firkowska, A., Ostrowska, A., Sokolowska, M., Stein, Z., Susser, M. & Wald, I. (1978). Cognitive development and social policy. *Science*, *200*, 1357–1362.

Fleck, L. (1979/1935). *The genesis and development of a scientific fact*. Chicago: University of Chicago Press.

Florida, R. (2002). *The rise of the creative class*. New York: Basic Books.

Flynn, J. R. (1984). The mean IQ of Americans: Massive gains 1932 to 1978. *Psychological Bulletin*, *95*, 29–51.

  (1987). Massive IQ gains in 14 nations: What IQ tests really measure. *Psychological Bulletin*, *101*, 171–191.

  (1991). *Asian Americans: Achievement beyond IQ*. Hillsdale, NJ: Erlbaum.

  (2007a). Arthur Jensen and John Stuart Mill. *Cato Unbound, November*(26). Retrieved from www.cato-unbound.org/2007/11/23/james-r-flynn/arthur-jensen-and-john-stuart-mill.

  (2007b). *What is intelligence?* Cambridge: Cambridge University Press.

  (2012a). *Are we getting smarter?* Cambridge: Cambridge University Press.

(2012b). *How to improve your mind: 20 keys to unlock the modern world.* Chichester: Wiley-Blackwell.

Foged, M. & Peri, G. (2015). Immigrants' effect on native workers: New analysis on longitudinal data. *American Economic Journal: Applied Economics, 8,* 1–34.

Fogel, R. W. (2007). Capitalism & democracy in 2040. *Dædalus, 136,* 87–95.

Foley, R. (1987). *Another unique species.* New York: Wiley.

Foy, P., Brossman, B. & Galia, J. (2012). Scaling the TIMSS and PIRLS 2011 achievement data. In M. O. Martin & I. V. S. Mullis (Eds.), *Methods and procedures in TIMSS and PIRLS 2011* (pp. 1–28). Chestnut Hill, MA: TIMSS & PIRLS International Study Center.

Frank, A. G. (1967). *Capitalism and underdevelopment in Latin America.* New York: Monthly Review Press.

Frankish, K. & Ramsey, W. (Eds.) (2012). *Cognitive science: An introduction to the science of the mind.* Cambridge: Cambridge University Press.

Franklin, B. (2004/1964). *The autobiography and other writings on politics, economics, and virtue.* Cambridge: Cambridge University Press.

Frazer, J. G. (1922/1890). *The Golden Bough: A study of magic and religion.* Adelaide: University of Adelaide.

Freedom House (2013). *Freedom in the world.* Washington. Retrieved from www.freedomhouse.org/sites/default/files/Territory%20Ratings%20and%20Status%2C%201973-2013%20%28final%29.xls.

Friedman, M. (1962). *Capitalism and freedom.* Chicago: University of Chicago Press.

Frost, P. (2010). The Roman state and genetic pacification. *Evolutionary Psychology, 8,* 376–389.

Frost, P. & Harpending, H. C. (2015). Western Europe, state formation, and genetic pacification. *Evolutionary Psychology, 13,* 230–243.

Fry, A. F. & Hale, S. (1996). Processing speed, working memory, and fluid intelligence: Evidence for a developmental cascade. *Psychological Science, 7,* 237–241.

Fuchs, Th. & Woessmann, L. (2007). What accounts for international differences in student performance? A re-examination using PISA data. *Empirical Economics, 32,* 433–464.

Fund for Peace (2014). *Fragile states index 2014.* Washington: Fund for Peace.

Fussell, P. (1983). *Class: A guide through the American status system.* New York: Touchstone.

Fylkesnes, K., Musonda, R. M., Sichone, M., Ndhlovu, Z., Tembo, F. & Monze, M. (2001). Declining HIV prevalence and risk behaviors in Zambia. *AIDS, 15,* 907–916.

Gächter, S. & Schulz, J. F. (2016). Intrinsic honesty and the prevalence of rule violations across societies. *Nature, 531,* 496–499.

Gagné, F. (2005). From noncompetence to exceptional talent. *Gifted Child Quarterly, 49,* 139–154.

Galton, F. (2005/1869). *Hereditary genius. An inquiry into its laws and consequences.* New York: Cosimo.

Gerschenkron, A. (1962). *Economic backwardness in historical perspective.* Cambridge, MA: Belknap Press.

Gerstmeyer, K. & Lehrl, S. (2004). Cataract-related changes of intelligence. An innovative aspect. *Der Ophthalmologe, 101,* 164–169.

Gigerenzer, G. (2004). Mindless statistics. *Journal of Socio-Economics*, *33*, 587–606.

Gignac, G. E. & Bates, T. C. (2017). Brain volume and intelligence. *Intelligence*, 64, 18–29.

Gilbert, G. M. (1947). *Nuremberg diary*. New York: Farrar, Straus.

Glaeser, E. L., La Porta, R., Lopez-de-Silanes, F. & Shleifer, A. (2004). Do institutions cause growth? *Journal of Economic Growth*, *9*, 271–303.

Glewwe, P. & King, E. (2001). The impact of early childhood nutritional status on cognitive development. *The World Bank Economic Review*, *15*, 81–113.

Glewwe, P. & Kremer, M. (2006). Schools, teachers, and education outcomes in developing countries. In E. A. Hanushek & F. Welch (Eds.), *Handbook of the economics of education* (II, pp. 945–1017). Amsterdam: North-Holland.

Goklany, I. M. (2007). *The improving state of the world. Why we are living longer, healthier, more comfortable lives on a cleaner planet*. Washington, DC: CATO Institute.

Goldman, D. P. & Smith, J. P. (2002). Can patient self-management help explain the SES health gradient? *Proceeding of the National Academy of Sciences*, *99*, 10929–10934.

Gonwouo, L. N. & Rödel, M.-O. (2008). The importance of frogs to the livelihood of the Bakossi people around Mount Manengouba, Cameroon, with special consideration of the Hairy Frog, Trichobatrachus robustus. *Salamandra*, *44*, 23–34.

Gordon, R. A. (1997). Everyday life as an intelligence test: Effects of intelligence and intelligence context. *Intelligence*, *24*, 203–320.

Gordon, R. J. (2016). *The rise and fall of American growth*. Princeton, NJ: Princeton University Press.

Gottfredson, L. S. (2003). g, jobs and life. In H. Nyborg (Ed.), *The scientific study of general intelligence. Tribute to Arthur R. Jensen* (pp. 293–342). Oxford: Pergamon.

  (2004a). Life, death, and intelligence. *Journal of Cognitive Education and Psychology*, *4*, 23–46.

  (2004b). Intelligence: Is it the epidemiologists' elusive "fundamental cause" of social class inequalities in health? *Journal of Personality and Social Psychology*, *86*, 174–199.

  (2010). Lessons in academic freedom as lived experience. *Personality and Individual Differences*, *49*, 272–280.

Gouguenheim, S. (2008). *Aristote au Mont-Saint-Michel*. Paris: Seuil.

Gould, S. J. (1981). *The mismeasure of man*. New York: Norton.

  (2000). The spice of life. *Leader to Leader*, *15*(Winter), 14–19.

Griaule, M. (1965/1948). *Conversations with Ogotemmeli*. Oxford: Oxford University Press.

Grill, B. (2005/2003). *Ach, Afrika. Berichte aus dem Inneren eines Kontinents.* [*Oh, Africa. Reports from inside a continent.*] Munich: Goldmann.

Groethuysen, B. (1968/1927). *The bourgeois. Catholicism vs. capitalism in eighteenth-century France*. New York: Holt.

Grondona, M. (2000). A cultural typology of economic development. In S. P. Huntington & L. E. Harrison (Eds.), *Culture matters* (pp. 44–55). New York: Basic Books.

Gross, P. R. & Levitt, N. (1994). *Higher superstition. The academic left and its quarrels with science*. Baltimore, MY: Johns Hopkins University.

Grudnik, J. L. & Kranzler, J. H. (2001). Meta-analysis of the relationship between intelligence and inspection time. *Intelligence, 29*, 523–535.

Gvosdev, N. (2006). Reimagining the Orthodox tradition. In L. E. Harrison & J. Kagan (Eds.), *Developing cultures. Essays on cultural change* (pp. 195–213). New York: Routledge.

Gwartney, J., Lawson, R. & Hall, J. (2013). *Economic freedom of the world. 2013 annual report.* Vancouver, BC: Fraser Institute. Retrieved from www.freetheworld.com/2013/EFW2013-complete.pdf. Dataset: www.freetheworld.com/2013/EFWdataset2013.xls.

Haasch, G. (Ed.) (2000). *Bildung und Erziehung in Japan.* [*"Bildung" and education in Japan.*] Berlin: Volker Spiess.

Habermas, J. (1984/1981). *The theory of communicative action. Reason and the rationalization of society.* Boston: Beacon.

Hadenius, A. (1992). *Democracy and development.* New York: Cambridge University Press.

Hadidjaja, P., Bonang, E., Suyardi, M. A., Abidin, S. A. N., Ismid, I. S. & Margono, S. S. (1998). The effect of intervention methods on nutritional status and cognitive function of primary school children infected with Ascaris lumbricoides. *American Journal of Tropical Medicine and Hygiene, 59*, 791–795.

Hafer, R. W. (2017). New estimates on the relationship between IQ, economic growth and welfare. *Intelligence, 61*, 92–101.

Hagenaars, S. P., Harris, S. E., Davies, G., Hill, W. D., Liewald, D. C. M., Ritchie, S. J., . . . Deary, I. J. (2016). Shared genetic aetiology between cognitive functions and physical and mental health in UK Biobank (*N*=112,151) and 24 GWAS consortia. *Molecular Psychiatry, 21*(11), 1624–1632.

Hajnal, J. (1965). European marriage patterns in perspective. In D. V. Glass & D. E. C. Eversley (Eds.), *Population in history* (pp. 101–143). London: Arnold.

Hallpike, Ch. R. (1980). *The foundations of primitive thought.* Oxford: Oxford University Press.

Halpern, C. T., Joyner, K., Udry, J. R. & Suchindran, Ch. M. (2000). Smart teens don't have sex (or kiss much either). *Journal of Adolescent Health, 26*, 213–225.

Hämäläinen, P., Saarela, K. L. & Takala, J. (2009). Global trend according to estimated number of occupational accidents and fatal work-related diseases at region and country level. *Journal of Safety Research, 40*, 125–139.

Hanushek, E. A. (2013). Economic growth in developing countries: The role of human capital. *Economics of Education Review, 37*, 204–212.

Hanushek, E. A. & Kimko, D. D. (2000). Schooling, labor-force quality, and the growth of nations. *American Economic Review, 90*, 1184–1208.

Hanushek, E. A. & Rivkin, S. G. (2006). Teacher quality. In E. A. Hanushek & F. Welch (Eds.), *Handbook of the economics of education* (II, pp. 1051–1078). Amsterdam: North-Holland.

Hanushek, E. A. & Woessmann, L. (2006). Does educational tracking affect performance and inequality? Differences-in-differences evidence across countries. *Economic Journal, 116*, C63–C76.

(2008). The role of cognitive skills in economic development. *Journal of Economic Literature, 46*, 607–668.

(2009). *Do better schools lead to more growth? Cognitive skills, economic outcomes, and causation.* Bonn: IZA DP No. 4575.

(2011). The economics of international differences in educational achievement. In E. A. Hanushek, S. Machin & L. Woessmann (Eds.), *Handbook of the economics of education, Volume III* (pp. 89–200). Amsterdam: Elsevier.

(2015a). *The knowledge capital of nations.* Cambridge, MA: MIT Press.

(2015b). *Universal basic skills.* Paris: OECD.

Hanushek, E. A., Peterson, P. E. & Woessmann, L. (2013). *Endangering prosperity.* Washington: Brookings.

Hanushek, E. A., Kain, J. F., Markman, J. M. & Rivkin, S. G. (2003). Does peer ability affect student achievement? *Journal of Applied Econometrics, 18,* 527–544.

Hanushek, E. A., Schwerdt, G., Wiederhold, S. & Woessmann, L. (2015). Returns to skills around the world: Evidence from PIAAC. *European Economic Review, 73,* 103–130.

Harber, K. D. (1998). Feedback to minorities: Evidence of a positive bias. *Journal of Personality and Social Psychology, 74,* 622–628.

Harrison, L. E. (2006). *The central liberal truth: How politics can change a culture and save it from itself.* New York: Oxford University Press.

(2013). *Jews, Confucians, and Protestants: Cultural capital and the end of multiculturalism.* Lanham, MD: Rowman & Littlefield.

Harrison, L. E. & Berger, P. L. (Eds.) (2006). *Developing cultures: Case studies.* New York: Routledge.

Harrison, L. E. & Huntington, S. P. (2000). *Culture matters: How values shape human progress.* New York: Basic Books.

Harrison, L. E. & Kagan, J. (Eds.) (2006). *Developing cultures. Essays on cultural change.* New York: Routledge.

Hart, B. & Risley, T. R. (1995). *Meaningful differences in the everyday experience of young American children.* Baltimore: Paul Brookes.

Hart, M. (2007). *Understanding human history. An analysis including the effects of geography and differential evolution.* Athens: Washington Summit.

Hattie, J. A. C. (2009). *Visible learning: A synthesis of over 800 meta-analyses relating to achievement.* London: Routledge.

Hatton, T. J. (2014). How have Europeans grown so tall? *Oxford Economic Papers, 66,* 349–372.

Hausmann, R., Tyson, L. D. & Zahidi, S. (2011). *Global gender gap report 2011.* Geneva: World Economic Forum.

Hawks, J., Wang, E. T., Cochran, G. M., Harpending, H. C. & Moyzis, R. K. (2007). Recent acceleration of human adaptive evolution. *Proceedings of the National Academy of Sciences, 104,* 20753–20758.

Hayek, F. A. (2011/1960). *The constitution of liberty.* Chicago: University of Chicago Press.

Hearnshaw, L. S. (1979). *Cyril Burt: Psychologist.* Ithaca, New York: Cornell University Press.

Hecht, R., Stover, J., Bollinger, L., Muhib, F., Case, K. & de Ferranti, D. (2010). Financing of HIV/AIDS programme scale-up in low-income and middle-income countries, 2009–31. *The Lancet, 376,* 1254–1260.

Heckman, J. J. (2000). Policies to foster human capital. *Research in Economics, 54*, 3–56.

Hegel, G. W. F. (1999/1807). *Phänomenologie des Geistes.* [*Phenomenology of spirit.*] Hamburg: Felix Meiner, major works in six books, book II.

(2001/1837). *The philosophy of history.* Kitchener: Batoche Books.

Helgason, A., Pálsson, S., Guðbjartsson, D. F., Kristjánsson, Þ. & Stefánsson, K. (2008). An association between the kinship and fertility of human couples. *Science, 319*, 813–816.

Heller, K. A. & Perleth, Ch. (2000). *Kognitiver Fähigkeits-Test (KFT 4-12+R).* [*CogAT test manual.*] Weinheim: Beltz.

Heller-Sahlgren, G. (2015a). Immigration helps explain Sweden's school trouble. *The Spectator, 10 August 2015.* Retrieved from http://blogs.spectator.co.uk/2015/08/immigration-helps-explain-swedens-school-trouble.

(2015b). *Real Finnish lessons.* London: Centre for Policy Studies.

(2015c). *Invandringen och Sveriges resultatfall i Pisa.* Stockholm: Institutet för Näringslivsforskning (IFN), IFN Policy Paper No. 71.

Helmke, A. & Schrader, F.-W. (2007). Entwicklung akademischer Leistungen. [Development of academic achievement.] In M. Hasselhorn & W. Schneider (Eds.), *Handbuch der Entwicklungspsychologie [Handbook of developmental psychology]* (pp. 289–298). Göttingen: Hogrefe.

Henneberg, M. & de Miguel, C. (2004). Hominins are a single lineage: Brain and body size variability does not reflect postulated taxonomic diversity of hominins. *Homo – Journal of Comparative Human Biology, 55*, 21–37.

Heron, W. T. (1941). The inheritance of brightness and dullness in maze learning ability in the rat. *Journal of Genetic Psychology, 58*, 41–49.

Herrnstein, R. J. (1973). *IQ in the meritocracy.* Boston: Atlantic Monthly Press.

Herrnstein, R. J. & Murray, Ch. (1994). *The bell curve. Intelligence and class structure in American life.* New York: Free Press.

Herrnstein, R., Nickerson, R., de Sanchez, M. & Swets, J. A. (1986). Teaching thinking skills. *American Psychologist, 41*, 1279–1289.

Heston, A., Summers, R. & Aten, P. (2012). *Penn World Table Version 7.1.* Philadelphia: Center for International Comparisons of Production, Income and Prices at the University of Pennsylvania.

Hirschi, T. & Hindelang, M. J. (1977). Intelligence and delinquency. *American Sociological Review, 42*, 571–587.

Hochman, A. (2013). Racial discrimination: How not to do it. *Studies in History and Philosophy of Biological and Biomedical Sciences, 44*, 278–286.

Hofer, D., Kornberger, I. & Lurz, E. (2010). *Migrantenkinder, Religion, Erziehung, Bildung und kognitive Kompetenz.* [*Immigrant children, religion, education and cognitive competence.*] Graz: Unpublished Student Thesis.

Hoppe, H.-H. (2001). *Democracy: The god that failed.* Rutgers: Transaction.

Horkheimer, M. (1997/1947). *Zur Kritik der instrumentellen Vernunft.* Frankfurt: Fischer.

Hornung, E. (2014). Immigration and the diffusion of technology: The Huguenot diaspora in Prussia. *American Economic Review, 104*, 84–122.

Horton, R. (1967). African traditional thought and western science: Part II. The 'closed' and 'open' predicaments. *Africa: Journal of the International African Institute, 37*, 155–187.

Houreld, K. (2009). African children denounced as "witches" by Christian pastors. *The Huffington Post, October 18, 2009*; Retrieved from www.huffingtonpost.com/2009/10/18/african-children-denounce_n_324943.html.

Howard, R. W. (1999). Preliminary real-world evidence that average intelligence really is rising. *Intelligence, 27*, 235–250.

Huckins, L. M., Boraska, V., Franklin, C. S., Floyd, J. A. B., Southam, L., GCAN, WTCCC, Sullivan, P. F., Bulik, C. M., Collier, D. A., Tyler-Smith, C., Zeggini, E. & Tachmazidou, I. (2014). Using ancestry-informative markers to identify fine structure across 15 populations of European origin. *European Journal of Human Genetics, 22*, 1190–1200.

Huebner, J. (2005). A possible declining trend for worldwide innovation. *Technological Forecasting and Social Change, 72*, 980–986.

Hungi, N., Makuwa, D., Ross, K., Saito, M., Dolata, S., Capelle, F. v., Paviot, L. & Vellien, J. (2010). *SACMEQ III Project Results: Pupil achievement levels in reading and mathematics*. Retrieved from www.sacmeq.org/downloads/sacmeqIII/WD01_SACMEQ_III_Results_Pupil_Achievement.pdf.

Hunt, E. (1995). *Will we be smart enough? A cognitive analysis of the coming workforce*. New York: Russell Sage Foundation.

(2012). What makes nations intelligent? *Perspectives on Psychological Science, 7*, 284–306.

Hunt, E. & Sternberg, R. J. (2006). Sorry, wrong numbers: An analysis of a study of a correlation between skin color and IQ. *Intelligence, 34*, 131–137.

Huntington, S. P. (1996). *The clash of civilizations*. New York: Simon & Schuster.

Innis, N. K. (1992). Tolman and Tryon: Early research on the inheritance of the ability to learn. *American Psychologist, 47*, 190–197.

Irwing, P. & Lynn, R. (2006). The relation between childhood IQ and income in middle age. *Journal of Social Political and Economic Studies, 31*, 191–196.

Irwing, P., Hamza, A., Khaleefa, O. & Lynn, R. (2008). Effects of Abacus training on the intelligence of Sudanese children. *Personality and Individual Differences, 45*, 694–696.

Itzkoff, S. W. (1994). *The decline of intelligence in America. A strategy for national renewal*. Westport: Praeger.

(2003). *2050: The collapse of the global techno-economy*. Ashfield: Paideia.

Jablonski, N. G. & Chaplin, G. (2000). The evolution of human skin coloration. *Journal of Human Evolution, 39*, 57–106.

Jacob, M. C. (1997). *Scientific culture and the making of the industrial west*. New York: Oxford University Press.

(2014). *The first knowledge economy. Human capital and the European economy, 1750–1850*. Cambridge: Cambridge University Press.

Jaensch, E. R. (1938). Grundsätze fur Auslese, Intelligenzprüfung und ihre praktische Verwirklichung. [Principles for selection, intelligence measurement and its application.] *Zeitschrift für angewandte Psychologie und Charakterkunde, 55*, 1–14.

Jahrbuch (2004). *Jahrbuch*. Munich: DTV.

Jardin-Botelho, A., Raff, S., Rodrigues, R. A., Hoffman, H. J., Diemert, J. H., Correa-Oliviera, R., Bethony, J. M. & Gazzinelli, M. F. (2008). Hookworm, Ascaris lumbricoides infection and polyparasitism associated with poor cognitive performance in Brazilian schoolchildren. *Tropical Medicine and International Health, 13*, 994–1004.

Jaspers, K. (1919). *Psychologie der Weltanschauungen. [Psychology of world views.]* Berlin: Springer.

Jedrychowski, W., Maugeri, U., Perera, F., Stigter, L., Jankowski, J., Butscher, M., Mroz, E., Flak, E., Skarupa, A. & Sowa, A. (2011). Cognitive function of 6-year old children exposed to mold-contaminated homes in early postnatal period. Prospective birth cohort study in Poland. *Physiology & Behavior, 104*, 989–995.

Jensen, A. R. (1969). How much can we boost IQ and scholastic achievement? *Harvard Educational Review, 39*, 1–123.

(1970). Race and the genetics of intelligence: A reply to Lewontin. *Bulletin of the Atomic Scientists, 26*, 17–23.

(1980). *Bias in mental testing.* London: Methuen.

(1983). Effects of inbreeding on mental-ability factors. *Personality and Individual Differences, 4*, 71–87.

(1998). *The g factor. The science of mental ability.* Westport, CT: Praeger.

(2006a). *Clocking the mind: Mental chronometry and individual differences.* Amsterdam: Elsevier.

(2006b). Comments on correlations of IQ with skin color and geographic-demographic variables. *Intelligence, 34*, 128–131.

Johnson, W. (2010). Understanding the genetics of intelligence: Can height help? Can corn oil? *Current Directions in Psychological Science, 19*, 177–182.

Jones, Ch. I. & Klenow, P. J. (2016). Beyond GDP? Welfare across countries and time. *American Economic Review, 106*, 2426–2457.

Jones, G. (2012). Cognitive skill and technology diffusion: An empirical test. *Economic Systems, 36*, 444–460.

(2016). *Hive mind: How your nation's IQ matters so much more than your own.* Stanford: Stanford University Press.

Jones, G. & Schneider, W. J. (2006). Intelligence, human capital, and economic growth: A Bayesian Averaging of Classical Estimates (BACE) approach. *Journal of Economic Growth, 11*, 71–93.

(2010). IQ in the production function: Evidence from immigrant earnings. *Economic Inquiry, 48*, 743–755.

Joynson, R. B. (1989). *The Burt affair.* London: Routledge.

Jürges, H., Schneider, K. & Büchel, F. (2005). The effect of central exit examinations on student achievement: Quasi-experimental evidence from TIMSS Germany. *Journal of the European Economic Association, 3*, 1134–1155.

Jussim, L. (2012). *Social perception and social reality: Why accuracy dominates bias and self-fulfilling prophecy.* Oxford: Oxford University Press.

Kanazawa, S. (2004). General intelligence as a domain-specific adaptation. *Psychological Review, 111*, 512–523.

(2012). *The intelligence paradox.* Hoboken, NJ: Wiley.

Kangasniemi, M., Mas, M. & Serrano, C. R. L. (2012). The economic impact of migration. *Journal of Productivity Analysis, 38*, 333–343.

Kant, I. (1996/1786). What does it mean to orient oneself in thinking? In A. W. Wood (Ed.), *Religion and rational theology.* (pp. 1–18). Cambridge: Cambridge University Press.

Kapur, D. & McHale, J. (2005). *Give us your best and brightest: The global hunt for talent and its impact on the developing world.* Washington: Center for Global Development.

Karabel, J. (2005). *The chosen: The hidden history of admission and exclusion at Harvard, Yale, and Princeton.* Boston: Houghton Mifflin.

Karlin, A. (2012a). Analysis of China's PISA 2009 results. *Anatoly Karlin Blog,* posted on August 13, 2012, http://akarlin.com/2012/08/13/analysis-of-chinas-pisa-2009-results.

   (2012b). Through a glass ceiling darkly. *Anatoly Karlin Blog,* posted on April 16, 2012, http://akarlin.com/2012/04/16/through-a-glass-ceiling-darkly-racial-iq-disparities-and-the-wealth-of-nations.

Kashamura, A. (1973). *Famille, sexualité et culture. Essai sur les moeurs sexuelles et les cultures des peuples des Grands Lacs africains.* Paris: Payot.

Kaufmann, D., Kraay, A. & Mastruzzi, M. (2010). *The worldwide governance indicators: A summary of methodology, data and analytical issues. The worldwide governance indicators, 2012 update.* Washington: World Bank Policy Research Working Paper No. 5430. Retrieved from http://info.worldbank.org/governance/wgi/wgidataset.xlsx.

Kaufmann, E. P. (2004). *The rise and fall of Anglo-America.* Cambridge, MA: Harvard University Press.

Kaufman, S. B., Reynolds, M. R., Liu, X., Kaufman, A. S. & McGrew, K. S. (2012). Are cognitive $g$ and academic achievement $g$ one and the same $g$? *Intelligence, 40,* 123–138.

Kendler, K. S. & Baker, J. H. (2007). Genetic influences on measures of the environment: A systematic review. *Psychological Medicine, 37,* 615–626.

Kendler, K. S., Turkheimer, E., Ohlsson, H., Sundquist, J. & Sundquist, K. (2015). Family environment and the malleability of cognitive ability: A Swedish national home-reared and adopted-away cosibling control study. *Proceedings of the National Academy of Sciences (PNAS), 112,* 4612–4617.

Kenny, Ch. (2005). Why are we worried about income? Nearly everything that matters is converging. *World Development, 33,* 1–19.

Keynes, J. M. (2010/1930). Economic possibilities for our grandchildren. In J. M. Keynes (ed.), *Essays in persuasion* (pp. 321–332). Cambridge: Cambridge University Press.

Kintsch, W. (1998). *Comprehension: A paradigm for cognition.* Cambridge: Cambridge University Press.

Kirkegaard, E. O. W. (2014a). Criminality and fertility among Danish immigrant populations. *Open Differential Psychology.* Retrieved from http://openpsych.net/ODP/wp-content/uploads/2014/03/criminality_fertility.pdf.

   (2014b). Criminality among Norwegian immigrant populations. *Open Differential Psychology.* Retrieved from http://openpsych.net/ODP/wp-content/uploads/2014/04/criminality_norway-final.pdf.

   (2015). Crime among Dutch immigrant groups is predictable from country level variables. *Open Differential Psychology.* Retrieved from http://openpsych.net/ODP/wp-content/uploads/2015/10/Kirkegaard2015DutchCrime.pdf.

Kirkegaard, E. O. W. & Becker, D. (2017). Immigrant crime in Germany 2012–2015. *Open Quantitative Sociology & Political Science,* 1–22.

Kirkegaard, E. O. W. & Fuerst, J. (2017). Admixture in Argentina. *Mankind Quarterly*, *57*, 542–580.

Kirkegaard, E. O. W. & Tranberg, B. (2015). Increasing inequality in general intelligence and socioeconomic status as a result of immigration in Denmark 1980–2014. *Open Differential Psychology, 4 March 2015*. Retrieved from http://openpsych.net/ODP/wp-content/uploads/2015/03/KirkegaardImmigration Inequality.pdf.

Kirsch, I., Braun, H. & Yamamoto, K. (2007). *America's perfect storm: Three forces changing our nation's future*. Princeton, NJ: Educational Testing Service (ETS).

Klauer, K. J. & Phye, G. D. (2008). Inductive reasoning: A training approach. *Review of Educational Research*, *78*, 85–123.

Koenen, K. C., Moffitt, T. E., Caspi, A., Taylor, A. & Purcell, S. (2003). Domestic violence is associated with environmental suppression of IQ in young children. *Development and Psychopathology*, *15*, 297–311.

Koerselman, K. (2013). Incentives from curriculum tracking. *Economics of Education Review*, *32*, 140–150.

Kohlberg, L. (1984). *Essays on moral development*. San Francisco: Harper & Row.
(1987). *Child psychology and childhood education. A cognitive-developmental view*. New York: Longman.

Komlos, J. & Baur, M. (2004). From the tallest to (one of) the fattest: The enigmatic fate of the American population in the 20th century. *Economics and Human Biology*, *2*, 57–74.

Komlos, J. & Kriwy, P. (2003). The biological standard of living in the two Germanies. *German Economic Review*, *4*, 493–507.

Komlos, J. & Snowdon, B. (2005). Measures of progress and other tall stories. From income to anthropometrics. *World Economics*, *6*, 87–135.

Koolwal, G. & van de Walle, D. (2010). *Access to water, women's work and child outcomes*. Washington: The World Bank, Policy Research Working Paper 5302.

Koopmans, R. (2014). *Religious fundamentalism and out-group hostility among Muslims and Christians in Western Europe*. Berlin: WZB Discussion Paper SP VI 2014–101.
(2016). Does assimilation work? Sociocultural determinants of labour market participation of European Muslims. *Journal of Ethnic and Migration Studies*, *42*, 197–216.

Kopiez, R. (2010). Vuvuzela. *Frankfurter Allgemeine Zeitung, 14–6-10*. Retrieved from www.faz.net/aktuell/sport/fussball/vuvuzela-trompeter-aller-vereine-vereinigt-euch-1998823.html.

Kovas, Y., Harlaar, N., Petrill, S. A. & Plomin, R. (2005). 'Generalist genes' and mathematics in 7-year-old twins. *Intelligence*, *33*, 473–489.

Kramer, D. A. (1983). Post-formal operations? *Human Development*, *26*, 91–105.

Kramer, J. (2009). General mental ability and occupational success in Germany. *Psychologische Rundschau*, *60*, 82–98.

Krapohl, E., Rimfeld, K., Shakeshaft, N. G., Trzaskowski, M., McMillan, A., Pingault, J.-B., Asbury, K., Harlaar, N., Kovas, Y., Daleg, P. S. & Plomin, R. (2014). The high heritability of educational achievement reflects many genetically influenced traits, not just intelligence. *PNAS*, *42*, 15273–15278.

Krauss, H. (2014). Islam in "Reinkultur". [Islam at its finest.] *Hintergrund-Verlag, 29.* August 2014. Retrieved from www.hintergrund-verlag.de/texte-islam-hartmut-krauss-islam-in-reinkultur-zur-antriebs-und-legitimationsgrundlage-des-islamischen-staates.html. Not authorized translation here: http://gatesofvienna.net/2014/09/pure-unadulterated-islam-part-two-mohammed-the-model.

Krebs, D. & Gillmore, J. (1982). The relationship among the first stages of cognitive development, role-taking abilities, and moral development. *Child Development, 53,* 877–886.

Krueger, A. B. (1999). Experimental estimates of education production functions. *Quarterly Journal of Economics, 114,* 497–532.

Kuhn, Th. S. (1962). *The structure of scientific revolutions.* Chicago: University of Chicago Press.

Kulik, J. A. & Kulik, C.-L. C. (1992). Meta-analytic findings on grouping programs. *Gifted Child Quarterly, 36,* 73–77.

Kuncel, N. R. & Hezlett, S. A. (2010). Fact and fiction in cognitive ability testing for admissions and hiring decisions. *Current Directions in Psychological Science, 19,* 339–345.

Kura, K., te Nijenhuis, J. & Dutton, E. (2015). Why do Northeast Asians win so few Nobel Prizes? *Comprehensive Psychology, 4,* 15.

Kuran, T. (2012). *The long divergence: How Islamic law held back the Middle East.* Princeton, NJ: Princeton University Press.

Kurian, G. T. (2001). *The illustrated book of world rankings.* Armonk, NY: Sharpe.

Kuznets, S. (1934). *National income, 1929–32. Letter from the acting secretary of commerce transmitting in response to senate resolution no. 220 (72d cong.). A report on national income, 1929–32.* Washington: United States Government Printing Office.

Lacey, P. R. (1970). A cross-cultural study of classificatory ability in Australia. *Journal of Cross-Cultural Psychology, 1,* 293–304.

La Griffe du Lion (2002). *The smart fraction theory of IQ and the wealth of nations.* Retrieved from www.lagriffedulion.f2s.com/sft.htm.

Lapointe, A. E., Askew, J. M. & Mead, N. A. (1992a). *The international assessment of educational progress: Learning science.* Princeton, NJ: Educational Testing Service.

Lapointe, A. E., Mead, N. A. & Askew, J. M. (1992b). *The international assessment of educational progress: Learning mathematics.* Princeton, NJ: ETS.

Land Berlin (2010). *Gesetz zur Regelung von Partizipation und Integration in Berlin.* [*Bill for regulation of participation and integration in Berlin.*] Retrieved May 25, 2012, from www.berlin.de/imperia/md/content/lb-integration-migration/publikationen/recht/partintg_bf.pdf?start&ts=1318346642&file=partintg_bf.pdf.

Landes, D. S. (1972/1969). *The unbound Prometheus.* Cambridge: Cambridge University Press.

(1983). *Revolution in time.* Cambridge: Belknap/Harvard.

(1998). *The wealth and poverty of nations.* New York: Norton.

(2006). Why Europe and the West? Why not China? *Journal of Economic Perspectives, 20,* 3–22.

Lanvin, B. & Evans, P. (2013). *The global talent competitiveness index 2013.* Singapore: Novus Media Solutions (INSEAD, Institut Européen d'Administration des Affaires).

Laqueur, W. (2007). *The last days of Europe*. New York: Dunne.

Lavy, V. (2015). Do differences in schools' instruction time explain international achievement gaps? *Economic Journal, 125*, F397–F424.

Lee, D. S. & Kun, L. S. (2014). As effective as a mother's kiss – Turtles in Traditional Chinese Medicine. *Radiata, 23*, 4–29.

Lee, J.-W. & Barro, R. J. (1997). *Schooling quality in a cross-section of countries*. New York. Retrieved November 18, 2004 from www.nber.org/papers/W6198.

(2001). Schooling quality in a cross-section of countries. *Economica, 68*, 465–488.

Legatum Institute (2013). *The 2013 Legatum Prosperity Index*. London: Legatum Institute. Retrieved from http://media.prosperity.com/2013/pdf/publications/PI2013Brochure_WEB.pdf.

Le Goff, J. (1980). *Time, work and culture in the Middle Ages*. Chicago: Chicago University Press.

(1993/1957). *Intellectuals in the Middle Ages*. Oxford: Blackwell.

Lehman, H. C. (1966). The most creative years of engineers and other technologists. *The Journal of Genetic Psychology, 108*, 263–277.

Lehrl, S. & Seifert, K. (2003). Does hearing loss in adults diminish intelligence? *HNO, 51*, 296–304.

LePan, D. (1989). *The cognitive revolution in Western culture*. London: Macmillan.

Leroi, A. M. (2005). A family tree in every gene. *Journal of Genetics, 84*, 3–6.

Levels, M., Dronkers, J. & Kraaykamp, G. (2008). Immigrant children's educational achievement in Western countries: Origin, destination, and community effects on mathematical performance. *American Sociological Review, 73*, 835–853.

Lévi-Strauss, C. (1952). *Race and history*. Paris: UNESCO.

Levine, R. (1997). *A geography of time*. New York: Basic Books.

Lévy-Bruhl, L. (1923/1922). *Primitive mentality*. London: George Allen.

Lewis, B. (2010). *Faith and power. Religion and politics in the Middle East*. New York: Oxford University Press.

Lewis, J. E., Degusta, D., Meyer, M. R., Monge, J. M., Mann, A. E. & Holloway, R. L. (2011). The mismeasure of science: Stephen Jay Gould versus Samuel George Morton on skulls and bias. *PLoS Biology, 9*(6), e1001071.

Lewontin, R. C. (1970). Race and intelligence. *Bulletin of the Atomic Scientists, 26*, 2–8.

Li, H., Loyalka, P., Rozelle, S. & Wu, B. (2017). Human capital and China's future growth. *Journal of Economic Perspectives, 31*, 25–48.

Lindsey, B. (2012). *Human capitalism: How economic growth has made us smarter – and more unequal*. Princeton, NJ: Princeton University Press.

Lipset, S. M. & Raab, E. (1995). *Jews and the New American Scene*. Cambridge: Harvard University Press.

List, F. (1909/1841). *The national system of political economy*. London: Longmans.

LLECE (2000). *Primer estudio internacional comparativo sobre lenguaje, matemática*. Santiago de Chile: UNESCO/Andros.

(2008). *Student achievement in Latin America and the Caribbean*. Santiago, Chile: Regional Bureau for Education.

Loeb, S., Bridges, M., Bassok, D., Fuller, B. & Rumberger, R. W. (2007). How much is too much? *Economics of Education Review, 26*, 52–66.

Loehlin, J. C. (1997). Dysgenesis and IQ. What evidence is relevant? *American Psychologist, 52*, 1236–1239.

Loveless, T. (2013). Attention OECD-PISA: Your silence on China is wrong. *Blog Brookings, December 11*. Retrieved from www.brookings.edu/blogs/brown-center-chalkboard/posts/2013/12/11-shanghai-pisa-scores-wrong-loveless.

Lukács, G. (1980/1954). *Destruction of reason*. London: Merlin.

Lukas, F. (2012). *Nikon D800/E outer AF sensor accuracy*. May 8, 2012, v1.0. Retrieved from www.falklumo.com/lumolabs/articles/D800Focus/OuterSensors.pdf.

Luria, A. R. (1976/1974). *Cognitive development. Its cultural and social foundations*. Cambridge, MA: Harvard University Press.

Lutz, W., Butz, W. P. & Kc, S. (Eds.). (2014). *World population and human capital in the twenty-first century*. Oxford: Oxford University Press.

Lykken, D. (1998). How can educated people continue to be radical environmentalists? Edge – *The Third Culture, 20. 6. 1998*, www.edge.org/3rd_culture/lykken/index.html.

Lynn, R. (1982). IQ in Japan and the United States shows a growing disparity. *Nature, 297*, 222–223.

(1987). The intelligence of the Mongoloids: A psychometric, evolutionary and neurological theory. *Personality and Individual Differences, 8*, 813–844.

(1990). The role of nutrition in secular increases in intelligence. *Personality and Individual Differences, 11*, 273–285.

(1996). *Dysgenics. Genetic deterioration in modern populations*. Westport, CT: Praeger.

(2006). *Race differences in intelligence: An evolutionary analysis*. Atlanta, GA: Washington Summit.

(2007). Race differences in intelligence, creativity and creative achievement. *Mankind Quarterly, 48*, 157–168.

(2008). *The global bell curve*. Augusta, GA: Washington Summit.

(2010). In Italy, north-south differences in IQ predict differences in income, education, infant mortality, stature, and literacy. *Intelligence, 38*, 93–100.

(2011). *The chosen people: A study of Jewish intelligence and achievement*. Whitefish: Washington Summit.

(2012). North-south differences in Spain in IQ, educational attainment, per capita income, literacy, life expectancy and employment. *Mankind Quarterly, 52*, 265–291.

(2013). Who discovered the Flynn effect? *Intelligence, 41*, 765–769.

Lynn, R. & Cheng, H. (2013). Differences in intelligence across thirty-one regions of China and their economic and demographic correlates. *Intelligence, 41*, 553–559.

Lynn, R. & Harvey, J. (2008). The decline of the world's IQ. *Intelligence, 36*, 112–120.

Lynn, R. & Vanhanen, T. (2002). *IQ and the wealth of nations*. Westport, CT: Praeger.

(2006). *IQ and global inequality*. Athens, GA: Washington Summit.

(2012). *Intelligence. A unifying construct for the social sciences*. London: Ulster Institute for Social Research.

Lynn, R. & Yadav, P. (2015). Differences in cognitive ability, per capita income, infant mortality, fertility and latitude across the states of India. *Intelligence, 49*, 179–185.

Lynn, R., Harvey, J. & Nyborg, H. (2009). Average intelligence predicts atheism rates across 137 nations. *Intelligence, 37*, 11–15.

Maas, H. L. J. v. d., Dolan, C. V., Grasman, R. P. P. P., Wicherts, J. M., Huizenga, H. M. & Raijmakers, M. E. J. (2006). A dynamical model of general intelligence: The positive manifold of intelligence by mutualism. *Psychological Review, 113*, 842–861.

MacArthur, R. H. & Wilson, E. O. (1967). *The theory of island biogeography.* Princeton, NJ: Princeton University Press.

MacDonald, K. (2002/1994). *A people that shall dwell alone.* San Jose, CA: Writers Club.

Maddison, A. (2001). *The world economy: A millennial perspective.* Paris: OECD.

(2007). *Contours of the world economy, 1–2030 AD: Essays in macro-economic history.* New York: Oxford University Press.

(2008). *Statistics on world population, GDP and per capita GDP, 1–2008 AD.* Retrieved from www.ggdc.net/maddison/Historical_Statistics/horizontal-file_02-2010.xls.

Maestas, N., Mullen, K. J. & Powell, D. (2014). The effect of population aging on economic growth. *RAND Working Papers, 1063.*

Makotschnig, N. (2010). Auswirkungen des Kindergartenbesuchs auf die kognitiven Fähigkeiten und das proschulische Verhalten bei Migrantenkindern. [Effects of kindergarten attendance on cognitive abilities and educational behaviour of migrants.] Graz: Unpublished Master's Thesis.

Makuwa, D. (2010). *What are the levels and trends in reading and mathematics achievement?* SACMEQ Policy Issues Series, 2. Retrieved from www.sacmeq.org/downloads/policy/002-SACMEQPolicyIssuesSeries-Pupilachievement.pdf.

Malinowski, B. (1954/1948). *Magic, science and religion.* Garden City, NY: Doubleday.

Malloy, J. (2013). HVGIQ: Cuba. *Human Varieties.* Posted on January 31, 2013, http://humanvarieties.org/2013/01/31/hvgiq-cuba.

(2014). HVGIQ: Vietnam. *Human Varieties.* Posted on June 19, 2014, http://humanvarieties.org/2014/06/19/hvgiq-vietnam.

Mani, A., Mullainathan, S., Shafir, E. & Zhao, J. (2013). Poverty impedes cognitive function. *Science, 341*, 976–980.

Mankiw, N. G. (2013). Defending the one percent. *Journal of Economic Perspectives, 27*, 21–34.

Mankiw, N. G., Romer, D. & Weil, D. N. (1992). A contribution to the empirics of economic growth. *Quarterly Journal of Economics, 107*, 407–437.

Manrique-Millones, D., Flores-Mendoza, C. & Millones-Rivalles, R. (2015). Intelligence in Peru: Students' results in Raven and its relationship to SES. *Intelligence, 51*, 71–78.

Manyika, J., Woetzel, J., Dobbs, R., Remes, J., Labaye, E. & Jordan, A. (2015). *Global growth: Can productivity save the day in an aging world?* New York: McKinsey Global Institute.

Maranto, R., Redding, R. E. & Hess, F. M. (Hrsg.). (2009). *The politically correct university.* Washington: AEI.

Marsh, H. W., Kong, C.-K. & Hau, K.-T. (2000). Longitudinal multilevel models of the Big-Fish-Little-Pond effect on academic self-concept. *Journal of Personality and Social Psychology, 78*, 337–349.

Marshall, M. G. (2013). *Major episodes of political violence (mepv) and conflict regions, 1946–2012.* Vienna, VA: Center for Systemic Peace. Retrieved from www.systemicpeace.org/inscr/MEPV2012.sav.

Marshall, M. G., Gurr, T. R. & Jaggers, K. (2013). *Polity IV project. Political regime characteristics and transitions, 1800–2012. Dataset users' manual*. Vienna, VA: Center for Systemic Peace.

Martin, M. O., Mullis, I. V. S., Gonzalez, E. J. & Chrostowski, S. J. (2004). *TIMSS 2003 international science report*. Chestnut Hill, MA: IES International Study Center.

Martin, M. O., Mullis, I. V. S. & Foy, P. (Eds.). (2008). *TIMSS 2007 international science report*. Chestnut Hill, MA: IEA Study Center.

Martin, M. O., Mullis, I. V. S., Foy, P. & Stanco, G. M. (2012). *TIMSS 2011. International results in science*. Chestnut Hill, MA: IEA International Study Center.

Martin, M. O., Mullis, I. V. S., Foy, P. & Hooper, M. (2016). *TIMSS 2015. International results in science*. Chestnut Hill, MA: International Study Center.

Martin, M. O., Mullis, I. V. S., Gonzalez, E. J., Smith, T. & Kelly, D. L. (1999). *School contexts for learning and instruction*. Chestnut Hill, MA: IEA International Study Center.

Martin, M. O., Mullis, I. V. S., Gregory, K. D., Hoyle, C. & Shen, C. (2000a). *Effective schools in science and mathematics: IEA's Third International Mathematics and Science Study (TIMSS)*. Chestnut Hill, MA: TIMSS International Study Center.

Martin, M. O., Mullis, I. V. S., Beaton, A. E., Gonzalez, E. J., Smith, T. & Kelly, D. L. (1997). *Science achievement in the primary school years*. Chestnut Hill, MA: International Study Center.

Martin, M. O., Mullis, I. V. S., Gonzalez, E. J., Gregory, K. D., Smith, T. A., Chrostowski, S. J., Garden, R. A. & O'Connor, K. M. (2000b). *TIMSS 1999 international science report*. Chestnut Hill, MA: International Study Center.

Mauro, P. (1995). Corruption and growth. *Quarterly Journal of Economics, 110*, 681–712.

Mayer, R. E. & Hegarty, M. (1996). The process of understanding mathematical problems. In R. J. Sternberg & T. Ben-Zeev (Eds.), *The nature of mathematical thinking* (pp. 29–53). Mahwah, NJ: Erlbaum.

Mayer, S. E. (1997). *What money can't buy: Family income and children's life chances*. Cambridge, MA: Harvard University Press.

Mbiti, I. M. (2016). The need for accountability in education in developing countries. *Journal of Economic Perspectives, 30*, 109–132.

McCloskey, D. N. (2006). *The bourgeois virtues: Ethics for an age of commerce*. Chicago: University of Chicago Press.

  (2010). *Bourgeois dignity: Why economics can't explain the modern world*. Chicago: University of Chicago Press.

  (2016). *Bourgeois equality: How ideas, not capital or institutions, enriched the world*. Chicago: The University of Chicago Press.

McDaniel, M. A. (2005). Big-brained people are smarter: A meta-analysis of the relationship between in-vivo brain volume and intelligence. *Intelligence, 33*, 337–346.

McNamee, S. (1977). Moral behaviour, moral development and motivation. *Journal of Moral Education, 7*, 27–31.

Meadows, D., Meadows, D., Randers, J. & Behrens, W. (1972). *The limits to growth*. New York: Universe.

Meisenberg, G. (2003). IQ population genetics: It's not as simple as you think. *Mankind Quarterly, 44,* 185–210.

(2007). Does multiculturalism promote income inequality? *Mankind Quarterly, 47,* 3–39.

(2009). Wealth, intelligence, politics and global fertility differentials. *Journal of Biosocial Science, 41,* 519–535.

(2010). The reproduction of intelligence. *Intelligence, 38,* 220–230.

(2014). Cognitive human capital and economic growth in the 21st century. In T. Abrahams (Ed.), *Economic growth in the 21ˢᵗ century* (pp. 49–106). New York: Nova Publishers.

(2015a). Do we have valid country-level measures of personality? *Mankind Quarterly, 55,* 360–382.

(2015b). *Trends of the world's intelligence: Past, present, and future.* Talk at the APS-Convention 2015 in New York, 21–24 May 2015.

Meisenberg, G. & Woodley, M. A. (2013). Are cognitive differences between countries diminishing? Evidence from TIMSS and PISA. *Intelligence, 41,* 808–816.

Meisenberg, G. & Woodley of Menie, M. A. (2014). Dysgenic trends in the United States during the 20th century. Talk at 13. December 2014 at the 15ᵗʰ Conference of the International Society for Intelligence Research (ISIR): Graz, Austria.

Meisenberg, G., Lawless, E., Lambert, E. & Newton, A. (2006). The social ecology of intelligence on a Caribbean island. *Mankind Quarterly, 46,* 395–433.

Mendieta, E. & Habermas, J. (1999). Über Gott und die Welt. [About God and the world.] *Jahrbuch Politische Theologie, 3,* 190–209.

Merriman, C. (1924). The intellectual resemblance of twins. *Psychological Monographs, 33,* i–57.

Merton, R. K. (1936). Puritanism, Pietism, and Science. *Sociological Review, 28,* 1–30.

Meyer, J. W. & Jepperson, R. L. (2000). The "actors" of modern society: The cultural construction of social agency. *Sociological Theory, 18,* 100–120.

Meyer, J. W., Boli, J. & Thomas, G. M. (1987). Ontology and rationalization in the western cultural account. In G. M. Thomas, J. W. Meyer, F. O. Ramirez & J. Boli (Hrsg.), *Institutional structure* (pp. 12–37). Newbury Park: Sage.

Meyer, J. W., Ramirez, F. O. & Soysal, Y. N. (1992). World expansion of mass education, 1870–1980. *Sociology of Education, 65,* 128–149.

Michael, J. S. (1988). A new look at Morton's craniological research. *Current Anthropology, 29,* 349–354.

Miguel, E. & Gugerty, M. K. (2005). Ethnic diversity, social sanctions, and public goods in Kenya. *Journal of Public Economics, 89,* 2325–2368.

Miguel, E. & Kremer, M. (2004). Worms: Identifying impacts on education and health in the presence of treatment externalities. *Econometrica, 72,* 159–217.

Miller, A. K. H. & Corsellis, J. A. N. (1977). Evidence for a secular increase in human brain weight during the past century. *Annals of Human Biology, 4,* 253–257.

Miller, E. M. (1991). Climate and intelligence. *Mankind Quarterly, 32,* 127–132.

Miller, G. (2009). *Spent: Sex, evolution and consumer behaviour.* New York: Viking.

Miller, T., Holmes, K. R. & Feulner, E. J. (2013). *2013 index of economic freedom.* Washington: The Heritage Foundation. Retrieved from www.heritage.org/index/pdf/2013/book/index_2013.pdf.

Michalopoulos, S. & Papaioannou, E. (2011). Divide and rule or the rule of the divided? Evidence from Africa. *NBER Working Paper, 17184.*

Mill, J. S. (2015/1859). *On liberty, utilitarianism and other essays.* Oxford: Oxford University Press.

(1977/1861). *Essays on politics and society.* Toronto: University of Toronto Press.

Mincer, J. (1958). Investment in human capital and personal income distribution. *Journal of Political Economy, 66,* 281–302.

Mingroni, M. A. (2007). Resolving the IQ paradox: Heterosis as a cause of the Flynn effect and other trends. *Psychological Review, 114,* 806–829.

Mises, L. v. (1996/1927). *Liberalism: The classical tradition.* New York: Cobden Press.

Moehler, E., Kagan, J., Brunner, R., Wiebel, A., Kaufmann, C. & Resch, F. (2006). Association of behavioral inhibition with hair pigmentation in a European sample. *Biological Psychology, 72,* 344–346.

Mokyr, J. (2005). The intellectual origins of modern economic growth. *Journal of Economic History, 65,* 285–351.

(2016). *A culture of growth: The origins of the modern economy.* Princeton, NJ: Princeton University Press.

Montesquieu, Ch.-L. (1989/1748). *The spirit of laws.* Cambridge: Cambridge University Press.

Moore, M. (2008). In France, prisons filled with Muslims. *Washington Post,* 29 April 2008, www.washingtonpost.com/wp-dyn/content/article/2008/04/28/AR2008042802560.html.

Moore, S. & Simon, J. L. (2000). *It's getting better all the time: 100 greatest trends of the last 100 years.* Washington: Cato.

Morris, I. (2013). *The measure of civilization: How social development decides the fate of nations.* Princeton, NJ: Princeton University Press.

Moser, P., Voena, A. & Waldinger, F. (2014). German Jewish émigrés and US invention. *American Economic Review, 104,* 3222–3255.

Muller, C. B., Ride, S. M., Fouke, J., Whitney, T., Denton, D. D. et al. (2005). Gender differences and performance in science. *Science, 307,* 1043.

Müller-Jentsch, D. (Ed.). (2008). *Die Neue Zuwanderung: Die Schweiz zwischen Brain-Gain und Überfremdungsangst. [New immigration.]* Zürich: Verlag Neue Züricher Zeitung.

Mullis, I., Martin, M. O., Gonzales, E. J. & Kennedy, A. M. (2003). *PIRLS 2001 international report.* Chestnut Hill, MA: IEA.

Mullis, I., Martin, M. O., Kennedy, A. M. & Foy, P. (2007). *PIRLS 2006 international report.* Chestnut Hill, MA: IEA/TIMSS & PIRLS International Study Center.

Mullis, I. V. S., Martin, M. O. & Foy, P. (2008). *TIMSS 2007 international mathematics report.* Chestnut Hill, MA: TIMSS & PIRLS Study Center.

Mullis, I. V. S., Martin, M. O., Foy, P. & Arora, A. (2012a). *TIMSS 2011. International results in mathematics.* Chestnut Hill, MA: IEA/TIMSS & PIRLS International Study Center.

Mullis, I. V. S., Martin, M. O., Foy, P. & Drucker, K. T. (2012b). *PIRLS 2011. International results in reading*. Chestnut Hill, MA: IEA/TIMSS & PIRLS International Study Center.

Mullis, I. V. S., Martin, M. O., Gonzalez, E. J. & Chrostowski, S. J. (2004). *TIMSS 2003 international mathematics report*. Chestnut Hill, MA: TIMSS & PIRLS International Study Center, Boston College.

Mullis, I. V. S., Martin, M. O., Beaton, A. E., Gonzalez, E. J., Kelly, D. L. & Smith, T. (1997). *Mathematics achievement in the primary school years*. Chestnut Hill, MA: TIMSS International Study Center.

Mullis, I. V. S., Martin, M. O., Gonzalez, E. J., Gregory, K. D., Garden, R. A., O'Connor, K. M., Chrostowski, S. J. & Smith, T. A. (2000). *TIMSS 1999 international mathematics report*. Chestnut Hill, MA: International Study Center.

Murdock, G. P. & Provost, C. (1973). Measurement of cultural complexity. *Ethnology, 12*, 379–392.

Murray, Ch. (2003). *Human accomplishment: The pursuit of excellence in the arts and sciences, 800 B.C. to 1950*. New York: Harper-Collins.

(2007). Jewish genius. *Commentary, 123*(10, April), 29–35.

Murray, Ch. J. L., Barber, R. M., Foreman, K. J., Ozgoren, A. A., Abd-Allah, F. et al. (2015). Global, regional, and national disability-adjusted life years (DALYs) for 306 diseases and injuries and healthy life expectancy (HALE) for 188 countries, 1990–2013. *Lancet, 386*, 2145–2191.

Must, O. & Must, A. (2013). Changes in test-taking patterns over time. *Intelligence, 41*, 780–790.

Nattrass, N. (2012). *The AIDS conspiracy: Science fights back*. New York: Columbia University Press.

NCD (NCD-RisC). (2016). A century of trends in adult human height. *eLife*, e13410.

Neal, D. (2006). Why has black-white skill convergence stopped? In E. A. Hanushek & F. Welch (Eds.), *Handbook of the economics of education* (I, pp. 511–576). Amsterdam: North-Holland.

(2009). The role of private schools in education markets. In M. Berends, M. G. Springer & D. Ballou (Eds.), *Handbook of research on school choice*. (pp. 447–460). New York: Routledge.

Needham, J. (1982). *Science in traditional China: A comparative perspective*. Cambridge, MA: Harvard University Press.

Neisser, U. (Ed.). (1998). *The rising curve*. Washington: APA.

Nelson, B. (1974). Sciences and civilizations, 'East' and 'West'. *Joseph Needham and Max Weber. Boston Studies in the Philosophy of Science, 11*, 445–492.

Nelson, R. R. & Phelps, E. S. (1966). Investment in humans, technological diffusion, and economic growth. *American Economic Review, 56*, 69–75.

Neumann, K. (2003). The late emergence of agriculture in Sub-Saharan Africa: Archaeobotanical evidence and ecological considerations. In K. Neumann, A. Butler & S. Kahlheber (Eds.), *Food, fuel and fields. Progress in African archaeobotany* (pp. 71–92). Köln: Heinrich Barth Institut.

New York Times (2011). Are they learning? *New York Times*, July 17, 2011, p. SR 11.

Nickell, S. & Quintini, G. (2002). The consequences of the decline in public sector pay in Britain. *Economic Journal, 112*, F107-F118.

Niebuhr, A. (2010). Migration and innovation: Does cultural diversity matter for regional R&D activity? *Papers in Regional Science, 89,* 563–585.

Nietzsche, F. (1997/1874). *Untimely meditations.* Cambridge: Cambridge University Press.

Nisbett, R. E. (2009). *Intelligence and how to get it. Why schools and cultures count.* New York: Norton.

Nordhaus, W. (2013). *The climate casino.* New Haven, CT: Yale.

Nores, M., Belfield, C. R., Barnett, W. S. & Schweinhart, L. J. (2005). Updating the economic impacts of the High/Scope Perry Preschool Program. *Educational Evaluation and Policy Analysis, 27,* 245–261.

North, D. C. (1990). *Institutions, institutional change and economic performance.* New York: Cambridge University Press.

North, D. C., Wallis, J. J. & Weingast, B. R. (2009). *Violence and social orders.* Cambridge, New York: Cambridge University Press.

Northstone, K., Joinson, C., Emmett, P., Ness, A. & Paus, T. (2012). Are dietary patterns in childhood associated with IQ at 8 years of age? *Journal of Epidemiology and Community Health, 66,* 624–628.

Nunn, N. (2014). Historical development. In Ph. Aghion & S. N. Durlauf (Eds.), *Handbook of economic growth* (Volume 2A, pp. 347–402). Amsterdam: Elsevier.

Nunnally, J. C. & Bernstein, I. H. (1994). *Psychometric theory.* New York: McGraw-Hill.

Nussbaum, M. C. (2011). *Creating capabilities. The human development approach.* Cambridge, MA: Belknap.

Nyborg, H. (2003). The sociology of psychometric and bio-behavioral sciences: A case study of destructive social reductionism and collective fraud in 20th century academia. In H. Nyborg (Ed.), *The scientific study of general intelligence. Tribute to Arthur R. Jensen* (pp. 441–502). Oxford: Pergamon.

(2009). The intelligence-religiosity nexus: A representative study of white adolescent Americans. *Intelligence, 37,* 81–93.

(2012). The decay of Western civilization: Double relaxed Darwinian selection. *Personality and Individual Differences, 53,* 118–125.

OECD (1999). *Classifying educational programmes.* Paris: OECD.

(2001). *The well-being of nations. The role of human and social capital.* Paris: OECD.

(2003). *Literacy skills for the world of tomorrow.* Paris: OECD.

(2004). *Learning for tomorrow's world.* Paris: OECD.

(2006). *PISA released items – reading.* Paris: OECD.

(2007). *PISA 2006. Volume 2: Data/Données.* Paris: OECD.

(2010a). *PISA 2009 results: What students know and can do (Volume I).* Paris: OECD.

(2010b). *PISA 2009 results: Overcoming social background equity in learning opportunities and outcomes (Volume II).* Paris: OECD.

(2010c). *PISA 2009 results: What makes a school successful? (Volume IV).* Paris: OECD.

(2012). *PISA 2009 technical report.* Paris: OECD.

(2013a). *How's life? Measuring well-being.* Paris: OECD.

(2013b). *OECD skills outlook 2013. First results from the survey of adult skills (PIAAC).* Paris: OECD.

(2013c). *PISA 2012 results: What students know and can do: Student performance in mathematics, reading and science (Volume I).* Paris: OECD.

(2013d). *PISA 2012 results: Excellence through equity: Giving every student the chance to succeed (Volume II).* Paris: OECD.

(2013e). *PISA 2012 results: What makes schools successful? Resources, policies and practices (Volume IV).* Paris: OECD.

(2014a). *Insights from the OECD Social Expenditure database (SOCX).* Paris: OECD.

(2014b). *Shifting gear: Policy challenges for the next 50 years.* Paris: OECD, Economics Department Policy Notes, No. 24.

(2016a). *PISA 2015 results (Volume I): Excellence and equity in education.* Paris: OECD.

(2016b). *PISA 2015 results (Volume II): Policies and practices for successful schools.* Paris: OECD.

(2016c). *Skills matter: Further results from the survey of adult skills (PIAAC).* Paris: OECD.

Oesterdiekhoff, G. W. (2007). Ancient sun cults: Understanding religious rites in terms of developmental psychology. *Mankind Quarterly, 48,* 99–116.

(2009a). The arena games in the Roman Empire: A contribution to the explanation of the history of morals and humanity. *Narodna Umjetnost, 46,* 177–202.

(2009b). Trials against animals: A contribution to the developmental theory of mind and rationality. *Mankind Quarterly, 49,* 346–380.

(2012a). Ontogeny and history. The leading theories reconsidered. *Cultural-Historical Psychology, 8,* 60–69.

(2012b). Was pre-modern man a child? The quintessence of the psychometric and developmental approaches. *Intelligence, 40,* 470–478.

(2012c). *Die geistige Entwicklung der Menschheit. [The cognitive development of humankind.]* Göttingen: Velbrück.

(2013). *Die Entwicklung der Menschheit von der Kindheitsphase zur Erwachsenenreife. [The development of humankind from childhood to adulthood.]* Berlin: Springer.

(2014a). The rise of modern, industrial society. The cognitive-developmental approach as a new key to solve the most fascinating riddle in world history. *Mankind Quarterly, LIV,* 262–312.

(2014b). Evolution of law and justice from ancient to modern times. *Journal on European History of Law, 5,* 54–64.

Oesterdiekhoff, G. W. & Rindermann, H. (2007). The spread of AIDS in developing countries: A psycho-cultural approach. *Journal of Social, Political and Economic Studies, 32,* 201–222.

Open Society Institute (Ed.). (2007a). *Muslims in Europe. Belgium.* New York: Open Soc. Inst.

(Ed.). (2007b). *Muslims in Europe. The Netherlands.* New York: Open Soc. Inst.

Oppenheimer, M. (2010). On a visit to the U.S., a Nigerian witch-hunter explains herself. *New York Times, May 22, 2010,* A11; Retrieved from www.nytimes.com/2010/05/22/us/22beliefs.html?_r=0.

O'Toole, B. I. & Stankov, L. (1992). Ultimate validity of psychological tests. *Personality and Individual Differences, 13,* 699–716.

Ott, A., Andersen, K., Dewey, M. E., Letenneur, L., Brayne, C., Copeland, J. R. M., Dartigues, J.-F., Kragh-Sorensen, P., Lobo, A., Martinez-Lage, J. M., Stijnen, T.,

Hofman, A. & Launer, L. J. (2004). Effect of smoking on global cognitive function in nondemented elderly. *Neurology, 62*, 920–924.

Ousley, S., Jantz, R. & Freid, D. (2009). Understanding race and human variation: Why forensic anthropologists are good at identifying race. *American Journal of Physical Anthropology, 139*, 68–76.

Palacios-Huerta, I. (Ed.). (2013). *In 100 years. Leading economists predict the future.* Cambridge, MA: MIT Press.

Panko, R. R. (1998). What we know about spreadsheet errors. *Journal of End-User Computing*, 10(2), 15–21. (Revised May 2008, http://panko.shidler.hawaii.edu/My%20Publications/Whatknow.htm).

Payton, A. (2009). The impact of genetic research on our understanding of normal cognitive ageing: 1995 to 2009. *Neuropsychology Review, 19*, 451–477.

Pellissier, H. (2012). Brain damage – 83 ways to stupefy intelligence. *Institute for Ethics and Emerging Technologies, January 9, 2012.* Retrieved from http://ieet.org/index.php/ieet/more/pellissier20120109.

(2013). Why is the IQ of Ashkenazi Jews so high? Twenty possible explanations. *Institute for Ethics and Emerging Technologies, December 11, 2013.* Retrieved from http://ieet.org/index.php/IEET/more/pellissier20131211.

Perissutti, Ch. & Rindermann, H. (2013). Cognitive competences of children and influential socio-economic status (SES) factors of parents. *Psychologie in Österreich, 33*, 232–240.

Perkins, A. (2016). *The welfare trait: How state benefits affect personality.* Basingstoke: Palgrave MacMillan.

Pesonen, A.-K., Raikkonen, K., Kajantie, E., Heinonen, K., Henriksson, M., Leskinen, J., Osmond, C., Forsen, T., Barker, D. J. P. & Eriksson, J. G. (2011). Intellectual ability in young men separated temporarily from their parents in childhood. *Intelligence, 39*, 335–341.

Pesta, B. J. & Poznanski, P. J. (2014). Only in America: Cold Winters Theory, race, IQ and well-being. *Intelligence, 46*, 271–274.

Pew Research Center (2015). *The future of world religions: Population growth projections, 2010–2050.* Washington: Pew Research Center.

Phelps, R. P. (2012). The effect of testing on student achievement, 1910–2010. *International Journal of Testing, 12*, 21–43.

Piaget, J. (1948/1932). *The moral judgment of the child.* Glencoe, NY: Free Press.
(2001/1947). *The psychology of intelligence.* London: Routledge.

Piaget, J. & Garcia, R. (1989/1983). *Psychogenesis and the history of science.* New York: Columbia.

Pietschnig, J. & Gittler, G. (2015). A reversal of the Flynn effect for spatial perception in German-speaking countries: Evidence from a cross-temporal IRT-based meta-analysis (1977–2014). *Intelligence, 53*, 145–153.

Pietschnig, J. & Voracek, M. (2015). One century of global IQ gains: A formal meta-analysis of the Flynn effect (1909–2013). *Perspectives on Psychological Science, 10*, 282–306.

Pietschnig, J., Penke, L., Wicherts, J. M., Zeiler, M. & Voracek, M. (2015). Meta-analysis of associations between human brain volume and intelligence differences: How strong are they and what do they mean? *Neuroscience and Biobehavioral Reviews, 57*, 411–432.

Piffer, D. (2013). Correlation of the COMT Val158Met polymorphism with latitude and a hunter-gather lifestyle suggests culture-gene coevolution and selective pressure on cognition genes due to climate. *Anthropological Science, 121,* 161–171.

Piffer, D. & Lynn, R. (2014). New evidence for differences in fluid intelligence between north and south Italy and against school resources as an explanation for the north-south IQ differential. *Intelligence, 46,* 246–249.

Piketty, Th. (2014/2013). *Capital in the twenty-first century.* Cambridge, MA: Belknap.

Pinker, S. (2011). *The better angels of our nature: Why violence has declined.* New York: Viking Adult.

Plomin, R. & Kovas, Y. (2005). Generalist genes and learning disabilities. *Psychological Bulletin, 131,* 592–617.

Plomin, R., DeFries, J. C., Knopik, V. S. & Neiderhiser, J. M. (2013a). *Behavioral genetics.* New York: Worth.

Plomin, R., Haworth, C. M., Meaburn, E., Price, Th. S., Wellcome Trust Case Control Consortium & Davis, O. S. (2013b). Common DNA markers can account for more than half of the genetic influence on cognitive abilities. *Psychological Science, 24,* 562–568.

Pollis, A. (1993). Eastern Orthodoxy and human rights. *Human Rights Quarterly, 15,* 339–356.

Potrafke, N. (2012). Intelligence and corruption. *Economics Letters, 114,* 109–112.

Prenzel, M., Baumert, J., Blum, W., Lehmann, R., Leutner, D., Neubrand, M., Pekrun, R., Rolff, H.-G., Rost, J. & Schiefele, U. (Eds.) (2004). *PISA 2003.* Münster: Waxmann.

Prince, M., Prina, M. & Guerchet, M. (2013). *World Alzheimer report 2013. Journey of caring.* London: Alzheimer's Disease International (ADI).

Pritchett, L. & Viarengo, M. (2009). Producing superstars for the economic mundial: The Mexican predicament with quality of education. In R. Hausmann, E. L. Austin & I. Mia (Eds.), *The Mexico competitiveness report 2009* (pp. 71–89). Genf/ Harvard: World Economic Forum.

Protzko, J., Aronson, J. & Blair, C. (2013). How to make a young child smarter: Evidence from the database of raising intelligence. *Perspectives on Psychological Science, 8,* 25–40.

Putnam, R. D. (2007). E pluribus unum: Diversity and community in the twenty-first century. *Scandinavian Political Studies, 30,* 137–174.

Quacquarelli Symonds (2012). *QS World University Rankings 2012.* Retrieved from www.topuniversities.com/university-rankings/world-university-rankings/2012.

Rahu, K., Rahu, M., Pullmann, H. & Allik, J. (2010). Effect of birth weight, maternal education and prenatal smoking on offspring intelligence at school age. *Early Human Development, 86,* 493–497.

Rampey, B. D., Dion, G. S. & Donahue, P. L. (2009). *NAEP 2008 trends in academic progress.* Washington: National Center for Education Statistics.

Randers, J. (2012). *2052: A global forecast for the next forty years.* White River Junction, VT: Chelsea.

Raven, J. (2000). The Ravens's Progressive Matrices: Change and stability over culture and time. *Cognitive Psychology, 41,* 1–48.

Rawls, J. (1999/1971). *A theory of justice.* Cambridge, MA: Belknap.

Reeve, C. L., Lyerly, J. E. & Peach, H. (2013). Adolescent intelligence and socio-economic wealth independently predict adult marital and reproductive behavior. *Intelligence, 41*, 358–365.

Reinikka, R. & Svensson, J. (2004). Local capture: Evidence from a central government transfer program in Uganda. *Quarterly Journal of Economics, 119*, 679–705.

Renfrew, C. (2008). Neuroscience, evolution and the sapient paradox: The factuality of value and of the sacred. *Philosophical Transactions of the Royal Society B: Biological Sciences, 363*, 2041–2047.

Rescher, N. (1988). *Rationality: A philosophical inquiry into the nature and the rationale of reason.* New York: Oxford University Press.

Richwine, J. (2009). *IQ and immigration policy.* Boston: Dissertation at Harvard University.

Rindermann, H. (2007a). The *g*-factor of international cognitive ability comparisons: The homogeneity of results in PISA, TIMSS, PIRLS and IQ-tests across nations. *European Journal of Personality, 21*, 667–706.

(2007b). The relevance of class ability for teaching and development of individual competences. *Unterrichtswissenschaft, 35*, 68–89.

(2008a). Relevance of education and intelligence at the national level for the economic welfare of people. *Intelligence, 36*, 127–142.

(2008b). Relevance of education and intelligence for the political development of nations: Democracy, rule of law and political liberty. *Intelligence, 36*, 306–322.

(2008c). Interaction between intelligence and society in the perspective of psychometric intelligence research. In G. W. Oesterdiekhoff & H. Rindermann (Eds.), *Culture and cognition: The contributions of psychometrics and Piaget-research for the understanding of cultural differences* (pp. 165–207). Münster: Lit. [in German]

(2011a). Increase of intelligence in childhood and youth. *Psychologie in Erziehung und Unterricht, 58*, 210–224.

(2011b). Results in the International Mathematical Olympiad (IMO) as indicators of the intellectual classes' cognitive-ability level. In A. Ziegler & Ch. Perleth (Eds.), *Excellence. Essays in honour of Kurt. A. Heller* (pp. 303–321). Münster: Lit.

(2012). Intellectual classes, technological progress and economic development: The rise of cognitive capitalism. *Personality and Individual Differences, 53*, 108–113.

(2013). African cognitive ability: Research, results, divergences and recommendations. *Personality and Individual Differences, 55*, 229–233.

Rindermann, H. & Baumeister, A. E. E. (2015). *Validating the interpretations of PISA and TIMSS tasks: A rating study.* International Journal of Testing.

Rindermann, H. & Ceci, S. J. (2009). Educational policy and country outcomes in international cognitive competence studies. *Perspectives on Psychological Science, 4*, 551–577.

(2018). Parents' education is more important than their wealth in shaping their children's intelligence: Results of 19 samples in seven countries at different developmental levels. *Journal for the Education of the Gifted.*

Rindermann, H. & Coyle, Th. R. (2014). Cognitive capitalism: Economic liberty increases the effects of cognitive competence on innovation and wealth. Poster for APS Convention 2014 in San Francisco, 22–25 May 2014.

Rindermann, H. & Heller, K. A. (2005). The benefit of gifted classes and talent schools for developing students' competences and enhancing academic self-concept. *Zeitschrift für Pädagogische Psychologie, 19*, 133–136.

Rindermann, H. & Meisenberg, G. (2009). Relevance of education and intelligence at the national level for health: The case of HIV and AIDS. *Intelligence, 37*, 383–395.

Rindermann, H. & Pichelmann, S. (2015). Future cognitive ability: US IQ prediction until 2060 based on NAEP. *PLoS ONE, 10*, e0138412.

Rindermann, H. & Thompson, J. (2011a). Cognitive capitalism: The effect of cognitive ability on wealth, as mediated through scientific achievement and economic freedom. *Psychological Science, 22*, 754–763.

(2011b). *Intelligence of the future and economic development.* Talk at 10. December 2011 at the 12th Conference of the International Society for Intelligence Research (ISIR) in Limassol, Cyprus.

(2013). Ability rise in NAEP and narrowing ethnic gaps? *Intelligence, 41*, 821–831.

(2016). The cognitive competences of immigrant and native students across the world: An analysis of gaps, possible causes and impact. *Journal of Biosocial Science, 48*, 66–93.

Rindermann, H., Baumeister, A. E. E. & Gröper, A. (2014). Cognitive abilities of Emirati and German engineering university students. *Journal of Biosocial Science, 46*, 199–213.

Rindermann, H., Becker, D. & Coyle, Th. R. (2016). Survey of expert opinion on intelligence: Causes of international differences in cognitive ability tests. *Frontiers in Psychology, 7*(399), 1–9.

Rindermann, H., Coyle, Th. R. & Becker, D. (2013). 2013 survey of expert opinion on intelligence. Talk at 14. December 2013 at the 14th Conference of the International Society for Intelligence Research (ISIR) in Melbourne, Australia.

Rindermann, H., Falkenhayn, L. & Baumeister, A. E. E. (2014). Cognitive ability and epistemic rationality: A study in Nigeria and Germany. *Intelligence, 47*, 23–33.

Rindermann, H., Flores-Mendoza, C. & Woodley, M. A. (2012). Political orientations, intelligence and education. *Intelligence, 40*, 217–225.

Rindermann, H., Hoang, Q. S. N. & Baumeister, A. E. E. (2013). Cognitive ability, parenting and instruction in Vietnam and Germany. *Intelligence, 41*, 366–377.

Rindermann, H., Kodila-Tedika, O. & Christainsen, G. (2015). Cognitive capital, good governance, and the wealth of nations. *Intelligence, 51*, 98–108.

Rindermann, H., Sailer, M. & Thompson, J. (2009). The impact of smart fractions, cognitive ability of politicians and average competence of peoples on social development. *Talent Development and Excellence, 1*, 3–25.

Rindermann, H., Schott, T. & Baumeister, A. E. E. (2013). FLynn effect in Turkey. *Intelligence, 41*, 178–180.

Rindermann, H., Woodley, M. A. & Stratford, J. (2012). Haplogroups as evolutionary markers of cognitive ability. *Intelligence, 40*, 362–375.

Robertson, K. F., Smeets, S., Lubinski, D. & Benbow, C. P. (2010). Beyond the threshold hypothesis. *Current Directions in Psychological Science, 19*, 346–351.

Rogers Commission (1986). *Report of the Presidential Commission on the Space Shuttle Challenger Accident.* Retrieved from http://history.nasa.gov/rogersrep/genindex.htm.

Romer, P. M. (1990). Human capital and growth: Theory and evidence. *Carnegie-Rochester Conference Series on Public Policy, 32,* 251–286.

Roth, B. M. (2014/2010). *The perils of diversity. Immigration and human nature.* Augusta, GA: Washington Summit.

Roth, T. C. & Pravosudov, V. V. (2009). Hippocampal volumes and neuron numbers increase along a gradient of environmental harshness: A large-scale comparison. *Proceedings of the Royal Society B: Biological Sciences, 276,* 401–405.

Roth, T. C., LaDage, L. D. & Pravosudov, V. V. (2010). Learning capabilities enhanced in harsh environments: A common garden approach. *Proceedings of the Royal Society B: Biological Sciences, 277,* 3187–3193.

Rothbard, M. N. (2000). *Egalitarianism as a revolt against nature, and other essays.* Auburn, AL: Ludwig von Mises Institute.

Rousseau, J. J. (1953/1782). *The confessions.* London: Penguin Classics.

Rowlatt, J. (2005). The risks of cousin marriage. *BBC-News,* 16. November 2005. Retrieved from http://news.bbc.co.uk/2/hi/programmes/newsnight/4442010.stm.

Rundquist, E. A. (1936). Intelligence test scores and school marks of high school seniors in 1929 and 1933. *School & Society, 43,* 301–304.

Rushton, J. P. (1985). Differential K theory: The sociobiology of individual and group differences. *Personality and Individual Differences, 6,* 441–452.

Rushton, J. Ph. (1997/1995). *Race, evolution, and behavior. A life history perspective.* New Brunswick, NJ: Transaction.

Rushton, J. Ph. & Ankney, C. D. (2009). Whole-brain size and general mental ability: A review. *International Journal of Neuroscience, 119,* 691–731.

Rushton, J. Ph., Cvorovic, J. & Bons, T. A. (2007). General mental ability in South Asians: Data from three Roma (Gypsy) communities in Serbia. *Intelligence, 35,* 1–12.

Sackett, P. R. & Walmsley, P. T. (2014). Which personality attributes are most important in the workplace? *Perspectives on Psychological Science, 9,* 538–551.

Sackett, P. R., Hardison, C. M. & Cullen, M. J. (2004). On interpreting stereotype threat as accounting for African American-White differences on cognitive tests. *American Psychologist, 59,* 7–13.

Sacerdote, B. (2011). Peer effects in education: How might they work, how big are they and how much do we know thus far? In E. A. Hanushek, S. Machin & L. Woessmann (Eds.), *Handbook of the economics of education.* Volume III (pp. 249–277). Amsterdam: Elsevier.

Sailer, S. (2007). *Diversity is strength! But...what about Finland?* 19-3-07. Retrieved from www.vdare.com/sailer/070319_diversity.htm.

Sala-i-Martin, X. (1997). I just ran two million regressions. *American Economic Review, 87,* 178–183.

Sala-i-Martin, X., Doppelhofer, G. & Miller, R. I. (2004). Determinants of long-term growth: A Bayesian averaging of classical estimates (BACE) approach. *American Economic Review, 94,* 813–835.

Salgado, J. F., Anderson, N., Moscoso, S., Bertua, C., De Fruyt, F. & Rolland, J. P. (2003). A meta-analytic study of general mental ability validity for different occupations in the European Community. *Journal of Applied Psychology, 88,* 1068–1081.

Salminen, S. (2015). *Immigrations and public finances in Finland. Part I: Realized fiscal revenues and expenditures. English summary.* Helsinki: Suomen Perusta.

Salter, F. K. (2007/2003). *On genetic interests.* New Brunswick, NJ: Transaction.

Salthouse, T. A. (2013). Within-cohort age-related differences in cognitive functioning. *Psychological Science, 24,* 123–130.

Sandefur, J. (2016). Internationally comparable mathematics scores for fourteen African countries. *Center for Global Development Working Paper, 444,* 1–51.

Sander, R. H. (2004). A systemic analysis of affirmative action in American law schools. *Stanford Law Review, 57,* 367–483.

Saroglou, V., Delpierre, V. & Dernelle, R. (2004). Values and religiosity: A meta-analysis of studies using Schwartz's model. *Personality and Individual Differences, 37,* 721–734.

Sarrazin, Th. (2014). Separate Duschen. Wie man in Berlin Polizist wird – und bleibt. *Weltwoche, 4.12.2014.* [How to become and remain constable in Berlin.] Retrieved from www.weltwoche.ch/weiche/hinweisgesperrt.html?hidID=552833.

Sarton, G. (1956). Arabic science and learning in the fifteenth century: Their decadence and fall. In *Homenaje a Millás-Vallicrosa,* II (pp. 303–324). Barcelona: Consejo Superior de Investigaciones Científicas.

Saunders, P. (1997). Social mobility in Britain: An empirical evaluation of two competing explanations. *Sociology, 31,* 261–288.

Scarr, S. (1992). Developmental theories for the 1990s: Development and individual differences. *Child Development, 63,* 1–19.

Scarr, S. & McCartney, K. (1983). How people make their own environments: A theory of genotype → environment effects. *Child Development, 54,* 424–435.

Schaub, H. & Zenke, K. G. (2004). *Wörterbuch Pädagogik.* Munich: DTV.

Scheerens, J. & Bosker, R. J. (1997). *The foundations of educational effectiveness.* Kidlington: Pergamon/Elsevier.

Schiefele, U., Artelt, C., Schneider, W. & Stanat, P. (Eds.) (2004). *Struktur, Entwicklung und Förderung von Lesekompetenz.* [*Structure, development and furtherance of reading literacy.*] Wiesbaden: VS.

Schmidt, F. L. (2012). Cognitive tests used in selection can have content validity as well as criterion validity. *International Journal of Selection and Assessment, 20,* 1–13.

Schmidt, F. L. & Hunter, J. E. (1998). The validity and utility of selection methods in personnel psychology. *Psychological Bulletin, 124,* 262–274.

Schmidt, F. L., Oh, I.-S. & Le, H. (2006). Increasing the accuracy of corrections for range restriction. *Personnel Psychology, 59,* 281–305.

Schmitt, D. P., Allik, J., McCrae, R. R., Benet-Martínez, V. & 123 co-authors. (2007). The geographic distribution of Big Five personality traits. *Journal of Cross-Cultural Psychology, 38,* 173–212.

Schneid, M., Isidor, R., Steinmetz, H., Kabst, R. & Weber, H. (2014). The influence of team diversity on team performance. A meta-analysis. *Die Betriebswirtschaft, 3,* 183–210.

Schoellman, T. (2016). Early childhood human capital and development. *American Economic Journal: Macroeconomics, 8,* 145–174.

Schopenhauer, A. (1974/1851). *Parerga und Paralipomena*. New York: Oxford University Press.

Schultz, Th. W. (1961). Investment in human capital. *American Economic Review, 51*, 1–17.

Schümer, G. (1998). Mathematikunterricht in Japan. [Mathematics education in Japan.] *Unterrichtswissenschaft, 26*, 195–228.

Schwekendiek, D. & Pak, S. (2009). Recent growth of children in the two Koreas: A meta-analysis. *Economics and Human Biology, 7*, 109–112.

Segerstråle, U. (2000). *Defenders of the truth. The sociobiology debate*. New York: Oxford University Press.

Sesardic, N. (2005). *Making sense of heritability*. Cambridge: Cambridge University Press.

  (2010). Race: A social destruction of a biological concept. *Biology and Philosophy, 25*, 143–162.

  (2013). Confusions about race: A new installment. *Studies in History and Philosophy of Biological and Biomedical Sciences, 44*, 287–293.

Sharkey, P. (2010). The acute effect of local homicides on children's cognitive performance. *Proceeedings of the National Academy of Sciences, 107*, 11733–11738.

Sharkey, P. T., Tirado-Strayer, N., Papachristos, A. V. & Raver, C. C. (2012). The effect of local violence on children's attention and impulse control. *American Journal of Public Health, 102*, 2287–2293.

Sharp, J. M. (2013). *U.S. foreign aid to Israel*. Washington: Congressional Research Service. Retrieved from www.fas.org/sgp/crs/mideast/RL33222.pdf.

Shavit, Y. (1990). Segregation, tracking and the educational attainment of minorities: Arabs and Oriental Jews in Israel. *American Sociological Review, 55*, 115–126.

Shayer, M. & Ginsburg, D. (2009). Thirty years on – a large anti-Flynn effect? *British Journal of Educational Psychology, 79*, 409–418.

Signer, D. (2004). *Die Ökonomie der Hexerei oder warum es in Afrika keine Wolkenkratzer gibt*. [*The economics of witchcraft or why there are no skyscrapers in Africa.*] Wuppertal: Peter Hammer.

Simola, H. (2005). The Finnish miracle of PISA: Historical and sociological remarks on teaching and teacher education. *Comparative Education, 41*, 455–470.

Simon, J. L. (1996). *The ultimate resource II*. Princeton, NJ: Princeton University Press.

Simonton, D. K. (1984). Leaders as eponyms: Individual and situational determinants of ruler eminence. *Journal of Personality, 52*, 1–21.

  (1988). Age and outstanding achievement: What do we know after a century of research? *Psychological Bulletin, 104*, 251–267.

Sirin, S. R. (2005). Socioeconomic status and academic achievement: A meta-analytic review of research. *Review of Educational Research, 75*, 417–453.

Skidelsky, R. & Skidelsky, E. (2012). *How much is enough? Money and the good life*. New York: Other.

Slezkine, Y. (2004). *The Jewish century*. Princeton, NJ: Princeton University Press.

Smith, A (2004/1759). *The theory of moral sentiments*. New York: Barnes & Noble.

Smith, A. (1982/1776). *An inquiry into the nature and causes of the wealth of nations*. New York: Penguin.

Smith, D. I. & Kirkham, R. W. (1982). Relationship between intelligence and driving record. *Accident Analysis and Prevention, 14,* 439–442.

Sokal, A. (2008). *Beyond the hoax. Science, philosophy and culture.* Oxford: Oxford University Press.

Sol, D., Duncan, R. P., Blackburn, T. M., Cassey, Ph. & Lefebvre, L. (2005). Big brains, enhanced cognition, and response of birds to novel environments. *Proceedings of the National Academy of Sciences, 102,* 5460–5465.

Solon, I. S. (2014). How intelligence mediates liberalism and prosociality. *Intelligence, 47,* 44–53.

Solzhenitsyn, A. (2009/2001). Two hundred years together. In E. E. Ericson & D. J. Mahoney (Eds.), *The Solzhenitsyn reader* (pp. 485–507). Wilmington, VA: ISI.

Sombart, W. (1998/1913). *The quintessence of capitalism: A study of the history and psychology of the modern business man.* [*Der Bourgeois.*] London: Routledge.

Sonnleitner, P., Keller, U., Martin, R. & Brunner, M. (2013). Students' complex problem-solving abilities. *Intelligence, 41,* 289–305.

Sowell, Th. (2004). *Affirmative action around the world: An empirical study.* New Haven, CT: Yale University Press.

Spearman, Ch. (1904). 'General intelligence', objectively determined and measured. *American Journal of Psychology, 15,* 201–292.

Spence, M. (1973). Job market signaling. *Quarterly Journal of Economics, 87,* 355–374.

Spengler, O. (1991/1918). *The decline of the West.* New York: Oxford University Press.

Spiegelberg, F. (1957/1956). *Living religions of the world.* Bath: Pitman.

Spolaore, E. & Wacziarg, R. (2013). How deep are the roots of economic development? *Journal of Economic Literature, 51,* 325–369.

Stadler, M., Becker, N., Gödker, M., Leutner, D. & Greiff, S. (2015). Complex problem solving and intelligence: A meta-analysis. *Intelligence, 53,* 92–101.

Stanat, P., Schipolowski, S., Rjosk, C., Weirich, S. & Haag, N. (Eds.). (2017). *IQB-Bildungstrend 2016.* Münster: Waxmann.

Standing, H. (1992). AIDS: Conceptual and methodological issues in researching sexual behaviour in sub-saharan Africa. *Social Science and Medicine, 34,* 475–483.

Stankov, L. (2009). Conservatism and cognitive ability. *Intelligence, 37,* 294–304.

Stanovich, K. E., Toplak, M. E. & West, R. F. (2016). *The rationality quotient: Toward a test of rational thinking.* Cambridge, Massachusetts: MIT Press.

Starke, K. (2007). Kinderwagen im Seminargebäude – Die Förderung von Studentinnen mit Kind in der DDR. [Support of female students with a child in the GDR.] In W. Cornelißen & K. Fox (Eds.), *Studieren mit Kind [To study with a child]* (pp. 79–91). Wiesbaden: VS Verlag.

Statistisches Bundesamt (2010). *Mikrozensus 2008. Neue Daten zur Kinderlosigkeit in Deutschland. Tabellen, Stand: Dezember 2010.* [*Micro-census 2008.*] Wiesbaden: Destatis.

Steele, C. M. & Aronson, J. (1995). Stereotype threat and the intellectual test performance of African Americans. *Journal of Personality and Social Psychology, 69,* 797–811.

Steinberg, L., Lamborn, S. D., Darling, N., Mounts, N. S. & Dornbusch, S. M. (1994). Over-time changes in adjustment and competence among adolescents from authoritative, authoritarian, indulgent, and neglectful families. *Child Development*, *65*, 754–770.

Steinhauser, K. (2010). *Qualität von Montessori-Kindergärten und traditionellen Kindergärten und ihre Effekte auf die kindliche Entwicklung.* [Quality of Montessori and traditional kindergartens and their effects on children's development.] Graz: Unpublished Master's Thesis.

Steinmetz, Ch. (2002). *German-Israeli armaments cooperation.* Berlin: Berlin Information Center for Transatlantic Security. Retrieved from www.bits.de/public/articles/cast06-02.htm.

Stelzl, I., Merz, F., Remer, H. & Ehlers, Th. (1995). The effect of schooling on the development of fluid and cristallized intelligence: A quasi-experimental study. *Intelligence*, *21*, 279–296.

Steppan, M. (2010). Protestantism and intelligence: Max Weber and the Rindermann-paradox. *The International Journal of Educational and Psychological Assessment*, *5*, 134–154.

Sternberg, R. J. (2013). The intelligence of nations – smart but not wise: Comment on Hunt (2012). *Perspectives on Psychological Science*, *8*, 187–189.

Stiglitz, J., Sen, A. & Fitoussi, J. P. (2010). *Report by the commission on the measurement of economic performance and social progress.* New York: Columbia University.

Stone, L. (1964). The educational revolution in England, 1560–1640. *Past and Present*, *28*, 41–80.

Stoolmiller, M. (1999). Implications of the restricted range of family environments for estimates of heritability and nonshared environment in behavior-genetic adoption studies. *Psychological Bulletin*, *125*, 392–409.

Storfer, M. (1999). Myopia, intelligence, and the expanding human neocortex. *International Journal of Neuroscience*, *98*, 153–276.

Strack, R., Baier, J., Marchingo, M. & Sharda, S. (2014). *The global workforce crisis: $10 trillion at risk.* Boston: Boston Consulting Group.

Strenze, T. (2013). Allocation of talent in society and its effect on economic development. *Intelligence*, *41*, 169–177.

Strumsky, D., Lobo, J. & Tainter, J. A. (2010). Complexity and the productivity of innovation. *Systems Research and Behavioral Science*, *27*, 496–509.

Stumm, S. v., Batty, G. D. & Deary, I. J. (2011). Marital status and reproduction. *Intelligence*, *39*, 161–167.

Summers, L. H. (2005, January 14). *Remarks at NBER conference on diversifying the science and engineering workforce.* Retrieved from www.harvard.edu/president/speeches/summers_2005/nber.php

Sundet, J. M., Barlaug, D. G. & Torjussen, T. M. (2004). The end of the Flynn effect? *Intelligence*, *32*, 349–362.

Tadmouri, G. O., Nair, P., Obeid, T., Ali, M. T. A., Khaja, N. A. & Hamamy, H. A. (2009). Consanguinity and reproductive health among Arabs. *Reproductive Health*, *6*, 1–9.

Täht, K., Must, O., Peets, K. & Kattel, R. (2014). Learning motivation from a cross-cultural perspective. *Educational Research and Evaluation*, *20*, 255–274.

Talhelm, T., Zhang, X., Oishi, S., Shimin, C., Duan, D., Lan, X. & Kitayama, S. (2014). Large-scale psychological differences within China explained by rice versus wheat agriculture. *Science*, *344*, 603–608.

Tang, H., Quertermous, T., Rodriguez, B., Kardia, S. L., Zhu, X., Brown, A., Pankow, J. S., Province, M. A., Hunt, S. C., Boerwinkle, E., Schork, N. J. & Risch, N. J. (2005). Genetic structure, self-identified race/ethnicity, and confounding in case-control association studies. *American Journal of Human Genetics*, *76*, 268–275.

Taylor, M. D., Hart, C. L., Davey-Smith, G., Starr, J. M., Hole, D. J., Whalley, L. J., Wilson, V. & Deary, I. J. (2003). Childhood mental ability and smoking cessation in adulthood. *Journal of Epidemiology and Community Health*, *57*, 464–465.

Teasdale, Th. W. & Owen, D. R. (2008). Secular declines in cognitive test scores: A reversal of the Flynn Effect. *Intelligence*, *36*, 121–126.

Templer, D. I. (2010). The comparison of mean IQ in Muslim and non-Muslim countries. *Mankind Quarterly*, *L*, 188–209.

(2013). Biological and cognitive correlates of murder and attempted murder in the Italian regions. *Mankind Quarterly*, *LIV*, 26–48.

Templer, D. I. & Arikawa, H. (2006). Temperature, skin color, per capita income, and IQ: An international perspective. *Intelligence*, *34*, 121–128.

te Nijenhuis, J. (2010). *Mean intelligence of immigrants from developing countries living in developed countries*. Presentation at the II Latin American Congress of Psychological Assessment. Belo Horizonte, 23-09-10.

te Nijenhuis, J. & van der Flier, H. (2013). Is the Flynn effect on *g*? A meta-analysis. *Intelligence*, *41*, 802–807.

te Nijenhuis, J., de Jong, M.-J., Evers, A. & van der Flier, H. (2004). Are cognitive differences between immigrant and majority groups diminishing? *European Journal of Personality*, *18*, 405–434.

Terracciano, A. et al. (2005). National character does not reflect mean personality trait levels in 49 cultures. *Science*, *310*, 96–100.

Thomas, K. J., Nicholl, J. P. & Coleman, P. (2001). Use and expenditure on complementary medicine in England: A population based survey. *Complementary Therapies in Medicine*, *9*, 2–11.

Times Higher Education (2013). *World university ranking 2012–2013*. Retrieved from www.timeshighereducation.co.uk/world-university-rankings/2012-13/world-ranking.

Tocqueville, A. d. (2010/1835). *Democracy in America. Historical-critical edition of De la démocratie en Amérique. Volumes I to IV*. Indianapolis, IA: Liberty Fund.

Toynbee, A. J. (1960). *A study of history*. Oxford: Oxford University Press

Trahan, L. H., Stuebing, K. K., Fletcher, J. M. & Hiscock, M. (2014). The Flynn effect: A meta-analysis. *Psychological Bulletin*, *140*, 1332–1360.

Transparency International (2012). *Corruption perceptions index 2012*. Berlin: Transparency International. Retrieved from www.transparency.org/cpi2012/results#myAnchor1.

Trut, L. N. (1999). Early canid domestication: The Farm-Fox Experiment. Foxes bred for tamability in a 40-year experiment exhibit remarkable transformations that suggest an interplay between behavioral genetics and development. *American Scientist*, *87*, 160–169.

Trzaskowski, M., Harlaar, N., Arden, R., Krapohl, E., Rimfeld, K., McMillan, A., Dale, P. S. & Plomin, R. (2014). Genetic influence on family socioeconomic status and children's intelligence. *Intelligence, 42*, 83–88.

Turkheimer, E. (2007). Race and IQ. *Cato Unbound, November*(26). Retrieved from www.cato-unbound.org/2007/11/21/eric-turkheimer/race-and-iq.

Turkheimer, E., Haley, A., Waldron, M., D'Onofrio, B. & Gottesman, I. I. (2003). Socioeconomic status modifies heritability of IQ in young children. *Psychological Science, 14*, 623–628.

UN (UN Department of Economic and Social Affairs, Population Division) (2011). *Population statistics and predictions, data tables*. Retrieved October 10, 2011, from http://esa.un.org/unpd/wpp/Excel-Data.

UN (United Nations, Department of Economic and Social Affairs, Population Division) (2013). *World population prospects: The 2012 revision*. Retrieved from http://esa.un.org/wpp.

UNAIDS/WHO (2003). *AIDS epidemic update*. Geneva: WHO/www.unaids.org.

UNAIDS (2013). *Global report. UNAIDS report on the global AIDS epidemic 2013*. Geneva: UNAIDS.

UNDP (United Nations Development Programme) & Arab Fund for Economic and Social Development (2003). *Arab Human Development Report 2003. Building a knowledge society*. New York: UNDP.

UNDP (2010). *Human development report 2010*. New York: United Nations.

UNESCO (1969/1950). *Four statements on the race question*. Paris: Unesco.

UNODC (2012). *Intentional homicide, count and rate per 100,000 population (1995–2011)*. Vienna: United Nations Office on Drugs and Crime.

UNSCEAR (2014). *UNSCEAR 2013 report. Sources, effects and risks of ionizing radiation*. New York: United Nations Scientific Committee on the Effects of Atomic Radiation.

Unz, R. (1981). *Preliminary notes on the possible sociobiological implications of the rural Chinese economy*. Cambridge, MA: Harvard, unpublished manuscript. Retrieved February 28, 2013 from www.ronunz.org/wp-content/uploads/2012/05/ChineseIntelligence.pdf.

    (2012). The myth of American meritocracy. How corrupt are Ivy League admissions? *The American Conservative, December*, 14–51.

    (2013). How Social Darwinism made modern China. A thousand years of meritocracy shaped the Middle Kingdom. *The American Conservative, March/April*, 16–27.

Ura, K., Alkire, S., Zangmo, T. & Wangdi, K. (2012). *An extensive analysis of GNH index*. Thimphu: The Centre for Bhutan Studies.

Uslucan, H.-H. (2007). *Expertise für das Familienministerium zum islamischen Religionsunterricht an deutschen Schulen. [Expertise for the the ministry for social and family affairs on Islam religious instruction in German schools.]* University Potsdam: Department of Psychology.

Van Damme, J., Liu, H., Vanhee, L. & Pustjens, H. (2010). Longitudinal studies at the country level as a new approach to educational effectiveness. *Effective Education, 2*, 53–84.

Vandenbussche, J., Aghion, P. & Meghir, C. (2006). Growth, distance to frontier and composition of human capital. *Journal of Economic Growth, 11*, 97–127.

Van Den Haag, E. (1969). *The Jewish mystique*. New York: Dell.

Van de Vijver, F. J. R. & Brouwers, S. A. (2009). Schooling and basic aspects of intelligence: A natural quasi-experiment in Malawi. *Journal of Applied Developmental Psychology, 30*, 67–74.

Vanhanen, T. (2011). IQ and international wellbeing indexes. *Journal of Social, Political and Economic Studies, 36*, 80–89.

    (2012). *Ethnic conflicts: Their biological roots in ethnic nepotism*. London: Ulster Institute for Social Research.

Vanhanen, T. & Åbo Akademi (2013). *Measures of democracy*. Tampere: Finnish Social Science Data Archive.

van IJzendoorn, M. H., Juffer, F. & Poelhuis, C. W. K. (2005). Adoption and cognitive development: A meta-analytic comparison of adopted and nonadopted children's IQ and school performance. *Psychological Bulletin, 131*, 301–316.

Vernon, M. (1968). Fifty years of research on the intelligence of deaf and hard-of-hearing children: A review of literature and discussion of implications. *Journal of Deaf Studies and Deaf Education, 10*, 225–231.

Victora, C. G., Horta, B. L., de Mola, C. L., Quevedo, L., Pinheiro, R. T., Gigante, D. P., Gonçalves, H. & Barros, F. C. (2015). Association between breastfeeding and intelligence, educational attainment, and income at 30 years of age. *The Lancet Global Health, 3*, e199–e205.

Vining, D. R. (1995). On the possibility of the reemergence of a dysgenic trend with respect to intelligence in American fertility differentials. *Personality and Individual Differences, 19*, 259–263.

Vinkhuyzen, A. A. E., Sluis, S. v. d., Maes, H. H. M. & Posthuma, D. (2012). Reconsidering the heritability of intelligence in adulthood: Taking assortative mating and cultural transmission into account. *Behavior Genetics, 42*, 187–198.

Virga, V. (2007). *Cartographia*. New York: Little Brown.

Wade, N. (2014). *A troublesome inheritance. Genes, race and human history*. New York: Penguin.

Wai, J. (2013). Investigating America's elite: Cognitive ability, education, and sex differences. *Intelligence, 41*, 203–211.

Walker, M. (2011). *PISA 2009 plus results. Performance of 15-year-olds in reading, mathematics and science for 10 additional participants*. Camberwell: ACER.

Wallerstein, I. (2004). *World-systems analysis: An introduction*. Durham, NC: Duke University Press.

Walsh, J. R. (1935). Capital concept applied to man. *Quarterly Journal of Economics, 49*, 255–285.

Walzer, M. (1983). *Spheres of justice*. New York: Basic Books.

    (2015). Islamism and the left. *Dissent, Winter 2015*. Retrieved from www.dissentmagazine.org/article/islamism-and-the-left

Wang, M., Fuerst, J. & Ren, J. (2016). Evidence of dysgenic fertility in China. *Intelligence, 57*, 15–24.

Wang, M., Rieger, M. O. & Hens, T. (2016). How time preferences differ: Evidence from 53 countries. *Journal of Economic Psychology, 52*, 115–135.

Watson, P. (2010). *The German genius. Europe's third Renaissance, the second scientific revolution, and the twentieth century*. New York: Harper.

Weber, E. & Weigand, R. (2016). Identifying macroeconomic effects of refugee migration to Germany. *IAB Discussion Paper, 20*, 1–13.

Weber, M. (2001/1905). The Protestant ethic and the spirit of capitalism. *[Die protestantische Ethik und der Geist des Kapitalismus.]* London: Routledge.

(1952/1919). *Ancient Judaism. [Das antike Judentum.]* New York: Free Press.

(1951/1920). *The religion of China. Taoism and Confucianism. [Konfuzianismus und Taoismus.]* New York: Free Press.

(1958/1921). *The religion of India. The sociology of Hinduism and Buddhism. [Hinduismus und Buddhismus.]* Glencoe, NY: Free Press.

(2007/1923). *General economic history. [Wirtschaftsgeschichte.]* New York: Cosimo.

(1978/1922). *Economy and society. [Wirtschaft und Gesellschaft.]* Berkeley: University of California Press.

Weede, E. (2008). Globalization and inequality. *Comparative Sociology, 7*, 415–433.

(2010). The rise of India: Overcoming caste society and permit-license-quota raj, implementing some economic freedom. *Asian Journal of Political Science, 18*, 129–153.

(2011). The capitalist peace. In Ch. J. Coyne & R. Mathers (Eds.), *The handbook on the political economy of war* (pp. 269–280). Cheltenham: Edward Elgar.

(2012). Liberty in comparative perspective. China, India, and the West. In F. McMahon (Hrsg.), *Towards a worldwide index of human freedom* (pp. 189–241). Vancouver, BC: Fraser Institute, Liberales Institut.

(2014). Economic development and growth. In M. Sasaki, J. Goldstone, E. Zimmermann & S. K. Sanderson (Eds.), *Concise encyclopedia of comparative sociology* (pp. 293–310). Leiden: Koninklijke Brill.

Weiss, V. (2007). The population cycle drives human history. *Journal of Social, Political and Economic Studies, 32*, 327–358.

Wellings, K., Collumbien, M., Slaymaker, E., Singh, S., Hodges, Z., Patel, D. & Bajos, N. (2006). Sexual behaviour in context: A global perspective. *The Lancet, 368*, 1706–1728.

Whaley, S. E., Sigman, M., Neumann, Ch., Bwibo, N., Guthrie, D., Weiss, R. E., Alber, S. & Murphy, S. P. (2003). The impact of dietary intervention on the cognitive development of Kenyan school children. *Journal of Nutrition, 133*, 3965–3971.

Whalley, L. J. & Deary, I. J. (2001). Longitudinal cohort study of childhood IQ and survival up to age 76. *British Medical Journal (BMJ), 322*, 1–5.

WHO (2013). *Global status report on road safety 2013*. Geneva: World Health Organization. Retrieved from www.who.int/iris/bitstream/10665/78256/1/9789241564564_eng.pdf.

Wicherts, J. M., Dolan, C. V. & Maas, H. L. J. v. d. (2010a). A systematic literature review of the average IQ of sub-Saharan Africans. *Intelligence, 38*, 1–20.

Wicherts, J. M., Borsboom, D. & Dolan, C. V. (2010b). Why national IQs do not support evolutionary theories of intelligence. *Personality and Individual Differences, 48*, 91–96.

Winship, Ch. & Korenman, S. (1997). Does staying in school make you smarter? The effect of education on IQ in The Bell Curve. In B. Devlin, S. E. Fienberg, D. P. Resnick & K. Roeder (Eds.), *Intelligence, genes and success* (pp. 215–234). New York: Springer.

WIPO (World Intellectual Property Organization) (2009). *Patent applications by patent office (1883–2007), by resident and non-resident.* Geneva. Retrieved June 22, 2009 from www.wipo.int/ipstats/en/statistics/patents.

Wober, M. (1969). Distinguishing centri-cultural from cross-cultural tests and research. *Perceptual and Motor Skills, 28,* 488.

(1974). Towards an understanding of the Kiganda concept of intelligence. In J. W. Berry & P. R. Dasen (Eds.), *Culture and cognition: Readings in cross-cultural psychology* (pp. 261–280). London: Methuen.

Wolf, C. (2010). Wie sicher ist meine Fluggesellschaft? [How safe is my airline?] www.aerointernational.de, *2,* 76–77.

(2011). Wie sicher ist meine Fluggesellschaft? [How safe is my airline?] www.aerointernational.de, *2,* 78–79.

Wongupparaj, P., Kumari, V. & Morris, R. G. (2015). A Cross-Temporal Meta-Analysis of Raven's Progressive Matrices: Age groups and developing versus developed countries. *Intelligence, 49,* 1–9.

Woodley, M. A. (2009). Inbreeding depression and IQ in a study of 72 countries. *Intelligence, 37,* 268–276.

(2010). Is Homo sapiens polytypic? Human taxonomic diversity and its implications. *Medical Hypotheses, 74,* 195–201.

(2012). The social and scientific temporal correlates of genotypic intelligence and the Flynn effect. *Intelligence, 40,* 189–204.

Woodley of Menie, M. A. (2015). How fragile is our intellect? Estimating losses in general intelligence due to both selection and mutation accumulation. *Personality and Individual Differences, 75,* 80–84.

Woodley, M. A. & Bell, E. (2013). Consanguinity as a major predictor of levels of democracy: A study of 70 nations. *Journal of Cross-Cultural Psychology, 44,* 263–280.

Woodley of Menie, M. A. & Fernandes, H. B. F. (2015). Do opposing secular trends on backwards and forwards digit span evidence the co-occurrence model? A comment on Gignac (2015). *Intelligence, 50,* 125–130.

Woodley, M. A., te Nijenhuis, J. & Murphy, R. (2013). Were the Victorians cleverer than us? The decline in general intelligence estimated from a meta-analysis of the slowing of simple reaction time. *Intelligence, 41,* 843–850.

Woodley, M. A., Rindermann, H., Bell, E., Stratford, J. & Piffer, D. (2014). The relationship between Microcephalin, ASPM and intelligence: A reconsideration. *Intelligence, 44,* 51–63.

Woodley of Menie, M. A., Fernandes, H. B. F., Figueredo, A. J. & Meisenberg, G. (2015). By their words ye shall know them: Evidence of genetic selection against general intelligence and concurrent environmental enrichment in vocabulary usage since the mid 19th century. *Frontiers in Psychology, 6*(361), 1–9.

Woodley of Menie, M. A., Figueredo, A. J., Sarraf, M. A., Hertler, S. C. & Fernandes, H. B. F. (2017). *The rhythm of the West.* Washington, DC: Council for Social and Economic Studies.

Woschek, R. (2005). *TIMSS 2 elaboriert. Eine didaktische Analyse von Schülerarbeiten im Ländervergleich Schweiz / Deutschland.* Universität Duisburg: Dissertation. Retrieved from http://deposit.ddb.de/cgi-bin/dokserv?idn=976119749.

Woessmann, L. (2001). Why students in some countries do better: International evidence of education policy. *Education Matters, 1,* 67–74.

(2002). *Central exams improve educational performance*. Kiel: Institut für Weltwirtschaft.

(2016). The importance of school systems: Evidence from international differences in student achievement. *Journal of Economic Perspectives, 30*, 3–31.

Wright, S. (1978). *Evolution and the genetics of populations. Vol. 4: Variability within and among natural populations*. Chicago: University of Chicago Press.

Zajenkowski, M., Stolarski, M. & Meisenberg, G. (2013). Openness, economic freedom and democracy moderate the relationship between national intelligence and GDP. *Personality and Individual Differences, 55*, 391–398.

Zakaria, F. (2011). *The post-American world*. New York: W.W. Norton.

Zimmerman, D. J. (2003). Peer effects in academic outcomes: Evidence from a natural experiment. *Review of Economics and Statistics, 85*, 9–23.

Zuckerman, H. (1996/1977). *Scientific elite: Nobel laureates in the United States*. New Brunswick, NJ: Transaction.

# Index